LIVING ✠ LITURGY™

LIVING ✤ LITURGY™

Spirituality, Celebration, and Catechesis for Sundays and Solemnities

Year B • 2021

Katy Beedle Rice
Orin E. Johnson
Verna Holyhead, SGS

with
John R. Donahue, SJ
Amy Ekeh
Dennis Gunn, CFC
and John W. Martens

LITURGICAL PRESS
Collegeville, Minnesota

www.litpress.org

ISSN 1547-089X

ISBN 978-0-8146-6463-6   ISBN 978-0-8146-6487-2 (ebook)

CONTENTS

CONTRIBUTORS

Katy Beedle Rice is a catechist and writer who lives with her husband and three children in Boise, Idaho. She is a formation leader for the National Association of the Catechesis of the Good Shepherd, training catechists who work with children ages three through six. Rice is also a contributing preacher for the Dominican Podcast *the Word* (https://word.op.org), writes for Celebration Publications, a division of the National Catholic Reporter Publishing Company, and blogs about motherhood, ministry, and the Eucharist at blessedbrokenshared.blogspot.com.

Orin E. Johnson has been director of music ministries at Sts. Joachim and Ann Parish in St. Charles, Missouri, since 2012. There, he directs a children's choir, a contemporary ensemble, a funeral choir, and a team of cantors, and supervises two other choirs and liturgical ministries at a K–8 parochial school. He was also coordinator of music and liturgy at the National Shrine of Our Lady of the Snows in Belleville, Illinois, from 1998 to 2012. He resides in St. Louis, Missouri, with his wife, Erin, and pet dog, Gracie.

Verna Holyhead, SGS (1933–2011), Australian Sister of the Good Samaritan of the Order of St. Benedict, wrote with an emphasis on biblical scholarship, liturgical insight, and pastoral challenge. She is the author of the three-volume collection *Welcoming the Word in Year A, B,* and *C*, published by Liturgical Press. Drawing from the wisdom of the community, her gospel reflections are included in this volume.

John R. Donahue, SJ, PhD, is the Raymond E. Brown Distinguished Professor Emeritus of New Testament Studies at St. Mary's Seminary and University in Baltimore. He is the author of *Life in Abundance: Studies of John's Gospel in Tribute to Raymond E. Brown, S.S.*, and *Hearing the Word of God: Reflections on the Sunday Readings*, published by Liturgical Press.

Amy Ekeh is the director of Little Rock Scripture Study. She is an instructor in the Catholic Biblical School in the Archdiocese of Hartford, where she also facilitates retreats and missions. She is the author of *Advent, Season of Divine Encounter*; *Lent, Season of Transformation*; and *Finding Peace, Letting Go of Stress and Worry*. Visit her blog at amyekeh.com.

Brother Dennis Gunn, CFC, PhD, has served as a teacher in K–12 education in various Catholic schools throughout the United States and South America. He is currently assistant professor in the Education Department at Iona College, New Rochelle, New York. He is the author of *Educating for Civic Dialogue in an Age of Uncivil Discourse*, published by Routledge.

John W. Martens, PhD, is professor of theology at the University of St. Thomas and director of the master of arts in theology program at St. Paul Seminary, School of Divinity, St. Paul, Minnesota. He is the author of three volumes of *The Word on the Street: Sunday Lectionary Reflections*, published by Liturgical Press, and *Paul, Pastoring God's People* in the Little Rock Scripture Study Alive in the Word series.

PREFACE

Purpose

As a premier Catholic publisher, Liturgical Press remains committed to offering liturgical, spiritual, and scriptural resources rooted in the Benedictine tradition. While these resources have changed and developed over the years, the commitment to sound theology and best pastoral practice remain hallmarks of our mission and ministry. *Living Liturgy*™ is one of our most loved and widely used incarnations of this commitment.

Living Liturgy™ will always help people prepare for liturgy and live a liturgical spirituality (that is, a way of living that is rooted in liturgy). The paschal mystery is the central focus of liturgy, of the gospels, and of this volume. *Living Liturgy*™ is more than a title. Rather, "living liturgy" is a commitment to a relationship with Jesus Christ, embodied in our everyday actions and interactions.

We hope this edition of *Living Liturgy*™ will continue to facilitate this relationship, making liturgical spirituality a lived reality.

Artwork

This latest edition of *Living Liturgy*™ features stunning new artwork from Ruberval Monteiro da Silva, OSB. Fr. Ruberval, a native of Brazil, resides in the Benedictine community of Sant'Anselmo in Rome. His colorful mosaics grace the walls of churches around the world, though he was eager to experiment with new mediums to fit within the pages of *Living Liturgy*™. His work is a labor of love and an outpouring of prayer, and will bring readers deeper into each gospel passage.

Reflecting on the Gospel

The gospel reflections in *Living Liturgy*™ draw from the prolific work of Verna Holyhead, SGS, whose commitment to the intersection of Scripture and liturgy provides rich and provocative fodder for reflection. Additional reflections drawing from the wisdom of our community are contributed by John R. Donahue, SJ; Amy Ekeh; Dennis Gunn, CFC; and John W. Martens. Each of their continued commitments to the liturgical life of the church is evident and inspiring.

Focusing the Gospel, Connecting the Gospel, Connecting the Responsorial Psalm, Prompts for Faith-Sharing, and Homily Points

Now in her third and, sadly, final year of writing for *Living Liturgy*™, Katy Beedle Rice's experience as a catechist shines through each of her contributions. Written in an accessible yet never simplistic style, Katy's work is carefully constructed, inviting readers to engage the parallels between Scripture, liturgy, and life.

Liturgy

As a liturgical musician, composer, and author, Orin Johnson brings intimate knowledge of the pastoral needs of the people of God. Orin's writing draws attention to some of the most timely realities of our church today through the lens of his own experience. For this edition, Orin suggested that each Sunday and solemnity in *Living Liturgy*™ have a different feature catechetical section. We're glad we agreed. His breadth of knowledge of liturgy will surely enhance yours.

ACKNOWLEDGMENTS *for Gospel Reflections*

Original "Reflecting on the Gospel" sections

Amy Ekeh
The Most Sacred Heart of Jesus
The Nativity of Saint John the Baptist
The Commemoration of All the Faithful Departed (All Souls' Day)
Thanksgiving Day

Dennis Gunn
Holy Thursday Evening Mass of the Lord's Supper
Good Friday of the Passion of the Lord
At the Easter Vigil in the Holy Night of Easter

John W. Martens
Saint Joseph, Spouse of the Blessed Virgin Mary
The Annunciation of the Lord

Adapted "Reflecting on the Gospel" sections

Days of the Lord: The Liturgical Year, Volume 1; Advent, Christmas, Epiphany (1991)
The Nativity of the Lord (Christmas), Vigil Mass
The Nativity of the Lord (Christmas), Mass at Dawn

John R. Donahue, *Hearing the Word of God: Reflections on the Sunday Readings, Year B (2002)*
The Nativity of the Lord (Christmas), Mass during the Night
Second Sunday of Lent
Seventh Sunday of Easter
Saints Peter and Paul, Apostles
Eighteenth Sunday in Ordinary Time

Verna Holyhead, *Welcoming the Word in Year B: Sowing the Seed (2008)*
First Sunday of Advent
Second Sunday of Advent
Fourth Sunday of Advent
The Nativity of the Lord (Christmas), Mass during the Day
Solemnity of Mary, the Holy Mother of God
The Epiphany of the Lord
The Baptism of the Lord
Second Sunday in Ordinary Time
Third Sunday in Ordinary Time

SEASON OF
ADVENT

SPIRITUALITY

GOSPEL ACCLAMATION
Ps 85:8

R∤. Alleluia, alleluia.
Show us, Lord, your love;
and grant us your salvation.
R∤. Alleluia, alleluia.

Gospel

Mark 13:33-37; L2B

**Jesus said to his disciples:
"Be watchful! Be alert!
You do not know when the time
will come.
It is like a man traveling abroad.
He leaves home and places his
servants in charge, each
with his own work,
and orders the gatekeeper to
be on the watch.
Watch, therefore;
you do not know when the
lord of the house is
coming,
whether in the evening, or at
midnight,
or at cockcrow, or in the morning.
May he not come suddenly and find you
sleeping.
What I say to you, I say to all:
'Watch!'"**

Reflecting on the Gospel

"Be watchful! Be alert!" are the first words with which Mark greets us at the beginning of this new year of the church. They are also the last words spoken by Jesus in Mark's gospel (Mark 13:37) before the vortex of violence begins to suck Jesus into the passion and death that he will conquer by his resurrection. So even as we begin Advent, we are reminded of the paschal mystery of Christ, the hub of the liturgical year.

Today's gospel is part of Mark 13, the chapter that is known as his "little apocalypse." Apocalypse is sometimes called the literature of the oppressed, as it usually arises from and is addressed to people in a time of uncertainty or suffering, present or imminent. Such was the situation of the Markan church, persecuted and unsure what the next day would bring in terms of fidelity to or betrayal of their faith.

In one sense, uncertainty is always the season of the church as we await the return of Jesus, the great Traveler, who has gone abroad from the home of his human presence with us, but will return at his Second Coming when human history has run its course. We are uncertain about the day or the hour of this, because it is known only to the Father; but we have the certainty of faith that there is an end for the world: a faith that Christ will come again to pour out upon the cosmos the extravagant love of God that will transform it into the new heaven and new earth. When the new impinges on our lives to threaten the established order, we often express our reaction to this in terms of cosmic collapse: "I felt as though my whole world was collapsing!" In the verses immediately before today's gospel, Jesus has spoken about the end of the old order in terms of the "passing away" of heaven and earth. The old order is the predictable, the ingrained habits, the mindless and often oppressive "business as usual." Jesus's words announce a new reality for which we must be awake and alert. Advent is our yearly reminder that, immersed in the present as we necessarily are, nonetheless we always stand on the edge of the future, secure in the words of Jesus which will not pass away but will help us journey into a new and hopeful transformation (cf. Mark 13:31-32).

Mark describes the "Jesus journey" through the parable of a man who goes abroad and leaves his servants in charge of his household. Just as each one of the servants in the parable is given specific work to do during his master's absence, so we, as members of God's household, are to be daily committed to our baptismal calling in our own circumstances, "evening, morning, cockcrow, dawn." Especially as "doorkeepers," we are to watch out for and open our personal and communal lives to the advent of God. Modern science speaks of the cosmos in terms of millennia of millennia, yet we know that this is not the scale of our own lifetime. The natural process of aging, perhaps the diagnosis of our own or our loved one's terminal illness, the sudden fatal accident, the ravages of natural disasters—all these are reminders of our much shorter time and our need to be prepared for that "personal parousia," Christ's advent in our death.

Today in our churches or homes we light the first candle on the Advent wreath: a small flame is struck on an evergreen circle, a simple ritual and symbol of the first flicker of hope in the One who is the Light of the World, who will lead us through every darkness to eternal life with God who is without beginning or end. "Marana tha," "Come, Lord," is our persistent Advent cry.

Focusing the Gospel

Key words and phrases: "Be watchful! Be alert!"

To the point: We begin each liturgical year with a passage near the end of one of the Synoptic Gospels. Jesus, shortly before his passion, death, and resurrection, speaks to his closest friends regarding the moment of his return. Each gospel offers Jesus giving subtly different instructions. In Matthew, Jesus urges his followers to "stay awake," in Luke they are to "be vigilant," and in our gospel for today (from Mark) we are told three times to "watch." As we enter into this Advent season of preparation and waiting, we might consider how to incorporate the spiritual practice of watching into our lives. In this moment in time, how can we attune our eyes to Jesus's presence in our world and to his eventual return in glory?

Connecting the Gospel

to the first reading: Jesus illustrates the need for watchfulness with the parable of a master leaving his servants in charge as he travels abroad, having placed a gatekeeper "on the watch." The prophet Isaiah seems to be utilizing the same imagery in today's first reading, pleading for God to "return for the sake of your servants" with the hope that "you might meet us doing right." While Jesus's parable seems to warn against becoming drowsy lest the day of his return catch his disciples unawares, Isaiah is eager for God to make his presence known again in the midst of his people, even if, in that moment he relates, "[Y]ou are angry, and we are sinful; / all of us have become like unclean people, / all our good deeds are like polluted rags."

to experience: How often in the spiritual life do we cry out to God seeking comfort and tenderness? Instead, Isaiah calls upon God's righteous anger and cleansing justice to turn the hearts of his people back to an existence where all are "mindful of you in our ways." We know our God is both perfect justice and perfect mercy. How might the justice of God be challenging you to greater fidelity and purity of heart this Advent?

Connecting the Responsorial Psalm

to the readings: Today's psalm matches the first reading in urgency and tone. The psalmist pleads with God to "[r]ouse your power, / and come to save us." In the gospel, Jesus calls his disciples to "[b]e watchful! Be alert!" But in the psalm, God is the one who is called upon to "hearken" to the cries of his people and to "look down from heaven and see." In the covenant, God, with consideration and patience, waits for our full and wholehearted response to his invitation to relationship. We are not forced, and at times it can seem as if God is far away, even when we know he is closer than our very breath.

to psalmist preparation: In your life of faith, when have you been most in need of God's strength and saving power?

PROMPTS FOR FAITH-SHARING

In the first reading we find the familiar refrain: "[W]e are the clay and you are the potter." How is God forming and molding you at this moment?

Throughout salvation history the people of God have prayed as in today's psalm, "Rouse your power, / and come to save us." Where is God's restoring power most needed in your community?

In his letter to the Corinthians, St. Paul writes, "[I]n [Christ] . . . you are not lacking in any spiritual gift." How would it change your family or faith community if this belief was lived out?

How is Jesus calling you to be watchful and alert this Advent season?

Model Penitential Act

Presider: We begin this season of Advent with Jesus's words from today's gospel: "Be watchful! Be alert!" For the times we have grown weary and apathetic in faith, let us ask for mercy and healing . . . *[pause]*

> Lord Jesus, you are the light of the world and the just judge come to save us: Lord, have mercy.
> Christ Jesus, in joyful hope we await your coming in glory: Christ, have mercy.
> Lord Jesus, mold us into a people after your own heart: Lord, have mercy.

Homily Points

• In the gospel parable, the master of the house goes abroad, leaving his servants in charge, "each with his own work." Jesus uses parables for many reasons throughout the gospels, but primarily to help his listeners understand the mystery of the kingdom of God. Today's parable is the final one Jesus gives in the Gospel of Mark. Intent upon preparing his closest friends for what is to come, Jesus explains the parable's meaning as a way to urge watchfulness in his followers, even when it seems like the master of the house is delayed in returning, or indeed might never be coming back at all.

• Nearly two thousand years later, we are still waiting for the time that has been promised, when Jesus will return in glory and the kingdom of God will be established in its fullness. It is not easy to wait—just ask an expectant couple two weeks away from their due date, or a five-year-old wondering why Christmas isn't here yet. It is even harder to wait, though, when we do not know the timeline for when our expectations will be fulfilled.

• Though it is of unknown duration, we are not left to our own devices in this time of waiting. Instead, we've been given the gift of work. We find ourselves as part of an unbroken chain stretching from the friends of Jesus, who heard these words directly from his lips, to now. It is our turn in history to carry out Jesus's commandment to be watchful and alert, and to attend to the work that is ours to do. In this way, through the grace of God, may the kingdom of God continue to grow until the moment when it reaches its fulfillment and the Master of the house returns home.

Model Universal Prayer (Prayer of the Faithful)

Presider: As we enter into Advent, a season of preparation and joyful hope, let us turn to God with hearts and minds intent on building his kingdom here on earth.

Response: Lord, hear our prayer.

For the church, may it be a force for good in the world, intent upon lifting up the lowly and comforting the brokenhearted . . .

For those who labor throughout the world, may the dignity of their work be upheld with safe conditions and a just wage . . .

For those who have wandered far from God's way of peace and justice, through conversion and penance may they be restored to right relationship with God and others . . .

For all gathered here, may we attune our senses to the presence of God in the world and dedicate our lives to carrying out his holy will . . .

Presider: Loving God, you are our father, our redeemer, and the one who forms us as a potter forms clay. Hear our prayers, that molded into the image and likeness of your son, we might hasten the arrival of his kingdom of peace and justice. We ask this through Christ our Lord. **Amen.**

COLLECT

Let us pray.

Pause for silent prayer

Grant your faithful, we pray, almighty God,
the resolve to run forth to meet your Christ
with righteous deeds at his coming,
so that, gathered at his right hand,
they may be worthy to possess the heavenly Kingdom.
Through our Lord Jesus Christ, your Son,
who lives and reigns with you in the unity of the Holy Spirit,
one God, for ever and ever. **Amen.**

FIRST READING

Isa 63:16b-17, 19b; 64:2-7

You, Lord, are our father,
    our redeemer you are named forever.
Why do you let us wander, O Lord, from your ways,
    and harden our hearts so that we fear you not?
Return for the sake of your servants,
    the tribes of your heritage.
Oh, that you would rend the heavens and come down,
    with the mountains quaking before you,
while you wrought awesome deeds we could not hope for,
    such as they had not heard of from of old.
No ear has ever heard, no eye ever seen,
    any God but you
    doing such deeds for those who wait for him.
Would that you might meet us doing right,
    that we were mindful of you in our ways!
Behold, you are angry, and we are sinful;
    all of us have become like unclean people,
    all our good deeds are like polluted rags;
we have all withered like leaves,
    and our guilt carries us away like the wind.
There is none who calls upon your name,
    who rouses himself to cling to you;
for you have hidden your face from us
    and have delivered us up to our guilt.
Yet, O Lord, you are our father;
    we are the clay and you the potter:
    we are all the work of your hands.

RESPONSORIAL PSALM
Ps 80:2-3, 15-16, 18-19

℟. (4) Lord, make us turn to you; let us see
   your face and we shall be saved.

O shepherd of Israel, hearken,
   from your throne upon the cherubim,
      shine forth.
Rouse your power,
   and come to save us.

℟. Lord, make us turn to you; let us see
   your face and we shall be saved.

Once again, O LORD of hosts,
   look down from heaven, and see;
take care of this vine,
   and protect what your right hand has
      planted,
   the son of man whom you yourself
      made strong.

℟. Lord, make us turn to you; let us see
   your face and we shall be saved.

May your help be with the man of your
      right hand,
   with the son of man whom you yourself
      made strong.
Then we will no more withdraw from you;
   give us new life, and we will call upon
      your name.

℟. Lord, make us turn to you; let us see
   your face and we shall be saved.

SECOND READING
1 Cor 1:3-9

Brothers and sisters:
Grace to you and peace from God our
      Father
   and the Lord Jesus Christ.

I give thanks to my God always on your
      account
   for the grace of God bestowed on you in
      Christ Jesus,
   that in him you were enriched in every
      way,
   with all discourse and all knowledge,
   as the testimony to Christ was
      confirmed among you,
   so that you are not lacking in any
      spiritual gift
   as you wait for the revelation of our
      Lord Jesus Christ.
He will keep you firm to the end,
   irreproachable on the day of our Lord
      Jesus Christ.
God is faithful,
   and by him you were called to
      fellowship with his Son,
   Jesus Christ our Lord.

About Liturgy
Active Waiting: Advent is perhaps the most difficult season for liturgical ministers to shape and form. No matter how well the liturgy and music are crafted and executed, it can feel, against the pervasive "Christmas Spirit" which imbues almost everything outside the church doors at this time of year, that these efforts are nearly meaningless. Another aspect of the Advent season that makes it so challenging for liturgical ministers is the need to hold together in peace the paradoxical elements of rushing and patience: in today's collect, we ask God for "the resolve to run forth to meet your Christ," while the Scripture passages urge us to patient waiting and watching for that coming of the same Son of God.

It would be wise to be attuned to how those in the assembly perceive what is happening in our liturgies, especially against the backdrop of their presumed experiences the other six days and twenty-three hours of the week. Notably, it can be quite challenging for any of us to recognize simple, quiet waiting as something active and preparatory, but so it is! In fact, sometimes stillness is the only and best thing we can do. While the Advent wreath helps us mark time, it also bids us "be patient," as only certain candles may be lit each week while the remaining candles, too, must patiently wait. This can also be echoed in other pieces of the art and environment: a set of four banners, with one more revealed each passing Sunday, or indeed in the pacing and music of the liturgies.

About Stillness
Intentional Tranquility: On various Sundays in this resource, you will find brief sections that examine liturgical postures, gestures, objects, and furnishings and their impact on our liturgical celebrations. As mentioned above, stillness is one of those challenging aspects of liturgy, particularly as Christmas draws near. At any time of year, it can be a challenge to set aside time for quiet stillness—and at times when it is most difficult to do so, we ought to set aside *even more* time for peaceful contemplation! The General Instruction of the Roman Missal (GIRM) instructs us to insert several moments of silence into the liturgy: during the penitential act, after the presider's invitation "let us pray," following each Scripture passage, after the homily, and following the distribution of Holy Communion. If these moments are not intentional at our liturgies, Advent is the perfect time to be more aware of the necessity for silence in prayerful liturgies. Elijah, we must remember, recognized the voice of God not in powerful winds, earthquakes, or fires, but in a gentle whisper.

About Music
Marking Time: It is wise to mark the changing of seasons with noticeable changes in the music of the liturgy. This can be through the selections of pieces themselves or through how they are presented: changes in the use of unisons and harmonies, the use of different tempos, and the use of (or resting of) certain instruments can be very effective in helping our assemblies mark the passing of time and the different characters of each liturgical season.

We should be mindful that, even though it is sometimes nicknamed "Little Lent," Advent should have "joyful, anxious anticipation" as a primary affect, not penitence. Still, it may be a good time to include a sung Kyrie Eleison, since the Gloria is omitted during Advent. A hymn that speaks well to the activity of Advent is "People, Look East," found in many hymnals; one that effectively paints the quietness of the season is John Foley's "Patience, People" (Oregon Catholic Press [OCP]). Consider using one of these as a common gathering hymn or sending hymn for the entire season.

✝ SPIRITUALITY

GOSPEL ACCLAMATION
Luke 3:4, 6

℟. Alleluia, alleluia.
Prepare the way of the Lord, make
straight his paths:
all flesh shall see the salvation of God.
℟. Alleluia, alleluia.

Gospel

Mark 1:1-8; L5B

**The beginning of the gospel of
Jesus Christ the Son of God.**

**As it is written in Isaiah the
prophet:**
*Behold, I am sending my
messenger ahead of you;
he will prepare your way.
A voice of one crying out in
the desert:
"Prepare the way of the
Lord,
make straight his paths."*
**John the Baptist appeared in the
desert
proclaiming a baptism of repentance
for the forgiveness of sins.
People of the whole Judean
countryside
and all the inhabitants of Jerusalem
were going out to him
and were being baptized by him in
the Jordan River
as they acknowledged their sins.
John was clothed in camel's hair,
with a leather belt around his waist.
He fed on locusts and wild honey.
And this is what he proclaimed:
"One mightier than I is coming after
me.
I am not worthy to stoop and loosen the
thongs of his sandals.
I have baptized you with water;
he will baptize you with the Holy
Spirit."**

Reflecting on the Gospel

The Liturgy of the Word puts the adult John before us today and next Sunday to block our view of "baby Jesus," and so remind us that the Advent–Christmas mystery is less about the child and more about the adult Coming One and the mystery of his life, death, and resurrection that he offers to us as our own mystery. We are called to make our way down to the Jordan with the hopeful and curious crowds to see this wilderness man.

John had accepted the hospitality that the desert had offered him. Cruncher of the desert food of bitter locusts sweetened with wild honey, he is satisfied with the food of the poor; clad in rough camel hair, he is dressed like a new Elijah (2 Kgs 1:5-8); tempered in his spirit by solitude, John, in his turn, welcomes the crowds with a bittersweet message in sparse words that are honed to a fine cutting edge for slicing through consciences and exposing them to the truth.

Son of a priest though he may be, John does not deliver his message in the temple or anywhere else in Jerusalem, but on the banks of the Jordan River. At this busy crossing place, so significant in the history of Israel's journey into the Promised Land (cf. Josh 3), John urges the people to cross over into God's forgiveness through the waters of a ritual baptism of repentance. The Baptist invites us, too, to honest mindfulness of the water—not of the Jordan, but of our baptism—and to examination of our consciousness about our fidelity to the Christ into whom we are baptized. Despite the crowds he draws, John's self-evaluation has nothing of self-exaltation. At this high point of his popularity he speaks directly to the people to point them away from himself to the stronger One who is coming, and declares that he is unworthy even to be a slave who would bend down and untie the sandals on the smelling and sweating feet of this Coming One. John resists the temptation of successful ministers: to allow our own popularity to become the main concern of our ministry. When we do this, we are proclaiming what we consider the good news of ourselves, not of Jesus.

In the Puerto Rican city of San Juan, named for John, there stands a huge stone sculpture of the precursor. It is located between the ocean and a main highway of this busy modern city. With the relentlessness of the stone from which he is carved, the Baptist stands with head bent and eyes looking down the highway. But one arm is raised high with a determined finger pointing to heaven. The statue expresses the gospel paradox of John the Baptist, the earthy man of both the wilderness and the Jordan crowds, and the heaven-directed prophet; the paradox of disengagement and engagement—and so the embodiment of the paradox of the Advent season. Day after day, as surely as the waves break on the shore, our lives must be directed to heaven, and yet we must also be involved in the rush and business of daily life. The former is almost certainly the more difficult during these weeks. But it can be done if we opt to deliberately turn off the TV, to unplug our ears from iPods or mobile phones and turn to a few moments of silent reflection about the hopes and promises of Advent. If we plug our listening into some quiet reading of Scripture (*lectio divina*), perhaps a reread of some of the Sunday texts; if we seize a few moments of prayerful repentance or awareness of the presence of God in our traveling companions along our highways or on public transport or while shopping—these are ways in which we can respond to Psalm 85 and "hear what God proclaims."

Focusing the Gospel

Key words and phrases: "Prepare the way of the Lord."

To the point: Mark's gospel begins with John the Baptist, "clothed in camel's hair," inviting the people of the Judean countryside to a baptism of repentance. In so doing, he fulfills Isaiah's prophecy of the "one who cries out in the desert: 'Prepare the way of the Lord.'" This preparation, which John invites us to, seems to be an internal work. By acknowledging our failings and downfalls, we are washed clean by the grace of God and prepared for the animating fire of the Holy Spirit.

Connecting the Gospel

to the first reading: For the people of Israel, Isaiah's prophecy meant something very different when it was first spoken. At the time they were living in exile in Babylon, and the words of the prophet heralded an imminent return to their homeland, when the Lord himself would lead them through the desert back to Jerusalem and their freedom would proclaim the glory of the Lord and God's presence among them.

to experience: For us today, these timeless words refocus our preparations for the fulfillment of God's kingdom, when "the glory of the Lord shall be revealed, / and all people shall see it together." Today's second reading reminds us that the Lord is not "delayed" in his return but rather is patient, "not wishing that any should perish / but that all shall come to repentance." Our lives as Christians follow a pattern of continual conversion. How are you embracing repentance this Advent season?

Connecting the Responsorial Psalm

to the readings: Our psalm response implores the Lord, "[L]et us see your kindness, and grant us your salvation." The kindness of the Lord is on display in each of today's readings. The prophet Isaiah proclaims a forgiving God, ready to save his captive people and return them to their homeland. In the second reading, kindness can be read into the very "delay" that has caused some to doubt Jesus's return. For those who require more time to come to repentance, God has allowed for an extended period of waiting for the day of the Lord. And in the gospel, God, in his goodness, sends a messenger, John the Baptist, to prepare the people to recognize Jesus when he comes to minister among them.

to psalmist preparation: In our own lives, the kindness of God surrounds and sustains us. The kindness of our Creator calls us to live lives that reflect God's glory and proclaim "peace to his people." How have you experienced God's kindness recently?

PROMPTS FOR FAITH-SHARING

In the first reading, Isaiah calls for every valley to be filled in and every mountain to be made low. What mountains and valleys need attention in your own life at this moment?

The psalmist proclaims that in the time of salvation, "Truth shall spring out of the earth." What is the place of truth in the spiritual life?

In the second letter of St. Peter, we are asked to consider "what sort of persons ought you to be, / conducting yourselves in holiness and devotion." What insight do you gain when considering what sort of person God is calling you to be?

John the Baptist tells the gathering crowds that the one who is coming "will baptize you with the Holy Spirit." Where in your life are you in need of the Holy Spirit's animating fire?

CELEBRATION

Model Penitential Act

Presider: In today's gospel, John the Baptist calls the people to repentance so that they might "prepare the way of the Lord." Knowing our own sinfulness, let us also turn our hearts to the Lord and ask for God's pardon and healing . . . *[pause]*

Lord Jesus, you are the shepherd who longs to restore us to your flock: Lord, have mercy.

Christ Jesus, your patience never wavers as you tirelessly seek out the lost: Christ, have mercy.

Lord Jesus, you are the mighty God who desires to lead us to lasting peace: Lord, have mercy.

Homily Points

• At the beginning of our second reading, we are reminded that God does not experience time in the same way that we do, for "with the Lord one day is like a thousand years / and a thousand years like one day." The second letter of St. Peter is believed to be the latest writing in the New Testament, most likely composed in the first half of the second century. At this time, the community of Christians faced new challenges as they dealt with the unrealized expectation that Christ would return in glory within the lifespan of the first apostles. Instead of a sprint, their collective waiting for the fulfillment of God's kingdom had turned into a marathon of unknown duration.

• We, too, find ourselves in a time of waiting. Advent calls to us to renew our own desire and longing for the "coming of the day of God," and each of today's readings offers insight into how we are called to prepare both individually and as a community for this moment.

• The prophet Isaiah invites us to turn our attention to the valleys and mountains that obscure our vision of God's glory. The epistle writer invokes us to "holiness and devotion," while John the Baptist calls us to repentance.

While these readings seem to promote interior reflection, today's psalm turns our attention outward, telling us, "Justice shall walk before [the Lord], / and prepare the way of his steps." After we have done the internal work of acknowledging sin, we are invited to consider how our actions affect the dignity and rights of others. The path of justice is one that leads us to right relationship with God and with all people. In our waiting there is plenty of work to be done.

Model Universal Prayer (Prayer of the Faithful)

Presider: In this time of preparation and anticipation for the coming of God's kingdom in its fullness, let us come before the Lord bringing our needs and the needs of our world.

Response: Lord, hear our prayer.

For bishops, priests, deacons, religious, and lay ministers, may they shepherd the people of God with holiness and devotion . . .

For politicians, diplomats, and peacekeepers, through their work may justice, peace, kindness, and truth flourish throughout the world . . .

For those nearing the end of life, may they be comforted and sustained by a loving community and know deeply the tenderness of God . . .

For all gathered here, formed by the Word of God, may we turn our hearts and minds to the work of preparing the way of the Lord . . .

Presider: God of truth and kindness, with love and mercy you call us forward on the path of conversion. Hear our prayers that we might answer your call with courage and live lives that proclaim your peace to all. We ask this through Christ our Lord. **Amen.**

I will hear what God proclaims;
    the LORD—for he proclaims peace to his
        people.
Near indeed is his salvation to those who
    fear him,
    glory dwelling in our land.

R̶⃗. Lord, let us see your kindness, and
    grant us your salvation.

Kindness and truth shall meet;
    justice and peace shall kiss.
Truth shall spring out of the earth,
    and justice shall look down from heaven.

R̶⃗. Lord, let us see your kindness, and
    grant us your salvation.

The LORD himself will give his benefits;
    our land shall yield its increase.
Justice shall walk before him,
    and prepare the way of his steps.

R̶⃗. Lord, let us see your kindness, and
    grant us your salvation.

SECOND READING
2 Pet 3:8-14

Do not ignore this one fact, beloved,
    that with the Lord one day is like a
        thousand years
    and a thousand years like one day.
The Lord does not delay his promise, as
    some regard "delay,"
    but he is patient with you,
    not wishing that any should perish
    but that all should come to repentance.
But the day of the Lord will come like a
    thief,
    and then the heavens will pass away
        with a mighty roar
    and the elements will be dissolved by
        fire,
    and the earth and everything done on it
        will be found out.

Since everything is to be dissolved in this
    way,
    what sort of persons ought you to be,
    conducting yourselves in holiness and
        devotion,
    waiting for and hastening the coming
        of the day of God,
    because of which the heavens will be
        dissolved in flames
    and the elements melted by fire.
But according to his promise
    we await new heavens and a new earth
    in which righteousness dwells.
Therefore, beloved, since you await these
    things,
    be eager to be found without spot or
        blemish before him, at peace.

About Liturgy

Navigating Connected Seasons: During the Advent season, liturgical and music ministers face the challenge of navigating the inherent connection between Advent and Christmas. Setting aside the concerns mentioned last week—those of how the secular world has, by now, been fully into Christmas mode for a few weeks—there is an additional element to be wary of: celebrating Advent, with its innate character, while being mindful that Advent has a relationship to Christmas, but is not itself Christmas.

We can sometimes fall into the trap of treating liturgical seasons and celebrations as nearly historical reenactments. This is understandable: many feasts are placed on the calendar with a mindfulness of the historical date on which they (might have) happened, and when possible, the Scripture passages bring us to, or at least inform us of, a particular historic time and place for certain celebrations. Yet today, and each and every time we celebrate liturgy, we must do so with the fullness of our salvation story and the paschal mystery in our minds and souls. Advent means so much more when we know the truth of Christmas that follows; Lent similarly is a shadow of itself if there is no knowledge of the Easter resurrection to come.

We obviously avoid some particular music as well as the art and environment of Christmastide during Advent, but that does not mean that some elements of the two seasons might not be the same, or perhaps undergo a transformation on Christmas Eve. For example, we might use the same Mass setting, music for the ordinary of the Mass, for both Advent and Christmas. At Christmas, we might expand the instrumentation of the setting, as described last week. The Advent wreath could be relocated and adorned with lights or white candles, in place of the violet and rose. Some communities also add a fifth candle, in the center of the wreath, symbolic of Christ. Many parishes take up some sort of collection during Advent: items for food pantries; winter jackets, hats, and gloves; or presents for area organizations that serve underprivileged youth. Advent "Giving Trees" are one way to do this: adorn a tree, in a lobby or gathering space, with gift tags that list special requests or items to donate. As the season progresses, tags are removed, and donations begin to grow. By Christmas, lights can be added to the tree and it can become a powerful symbol of your community's witness to celebrating fully Christ's birth and presence in the world today.

About Music

A Common Repertoire: Last week, this space suggested using the same hymn at all seasonal liturgies to help delineate the season of Advent. This can be a powerful technique, if a piece of music is chosen well and, when possible, connects to the art and environment of the season and other notable elements of the liturgy.

Taking this approach would also allow a bit more rehearsal time for choirs and ensembles to prepare for Christmastide during this busy time of year. And it might be easier on your assembly to sing the music of this season for these four weeks (and then never again, at least not until next Advent).

There is such a richness, however, in the Advent repertoire, and repeating one hymn for several weeks would mean neglecting a few others. This may be a trade-off we are not willing to make. Today's readings especially are likely inspiration for many of our favorite hymns; which one would we be willing to omit?

GOSPEL ACCLAMATION
cf. Luke 1:28

℟. Alleluia, alleluia.
Hail, Mary, full of grace, the Lord is with you;
blessed are you among women.
℟. Alleluia, alleluia.

Gospel

Luke 1:26-38; L689

The angel Gabriel was sent from God
  to a town of Galilee called Nazareth,
  to a virgin betrothed to a man named
    Joseph,
  of the house of David,
  and the virgin's name was Mary.
And coming to her, he said,
  "Hail, full of grace! The Lord is with
    you."
But she was greatly troubled at what
    was said
  and pondered what sort of greeting
    this might be.
Then the angel said to her,
  "Do not be afraid, Mary,
  for you have found favor with God.
Behold, you will conceive in your womb
    and bear a son,
  and you shall name him Jesus.

Continued in Appendix A, p. 259.

See Appendix A, p. 259 for the other readings.

Reflecting on the Gospel

The feast of the Immaculate Conception developed in the history and life of the church, not simply from Scripture, but from the reflections of the faithful in the church on Mary and her role in salvation history. It was the lived faith of the church that led to the understanding of the immaculate conception of Mary and, secondarily, the writings of theologians reflecting on Scripture and the tradition of the church. These reflections took place over many centuries before being promulgated as a doctrine of the church. The doctrine arose from this lived faith, already accepted within the church by numerous faithful, and contemplation of the requisite holiness necessary for the task to which Mary had been chosen, her sinlessness, and the challenge her sinlessness posed to the doctrine on original sin.

The key line perhaps in all of Scripture regarding Mary's unique status is in Luke 1:28, in which the Douay-Rheims translates Gabriel's greeting to Mary as "Hail, full of grace, the Lord is with thee." Questions about the traditional rendering of this verse abound, as seen in the NRSV translation, "Greetings, favored one! The Lord is with you." While I think the NRSV translation is weak—does Luke wish to say only that Mary had gained favor?—it raises issues as to how much theological weight should be placed on a simple Greek perfect participle.

The traditional rendering of this perfect participle has understood that Mary had already been graced, that is, the angel Gabriel is acknowledging something about Mary's unique nature. The word "grace" should appear in the translation, but it is still fair to ask, what does "full of grace" mean? It does not clearly indicate on its own and cannot be pressed to indicate on its own linguistically, that Mary was born free of the stain of original sin.

But it is precisely here where the church—reflecting on the theological reality of Mary expressed by the relevant biblical passages, a significant noncanonical text of the early church, the teachings of the ecumenical council at Ephesus (431) that Mary was the *theotokos*, and the theological developments throughout ecclesiastical history—claims the authority to pronounce on the reality of Mary's sinlessness. The teaching of Mary's immaculate conception developed in the living tradition of the church as it reflected on the holiness necessary for the task to which she had been called and the Scriptures that occasioned this reflection. We should continue to reflect on Mary's holiness, too, for it was through her being prepared to receive the Son of God that the Second Person of the Trinity became incarnate. In order for her to do so it was necessary that she be "full of grace," free from all stain of sin, open to be the handmaiden of the Word so that all the world could encounter the Word in the flesh.

Focusing the Gospel
Key words and phrases: "The Lord is with you."

To the point: Some seven hundred years before Gabriel's visit to Mary, Isaiah prophesied, "[T]he young woman, pregnant and about to bear a son, shall name him Emmanuel" (Isa 7:14; NABRE). This name (and prophecy) is repeated in the Gospel of Matthew's story of Jesus's nativity where the evangelist cites Jesus as the fulfillment of Isaiah's words, adding in the meaning of the name Emmanuel as "God is with us" (Matt 1:23; NABRE). Gabriel greets Mary in a similar way, hailing her as "full of grace! The Lord is with you!" Within Mary, God finds the perfect human partner in bringing about his plan of redemption, in which God himself takes on human flesh to truly be "God with us" in the person of Jesus.

Model Penitential Act

Presider: In today's first reading, ashamed and fearful, Adam attempts to hide from God. For the ways sin and shame have touched our own lives, let us turn to God for healing and mercy . . . *[pause]*

Lord Jesus, in you we were chosen by God before the foundation of the world: Lord, have mercy.

Christ Jesus, through you we have been adopted as God's own sons and daughters: Christ, have mercy.

Lord Jesus, with you we are called to holiness and everlasting life: Lord, have mercy.

Model Universal Prayer (Prayer of the Faithful)

Presider: On this feast of the Immaculate Conception, let us, together with our Blessed Mother, place all of our needs before the Lord, knowing that with God nothing is impossible.

Response: Lord, hear our prayer.

For the church, in all it does may it stand with the vulnerable, the weak, and the disenfranchised . . .

For the poor throughout the world, may they receive access to education, medical care, and clean water . . .

For those who are burdened with mental and spiritual illness, may they find solace and peace in God's unfailing love and mercy . . .

For all gathered here, through the intercession of Mary may we grow in holiness each day . . .

Presider: God of mercy and love, in Mary you have given us a model of discipleship and grace. Hear our prayers, that all we do might further your dream of peace and joy for all people and all nations. We ask this through Christ our Lord. **Amen.**

About Liturgy

Choosing the Right Words: When we are speaking about the liturgy, we should always take care to choose just the right words. Mark Twain once offered this advice: "The difference between the almost right word and the right word is really a large matter—'tis the difference between the lightning-bug and the lightning."

Regarding the Solemnity of the Immaculate Conception, or many other dates of the liturgical calendar, we might be asked by a parishioner, "Is *such and such* a holy day?" In most cases, we know what the questioner is really asking: is there an obligation coming up to attend a midweek Mass? The question is understandable, because it can all get confusing very quickly.

In any case, "Is *such and such* a holy day?" while being the wrong question, can still present a brief moment of catechesis for us to share. "Immaculate Conception is indeed a holy day every year," one might respond, "and this year it does carry the obligation to attend Mass." It's a longer answer than the asker expects to hear, but it may also make that person think more deeply about the liturgical calendar and the practice of his or her faith.

COLLECT

Let us pray.

Pause for silent prayer

O God, who by the Immaculate Conception of
   the Blessed Virgin
prepared a worthy dwelling for your Son,
grant, we pray,
that, as you preserved her from every stain
by virtue of the Death of your Son, which you
   foresaw,
so, through her intercession,
we, too, may be cleansed and admitted to your
   presence.
Through our Lord Jesus Christ, your Son,
who lives and reigns with you in the unity of
   the Holy Spirit,
one God, for ever and ever. **Amen.**

FOR REFLECTION

• Has there been a time in your life when, like Adam, you were tempted to hide from God out of fear or shame?

• The psalmist calls us to "[s]ing to the Lord a new song." Over the past year, where have you experienced "newness" in your relationship with God?

• Where in your life are you in need of the angel's words to Mary, "Do not be afraid"?

Homily Points

• In Advent we enter into a time of waiting and preparation, both for the feast of Christmas and for the eventual return of Christ in glory. We can look to Mary as a model for our waiting and our preparation. Though this miraculous pregnancy will disrupt her life in unknown ways, she trusts in God's providence and agrees to bear the one who will be "called holy, the Son of God."

• In Raymond Brown's *A Coming Christ in Advent,* the Scripture scholar writes of Mary's fiat: "Her readiness is possible for her because by God's grace she has said yes to Him before. Thus Mary's discipleship does not exhibit conversion but consistency." In our own waiting and preparation, let us practice this same consistency, saying yes to God in small, ordinary ways that will prepare us to welcome Christ fully.

SPIRITUALITY

GOSPEL ACCLAMATION
Isa 61:1 (cited in Luke 4:18)

R⁊. Alleluia, alleluia.
The Spirit of the Lord is upon me,
because he has anointed me
to bring glad tidings to the poor.
R⁊. Alleluia, alleluia.

Gospel   John 1:6-8, 19-28; L8B

A man named John was sent from God.
He came for testimony, to testify to the
    light,
    so that all might believe through him.
He was not the light,
    but came to testify to the light.

And this is the testimony of John.
When the Jews from Jerusalem sent priests
        and Levites to him
    to ask him, "Who are you?"
    he admitted and did not deny it,
    but admitted, "I am not the Christ."
So they asked him,
    "What are you then? Are you Elijah?"
And he said, "I am not."
"Are you the Prophet?"
He answered, "No."
So they said to him,
    "Who are you, so we can give an answer
        to those who sent us?
What do you have to say for yourself?"
He said:
    "I am *the voice of one crying out in the
        desert,*
    'make straight the way of the Lord,'
    as Isaiah the prophet said."
Some Pharisees were also sent.
They asked him,
    "Why then do you baptize
    if you are not the Christ or Elijah or the
        Prophet?"
John answered them,
    "I baptize with water;
    but there is one among you whom you do
        not recognize,
    the one who is coming after me,
    whose sandal strap I am not worthy to
        untie."
This happened in Bethany across the Jordan,
    where John was baptizing.

Reflecting on the Gospel

Christians read the Old Testament today, understandably, in light of Christ's fulfillment of the promises and prophecies found there. It is a simple thing to do, since the early church read the Old Testament in the context of Jesus's incarnation and teaching and the experience of Easter, and then formalized these readings and understandings in the texts of the New Testament.

But what if you were a Jew in the first century, eagerly hoping for the Messiah, a successor to David? These hopes, shared with the whole nation, had been growing since the return from Babylonian exile. As you searched through the panoply of prophecies, you began to wonder, when will these hopes be fulfilled? Who do you look for and where do you start looking? It would be like reading a mystery novel, knowing every clue, studying every sign, but seeing only in retrospect how the whole fits together.

Isaiah 61, for instance, is most often dated to the period just after the return from Babylonian exile, and the author of the passage is generally considered to be the speaker in the text. This prophetic passage emerged, therefore, some five centuries before the birth of Christ. In it the speaker says, "The spirit of the Lord GOD is upon me, / because the LORD has anointed me; / he has sent me to bring glad tidings to the poor, / to heal the brokenhearted, / to proclaim liberty to the captives / and release to the prisoners." In its original historical context and literal meaning, the author speaks of the conditions that the returning Babylonian exiles found, especially when he promises that those returning exiles "shall rebuild the ancient ruins, / the former wastes they shall raise up / And restore the desolate cities, / devastations of generation upon generation" (v. 4; NABRE). It also seems that the postexilic prophet is speaking of his own role in the restoration of Jerusalem when he says, "The spirit of the Lord GOD is upon me."

Yet there is also an eschatological edge to the hopes imagined, especially in the proclamation of "a year of favor from the LORD," an event still to come. Christians see the spiritual fulfillment of these proclamations in the person and ministry of Jesus, centuries after they were uttered. The reason is simple: Jesus himself read this passage, according to Luke 4, in the synagogue in Nazareth.

There Jesus says of the Isaian passage, "Today this scripture passage is fulfilled in your hearing" (Luke 4:21; NABRE). This we might identify with what Catholic biblical scholarship has called the *sensus plenior*, or "fuller sense," since it does not obviate the original historical meaning and context but points to a fulfillment of which the original human author was unaware.

This is why the questioning of John the Baptist in today's gospel reading by some representatives of the Pharisees makes historical and theological sense. The Pharisees, like most Jews of this period, were awaiting the Messiah. Because of the attractiveness of John's prophetic message of repentance to the people, and his popularity, he was someone who had to be examined. They asked, "Who are you?" In response, John confesses that he is not the Messiah, not Elijah, not the prophet and cites Isaiah 40:3, a passage dated to the end of the Babylonian exile: "I am *the voice of one crying out in the desert, / 'make straight the way of the Lord.'"* John identifies himself not as the Messiah, but as the fulfillment of long-ago prophecies, as the one who prepares the way for the coming Messiah.

But the questions still remained, even for John. Who ever thought that it would happen through a young, unmarried woman, that God would look with favor "upon his lowly servant," Mary? God asks that as we wait for fulfillment, we be prepared for God to do new things, unexpected things, and be ready for the unlikeliest of answers.

Focusing the Gospel

Key words and phrases: "[T]here is one among you whom you do not recognize."

To the point: Again, in today's gospel, we hear the preaching of John the Baptist, this time from John's gospel. When the priests and Levites question John about his identity, he points instead to one who is coming after him, one whom they "do not recognize." As mysterious as these words must have been for the people who first heard them, they also hold a mystery for us. Near the end of Matthew's gospel, Jesus offers a parable about the end of time when he will confront his followers, telling them, "[W]hat you did not do for one of these least ones, you did not do for me" (25:45; NABRE). How is Christ in our midst, right here, right now, and we do not recognize him?

Connecting the Gospel

to the first reading: In John the Baptist we find the ultimate prophet. He points to Jesus in all that he does. The first reading from Isaiah describes what a prophet truly is: one who has been anointed by God to proclaim "glad tidings to the poor," healing to the brokenhearted, and freedom to those imprisoned.

to experience: In baptism we have each been anointed as "priest, prophet, and king." The mantle of proclaiming "glad tidings" to those beaten down by life has been passed to us. How do the words you speak and the life you lead bring the good news of Jesus to others?

Connecting the Responsorial Psalm

to the readings: For Gaudete (Latin for "Rejoice") Sunday, our "psalm" comes from Mary's own song of praise to her Creator, the *Magnificat.* In the first reading, the responsorial psalm, and the second reading we find today's theme of joy expounded upon. The prophet Isaiah proclaims, "I rejoice heartily in the Lord, / in my God is the joy of my soul." Mary responds to Elizabeth's claim that Mary herself is "blessed" by singing out the source of all blessing: "My soul proclaims the greatness of the Lord; / my spirit rejoices in God my savior." And St. Paul exhorts the Thessalonians to "[r]ejoice always." Our readings leave no doubt that joy is a central part of any Christian's life and not an optional attitude to be adopted only when we are naturally inclined to happiness.

to psalmist preparation: As you prepare to lead the assembly in praying Mary's treasured words, pause to consider the place of joy in your own faith journey. How do you strive to embody this joy in your ministry and in your daily life?

PROMPTS FOR FAITH-SHARING

The prophet Isaiah proclaims, "I rejoice heartily in the Lord." How do you experience God as "the joy of [your] soul"?

Isaiah prophesies that just as "the earth brings forth its plants," God will "make justice and praise / spring up before all nations." Where do you see justice and peace growing in the world?

In his letter to the Thessalonians, St. Paul writes, "[T]he one who calls you is faithful." When was a time in your life that you experienced deeply the faithfulness of God?

In the gospel, John the Baptist is described as one who came to "testify to the light." How does the way you live your life testify to the light of Christ?

Model Penitential Act

Presider: On this Third Sunday of Advent, we hear the call to "rejoice always." For the ways that our spirits have grown weary and for the sorrows that keep us from joy, let us turn to the Lord for healing and mercy . . . *[pause]*

Lord Jesus, you are the light that illuminates all darkness: Lord, have mercy.

Christ Jesus, you heal the brokenhearted: Christ, have mercy.

Lord Jesus, you call us to fullness of life: Lord, have mercy.

Homily Points

• Today's gospel tells us that John the Baptist was born into the world for a singular purpose, "to testify to the light." And not just any light, but "the light of the human race" (John 1:4; NABRE), "the light [that] shines in the darkness," that the darkness can never overpower (1:5). One of the reasons the feast of Christmas was originally placed on December 25 was to highlight the symbolism of celebrating the birth of the one who proclaimed himself "the light of the world" (John 8:12) during the darkest days of the Northern Hemisphere's winter.

• Whether we find ourselves in the Northern or Southern Hemisphere on this Gaudete Sunday, there is plenty of darkness to be encountered: poverty, war, violence, hatred, greed, and all manners of evil. When we turn our gaze to our own suffering and that of others, it is easy to become discouraged. How can any light possibly brighten this darkness?

• As Christians, we could say that we have all been born into the world with the same vocation as John the Baptist: to testify to the light, to be hope in the world by fully living our belief in and relationship with Jesus Christ. This is the source of our gladness, and the reason St. Paul urges all of us to "[r]ejoice always." As the feast of Christ's nativity draws nearer, we pause to ask ourselves, How do we live our vocation to joy? How are we being called, at this moment in human history, to testify to the light that no darkness can overcome?

Model Universal Prayer (Prayer of the Faithful)

Presider: As we draw closer to the feast of Christmas when we celebrate the light of Christ being born into the world, let us lift up to God all the places of darkness in our own lives and in our world. With hope and joy, let us bring our needs before the Lord.

Response: Lord, hear our prayer.

For all who preach the gospel, may their words bring glad tidings to the poor, heal the brokenhearted, and proclaim liberty to captives . . .

For leaders of nations, in their policies and decisions may they work tirelessly to ensure support and care for the hungry, homeless, and ailing . . .

For all those who grieve, may they know the tender compassion of God and find joy and peace in the midst of sorrow . . .

For all gathered in this place, having encountered the light of Christ in word and sacrament, may we in turn bring this light to others . . .

Presider: God of joy, in times of darkness, grief, and sorrow, you send us the light of your mercy and compassion. Hear our prayers that all of creation might be enlightened by your love and our world transformed by your justice. We ask this through Christ our Lord. **Amen.**

COLLECT

Let us pray.

Pause for silent prayer

O God, who see how your people
faithfully await the feast of the Lord's
    Nativity,
enable us, we pray,
to attain the joys of so great a salvation
and to celebrate them always
with solemn worship and glad rejoicing.
Through our Lord Jesus Christ, your Son,
who lives and reigns with you in the unity
    of the Holy Spirit,
one God, for ever and ever. **Amen.**

FIRST READING

Isa 61:1-2a, 10-11

The spirit of the Lord GOD is upon me,
    because the LORD has anointed me;
he has sent me to bring glad tidings to the
        poor,
    to heal the brokenhearted,
to proclaim liberty to the captives
    and release to the prisoners,
to announce a year of favor from the LORD
    and a day of vindication by our God.

I rejoice heartily in the LORD,
    in my God is the joy of my soul;
for he has clothed me with a robe of
        salvation
    and wrapped me in a mantle of justice,
like a bridegroom adorned with a diadem,
    like a bride bedecked with her jewels.
As the earth brings forth its plants,
    and a garden makes its growth spring
        up,
so will the Lord GOD make justice and
        praise
    spring up before all the nations.

RESPONSORIAL PSALM
Luke 1:46-48, 49-50, 53-54

R̂. (Isa 61:10b) My soul rejoices in my God.

My soul proclaims the greatness of the
    Lord;
    my spirit rejoices in God my Savior,
for he has looked upon his lowly servant.
    From this day all generations will call
        me blessed:

R̂. My soul rejoices in my God.

The Almighty has done great things for
    me,
    and holy is his Name.
He has mercy on those who fear him
    in every generation.

R̂. My soul rejoices in my God.

He has filled the hungry with good things,
    and the rich he has sent away empty.
He has come to the help of his servant
    Israel
    for he has remembered his promise of
        mercy.

R̂. My soul rejoices in my God.

SECOND READING
1 Thess 5:16-24

Brothers and sisters:
Rejoice always. Pray without ceasing.
In all circumstances give thanks,
    for this is the will of God for you in
        Christ Jesus.
Do not quench the Spirit.
Do not despise prophetic utterances.
Test everything; retain what is good.
Refrain from every kind of evil.

May the God of peace make you perfectly
    holy
    and may you entirely, spirit, soul, and
        body,
    be preserved blameless for the coming
        of our Lord Jesus Christ.
The one who calls you is faithful,
    and he will also accomplish it.

About Liturgy

A Joyful Paradox: Our attention this Advent, beginning last week and continuing into this week, turns to John the Baptist. This Sunday is also called "Gaudete Sunday"—or "Rejoice Sunday"—acknowledging the prescribed entrance antiphon of the day, with its text from the Epistle to Philemon: "Rejoice in the Lord always; again I say, rejoice. / Indeed, the Lord is near." The collect of the liturgy also refers to "the joys of so great a salvation," and the Old Testament, the Psalm, and the epistle readings each call us to rejoicing as well. The rose candle on the wreath, lighter and perhaps cheerier than the violet ones, is lit today, and the presider may wear rose-colored vestments if desired.

Yet John the Baptist is not a figure one might describe, generally, as cheerful or joyful. There is a natural tension here: the precursor of the Messiah, a man who wore burlap, ate insects, and with fiery language rebuked Pharisees, is the dominant figure on a weekend of joy and glad tidings. The gospel here, at first hearing, seems at best to be a mismatch.

On closer inspection though, our faith, and therefore our celebrations of it, are filled with paradox. Christian paradox is perhaps best expressed in mystery—God's truth beyond all human understanding. Said more simply, it is the word "and." In our Scriptures, these paradoxes abound: both greatness and lowliness, strength and weakness, light and darkness, first and last, humanity and divinity, life and death, one and many. One does not replace the other, nor does one become the other; both exist side by side, in mystery—the paschal mystery.

In the liturgy, we've already explored how patient and prayerful silence might be the most intensely active thing one can do this season. Today, John the Baptist, while decidedly unjoyful, calls us to a most joyful pursuit: following the one true light in the darkness, which the darkness could not overcome.

About the Altar (Part I)

A Place of Unity: Built of Living Stones tells us this about the altar: "At the Eucharist, the liturgical assembly celebrates the ritual sacrificial meal that recalls and makes present Christ's life, death and resurrection, proclaiming "the death of the Lord until he comes." The altar is "the center of thanksgiving that the Eucharist accomplishes" and the point around which the other rites are in some manner arrayed" (BLS 56).

The altar, then, embodies the whole of the mystery and paradox that is the liturgical celebration of our faith: the Eucharist is both sacrifice and meal; the sacrificial altar is simultaneously a dinner table and, in the celebration of Eucharist, is past, present, and future in a single moment. It is the place where we, though many, are all one in Christ Jesus.

Further, not only is the altar Christ's cross on Calvary, the church teaches us that it is Christ himself (BLS 56). This is why we take care to adorn the altar carefully and appropriately, and offer it reverence, especially in the liturgy itself.

About Music

Hymns of Dynamic Joy: There are many pieces that can reinforce the words and activity of John the Baptist from the gospel reading. For a contemporary feel, look to Curtis Stephan's "Ready the Way" (OCP), but make sure not to take the piece at too brisk a tempo! Ed Bolduc's "Awake to the Day" (World Library Publications [WLP]) also has a contemporary feel with a text calling to mind the season's urgings to stay awake and prepare.

DECEMBER 13, 2020
THIRD SUNDAY OF ADVENT

SPIRITUALITY

GOSPEL ACCLAMATION
Luke 1:38

℟. Alleluia, alleluia.
Behold, I am the handmaid of the Lord.
May it be done to me according to your word.
℟. Alleluia, alleluia.

Gospel   Luke 1:26-38; L11B

The angel Gabriel was sent from God
   to a town of Galilee called Nazareth,
   to a virgin betrothed to a man named
      Joseph,
   of the house of David,
   and the virgin's name was Mary.
And coming to her, he said,
   "Hail, full of grace! The Lord is with you."
But she was greatly troubled at what was
      said
   and pondered what sort of greeting this
      might be.
Then the angel said to her,
   "Do not be afraid, Mary,
   for you have found favor with God.

"Behold, you will conceive in your womb
      and bear a son,
   and you shall name him Jesus.
He will be great and will be called Son of
      the Most High,
   and the Lord God will give him the throne
      of David his father,
   and he will rule over the house of Jacob
      forever,
   and of his kingdom there will be no end."
But Mary said to the angel,
   "How can this be,
   since I have no relations with a man?"
And the angel said to her in reply,
   "The Holy Spirit will come upon you,
   and the power of the Most High will
      overshadow you.
Therefore the child to be born
   will be called holy, the Son of God.
And behold, Elizabeth, your relative,
   has also conceived a son in her old age,
   and this is the sixth month for her who
      was called barren;
   for nothing will be impossible for God."
Mary said, "Behold, I am the handmaid of
      the Lord.
May it be done to me according to your word."
Then the angel departed from her.

Reflecting on the Gospel

The heavens have been torn open; God has come down, not with mountain quaking and fire burning, but in the gentle descent of the Spirit who broods over the womb of Mary of Nazareth. And as at the first creation life was called forth, so now the first cell of the new creation is conceived. The Shekinah, the cloud of the presence of the Most High, overshadows Mary (cf. Exod 40:35), and the Son of God is at home among us. During Advent the Liturgy of the Word tells us that we bump into God in strange places: in the poor, in crowds, and, strangest of all, in the obscure village of Nazareth and one of its backwater young women. Mary is a powerless female in a world ruled by males; poor, in a highly stratified society; found to be pregnant before she cohabits with her husband, and so obviously not carrying his child to validate her existence. That she would have "found favor with God" is hugely surprising, especially to Mary!

The Lukan biblical imagination has captured the imagination of artists down through the centuries. With their own prophetic insight, they have set the extraordinary faith of Mary among familiar things: a half-read book, a meal in preparation, a door opened on children and animals at play, people passing by. One of the more unusual depictions is that by Henry Ossawa Tanner, an African American painter (1859–1937). In a Middle Eastern-style bedroom, Mary sits enfolded in the heavy drapes of bedclothes and her own robe, her gaze attentive. All is simplicity, not luxury, and there is no winged angel. What Mary's gaze is fixed on is a tall, thin pillar of white cloud at the end of her bed. Perhaps Tanner is remembering the presence of God, the "angel" of Exodus 14:19, described as a cloud, that led the Israelites into their future, would lead Mary into hers, and will lead us through the ordinary and familiar events and places where God is present—if we will only recognize him and respond with our own, "Behold, I am the handmaid of the Lord. May it be done to me according to your word."

Every Advent we are challenged to have the attentiveness of Mary to the flutter of Christ-life that stirs in the womb of our complacency. So often our world seems starved of stars; and so often we watch or participate in rituals of mourning for acts of terrorism, natural disaster, the local tragedies of road deaths, or other dark events. Usually in these rituals there are candles: small pieces of self-consuming wax and flame that say light has more right to exist in our world than darkness. This is the message, too, of our Advent wreath as we light the last of its four candles. But those candles, like all ritual candles, will burn out. It is up to us, disciples of the Light of the World, to catch fire from Christ's mystery and bring something of this fire and light into our own lives and, especially, into the lives of those for whom Christmas may not be a feast of joy but a time of darkness that stirs painful memories of those with whom they can no longer celebrate because of death, separation, divorce, family quarrels. For the friendless, the homeless, the abused, Christmas may arouse bitter comparisons and regrets. The fire we catch from Christ, our readiness to be consumed like him in the flame of loving service of our sisters and brothers, may be as simple a gift as a visit, a letter, a phone call, an invitation to a meal, a present on the parish "Giving Tree." But it will mean that, together, we will truly celebrate something of a "Happy Christmas."

Focusing the Gospel
Key words and phrases: "[O]f his kingdom there will be no end."

To the point: Throughout the gospels, Jesus preaches the imminence of the kingdom of God and calls for those "with ears to hear" to "repent and believe." We could say the first person to hear of and draw near to this kingdom is Mary. Gabriel tells her that the child she will bear "will be called holy, the Son of God." In Mary's reliance and trust in God's word, the kingdom takes root in her, just as it wishes to take root in each of us.

Connecting the Gospel
to the first reading: In the first reading, God chastises David, the king, for believing it is up to him to build a house for God to dwell in. And yet, in the gospel, we find God gladly choosing to make a home in Mary, the young woman from Nazareth. This is the kind of dwelling that God desires—not one made of stone, brick, or marble, but within the hearts of his people.

to experience: Mary's words of assent, "May it be done to me according to your word," offer us a challenging model of trust and collaboration with God. Mary's "yes" to God's will in her life changes everything, not only for her, but within the history of salvation. Each day we are invited to cooperate in God's desire to bring us to fullness of life. How will we answer this invitation today?

Connecting the Responsorial Psalm
to the readings: Today's psalm seems to convey joy, praise, and thanksgiving, so it might be surprising to discover it is titled as "[a] Lament over God's Promise to David" in the New American Bible Revised Edition. Many verses after the ones proclaimed today found the reason for lamentation: "But now you have rejected and spurned, / been enraged at your anointed . . . You have exalted the right hand of his foes, / have gladdened all his enemies" (vv. 39, 43; NABRE). It is noteworthy that the words of praise and trust that we pray today were first sung in the context of defeat rather than victory. It is one thing to praise God in times of peace and abundance, and quite another to say, "For ever I will sing the goodness of the Lord" when facing ruin and uncertainty. Perhaps this is the only kind of faith strong enough to span from one generation to another.

to psalmist preparation: In preparing to cantor today's psalm, how does it change your understanding of the words to know that it was first sung in a time of sorrow and looming despair? Where, within your community or within the wider world, is the hope of the psalmist most needed?

PROMPTS FOR FAITH-SHARING

In the first reading God promises David, "Your house and your kingdom shall endure forever." How do you see God's hand at work building up your family throughout past generations and up to this point?

Our psalm response is, "For ever I will sing the goodness of the Lord." How are you singing God's goodness in your life at this moment?

In his letter to the Romans, St. Paul names God as "him who can strengthen you." Which events, hardships, or trials might God be calling you to turn over to his strengthening power?

Gabriel greets Mary, "Hail, full of grace! The Lord is with you." What is your reaction if you consider these words as directed toward you?

CELEBRATION

Model Penitential Act

Presider: Mary responds to Gabriel's proclamation that she will become the mother of Jesus, with the words, "May it be done to me according to your word." For the times we have not embraced the word of God in our own lives, let us ask for pardon and mercy . . . *[pause]*

Lord Jesus, you are the Son of the Most High whose kingdom is everlasting: Lord, have mercy.

Christ Jesus, true God and true man, you intercede for us at the right hand of the Father: Christ, have mercy.

Lord Jesus, son of the humble handmaid, you came to seek the lost: Lord, have mercy.

Homily Points

• Although Mary was conceived and lived without sin, as a fully human member of the Body of Christ, she experienced human emotions and difficulties. Before she assents to Gabriel's proclamation that she will become the mother to God's own son, Mary is said to be "troubled" and questions how this event can possibly come to be. Gabriel responds, "Do not be afraid . . . for nothing will be impossible for God." As disciples of Christ and spiritual children of Mary, we are called to take these words to heart in our own lives.

• Being faithful to God's call will very likely lead us to places of discomfort, hardship, and even fear. In his book *Ave Maria,* Pope Francis writes, "If a young man of today, a young woman of today, hears a special call from the Lord and is not afraid, that means something is missing. However, when along with enthusiasm for that call there is also the experience of fear, then we can move forward, because God calls us to great things."

• In the words of Gabriel we see a pattern for God's action and invitation in human lives. God desires to bring us to a fullness of life beyond our wildest imaginings. To become his collaborators, like Mary, we must both believe in the God of possibilities and be willing to face our fears. Today, as we ponder the message spoken to a young Jewish woman nearly two thousand years ago, we might ask, In our own lives of faith do we dare respond to God's invitation by echoing Mary's words of courage and trust, "[B]e it done to me according to your word"?

Model Universal Prayer (Prayer of the Faithful)

Presider: Gabriel tells Mary, "Do not be afraid, for you have found favor with God." With trust in our God's never-ending love and merciful compassion, let us place our needs before him.

Response: Lord, hear our prayer.

For the church throughout the world, may it grow in fidelity to God's will, adopting the prayer of Mary, "May it be done according to your word" . . .

For those who hold elected office, with humility and integrity may they listen to the people they serve while also caring for society's most vulnerable members . . .

For all women who are anticipating the birth of a child and especially for those in crisis and high-risk pregnancies, may they receive abundant support . . .

For all gathered here, may our faith be strengthened as we contemplate the words of the angel Gabriel, "[F]or nothing will be impossible for God" . . .

Presider: God of creation, you called the Virgin Mary to be the mother of your son and our mother. Hear our prayer that in following her example we might also let our lives be instruments of your grace. We ask this through Christ our Lord. **Amen.**

COLLECT

Let us pray.

Pause for silent prayer

Pour forth, we beseech you, O Lord,
your grace into our hearts,
that we, to whom the Incarnation of Christ your Son
was made known by the message of an Angel,
may by his Passion and Cross
be brought to the glory of his Resurrection.
Who lives and reigns with you in the unity of the Holy Spirit,
one God, for ever and ever. **Amen.**

FIRST READING
2 Sam 7:1-5, 8b-12, 14a, 16

When King David was settled in his palace,
    and the LORD had given him rest from his enemies on every side,
    he said to Nathan the prophet,
    "Here I am living in a house of cedar,
    while the ark of God dwells in a tent!"
Nathan answered the king,
    "Go, do whatever you have in mind,
    for the LORD is with you."
But that night the LORD spoke to Nathan and said:
    "Go, tell my servant David, 'Thus says the LORD:
    Should you build me a house to dwell in?'

"'It was I who took you from the pasture
    and from the care of the flock
    to be commander of my people Israel.
I have been with you wherever you went,
    and I have destroyed all your enemies before you.
And I will make you famous like the great ones of the earth.
I will fix a place for my people Israel;
    I will plant them so that they may dwell in their place
    without further disturbance.
Neither shall the wicked continue to afflict them as they did of old,
    since the time I first appointed judges over my people Israel.
I will give you rest from all your enemies.
The LORD also reveals to you
    that he will establish a house for you.
And when your time comes and you rest with your ancestors,
    I will raise up your heir after you,
    sprung from your loins,
    and I will make his kingdom firm.

I will be a father to him,
   and he shall be a son to me.
Your house and your kingdom shall
   endure forever before me;
   your throne shall stand firm forever.'"

RESPONSORIAL PSALM
Ps 89:2-3, 4-5, 27, 29

R̞. (2a) For ever I will sing the goodness of
   the Lord.

The promises of the LORD I will sing
   forever;
   through all generations my mouth shall
      proclaim your faithfulness.
For you have said, "My kindness is
   established forever";
   in heaven you have confirmed your
      faithfulness.

R̞. For ever I will sing the goodness of the
   Lord.

"I have made a covenant with my chosen
   one,
   I have sworn to David my servant:
forever will I confirm your posterity
   and establish your throne for all
      generations."

R̞. For ever I will sing the goodness of the
   Lord.

"He shall say of me, 'You are my father,
   my God, the rock, my savior.'
Forever I will maintain my kindness
   toward him,
   and my covenant with him stands firm."

R̞. For ever I will sing the goodness of the
   Lord.

SECOND READING
Rom 16:25-27

Brothers and sisters:
To him who can strengthen you,
   according to my gospel and the
      proclamation of Jesus Christ,
   according to the revelation of the
      mystery kept secret for long ages
but now manifested through the
   prophetic writings and,
   according to the command of the
      eternal God,
   made known to all nations to bring
      about the obedience of faith,
to the only wise God, through Jesus
   Christ
be glory forever and ever. Amen.

About Liturgy

Mary as Model: The end of the Advent season always brings the faithful to reflect on Mary and her role in the birth of Christ and our salvation. In this year's gospel passage, Mary is described as someone who, when visited by the angel Gabriel, is troubled and pensive, who has questions about what she is being told, and who, after consideration, is able to say "Yes" to the Lord's calling to her and her life.

Mary is often called "the first disciple" because of her relationship to Christ, her son. The words "disciple" and "discipline" have the same etymological root, referring to someone who learns, who studies, who follows a certain teacher or set of teachings. It seems that even before Mary knew of her calling to become the mother of God incarnate, she must have already learned her faith well: from her parents, from rabbis and other holy men and women, and perhaps even from the ritual practices of her faith.

Liturgy is meant to be catechetical, if not explicitly, but that is only half the work of forming disciples. To fully be a disciple, one must not be solely a student but be in relationship with the teacher. Our liturgies fall short if they—through the prescribed texts, through the music, and through the preaching—strive only to be catechetical and do not give space for the faithful, like Mary, to at times be troubled and pensive, and to even have questions about what the liturgy is expressing of our shared faith. If we do not allow room for such experiences, we can't truly expect people to be or become the fullest expression of what it means to be a disciple. We will explore these themes in more detail, after Christmastide.

About Music

Components of Rehearsals: As the number of days until Christmas grow shorter and shorter, choir directors may become more and more tempted to utilize every last second of rehearsal time refining the music, making sure each chord is in tune, that each meaningful text is correctly and carefully sung, and that everyone knows precisely what to wear, which chair to sit in, and what time to arrive on Christmas Eve. While these are truly important details, they should never take the place of three important elements of every choir rehearsal, even at the busiest times of year. Here are those three elements:

1. Warm-up time—This time at the beginning of rehearsal is important for at least a couple reasons. Good choir directors know they can teach practical skills during warm-ups that become habitual, saving time elsewhere in rehearsals. Also, this time provides a necessary transition for choir members as they leave the concerns of their daily lives and move into a period of learning and, hopefully, prayer.

2. Prayer—Time should be set aside for prayer, usually at the beginning or end of the rehearsal. Prayer helps frame the work of the evening and helps those praying to be formed into a small faith community.

3. Theological reflection—Singers need breaks at times during rehearsals, and it's important, too, to keep voices focused on the words they are singing. When we're busy focusing on little details, we can overlook the profound message of the text being sung. It's even possible that someone doesn't understand the relatively obtuse and obscure language of a song. Take a few moments, every now and then, to talk through some of your sung texts with your music ministers.

SEASON OF CHRISTMAS

The Lord entered her, and became a servant;
the Word entered her, and became silent within her;
thunder entered her, and his voice was still;
the Shepherd of all entered her;
he became a Lamb in her, and came forth bleating.

—St. Ephrem the Syrian

SPIRITUALITY

The Vigil Mass

GOSPEL ACCLAMATION
R/. Alleluia, alleluia.
Tomorrow the wickedness of the earth will be
destroyed:
the Savior of the world will reign over us.
R/. Alleluia, alleluia.

Gospel

Matt 1:1-25; L13ABC

The book of the genealogy of Jesus
    Christ,
    the son of David, the son of
        Abraham.

Abraham became the father of Isaac,
    Isaac the father of Jacob,
    Jacob the father of Judah and his
        brothers.
Judah became the father of Perez and
    Zerah,
    whose mother was Tamar.
Perez became the father of Hezron,
    Hezron the father of Ram,
    Ram the father of Amminadab.
Amminadab became the father of
    Nahshon,
    Nahshon the father of Salmon,
    Salmon the father of Boaz,
    whose mother was Rahab.
Boaz became the father of Obed,
    whose mother was Ruth.
Obed became the father of Jesse,
    Jesse the father of David the king.

David became the father of Solomon,
    whose mother had been the wife of
        Uriah.
Solomon became the father of
    Rehoboam,
    Rehoboam the father of Abijah,
    Abijah the father of Asaph.

*Continued in Appendix A, p. 260, or
Matt 1:18-25 in Appendix A, p. 260.*

See Appendix A, p. 261, for the other readings.

Reflecting on the Gospel

The Mass suggested for the evening of December 24—either before or after the first vespers of the solemnity—has the liturgical spirit of a Christmas vigil. If this Mass is not celebrated, its readings can be used for prayer and meditation in preparing for the celebration of the feast. "Today you will know that the Lord will come, and he will save us, / and in the morning you will see his glory," the church prays in this evening's entrance antiphon. It is a quiet waiting that ends with the sudden cry of joy that bursts forth at the beginning of the Office for Christmas Day: "Christ is born for us; come let us adore him" (invitatory refrain).

Biblical genealogy is a literary genre whose aim must be understood lest one be misled. To regard these lists as archival documents is to open oneself to endless questions that have no firm answers. They must be read as a way to understand and recapitulate the ancient prophecies, a way of interpreting events rather than merely recounting them. Their value is thus more homiletic than historical.

These genealogies are undoubtedly composed of symbolic elements—coded messages?—that elude our grasp today. In Matthew's genealogy of Jesus, we can note, for example, that of the four women mentioned, three are foreigners: Rahab, Ruth, and "the wife of Uriah," who, we are told, gave birth under irregular conditions. Is this a lesson in the universality of grace?

Matthew's genealogy insists on the Davidic line of "Jesus Christ, the son of David, the son of Abraham." This legitimacy seems to be compromised, since Jesus's origin is directly from Mary. This is not the case, however, since a new protagonist intervenes: the Holy Spirit. Moreover, Joseph, himself a "son of David," must give the name to the child thus conceived and, by doing so, he must integrate him into the line from which he himself descends. Joseph did not beget Jesus. But by giving him the name revealed by the angel and taking Mary into his home to be his wife, he has assumed the role and mission of being the indispensable link to the line of David, to which the Messiah must belong.

However it may appear at first glance, Matthew's beginning does not limit itself to Jesus's origins, his genealogy, and manner of conception. It is truly concerned with the Gospel, that is, with the Good News given to the community that Matthew is addressing.

Jesus is the summit toward which past sacred history converges, as does our history, which begins with his birth. From beginning to end, this history is lived out by men and women from generation to generation.

In some way, Joseph and Mary show the road to follow by outlining the general path, which will become specific in the lives of all people according to the way they respond to their vocation. We can recognize ourselves in one or another of Jesus's ancestors, in the sinners that the list mentions; but we are all asked to relate ourselves to Christ, to enter into his line. Salvation history knows no other continuity. It is the duty of each person to find his or her proper place in it. In a way certainly different from Joseph's, but no less real, we have an irreplaceable role to fulfill. God waits for us to do what he tells us, not by the voice of an angel, but by that of Scripture and the church at first, and later through unexpected situations and people who come into our lives. Jesus receives the name that Joseph gives him. We have to acknowledge it and pass it on.

Then, as we pray in this evening's communion antiphon, "The glory of the Lord will be revealed, / and all flesh will see the salvation of our God." Let us rise up, let us go forward with songs of joy. The celebration of Christmas is about to begin.

SPIRITUALITY

Mass during the Night

GOSPEL ACCLAMATION
Luke 2:10-11

R7. Alleluia, alleluia.
I proclaim to you good news of great joy:
today a Savior is born for us,
Christ the Lord.
R7. Alleluia, alleluia.

Gospel

Luke 2:1-14; L14ABC

In those days a decree went out from
    Caesar Augustus
  that the whole world should be
    enrolled.
This was the first enrollment,
  when Quirinius was governor of
    Syria.
So all went to be enrolled, each to his
    own town.
And Joseph too went up from Galilee
    from the town of Nazareth
  to Judea, to the city of David that is
    called Bethlehem,
  because he was of the house and
    family of David,
  to be enrolled with Mary, his be-
    trothed, who was with child.
While they were there,
  the time came for her to have her
    child,
  and she gave birth to her firstborn
    son.
She wrapped him in swaddling clothes
    and laid him in a manger,
  because there was no room for them
    in the inn.

Continued in Appendix A, p. 261.

See Appendix A, p. 262, for the other readings.

Reflecting on the Gospel

Luke's story of the birth and initial revelation of Jesus is filled with paradox. Jesus's birth takes place during the reign of Caesar Augustus (27 BC to AD 14), who rules over "the whole world" and was known for bringing peace after years of civil strife. An ancient inscription celebrates the birthday of Augustus as "good news for the whole world." Yet Jesus, whose parents are from the little-known town of Nazareth on the fringe of Augustus's empire, and who is laid in a manger, is Messiah and Lord and will bring peace to those "on whom his favor rests" (Luke 2:14). His birth is not announced in city squares throughout the empire but to shepherds, a group often scorned by the religious elite of the day.

The beauty of Luke's narrative and its influence on Christian art, literature, and music remind us that through the incarnation, the human condition is now suffused with God's beauty. Still, the contemporary marketing of Christmas can mask the stark reality of Jesus's birth. St. Ignatius instructs us in his *Spiritual Exercises* that when contemplating the nativity, we are to see how the persons in the scene are laboring so that "Jesus may be born in greatest poverty; and that after so many hardships of hunger, thirst, heat, cold, injuries, and insults, he may die on the cross." Luke may be hinting at this by his use of the same term for the "inn" (Luke 2:7) that did not welcome Mary and Joseph and for the "guest room" (Luke 22:11, *katalyma*) where Jesus celebrates his final supper and speaks of his body, which will be given "for you" and his blood shed "for you." The shadow of the cross falls even upon the crèche of Bethlehem.

Taken together, Luke's narrative that we read this Christmas night and the gospel reading for tomorrow's Christmas Mass during the Day, John's hymn (1:1-18), emphasize the paradox of Christian faith in the incarnation: truly human, truly divine; eternal Word, a life unfolding in history. This paradox is also a tension. The "high Christology" of John can envelop the human Jesus; neglect of the transcendent Word made flesh can reduce Jesus to a compassionate social prophet or innocent martyr. There is another paradox. When Christians gather to pray at Christmas, they must recall that Jesus's life and death are not only "for us" but through the Word now incarnate "was life, / and this life was the light of the human race" (John 1:4; NABRE). The human condition has been radically changed by the coming of Christ, and this is cause for—to borrow the words of the angel in tonight's gospel reading—"good news of great joy."

SPIRITUALITY

Mass at Dawn

GOSPEL ACCLAMATION
Luke 2:14

℟. Alleluia, alleluia.
Glory to God in the highest,
and on earth peace to those
on whom his favor rests.
℟. Alleluia, alleluia.

Gospel   Luke 2:15-20; L15ABC

When the angels went away from them
   to heaven,
   the shepherds said to one another,
   "Let us go, then, to Bethlehem
   to see this thing that has taken place,
   which the Lord has made known
      to us."
So they went in haste and found Mary
   and Joseph,
   and the infant lying in the manger.
When they saw this,
   they made known the message
   that had been told them about this
      child.
All who heard it were amazed
   by what had been told them by the
      shepherds.
And Mary kept all these things,
   reflecting on them in her heart.
Then the shepherds returned,
   glorifying and praising God
   for all they had heard and seen,
   just as it had been told to them.

See Appendix A, p. 262, for the other readings.

Reflecting on the Gospel

The gospel of the Nativity of the Lord does not end with the song of the angelic choir. Luke recounts what the shepherds did after the angels left them. These simple folk did not doubt the extraordinary revelation that was given them: "good news," "great joy," "savior." Nor were they scared away by the light that shone about them. They went to Bethlehem "in haste," just as Mary had gone to her cousin Elizabeth's house. They saw for themselves that it was not a dream: they found "the infant lying in a manger." It was exactly as they had been told. "When they saw this, they made known the message that had been told them about this child." Having been the first to receive the Good News, as the first witnesses of the event, they also became the first evangelists.

"All who heard it were amazed by what had been told them by the shepherds." In writing this, Luke is no doubt thinking of all those who have received the gospel message. And who would they be, those who accept the witness of the shepherds, if not simple people like themselves? Luke feels no need to be more precise: he has seen such things happen in the apostles' preaching. His book of the Acts of the Apostles emphasizes the point.

People "were amazed." According to Luke, this is a reaction that Jesus frequently inspired, from his first preaching in the synagogue at Nazareth (Luke 22), by his words, authority, and miracles. This reaction may be merely superficial. In any case, it does not foretell what will come of it. Is it not typical that after wondrous sights and events, we often find ourselves quickly returning to our mundane preoccupations? Is this kind of astonishment the trigger that begins our search for the meaning of the event? Will it evolve, much later, into faith? Anything is possible. Even after piously celebrating the feast of Christmas, one follows the same road as before.

In contrast with this astonishment, which often defies definition, we find the attitude of Mary. She "kept all these things, reflecting on them in her heart." Doubtless, she did not at first perceive the full depth and meaning of her experience. Everyone, including Mary, enters gradually into this mystery, listening attentively to her son's teaching and examining the meaning of his behavior and miracles, beginning with that of Cana. She must confront the "why" of the life of faith, from the day when Jesus remained in Jerusalem because he had to be in his Father's house (Luke 2:41-53) to Calvary where, surrounded by his friends, she watched her son die on the cross (Luke 23:49). The gospels say nothing about it, but Mary's faith must undoubtedly have come to fruition with the resurrection of the Lord. In any case, Luke mentions her as being among the faithful who were earnestly united in prayer when the Spirit descended on them (Acts 1:14). From that point on, he says nothing more about her. Mary has followed and meditated on the various phases of the mystery. She has seen with her own eyes the vitality of the first Christian community after Pentecost. Nothing remains but for her to enter into glory, to follow her son, to experience at his side the blessedness of those who hear the word and keep it (Luke 11:28).

Though unique, this itinerary of the "privileged of God" maps out the road that all believers must follow. Faith is nourished by listening to Scripture and by meditating on all the events in which God comes to us.

SPIRITUALITY

Mass during the Day

GOSPEL ACCLAMATION
R7. Alleluia, alleluia.
A holy day has dawned upon us.
Come, you nations, and adore the Lord.
For today a great light has come upon the earth.
R7. Alleluia, alleluia.

Gospel

John 1:1-18; L16ABC

In the beginning was the Word,
    and the Word was with God,
    and the Word was God.
He was in the beginning with God.
All things came to be through him,
    and without him nothing came to be.
What came to be through him was life,
    and this life was the light of the human
        race;
the light shines in the darkness,
    and the darkness has not overcome it.

A man named John was sent from God.
He came for testimony, to testify to the
        light,
    so that all might believe through him.
He was not the light,
    but came to testify to the light.
The true light, which enlightens everyone,
    was coming into the world.
He was in the world,
    and the world came to be through him,
    but the world did not know him.
He came to what was his own,
    but his own people did not accept him.

But to those who did accept him
    he gave power to become children of
        God,
    to those who believe in his name,
    who were born not by natural
        generation
    nor by human choice nor by a man's
        decision
    but of God.

Continued in Appendix A, p. 263, or
John 1:1-5, 9-14 *in Appendix A, p. 263.*

See Appendix A, p. 263, for the other readings.

Reflecting on the Gospel

In the first reading, the prophet Isaiah allows us to hear a chorus of voices that sings the joy so appropriate to this festival: the glad Good News of peace and the arrival of a king. And yet it will take a longer journey through hundreds of years of fidelity and infidelity, exile and return after the time of Isaiah, before the definitive King will return to his people and tabernacle among us.

Today we remember this God who pitches his presence among us, not as he tented with his people in the desert or in the Jerusalem temple, but in bared human flesh like our own. At the end of his gospel, John tells us his reason for writing: "that you may [come to] believe that Jesus is the Messiah, the Son of God, and that through this belief you may have life in his name" (John 20:31; NABRE). But the beginning of his gospel, the Prologue that is proclaimed at this Mass, asserts John's conviction that to believe in Jesus we must understand the entire journey of the Word: his beginning in eternity, his becoming flesh among us to open heaven for us, and his return to heaven, "at the Father's side" (John 1:18). The movement of the Prologue to John's gospel is like a pendulum swinging: from the glory of the Word in eternity who was with God and was God, arcing down into our world, and then again swinging upwards through death and resurrection into the glory of the Father, and catching us up with him.

John names Jesus as the Word. When a word is spoken it is the extension of something of the inner person into the outer environment. In this sense, God most truly speaks God into the world through the Word made flesh whose mission is that we might understand, most clearly and most humanly, the overwhelming love of God that offers us eternal life (cf. John 3:16). "In the beginning" of Genesis 1:1, there was the moment of the first creation called into existence by the word of God. The coming of the Word made flesh into the world is another beginning, a renewing creation of life and light that no darkness can overcome. Jesus the Word, although without sin, is not remote from the darkness of our world, from the human sinfulness that will raise him on a cross, but from which he will draw all people to himself and to his Father (cf. John 12:32).

As if to make sure that we do understand the mystery of the Word as grounded in time and place, John the Baptist makes what we may at first regard as a surprising appearance in the Prologue as a witness to the light. Witnessing is the way the Word is still made known by each one of us in our own worlds of family, friendship, workplace, and leisure. The Baptist comes as a voice for a time; Jesus is the Word for all eternity. The Word is the radiance of the Father's glory; the Baptist is the lamp-carrier who becomes unnecessary when the Light is among us. And John the Baptist is humbly content to be only voice and lamp. Such humble witness to the Word, and not to ourselves, is the privilege of all who accept the Word into their lives. It is not an optional extra for those who have heard the Word and seen the Light.

That the Word "became flesh and made his dwelling among us" (more literally from the Greek: "set up his tent among us") recalls the tenting of God's presence in the portable wilderness tabernacle (Exod 40:34) and the pitching of Wisdom's tent in the midst of the people (Sir 24:8). In the Word, the glory and wisdom of God are now present in humankind to reveal God's truth. In this gospel we are given a vocabulary with which to name the mystery: Word, life, light, glory. Its effects are the actions of revealing, birthing, overcoming, living.

Model Penitential Act

Presider: We have gathered to celebrate the nativity of Jesus, the one who is "God with us." Let us pause to prepare our hearts to welcome him by bringing to God all the places in our lives in need of his healing and mercy . . . *[pause]*

> Lord Jesus, you are named "Wonder-Counselor, God-Hero, / Father-Forever, Prince of Peace": Lord, have mercy.
>
> Christ Jesus, you are the reason for our joy and the sure foundation of our hope: Christ, have mercy.
>
> Lord Jesus, we are blessed to walk in your light: Lord, have mercy.

Model Universal Prayer (Prayer of the Faithful)

Presider: Our joy overflows as we celebrate the holy night on which our savior was born. With hearts eager to meet him when he returns in glory, let us bring our needs before the Lord.

Response: Lord, hear our prayer.

For God's holy church, in celebrating the feast of the Nativity may it be purified by the light of Christ's glory and strengthened through his humble authority . . .

For children throughout the world, may they be provided with the love, support, and resources necessary to grow in wisdom and grace . . .

For all those seeking asylum and refuge far from their homelands due to war, natural disaster, and poverty, may they find welcome, comfort, and safety . . .

For all gathered here, may we continue to grow in justice and compassion, eager in all things to do what is good . . .

Presider: God who enlightens all darkness, you sent your only begotten son to dwell among us and to lead us to you. Hear our prayers that with humility and joy we might give witness to your light in both our words and our deeds. We ask this through Christ our Lord. **Amen.**

About Liturgy

How We've Always Done It: Frequently, the rites, the music, and the art and environment of Christmastide are all holdovers from previous years—or even previous decades—of practice. "Well, this is the way we've always done it." Sometimes there is wisdom in that. Yet, often, our expressions of faith need to be approached anew, for a particular time and place, and indeed for a community that has likely shifted somehow over the years: by age, ethnicity, language, size, and countless other details.

Consider your Christmas tree at home. Is it always set up in the same location? Is it even always the same tree? Perhaps each year you choose different lights to string on it. What guides your choices of "not these, but those" as you hang up precious memories and create new ones?

So it can be with various liturgical elements: it is important to cling to certain traditions, though we also ought to avoid crafting an experience of worship that is motivated by our ease or even apathy. Liturgically, which way of celebrating the rites, which pieces of music, which elements of the art and environment will "remain on the Christmas tree" this year, and which might it be time to reconsider?

COLLECT

(from the Mass during the Day)

Let us pray.

Pause for silent prayer

O God, who wonderfully created the dignity
  of human nature
and still more wonderfully restored it,
grant, we pray,
that we may share in the divinity of Christ,
who humbled himself to share in our humanity.
Who lives and reigns with you in the unity of
  the Holy Spirit,
one God, for ever and ever. **Amen.**

FOR REFLECTION

• In the vigil gospel reading, Matthew quotes the prophet Isaiah, "[T]hey shall name him Emmanuel, / which means 'God is with us.'" How have you experienced Jesus as "Emmanuel" this past year?

• In Luke's gospel (read at the Mass during the night and Mass at dawn), Jesus is proclaimed the savior of all the world who is to be found in a feed box since there is no room at the inn. This past year, where have you found Jesus in the poor?

• In John's gospel (read at the Mass during the day) Jesus is named "the light [that] shines in the darkness." As a follower of Christ, how are you seeking to bear his light to those around you?

Homily Points

• Throughout the Christmas liturgies, there is a strong theme of light and darkness. At the Mass during the night Isaiah proclaims, "The people who walked in darkness / have seen a great light." And in the gospel for the Mass during the day we hear, "[T]he light shines in the darkness, / and the darkness has not overcome it."

• For us Christians, the light is a concept, but even more, it is a person. In Jesus's life all darkness is dispelled. He is the fullness of light that our God longs to give each one of us. As the Body of Christ, we are called to proclaim with our lives that no matter how strong the darkness may seem, the light is always stronger.

SPIRITUALITY

GOSPEL ACCLAMATION
Heb 1:1-2

℟. Alleluia, alleluia.
In the past God spoke to our ancestors through
    the prophets;
in these last days, he has spoken to us through
    the Son.
℟. Alleluia, alleluia.

or:

Col 3:15a, 16a

℟. Alleluia, alleluia.
Let the peace of Christ control your hearts;
let the word of Christ dwell in you richly.
℟. Alleluia, alleluia.

Gospel

Luke 2:22-40; L17B

**When the days were completed
    for their purification
    according to the law of
        Moses,
    the parents of Jesus took him
        up to Jerusalem
    to present him to the Lord,
    just as it is written in the law of the
        Lord,
    *Every male that opens the womb
        shall be consecrated to the Lord,*
    and to offer the sacrifice of
    *a pair of turtledoves or two young
        pigeons,*
    in accordance with the dictate in the
        law of the Lord.**

**Now there was a man in Jerusalem
    whose name was Simeon.
This man was righteous and devout,
    awaiting the consolation of Israel,
    and the Holy Spirit was upon him.
It had been revealed to him by the Holy
    Spirit
    that he should not see death
    before he had seen the Christ of the
        Lord.**

Continued in Appendix A, p. 264, or
Luke 2:22, 39-40 *in Appendix A, p. 264.*

Reflecting on the Gospel

"The child's father and mother were amazed at what was said about him." (Luke 2:33)

The truth of the supposedly clichéd phrase "every child is a miracle" hits home for most people when a child is born to them or an adopted child is welcomed into the family. The instantaneous recognition of the child never before seen is a spiritual experience made tactile as a mother takes the newborn in her arms and a father gazes at an infant who evokes on sight the deepest of loves.

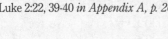

We tend to think of childbirth, especially today, as something that is simple and straightforward. It is certainly natural; and for many people, both in conception and at delivery, it poses no problems. Yet, there are many others for whom having a child is a struggle. We have no idea why some couples have no children and other families have one, why some women have miscarried numerous times or had ectopic pregnancies that threaten the lives of mother and child. We should never judge the size of a family, for we have no knowledge of the hidden burdens that many women and men carry. Many of the model families throughout the Bible were overjoyed that God blessed them with one child, a child they had long desired.

The miraculous nature of conception and childbirth is a theme that runs through the Old Testament and is often seen in families that have only one child. Numerous women who were considered "barren" give birth to a child of hope, often when it seemed such hope was out of reach. In this number we count Rebekah, Hannah, and the mother of Samson, all blessed with children when it seemed it could never happen. But the preeminent example is the first one we see in Genesis: Sarah.

Sarah was too old, as was Abram, to have and raise a child. But God gave them Isaac, a child of promise and hope for Abram, now called Abraham, and Sarah and for the future of a promised nation. The promised Messiah would come from this lineage and be given miraculously to Mary, which reveals another part of the equation: never having engaged in sexual intercourse, she was given a child by God—a child given to this new mother and her husband-to-be, but a child of hope for the whole world.

Yet the stories of the matriarchs, Mary, and their unique children indicate to us the miraculous nature of every birth. True, our children will probably not be patriarchs of a nation, as Isaac was for Israel; and certainly none can be Jesus, the Messiah, the Savior, both God and man. But the mothers were real mothers, just like women today, who raise many children or one child, or yearn for a child. And their children were real children, who had to be loved and raised. God chose to work his miracles not in opposition to nature but through the most natural of ways: childbirth.

But every family, whether gifted with many children or none or one, has a role to play in God's dramatic story of salvation and shares in the miraculous gift of hope children represent. Each child has been willed by God to serve a unique purpose.

And it was through the birth of one child that all of us share in the hope of salvation. As Simeon says in Luke's gospel of the newborn baby boy Jesus, "my eyes have seen your salvation, / which you prepared in sight of all the peoples, / a light for revelation to the Gentiles, / and glory for your people Israel."

Mary and Joseph were "amazed at what was said about him," for he was the fulfillment of all hopes. But in the reality of the Holy Family, we see the miraculous nature of every child and every family reflected.

Focusing the Gospel

Key words and phrases: "[M]y eyes have seen your salvation."

To the point: Within the simple family from Nazareth, Simeon recognizes the consolation and salvation he has been awaiting his entire life. We could ponder what it was about this child, these parents, that prompted Simeon to utter, "Now, Master, you may let your servant go / in peace." Only through the power of the Holy Spirit is Simeon given eyes to perceive the light of the world enfleshed in the newborn Jesus. Christ is present in our daily lives as well, in the people we meet inside and outside of our homes. Through the revelation of the Holy Spirit may we, too, be able to recognize him and serve him.

Connecting the Gospel

to the second reading: Today's gospel ends with the image of the child Jesus growing and becoming strong as he is brought up by Mary and Joseph in Nazareth. Within their daily lives from the time of Jesus's conception until the beginning of his public ministry, Mary and Joseph physically dwelt with the word of God, attending to his needs, teaching him, and learning from him. In his letter to the Colossians, St. Paul urges the community to "[l]et the word of Christ dwell in you richly." Only through constant and dedicated reflection and meditation on this word could the Colossians hope to be reflections of Christ in the world.

to experience: We come to know Jesus through both word and sacrament. The words of the Bible illuminate our minds and lift our spirits to consider things not as human beings do but from the perspective of our divine and heavenly God: Father, Son, and Holy Spirit. In considering the life of the Holy Family in Nazareth, we might ponder, How can we also look at the events of our days as a constant living with the word of God? How do we make room and space for this word to dwell within us richly?

Connecting the Responsorial Psalm

to the readings: Forty days after the birth of Jesus, Mary and Joseph leave Bethlehem to begin the trek back home to Nazareth. On the way, they stop at the temple in Jerusalem to fulfill "the dictate in the law of the Lord." In Luke's gospel, this is the first journey that Mary and Joseph undertake with their newborn son. Today's psalm response also calls to mind a journey. We are told, "Blessed are those who fear the Lord and walk in his ways." Just as traveling with a newborn requires parents to be attentive to the rhythms and needs of their child, entering into the journey of faith calls us to be attentive to the actions and voice of God prompting us forward or holding us back.

to psalmist preparation: In the spiritual life, how do you seek to walk in the "ways" of God?

PROMPTS FOR FAITH-SHARING

The writer of Sirach upholds caring for the elderly as an essential and honored duty. How are the elders in your community respected, cared for, and listened to?

The psalm refrain for today tells us we are blessed when we "walk in [God's] ways." How does this image of walking with God and keeping his ways relate to your faith journey?

St. Paul urges the Colossians to "[p]ut on . . . heartfelt compassion, kindness, humility, gentleness, and patience." What situations in your life are in need of this approach?

In the gospel, we hear the promised Messiah referred to as "the consolation of Israel." How do you experience Jesus as consolation and comfort?

CELEBRATION

Model Penitential Act

Presider: Today we celebrate the Holy Family of Jesus, Mary, and Joseph. For the times our words and actions have sown discord instead of unity and peace within our own families and the family of the church, let us ask for pardon and mercy . . . *[pause]*

Lord Jesus, you are our light and our salvation: Lord, have mercy.

Christ Jesus, in you we are consecrated to God, the Father: Christ, have mercy.

Lord Jesus, purify us that we might live in righteousness and truth: Lord, have mercy.

Homily Points

• Following the birth of Jesus, Mary and Joseph do what countless generations did before them (and which parents continue to do today): they present their baby to God in a spirit of thanksgiving. There is a longing in the human heart to give our best gifts back to God, and what greater gift in the life of a parent is there than the life of their child? Of course, in Mary and Joseph's case, this is compounded by the fact that the newborn child they bring to the temple is not only the greatest gift of their lives, but also the greatest gift of God to all humanity.

• While the Holy Family is often considered a unit unto itself, throughout their earthly lives, Mary, Joseph, and Jesus encountered many people and doubtless looked to some for support and guidance. At the temple, Anna and Simeon join Mary and Joseph in rejoicing at the child's birth, and also in anticipating the trajectory of his life and his role within the history of salvation as "a light for revelation to the Gentiles, / and glory for your people Israel."

• As parts of the Body of Christ, we are also members of the Holy Family of God. At times our role might be to tend the young, the sick, or the elderly in our own biological family units. At other times, we might be privileged to offer support to a young or struggling family. In his letter to the Colossians, St. Paul tells us how we are to tend the bonds of love that unite us in Christ, by putting on "compassion, kindness, humility, gentleness, and patience." In this way, we offer our lives to God in thanksgiving and help to build and nurture his Holy Family.

Model Universal Prayer (Prayer of the Faithful)

Presider: As beloved sons and daughters of God, let us bring our needs, and the needs of the world, before the Lord.

Response: Lord, hear our prayer.

For the family of the universal church, by putting on the compassion, kindness, and humility of Christ may we be united in all that we do . . .

For leaders of nations, may they receive wisdom and clarity in making decisions and implementing policies to support the most vulnerable . . .

For all those who have been harmed by domestic violence and abuse, may God's love heal and strengthen their bodies, minds, and souls . . .

For all gathered here, in our prayer and work may we carry the light of Christ to all those we meet . . .

Presider: Everlasting Father and creator God, we praise you, for all your deeds are wonderful. Hear our prayers that through the intercession of the Holy Family, we might be united by the bonds of love and empowered to serve you in our brothers and sisters. We ask this through Christ our Lord. **Amen.**

COLLECT

Let us pray.

Pause for silent prayer

O God, who were pleased to give us
the shining example of the Holy Family,
graciously grant that we may imitate them
in practicing the virtues of family life and
    in the bonds of charity,
and so, in the joy of your house,
delight one day in eternal rewards.
Through our Lord Jesus Christ, your Son,
who lives and reigns with you in the unity
    of the Holy Spirit,
one God, for ever and ever. **Amen.**

FIRST READING

Sir 3:2-6, 12-14

God sets a father in honor over his
    children;
    a mother's authority he confirms over
        her sons.
Whoever honors his father atones for sins,
    and preserves himself from them.
When he prays, he is heard;
    he stores up riches who reveres his
        mother.
Whoever honors his father is gladdened
        by children,
    and, when he prays, is heard.
Whoever reveres his father will live a long
        life;
    he who obeys his father brings comfort
        to his mother.

My son, take care of your father when he
        is old;
    grieve him not as long as he lives.
Even if his mind fail, be considerate of
        him;
    revile him not all the days of his life;
kindness to a father will not be forgotten,
    firmly planted against the debt of your
        sins
    —a house raised in justice to you.

RESPONSORIAL PSALM

Ps 128:1-2, 3, 4-5

℟. (cf. 1) Blessed are those who fear the
    Lord and walk in his ways.

Blessed is everyone who fears the LORD,
    who walks in his ways!
For you shall eat the fruit of your
        handiwork;
    blessed shall you be, and favored.

℟. Blessed are those who fear the Lord
    and walk in his ways.

Your wife shall be like a fruitful vine
   in the recesses of your home;
your children like olive plants
   around your table.

R℣. Blessed are those who fear the Lord
   and walk in his ways.

Behold, thus is the man blessed
   who fears the LORD.
The LORD bless you from Zion:
   may you see the prosperity of
      Jerusalem
   all the days of your life.

R℣. Blessed are those who fear the Lord
   and walk in his ways.

SECOND READING
Col 3:12-21

Brothers and sisters:
Put on, as God's chosen ones, holy and
      beloved,
   heartfelt compassion, kindness,
         humility, gentleness, and patience,
   bearing with one another and forgiving
      one another,
   if one has a grievance against another;
   as the Lord has forgiven you, so must
      you also do.
And over all these put on love,
   that is, the bond of perfection.
And let the peace of Christ control your
      hearts,
   the peace into which you were also
         called in one body.
And be thankful.
Let the word of Christ dwell in you richly,
   as in all wisdom you teach and
         admonish one another,
   singing psalms, hymns, and spiritual
         songs
   with gratitude in your hearts to God.
And whatever you do, in word or in deed,
   do everything in the name of the Lord
      Jesus,
   giving thanks to God the Father
         through him.

Wives, be subordinate to your husbands,
   as is proper in the Lord.
Husbands, love your wives,
   and avoid any bitterness toward them.
Children, obey your parents in everything,
   for this is pleasing to the Lord.
Fathers, do not provoke your children,
   so they may not become discouraged.

or Col 3:12-17 in Appendix A, p. 264.

See Appendix A, p. 265, for optional readings.

About Liturgy

Out of Order: Several years ago, there was a photocopier at my workplace dedicated to the ministries of the pastoral team, of which I was a member. It was an amazing piece of technology: it collated, stapled, scanned—it did everything we needed it to do.

One day I arrived at work and found an "out of order" sign hung on the machine. I did some asking around and learned that one of the "feet" on the copier had broken, and without it, the whole copier leaned just a little bit in that direction. "What does that matter?" I asked myself.

Shortly thereafter, I discovered that if the copier wasn't oriented very close to level, several problems would arise: it would put strain on the motor that ran the light across the glass, the copier would have trouble feeding the paper out of the drawers, the toner might settle in the wrong part of the cartridge, and probably a few other things that have since left my memory.

That is, if the copier's foot was broken, the whole copier fell into disarray and couldn't function, even though the only tangible issue was that it leaned over an inch or less.

Today's celebration speaks to us of order in a family, however one wishes to define that—be it the so-called nuclear family, a family of faith, or many other types of family. Of course, our liturgies too are ordered, given a structure and set of directives, intended to keep celebrations more or less consistent from place to place, though with enough leeway for pastoral adaptations when truly needed.

Consider the familiar passage from Paul's first epistle to the Corinthians: that we are many parts yet all one body, and that when one part of that body suffers, the whole body suffers with it. As we consider "order" today, is there an aspect of our liturgical practices that is suffering and in turn affecting the whole "body" of the liturgy? Perhaps lectors or servers are not well trained? Is the person who coordinates art and environment not well formed to the intricacies of that ministry? How can issues like these be addressed, for the betterment of the liturgy and the community?

About the Chair of the Priest Celebrant

Qualities of a Leader: The GIRM tells us that the "chair of the Priest Celebrant" is a symbol of presiding over the assembly and of directing prayer (310). Further, BLS instructs that the chair "reflects the dignity of the one who leads the community in the person of Christ, but is never intended to be remote or grandiose" (63). Indeed, the one who presides at prayer ought to approach that role as a servant-leader: servant to the liturgy, and servant to the people of God. Humility, surrender, and dedication are the attributes Christ requires of all disciples but most especially of those who would lead the church. Perhaps transparency is most required in the presidential ministry. On this Sunday when we consider the value of "order," let us also consider the qualities that leaders of prayer should possess.

About Music

Growing in Holiness: In addition to continuing the music of Christmastide, we can give particular attention to pieces whose texts speak of family life and specifically the sparse bits of Jesus's upbringing we hear of in Scripture. An underutilized tune and text is "Once in Royal David's City." In *Psallite* (Liturgical Press), we can find helpful pieces like "Teach Me Your Path" and "I Will Dwell with You," which both speak of God being in a familial relationship with us, God's adopted sons and daughters.

DECEMBER 27, 2020
THE HOLY FAMILY OF JESUS, MARY, AND JOSEPH

GOSPEL ACCLAMATION

Heb 1:1-2

R7. Alleluia, alleluia.

In the past God spoke to our ancestors through the prophets;

in these last days, he has spoken to us through the Son.

R7. Alleluia, alleluia.

Gospel

Luke 2:16-21; L18ABC

The shepherds went in haste to Bethlehem and found Mary and Joseph,

and the infant lying in the manger.

When they saw this, they made known the message that had been told them about this child.

All who heard it were amazed by what had been told them by the shepherds.

And Mary kept all these things, reflecting on them in her heart.

Then the shepherds returned, glorifying and praising God for all they had heard and seen, just as it had been told to them.

When eight days were completed for his circumcision, he was named Jesus, the name given him by the angel before he was conceived in the womb.

See Appendix A, p. 265, for the other readings.

Reflecting on the Gospel

In today's gospel there is excitement as the shepherds hurry into Bethlehem to pour out what they have heard and seen to anyone who would listen to them. But at the center of this movement and ferment is Mary, the still point around which it all revolves. She says nothing, but in her heart she treasures and ponders all that is happening. The word that Luke uses here for "reflecting on" is *symballo*, a word in the Greek that literally means to "throw together." With Joseph at her side and her child lying in a manger wrapped in the swaddling cloths that bind both king and commoner (cf. Wis 7:4), Mary, the contemplative woman, silently holds and "throws together" in her heart the events of divine conception and human birth, heavenly hosts and hillside shepherds. Years of seeking to understand lie ahead of her as the first and most faithful of the disciples of Jesus. In her pondering and remembering, Mary is a model for our *lectio divina*, our reading of the Word of God and the conversation between that Word and events of our own lives.

As we gaze on this peaceful woman, we can appreciate how appropriate it is that January 1 has been chosen by the church as the day on which we pray for world peace. Like her, we are called to gaze on the child who is the Prince of Peace. It is his reign, not the Pax Romana, not the Pax Americana, nor any other political maneuvering, that will make the words of the responsorial Psalm 67 a reality in our hearts and in our world, so that God's way is known upon earth and all nations will learn God's saving power. Then humanity will be a people of praise, and all the nations will "be glad and exult." The responsibility for peace is now in our hands.

The second focus of this day is the child's circumcision and naming. The rite of circumcision, celebrated eight days after birth, is called the "covenant of circumcision," and marks the male child's formal entry into the covenantal Jewish community (Gen 17:10-11). The covenant made in his flesh, the blood shed for the first time from his foreskin, will one day flow from raw wounds of the crucified Savior for the salvation of the world.

At the same time as circumcision, the naming of the child is celebrated. For a Jewish family, the name of the child is both a remembrance of previous generations and a hope for those yet to be born. We have no record of what words were spoken in the first-century rite, but the contemporary prayer is that God will: "give a pure and holy heart to N., a heart wide open to comprehend Thy Holy Law, that he may learn and teach, keep and fulfill Thy Laws." However the rite was expressed in Jesus's time, he was the most excellent son of his ancestors, the most obedient to God's Holy Law and, as "savior," the ultimate expression of his Name for the sake of the world.

The reading from the book of Numbers is twinned with the gospel because of the emphasis on the name of the Lord that is three times called down or "invoked upon" the people of Israel in the priestly blessing given by the descendants of Aaron. The people are known to God and know themselves as God's people in an intimate relationship. This blessing is a gift from God, but is infinitely surpassed by that gift which is named Jesus, Savior.

Focusing the Gospel

Key words and phrases: [G]lorifying and praising God / for all they had heard and seen.

To the point: Mary's role as Jesus's mother renders her a unique witness to the life of the Messiah. She knows of him from Gabriel's words before he is conceived in her womb, she participates in his birth, and she cares for him as an infant, child, and adolescent. Throughout these intense years of mothering the son of God, she must have heard and seen many things. In Mary we find a model of discipleship and also a model of glorifying and praising God with the entirety of her body, mind, soul, and spirit. In reflecting on all she has heard and seen within her heart, she shows us a way of living deeper each day into the mystery of the incarnation.

Model Penitential Act

Presider: Gathering at the beginning of this new calendar year, we pause to consecrate it and ourselves anew to the Lord of life by first asking for God's pardon, mercy, and healing . . . *[pause]*

Lord Jesus, in you all nations of the earth find blessing: Lord, have mercy.
Christ Jesus, you are son of God and son of Mary: Christ, have mercy.
Lord Jesus, by your life, death, and resurrection, we are saved: Lord, have mercy.

Model Universal Prayer (Prayer of the Faithful)

Presider: Through the intercession of Mary, Mother of God and our mother, let us bring our needs before the Lord.

Response: Lord, hear our prayer.

For God's holy church spread throughout the world, may it be a beacon of light and a blessing for all the peoples of the earth . . .

For civil leaders, with humble authority may they lead their communities in peace and prosperity . . .

For the poor, hungry, and homeless throughout the world, may their lives be safeguarded through compassionate and respectful care and support . . .

For all gathered here around the table of the Lord, may this coming year be a time of growth, healing, and renewal . . .

Presider: God of abundant blessings, in you we move and live and have our being. Hear our prayers this day that in the coming year we might serve you with joyful hearts and willing spirits. We ask this through Christ our Lord. **Amen.**

About Liturgy

Mary and the World Day of Peace: In addition to celebrating the *Theotokos*, the "God-bearer" today, many hymnals and missalettes will still remind us that January 1 is also the World Day of Peace, as instituted by Pope Paul VI. We would be wise to recall on this day how Mary herself is a shining example of peace, justice, and dignity.

Are we like Mary, who took time to reflect on the events of the nativity in her heart? Do we set aside times of stillness and peace, time to pray for and reflect on the coming of God's reign of justice? Do we accept spoken prayers and lyrics of social justice as an integral part of our liturgical prayer?

Are we like Mary, who welcomed the lowly shepherds to witness the birth of the Messiah? Do we truly welcome the lowly and outcast among us into our celebrations? Do we perhaps say we do but then offer nothing as a practical manifestation of that welcome?

As we celebrate the God-bearer today, let us also recommit ourselves and our liturgical ministries to the example given us by the Blessed Mother in prayer, contemplation, and action.

COLLECT

Let us pray.

Pause for silent prayer

O God, who through the fruitful virginity of
    Blessed Mary
bestowed on the human race
the grace of eternal salvation,
grant, we pray,
that we may experience the intercession of her,
through whom we were found worthy
to receive the author of life,
our Lord Jesus Christ, your Son.
Who lives and reigns with you in the unity of
    the Holy Spirit,
one God, for ever and ever. **Amen.**

FOR REFLECTION

• In the first reading, God instructs Aaron on how to bless the people. How have you experienced God's blessing this past year?

• In the gospel the shepherds go "in haste" to visit the newborn baby Jesus. Their excitement and curiosity lead them to the manger. What aspect of faith has you excited and curious at this moment?

• "Mary kept all these things, reflecting on them in her heart." How do you make time for contemplative prayer in your faith life?

Homily Points

• We begin our new calendar year with the blessing from the book of Numbers: "The Lord bless you and keep you! / The Lord let his face shine upon you, and be gracious to you! / The Lord look upon you kindly and give you peace!" Oftentimes, the New Year's holiday is synonymous with resolutions and focusing on the actions we might take to improve or thrive in the coming months.

• The Scriptures invite us to look to the presence and action of God in our lives. When we are attentive to the one in whom "we live and move and have our being" (Acts 17:28; NABRE), everything falls into place. How is God hoping to bless you in this coming year, and how might you be an instrument of God's blessing in the lives of others?

SPIRITUALITY

GOSPEL ACCLAMATION
Matt 2:2

℟. Alleluia, alleluia.
We saw his star at its rising
and have come to do him homage.
℟. Alleluia, alleluia.

Gospel

Matt 2:1-12; L20ABC

When Jesus was born in
    Bethlehem of Judea,
  in the days of King Herod,
  behold, magi from the east
      arrived in Jerusalem,
      saying,
  "Where is the newborn king of
      the Jews?
We saw his star at its rising
  and have come to do him
      homage."
When King Herod heard this,
  he was greatly troubled,
  and all Jerusalem with him.
Assembling all the chief priests
    and the scribes of the people,
  he inquired of them where the Christ
      was to be born.
They said to him, "In Bethlehem of
    Judea,
  for thus it has been written through
      the prophet:
  *And you, Bethlehem, land of
      Judah,*
    *are by no means least among
        the rulers of Judah;*
    since from you shall come a ruler,
      *who is to shepherd my people
          Israel."*
Then Herod called the magi secretly
  and ascertained from them the time
      of the star's appearance.
He sent them to Bethlehem and said,
  "Go and search diligently for the child.
When you have found him, bring me
      word,
  that I too may go and do him homage."

Continued in Appendix A, p. 266.

Reflecting on the Gospel

The first human word spoken in Matthew's gospel is the one the wise men address to Herod: "Where . . . ?" It is also the response of Herod when he summons the chief priests and scribes and his Jerusalem supporters (generalized to "all Jerusalem"). But the two questions are spoken from very different hearts. Herod is panic-stricken at the thought of losing his power to another "king of the Jews," and is desperate to know "where" this threat lurks. It is some of the same coterie that Matthew will later describe Herod as summoning to help him to plot the death of Jesus, and who will mock him on the cross (Matt 26:3-4; 27:41-43). In contrast, the wise men, Gentile (perhaps Persian) seekers and aristocratic scholars, have no concern with status or ethnicity; their "Where . . .?" is a sign of their genuine search for the new king so that they may come to pay him homage. They also have the humility to come to Jerusalem to add to their foreign and pagan wisdom the wisdom of the Hebrew Scriptures to help them in their search. In the wolfish company of Herod and his cohorts, Matthew sees the wise men as witnesses to the later call of Jesus for all his disciples to be "shrewd as serpents and simple as doves" (Matt 10:16; NABRE).

The search of the wise men from the East begins with a sign in the skies and the guiding wisdom of pagan astrology; it ends with a Child of earth to whom they are led by both the star and the light of the Hebrew Scriptures. Whether Matthew intended it or not, later tradition has seen in the gifts the magi bring a hint of the paschal mystery: the myrrh for embalming, the frankincense for fragrancing of sacrifices and burning before the holy of holies, the gold a fitting gift for a king.

Their human "dreams" fulfilled by their visit to the Child, God touches their spirit in a dream that warns them of Herod's hypocrisy so that they do not return to Jerusalem to tell him the "where" of Jesus, but return to their own country by another way.

When we place the magi in our Christmas crib, they are usually dressed in opulent robes and have black, yellow, and brown faces. For the number or the physical appearance of the wise men we have no biblical evidence, but the truth that their visit declares, and the symbolism that their presence in the crib proclaims, is the gospel truth that Jesus is king for all the nations of the earth. This is what we pray for in the words of the responsorial Psalm 72: the establishment of God's kingdom of justice and peace throughout the world so that the rights of the poor and helpless are respected and the cries of the needy are answered.

In the story of the revelation of Jesus to the magi, what is revealed to us about our own eagerness or reluctance to seek God? What is our own ability to listen to the Word of God, our own discernment of hypocrisy and hunger for power, in ourselves, our world, our church? What is our own attitude to strangers and our appreciation of their wisdom? Do we make the refugees and asylum seekers welcome in the parish or as neighbors, or do we regard them as a threat to jobs, property values, national security, our own comfortable and myopic spiritual wisdom? How do we respond to the young people who are searching for their own stars to guide them in their "where" and "when" of something more in their lives? Where and when must there be both a "birth" and a "death" in our Christian lives as we gaze on the Christmas Child and recognize the mystery of the adult Christ for adult Christians?

Focusing the Gospel

Key words and phrases: They opened their treasures / and offered him gifts of gold, frankincense, and myrrh.

To the point: The magi arrive in Bethlehem intent upon finding the "newborn king of the Jews" who has been revealed to them by the light of a star. Upon encountering him with his mother, Mary, they are not content to only fall down in worship; they also desire to offer something tangible to the child. From their treasures they present him with gifts of gold, frankincense, and myrrh. In our own unique ways, we too have encountered the child of Bethlehem. We find him in the faces of those we hold dear, within the bread and wine of the Eucharist, and within our very hearts. In what ways might we respond, both in homage and through gifts, to the revelation of Christ within our midst?

Connecting the Gospel

to the first and second readings: The magi are the first formal visitors Jesus receives from outside the land of Israel. They are drawn to him by the revelation of creation itself in the light of a star. Within the story of the magi, we see a fulfillment of Isaiah's prophecy that "[n]ations shall walk by your light, / and kings by your shining radiance." In the second reading, St. Paul reflects on the inclusivity of God's plan by affirming that the "Gentiles are coheirs, members of the same body" along with his fellow Jews.

to experience: While we find within the gospel and the epistle historical events in which Jews and Gentiles (signifying all the people of the world) are brought together by the light of Christ, we are still waiting for the fullness of Isaiah's prophecy to take place in which the radiance of God's peace will eradicate the darkness of violence, war, and bloodshed. As we wait for the fullness of God's kingdom, we are invited to work for the peace and unity that God dreams for the world.

Connecting the Responsorial Psalm

to the readings: Today's psalm gives us more images for what the fullness of God's kingdom will look like when "every nation on earth will adore" the Creator. We are told that this will be a time of justice and "profound peace, till the moon be no more." This time is also set apart by care for the poor whose lives God "shall save."

to psalmist preparation: With its images of peace and justice, today's psalm is one of comfort, hope, and also of challenge. When we look at the world, we can see many places where this peace and justice do not yet reign, areas where the lives of the poor are endangered and threatened. As you prepare to lead the people of God in prayer, consider how you are attending to the work of peace and justice and care for the poor in your own life.

PROMPTS FOR FAITH-SHARING

In all three of today's readings we hear of different nations and different faiths coming together. How does your faith community reach out to those of different religions and different nationalities?

It was challenging for the early church to navigate the inclusion of both Gentile and Jewish followers of Christ. In your own parish, what groups have difficulty interacting with each other? How might they enjoy greater unity?

The newborn king of the Jews is not found in the palace in Jerusalem but in a humble home in Bethlehem. How do you recognize Jesus in the poor and the vulnerable?

Upon encountering Jesus, the magi respond by offering him gifts from amongst their "treasures." What treasures (either material or spiritual) are you being called to place at the service of Christ?

CELEBRATION

Model Penitential Act

Presider: On the feast of the Epiphany, Jesus is revealed as the savior of all who bring peace, justice, and mercy. Let us pause to recall the times we have not lived in the light of his peace and ask our Lord for healing . . . *[pause]*

Lord Jesus, you are the light of the nations: Lord, have mercy.

Christ Jesus, you are worthy of all glory and praise: Christ, have mercy.

Lord Jesus, you hear and answer the cry of the poor: Lord, have mercy.

Homily Points

• In their search for the newborn king of the Jews, the magi travel first to the place where one could plausibly expect to find a royal child—the royal city of Jerusalem. But they do not find Jesus among the wealthy, powerful, and elite. Instead, they are sent by the chief priests and scribes to Bethlehem, a small town that is a fitting birthplace for one who will use his authority to "shepherd" his people rather than rule over them with military power and coercive control.

• On the final Sunday of each liturgical year, we celebrate Jesus as the "king of the universe." Within this title we find a truth proclaimed about the Lord: He is powerful and mighty, deserving of all honor and praise. As Christians, however, we must always hold in tension this identity of Jesus with the equally true revelation of him as a helpless and humble child born far from the opulence and protection of a royal household. God did not choose for his son to be raised with ease and privilege, and as an adult Jesus did not perform miracles to impress or to exert power over others.

• In Jesus we find the marriage of total power with complete humility and vulnerability. The epiphany is a revelation of the person of Christ and a revelation of who we are called to be as Christians. The magi, well known, respected, and revered in their own country, come to Bethlehem to kneel at the feet of a peasant child whom they recognize as a king greater than any they have ever known. May we also find Jesus and be ready to serve him in the weak and the poor, for in our humility we become like Christ, the shepherd king.

Model Universal Prayer (Prayer of the Faithful)

Presider: Together with the universal church spread throughout the world, let us turn to our faithful God knowing that he hears and answers the prayers of those in need.

Response: Lord, hear our prayer.

For bishops, priests, deacons, religious, and lay ministers, in pondering the word of God may they be strengthened to humbly lead the people they serve . . .

For leaders of nations, together may they strive to protect the beauty and the resources of the earth for future generations . . .

For those who suffer from religious persecution throughout the world, may the fruit of inter-religious dialogue and ecumenism lead to safety of worship for all . . .

For all gathered here, may we worship the Lord in truth and eagerly offer him the best of our spiritual and material treasures . . .

Presider: God of creation, by the light of a star the magi sought and found Jesus, the savior of the world. Hear our prayers that in being attentive to your presence and grace in our own lives, we might be a source of light for others. We ask this through Christ our Lord. **Amen.**

COLLECT
Let us pray.

Pause for silent prayer

O God, who on this day
revealed your Only Begotten Son to the
    nations
by the guidance of a star,
grant in your mercy
that we, who know you already by faith,
may be brought to behold the beauty of
    your sublime glory.
Through our Lord Jesus Christ, your Son,
who lives and reigns with you in the unity
    of the Holy Spirit,
one God, for ever and ever. **Amen.**

FIRST READING
Isa 60:1-6

Rise up in splendor, Jerusalem! Your light
    has come,
    the glory of the Lord shines upon you.
See, darkness covers the earth,
    and thick clouds cover the peoples;
but upon you the LORD shines,
    and over you appears his glory.
Nations shall walk by your light,
    and kings by your shining radiance.
Raise your eyes and look about;
    they all gather and come to you:
your sons come from afar,
    and your daughters in the arms of their
        nurses.

Then you shall be radiant at what you see,
    your heart shall throb and overflow,
for the riches of the sea shall be emptied
        out before you,
    the wealth of nations shall be brought
        to you.
Caravans of camels shall fill you,
    dromedaries from Midian and Ephah;
all from Sheba shall come
    bearing gold and frankincense,
    and proclaiming the praises of the LORD.

RESPONSORIAL PSALM
Ps 72:1-2, 7-8, 10-11, 12-13

℟. (cf. 11) Lord, every nation on earth will
   adore you.

O God, with your judgment endow the
   king,
   and with your justice, the king's son;
he shall govern your people with justice
   and your afflicted ones with judgment.

℟. Lord, every nation on earth will adore
   you.

Justice shall flower in his days,
   and profound peace, till the moon be no
      more.
May he rule from sea to sea,
   and from the River to the ends of the
      earth.

℟. Lord, every nation on earth will adore
   you.

The kings of Tarshish and the Isles shall
   offer gifts;
   the kings of Arabia and Seba shall
      bring tribute.
All kings shall pay him homage,
   all nations shall serve him.

℟. Lord, every nation on earth will adore
   you.

For he shall rescue the poor when he cries
   out,
   and the afflicted when he has no one to
      help him.
He shall have pity for the lowly and the
   poor;
   the lives of the poor he shall save.

℟. Lord, every nation on earth will adore
   you.

SECOND READING
Eph 3:2-3a, 5-6

Brothers and sisters:
You have heard of the stewardship of
   God's grace
   that was given to me for your benefit,
   namely, that the mystery was made
      known to me by revelation.
It was not made known to people in other
   generations
   as it has now been revealed
to his holy apostles and prophets by the
   Spirit:
   that the Gentiles are coheirs, members
      of the same body,
   and copartners in the promise in Christ
      Jesus through the gospel.

About Liturgy

Processing Different Gifts: Beyond the blessings over doorways with "C+M+B 2021" and the requisite singing of "We Three Kings," some choose to, at liturgy, in either the entrance procession or at the preparation of the gifts, process with gold, frankincense, and myrrh, the three gifts mentioned in today's gospel. Without care, this sort of moment might be viewed as nothing more than a photo opportunity or meaningless ritual. It's not called for in the rubrics, after all. Take time to consider why you might include such a procession. Care should be taken to integrate it into the rites somehow: is the gold processed a gold paten, the frankincense some incense used at Mass, or is the "myrrh" the oil of the sick? Are these elements and their symbolisms of kingship, divinity, and death preached about during the homily? Unless a strong case can be made for inclusion, this is probably a liturgical addition to avoid.

About Processing

Faith Is a Journey: On Epiphany, we celebrate, in the Western church, the visitation of the magi to the Christ Child. We hear very little about the journey they must have taken: we know not from where they came and to where they returned, for instance. But it is helpful to consider their journey as a procession.

At eucharistic liturgies, there typically are several processions: at the entrance, with the book of the gospels, the presentation of the gifts, the communion procession, and the recessional. There are others scattered throughout the year, like the Passion Sunday procession, the Holy Thursday procession to the altar of repose; there, too, are devotional processions in our faith, like the Stations of the Cross or Corpus Christi processions. Some would teach us that the first procession of Mass is each member of the assembly leaving their homes and journeying to the church.

Processions remind us that faith is a journey: like Israelites traveling through the desert, we journey, escaping bondage and passing through waters of rebirth to new life. We recall that the ground we walk on is holy ground and that the church to which we belong is rarely stationary but is active and in motion, from east to west, from sunrise to sunset, from birth to rebirth.

If, liturgically, we have neglected some processions of the various rites, it is worth considering the value of them, as a church prays together and is formed not only by words spoken and heard, but by the prayer of our whole bodies.

About Music

More than Dates: In this era of calendars—on our personal digital devices and synced to the cloud, as to be accessible in any given moment and place—some may not see the value of including the sung proclamation the "Announcement of Easter and the Movable Feasts" in the day's festivities. A quick internet search, if Easter is not already in our calendar, will tell us what most people would want to know, at least logistically.

This proclamation, though, conveys something more than just dates and holidays. It reminds the faithful, as the days of Christmastide continue, that there is a connection between the nativity and the resurrection, and that the whole of the Christian year—the whole of our Christian lives—orbits the day of resurrection. Perhaps someone in the pews this day also heard its "sister proclamation" on Christmas, "The Nativity of our Lord Jesus Christ," and is well-suited then to place the resurrection event more completely in the context of salvation history.

Don't overlook this seemingly perfunctory and arcane bit of liturgy! It can have a powerful effect and communicate much when sung well (by a deacon or cantor) and approached with understanding and care.

JANUARY 3, 2021
THE EPIPHANY OF THE LORD

SPIRITUALITY

R̸. Alleluia, alleluia.
John saw Jesus approaching him, and said:
Behold the Lamb of God who takes away the
    sin of the world.
R̸. Alleluia, alleluia.

or:

cf. Mark 9:7

R̸. Alleluia, alleluia.
The heavens were opened and the voice of the
    Father thundered:
This is my beloved Son, listen to him.
R̸. Alleluia, alleluia.

Gospel

Mark 1:7-11; L21B

This is what John the Baptist
    proclaimed:
  "One mightier than I is
      coming after me.
I am not worthy to stoop and
    loosen the thongs of his
    sandals.
I have baptized you with water;
  he will baptize you with the Holy
    Spirit."

It happened in those days that Jesus
    came from Nazareth of Galilee
  and was baptized in the Jordan by
    John.
On coming up out of the water he saw
    the heavens being torn open
  and the Spirit, like a dove,
      descending upon him.
And a voice came from the heavens,
  "You are my beloved Son; with you I
    am well pleased."

Reflecting on the Gospel

John the Baptist is part of the stirring excitement of a new beginning of the Good News that Mark announces in the first verse of his gospel. He is the precursor, the one going before Jesus to prepare his way.

Mark describes Jesus's arrival from the humble and unimportant village of Nazareth, in Galilee, in case anyone doesn't know it. Although he is without sin (cf. 2 Cor 5:21), Jesus puts himself in solidarity with the crowd and with sinful humanity. He bares his human body and at this, his first public appearance, chooses to go down into the waters of the Jordan to be baptized by John as a representative of our collective guilt. As he rises up, the heavens are torn open, and the action of God is manifested in the descent of the Spirit "like a dove" and the voice addresses Jesus as "my beloved Son; with you I am well pleased." In the person of Jesus, this is the beginning of a new age, a new relationship of earth and heaven, of the whole of creation and our human condition. As Joel Marcus comments: "God has ripped the heavens apart irrevocably at Jesus' baptism, never to shut them again. Through this gracious gash in the universe, he has poured forth his Spirit into the earthly realm" (*Mark 1–8*, The Anchor Bible 27). Here is the answer to the cry of the exiles to God: "Oh, that you would rend the heavens and come down" (Isa 64:1)! But there is no mountain quaking, no violent cosmic disturbances in this rending; it is a "gracious gash." The symbolism of "like a dove" is perhaps a memory of the spirit/wind of God that brooded birdlike over the face of the primeval waters at the first creation (Gen 1:2). It is also a witness to the gentle action of God that descends upon Jesus to empower him, like the prophets, with gentle service of the poor (e.g., Isa 42:1-5; 61:1) and our humanity that is impoverished by our sinfulness.

The word spoken by the Father at the baptism of Jesus is addressed to Jesus, not the Baptist or the crowd. The voice of God affirms Jesus as "my Son," with memories of Psalm 2:7, a royal coronation psalm, and then as "the Beloved" upon whom God's favor rests. In the humble setting of the Jordan River, a humble man from a humble Galilean village is baptized by the humble precursor and proclaimed by God as one with royal dignity. Three times in the testing of faith at Mount Moriah, Abraham refers to Isaac as his "beloved son" as Isaac and he face the sacrificial knife out of obedience to God (Gen 22:2, 12, 16, LXX). The cost of Jesus's allegiance to his Father as yet hovers only as gently as a dove; in the not-too-distant future it is the carrion crow of death that will descend upon Jesus before he is unbound in the resurrection because of his obedient love of his Father.

This gospel is a declaration of who Jesus is to Mark's church, a statement of their self-understanding as disciples of the new messianic times who are sons and daughters of the Father because they are baptized into the Spirit-filled and Beloved Son, and commissioned to serve in his name. Throughout Mark's gospel, those who follow Jesus will struggle to understand and accept the implications of accepting one who is Son and Beloved, to understand what is revealed to Jesus as he rises from the waters: that humanity, despite its sinfulness, is loved with the prodigal love of God. The first human being in this gospel who professes faith in Jesus as the Son of God and recognizes the heavens torn open in the torn body of the crucified One is the Gentile centurion. We are caught up in this same struggle of faith. Baptism demanded everything of Jesus—as it does of us.

Focusing the Gospel
Key words and phrases: "He will baptize you with the Holy Spirit."

To the point: At the time of John the Baptist, baptism was performed as a ritual of cleansing and repentance. The one who entered into the waters was publicly proclaiming his or her sin and the desire to be washed clean of its effects. In today's gospel, John identifies the difference between the baptism he performs and the one that will be offered by Jesus. In Jesus, there is not only the cleansing from sin but also newness of life. In our Christian baptism, we enter into the death and resurrection of Jesus and through the power of the Holy Spirit become a new creation in Christ.

Connecting the Gospel
to the first reading: Today's first reading contains the first of four "Servant Songs" found in the book of the prophet Isaiah. While the other three servant songs are often interpreted as referring to an individual, this one seems to have been alluding to the entire people of Israel. One reason for this interpretation is that in the previous chapter, God addresses his people as "[Y]ou, Israel, my servant" (41:8; NABRE). When we, as Christians, read this hymn to a servant of God who will be "a light for the nations, / to open the eyes of the blind, / to bring prisoners out of confinement," we immediately think of Jesus, who has been revealed to us as the light of the world and did indeed open the eyes of the blind and proclaim liberty to captives. As the Body of Christ in the world, we might be served by considering these words as not only proclaiming a truth about who Jesus is but also a truth about who we are called to be.

to experience: Take a moment to consider the first reading as directed toward you as an individual and then directed toward your parish community. How have you and your community been able to fulfill these words so far in your journey of faith? How might God be inviting you to embody them more fully?

Connecting the Responsorial Psalm
to the readings: When Jesus comes out of the waters, he witnesses "the Spirit, like a dove, descending upon him." In the dove we find a symbol of peace, hearkening back to the dove who brought Noah an olive branch to signal the end of the great flood and a new covenant between God and humans. In this covenant, God promised to never again "strike down every living being, as I have done" (Genesis 8:21; NABRE). At the beginning of his public ministry, Jesus receives an affirmation of his identity as God's beloved Son who is anointed to bring God's spirit of peace and love to all people. Today's psalm once again proclaims God's deep desire to "bless his people with peace."

to psalmist preparation: Where in your life are you in need of the peace of God, which casts out all anxieties, doubts, and fears?

PROMPTS FOR FAITH-SHARING

Today's feast calls to mind the day of our own baptism. What do you remember or what stories have you heard about the day you were baptized?

In the first reading the servant of the Lord is described as one who will "bring out prisoners from confinement." Where in your life are you in need of Jesus's freeing touch?

In the Acts of the Apostles, Peter tells the gathered community, "God shows no partiality." In your family, faith community, or city do you see some individuals or groups receive particular acclaim or censure due to their race, gender, or religious creed? How can you challenge these biases when you encounter them?

John the Baptist proclaims that Jesus will baptize "with the Holy Spirit." What does this mean to you? How have you experienced the actions of the Holy Spirit most recently in your life?

CELEBRATION

Model Rite for the Blessing and Sprinkling of Water

Presider: At his baptism, Christ is named as the beloved Son of God and commissioned to begin his public ministry. May these holy waters remind us of the grace of our own baptism when we, too, were claimed as God's beloved and anointed to serve him . . . *[pause]*

[*continue with* The Roman Missal, *Appendix II*]

Homily Points

• On the banks of the Jordan river, John the Baptist tells the gathered crowd that there is one who is coming after him who will baptize not with mere water but "with the Holy Spirit." The men and women who have presented themselves for John's baptism of repentance are ready for a newness of life. They desire to be washed clean from the old habits and sins that have kept them captive and to enjoy the freedom of a forgiven child of God. If the water of the Jordan could produce those effects, what then can we expect from a baptism of the Holy Spirit—a plunging not only into rushing water but into the very life of God?

• Today's second reading gives us an idea of what being baptized in the Holy Spirit is meant to bring about. Peter tells us that after "God anointed Jesus of Nazareth / with the Holy Spirit and power . . . He went about doing good / and healing all those oppressed by the devil, / for God was with him." The prophet Isaiah also offers clues, describing the servant on which God has "put [his] spirit" as one who "shall bring forth justice," "open the eyes of the blind . . . and bring out prisoners from confinement."

• In our Christian tradition, baptism is not only for repentance but also an entry into the death and resurrection of Jesus. We are baptized in the name of the Father, Son, and Holy Spirit and anointed as "priest, prophet, and king" to bear the light and life of God to the lost and the brokenhearted. Today, as we celebrate the baptism of the Lord may the grace of our own baptism be stirred anew within us so we might continue to be transformed by the power of the Holy Spirit prompting us to do what is good, bring forth justice, and seek the lost.

Model Universal Prayer (Prayer of the Faithful)

Presider: In baptism we were each anointed priest, prophet, and king. Let us, together, lift our voices to our God, entrusting to him our needs and the needs of our world.

Response: Lord, hear our prayer.

For all who minister to the people of God, strengthened by the grace of their baptism, may they testify to the light of Christ in word and deed . . .

For areas of the world suffering due to drought and a lack of clean drinking water, may scientists and politicians come together to propose solutions and offer aid . . .

For all those who are incarcerated, may they know the support of a forgiving and loving community, and encounter opportunities for growth and healing . . .

For all gathered here, nourished by the word of God, may we be renewed in mind, body, and spirit to bring Christ's merciful love to all we meet . . .

Presider: God of compassion, despite our weaknesses and our sinfulness, you look upon each of us as a beloved child. Hear our prayers that through the power of the Holy Spirit we might serve you with fidelity all the days of our lives. We ask this through Christ our Lord. **Amen.**

RESPONSORIAL PSALM
Ps 29:1-2, 3-4, 3, 9-10

R/. (11b) The Lord will bless his people with peace.

Give to the LORD, you sons of God,
  give to the LORD glory and praise,
give to the LORD the glory due his name;
  adore the LORD in holy attire.

R/. The Lord will bless his people with peace.

The voice of the LORD is over the waters,
  the LORD, over vast waters.
The voice of the LORD is mighty;
  the voice of the LORD is majestic.

R/. The Lord will bless his people with peace.

The God of glory thunders,
  and in his temple all say, "Glory!"
The LORD is enthroned above the flood;
  the LORD is enthroned as king forever.

R/. The Lord will bless his people with peace.

SECOND READING
Acts 10:34-38

Peter proceeded to speak to those gathered
  in the house of Cornelius, saying:
  "In truth, I see that God shows no
    partiality.
Rather, in every nation whoever fears him
    and acts uprightly
  is acceptable to him.
You know the word that he sent to the
    Israelites
  as he proclaimed peace through Jesus
    Christ, who is Lord of all,
  what has happened all over Judea,
  beginning in Galilee after the baptism
  that John preached,
  how God anointed Jesus of Nazareth
  with the Holy Spirit and power.
He went about doing good
  and healing all those oppressed by the
    devil,
  for God was with him."

Other readings may also be used.
See Appendix A, p. 266.

About Liturgy

"The Work of Christmas": There is a brief poem by Howard Thurman that comes to mind as the Christmas season reaches its last day. It is titled "The Work of Christmas" (in *The Mood of Christmas and Other Celebrations*): "When the song of the angels is stilled, / When the star in the sky is gone, / When the kings and princes are home, / When the shepherds are back with their flock, / The work of Christmas begins: / To find the lost, / To heal the broken, / To feed the hungry, / To release the prisoner, / To rebuild the nations, / To bring peace among brothers, / To make music from the heart."

It is difficult to imagine a more perfect and concise text for this celebration. Celebrating the baptism of Jesus is more than a liturgical remembrance of an historical event: like all liturgy, it binds past, present, and future together as one. In this case, our celebration reminds us of our own baptism and what that means for us as we go about our day-to-day lives. Consider including a sprinkling rite, supplanting the penitential act near the beginning of the celebration, and ensuring that the other variable parts of this liturgy strongly link Jesus's earthly mission (one description of which he once proclaimed himself from the prophecy of Isaiah) to our own, as mentioned in this wonderful poem.

About Water

Ubiquitous Paradox: Water is one of the symbols of our faith steeped in paradox. It is, in a way, our first home—for all of us began life in our mother's womb—yet it is for some of us our death and tomb. While it cleans and purifies, water can also be the bearer of illness and disease. While in some places it is as common as rain or the seashore, in other places it is rarely seen in nature.

Water is, principally for the faithful, death and life simultaneously. If designed well, the font in our church reminds us of womb and tomb, with the water itself prominent and obvious (BLS 68). Further, as baptism itself is the sacramental entry into the life of the church, it is desirable that the font and its water be located near the entry doors to the church, and indeed set "on an axis with the altar" to "symbolize the relationship between the various sacraments as well as the importance of the Eucharist within the life and faith development of the members" (BLS 69).

Water is what, sacramentally, makes us God's people, each of us an adopted heir, baptized as priest, prophet, and king, raised by symbolic death to new life.

About Music

Christmas and Mission: As mentioned above, this celebration is an ideal time to include a sprinkling rite at liturgy. There is no shortage of appropriate music for the ritual, but consider "Come to Me and You Shall Never Hunger" from *Psallite* (Liturgical Press) or "Spirit, Move Upon the Waters" to the familiar NETTLETON tune (WLP). We should also note that the church is still in Christmastide today, and therefore we should still include some music of the season.

Additionally, "Songs of Thankfulness and Praise" has a wonderful text about several manifestations of Jesus's divinity, referencing not only Jesus's baptism but also the visit of the magi, Jesus's first miracle at Cana, and other miracles. These first three, in the Eastern church, are known as the "Theophany" and remind each of us not only of Christ's divinity but of the mission that is given to us as disciples at our own baptism, and the last verse of this hymn calls us to that imitation of Christ.

ORDINARY
TIME I

SPIRITUALITY

GOSPEL ACCLAMATION
John 1:41, 17b

℟. Alleluia, alleluia.
We have found the Messiah:
Jesus Christ, who brings us truth and
    grace.
℟. Alleluia, alleluia.

Gospel

John 1:35-42; L65B

**John was standing with two of his
    disciples,
  and as he watched Jesus walk
    by, he said,
"Behold, the Lamb of God."
The two disciples heard what he
    said and followed Jesus.
Jesus turned and saw them fol-
    lowing him and said to them,
"What are you looking for?"
They said to him, "Rabbi"—which
    translated means Teacher—,
"where are you staying?"
He said to them, "Come, and you
    will see."
So they went and saw where Jesus was
    staying,
  and they stayed with him that day.
It was about four in the afternoon.
Andrew, the brother of Simon Peter,
  was one of the two who heard John
    and followed Jesus.
He first found his own brother Simon
    and told him,
"We have found the Messiah"—which
    is translated Christ.
Then he brought him to Jesus.
Jesus looked at him and said,
"You are Simon the son of John;
  you will be called Cephas"—which is
    translated Peter.**

Reflecting on the Gospel

As we begin our journey through Ordinary Time, the gospel begins with looking and gazing and responding to the call to discipleship. John the Baptist
stands with two of his disciples, ready to decrease in personal significance so
that Jesus may increase (cf. John 3:30). After his testimony there will be no hanging onto or hankering for his former disciples. John watches Jesus pass by; the
eyes of John's heart penetrate to the reality of
this man, and he points him out to his disciples
as the Lamb of God. The Jewish religious experience of the lamb was as the sacrificial offering
that overcame the alienation of sin and created
unity between the people and God. In whatever
way the Baptist's disciples understood his words,
they were spoken with an urgency that made
them leave John and follow Jesus. Jesus himself
turns and sees them. The word the evangelist
uses for "saw" (*theásthai*) has the sense of gazing contemplatively and engagingly at these two
followers. Jesus then asks them his first question
in the fourth gospel: "What are you looking for?"
It is a question that will persist throughout this
gospel, from this first chapter to the garden of
the resurrection morning, but by then the "What"
has become "Whom" in the intimate encounter of
Jesus and Mary Magdalene (John 20:15).

    The two disciples ask Jesus, the Teacher
(Rabbi), where he is staying, and he responds
by inviting them to "Come, and you will see." Their question is about a place;
their experience is about abiding for the rest of the day in a relationship with
a person, about the beginning of a new communion between the people and
this Lamb of God. The "where" is not as important as the "with whom." The
pattern of discipleship is established: through witness (of the Baptist), others
follow and experience Jesus's truth for themselves. They in turn bring others to
Jesus. One of the first two who followed Jesus remains anonymous, perhaps as
a Johannine invitation to future readers to see a challenge to themselves in the
following, seeking pattern of discipleship. The other is later named as Andrew,
who announces to his brother, Simon Peter, that he has found the Messiah. Like
the first disciples, we all see something different in this same Jesus, and Jesus
recognizes the truth in us, just as in this first chapter of the fourth gospel,
Jesus's insight into Simon's role in the community of the disciples suggests his
renaming as Cephas (in Aramaic, *kepha*; in Greek, *petra*; in English, *rock*).

    This gospel proclaims that all discipleship is an active and involving relation-
ship with Jesus: a following, seeking, staying, finding, and dialoguing with him.
We hear how each decision to follow Jesus is a response to a statement about
Jesus's identity as Lamb of God, Rabbi, Messiah, by people whose ears and
hearts are open to the Word of God, who hear his invitation through the words
of friend or stranger, through events of joy or sorrow, or who discern a moment
of religious significance in the everyday. As the nineteenth-century English
poet Matthew Arnold wrote in his haunting poem "The Buried Life":

    But often, in the world's most crowded streets,
    But often in the din of strife,

There rises an unspeakable desire
After the knowledge of our buried life;
A thirst to spend our fire and restless force
In tracking out our true, original course,
A longing to enquire
Into the mystery of this heart which beats
So wild, so deep in us—to know
Whence our lives come and whence they go.

Focusing the Gospel

Key words and phrases: "Behold, the Lamb of God."

To the point: John's proclamation about Jesus is ripe with theological significance. In naming Jesus the "Lamb of God," he emphasizes not only that Jesus is consecrated and set apart for a holy purpose, but also that Jesus's life will end in sacrifice to save others, calling to mind the blood of the lambs spread above the doorways of the Hebrew people in the land of Egypt so the angel of death might pass over them. Hearing John's words, two of his own disciples are intrigued enough to approach Jesus and then follow him to where he is staying. These first steps are the beginning of a path that will eventually lead them to the agony of the cross and then, finally, to the joy of the empty tomb.

Connecting the Gospel

to the first reading: In the first reading, we encounter another story of an invitation accepted and a life changed. The youth Samuel hears a voice calling to him in the night. At first he is confused about who is summoning him, but after receiving direction from his mentor, Eli, he responds to God's call, saying, "Speak, for your servant is listening." In the reading we hear that "[a]t that time Samuel was not familiar with the Lord, / because the Lord had not revealed anything to him as yet."

to experience: Both Samuel and the two disciples from the gospel begin a journey that will change the trajectory of their lives and bring them to the limits of their abilities, demanding all of who they are and even, in the case of Andrew and Peter, their very lives. They do not walk the road alone, however. In each stage they are guided and fortified by the light and life of God. Though we cannot see where our own journey of faith is leading, we can be assured of the presence and friendship of the same divine companion walking ahead of us to show us the way.

Connecting the Responsorial Psalm

to the readings: In today's readings we are given two similar prayers with which to ponder the life of discipleship. The psalm refrain "Here am I, Lord; I come to do your will" is very similar to Samuel's response to the divine voice calling him by name: "Speak, Lord, for your servant is listening." Both express an awareness of God's presence and also complete trust in God's plan and action in their lives. As the psalmist recounts, however, the life of discipleship is not always straightforward and can require a good deal of patience ("I have waited, waited for the Lord").

to psalmist preparation: This week, take time to pray with the words from the psalm response. What does it mean to show up each day in your relationship with God and to be eager to do God's will?

PROMPTS FOR FAITH-SHARING

In the first reading, Samuel hears God's voice calling to him as he sleeps. How do you experience the voice of God calling to you?

The psalm response for today echoes Samuel's answer to the voice calling to him in the night, "Here I am." How do you practice being present to God and to those who share your life?

St. Paul writes to the Corinthians, "Do you not know that your body / is a temple of the Holy Spirit within you?" How would you answer Paul's question?

In today's gospel Jesus is identified as the Lamb of God, as Teacher, and as Messiah. What do these titles tell you about Jesus's identity?

Model Penitential Act

Presider: In today's first reading Samuel hears the voice of God calling in the night and responds, "Speak, for your servant is listening." For the times we have failed to respond to God's call in our own lives, let us ask for pardon and mercy . . . *[pause]*

Lord Jesus, you are the Messiah, the anointed one of God: Lord, have mercy.

Christ Jesus, you are the true Teacher who shows the way to everlasting life: Christ, have mercy.

Lord Jesus, you are the Lamb of God, who takes away the sins of the world: Lord, have mercy.

Homily Points

• Following the anticipation and excitement of Advent and Christmas, we find ourselves in Ordinary Time. This liturgical year, the majority of the gospel readings in Ordinary Time will come from Mark. One of the exceptions is the gospel for this Sunday, where we read from the first chapter of John. Two disciples of John the Baptist, hearing John's proclamation "Behold, the Lamb of God" as Jesus walked by are intrigued. They approach Jesus and ask him, "Where are you staying?" Instead of answering directly, Jesus responds, "Come, and you will see."

• As readers of this story, we do not learn where Jesus is staying, but we are told that the men follow Jesus there and then stay with him that day. In each of the gospels, Jesus's closest followers share his days, moving throughout the land of Israel preaching, healing the sick, and eating with sinners and outcasts. They come to know Jesus not only through his words but more importantly through his actions. In his book *Into His Likeness,* Edward Sri writes that in Jesus's time "disciples were known for walking behind their rabbi, following him so closely that they would become covered with the dust kicked up from his sandals. . . . Disciples were expected to follow their rabbi so closely that they would be covered with their master's whole way of thinking, living, and acting."

• As we enter into the season of Ordinary Time, we are also invited to live deeper into our relationship with Jesus by sharing our days with him. And we're welcomed to live the gospel once again along with Jesus's closest disciples as they follow in his footsteps and answer his invitation to "come, and you will see."

Model Universal Prayer (Prayer of the Faithful)

Presider: Trusting in the limitless compassion of our God and his care for all of creation, let us bring our needs and the needs of the world before him.

Response: Lord, hear our prayer.

For the church throughout the world, in prayer and worship may it listen for the voice of God calling it to fidelity and holiness . . .

For all who serve as teachers and educators, may they be inspired to provide the best instruction, care, and support to their pupils . . .

For all who are seeking employment, may they find meaningful work and a just wage to support themselves and their families . . .

For all gathered here, by encountering Jesus, the Messiah, in word and sacrament, may we be emboldened to follow where he leads . . .

Presider: Loving God, you call us by name and desire to bring us to the fullness of life. Hear our prayers that with ears attuned to your voice, we might listen for your call and answer, "Here am I, Lord, I come to do your will." We ask this through Christ our Lord. **Amen.**

COLLECT

Let us pray.

Pause for silent prayer

Almighty ever-living God,
who govern all things,
both in heaven and on earth,
mercifully hear the pleading of your
people
and bestow your peace on our times.
Through our Lord Jesus Christ, your Son,
who lives and reigns with you in the unity
of the Holy Spirit,
one God, for ever and ever. **Amen.**

FIRST READING
1 Sam 3:3b-10, 19

Samuel was sleeping in the temple of the LORD
where the ark of God was.
The LORD called to Samuel, who answered,
"Here I am."
Samuel ran to Eli and said, "Here I am.
You called me."
"I did not call you," Eli said. "Go back to
sleep."
So he went back to sleep.
Again the LORD called Samuel, who rose
and went to Eli.
"Here I am," he said. "You called me."
But Eli answered, "I did not call you, my
son. Go back to sleep."

At that time Samuel was not familiar with
the LORD,
because the LORD had not revealed
anything to him as yet.
The LORD called Samuel again, for the
third time.
Getting up and going to Eli, he said, "Here
I am. You called me."
Then Eli understood that the LORD was
calling the youth.
So he said to Samuel, "Go to sleep, and if
you are called, reply,
Speak, LORD, for your servant is
listening."
When Samuel went to sleep in his place,
the LORD came and revealed his
presence,
calling out as before, "Samuel, Samuel!"
Samuel answered, "Speak, for your
servant is listening."

Samuel grew up, and the LORD was with
him,
not permitting any word of his to be
without effect.

RESPONSORIAL PSALM

Ps 40:2, 4, 7-8, 8-9, 10

R̸. (8a and 9a) Here am I, Lord; I come to
   do your will.

I have waited, waited for the LORD,
   and he stooped toward me and heard
      my cry.
And he put a new song into my mouth,
   a hymn to our God.

R̸. Here am I, Lord; I come to do your will.

Sacrifice or offering you wished not,
   but ears open to obedience you gave me.
Holocausts or sin-offerings you sought not;
   then said I, "Behold I come."

R̸. Here am I, Lord; I come to do your will.

"In the written scroll it is prescribed for
   me,
to do your will, O my God, is my delight,
   and your law is within my heart!"

R̸. Here am I, Lord; I come to do your will.

I announced your justice in the vast
   assembly;
   I did not restrain my lips, as you, O
      LORD, know.

R̸. Here am I, Lord; I come to do your will.

SECOND READING

1 Cor 6:13c-15a, 17-20

Brothers and sisters:
The body is not for immorality, but for the
   Lord,
   and the Lord is for the body;
   God raised the Lord and will also raise
      us by his power.

Do you not know that your bodies are
   members of Christ?
But whoever is joined to the Lord becomes
   one Spirit with him.
Avoid immorality.
Every other sin a person commits is
   outside the body,
   but the immoral person sins against his
      own body.
Do you not know that your body
   is a temple of the Holy Spirit within
      you,
   whom you have from God, and that you
      are not your own?
For you have been purchased at a price.
Therefore glorify God in your body.

CATECHESIS

About Liturgy

Liturgical Evangelization: In today's Old Testament and gospel readings, God's calls reach the ears, and indeed the very souls, of people not expecting it. Further, we might not expect God's call to be given to ones such as these: an eleven-year-old, Samuel, apparently working as a sort of sacristan in the temple, and two men who are already disciples of another: John the Baptist.

Our liturgical work includes elements of evangelization and catechesis. That is, we are charged with bringing people to the liturgies themselves and sharing the Good News, as well as forming and educating them on matters of faith. More simply, we are charged with calling and fashioning new disciples. Over these few weeks of Ordinary Time, let us take a few moments each week to dig deeper into these facets of our ministries.

First, evangelization. How do we preach the Good News to those who most need to hear it? Is that message of hope and salvation brought outside the church doors somehow? Are those who have fallen away from the faith invited to return? Many parishes have "Evangelization Committees" whose ministry is just that: reaching out to those who, for instance, are registered in the parish but who have not been seen in the pews recently; spending time at public events, just being a faith-filled presence, ready for conversations about faith, community, and Christ; welcoming those who, by these efforts or others, have found their way again to the church building, curious about becoming "church" themselves.

Our Jewish brothers and sisters name this welcoming the stranger "Hachnasat Orchim." Abraham is held as the prime example of such hospitality, by his reception of wayfarers in Genesis 18. Some even note that his standing at the entrance of his tent is perhaps proactive, not waiting for others to come to him, but eagerly seeking out those who need welcome. It's worth noting that Scripture tells us that because of Abraham's "Hachnasat Orchim," he and Sarah were blessed with future generations (beginning with Isaac, father of Jacob, the patriarch of Israel), even though they were both advanced in age and had no reason to expect any new family members. Might our church families also be blessed by eagerly seeking out the lost and finding new ways to evangelize?

About Music

Behold the Lamb: John the Baptist begins today's gospel passage with the iconic phrase "Behold, the Lamb of God" (John 1:35). These words we know well; they are a part of every eucharistic celebration, words of the priest just after the congregation sings of that same Lamb of God, who takes away the sins of the world.

Many of us are familiar with Martin Willett's "Behold the Lamb" (OCP), with its strong connection to Eucharist and eucharistic living. Although we just finished celebrating Christ's nativity, the phrase "Lamb of God" should remind us of the purpose for which Christ was born—to be our paschal sacrifice. Bob Dufford's "Behold the Lamb of God" (OCP) may also spring instantly to mind and might not be as out of place as it initially seems, as we integrate our beliefs about the Messiah: the child of the cradle is also our Passover lamb. Paul Hillebrand has written a piece titled "Eucharistic Litany" (WLP), which effectively begins each verse, "Behold," to elaborate further on who the Christ we consume is: nourishment, strength, and unifier of humanity.

The themes of calling and following persist into next week's Scripture passages; for those looking for related music suggestions, look a few pages ahead!

SPIRITUALITY

GOSPEL ACCLAMATION
Mark 1:15

R̸. Alleluia, alleluia.
The kingdom of God is at hand.
Repent and believe in the Gospel.
R̸. Alleluia, alleluia.

Gospel

Mark 1:14-20; L68B

After John had been arrested,
  Jesus came to Galilee
      proclaiming the gospel of
      God:
"This is the time of fulfillment.
The kingdom of God is at hand.
Repent, and believe in the
    gospel."

As he passed by the Sea of
    Galilee,
he saw Simon and his brother
    Andrew casting their nets
    into the sea;
they were fishermen.
Jesus said to them,
"Come after me, and I will make you
    fishers of men."
Then they abandoned their nets and
    followed him.
He walked along a little farther
    and saw James, the son of Zebedee,
    and his brother John.
They too were in a boat mending their
    nets.
Then he called them.
So they left their father Zebedee in the
    boat
    along with the hired men and
      followed him.

Reflecting on the Gospel

In the wilderness Jesus has withstood Satan's temptation, and, strengthened in spirit by this personal combat, he comes into Galilee, the "springtime" place of first preaching, first ministry, first calling of disciples. Yet there has also been a winter: the arrest and imprisonment of John the Baptist, which add urgency to Jesus's first spoken words in Mark's gospel. The time of God's reigning presence is at hand, and this Good News of God demands a response. "Repent, and believe in the gospel" may have been repeated as an early Christian baptismal call to the catechumens (the elect) as they descended into the Easter waters to rise up as God's new creation. At infant baptism our parents and our faith community made this response for us; the challenge is for us to say our own continuing adult "Yes" to this call and grow in our discipleship.

Urged on by his sense of mission, Jesus passes along the lakeside, the Sea of Galilee. He "saw" Peter and Andrew, with a seeing that penetrates to their deepest selves and their future potential as his disciples whom, with all their successes and failures, he will make fishers of people to draw others into the kingdom. All that Simon and Andrew will become will be because of Jesus and, with contagious gospel urgency, "they abandoned their nets"—the source of their income—and follow him. A little further on another two brothers, James and John, sons of Zebedee, are called while they are involved in their fishermen's task of mending nets. Once again the call and response is immediate and the dispossession is radical when they follow Jesus. It is significant that the first disciples whom Jesus calls are people who must leave what is indicative of their success in a brotherly and family venture: boats, nets, hired servants, parent. They follow Jesus, not hoping for a better lifestyle, but urged by his words to an unconditional obedience to him. From the beginning of his ministry, Jesus gathers a community around himself in a relationship of "brotherliness" that the call of two sets of brothers may also suggest.

Whereas our consumer society has to package and market every commodity, every offer has to have a good sales pitch, even in some megachurches and by some TV evangelists, Mark's narrative of Jesus's call is stark and unadorned. Like any relationship, this is the "honeymoon" period (the terminology of Joel Marcus in *Mark 1–8*, The Anchor Bible 27). Much of what they understand at this moment they will progressively forget, and compromises, obtuseness, status-seeking will replace following until, on the eve of Jesus's passion and death, the disciples leave everything to run away from him (Mark 14:50-51). The traditional prophetic calling accounts, such as that of Samuel or Elisha's call by Elijah (1 Kgs 19:19-21), are transformed because now it is Jesus who calls. Jesus does not issue orders to his followers like a charismatic military leader (e.g., Judg 3:28; 1 Sam 11:6-7); he offers no rallying call to a revolutionary war (1 Macc 2:27-28), but he does make promises. Do we live as though we believe these promises? How constant, how radical are we in our following of Jesus to which we are invited by our baptism? How discerning of its demands are we in our contemporary society, and has Jesus priority in our lives? Do we continually try to launch out into a shared mission with Jesus that will transform us from day to day and draw other people into a relationship with him, or do we cling to the safe and familiar?

Focusing the Gospel

Key words and phrases: "Come after me, and I will make you fishers of men."

To the point: Jesus approaches his first disciples, Simon and Andrew, with an interesting proposition: leave your fishing nets and lives by the sea and turn your attention toward catching people in the net of God's love. In some ways, calling fishermen to his work seems like an odd choice and yet the skills needed for catching fish (patience, perseverance, hard work, ability to weather storms) would likely come in handy when fishing for people. Within the gospel, Jesus chooses ordinary people with everyday occupations to be his closest collaborators. Though they were not the obvious choices for founding his church, in following Jesus the disciples gained the knowledge, wisdom, and understanding to carry forth Jesus's mission after his death and resurrection. Today, Jesus continues to call ordinary, everyday people to be "fishers of men." How will we respond?

Connecting the Gospel

to the first reading: In the gospel, Jesus begins his public ministry by calling the people to "[r]epent, and believe in the gospel," and in the first reading we find an extreme example of repentance. The book of Jonah has been considered many different genres including satire, parable, and fable. In this story, many surprising things occur that would have startled and shocked the original readers, including that Nineveh (the ancient enemy of Israel) responds to Jonah's lackluster preaching with such total and immediate repentance that even their animals join in, dressed in sackcloth and ashes (4:7).

to experience: There are many different messages that can be gleaned from the book of Jonah. One could be that repentance (even for those we consider our greatest enemies and who have committed the most intolerable evil) is always possible.

Connecting the Responsorial Psalm

to the readings: God's loving compassion is affirmed by the psalmist who proclaims, "Good and upright is the Lord; / thus he shows sinners the way." This truth can be comforting when we apply it to ourselves and our own sinfulness, but challenging when we consider this boundless compassion enveloping those who have hurt us. Though the first reading offers only a portion of the book of Jonah, we know how this story ends. The Ninevites, who had crushed the northern kingdom of Israel and then ravaged Jerusalem in 701 BC, repent of their evil ways and are forgiven by God. Although this tale is fiction, it would have been difficult for the Israelites to swallow. We could place ourselves in this tale by thinking of the Ninevites as a nation or ideological group that has waged war or acts of terror on our own nation or members of our religion.

to psalmist preparation: Our responsorial psalm asks, "Teach me your ways, O Lord." One of these ways is God's unconditional love and forgiveness. How can you live deeper into this attribute of God this week?

PROMPTS FOR FAITH-SHARING

The responsorial psalm implores, "Teach me your ways, O Lord." Who have been the spiritual mentors and guides who have helped you learn the ways of God?

St. Paul tells the Corinthians, "[T]he world in its present form is passing away." What are the greatest changes you see within the world at this moment? How are we called to respond to these changes as people of faith?

Jesus calls Simon and Andrew to follow him and become "fishers of men." How does your parish community live out this call?

In today's gospel the disciples are called in pairs and together they leave their livelihoods and families to follow Jesus. Who are your closest collaborators and partners in living out the Christian life?

49

Model Penitential Act

Presider: In today's gospel Jesus proclaims, "The kingdom of God is at hand. / Repent, and believe in the gospel." Let us answer Jesus's invitation by taking a moment to call to mind our own sins and to ask God for healing and forgiveness . . . *[pause]*

    Lord Jesus, you are the voice calling us to fullness of life: Lord, have mercy.

    Christ Jesus, you are the way that leads to the Father: Christ, have mercy.

    Lord Jesus, you desire to gather all people to yourself: Lord, have mercy.

Homily Points

• Today we read Jesus's first spoken words in the Gospel of Mark: "This is the time of fulfillment. / The kingdom of God is at hand. / Repent, and believe in the gospel." Within these three statements we find the general thesis for the whole of Jesus's preaching. First, Jesus declares the time of fulfillment. While Jesus might be speaking of his life, when the Son of God has come to earth and a new moment in the history of salvation has begun, we can also find within these words a message of hope and challenge for us in the twenty-first century. In each moment our God is actively reaching for us, inviting us to join him. It is never too late or too early to respond to his invitation.

• In his translation of the New Testament, David Bentley Hart renders the next two sentences this way: "[T]he Kingdom of God has drawn near; change your hearts and have faith in good tidings." The theme of God's kingdom will dominate much of Jesus's preaching throughout the gospels. Rather than a place or a time, we could say the kingdom of God is a phenomenon that breaks forth whenever God's lordship is met with perfect trust, faith, and cooperation.

• Like John the Baptist, Jesus calls his listeners to repentance. The Greek word for repentance, "metanoia," evokes more than just a sorrow for individual sins, but an actual turning of one's whole being toward the Lord. As we continue on our journey of faith, returning to Jesus's first words in the gospel can help orient us to the heart of Jesus's preaching: Now is the time; be a part of the kingdom; turn your whole lives toward God.

Model Universal Prayer (Prayer of the Faithful)

Presider: Knowing that our God's compassion is from of old and his love is never-ending, let us confidently place before him our needs and our petitions.

Response: Lord, hear our prayer.

For God's holy church, may it carry out the mission of the earliest disciples by proclaiming the good news of Jesus Christ and searching for the lost . . .

For leaders of nations, may they work together to safeguard basic human rights for all people from conception to natural death . . .

For those who are imprisoned by addiction, through the grace of God may they be freed from illness of body, mind, and soul . . .

For all gathered here, may we hearken to Jesus's call for ongoing conversion and ever-deepening belief in the gospel . . .

Presider: God, Father of mercy and healer of souls, you never cease to invite us into closer relationship with you. Hear our prayers that in each action and word we might testify to your goodness and love. We ask this through Christ our Lord. **Amen.**

COLLECT

Let us pray.

Pause for silent prayer

Almighty ever-living God,
direct our actions according to your good
    pleasure,
that in the name of your beloved Son
we may abound in good works.
Through our Lord Jesus Christ, your Son,
who lives and reigns with you in the unity
    of the Holy Spirit,
one God, for ever and ever. **Amen.**

FIRST READING
Jonah 3:1-5, 10

The word of the LORD came to Jonah,
    saying:
    "Set out for the great city of Nineveh,
    and announce to it the message that I
        will tell you."
So Jonah made ready and went to Nineveh,
    according to the LORD's bidding.
Now Nineveh was an enormously large
    city;
    it took three days to go through it.
Jonah began his journey through the city,
    and had gone but a single day's walk
        announcing,
    "Forty days more and Nineveh shall be
        destroyed,"
    when the people of Nineveh believed
        God;
    they proclaimed a fast
    and all of them, great and small, put on
        sackcloth.

When God saw by their actions how they
    turned from their evil way,
    he repented of the evil that he had
        threatened to do to them;
    he did not carry it out.

RESPONSORIAL PSALM

Ps 25:4-5, 6-7, 8-9

℟. (4a) Teach me your ways, O Lord.

Your ways, O LORD, make known to me;
    teach me your paths,
guide me in your truth and teach me,
    for you are God my savior.

℟. Teach me your ways, O Lord.

Remember that your compassion, O LORD,
    and your love are from of old.
In your kindness remember me,
    because of your goodness, O LORD.

℟. Teach me your ways, O Lord.

Good and upright is the LORD;
    thus he shows sinners the way.
He guides the humble to justice
    and teaches the humble his way.

℟. Teach me your ways, O Lord.

SECOND READING

1 Cor 7:29-31

I tell you, brothers and sisters, the time is
    running out.
From now on, let those having wives act
    as not having them,
    those weeping as not weeping,
    those rejoicing as not rejoicing,
    those buying as not owning,
    those using the world as not using it
        fully.
For the world in its present form is
    passing away.

About Liturgy

Evangelization Through Welcoming: As we continue exploring the ways that liturgy enters into welcoming and catechesis, we hear in the first reading this weekend about Jonah's testimony in Nineveh, a forerunner of Jesus's proclamation of the coming reign of God.

You remember Jonah, don't you? While we hear today of his successful preaching, Jonah was not always so keen on answering God's call affirmatively. Jonah did his best to run away from the Lord at first, only to be thrown into a stormy sea, swallowed by a whale, vomited up onto dry land, and called to a second time.

Even if our evangelization and welcome have been effective, those who may be sitting in our pews on Sunday, for the first time or for the first time in a long time, could still have significant reservations and doubts about their presence in church. They might have feelings of unworthiness, they might feel like a fish out of water, and they could perhaps be second-guessing why they even got out of bed that morning.

Those of us responsible for preparing and executing our church's public prayer can be mindful of many things in the liturgy to ensure we are welcoming to those who are joining us for the first time, or the first time in a long time.

• Is there a greeting of the assembly from a lector or music minister prior to liturgy? Is it delivered in a clear, pleasing, and joy-filled tone?

• Are we thoughtful when we ask congregants to greet those around them? Are we careful to avoid singling out first-time visitors, who may feel uncomfortable having attention drawn to them during Mass?

• Are hymn numbers visibly posted or clearly announced? What about the Gloria and other music of the Ordinary of the Mass? Is everything readily and obviously available that someone sitting in the pews for the first time would need to fully participate in the liturgy?

• More broadly, while there are many immutable texts of our liturgies, are we paying enough attention to the changeable ones: hymn texts, preaching, intercessions, and the like? Do our spoken and sung prayers of our own choosing leave room for mystery, for doubt, for questions?

To break open that last point just a bit more: one need only do an internet search for any recent Pew Research study about religion to learn that many people, both those who call themselves still faithful and those who have left their faith, struggle greatly with many aspects of that faith. Our ministry, like Christ's, must be one that meets people where they are and offers loving invitations to form deeper relationships with God and with the Christian community. To try to do ministry in any other way is inauthentic and may not be the love that God is and that God calls us to. Love can never force another person to a certain belief, a certain way of life, a certain holiness. Love is constant, love pursues, but ultimately love only offers, only invites: Come, enter into the mystery. Journey with me; let us meet God together.

About Music

Come, Come, Come . . . : Today's gospel presents Jesus inviting fishermen, "Come after me . . ." (Mark 1:17). This is an invitation to discipleship and should call to mind countless songs: "The Summons" (GIA Publications [GIA]), "Come Follow Me and Live" (OCP), and "Pescador de Hombres" to name but a few. In *Psallite* (Liturgical Press) there are no fewer than seven chants that begin with the word "Come," notably "Come, All You Good and Faithful Servants."

✠ SPIRITUALITY

GOSPEL ACCLAMATION
Matt 4:16

R⁊. Alleluia, alleluia.
The people who sit in darkness have seen a great
    light;
on those dwelling in a land overshadowed by
    death,
light has arisen.
R⁊. Alleluia, alleluia.

Gospel

Mark 1:21-28; L71B

Then they came to
    Capernaum,
  and on the sabbath
      Jesus entered the
      synagogue and
      taught.
The people were
    astonished at his
    teaching,
  for he taught them as one
      having authority and
      not as the scribes.
In their synagogue was a man
    with an unclean spirit;
  he cried out, "What have you to do
      with us, Jesus of Nazareth?
Have you come to destroy us?
I know who you are—the Holy One of
    God!"
Jesus rebuked him and said,
  "Quiet! Come out of him!"
The unclean spirit convulsed him and
    with a loud cry came out of him.
All were amazed and asked one
    another,
  "What is this?
A new teaching with authority.
He commands even the unclean spirits
    and they obey him."
His fame spread everywhere
    throughout the whole region of
    Galilee.

Reflecting on the Gospel

We are all formally students for some time in our lives, and it is best to remain informal students throughout our lives, for there is no point at which there is not something we can learn. At the same time, most of us function as teachers at many points in our lives, some of us professionally but most of us casually, guiding and directing people in ways that might even escape us. We teach by how we live, how we treat people, how we respond under stress, how we reprimand a child, how we help a neighbor, as well as by more concrete and direct ways of teaching.

Some of us, by training and vocation, teach religion and theology, and it is those of us engaged in this vocation who must always remain students in our area of expertise, for Jesus says, "You are not to be called rabbi, for you have one teacher, and you are all students. And call no one your father on earth, for you have one Father—the one in heaven. Nor are you to be called instructors, for you have one instructor, the Messiah" (Matt 23:8-10; NRSV). This teaching is directed at all Christians, but it is a difficult teaching for those called upon to be teachers and instructors, for it is easy to forget that in the things of God we are always students.

It is telling, and especially humbling for biblical scholars, to remember that Jesus did not choose his apostles from among the biblical interpreters or experts in Jewish Halakah (roughly equivalent to canon lawyers today) but from among the fishermen. How could fishermen be teachers in the Bible and Jewish law when they had not been formally trained? What did they know that the experts did not?

What the fishermen knew, or were willing to encounter, was the only true subject: God. The unschooled fishermen knew Jesus, spent time with Jesus, and were willing to learn from Jesus what they did not know. It was not technical expertise that Jesus sought in his apostles but the willingness to encounter the word of God as life-changing and life-giving.

It was the encounter with truth that led the students, the crowds of ordinary people in Galilee, Judea, and elsewhere, to throng around the teacher Jesus; they responded as people hungry to learn the deepest reality about God and themselves. So, "on the sabbath Jesus entered the synagogue and taught. The people were astonished at his teaching, for he taught them as one having authority and not as the scribes." The religious experts, the scribes, are mentioned, though it seems they are not present, as a contrast to Jesus's authority. Perhaps the experts hung back, wary of how Jesus's teaching might affect their livelihood or authority, or because they disagreed that Jesus's authority was grounded in the Scriptures or God.

Yet, Jesus's final act in the Capernaum synagogue is the demonstration of the divine ground of his teaching authority, for "[i]n their synagogue was a man with an unclean spirit; he cried out, 'What have you to do with us, Jesus of Nazareth? Have you come to destroy us? I know who you are—the Holy One of God!'" Jesus healed the man of the unclean spirit, and the people were again "amazed," referring to this action of Jesus as a "teaching": "[They] asked one another, 'What is this? A new teaching with authority.'" It is God's presence and power that is the lesson not only to learn but to encounter.

It is necessary to have teachers in all areas of knowledge, and this includes theology and biblical studies. Expertise and properly ordered authority are essential for all fields. But ultimately we are all students of the one teacher, whose authority is ordered to our salvation and joy. From this school we never graduate; this teacher is always guiding us. This education is perfected for our final purpose: to know God.

Focusing the Gospel
Key words and phrases: [P]eople were astonished at his teaching.

To the point: Unlike in Luke's gospel when Jesus attends the synagogue in Nazareth, reads from the scroll of Isaiah, and tells the people, "Today this scripture passage is fulfilled in your hearing" (4:21; NABRE), we don't know exactly what Jesus preached in Capernaum. The only detail we are given is the people's reaction to his words: astonishment. In particular, they compare his teaching to that of the scribes and remark on the "authority" Jesus displays. As the complete revelation of God, Jesus is named at the beginning of John's gospel as the "Word," and we continue to draw close to him whenever the Scriptures are proclaimed. May we also open ourselves to the shocking and challenging nature of Jesus's preaching.

Connecting the Gospel
to the first reading: The people of Israel gather at the foot of Mount Sinai on the day Moses is given the Ten Commandments. While they watch and wait, Moses goes to the mountaintop to converse with God, and though God's face is obscured in a "dense cloud" (Exod 19:9; NABRE), the people witness "thunder and lightning, the blast of the shofar and the mountain smoking" (Exod 20:18; NABRE). It's no surprise that after seeing such a spectacle the people implore, "Let us not again hear the voice of the LORD, our God / nor see this great fire any more, lest we die." Thousands of years later, the people again experience a direct revelation of God when Jesus of Nazareth enters into the synagogue in Capernaum to preach. Both Jesus's words and actions cause amazement and the people gathered recognize he possesses "a new teaching with authority."

to experience: Like the people gathered at the synagogue in Capernaum, we, too, gather to listen to the word of the Lord and to draw near to him in his body and blood. How do you find amazement in the words and actions of Jesus at this moment on your faith journey?

Connecting the Responsorial Psalm
to the readings: Today's psalm calls to mind another event from the exodus: when the Israelites, freed from slavery in Egypt but before meeting God at Mount Sinai, grumble to Moses due to their thirst. They even go so far as to ask him, "Why then did you bring us up out of Egypt? To have us die of thirst with our children and our livestock?" (Exod 17:3; NABRE). Although the people had seen the power of the Lord at work in their escape from Egypt, they do not yet believe that God will continue to provide for all of their needs. In doubt and bitterness they quarrel and test the Lord, asking, "Is the Lord in our midst or not?" (Exod 17:7; NABRE).

to psalmist preparation: The psalmist invites us, even as we encounter our own trials and temptations, to "harden not your hearts." How is God calling you to trust in his goodness?

PROMPTS FOR FAITH-SHARING

In the first reading God promises to raise up a prophet to speak his words to the people. Who are our modern-day prophets who call us to walk in the ways of the Lord?

The psalmist counsels, "If today you hear his voice, harden not your hearts." What message is God inviting you to be open to this day?

St. Paul urges the Corinthians to be free of anxieties and distractions. What spiritual practices help you to be firmly centered in God's peace?

In the gospel we hear that the people of Capernaum "were astonished" at Jesus's teaching. What words of Jesus in the gospels do you find astonishing or even shocking?

Model Penitential Act

Presider: In today's gospel the people of Capernaum are astonished by Jesus's authoritative teaching. For the times when our ears have been deaf to the precious words of Christ, let us ask God for pardon and mercy . . . *[pause]*

Lord Jesus, you have the words of everlasting life: Lord, have mercy.

Christ Jesus, you are the Good Shepherd who calls us each by name: Christ, have mercy.

Lord Jesus, in you we find true peace and rest: Lord, have mercy.

Homily Points

• In the first reading from Deuteronomy we hear how the people of Israel asked God for a mediator, a prophet who would speak God's word so they would not be overcome by his direct presence, "lest we die." From the moment of being called by name in the burning bush, Moses has been God's mouthpiece and at this moment he assures the people that when he is gone, the Lord will raise up "a prophet like me" who will speak God's word to the people.

• There are many prophets who follow in the tradition of Moses. In loving God with the entirety of their selves and in listening to his voice, they are empowered to speak his words to the people, to preach compassion and hope, and also to call the people away from sin and back to the covenant. And then, in the fullness of time, God sends a new mouthpiece—one who is fully human and fully God, the perfect mediator between heaven and earth.

• In today's gospel reading, the people of Capernaum hear the one who embodies the word of God speaking directly to them and they are "astonished at his teaching." In Jesus we find the revelation of God in flesh and blood. During his earthly life, people look upon his face, touch the hem of his robe, and listen to his voice, all without fear of death. When we come to Mass we also encounter the risen Lord, truly present with us in word, body, and blood. In wonder and awe, let us draw close to him and may we never cease to be astonished at the beauty of this mystery.

Model Universal Prayer (Prayer of the Faithful)

Presider: Today's psalm reminds us that our God cares for us as a shepherd watches over his flock. Confident in his everlasting kindness, let us bring our needs before him.

Response: Lord, hear our prayer.

For all who proclaim and teach the word of God, in truth and humility may they preach the gospel and draw others to Christ . . .

For diplomats and peacekeepers, may they be committed to finding just and nonviolent solutions to international conflicts . . .

For all who suffer from mental illness, may they know the love of God that surrounds them continually and be sustained in faith and hope . . .

For all gathered here, may we be freed from all anxieties and distractions that keep us from living joyfully in God's presence . . .

Presider: God of salvation, you sent your son to walk among us and teach us with authority about your ways. Hear our prayers that we might heed his voice and be fashioned into a people after your own heart. We ask this through Christ our Lord. **Amen.**

Let us pray.

Pause for silent prayer

Grant us, Lord our God,
that we may honor you with all our mind,
and love everyone in truth of heart.
Through our Lord Jesus Christ, your Son,
who lives and reigns with you in the unity
    of the Holy Spirit,
one God, for ever and ever. **Amen.**

FIRST READING
Deut 18:15-20

Moses spoke to all the people, saying:
    "A prophet like me will the LORD, your
        God, raise up for you
    from among your own kin;
    to him you shall listen.
This is exactly what you requested of the
        LORD, your God, at Horeb
    on the day of the assembly, when you
        said,
    'Let us not again hear the voice of the
        LORD, our God,
    nor see this great fire any more, lest we
        die.'
And the LORD said to me, 'This was well
        said.
I will raise up for them a prophet like you
        from among their kin,
    and will put my words into his mouth;
    he shall tell them all that I command
        him.
Whoever will not listen to my words
        which he speaks in my name,
    I myself will make him answer for it.
But if a prophet presumes to speak in my
        name
    an oracle that I have not commanded
        him to speak,
    or speaks in the name of other gods, he
        shall die.'"

RESPONSORIAL PSALM
Ps 95:1-2, 6-7, 7-9

℟. (8) If today you hear his voice, harden
   not your hearts.

Come, let us sing joyfully to the LORD;
   let us acclaim the rock of our salvation.
Let us come into his presence with
      thanksgiving;
   let us joyfully sing psalms to him.

℟. If today you hear his voice, harden not
   your hearts.

Come, let us bow down in worship;
   let us kneel before the LORD who made
      us.
For he is our God,
   and we are the people he shepherds, the
      flock he guides.

℟. If today you hear his voice, harden not
   your hearts.

Oh, that today you would hear his voice:
   "Harden not your hearts as at Meribah,
   as in the day of Massah in the desert,
where your fathers tempted me;
   they tested me though they had seen
      my works."

℟. If today you hear his voice, harden not
   your hearts.

SECOND READING
1 Cor 7:32-35

Brothers and sisters:
I should like you to be free of anxieties.
An unmarried man is anxious about the
      things of the Lord,
   how he may please the Lord.
But a married man is anxious about the
      things of the world,
   how he may please his wife, and he is
      divided.
An unmarried woman or a virgin is
      anxious about the things of the Lord,
   so that she may be holy in both body
      and spirit.
A married woman, on the other hand,
   is anxious about the things of the
      world,
   how she may please her husband.
I am telling you this for your own benefit,
   not to impose a restraint upon you,
   but for the sake of propriety
   and adherence to the Lord without
      distraction.

About Liturgy

The Medium Is the Message?: Last week, this space urged readers to ensure that any particular liturgical ministry we offer "meets people where they are and offers loving invitations . . ." This and the rest of last week's writings could be seen, potentially, as oppositional to a faith and a liturgical practice of it that speaks and lives truth (or *Truth*, with a capital T). We hear of prophets this week in the liturgy of the word: Moses, himself a prophet, tells the people that more prophets will come, more who speak divine truth, and that we must be attentive to them.

The love that was spoken of last week and the truth that is spoken of this week are of course not oppositional at all—God *is* love, and God *is* truth, after all. I might suggest that those who perhaps find contradictions here are concerned too much with content and perhaps not concerned enough with the manner of delivery.

In 1964, Marshall McLuhan coined the phrase "The medium is the message," and the world has been unpacking that ever since. While the deposit of faith left to us from our Scriptures and tradition is indeed vast and profound, it is a message sometimes not communicated well to the next generation of believers.

Having already quoted Mark Twain once, here is another useful image from him: "We should be careful to get out of an experience only the wisdom that is in it—and stop there; lest we be like the cat that sits down on a hot stove-lid. She will never sit down on a hot stove-lid again—and that is well; but also she will never sit down on a cold one any more" (*Pudd'nhead Wilson's New Calendar*). As we continue to ponder how our liturgical ministries invite, welcome, and begin to form disciples, let us be mindful that our liturgies could include, perhaps even unbeknownst to us and only happening one time, some moment that gives someone the idea that it's not worth returning to the eucharistic table again. Most of the time, if there is that moment, it's not the message—it's the medium. Said another way, such a moment wouldn't be caused by the truth itself, but by the lack of love in passing on that truth to one another.

About the Ambo

Altar of the Word: "The central focus of the area in which the word of God is proclaimed during the liturgy is the ambo," it says in *Built of Living Stones* (61), and it is the place where "the Christian community encounters the living Lord in the word of God and prepares itself for the 'breaking of the bread' and the mission to live the word that will be proclaimed." It is the altar of the Word, where Scripture is broken open and shared: the GIRM tells us, "When the Sacred Scriptures are read in the Church, God himself speaks to his people, and Christ, present in his word, proclaims the Gospel" (29). While many of us are hopefully aware of the ambo's sacred purpose, it often becomes a place—owing to its visibility and, frequently, its microphone—for many other verbal utterances. Much like we wouldn't dream of celebrating "Donut Sunday" from the consecrated altar, we should be careful to only use the ambo for its sacred purpose as well.

About Music

A Human Struggle: Music that speaks to us of truth, love, and the struggle we all have at times in seeking and understanding these facets of our faith would serve the liturgy well this weekend. This author's "To Know Darkness" (GIA) speaks well to this challenge, as does Bernadette Farrell's wonderful paraphrase of Psalm 139, "O God, You Search Me" (OCP).

SPIRITUALITY

GOSPEL ACCLAMATION
Matt 8:17

℟. Alleluia, alleluia.
Christ took away our infirmities
and bore our diseases.
℟. Alleluia, alleluia.

Gospel

Mark 1:29-39; L74B

**On leaving the synagogue
  Jesus entered the house of
    Simon and Andrew with
    James and John.
Simon's mother-in-law lay sick
  with a fever.
They immediately told him
  about her.
He approached, grasped her
  hand, and helped her up.
Then the fever left her and she
  waited on them.**

**When it was evening, after
  sunset,
  they brought to him all who
    were ill or possessed by demons.
The whole town was gathered at the
  door.
He cured many who were sick with
  various diseases,
  and he drove out many demons,
  not permitting them to speak because
    they knew him.**

**Rising very early before dawn, he left
  and went off to a deserted place,
    where he prayed.
Simon and those who were with him
  pursued him
  and on finding him said, "Everyone is
    looking for you."
He told them, "Let us go on to the
  nearby villages
  that I may preach there also.
For this purpose have I come."
So he went into their synagogues,
  preaching and driving out demons
    throughout the whole of Galilee.**

Reflecting on the Gospel

In the gospel, God's remembrance of and compassion for suffering humanity comes most tangibly and radically in the healing presence of Jesus. From the religious service in the synagogue Jesus moves immediately into the house of Simon and Andrew, accompanied by James and John, disciples who are having a busy apprenticeship. In the healing of Simon's mother-in-law we have a vignette of the mission of Jesus, the free man, who cares nothing for taboos that prohibited the touching of a woman not one's wife, and especially on the Sabbath. Jesus has healed the tormented man in the synagogue, and he will make no discrimination between male and female, even though to hold the hand of the sick woman could earn him the accusation of ritual uncleanness. Compassion has a more urgent hold on Jesus, and his raising of her is by the same power that God will manifest in raising Jesus from the dead. The response of Simon's mother-in-law to her healing is to *serve* (*diēkonei*, which the Lectionary translates as "she waited on them") Jesus and his companions. The last use of this word in Mark's gospel is in Mark 15:41, and here it is again with reference to women who followed and served him, so framing the mission of Jesus from its beginning to his death with the service of women. It is a reminder, too, that all who have experienced the healing power of Jesus, in the flesh and in the Spirit, should respond with service of others.

Even though Jesus did not subject himself to Sabbath restraints, the crowds wait until "after sunset" when the Sabbath was over to bring those who are sick in body and mind to him. Jesus responds to the universal longing for wholeness and healing, vanquishing the reign of evil, yet commanding the evil spirits not to speak of him because not until his death will his true messianic identity be revealed. Before that, such a revelation, especially by the proclamation of the formerly possessed, could be manipulated by Jesus's enemies into false charges of his being on the side of the kingdom of evil (see Mark 3:22-27).

The one to whom Jesus is first accountable, however, is not the sick or possessed person, not Simon or his companions. Jesus's life is above all directed to God who is acting in him and through him, so early the next morning he seeks a place where he can be alone with God in prayer. Simon and some of his companions are described not as Jesus's "followers," but as those who "pursue" Jesus. There is a note of accusation and misunderstanding in Simon's words: "Everyone is looking for you" (including us!). There is no appreciation of Jesus's own need to search for his God in prayer. What Jesus has heard in his prayer is the call to proclaim the reigning presence of God in other towns, to move on from the enthusiastic reception of yesterday, because that is why he came. How often are we tempted to stay with the "yesterdays" of success and acclamation and hesitate to go forward to the largely unknown "tomorrows" to which God is calling us? And how important is prayer in our discernment of God's call?

Focusing the Gospel

Key words and phrases: He approached, grasped her hand, and helped her up.

To the point: Jesus's day in Capernaum is punctuated by healings. Last week we read in the gospel of how, while at synagogue, he frees a man from an unclean spirit by rebuking the spirit, saying, "Quiet! Come out of him!" Immediately after leaving the synagogue, Jesus encounters another person who is ailing, this time from an illness of the body rather than the spirit. Whereas before Jesus had used the power of his words to command the unclean spirit, now Jesus draws physically near to Simon's mother-in-law, takes her hand, and helps her from her sickbed. In both instances Jesus's presence restores health and wellness. Word of these healings spreads quickly and by nightfall "the whole town" is pressing in upon Jesus's door, eager to be near the one who has the ability to make the broken whole.

Connecting the Gospel

to the first reading: The first reading from Job gives us the words of one who is suffering acutely. Job's plight is well-known: having lost his children, servants, and livestock, he is then struck with "severe boils from the soles of his feet to the crown of his head" (Job 2:7; NABRE). Most of the book of Job's forty-two chapters consist of a dialogue between Job and three friends who come to comfort and counsel him. Today's reading is Job's response to his friend Eliphaz's suggestion that Job continue to trust in God's mercy.

to experience: While Job's despairing words seem to deny all hope, they are a true rendering of the pain that can overtake human life when unthinkable tragedy strikes. We can affirm the presence of suffering and evil in our world, but at the same time also proclaim the presence of Jesus, who desires to be with us in illness and sorrow, and to restore us to complete joy and fullness of life.

Connecting the Responsorial Psalm

to the readings: Today's psalm references God's mighty acts of mercy and compassion in returning the people of Israel to their land after the Babylonian exile. After seeing their country ravaged and the temple destroyed, it would not be an overstatement to say the people's hearts had been collectively broken as they were taken away into exile as the spoils of conquest. Much like the story of Job, it seems like this is the worst that a country or an individual could face. And yet, the psalmist stresses that the people are not alone. Though the temple—the particular place of encounter with God—is no more, their God accompanies them into exile, tends to their broken hearts, and finally leads them home again.

to psalmist preparation: How have you experienced God as a healer to the brokenhearted?

PROMPTS FOR FAITH-SHARING

In the first reading Job laments, "My days . . . come to an end without hope." Have you ever found yourself in a similar position of despair? What sustained you?

Today's responsorial psalm calls us to "[p]raise the Lord, who heals the brokenhearted." How has God's healing action tended your own heart through life's struggles and sorrows?

St. Paul writes to the Corinthians of all that he does "for the sake of the gospel." How do you proclaim the gospel in word and deed?

Jesus rises early and goes off "to a deserted place" to pray. Where and when do you find silence and solitude to be with God?

CELEBRATION

Model Penitential Act

Presider: Throughout his ministry in Israel, Jesus tirelessly healed spiritual and physical infirmities. Knowing his goodness and desire to make us whole, let us bring our own brokenness before the Lord to ask for his healing and mercy . . . *[pause]*

Lord Jesus, you tend the brokenhearted: Lord, have mercy.

Christ Jesus, you sustain the lowly and set the captive free: Christ, have mercy.

Lord Jesus, you show the sinner the way of salvation: Lord, have mercy.

Homily Points

• In the middle of today's gospel we hear of a rather striking scene: "When it was evening, after sunset, / they brought to him all who were ill or possessed by demons. / The whole town was gathered at the door." It seems as if everyone in Capernaum has been touched in some way by sickness. Whether ill themselves, or the friend or family member of someone who is ailing, all the townspeople have drawn near to the healer and wonder-worker who just that morning spoke in the synagogue with authority and astonished many with his teaching.

• Mark's gospel is the shortest of the four canonical gospels. Although at times we are given passages where Jesus speaks, often we can infer what he is about by his actions. After proclaiming the kingdom of God is at hand and then calling his first four disciples to follow him, Jesus devotes himself to making whole those who have been broken by spiritual or physical illness. He does not shy away from the dark places within humanity but instead seems to seek out those who are most in need of his light.

• His works of healing prove to be the best possible way of spreading the good news that God's reign has drawn near. By the end of just one day in Capernaum the entire town is gathered at Jesus's doorstep, eager to listen to his words and come close to the power of his healing. As Christians we, too, are called to be healers and to bring Jesus's mercy to the broken places in our society. May we proclaim in our actions that Jesus is "Emmanuel," God who desires to be with us always, not only or even primarily in places of joy and peace but also where we find the deepest pain and suffering.

Model Universal Prayer (Prayer of the Faithful)

Presider: We know that our God is mighty in power and always ready to come to the aid of those in need. With trust, let us bring our petitions before him.

Response: Lord, hear our prayer.

For ordained and lay ministers, may they bring hope to the despairing and be agents of healing for those in mental, emotional, and spiritual pain . . .

For leaders of nations, may they be inspired to find and implement solutions to raise families out of poverty . . .

For all those suffering from chronic and acute illness and for their caregivers, may they be comforted and upheld by Jesus the healer . . .

For all gathered here, in our daily lives may we find moments of silence and solitude to dwell with the Lord in prayer . . .

Presider: God of creation, in you the restless, anxious, and despairing find peace and hope. Hear our prayers that by clinging to you we might be healed from every infirmity and strengthened to serve you in the poorest of the poor. We ask this through Christ our Lord. **Amen.**

COLLECT

Let us pray.

Pause for silent prayer

Keep your family safe, O Lord, with
   unfailing care,
that, relying solely on the hope of
   heavenly grace,
they may be defended always by your
   protection.
Through our Lord Jesus Christ, your Son,
who lives and reigns with you in the unity
   of the Holy Spirit,
one God, for ever and ever. **Amen.**

FIRST READING
Job 7:1-4, 6-7

Job spoke, saying:
   Is not man's life on earth a drudgery?
      Are not his days those of hirelings?
   He is a slave who longs for the shade,
      a hireling who waits for his wages.
   So I have been assigned months of
      misery,
      and troubled nights have been
         allotted to me.
   If in bed I say, "When shall I arise?"
      then the night drags on;
      I am filled with restlessness until the
         dawn.
   My days are swifter than a weaver's
      shuttle;
      they come to an end without hope.
   Remember that my life is like the wind;
      I shall not see happiness again.

RESPONSORIAL PSALM
Ps 147:1-2, 3-4, 5-6

R℣. (cf. 3a) Praise the Lord, who heals the
   brokenhearted.
   or:
R℣. Alleluia.

Praise the LORD, for he is good;
   sing praise to our God, for he is gracious;
   it is fitting to praise him.
The LORD rebuilds Jerusalem;
   the dispersed of Israel he gathers.

R℣. Praise the Lord, who heals the
   brokenhearted.
   or:
R℣. Alleluia.

He heals the brokenhearted
   and binds up their wounds.
He tells the number of the stars;
   he calls each by name.

R℣. Praise the Lord, who heals the
   brokenhearted.
   or:
R℣. Alleluia.

Great is our Lord and mighty in power;
   to his wisdom there is no limit.
The LORD sustains the lowly;
   the wicked he casts to the ground.

R℣. Praise the Lord, who heals the
   brokenhearted.
   or:
R℣. Alleluia.

SECOND READING
1 Cor 9:16-19, 22-23

Brothers and sisters:
If I preach the gospel, this is no reason for
      me to boast,
   for an obligation has been imposed on
      me,
   and woe to me if I do not preach it!
If I do so willingly, I have a recompense,
   but if unwillingly, then I have been
      entrusted with a stewardship.
What then is my recompense?
That, when I preach,
   I offer the gospel free of charge
   so as not to make full use of my right in
      the gospel.
Although I am free in regard to all,
   I have made myself a slave to all
   so as to win over as many as possible.
To the weak I became weak, to win over
      the weak.
I have become all things to all, to save at
      least some.
All this I do for the sake of the gospel,
   so that I too may have a share in it.

About Liturgy

Recognizing God's Presence: I have been involved with a Catholic teen summer camp called Youth Sing Praise for more than twenty years. Sacraments are a portion of the prayer life of the week: Mass twice and an opportunity for reconciliation as well. When I first became involved with the program, the reconciliation service had become a bit warped. To wit: participants would sometimes come to the service excited solely because it would be an opportunity to cry, and to cry hard. There were other curious things wrong with the service, but this isn't the time or place for those details.

This experience of encountering Christ and the graces bestowed in the sacrament had given way to something much more human and, in most cases, quite far from the ideal. That's not to say that for some people, it wasn't an encounter with God's boundless love which led them to holy tears; I'm sure that happened for some. For others, though, I'm quite certain the experience became merely a reason to let go of emotions in perhaps an unnecessary and unhealthy way.

Then there were always a couple youth each year who worried that their experience of the sacrament was incomplete. "But I didn't cry . . ." became a familiar complaint: both from those who really wanted to but for some reason didn't, and from those who were not moved by God's presence to do so. I have heard similar reactions from others experiencing group adoration for the first time, especially when many react to that presence of the Lord in emotional and profound ways.

Knowing what to do when in the presence of the Lord, be it sacramentally or otherwise, can be challenging—especially if it's our first time with a profound awareness of that presence. Further, knowing that we are in the presence of the Lord can sometimes be even more of a challenge, particularly for those we have been considering in recent weeks: people coming to church for the first time, or people returning after an extended absence. We should, too, consider regular church attendees who may at times feel like Job, in today's first reading, completely unaware of the sacred presence surrounding them. Ignatian spirituality invites us to "see God in everything." That's not necessarily a good place to start for those who have some difficulty knowing God's presence; it is, though, a reality that is amazing when we can finally come to it.

To circle back: after a few years of this devolved reconciliation service, we had to "rip the bandage off" so to speak and start again. A new time, a new location, a new way to encounter the Lord. There were many not happy about that, and some who were. Change promises to be unpleasant for a moment, but is there some bandage you need to rip off of your liturgical practices, for a fresh start? Perhaps you are unaware of any, but someone else, perhaps even an unexpected someone sitting in the pews, might be. How can we all help those in our pews be more aware of the presence of the Lord, right now, today?

About Music

Comfort in Despondency: A more recent song that speaks to both Job's desolation and the hope and healing that Christ brings into our lives, found in today's gospel, is "Make Your Home in Me" by Ben Walther (OCP). Marty Haugen's "O God, Why Are You Silent?" (GIA) is a profound and prayerful lament. "There Is a Balm in Gilead" is a well-known hymn of comfort and healing, perfect for today's Scriptures as well.

FEBRUARY 7, 2021
FIFTH SUNDAY IN ORDINARY TIME

SPIRITUALITY

GOSPEL ACCLAMATION
Luke 7:16

R⁷. Alleluia, alleluia.
A great prophet has arisen in our
    midst,
God has visited his people.
R⁷. Alleluia, alleluia.

Gospel

Mark 1:40-45; L77B

**A leper came to Jesus and
    kneeling down begged
    him and said,
"If you wish, you can make
    me clean."
Moved with pity, he stretched
    out his hand,
touched him, and said to
    him,
"I do will it. Be made
    clean."
The leprosy left him
    immediately, and he was
    made clean.
Then, warning him sternly, he
    dismissed him at once.**

**He said to him, "See that you tell no
    one anything,
but go, show yourself to the priest
and offer for your cleansing what
    Moses prescribed;
that will be proof for them."**

**The man went away and began to
    publicize the whole matter.
He spread the report abroad
so that it was impossible for Jesus to
    enter a town openly.
He remained outside in deserted
    places,
and people kept coming to him from
    everywhere.**

Reflecting on the Gospel

The leprosy about which the first reading and the gospel speak today is not to be confused with contemporary Hansen's disease, medically identified only in 1868 by the Norwegian scientist Gerhard Hansen. A number of conditions, especially those with the signs of scaly skin, swellings, and exuding bodily fluids, are described as "leprosy" in this Sunday's first reading from the book of Leviticus. Skin that flaked off, fluids that were unnaturally exuded from the body, were considered to be conditions that violated religious-cultural boundaries connected with the integrity, and therefore holiness, of the human body, and so were considered to diminish the worth of the person. People with such conditions were banished from the community, compelled to cry "Unclean!" and make themselves obviously disheveled so that others would avoid them. To be "unclean" was also regarded as a moral failing and therefore sinful. The person who came into contact with such an afflicted one was regarded as contaminated and as ritually unclean and as adding to the moral pollution of the very gregarious Middle Eastern society.

Leprosaria and Hansen's disease still exist in some parts of the world, but social and religious alienation because of other causes is sadly much more familiar. Who are today's "lepers," people whom some consider as "polluting" the homogeneous and often exclusive society by their differences in race, culture, social mores, or physical and intellectual disabilities? The attitudes of the Nazis to the Jews, the Hutus to the Tutsis, the second people to the first and indigenous people of a land, are bred by a "leper" mindset. What are our attitudes to those we might consider as weakening the moral fiber of society—the drug addicts, the HIV/AIDS sufferers, those in prison? Are we on the side of harsh, punitive justice or compassionate restorative justice? And do we consider that the pollution of our planet, by us, can be sinful?

In the gospel, Jesus is approached by a leper. He makes no attempt to move away from him. What he is moved by is compassion, the deep gut-wrenching response that identifies with the suffering of another, and his hand stretches out to touch the man and affirm his choice to heal him. How long had it been since the leper had felt the touch of another human being on his diseased flesh, had heard words of affirmation rather than insult? We should be more enlightened about the importance of touch—the holding of the hand of the seriously ill or dying person, the silent embrace of the bereaved. Yet for some people there is the almost hysterical avoidance of touching the HIV/AIDS sufferer, or of drinking from the communion chalice lest, contrary to all medical opinion, one might be infected by this. Jesus's compassion and humanity bridge the gap between the holy and the unclean, freedom and taboos, sickness and health.

Jesus tells the man to observe the Mosaic Law by showing himself to a priest for the confirmation of his healing, and to offer a public sacrifice, an act of worship from which his leprosy had excluded him. By this instruction Jesus shows that he respects the Mosaic teaching, even though he will soon clash with some of the scribes' interpretation of this. Ironically, the man now goes around publicly and freely, while Jesus must leave the town and go into the country to escape his unwanted publicity. Because he has touched the leper, according to the Law Jesus is also regarded as unclean and excluded. He has taken upon himself another's infirmity; in his passion and death he will be the Suffering Servant who bears all our infirmities and transgressions for the sake of our salvation (cf. Isa 53:4-5). Yet people still come to him, caring nothing for his "infection" and everything for his miraculous power. As those who come to Jesus, what are we seeking from him? Do we want to be infected with his compassion or with the miraculous? How does Jesus touch us—and how do we touch others?

Focusing the Gospel

Key words and phrases: Moved with pity, he stretched out his hand, / touched him.

To the point: Jesus reaches out to touch the leper, one who had been rendered ritually impure or "unclean" due to his skin infection. There are many aspects to the ritual purity system in place at the time of Jesus. One effect of the system, as explained by Jewish scholar Jonathan Klawans, was to "force a separation between the experience of encountering God's sanctity and matters pertaining to death . . . Because God is eternal, God does not die . . . by following the ritual purity regulations ancient Israelites separated themselves from what made them least God-like" (*The Jewish Study Bible,* "Concepts of Purity in the Bible," 2,044). In Jesus, true God and true man, we find a perfect marriage of the human and the divine. Jesus, Son of God, the source of all purity, touches the man, heals his leprosy, and restores him to health and to his place in the community. Again, Jesus reveals himself as the savior, sent by the Father not to condemn the world but to redeem it (John 3:17).

Connecting the Gospel

to the first reading: In the first reading from Leviticus we find some of the rules and regulations put in place to protect the community as a whole from becoming ritually impure due to contact with a person rendered "unclean" by leprosy. The reading from Leviticus ends with the declaration that any person determined to be unclean from a skin ailment "shall dwell apart, making his abode outside the camp." In the gospel, Jesus heals the man with leprosy and restores him to the community, but at the end it is Jesus who must dwell apart "in deserted places" due to the publicity that the healing has generated.

to experience: Throughout his life, Jesus seeks out and draws near to those on the margins. How does your faith community minister to those who dwell on the edges of society and who are in the greatest need of support and inclusion?

Connecting the Responsorial Psalm

to the readings: The leper approaches Jesus and tells him, "If you wish, you can make me clean." In these simple words the man names both who he is and who he believes Jesus to be. He acknowledges his own affliction while also asserting Jesus's power to cleanse and to heal. Today's psalm offers us much the same framework for reconciliation, first in revealing oneself truthfully to God ("I acknowledged my sin to you / my guilt I covered not") and then lifting up God's power to restore ("you took away my guilt").

to psalmist preparation: The season of Lent will soon be upon us; what sin or weakness is God calling you to bring before him so that he might take it away and bring healing?

PROMPTS FOR FAITH-SHARING

In the first reading from Leviticus we hear of people with leprosy being ostracized from the community due to fear over their disease. Which groups in your community face ostracism and isolation due to fear?

The responsorial psalm lifts up the joy to be found in the Lord, even in the midst of trouble. Where do you experience the most joy in your life at this moment?

St. Paul urges the Corinthians to "do everything for the glory of God." How does your parish community live out this command?

We hear that Jesus is "moved with pity" at the plight of the leper and reaches out to touch him, breaking the law of the time. How as Christians shall we respond when laws, rules, or regulations stand in the way of compassion?

CELEBRATION

Model Penitential Act

Presider: In today's second reading, St. Paul instructs the Corinthians, "[D]o everything for the glory of God." For the times we have not glorified God in our words, thoughts, and actions, let us pause to ask for pardon and mercy . . . *[pause]*

Lord Jesus, you are worthy of all honor and praise: Lord, have mercy.

Christ Jesus, you call us to the joy of salvation: Christ, have mercy.

Lord Jesus, you desire to cleanse us from our iniquity and wash us from our sin: Lord, have mercy.

Homily Points

• In just a few days we will enter into the season of Lent, a time of preparation, penance, and purification as we look toward our holiest days of the year when we celebrate in a particular way Jesus's passion, death, and resurrection. In today's gospel, a leper approaches Jesus and says, "If you wish, you can make me clean." It is interesting that the leper does not ask Jesus a question: "Can you make me clean?" Or implore him for a favor: "Will you make me clean?" Instead, he comes to Jesus with a statement of faith: "If you wish, you can make me clean." Perhaps this man has heard of the healings Jesus performed in Capernaum, or maybe he has an intuitive sense of Jesus's closeness to God; in any case, the leper is emboldened to name Jesus as the one who possesses power over sickness.

• In Jesus's time people with certain diseases were viewed as "unclean" in the eyes of the community. To protect others from infection, they were isolated from society. When Jesus responds to the man's statement by telling him, "I do will it," he is affirming his desire to bring health and wholeness to both individuals and communities broken and separated by disease and fear.

• As we prepare for the beginning of Lent on Ash Wednesday, let us take a moment to consider the broken and sinful places in our own lives and in the life of our community. What affliction—whether of mind, body, or spirit—might God be calling us to turn over to him and his infinite mercy? Do we have the faith to say to Jesus, "If you wish, you can make me clean"?

Model Universal Prayer (Prayer of the Faithful)

Presider: Just as Jesus was moved with pity at the plight of the leper who approaches him in today's gospel reading, we know our God is one of boundless compassion. Secure in his desire to restore and heal, let us bring our needs before the Lord.

Response: Lord, hear our prayer.

For God's holy church, strengthened by the kindness and empathy of God, may we be a community where all are welcome to worship in joy and peace . . .

For medical workers throughout the world who place themselves at risk to care for others, may they be protected and renewed in mind, body, and spirit . . .

For those who have been ostracized and isolated from others due to illness or prejudice, may they find community and know their worth as children of God . . .

For all gathered here, even in the midst of struggle and suffering, may we know the joy of living life in Christ . . .

Presider: Almighty God, we have been created in your image and likeness, and we are restless until we rest in you. Hear our prayers that we might give you glory with our words and actions and so build the kingdom of God here on earth. We ask this through Christ our Lord. **Amen.**

COLLECT
Let us pray.

Pause for silent prayer

O God, who teach us that you abide
in hearts that are just and true,
grant that we may be so fashioned by
    your grace
as to become a dwelling pleasing to you.
Through our Lord Jesus Christ, your Son,
who lives and reigns with you in the unity
    of the Holy Spirit,
one God, for ever and ever. **Amen.**

FIRST READING
Lev 13:1-2, 44-46

The LORD said to Moses and Aaron,
    "If someone has on his skin a scab or
        pustule or blotch
    which appears to be the sore of leprosy,
    he shall be brought to Aaron, the priest,
    or to one of the priests among his
        descendants.
If the man is leprous and unclean,
    the priest shall declare him unclean
    by reason of the sore on his head.

"The one who bears the sore of leprosy
    shall keep his garments rent and his
        head bare,
    and shall muffle his beard;
    he shall cry out, 'Unclean, unclean!'
As long as the sore is on him he shall
        declare himself unclean,
    since he is in fact unclean.
He shall dwell apart, making his abode
        outside the camp."

RESPONSORIAL PSALM
Ps 32:1-2, 5, 11

R⁄. (7) I turn to you, Lord, in time of
    trouble, and you fill me with the joy
    of salvation.

Blessed is he whose fault is taken away,
    whose sin is covered.
Blessed the man to whom the LORD
    imputes not guilt,
    in whose spirit there is no guile.

R⁄. I turn to you, Lord, in time of trouble,
    and you fill me with the joy of
    salvation.

Then I acknowledged my sin to you,
    my guilt I covered not.
I said, "I confess my faults to the LORD,"
    and you took away the guilt of my sin.

R⁄. I turn to you, Lord, in time of trouble,
    and you fill me with the joy of
    salvation.

Be glad in the LORD and rejoice, you just;
    exult, all you upright of heart.

R⁄. I turn to you, Lord, in time of trouble,
    and you fill me with the joy of
    salvation.

SECOND READING
1 Cor 10:31–11:1

Brothers and sisters,
whether you eat or drink, or whatever you
    do,
    do everything for the glory of God.
Avoid giving offense, whether to the Jews
    or Greeks or the church of God,
    just as I try to please everyone in every
        way,
    not seeking my own benefit but that of
        the many,
    that they may be saved.
Be imitators of me, as I am of Christ.

About Liturgy

Healing and Curing: Jesus continues this week with his healing ministry, through which he shows God's love, announces the reign of God, and preaches by actions the Good News of salvation. In fact, this particular ministry becomes so successful and widely known that Jesus encounters crowds wherever he goes, even when he's purposefully remaining in desolate areas.

Some parishes include anointing of the sick in Mass once or twice a year, and it's sensical to plan those celebrations for Sundays like this one (or last weekend's), when gospel passages of physical healing are part of the Liturgy of the Word.

The sacrament of anointing of the sick is not well understood among the faithful. Many confuse it with last rites and Viaticum, the prayers surrounding someone about to die. While this anointing is often performed near death, usually that is because of a sudden illness or injury that precipitates need for the sacrament, which might not have been needed prior. But a person need not be dying to receive the sacrament: "The anointing of the sick is not a sacrament for those only who are at the point of death. Hence, as soon as anyone of the faithful begins to be in danger of death from sickness or old age, the fitting time for him to receive this sacrament has certainly already arrived" (*Catechism of the Catholic Church* 1514). Further, canon law tells us: "The anointing of the sick can be administered to a member of the faithful who, having reached the use of reason, begins to be in danger due to sickness or old age. This sacrament can be repeated if the sick person, having recovered, again becomes gravely ill or if the condition becomes more grave during the same illness. This sacrament is to be administered in a case of doubt whether the sick person has attained the use of reason, is dangerously ill, or is dead. This sacrament is to be conferred on the sick who at least implicitly requested it when they were in control of their faculties" (c. 1004–1006).

The definitions above are certainly open to some amount of interpretation, but care should be given to catechize the faithful about the sacrament, its purpose, and who ought to receive it before incorporating the rite into a Sunday Eucharist. In such catechesis, it is important to distinguish related but often conflated terms: "healing" and "curing." The recipient of the sacrament should not expect a miraculous *cure* from the rite, though unexplained and miraculous cures are known to have happened for God's faithful. The sacrament offers "the restoration of health, if it is conducive to the salvation of his soul" (*Catechism* 1532), which seems, in general, to be an unlikely circumstance. If the sacrament offers a more likely *healing*, it is perhaps for an anxious spirit that is given strength, peace, and courage (*Catechism* 1520). It also unites us with Christ and bestows grace (as do all sacraments) and, should it be time, prepares us for "the final journey," forgiving sins (if the person is not able to celebrate the sacrament of penance) and preparing us for our passing to eternal life (*Catechism* 1521–23).

About Music

Music of Restoration: David Haas's "Heal Us, Jesus" (GIA) is a beautiful and simple melody for Mass or for use during a communal anointing of the sick service. Marcy Weckler's "In the Arms of the Shepherd" (WLP) is a touching paraphrase of Psalm 23. Consider, too, the *Psallite* refrain "Heal Me in Your Mercy" (Liturgical Press).

SEASON OF LENT

GOSPEL ACCLAMATION
See Ps 95:8

If today you hear his voice,
harden not your hearts.

Gospel   Matt 6:1-6, 16-18; L219

Jesus said to his disciples:
   "Take care not to perform righteous
      deeds
   in order that people may see them;
      otherwise, you will have no recompense
         from your heavenly Father.
When you give alms,
   do not blow a trumpet before you,
   as the hypocrites do in the synagogues
      and in the streets
   to win the praise of others.
Amen, I say to you,
   they have received their
      reward.
But when you give alms,
   do not let your left hand
      know what your right
      is doing,
   so that your almsgiving may be secret.
And your Father who sees in secret will
   repay you.

"When you pray,
   do not be like the hypocrites,
   who love to stand and pray in the
      synagogues and on street corners
   so that others may see them.
Amen, I say to you,
   they have received their reward.
But when you pray, go to your inner room,
   close the door, and pray to your Father in
      secret.
And your Father who sees in secret will
   repay you.

"When you fast,
   do not look gloomy like the hypocrites.
They neglect their appearance,
   so that they may appear to others to be
      fasting.
Amen, I say to you, they have received their
   reward.
But when you fast,
   anoint your head and wash your face,
   so that you may not appear to be fasting,
   except to your Father who is hidden.
And your Father who sees what is hidden
   will repay you."

See Appendix A, p. 267, for the other readings.

Reflecting on the Gospel

If the drama of the liturgy is respected, when the catechumens who are to be baptized at Easter celebrate the rite of acceptance they are marked with the sign of the cross, not just on their foreheads, but on their heart, hands, and feet. It is as embodied men and women that we journey to God, and as Christians whose humanity is enveloped in our only boast, the cross of Christ (cf. Gal 6:14), that we come to share his risen life. During this rite the catechumens are also given a cross—not as a fancy piece of jewelry (one actress is reported to own four hundred cross accessories!), but as a reminder of the way they have started to walk in company with their crucified and risen Lord into whose death all disciples are baptized. To have the catechumens in our midst during Lent, on the last stage of their journey to baptism, is the most significant reminder for a community of the grace of our own baptism and the responsibility we have to continue our own journey of discipleship and witness to its joy.

On Ash Wednesday, we too are marked with the cross of ash as we begin our annual Lenten journey. It is a day that seems to draw more people than usual, a day when even those who are irregular church attenders seem to sense that they can line up without any feeling of unworthiness, presenting themselves (as the alternative ritual words announce) to: "Remember that you are dust, and to dust you shall return." With all the other Christians whose spirits are dusty and grimy, we affirm our shared need to turn away from sin and believe the Good News, and are marked with this identity.

We are familiar with ashes. On our TV screens they come into our homes on the agonizing faces of victims of war and terrorism against the backdrop of their burned-out buildings, and on the irreverent tongues of those who threaten violence that reduces hope to ashes. In contrast, on the faces of heroic firefighters and emergency workers, ash has new dignity, a humble witness to self-sacrifice and love of neighbor. Since the last Ash Wednesday, something has almost certainly and personally turned to "ash" for us: when illness struck, when a loved one died, when friendship was betrayed, when illusions about ourselves or others were destroyed . . . so much ash.

And yet ash is also fertile and protective. After a bushfire ravages the countryside, new life springs from cracked seeds and mulched branches; to keep the embers in the hearth warm until morning, there was an old Irish ritual of *grieshog*. The woman of the house would cover the last embers at night with a soft blanket of ash to keep them warm until morning when she would then brush away the ash and rekindle the fire with her breath.

Ash Wednesday calls us into the Lenten weeks of keeping warm the embers of our Christian discipleship through a renewed commitment to prayer, to fasting, and to almsgiving, so that the breath of the Easter Jesus may rekindle in us the fire of our baptism, and "Alleluia" may truly be our song of praise for what God has done, is doing, and will do for us in Christ. The Sundays of Lent retain their character of "Sundays," of commemorations of the resurrection of the Lord, and so the reminder that Lent is a preparation for the celebration of Easter is woven like a golden thread through the season's darker days.

Focusing the Gospel

Key words and phrases: "[T]o win the praise of others . . . so that others may see them . . . so that they may appear to others . . ."

To the point: In today's gospel Jesus gets to the heart of humanity's great temptation to seek praise, fame, and glory in what we do and in who we are. When we are motivated by the desire for others' approval, Jesus tells us we have "received [our] reward." Oftentimes, this "reward" is greed and bitterness since in the end the acclaim of other human beings cannot satisfy the deepest desires of our hearts to be loved, accepted, and known. Only in God can we find the peace and meaning we seek. This Lent, let us free ourselves from anxiety over how we appear to others and instead focus on our relationship with God.

Model Universal Prayer (Prayer of the Faithful)

Presider: In the second reading St. Paul writes to the Corinthians, "Behold, now is a very acceptable time; / behold, now is the day of salvation." Trusting in our God's mercy and eternal love throughout the ages, let us bring the needs of today before the Lord.

Response: Lord, hear our prayer.

For God's holy church, in this season of Lent may it be purified, strengthened, and renewed in faith, love, and charity . . .

For areas of the world affected by famine and drought, may the fasting of those who have plenty aid in caring for those with less . . .

For those who have wandered far from God's grace due to sin and despair, by repentance and reconciliation may they return to the one who calls them by name . . .

For all gathered here, may we grow in holiness by undertaking the Lenten practices of prayer, fasting, and almsgiving . . .

Presider: God of abundant grace, you sent your son Jesus to seek out the lost and to show sinners the way. Hear our prayers that nourished by your word and fed at your table, we might bring hope to the despairing and light to places of darkness. We ask this through Christ our Lord. **Amen.**

About Liturgy

An Idol of Faith: We have reached the season of Lent, the time for all things sad and repentant and morose and sackcloth and ashes and everything else depressing, right? No! Lent need not be those things, at least not overly so. We ought to be repentant for our sinfulness, yes, and further, knowing our sinfulness led Jesus to his suffering and death on the cross can lead us to be sad and even grieve these things.

But to do so without also knowing there's more to the story is to, in a sense, make an idol out of one tiny facet of our faith. During Lent we should not only remember repentance, suffering, and death. We should also, while celebrating these things, remember that new life arises from these very things—there is joy and even more celebrating to come.

Lent is only one part of a broader story, a broader mystery, which as a whole tells us where we've come from, who we are now and who we should strive to be, and the future that awaits us all if we help each other grow in faith and holiness.

COLLECT

Let us pray.

Pause for silent prayer

Grant, O Lord, that we may begin with holy
    fasting
this campaign of Christian service,
so that, as we take up battle against spiritual
    evils,
we may be armed with weapons of self-restraint.
Through our Lord Jesus Christ, your Son,
who lives and reigns with you in the unity of
    the Holy Spirit,
one God, for ever and ever. **Amen.**

FOR REFLECTION

• The prophet Joel tells us, "Rend your hearts, not your garments, / and return to the Lord, your God." In what elements in your life have you wandered from God's presence? How are you being called to return?

• St. Paul writes to the Corinthians, "Behold, now is a very acceptable time." How is this moment in your life "an acceptable time" for reconciliation with God and others?

• Jesus warns us "not to perform righteous deeds / in order that people may see them." Where in your life have you been particularly attuned to the approval of other people?

Homily Points

• In today's psalm we find this prayer: "A clean heart create for me, O God, / and a steadfast spirit renew within me." No matter how faithfully we might attempt to live the Christian life, as human beings we are always in need of a savior. Although our desire to do good might be strong, like St. Paul we will inevitably find ourselves at some point realizing, "I do not do the good I want, but I do the evil I do not want" (Rom 7:19; NABRE). This should not lead us to despair, however.

• Even in the season of Lent, which we might think of as the most somber within the liturgical year, the good news of the gospel dominates all else. We are loved even in our sinfulness, and our God never tires of cleansing our hearts and renewing our spirits.

SPIRITUALITY

GOSPEL ACCLAMATION
Matt 4:4b

One does not live on bread alone,
but on every word that comes forth from the
mouth of God.

Gospel

Mark 1:12-15; L23B

**The Spirit drove Jesus out into the
desert,
and he remained in the desert for
forty days, tempted by Satan.
He was among wild beasts,
and the angels ministered to him.**

**After John had been arrested,
Jesus came to Galilee proclaiming
the gospel of God:
"This is the time of fulfillment.
The kingdom of God is at hand.
Repent, and believe in the gospel."**

Reflecting on the Gospel

Every year on the First Sunday of Lent, the gospel proclaimed is the wilderness temptation of Jesus. Mark's account is honed to three short verses following immediately and urgently after the baptism of Jesus. The Spirit "drove" Jesus into the wilderness, says Mark. We often describe people as "driven"—by ambition, lust, desperation—but what drives Jesus is the Holy Spirit. He is tossed into the physical and spiritual space where, before he begins his public ministry, before he proclaims one word of the Good News, he must struggle with two consequences of his baptism: his naming as Son of the Father and his solidarity with sinful humanity represented by the crowds on the Jordan's banks who were called by John to a baptism of repentance. Now there are no crowds; Jesus is alone with the Spirit of God and the spirit of evil, with the wild beasts and the angels, with communion and conflict, with the struggle—that will persist throughout his life and death—to be the faithful Son. He is alone with the memory of his ancestors and their wilderness wandering in what for them was not only a place of God's revelation and promises, but also a place of their temptations and failures. Jesus will show himself to be the most faithful Israelite. The opposition between human sin and divine presence, between the "angelic" and the "beastly," was starkly exposed in Jesus's own psyche. And if we are honest and mindful, we know them in ourselves and in our own struggles to be faithful sons and daughters of our same Father.

The English artist Stanley Spencer (1891–1959) painted a "wilderness series" about the life of Christ. In one of these paintings he depicts Jesus sitting on the desert sands with a "wild beast." But the beast is not a roaring lion or a skulking tiger. In his cupped hands he holds a small but deadly scorpion. Jesus is no wraith-like ascetic, but very much a plump "flesh of our flesh" man. Spencer may be suggesting that the really dangerous beasts are those small ones that can slither insidiously into our lives; the persistent sins and small infidelities that, almost unnoticed, can inject a paralyzing venom into our discipleship. Alternatively, we might read Spencer's painting, and Mark's account, positively: as a vision of peace and harmony in a restored creation in the hands of the New Adam on whom angels wait in service.

Jesus comes out from his wilderness experience strengthened for praise and pain and mission. The arrest of John the Baptist is the first storm that breaks over Mark's gospel, but over it rises a Galilean rainbow of hope as Jesus proclaims his first words: "This is the time of fulfillment. The kingdom of God is at hand. Repent, and believe in the gospel." On Ash Wednesday, the last words of that proclamation were an alternative that was pronounced as we were signed as baptized disciples of the tempted One and called to Lenten mindfulness of the struggle between sin and grace, success and failure, into which we too are tossed.

The desert sand is not under our feet but in our hearts. Its grit is the daily irritations and indefinable loneliness we often feel. We need these Lenten weeks of heightened awareness of the importance of uncluttered spiritual and physical space where we can come to grips with our pain, where we can discover the beauty of God and our sisters and brothers under the surface sands of our busy lives, and where we can allow our ears to be "dug out" (Ps 40:6; God's Word Translation) by closer listening to the word of God in our Sunday liturgy. We may then become much wiser about the spiritual baggage that we, as wilderness travelers, need to keep or discard in the trek toward Easter.

Focusing the Gospel

Key words and phrases: [T]he Spirit drove Jesus out into the desert.

To the point: Before his public ministry begins, Jesus spends forty days alone with wild beasts and angels. For the people of Israel, the desert hearkened back to the time of the Exodus when God led them in the wilderness, feeding them with manna, and finally revealing himself to them on the top of Mount Sinai. In the desert the people learned to rely on God as they were formed into his chosen people through the gift of the Torah. Jesus's time in the desert is the last step in his preparation to begin his public ministry. Having withstood temptation and received the ministrations of angels, he is finally ready to proclaim the "gospel of God."

Connecting the Gospel

to the first reading: While in the gospel Jesus dwells among wild beasts in the desert, in the first reading Noah and his family are the ones who are surrounded by animals. The account of the flood in Genesis (and the retelling of it in today's second reading from the first letter of St. Peter) records that only eight people survived the rising waters that destroyed the rest of creation. Along with these eight people, however, are a pair "of the clean animals and the unclean, of the birds, and of everything that crawls on the ground" (Gen 7:8; NABRE). When God makes the covenant with Noah and his family, it extends also to "every living creature" that accompanied them on the ark, indeed to "all living beings."

to experience: In the gospels we don't often hear of Jesus interacting with animals. His time of preparation in the desert appears to be not only a time to commune with God, but to also live within God's creation. The covenant with Noah and his family can remind us that, though among the creatures, we are the only ones who have been created in "the image and likeness of God"; every living being is precious in his sight.

Connecting the Responsorial Psalm

to the readings: The book of Genesis tells us, "[W]hen the waters had swelled on the earth for one hundred and fifty days, God remembered Noah" (7:24–8:1; NABRE) and the waters begin to subside. Today's psalm also speaks of God's remembrance: "In your kindness remember me, / because of your goodness, O Lord." In today's first reading, God offers a sign of the covenant he has made with Noah's family and with all of creation: "When I bring clouds over the earth, / and the bow appears in the clouds, / I will recall the covenant I have made."

to psalmist preparation: At times in our lives a sign, symbol, or experience might have a profound impact on us and help call to mind our covenant with God, and with each other to live as children of God. This Lenten season, what sign or symbol might help you live more deeply into this covenant?

PROMPTS FOR FAITH-SHARING

In the first reading God institutes a covenant between himself and the earth. What role do you see creation playing in our relationship with God?

The psalmist says, "Your ways, O Lord, are love and truth to those who keep your covenant." How would you like to grow in love and truth this Lenten season?

Today's verse before the gospel reminds us, "One does not live on bread alone, but on every word that comes forth from the mouth of God." What nourishment have you received from God's word recently?

After Jesus's baptism, the Spirit drives "Jesus out into the desert." Where do you find solitude and quiet to be with God?

Model Penitential Act

Presider: In today's gospel Jesus proclaims, "This is the time of fulfillment. / The kingdom of God is at hand. / Repent, and believe in the gospel." Let us take a moment to heed Jesus's call to repentance and to ask our merciful God for forgiveness . . . *[pause]*

    Confiteor: I confess . . .

Homily Points

• Several weeks ago, on the Third Sunday of Ordinary Time, the gospel began with the verses that end today's gospel, Jesus's first words of preaching: "This is the time of fulfillment. / The kingdom of God is at hand. / Repent and believe in the gospel." They are apt words to reflect on again as we enter into this season of Lent.

• Our liturgical year offers us rhythms for living out the life of faith. There are times to live and grow in knowledge and wisdom (Ordinary Time), a time to celebrate that God entered into human history to draw us closer to himself (Christmas season), a time to live into the mystery of God's victory over death (Easter season), and times for preparation, repentance, and purification (Advent and Lent). Throughout the liturgical year, we enter into the life of Christ from conception to ascension, and we also live out the peculiarities of the human condition.

• As humans, we crave meaningful work, but also times of celebration and repose. The liturgical year offers us all of this, and also something else—time for reconciliation and healing. Each one of us is a sinner. Despite our best intentions and resolve, we will do things that hurt our relationship with God and our relationship with others. Because of this truth, repentance is not an optional undertaking for those guilty of serious social sin, but a necessary practice for all children of God. In Lent we are given the opportunity together to accept Jesus's invitation anew to "[r]epent and believe in the gospel." As with all seasons, this one will draw to a close. How will you enter into these weeks of penance and purification that will prepare us for Easter joy?

Model Universal Prayer (Prayer of the Faithful)

Presider: In today's reading from Genesis we hear of how God first establishes a covenant with the earth following the great flood. Confident in God's promise to never forget this covenant, let us bring the needs of our world before the Lord.

Response: Lord, hear our prayer.

For bishops, priests, deacons, religious, and lay ministers, may they renounce every temptation of power and gratification in favor of the cross of Christ . . .

For leaders of nations, together may they commit themselves to the preservation of the environment and protection of endangered species . . .

For victims of violent crime and for their assailants, may the grace of God bring about repentance, reconciliation, and peace . . .

For all gathered here, as we journey with the catechumens toward the waters of baptism, may we always strive to live as children of the light . . .

Presider: God of creation, you are the source of salvation and the font of living water that calls us to new life. Hear our prayers that in this season of Lent we may be cleansed, purified, and brought closer to you in our acts of prayer, fasting, and almsgiving. We ask this through Christ our Lord. **Amen.**

COLLECT

Let us pray.

Pause for silent prayer

Grant, almighty God,
through the yearly observances of holy Lent,
that we may grow in understanding
of the riches hidden in Christ
and by worthy conduct pursue their effects.
Through our Lord Jesus Christ, your Son,
who lives and reigns with you in the unity
of the Holy Spirit,
one God, for ever and ever. **Amen.**

FIRST READING

Gen 9:8-15

God said to Noah and to his sons with him:
"See, I am now establishing my covenant
with you
and your descendants after you
and with every living creature that was
with you:
all the birds, and the various tame and
wild animals
that were with you and came out of the ark.
I will establish my covenant with you,
that never again shall all bodily
creatures be destroyed
by the waters of a flood;
there shall not be another flood to
devastate the earth."
God added:
"This is the sign that I am giving for all
ages to come,
of the covenant between me and you
and every living creature with you:
I set my bow in the clouds to serve as
a sign
of the covenant between me and the earth.
When I bring clouds over the earth,
and the bow appears in the clouds,
I will recall the covenant I have made
between me and you and all living
beings,
so that the waters shall never again
become a flood
to destroy all mortal beings."

RESPONSORIAL PSALM
Ps 25:4-5, 6-7, 8-9

R⃓. (cf. 10) Your ways, O Lord, are love
    and truth to those who keep your
    covenant.

Your ways, O LORD, make known to me;
    teach me your paths,
guide me in your truth and teach me,
    for you are God my savior.

R⃓. Your ways, O Lord, are love and truth
    to those who keep your covenant.

Remember that your compassion, O LORD,
    and your love are from of old.
In your kindness remember me,
    because of your goodness, O LORD.

R⃓. Your ways, O Lord, are love and truth
    to those who keep your covenant.

Good and upright is the LORD,
    thus he shows sinners the way.
He guides the humble to justice,
    and he teaches the humble his way.

R⃓. Your ways, O Lord, are love and truth
    to those who keep your covenant.

SECOND READING
1 Pet 3:18-22

Beloved:
Christ suffered for sins once,
    the righteous for the sake of the
        unrighteous,
    that he might lead you to God.
Put to death in the flesh,
    he was brought to life in the Spirit.
In it he also went to preach to the spirits
        in prison,
    who had once been disobedient
    while God patiently waited in the days
        of Noah
    during the building of the ark,
    in which a few persons, eight in all,
    were saved through water.
This prefigured baptism, which saves you
        now.
It is not a removal of dirt from the body
    but an appeal to God for a clear
        conscience,
    through the resurrection of Jesus Christ,
    who has gone into heaven
    and is at the right hand of God,
    with angels, authorities, and powers
        subject to him.

About Liturgy

About the Liturgy of the Hours: The General Instruction of the Liturgy of the Hours (GILH) serves as a great resource for anyone wishing to grow in understanding of this lesser known, and still underutilized, form of prayer.

More and more parishes are using the Liturgy of the Hours, sometimes on weekday mornings when a priest cannot be available to celebrate Mass, and, frequently, seasonally—during Advent and Lent for instance, perhaps on Sunday evenings, the mornings of the Triduum, or other convenient times. Sometimes this is due to a diminishing number of priests, and sometimes one might attribute the slowly rising interest in this form of prayer to a desire from some of the faithful for more chant, more contemplative prayer experiences, and an opportunity to pray in gathered ways outside of the eucharistic liturgy.

As the GILH tells us, Christians gathering to pray at fixed times of day is an ancient practice (1), and one that has continued, principally in monasteries and convents, to the present day. Like a eucharistic liturgy, this liturgy is also a "[p]ublic and common prayer" (1), and links us with Christ, is Christ's own prayer, and is prayer by Christ's command (3–6).

Quoting *Lumen Gentium*, it continues: "Christ's priesthood is also shared by the whole Body of the Church, so that the baptized are consecrated as a spiritual temple and holy priesthood through the rebirth of baptism and the anointing by the Holy Spirit and are empowered to offer the worship of the New Covenant, a worship that derives not from our own powers but from Christ's merit and gift" (7). Later, when describing who ought to pray the Liturgy of the Hours, the list leaves no one out, mentioning those in religious life, but also being sure to include groups of lay faithful and the domestic church (27).

There are many ways in which to pray this liturgy, but the core of the prayer is psalms and canticles (songs in Scripture outside of the psalms). The instruction envisions them to be sung (100, 103–4) and if one is unfamiliar, the psalms of this liturgy are structured differently than the responsorial psalms of the Mass. These are much longer, frequently whole psalms, for all to pray together—often in alternation side to side, or men, women, etc.—with an antiphon only at the beginning or end. Often, too, one encounters psalms that are less familiar, if the ones principally known are those that regularly appear at Sunday Mass. The whole of the psalter is prayed through, various times each day, day by day, week by week. There are also other familiar parts of communal prayer: hymns, a Scripture reading (or perhaps a reading from a saint's writings or a patriarch's homily), intercessions, and the Lord's Prayer to name a few.

A popular website and smartphone app with the texts for each celebration can be found at universalis.com, and many publishers offer resources with orders of worship and music for the hymns, chants, psalms, and canticles of the various liturgies.

As Lent begins this year, consider whether some form of the Liturgy of the Hours would be a positive contribution to the prayer life of your community!

About Music

Concerning Covenant: The Old Testament passage about Noah and his family seeing the rainbow at the end of the great flood is the first of many readings in this cycle of the Lenten readings regarding covenant. "God of the Covenants" (WLP), by this author, speaks directly to these readings and the varied theological concepts of covenant that are so strong these next few weeks.

SPIRITUALITY

GOSPEL ACCLAMATION
cf. Matt 17:5

From the shining cloud the Father's voice is
    heard:
This is my beloved Son, listen to him.

Gospel

Mark 9:2-10; L26B

Jesus took Peter, James, and John
    and led them up a high
        mountain apart by
        themselves.
And he was transfigured before
    them,
    and his clothes became
        dazzling white,
    such as no fuller on earth could
        bleach them.
Then Elijah appeared to them
    along with Moses,
    and they were conversing with
        Jesus.
Then Peter said to Jesus in reply,
    "Rabbi, it is good that we are here!
Let us make three tents:
    one for you, one for Moses, and one
        for Elijah."
He hardly knew what to say, they were
    so terrified.
Then a cloud came, casting a shadow
    over them;
    from the cloud came a voice,
    "This is my beloved Son. Listen to
        him."
Suddenly, looking around, they no
    longer saw anyone
    but Jesus alone with them.

As they were coming down from the
    mountain,
    he charged them not to relate what
        they had seen to anyone,
    except when the Son of Man had
        risen from the dead.
So they kept the matter to themselves,
    questioning what rising from the
        dead meant.

Reflecting on the Gospel

The readings present a compendium of themes that shape the Lenten season. The first reading concludes the cycle of narratives about Abraham (Gen 12–23), which unfold from his call, with the promise that he and Sarah will be the parents of many nations, through the covenant and the birth of a son, the bearer of the promise (Isaac), and reaches its pinnacle in God's command that Abraham offer Isaac as a holocaust. As one of the most treasured subjects of Christian art, the denouement of the story is familiar. At the last moment "the LORD's messenger" intervenes; Isaac is spared, and the promise is renewed: "[B]ecause you acted as you did in not withholding from me your beloved son, I will bless you abundantly" (Gen 22:16-17).

In both Judaism and Christianity Abraham is a paradigm of faith who "when tested was found loyal" (Sir 44:20), who "hop[ed] against hope" (Rom 4:18), and who "[b]y faith, . . . when put to the test, offered up Isaac" because he believed in a God who could raise up the dead (Heb 11:17-19). Also in Jewish tradition Isaac is transformed into a model of self-sacrifice who went willingly to his death, which is adopted by Christians for Jesus, "the Son of God who has loved me and given himself up for me" (Gal 2:20; all NABRE).

"Transformation" would be a better term to describe today's gospel story, since Jesus, though in the form of God, took on the "*form* of a slave" (Phil 2:6-7; NABRE), and is now transformed and seen as an exalted member of the heavenly court. The narrative is dense with biblical allusions. The dazzling white clothes are a symbol of divine presence in Daniel 7:9, while the presence of Elijah and Moses has been interpreted in a number of ways. They are symbols of the prophets and the Law; both are people who did not taste death but were exalted to heaven (Elijah in 2 Kgs 2:1-12; Moses in extra-biblical tradition); they are faithful prophets who suffered because they followed God's word.

The deeper focus of the account emerges from the divine voice: "This is my beloved Son. Listen to him" (Mark 9:7). The transformation follows the first of three predictions by Jesus of his death by crucifixion, which the disciples consistently resist. Peter's desire for three booths seems an attempt to substitute divine presence for the way of the cross. The same three disciples who witness Jesus's transformation fail to watch with him during his agony in the garden (Mark 14:32-42). Mark's readers and we ourselves are to hear the voice of a Jesus who says that the way to glory is only through the cross.

The narrative is also followed by one of the most dramatic stories in the gospel (Mark 9:14-29), the exorcism from a young boy of a destructive demon which the disciples of Jesus are powerless to combat. Raphael's magnificent panorama "The Transfiguration," which greets visitors to the Vatican museums, captures the sequence perfectly. While Jesus and the heavenly companions are illumined in resplendent colors, the fruitless struggle of the disciples with the demon occupy the lower right-hand corner. The eye cannot help but behold the chaos of earthly evil when looking at heavenly glory.

The transfiguration is not, as some homilists state, a kind of midpoint encouragement to the disciples, since they will continue to misunderstand Jesus and will flee at his arrest; and Peter denies him. The deeper meaning of the narrative for Mark and for us during Lent is that even after moments of transcendence and transformation, we must come back to earth, continue to hear the voice of Jesus, and follow him on the way to the cross. Experience of transcendence is juxtaposed with the struggle against evil.

The readings today encourage deep faith and trust in God.

Focusing the Gospel
Key words and phrases: [Q]uestioning what rising from the dead meant.

To the point: The transfiguration takes place only a few days after Jesus makes his first passion prediction to the disciples, telling them how "the Son of Man must suffer greatly and be rejected by the elders, the chief priests, and the scribes, and be killed, and rise after three days" (Mark 8:31; NABRE). For the first disciples, Jesus's words must have sounded nonsensical. To rise from the dead was not something anyone in the history of salvation had done before. What did it entail? How was it brought about? Despite their confusion, the disciples continue to follow Jesus on the road to Jerusalem. Only in living the paschal mystery with Jesus will they begin to perceive the immensity of the resurrection.

Connecting the Gospel
to the first reading: In the first reading Abraham also receives an absurd, and disquieting, request from God. Even though he has been promised that he will "become the father of a multitude of nations" (Gen 17:4; NABRE), now God instructs him to offer his only descendant, Isaac, up "as a holocaust." Just as Abraham is about to carry out the request, he is stopped by a voice calling him twice by name, telling him, "Do not lay your hand on the boy . . . Do not do the least thing to him." At this time, the nations around the land of Israel practiced human sacrifice as a form of worship. Although this reading can be difficult for us to encounter, within it we find an affirmation not of death, but of life. God does not desire child sacrifice, or indeed, any harm to come to a son or daughter.

to experience: We believe in a God who brings life from death. How have you experienced this in your life?

Connecting the Responsorial Psalm
to the readings: As Christians, we find in today's psalm response another affirmation of the resurrection promised to us in Jesus: "I will walk before the Lord, in the land of the living." A few chapters after the account of the transfiguration in Mark's gospel, Jesus will tell the Sadducees—a religious group who denied the resurrection of the dead—that God "is not God of the dead but of the living" by citing the passage in Exodus where God tells Moses, "I am the God of Abraham, [the] God of Isaac, and [the] God of Jacob" (Mark 12:26-27; NABRE).

to psalmist preparation: Our Lenten journey will lead us to the foot of the cross and then on to the joy of the empty tomb and the waters of baptism that bring us to new birth and a life in Christ that will never end. How are you preparing yourself—body, mind, and spirit—to live these mysteries anew?

PROMPTS FOR FAITH-SHARING

In the first reading, God tells Abraham, "Do not lay your hand on the boy . . . Do not do the least thing to him." How does your community teach and embrace nonviolence?

The psalmist tells us, "I believed, even when I said, / 'I am greatly afflicted.'" When have you persevered in faith despite difficulty or suffering?

St. Paul asks, "If God is for us, who can be against us?" What fears do you experience in the spiritual life that this statement could help counteract?

In the gospel, a voice from the cloud says, "This is my beloved Son. Listen to him." How do you take time in prayer not only to talk, but also to listen to Jesus?

Model Penitential Act

Presider: In the transfiguration, Peter, James, and John have their eyes opened to the glory of Jesus as the beloved Son of God. For the times we have not recognized Christ in our midst, let us pause to ask for mercy and pardon . . . *[pause]*

    Confiteor: I confess . . .

Homily Points

• On the mountain Jesus is transfigured in front of Peter, James, and John and they hear a voice from the cloud telling them, "This is my beloved Son. Listen to him." We know that later on in the gospel, Jesus will commission the disciples, "Go into the whole world and proclaim the gospel to every creature" (Mark 16:15; NABRE), but at this moment he instead cautions Peter, James, and John "to not relate what they had seen to anyone."

• This is a particular theme in the Gospel of Mark. Often, after someone has experienced a healing, Jesus tells that person, "[S]ee that you tell no one anything" (1:44; NABRE). This can seem very strange to us. If Jesus's mission was to come into the world to preach the kingdom of God and to draw all peoples to himself, certainly being known as a healer, miracle worker, and the one who is proclaimed by God as "my beloved Son" would only help, right? But Jesus is concerned with people receiving the full revelation of who he is, not just as a healer, miracle worker, or even the beloved Son of God, but also as the fully human person of the divine who will undergo suffering and death.

• Only a few verses before the transfiguration, Peter answers Jesus's question, "But who do you say that I am?" with his proclamation: "You are the Messiah" (Mark 8:29; NABRE). Immediately, we are told, "[Jesus] began to teach them that the Son of Man must suffer greatly and be rejected by the elders, the chief priests, and the scribes, and be killed, and rise after three days" (8:31; NABRE). As followers of Christ, we are called to constantly keep in tension Jesus's power and his vulnerability. We can understand his glory only through the lens of the cross.

Model Universal Prayer (Prayer of the Faithful)

Presider: In today's second reading, St. Paul writes, "If God is for us, who can be against us?" Secure in the love of our merciful Father, let us turn to him with our needs and petitions.

Response: Lord, hear our prayer.

For all who preach the gospel, may they live their lives with ears always open to the voice of Jesus, God's beloved Son, leading and guiding them . . .

For children throughout the world, may they dwell in safety and security, knowing the love and support of family, friends, and community . . .

For all who live in a prison made of their own fear and scruples, may the love of Christ and the mercy of God free them to live in joy and peace . . .

For all gathered here, enlightened by the word of God, may we find and serve Christ in the poor and vulnerable among us . . .

Presider: Faithful and compassionate God, in the transfiguration you reveal Jesus's identity as your beloved Son and you instruct us to "[l]isten to him." Hear our prayers that infused by his teaching, we might bear Christ into the world through our own words and actions. We ask this through Christ our Lord. **Amen.**

COLLECT

Let us pray.

Pause for silent prayer

O God, who have commanded us
to listen to your beloved Son,
be pleased, we pray,
to nourish us inwardly by your word,
that, with spiritual sight made pure,
we may rejoice to behold your glory.
Through our Lord Jesus Christ, your Son,
who lives and reigns with you in the unity
    of the Holy Spirit,
one God, for ever and ever. **Amen.**

FIRST READING
Gen 22:1-2, 9a, 10-13, 15-18

God put Abraham to the test.
He called to him, "Abraham!"
"Here I am!" he replied.
Then God said:
    "Take your son Isaac, your only one,
        whom you love,
    and go to the land of Moriah.
There you shall offer him up as a
    holocaust
    on a height that I will point out to you."

When they came to the place of which
    God had told him,
    Abraham built an altar there and
        arranged the wood on it.
Then he reached out and took the knife to
    slaughter his son.
But the LORD's messenger called to him
    from heaven,
    "Abraham, Abraham!"
"Here I am!" he answered.
"Do not lay your hand on the boy," said the
    messenger.
"Do not do the least thing to him.
I know now how devoted you are to God,
    since you did not withhold from me
        your own beloved son."
As Abraham looked about,
    he spied a ram caught by its horns in
        the thicket.
So he went and took the ram
    and offered it up as a holocaust in place
        of his son.

Again the LORD's messenger called to
    Abraham from heaven and said:
    "I swear by myself, declares the LORD,
    that because you acted as you did
    in not withholding from me your
        beloved son,
I will bless you abundantly
    and make your descendants as
        countless
    as the stars of the sky and the sands of
        the seashore;

your descendants shall take possession
of the gates of their enemies,
and in your descendants all the nations
of the earth shall find blessing—
all this because you obeyed my
command."

RESPONSORIAL PSALM
Ps 116:10, 15, 16-17, 18-19

R̸. (116:9) I will walk before the Lord, in
the land of the living.

I believed, even when I said,
"I am greatly afflicted."
Precious in the eyes of the LORD
is the death of his faithful ones.

R̸. I will walk before the Lord, in the land
of the living.

O LORD, I am your servant;
I am your servant, the son of your
handmaid;
you have loosed my bonds.
To you will I offer sacrifice of
thanksgiving,
and I will call upon the name of the
LORD.

R̸. I will walk before the Lord, in the land
of the living.

My vows to the LORD I will pay
in the presence of all his people,
in the courts of the house of the LORD,
in your midst, O Jerusalem.

R̸. I will walk before the Lord, in the land
of the living.

SECOND READING
Rom 8:31b-34

Brothers and sisters:
If God is for us, who can be against us?
He who did not spare his own Son
but handed him over for us all,
how will he not also give us everything
else along with him?

Who will bring a charge against God's
chosen ones?
It is God who acquits us. Who will
condemn?
Christ Jesus it is who died—or, rather, was
raised—
who also is at the right hand of God,
who indeed intercedes for us.

About Liturgy

From the Rising of the Sun . . . : On this Sunday of Lent, we always, in each lectionary cycle, hear about the transfiguration of the Lord, one of the few passages found in all three Synoptic Gospels and a moment even alluded to in Peter's second epistle. Jesus's clothes become dazzlingly white, Mark tells us, and Luke's gospel adds that Jesus's face shone brightly like the sun. Light, considered together with darkness, is an always present sign and symbol of our faith. There is no darkness the light cannot overcome, John's beautiful prologue reminds us.

A hopefully familiar line in Eucharistic Prayer III says, "[S]o that from the rising of the sun to its setting / a pure sacrifice may be offered to your name." There is that presence of light and darkness again. At first hearing, one might assume this phrase describes a length of time, the duration that the sun shines in any particular spot on the earth. One can quickly determine this must not be the case, however: otherwise this would be prescribing that Masses ought not be offered, anywhere, after sundown.

Instead of a statement of only light and darkness, this phrase is rather a geographical one. The previous English translation of this phrase used the words "so that from east to west," which indicates perhaps more clearly that it is all over the world people are gathered unto the Lord to worship and give thanks. Indeed, somewhere on earth the sun is always shining. The divine light is always piercing the darkness, one way or another. Christ's light fills the earth at all times, even if reflected by the moon, making it impossible for the darkness to ever achieve final victory.

About the Altar (Part II)

On This Mountain: The altar has a such a rich history and so many multivalent meanings that some very few words will not do it justice. Yet, let us recall here that "[a]t the Eucharist, the liturgical assembly celebrates the ritual sacrificial meal that recalls and makes present Christ's life, death and resurrection, proclaiming 'the death of the Lord until he comes'" (BLS 56). The altar is a "both/and" of our faith: it is both an altar of sacrificial offering and a table for a memorial meal. It is not helpful to be mindful of one of these things without holding the other with it—both give the other meaning and vitality they would not have on their own. Abraham brings Isaac to an altar, intending to offer sacrifice, and in fact eventually does, with a ram in place of his son. In a verse omitted from the Lectionary, we learn that "Abraham named that place Yahweh-yireh; hence people today say, 'On the mountain the LORD will provide'" (Gen 22:14; NABRE). Thus this altar became both one of sacrifice and a place where the Lord provided a rich bounty.

About Music

God's Revelation: We likely can rapidly name, off the top of our heads, five or six pieces of music through which the transfiguration narrative is told or allowed to unfold and be unpacked, or hymns with light as a central focus of the text. Instead of suggesting any of these, it might be valuable to note that this gospel is paired with the Old Testament reading of the near-sacrifice of Isaac and that these texts, along with the psalm and epistle, all include strong elements of God's direct revelation of faithfulness to us as we learn to trust God's will and eternal love of us. We would be wise to include music that speaks to these facets of our faith, like Bernadette Farrell's "All That Is Hidden" (OCP) or the Taizé community's "Eat This Bread" (GIA), which also points the singer's heart and mind toward the coming journey to Jerusalem.

SPIRITUALITY

GOSPEL ACCLAMATION

John 3:16

God so loved the world that he gave his only Son,
so that everyone who believes in him might have
eternal life.

Gospel John 2:13-25; L29B

Since the Passover of the Jews
    was near,
    Jesus went up to Jerusalem.
He found in the temple area those
    who sold oxen, sheep, and
    doves,
    as well as the money changers seated
        there.
He made a whip out of cords
    and drove them all out of the
        temple area, with the sheep
        and oxen,
    and spilled the coins of the money
        changers
    and overturned their tables,
    and to those who sold doves he
        said,
    "Take these out of here,
    and stop making my Father's house a
        marketplace."
His disciples recalled the words of
    Scripture,
    Zeal for your house will consume me.
At this the Jews answered and said to
    him,
    "What sign can you show us for doing
        this?"
Jesus answered and said to them,
    "Destroy this temple and in three days
        I will raise it up."
The Jews said,
    "This temple has been under
        construction for forty-six years,
    and you will raise it up in three days?"

Continued in Appendix A, p. 267.

*Year A readings may be used, see Appendix A,
pp. 268–270.*

Reflecting on the Gospel

We find it easy to admire—even if we do not imitate—the compassionate Jesus, but an angry Jesus armed with a corded whip, driving traders and moneychangers out of the Jerusalem temple and upturning their tables, may shock us. This gospel does not actually use the word "angry," but Jesus's actions are played out against the backdrop of the "zeal" of Psalm 69:10, and the burning passion of the psalmist for God and the house of God, the Temple, that Mark places in the mouth of Jesus. This is the zeal that will consume Jesus in the hot noon of Calvary.

The cause of Jesus's anger is not so much the money exchange or animal trading in the outer court of the temple. Foreign coinage that bore pagan or imperial images could not be accepted for the half-shekel tax for the upkeep of the temple sanctuary, and so it had to be exchanged for acceptable temple currency with which to pay this tax and also buy sacrificial animals. John writes that "the Passover of the Jews was near," and so those flocking to Jerusalem to celebrate this feast from all over the Roman Empire needed to buy the animals required for participation in the temple worship and the domestic rituals. They could do this most conveniently at the temple. Jesus is not unaware of the need for the money exchange, nor so naïve as not to know that petty pilfering and profiteering can be involved in these transactions. Something much more radical is happening: the reclamation of the holy place from marketplace to his Father's house; from empty, atrophied ritual to living worship.

By his "parable in action," Jesus momentarily terminates the temple worship, reclaims it from chaos and commerce, and cleanses the privileged piece of creation that is his Father's house of prayer. No doubt a few hours later the tables were again in place, animals led back in, coins exchanged—with plenty to talk about!

Yet the disturbing Jesus does not disappear from the scene; he has more "table turning" to do. He stays to answer the criticism of his opponents who can see no further than the temple built over forty-six years by human hands or who refuse to imagine or tolerate any alternatives to the religious practices and institutions that they consider faultless and unchangeable. In this Jesus stands in the line of the Hebrew prophets like Isaiah, Jeremiah, Hosea, and Amos, who angrily and zealously denounced triumphalism and absolutism in worship (e.g., Isa 58:6-9; Jer 7:4-7; Hos 6:6; Amos 5:21-24). Jesus, too, will suffer the fate of so many prophets before and after him: rejection, persecution, even death. Jesus dares to name himself as the new and living temple in which the divine presence dwells. Ultimately, the sanctuary of his body will be destroyed in his passion and death, only to be raised again in three days. It is only after these events that his disciples will remember and understand Jesus's words.

The contemporary church cannot consider itself beyond the reach of Jesus's whip or overturning hands. When church leaders connive with unjust and tyrannical civil leaders, when fundraising takes precedence over faith raising, when we refuse to tolerate or even imagine alternatives to religious practices and institutions (even when some of these are obviously in their death throes), when nostalgia for past liturgical practice resists the leading of the Holy Spirit into the future envisaged by Vatican II, then ecclesial "cleansing" is needed by prophets driven by that Spirit of Jesus. And like Jesus, these men and women may often be torn down and destroyed—but ultimately raised up by him. For us who are living stones in the temple of Christ's Body, Lent is also a time for cleansing the deep personal sanctuary of our hearts, for driving out of our lives whatever clutters our discipleship, blocks our ears to the word of God and the prophets, and distracts us from trading justly and lovingly with the gifts God has given us.

Focusing the Gospel

Key words and phrases: Zeal for your house will consume me.

To the point: In watching Jesus drive the money changers and the merchants from the temple, his disciples remember the verse from the book of Psalms: "[Z]eal for your house has consumed me" (69:10; NABRE). In John's gospel, Jesus's cleansing of the temple is at the beginning of the gospel instead of the end, where the synoptic gospels place it. We find within this account another revelation of who Jesus is as the true temple of the Lord—a temple that, even when destroyed, will be raised "in three days."

Connecting the Gospel

to the first reading: After leading the people out of captivity in Egypt, Moses meets God on Mount Sinai and is given the Ten Commandments. The first three of these commandments explore what we are called to in our relationship with God, while the following seven lay out how we are to interact with other humans. To God, we are called to give fidelity, reverence, and also time. One day of the week is set apart in particular for worship and repose, the Sabbath day. In ancient Israel the temple was the privileged place of encounter with and worship of God and in his cleansing of it, Jesus claims it again as a place of fidelity and reverence where commerce, wealth, and greed have no place.

to experience: As Christians, we are still called to set aside time for God within our week, to draw near to him in reverence and love. How do you strive to "keep holy the Sabbath day"?

Connecting the Responsorial Psalm

to the readings: Today's psalm is a litany of praise for the words and laws of the Lord. In their essence, the commandments given on Mount Sinai are not a restriction placed upon us, but a way that leads to the fullness of life in God's kingdom. In them we find refreshment, joy, and perfection. In the second reading from St. Paul's first letter to the Corinthians, we are told that the wisdom of the law finds its fulfillment in Jesus.

to psalmist preparation: In the final verse of today's psalm we proclaim of God's words, "They are more precious than gold, / than a heap of purest gold." These words of God contained in the Bible, and the Word of God made present in Jesus Christ, are our greatest treasure. How do you relish these gifts of God in your own life?

PROMPTS FOR FAITH-SHARING

In the first reading we hear how God "has blessed the sabbath day and made it holy." How do you set apart a day for God in your week?

Today's psalm reminds us, "The precepts of the Lord are right, rejoicing the heart." How does following God's law bring joy to your life?

St. Paul writes to the Corinthians, "[W]e proclaim Christ crucified." How does this mystery—that the living God became man and died on a cross—inform your faith?

In the gospel Jesus purifies the temple. How does your faith community maintain a sacred and holy space for the people of God to worship?

Model Penitential Act

Presider: In today's first reading God gives the Ten Commandments to the people of Israel. For the times we have not upheld God's law and followed in his ways, let us ask for pardon and mercy . . . *[pause]*

Confiteor: I confess . . .

Homily Points

• We know that God cannot be contained in space and time but lives outside of these constructs and so we can say he is present in every time and every place. And yet for us as humans, very much constricted by the confines of space and time, it is important to have particular places to encounter the living God. For this need we have been given the Sabbath, a day each week set apart for rest and reconnection with God. Ever since the beginning of God's covenant with Abraham, human beings have dedicated physical spaces for worship—from altars built by the nomads, to the ark of the covenant carried with the people as they journeyed to the promised land, and then finally the temple constructed in Jerusalem.

• In our time, we also have places of meeting with God. Our churches hold not only holy artwork and space for us to gather as the Body of Christ, but also the Body of Christ itself in the bread and wine of the Eucharist. In his Body and Blood we find the risen Lord is made present to us and we are invited to make ourselves truly present to him in all that we are.

• The final verses from today's gospel tell us that we need not be afraid to draw near to God due to our sin and failing, for Jesus "did not need anyone to testify about human nature. He himself understood it well." In his person, Jesus redeems human nature, intimately marrying it with the divine. We gather together around the altar of the Lord each week desiring to be cleansed from all that separates us from God, knowing that he also desires to be in communion with us.

Model Universal Prayer (Prayer of the Faithful)

Presider: Knowing God's love and compassion for all he has created, let us confidently place before him our needs and our petitions.

Response: Lord, hear our prayer.

For those who offer pastoral ministry to the people of God and all who care for church structures and buildings, may their efforts bear abundant fruit . . .

For faith leaders throughout the world, may they model interreligious dialogue and civil discourse that lead to understanding and peace among peoples . . .

For victims of human trafficking, may those in slavery be freed and their physical, emotional, and spiritual wounds tended to by compassionate and experienced caregivers . . .

For all gathered here, each day may we grow in fidelity to God's law of love and mercy . . .

Presider: Father of all and giver of every good gift, in your son, Jesus, you call us to worship you in holiness and truth. Hear our prayers that by following his example, we might keep your ways and be strengthened against every evil. We ask this through Christ our Lord. **Amen.**

COLLECT

Let us pray.

Pause for silent prayer

O God, author of every mercy and of all
    goodness,
who in fasting, prayer and almsgiving
have shown us a remedy for sin,
look graciously on this confession of our
    lowliness,
that we, who are bowed down by our
    conscience,
may always be lifted up by your mercy.
Through our Lord Jesus Christ, your Son,
who lives and reigns with you in the unity
    of the Holy Spirit,
one God, for ever and ever. **Amen.**

FIRST READING
Exod 20:1-17

In those days, God delivered all these
    commandments:
  "I, the LORD, am your God,
  who brought you out of the land of
     Egypt, that place of slavery.
You shall not have other gods besides me.
You shall not carve idols for yourselves
  in the shape of anything in the sky
    above
  or on the earth below or in the waters
    beneath the earth;
  you shall not bow down before them or
    worship them.
For I, the LORD, your God, am a jealous
    God,
  inflicting punishment for their fathers'
    wickedness
  on the children of those who hate me,
  down to the third and fourth generation;
  but bestowing mercy down to the
    thousandth generation
  on the children of those who love me
    and keep my commandments.

"You shall not take the name of the LORD,
    your God, in vain.
For the LORD will not leave unpunished
  the one who takes his name in vain.

"Remember to keep holy the sabbath day.
Six days you may labor and do all your
    work,
  but the seventh day is the sabbath of
    the LORD, your God.
No work may be done then either by you,
  or your son or daughter,
  or your male or female slave, or your
    beast,
  or by the alien who lives with you.

In six days the LORD made the heavens and
    the earth,
    the sea and all that is in them;
    but on the seventh day he rested.
That is why the LORD has blessed the
    sabbath day and made it holy.

"Honor your father and your mother,
    that you may have a long life in the land
    which the LORD, your God, is giving you.
You shall not kill.
You shall not commit adultery.
You shall not steal.
You shall not bear false witness against
    your neighbor.
You shall not covet your neighbor's house.
You shall not covet your neighbor's wife,
    nor his male or female slave, nor his ox
      or ass,
    nor anything else that belongs to him."

or

Exod 20:1-3, 7-8, 12-17

In those days, God delivered all these
    commandments:
    "I, the LORD, am your God,
    who brought you out of the land of
      Egypt, that place of slavery.
You shall not have other gods besides me.

"You shall not take the name of the LORD,
    your God, in vain.
For the LORD will not leave unpunished
    the one who takes his name in vain.

"Remember to keep holy the sabbath day.
Honor your father and your mother,
    that you may have a long life in the land
    which the LORD, your God, is giving you.
You shall not kill.
You shall not commit adultery.
You shall not steal.
You shall not bear false witness against
    your neighbor.
You shall not covet your neighbor's house.
You shall not covet your neighbor's wife,
    nor his male or female slave, nor his ox
      or ass,
    nor anything else that belongs to him."

RESPONSORIAL PSALM
Ps 19:8, 9, 10, 11

SECOND READING
1 Cor 1:22-25

See Appendix A, p. 268.

About Liturgy

About Reverence—"Are You God?": Sometime near the beginning of each school year, at the parish where I am music director, we gather the entire student body, pre-K through eighth grade, in the church to go over some music we'll be using at upcoming Masses. One of those times, a few years ago, I had a brief conversation with one of the new pre-K students. This group was the first to arrive in church that day, as they were still learning how to get from place to place, how to behave reverently in church, and so many other things. So, while waiting for the other students to arrive, I sat down next to a young girl. She looked up at me and quite matter-of-factly asked, "Are you God?"

There was no particular sense of awe in her voice or on her face; she didn't seem scared, curious, bewildered, or any other particular adjective. It just seemed like someone, a parent or a teacher probably, had told her something like "Church is God's house," and, well, there I was.

"Are you God?"

"No," I eventually answered, "I'm not God."

"Well, where is God?" she continued.

I tried to start answering, after a moment's thought, with how God is everywhere, in everything God ever created . . . But then a boy in the class, a couple seats down, pointed up to the large crucifix mounted on the wall. "That's God, up there!" he exclaimed.

At that point, the pre-K teacher walked past. "Yes, Jesus is God," she said, on her way to attend to another student's needs, "but we'll get into that later on."

Jesus is God, and in today's gospel passage, God's righteous anger fills the temple, desecrated by money changers and those who would unfairly sell animals for sacrificial offerings. God's temple should be a house of prayer, other gospels tell us; and Jesus, with zealous authority and power, drives out the evildoers.

This can be a jarring image of the Lord, when we are more accustomed to images like a watchful shepherd, a prince of peace, or a loving brother. It is helpful at times to approach God the way the young student I mentioned above did, without any definition or limit of who God actually is. It's good of course to have a sense of awe and respect and wonder in the presence of the Lord—and the building itself, the dwelling of the Most High—but only so much. If we only ever see our God as Creator, Universal Ruler, and Almighty and Powerful Master—but never as parent, brother, friend—then we limit who God is, ignoring much of who God has revealed to us that God is.

Part of that revelation is revealed to us in Jesus Christ, fully God and fully human, a sacrifice of love to the point of death on a cross. Sometimes we consider Jesus Christ as but one of those at the expense of the other, when it is of course most important that Jesus Christ was and is both divine and human at the same time and through all time.

The Holy Spirit proceeds, we believe, from Father and Son (some say through the love that flows between the two) and permeates all of creation if we perceive the universe with eyes of faith. Can you see God in everything? asks a certain Jesuit spirituality. So, while I am in fact not God—and neither are you—how is it that we approach God and help our worshipers do the same: Is it with a childlike faith? How, when, and where are we aware of God, present in our midst? Are we aware, as best as we can be, of the fullness of who God is, in each moment of our lives?

SPIRITUALITY

GOSPEL ACCLAMATION
John 3:16

God so loved the world that he gave his only Son,
so everyone who believes in him might have
eternal life.

Gospel

John 3:14-21; L32B

Jesus said to Nicodemus:
"Just as Moses lifted up the
serpent in the desert,
so must the Son of Man be
lifted up,
so that everyone who
believes in him may
have eternal life."

For God so loved the world
that he gave his only Son,
so that everyone who
believes in him might
not perish
but might have eternal life.
For God did not send his Son into the
world to condemn the world,
but that the world might be saved
through him.
Whoever believes in him will not be
condemned,
but whoever does not believe has
already been condemned,
because he has not believed in the
name of the only Son of God.
And this is the verdict,
that the light came into the world,
but people preferred darkness to light,
because their works were evil.
For everyone who does wicked things
hates the light
and does not come toward the light,
so that his works might not be exposed.
But whoever lives the truth comes to
the light,
so that his works may be clearly seen
as done in God.

*Year A readings may be used, see Appendix A,
pp. 270–272.*

Reflecting on the Gospel

Today we hear one of the most well-known and best-loved verses in the whole of John's gospel, a verse that proclaims "God so loved the world that he gave his only Son, so that everyone who believes in him might not perish but might have eternal life." These words are spoken in the context of the night visit of Nicodemus to Jesus. Nicodemus, a Pharisee and Jewish leader and teacher, avoids the daylight that might reveal him as associating with a man who is unpopular with the religious institution, and so arouse suspicion of Nicodemus's own motives and stance. To be unafraid or un-ashamed of professing our friendship with Jesus by the way we live every day always brings hard demands. The German theologian Eugen Drewermann gives us a memorable image of ourselves when, in the words of the gospel, we have "preferred darkness to light," to that light which is the only Son of God, given for its salvation to the world that God loves so much: "It can happen that we become like bats, like night-flying creatures who are so accustomed to the dark that our whole biorhythm is attuned to these shadowy periods, as if our eyes would be hurt and our whole lives would be turned inside out if we were dragged out of our caves and the hidden and fearful forms of our existence were exposed to the quiet regions of light and the brightness of day" (*Dying We Live: Meditations for Lent and Easter*).

But we often prefer the false safety of darkness to the light of Christ that exposes, for example, our selfish, racist, sexist, or violent selves. We all have our own caves that we need to name. Lent is designed to drag us out of their darkness into the Easter light of Christ through prayer, fasting, and the "alms-giving" of the gift of ourselves as well as the offer of material assistance to our sisters and brothers in many kinds of need.

To help the night visitor, Nicodemus, to come into the light of understanding something of his mystery and mission, Jesus uses a good catechetical approach: he talks the language of his listener. He reminds this "teacher of Israel" (John 3:10; NABRE), who is very much in the dark, of a story from their own Hebrew Scriptures (Num 21:4-9). In the wilderness, the people grumble against God and are struck with a plague of serpents whose bite could cause death. The people come to Moses, admit their sinfulness, and ask him to intercede for them with God. When he does so, God tells Moses to forge a bronze serpent, fix it and raise it up before those who are stricken. If they gaze on it, they will be saved. This seems a great paradox: healing and life from gazing on a creature of death! But they obey and are healed.

In our humanity, we are all bitten by death; yet, Jesus tells Nicodemus, the God who is love wants to give us life that never ends. And so the flesh of the Son of Man will be brutally, senselessly twisted around the wood of the cross, forged by the fire of his passion and death, and raised up for our salvation. In John's gospel, "raising" or "lifting up" always has the double sense of crucifixion and exaltation, death and resurrection, for the two movements are inseparable. To gaze with the eyes of faith on this mystery and commit ourselves to it will mean eternal life. Jesus does not come to judge, but just as turning on a light exposes what is hidden in darkness, so it is when the light of Christ shines upon us to expose both good and evil. The cross that will be raised up and venerated on Good Friday will give way at the Easter Vigil to the raised Easter candle, marked with the cross of fragrant "nails" of incense, from which we catch fire and rekindle our baptismal commitment to the saving and universal love of Jesus Christ.

Focusing the Gospel

Key words and phrases: "Just as Moses lifted up the serpent in the desert, / so must the Son of Man be lifted up."

To the point: Today's gospel refers to an event that occurred as the people of Israel sojourned in the desert after their escape from slavery in Egypt and before entering into the Promised Land. The people, weary from their travel, complain bitterly against God and Moses: "Why have you brought us up from Egypt to die in the wilderness, where there is no food or water? We are disgusted with this wretched food!" (Num 21:5; NABRE). The people are punished for their complaints with serpent bites, and then saved from their punishment when God commands Moses, "Make a seraph and mount it on a pole, and everyone who has been bitten will look at it and recover" (Num 21:8; NABRE). And now, in today's gospel, Jesus is compared to this "sign of salvation" (Wis 16:6; NABRE), for when he is lifted up, "everyone who believes in him may have eternal life."

Connecting the Gospel

to the first and the second readings: In today's gospel we find the oft-quoted line, "For God so loved the world that he gave his only Son, so that everyone who believes in him might not perish / but might have eternal life." The first and second reading echo this theme of God's unfailing mercy. The narrator from the second book of Chronicles tells us, "Early and often did the Lord, the God of their fathers, / send his messengers" to his wayward people. Though they had been unfaithful even to the point of "polluting the Lord's temple" and practicing "abominations," God still has "compassion on his people and his dwelling place." We see God's grace at work calling the people of Israel who had been exiled from their homeland to return once more to Jerusalem to rebuild his house. Similarly, St. Paul writes to the Ephesians that they have been saved through no merit of their own but purely through "the gift of God."

to experience: As St. Paul writes, our God is "rich in mercy" and in Jesus we receive the greatest gift of his mercy—that even in our sinfulness, Jesus did not come to condemn but to save. How is God calling you to accept this mercy in your life and also to extend it to others?

Connecting the Responsorial Psalm

to the readings: While today's first reading gives a synopsis of the Babylonian exile, the psalm gives voice to the captives' sorrow. In this time of exile the people of God enter into their faith in a new way. Though the temple has been destroyed and the holy city of Jerusalem ransacked, the people are sustained by their memories and also in the sure knowledge that their God is still with them.

to psalmist preparation: Even in exile, the people learn how to "sing a song of the Lord / in a foreign land." What has brought you comfort in times of grief or struggle?

PROMPTS FOR FAITH-SHARING

In the first reading we hear that "early and often did the Lord . . . send messengers to them" to call the people back to the covenant. Which saints throughout the ages have inspired your spiritual journey?

Today's psalm asks, "How could we sing a song to the Lord / in a foreign land?" When in your life (either physically or spiritually) have you experienced being far from home and what sustained you in that time?

St. Paul writes to the Ephesians that we are God's "handiwork." Where do you see the handiwork of God flourishing in your family and community?

In today's gospel, Jesus tells Nicodemus, "[T]he light came into the world, / but people preferred darkness to light." Where do you perceive light encountering darkness in your community at this moment?

CELEBRATION

Model Penitential Act

Presider: In today's gospel, Jesus tells Nicodemus, "[T]he light came into the world, / but people preferred darkness." For all the times and ways that we have preferred darkness to the light of Christ, let us ask for mercy and pardon . . . *[pause]*

    Confiteor: I confess . . .

Homily Points

• Shortly after cleansing the temple Jesus enters into a discourse with Nicodemus, a Pharisee, who comes at night to talk to him. Today's gospel is the second half of their conversation. While Nicodemus begins by stating, "Rabbi, we know that you are a teacher who has come from God, for no one can do these signs that you are doing unless God is with him" (John 3:2; NABRE), it seems that Nicodemus's faith is not complete enough for Jesus. In the verses we read from today, Jesus alludes to the crucifixion, when he will be "lifted up," as well as to his identity as the savior and light of the world.

• In his discourse with Nicodemus, Jesus offers us a powerful tool for discernment as we travel along the journey of faith. He tells us, "[T]he light came into the world, / but the people preferred darkness to light, / because their works were evil." While certainly not condemning Nicodemus as wicked, Jesus's words could cast some judgment on Nicodemus for choosing to come to him at night. Despite his words of affirmation when he greets Jesus, does Nicodemus fear being seen and associated with this zealous preacher?

• In Lent we enter into a time of purification and penance. It is an apt time to ask ourselves, In what ways have we preferred the cover of darkness to the illuminating power of the light? We need not fear the brightness of Christ, for as St. Paul writes to the Ephesians we were brought "to life with Christ," even when we were "dead in our transgressions." God's grace is a gift offered freely and abundantly. We only need accept it.

Model Universal Prayer (Prayer of the Faithful)

Presider: In today's gospel, Jesus assures Nicodemus, "For God did not send his Son into the world to condemn the world, / but that the world might be saved through him." Trusting in Christ's desire to save and redeem, let us bring our needs and petitions before him.

Response: Lord, hear our prayer.

For God's holy church, may God raise up prophets and preachers to call his people to renewed fidelity and away from sin . . .

For all who are caught up in the darkness of greed and violence, may the light of Christ allow charity and peace to reign in their hearts . . .

For refugees and immigrants who find themselves far from their homeland, may they be sustained by a welcoming community . . .

For all gathered here as we continue on our Lenten journey, may our faith be strengthened and our lives transformed in Christ . . .

Presider: God of light and life, you sent your son Jesus as our savior and redeemer. Hear our prayers that we might share your mercy and love with all we encounter. We ask this through Christ our Lord. **Amen.**

COLLECT

Let us pray.

Pause for silent prayer

O God, who through your Word
reconcile the human race to yourself in a
    wonderful way,
grant, we pray,
that with prompt devotion and eager faith
the Christian people may hasten
toward the solemn celebrations to come.
Through our Lord Jesus Christ, your Son,
who lives and reigns with you in the unity
    of the Holy Spirit,
one God, for ever and ever. **Amen.**

FIRST READING
2 Chr 36:14-16, 19-23

In those days, all the princes of Judah, the
    priests, and the people
    added infidelity to infidelity,
    practicing all the abominations of the
        nations
    and polluting the Lord's temple
    which he had consecrated in Jerusalem.

Early and often did the Lord, the God of
    their fathers,
    send his messengers to them,
    for he had compassion on his people
        and his dwelling place.
But they mocked the messengers of God,
    despised his warnings, and scoffed at
        his prophets,
    until the anger of the Lord against his
        people was so inflamed
    that there was no remedy.
Their enemies burnt the house of God,
    tore down the walls of Jerusalem,
    set all its palaces afire,
    and destroyed all its precious objects.
Those who escaped the sword were
        carried captive to Babylon,
    where they became servants of the king
        of the Chaldeans and his sons
    until the kingdom of the Persians came
        to power.
All this was to fulfill the word of the Lord
    spoken by Jeremiah:
    "Until the land has retrieved its lost
        sabbaths,
    during all the time it lies waste it shall
        have rest
    while seventy years are fulfilled."

In the first year of Cyrus, king of Persia,
in order to fulfill the word of the LORD
spoken by Jeremiah,
the LORD inspired King Cyrus of Persia
to issue this proclamation throughout
his kingdom,
both by word of mouth and in writing:
"Thus says Cyrus, king of Persia:
All the kingdoms of the earth
the LORD, the God of heaven, has given
to me,
and he has also charged me to build him
a house
in Jerusalem, which is in Judah.
Whoever, therefore, among you belongs to
any part of his people,
let him go up, and may his God be with
him!"

RESPONSORIAL PSALM
Ps 137:1-2, 3, 4-5, 6

R⁊. (6ab) Let my tongue be silenced, if I
ever forget you!

By the streams of Babylon
we sat and wept when we remembered
Zion.
On the aspens of that land
we hung up our harps.

R⁊. Let my tongue be silenced, if I ever
forget you!

For there our captors asked of us
the lyrics of our songs,
and our despoilers urged us to be joyous:
"Sing for us the songs of Zion!"

R⁊. Let my tongue be silenced, if I ever
forget you!

How could we sing a song of the LORD
in a foreign land?
If I forget you, Jerusalem,
may my right hand be forgotten!

R⁊. Let my tongue be silenced, if I ever
forget you!

May my tongue cleave to my palate
if I remember you not,
if I place not Jerusalem
ahead of my joy.

R⁊. Let my tongue be silenced, if I ever
forget you!

SECOND READING
Eph 2:4-10

See Appendix A, p. 270.

About Liturgy

Practicing Sacred Time: The Old Testament passage for today paints a dire picture of the misdeeds of God's people: defiling the temple, mocking prophets, and rousing the anger of a compassionate and loving God. It's worth noting that the passage says nothing about God bringing retribution directly; rather, it's the "enemies" of God's people that ravage them, their lands, and the holy temple. The Babylonian exile then begins, as the people of God are led away in captivity.

The psalmist decries, "Let my tongue be silenced, if I ever forget you!" (Ps 137:6ab). We previously discussed the importance of stillness and silence in the liturgy. What deserves further contemplation is how to help our assemblies become proficient in utilizing times of sacred silence. We are in a world that, more and more each passing day, bombards us with a variety of smartphone alerts, breaking news chyrons, and bright flashing billboards demanding our attention and reaction. We are pulled hour by hour, minute by minute, in eighteen different directions. Frequently, the only "downtime" we get is not by our own choosing, but rather comes only if the power goes out or our phone battery dies.

The axiom states "You get good at what you practice." That is step one—making sure that silences at liturgy are not an occasional thing, but an every-Mass thing. They are expected, consistent, and obviously intentional. Give the assembly that time and space.

Next is helping them truly use the sacred time well. It can be easy to immediately fill such silences with a myriad of quasi-liturgical activities: finding the next hymn in the book, reading a bit of the bulletin, and the like. One might even fill the moment with activities that take one out of kairos: checking a watch, recalling the rest of the day's activities that lie ahead, and so many more "human" pursuits.

Consider a bulletin column series, perhaps a pre-Mass announcement, or possibly even incorporating into today's homily catechesis on effectively using silent time. Silence is an opportunity to watch and listen, both with our eyes and with our hearts, to the sacred space around us. It's important, to begin, that we not bother with questions like "why" or "how," but rather just observe and notice. Most church buildings are so detailed that one could spend endless Sundays noticing bits of architecture, stained glass windows, or statuary and find details previously overlooked. We can hear the smallest features in the organ playing during the preparation of the gifts: the colors of the tones, the harmonies shifting, the melody floating toward the heavens. We can begin, after observing the prayerful environment around us, to contemplate in our hearts what it is that God is speaking to us and how it is we will choose to respond to a loving God, in word and in deeds.

About Music

The Music of Incarnation: This Sunday's gospel contains one of the most well-known passages in all of Scripture, John 3:16. If you haven't lately, consider singing a piece of music, for instance during the preparation of the gifts, for the assembly to remain still and listen to these profound words—especially if the advice above on utilizing silence and stillness is taken to heart. Robert Farrell has an approachable setting for SATB choir and keyboard (OCP).

Alternatively, it would also be good to place on the assembly's lips a text that breaks open the significance of this passage. A wonderful text by J. Michael Thompson is titled "God of Love" (WLP, also in Liturgical Press's *Sacred Song*), which can be sung to BEACH SPRING among other favorite hymn tunes.

MARCH 14, 2021
FOURTH SUNDAY OF LENT

GOSPEL ACCLAMATION
Ps 84:5

Blessed are those who dwell in your house,
O Lord;
they never cease to praise you.

Gospel

Luke 2:41-51a; L543

Each year Jesus' parents went
to Jerusalem for the feast of
Passover,
and when he was twelve years old,
they went up according to
festival custom.
After they had completed its days,
as they were returning,
the boy Jesus remained behind
in Jerusalem,
but his parents did not know it.
Thinking that he was in the caravan,
they journeyed for a day
and looked for him among their
relatives and acquaintances,
but not finding him,
they returned to Jerusalem to
look for him.
After three days they found him in
the temple,
sitting in the midst of the teachers,
listening to them and asking them
questions,
and all who heard him were astounded
at his understanding and his answers.
When his parents saw him,
they were astonished,
and his mother said to him,
"Son, why have you done this to us?
Your father and I have been looking for
you with great anxiety."
And he said to them,
"Why were you looking for me?
Did you not know that I must be in my
Father's house?"
But they did not understand what he said
to them.
He went down with them and came to
Nazareth,
and was obedient to them.

or Matt 1:16, 18-21, 24a in Appendix A, p. 272.

*See Appendix A, pp. 272–273 for the other
readings.*

Reflecting on the Gospel

St. Joseph is an ordinary saint, comparable to many of the ordinary heroes of daily and family life, who behave dutifully, and with kindness, often behind the scenes, not drawing attention or praise to themselves, but fulfilling the work assigned to them without complaint. When Joseph found that his betrothed Mary was pregnant, his first reaction was not anger, or a desire to see her punished by stoning for adultery, but "since he was a righteous man, yet unwilling to expose her to shame," he "decided to divorce her quietly."

This would have been an act of kindness on Joseph's part, but a different task was assigned to him in a revelatory dream. Joseph was not to divorce his betrothed wife Mary, but to understand that she was pregnant through the Holy Spirit. This would not be an easy thing for anyone to accept, but Joseph did it. When he woke up, he accepted God's word to him and did what he was commanded.

Joseph's role is not great in many ways, but it is fundamental to human salvation. Mary—the Mother of God, *theotokos* as the church would come to call her—would bear the son. That son, Jesus, would "save his people from their sins." Joseph's task was to accept that this was God's will and "to name him Jesus." In Greek, the verb to name is in the second person singular, "you, Joseph, are to name him Jesus." Joseph did not have a major role in saving the world, but he supported them with his necessary and essential role, even if it was simply remaining with his wife and naming the son.

Yet, this ordinary human history is where our salvation is played out. Joseph, whose day-to-day life is hidden from us for the most part, helped raise Jesus and taught him the work of the carpenter and craftsman, as fathers had for generations trained their sons to enter their own craft. Certainly, Joseph also took Jesus to the local synagogue to hear and learn to read Scripture, bringing him up in the Torah and the commandments of God, as a child of Israel.

And while history has as its goal the glory of God's kingdom, established by the Son of David, God's son, most of us participate in this goal not through heroic acts or by being the center of attention, but by remaining faithful to God's call, by listening to God's word, by carrying out daily, mundane tasks just like Joseph. We labor in the background doing what is asked of us because it is in the ordinariness of everyday life that most of us build up the kingdom and seek righteousness, just like Joseph. Like him, we are called by God to do our part that is essential and necessary, even if often unseen and unheralded.

Focusing the Gospel

Key words and phrases: [H]is parents did not know it.

To the point: Mary and Joseph are in a position familiar to anyone who has parented an adolescent. Their child, who has entered into a new phase of freedom and self-determination, uses this freedom in a way they had not foreseen or intended. Instead of returning home with his family in the safety of their caravan, the twelve-year-old Jesus remains in the holy city of Jerusalem, eager to learn from and speak with the teachers in the temple. We can only imagine Joseph and Mary's frenzy and panic as they scour the streets of Jerusalem looking for their child. In their distress, we can find a companion for our own lives. We do not always understand the ways of God (much less the ways of the people we share our lives with), and yet we are called to faith and trust.

Model Penitential Act

Presider: St. Joseph trusted God in all things, taking the Virgin Mary as his wife and caring for the child she conceived of by the Holy Spirit as his own. For the times our faith has not lived up to the model of St. Joseph's, let us ask God for pardon and mercy . . . *[pause]*

Lord Jesus, you are descended from the family of David: Lord, have mercy.
Christ Jesus, you are Son of God and son of Mary: Christ, have mercy.
Lord Jesus, your kingdom shall have no end: Lord, have mercy.

Model Universal Prayer (Prayer of the Faithful)

Presider: Through the intercession of St. Joseph, spouse of the blessed Virgin Mary and foster father of Jesus, let us bring our needs before the Lord.

Response: Lord, hear our prayer.

For all who take on the role of spiritual father among the faithful, may they be refreshed in their ministry and renewed to share the love of God with others . . .

For leaders of nations, may they construct policies and enact legislation to support families in crisis . . .

For adolescents as they traverse the years from childhood to adulthood, may they be blessed with role models and mentors to assist their growth and safeguard their innocence . . .

For all gathered here, may we recognize each other as brothers and sisters in the Lord and build a community intent upon discipleship and reconciliation . . .

Presider: God of wonder and might, you called St. Joseph to live in the communion of the Holy Family with Jesus and Mary. Hear our prayers that following in his footsteps, we might protect the vulnerable and serve the lowly. We ask this through Christ our Lord. **Amen.**

About Liturgy

A Weekday Sunday: We arrive at a bit of a Lenten oasis, the solemnity of St. Joseph, made even more of a relief perhaps by the date of the celebration falling on a Friday this year. "Solemnities are counted among the most important days, whose celebration begins with First Vespers (Evening Prayer I) on the preceding day" (Universal Norms on the Liturgical Year and the General Roman Calendar 11). Mass is celebrated then as if on a Sunday, with Gloria and Creed. In some parts of the world, Mass attendance on this solemnity is obligatory.

Further, canon law tells us, "Abstinence from meat, or from some other food as determined by the Episcopal Conference, is to be observed on all Fridays, unless a solemnity should fall on a Friday" (c. 1251). Just as certain penitential practices are "suspended" on Sundays of Lent, they are also lifted on solemnities, even when falling on a Friday.

So, take the opportunities, both inside and outside the church building, to celebrate this silent, holy man! St. Joseph, pray for us!

FOR REFLECTION

• In the first reading, God promises David that his "house . . . and kingdom shall endure forever before me." How far back can you trace your ancestry in faith? What spiritual gifts have you received from your ancestors?

• In the second reading St. Paul lifts up Abraham's "righteousness that comes from faith." Where are you being called to grow in faith?

• Along with Jesus and Mary, St. Joseph is a member of the Holy Family. How does your family take inspiration from this simple family of Nazareth?

Homily Points

• Today's second reading focuses on Abraham, our father in faith. In St. Joseph we are given another father in faith. Like Abraham, Joseph left what he expected from his life as the husband of Mary, a maiden from Nazareth, to be the spouse of the Mother of God and to protect and nurture her child.

• The gospel gives a small glimpse into the life of the family from Nazareth when Mary and Joseph search for Jesus for three days only to find him in the temple, his "Father's house." Joseph's vocation was to serve God in the child Jesus, providing for him, teaching him, loving him. We are called to follow in his footsteps, offering service to Christ within those we meet and trusting in the God who calls us beyond what is known to the fullness of life.

SPIRITUALITY

GOSPEL ACCLAMATION
John 12:26

Whoever serves me must follow me, says the Lord;
and where I am, there also will my servant
be.

Gospel

John 12:20-33; L35B

Some Greeks who had come to
worship at the Passover Feast
came to Philip, who was from
Bethsaida in Galilee,
and asked him, "Sir, we would like
to see Jesus."
Philip went and told Andrew;
then Andrew and Philip went and
told Jesus.
Jesus answered them,
"The hour has come for the Son of
Man to be glorified.
Amen, amen, I say to you,
unless a grain of wheat falls to the
ground and dies,
it remains just a grain of wheat;
but if it dies, it produces much fruit.
Whoever loves his life loses it,
and whoever hates his life in this world
will preserve it for eternal life.
Whoever serves me must follow me,
and where I am, there also will my
servant be.
The Father will honor whoever serves
me.

"I am troubled now. Yet what should I
say?
'Father, save me from this hour'?
But it was for this purpose that I came to
this hour.
Father, glorify your name."
Then a voice came from heaven,
"I have glorified it and will glorify it
again."

Continued in Appendix A, p. 273.

Year A readings may be used, see Appendix A,
pp. 273–275.

Reflecting on the Gospel

The gospel of this Sunday proclaims the paradoxical wisdom of emptying in order to become full, of dying so that we may be raised to new life. This is the "hour" of radical obedience and exaltation for which, from Cana, through controversies, festivals, and miraculous signs, Jesus has been waiting: an hour that in today's gospel sees Jesus sought by new "first disciples," those beyond Israel, to whom the evangelist refers as "[s]ome Greeks."

They were probably Greek-speaking Jews who had come up to Jerusalem to celebrate the Passover. They approach Andrew and Philip, two of Jesus's original disciples who are apparently approachable and good at bringing others to Jesus. (Remember Peter, Nathanael, and the boy with five barley loaves and two fish.) Although these seekers may have been Jews from far-flung places, John uses this episode on the threshold of Jesus's "hour" to suggest the call of the Gentiles. Many nations who eagerly seek Jesus will be drawn into his mystery when he is lifted up from the earth on a cross; all those who will belong to the church that is meant to be multiracial and multicultural.

To explain the meaning of his "hour," Jesus tells the parable of a grain of wheat. When it is dropped into the earth, the seed shrinks, empties itself, and dies. But in the warmth and moisture of the earth new life breaks out of the husk and bears much fruit. "Fruit" in John's gospel means "life," and the hour is at hand when Jesus will be buried in the heart of the earth and rise from there to transformed and transforming life.

The larger world beyond Israel now includes us. If we wish not only to see but also to follow Jesus, we must choose to empty ourselves of self-centeredness, of the instinct for self-preservation at the expense of our sisters and brothers. Those insulated from others' suffering, eager for good connections, popularity, and status, rather than finding and following Jesus, will lose their lives. From seeds buried in the warm love and service of others, and watered by fidelity to our baptismal commitment, the Christian community grows into the mystery of the death and resurrection of Jesus. This is not easy; it was painful for Jesus, and it is painful for us. Jesus's soul was troubled, we hear, but he embraces his hour of his own free will. He has already told the crowds, "No one takes it [my life] from me, but I lay it down on my own. I have power to lay it down, and power to take it up again. This command I have received from my Father" (John 10:18; NABRE). What Jesus has done, he proclaims, has always been for the glory of his Father, and he will die because of the way he lived. The Father's voice affirms Jesus's proclamation, declaring that Jesus is giving glory to God, and will be glorified because of this. It is a voice, says Jesus, that speaks not so much to reassure Jesus himself, but to bring faith and encouragement to the bystanders.

We are now the crowd assembled around Jesus. Do we understand his words or the Father's voice? Can we recognize his saving cross at the epicenter of the tragedies that are born of sin, planted on the seismic fault lines that threaten to open and crack our world apart: the divides between rich and poor, peace and violence, north and south, east and west? Even more important, can we allow ourselves to be drawn to the exalted cross of Christ so that we ourselves may offer from the "right place" of the cross the fruit of healing reconciliation for the glory of God?

Focusing the Gospel

Key words and phrases: "The hour has come for the Son of Man to be glorified."

To the point: As he did in last week's gospel, Jesus once again reveals that he will be "lifted up." In speaking with Nicodemus, Jesus said, "[T]he Son of Man must be lifted up / so that everyone who believes in him may have eternal life." In today's gospel he proclaims, "[W]hen I am lifted up from the earth, / I will draw everyone to myself." Even though Jesus's body will eventually be "lifted up" on a cross, a tool of torture and death, in John's gospel the crucifixion is the moment of Jesus's complete glorification. Each day we draw closer to the holiest days of our year when we live in a particular way Jesus's passion, death, and resurrection. Let us also prepare ourselves to give glory to our crucified and risen Lord who draws everyone to himself.

Connecting the Gospel

to the second reading: The second reading from the letter to the Hebrews focuses more on Jesus's suffering in the crucifixion than on his glory. Today's reading ends with the proclamation that Jesus "became the source of eternal salvation for all who obey him." In his obedience to God, Jesus endures death on a cross and in his suffering, the epistle writer states, "[H]e was made perfect." Once again, we find the tension of Jesus's divine and human nature. In John's gospel Jesus appears to know everything that will occur to him and has no desire to pray, "Father, save me from this hour." Instead he states, "Father, glorify your name," a proclamation that is met with divine approval via a thundering voice from heaven.

to experience: At different times in our lives, we might be attracted more to the suffering Jesus or to the glorified and authoritative Jesus. Both are true revelations of who Christ is, and yet neither is complete without the other. At this moment on your journey of faith, are you drawn more to Jesus the crucified or Jesus the victor?

Connecting the Responsorial Psalm

to the readings: The prophet Jeremiah lived during the bleakest period of Israel's history, when the southern kingdom of Judah was conquered by the Babylonians, Jerusalem and the temple destroyed, and the people taken off into exile. Today's first reading occurs near the end of the prophetic book when Jeremiah turns from condemnation to consolation. Though the people have broken the covenant time and time again, God is planning a new covenant that will be written not on stone tablets but instead upon the hearts of his people. Today's psalm implores the Lord to "[c]reate a clean heart in me, O God." This pure heart is one that is not divided by guilt, sin, or offense, but one dedicated solely to the Lord.

to psalmist preparation: As we draw closer to Holy Week, how are you in need of God's renewing and restoring action in your heart?

PROMPTS FOR FAITH-SHARING

In the first reading God declares through Jeremiah, "I will forgive their evildoing and remember their sin no more." How have you experienced God's forgiveness this Lent?

The psalmist implores God, "Create a clean heart in me." What attributes do you think of when considering a "clean heart"?

The second reading from the letter to the Hebrews offers the image of Christ being "perfected" through suffering. Have there been moments of suffering in your life that have led to spiritual growth?

Jesus tells his disciples, "[U]nless a grain of wheat falls to the ground and dies, / it remains just a grain of wheat; / but if it dies, it produces much fruit." How have you encountered this mystery that death leads to even more abundant life?

CELEBRATION

Model Penitential Act

Presider: In today's first reading, God declares through Jeremiah, "I will forgive their evildoing and remember their sin no more." Confident in God's unfailing mercy, let us pause to call to mind our sins . . . *[pause]*

Confiteor: I confess . . .

Homily Points

• Today's gospel reading takes place only a few days before Jesus's crucifixion and death. In John's gospel, Jesus speaks of this moment as the hour when the Father will truly "glorify [God's] name," for "when I am lifted from the earth, / I will draw everyone to myself." Despite this focus on God's glory, Jesus uses a rather mundane image to explain what will occur. The power and authority of God over evil and death can be seen in the simple power of a seed, which planted in the ground eventually bears "much fruit."

• The language Jesus uses is odd. We don't usually say when gardening that we are causing seeds to "die." And yet, it is true that in the process of planting and growing, the seed will cease to be. Its life goes into the plant it becomes—a plant that, allowed to grow to fruition, will produce many seeds of its own.

• In Jesus's crucifixion, we are freed from the chains of death and powers of evil, and this is all accomplished in the most peaceful and nonviolent manner possible. Jesus offers no resistance to the crowd that demands his death. Despite his ability to feed five thousand people with only a few loaves and fishes and his power to calm a storm with a word, Jesus uses no spiritual force to climb down from the cross he has been raised up on. Instead, as we read every Good Friday from John's gospel, when the time of his death arrives, he proclaims, "It is finished," bows his head, and hands over his spirit (19:30; NABRE). In all he does, Jesus has faith in God who can bring life from death, and does so each day in the fruits of creation.

Model Universal Prayer (Prayer of the Faithful)

Presider: As we draw closer to Holy Week and the season of Easter joy, let us bring our prayers before the Lord who hears and answers the cries of his people.

Response: Lord, hear our prayer.

For God's holy church, inspired by the sacrifice of the martyrs throughout the ages, may it continue to boldly preach the good news of Jesus Christ . . .

For leaders of nations, may they come together to end the production of weapons of mass destruction and craft a vision for world peace . . .

For those who are imprisoned due to political and religious beliefs, may their freedom be secured and their human rights safeguarded . . .

For all gathered here, may any suffering we encounter serve to strengthen and perfect us in faith . . .

Presider: God of redemption, in the death of your Son you brought about even more abundant life for him and for all who follow in his way. Hear our prayers that in our hope of the resurrection, we might proclaim in both word and action that life is stronger than death. We ask this through Christ our Lord. **Amen.**

COLLECT

Let us pray.

Pause for silent prayer

By your help, we beseech you, Lord our
   God,
may we walk eagerly in that same charity
with which, out of love for the world,
your Son handed himself over to death.
Through our Lord Jesus Christ, your Son,
who lives and reigns with you in the unity
   of the Holy Spirit,
one God, for ever and ever. **Amen.**

FIRST READING

Jer 31:31-34

The days are coming, says the LORD,
   when I will make a new covenant with
      the house of Israel
   and the house of Judah.
It will not be like the covenant I made with
      their fathers
   the day I took them by the hand
   to lead them forth from the land of
      Egypt;
   for they broke my covenant,
   and I had to show myself their master,
      says the LORD.
But this is the covenant that I will make
   with the house of Israel after those
      days, says the LORD.
I will place my law within them and write
   it upon their hearts;
   I will be their God, and they shall be my
      people.
No longer will they have need to teach
   their friends and relatives
   how to know the LORD.
All, from least to greatest, shall know me,
   says the LORD,
   for I will forgive their evildoing and
      remember their sin no more.

RESPONSORIAL PSALM

Ps 51:3-4, 12-13, 14-15

R̸. (12a) Create a clean heart in me, O God.

Have mercy on me, O God, in your
goodness;
in the greatness of your compassion
wipe out my offense.
Thoroughly wash me from my guilt
and of my sin cleanse me.

R̸. Create a clean heart in me, O God.

A clean heart create for me, O God,
and a steadfast spirit renew within me.
Cast me not out from your presence,
and your Holy Spirit take not from me.

R̸. Create a clean heart in me, O God.

Give me back the joy of your salvation,
and a willing spirit sustain in me.
I will teach transgressors your ways,
and sinners shall return to you.

R̸. Create a clean heart in me, O God.

SECOND READING

Heb 5:7-9

In the days when Christ Jesus was in the
flesh,
he offered prayers and supplications
with loud cries and tears
to the one who was able to save him
from death,
and he was heard because of his
reverence.
Son though he was, he learned obedience
from what he suffered;
and when he was made perfect,
he became the source of eternal
salvation for all who obey him.

About Liturgy

Building a Church: Today's Lectionary brings our Lenten journey, nearing its end once again, in some ways back to where we began. You will recall that this particular Lenten cycle is one of covenants: first Noah, then Abraham, and others. On this Sunday, we hear that there are days coming when God will make a new covenant, where God's laws will not be handed on to us externally, like the Ten Commandments on tablets, but will be written on our hearts. In the gospel, we are told of God's thunderous voice, much like the voice at the transfiguration. Everything is seeming to return us to where the journey began: Jesus's proclamation that the kingdom of God is at hand.

In our various ministries, it can frequently feel like we are running in circles, especially if we lose sight of the reasons for our ministry, our love of it and the people of God, or if we feel unsupported: by our peers, by those in leadership roles, or by the very people we believe we have been called to serve. Particularly as Holy Week approaches, days can grow very long and stressful with the many different preparations demanded of us.

A modern-day parable—not an original one—may be helpful in this circumstance. It seems, one day, a man came upon a group of laborers, stone masons. He approached the first to ask what he was doing that day. Barely looking up from his work, the man grumbled, "I'm laying bricks," and with a sigh continued his labors. Approaching a second worker, the man asked him this same question. "I'm making a wall," the worker said, pausing to look left and right at the long expanse already partially created. Then the man walked up to the third worker. "What are you doing today?" he asked him. Putting down his tools, the mason gestured that the man should follow him a few steps away. Turning back around to his work, the laborer spread his arms wide and exclaimed, "I'm building a church!"

So it is with our ministries, if we pause a few moments to ponder our work in the vineyard. What is the expression, if we don't have ten minutes a day during which we can pray, we should pray for twenty minutes? Find some time these next couple weeks to contemplate during all the busyness—which can at times seem like we are simply fortifying a wall or even just moving heavy stones from point A to point B—how we are in fact building a church: a sacred assembly of God's holy people, the Body of Christ present in the world.

About Music

Embracing the Cross: If we have planned music well thus far, we have noticed that the season of Lent is largely not one about suffering and death, at least not until reaching last Sunday, this Sunday, and of course Passion Sunday. Music of repentance and discipleship gives way now to music of redemption, of sacrifice, and of the cross itself.

Jaime Cortez has a recent "Take Up Your Cross" (OCP) that weds discipleship and sacrifice well. There is, too, a more "traditional" hymn by the same name in most hymnals, which also carries a similar message. From the "Praise and Worship" genre, "Above All" (Le Blanc and Baloche) is a powerful and prayerful reflection on the crucifixion Jesus foretells in today's gospel.

GOSPEL ACCLAMATION
John 1:14ab

The Word of God became flesh and made his
dwelling among us;
and we saw his glory.

Gospel   Luke 1:26-38; L545

The angel Gabriel was sent from God
    to a town of Galilee called Nazareth,
    to a virgin betrothed to a man named
        Joseph,
    of the house of David,
    and the virgin's name was Mary.
And coming to her, he said,
    "Hail, full of grace! The Lord is with
        you."
But she was greatly troubled at what was
        said
    and pondered what sort of greeting this
        might be.
Then the angel said to her,
    "Do not be afraid, Mary,
    for you have found favor with God.
Behold, you will conceive in your womb and
        bear a son,
    and you shall name him Jesus.
He will be great and will be called Son of
        the Most High,
    and the Lord God will give him the throne
        of David his father,
    and he will rule over the house of Jacob
        forever,
    and of his Kingdom there will be no end."
But Mary said to the angel,
    "How can this be,
    since I have no relations with a man?"
And the angel said to her in reply,
    "The Holy Spirit will come upon you,
    and the power of the Most High will
        overshadow you.
Therefore the child to be born
    will be called holy, the Son of God.
And behold, Elizabeth, your relative,
    has also conceived a son in her old age,
    and this is the sixth month for her who
        was called barren;
    for nothing will be impossible for God."
Mary said, "Behold, I am the handmaid of
        the Lord.
May it be done to me according to your
        word."
Then the angel departed from her.

See Appendix A, p. 276, for the other readings.

Reflecting on the Gospel

Girls in the ancient world were married at young ages, often between thirteen
and seventeen. When Isaiah prophesied centuries before the birth of Jesus that
"the virgin shall be with child, and bear a son, and shall name him Emmanuel,
which means 'God is with us!,'" it was a prophecy in the first place directed
toward King Ahaz of Judah in the eighth century BC. This sign of
a young woman giving birth was to assure Ahaz that the Syrian
armies would not destroy the kingdom of David in Judah. But why
do I say that the sign was of a young woman giving birth and
not a virgin? In the original Hebrew, the word used by Isaiah to
describe the girl was *'almah*, a girl of marriageable age or a girl
having reached puberty. When the Hebrew Bible was translated
into Greek in a text we now know as the Septuagint (LXX), the
word used to translate *'almah* was *parthenos*, virgin, which in
ancient Greece could also designate a young girl of marriageable age. Isaiah's initial prophecy, therefore, did not clearly
designate a virgin.

Yet, Isaiah 7:14 was cited in Matthew 1:23 when trying
to explain Jesus's miraculous virgin birth and Matthew relied on the LXX and cited its version in which a virgin gives
birth. The prophecy had a fuller sense, in which a historically
grounded sign about David's kingdom in the eighth century
BC had implications the prophet Isaiah could not imagine over
seven hundred years later. The prophecy referred to an actual
virgin giving birth to the Messiah Jesus who, as the Son of David,
would establish God's kingdom eternally. The name that Isaiah
prophesied, Emmanuel, "God is with us," referred to the incarnation of God on earth through the virgin birth.

Who could believe such a prophecy? It fell upon a young girl not
only to believe it but to give her yes to allow it to take place according
to God's word. It fell upon Mary to hear God's word from the angel Gabriel and
to conquer her fear. What the angel told her must have been nearly incomprehensible: Mary would conceive a child in her womb even though she had never
had sexual intercourse. Even more, she would miraculously give birth to the son
of God, the ruler of God's kingdom.

Truly, this would be a moment to question what was taking place, even for
one called and prepared for a unique role in salvation history, even knowing
that, as the angel Gabriel said, "nothing will be impossible for God." But Mary
opened herself to God's work in history, opened herself to God's will, and said
yes. And because of Mary's yes to God, all of us are able to share in God's saving work and in our own way say yes to God's work in our lives, however baffling or confusing it might seem, to act with the courage of the young girl Mary
and to play our own part in the story of "God is with us."

Focusing the Gospel

Key words and phrases: "[F]or nothing will be impossible for God."

To the point: In today's reading we find two unexpected pregnancies.
Elizabeth, who was thought too old to conceive a child, is now bearing John
the Baptist, and Mary, a virgin, agrees to conceive Jesus by the Holy Spirit and
bring to birth the Son of God. God is able to bring forth life in improbable and

impossible situations. In our own lives of faith, do we believe in the God of possibilities? How do we live out this belief?

Model Penitential Act

Presider: Mary, the Mother of God and our mother, told God, "May it be done to me according to your will." For the times we have failed to do the will of God, let us ask for mercy and healing . . . *[pause]*

Lord Jesus, you are the Word of God: Lord, have mercy.

Christ Jesus, you came to do the Father's will: Christ, have mercy.

Lord Jesus, you are Emmanuel, God with us: Lord, have mercy.

Model Universal Prayer (Prayer of the Faithful)

Presider: In Mary, the word of God took on flesh and she bore him to the world. Through her intercession and strengthened by her faith, may we bring our petitions to the Lord.

Response: Lord, hear our prayer.

For women who serve God as religious sisters, lay ministers, lectors, and extraordinary ministers of Holy Communion, may their gifts be welcomed and treasured by the church . . .

For elected officials, may they humbly serve their people while standing in solidarity with the poor and vulnerable . . .

For expectant mothers, especially those in crisis pregnancies, may they receive an abundance of medical, emotional, and spiritual support . . .

For all gathered here, like Mary may we have the faith and courage to say to God, "May it be done to me according to your will" . . .

Presider: God of glory, you never cease to cast down the powerful and lift up the lowly. Hear our prayers that in communion with Mary our mother we might devote ourselves to the care and protection of those most in need. We ask this through Christ our Lord. **Amen.**

About Liturgy

Liturgical Math, Human Life: Inasmuch as the liturgical calendar and its various celebrations do not place us in a specific historical moment of time (that is, as mentioned previously, we don't celebrate Good Friday as if we are unaware that Easter is coming soon), there is still a beautiful logic and "humanness" to the calendar at times.

March 25 as the date for this solemnity might seem a bit arbitrary, though today's gospel passage does indicate that the event happened sometime in the sixth month of the Hebrew calendar. However, let us ponder more of the liturgical year, principally that Christmas falls on December 25, nine months of pregnancy from today suddenly making Mary seem that much more human. Further, we are told that Elizabeth, Mary's elder cousin, is already in her sixth month of carrying John the Baptist in her womb. So, it's sensical that the feast of the Nativity of John the Baptist is June 24. Note, too, that the feast of the birth of Mary is on September 8, nine months following the solemnity of the Immaculate Conception (which can be a helpful aid in the annual explaining of what the immaculate conception itself was!).

FOR REFLECTION

• The first reading from Isaiah includes the prophecy of a child named "Emmanuel, which means 'God is with us!'" Where is your community most in need of God's presence?

• The angel greets Mary as "full of grace." What people in your life do you experience as filled with the grace of God?

• Mary responds to the angel's proclamation, "May it be done to me according to your word." Where is God calling you to greater faith at this moment?

Homily Points

• In the gospel we find the fulfillment of the prophecy from Isaiah: "[T]he virgin shall be with child, and bear a son." In her book *The Reed of God,* Caryll Houselander meditates on the implication of Mary's virginity, going beyond just the physical nature of it: "Virginity is really the whole offering of soul and body to be consumed in the fire of love and changed into the flame of its glory. The virginity of Our Lady is the wholeness of Love through which our own humanity has become the bride of the Spirit of Life."

• In this sense, all of us are called to emulate the Blessed Virgin Mary in offering the wholeness of who we are to the service of God's love, and in so doing, bear Christ to the world in our own lives.

SPIRITUALITY

GOSPEL ACCLAMATION
Phil 2:8-9

Christ became obedient to the point of death,
even death on a cross.
Because of this, God greatly exalted him
and bestowed on him the name which is above
        every name.

Gospel at the procession with palms

Mark 11:1-10; L37B (John 12:12-16 may also
be read.)

When Jesus and his disciples drew
        near to Jerusalem,
    to Bethphage and Bethany at the
        Mount of Olives,
    he sent two of his disciples
        and said to them,
"Go into the village
        opposite you,
    and immediately on
        entering it,
    you will find a colt
        tethered on which
            no one has ever sat.
Untie it and bring it here.
If anyone should say to
        you,
    'Why are you doing
        this?' reply,
    'The Master has need of it
    and will send it back here at once.'"
So they went off
    and found a colt tethered at a gate
        outside on the street,
    and they untied it.

Continued in Appendix A, p. 276.

Gospel at Mass   Mark 14:1–15:47; L38B
or Mark 15:1–39; L38B *in Appendix A,
pp. 276–280.*

Reflecting on the Gospel

If the gospel accounts stopped just after Jesus's entry into Jerusalem on Palm Sunday, how would you imagine the next few days playing out? The scene could easily be imagined as a hero's entry in advance of his great triumph soon to follow.

When Jesus entered Jerusalem, his disciples must have felt the same weight of expectations, the portent of what Jesus's entry meant, not just for themselves, but for everyone. If Jesus was the promised Messiah, the events to come were not just concerned with the realities of one Passover in Jerusalem or the fate of the people of Judah but with the world and, yes, the world to come. What could one do but wait with sharp expectancy for events to unfold?

And yet one unnamed woman does more than wait. Her actions interpret not only Jesus's entry as the expected king, but the sort of king Jesus must be. After his entrance into Jerusalem, Jesus went to Bethany. In Bethany, "a woman came with an alabaster jar of perfumed oil, costly genuine spikenard. She broke the alabaster jar and poured it on his head." In this action, she simply supports the reception accorded Jesus as he entered Jerusalem as the king. The *mashiach* (Greek, *christos*) is the "anointed one," and her actions tell us that she not only understands that Jesus is the anointed one but that she has a need or responsibility to anoint him. But who is she to anoint a king?

The people gathered around Jesus, however, ask a different question: "'Why has there been this waste of perfumed oil? It could have been sold for more than three hundred days' wages and the money given to the poor.' They were infuriated with her." Their question is not without merit, for in scolding her they probably were attempting to voice Jesus's concern for the poor seen throughout his ministry. Jesus asks another question, "Let her alone. Why do you make trouble for her?"

Somehow the concerned disciples have missed something. "She has done a good thing for me. The poor you will always have with you, and whenever you wish you can do good to them, but you will not always have me." Jesus's response is not an attempt to mark out the permanence of poverty as a social problem but to note that her "good thing for me" has focused proper attention on him. Whether or not she knows the full implications of what she has done, she has directed those present to see Jesus as the Messiah, to grasp his christological identity.

Her identification of Jesus as the Christ by anointing went deeper, however, than even she knew, for she could not have known that she had "anticipated anointing [Jesus's] body for burial." Faithful women will later seek to care for Jesus's broken body after his death in order to anoint it with burial spices, but they would not find a body. The unnamed woman, though, already had anointed Jesus not only as a king but as the humble King who emptied himself out in death.

The humility of Jesus is reflected by the generosity of this woman, who pours out all that she has as a witness for him. Who is she to anoint a king? Given the universal significance of Jesus's passion week, her anointing might seem a little thing, but it is the most any of us can do: she recognizes Jesus, and gives all she has for him, not understanding completely that her actions helped to prepare the King, first for his death and then for his triumph, but knowing somehow he is the Messiah.

The significance of her actions is felt when Jesus says, "Amen, I say to you, wherever the gospel is proclaimed to the whole world, what she has done will be told in memory of her." We, too, are called to recognize Jesus the Messiah in faith, not simply as a conquering hero but as a servant willing to give himself up to death for us.

Focusing the Gospel
Key words and phrases: "Truly this man was the Son of God!"

To the point: The passion narratives were the first part of each gospel to be written. They form the beating heart of what we believe about Jesus, the suffering servant of God, who made of his life a gift to God and to others—giving of himself in every moment through his healing, preaching, and welcoming the excluded until finally, on the cross, he gave his very life. Witnessing Jesus's last breath on the cross was enough for a centurion soldier to proclaim, "Truly this man was the Son of God!" May our own participation in the paschal mystery lead us to ever stronger faith in Jesus, the Son of the Blessed One.

Connecting the Gospel
to the second reading: Paradoxically, in the vulnerability and frailty of Jesus on the cross we find the power of God displayed. Passersby, knowing Jesus's reputation as a wonder-worker, taunted him by saying, "[S]ave yourself by coming down from the cross." In this moment we don't witness Jesus's power to free himself from the grip of his tormentors, but instead the power to stay on the cross. The resolve to die. Today's second reading offers us a beautiful hymn to Christ's humility and his glory. In becoming "obedient to the point of death, / even death on a cross," Jesus is "greatly exalted."

to experience: How do you harness the power of vulnerability in your own life? Who are models for you as you seek to walk the path of Christ that leads to the cross and then to the triumph of life over death in the resurrection?

Connecting the Responsorial Psalm
to the readings: Today, we pray using the psalm that Jesus spoke on the cross: "My God, my God, why have you abandoned me?" In taking on human form, God, in the person of Jesus, took on the fullness of human experience. Being sinless did not deliver Jesus from knowing the complexities of emotion, from joy and love to grief and despair. In this psalm, however, we notice another type of death and resurrection. At the beginning, the faith of the psalmist seems to be a casualty of the peril he now finds himself in. Surrounded by his enemies, mocked and tormented, he experiences anguish that is compounded by the distance he perceives between himself and God, the deliverer. And yet, by the end of the psalm his hope has returned. He proclaims, "I will live for the Lord; / my descendants will serve you." Just as death leads to life, it seems that in the Lord despair can lead to hope.

to psalmist preparation: The psalms embrace the fullness of human emotion, reminding us that there is nothing we cannot bring to God in prayer. How are you being called to entrust God with the whole of your life experience?

PROMPTS FOR FAITH-SHARING

The prophet Isaiah proclaims, "The Lord God has given me / a well-trained tongue, / that I might know how to speak to the weary / a word that will rouse them." How do homilies in your parish serve to "rouse the weary"?

Today's psalm echoes the words of Jesus on the cross: "My God, why have you abandoned me?" How do you strive to reach out to those who might feel abandoned?

At the Mount of Olives, Jesus tells the disciples, "All of you will have your faith shaken." What role does questioning or doubt have in the spiritual life?

After his death, a centurion says of Jesus, "Truly this man was the Son of God!" What has Jesus done in your life that inspires you to say the same?

Model Penitential Act

Presider: As we begin the holiest days of our church year, let us pause to call to mind our sins and ask God for healing, mercy, and pardon . . . *[pause]*

    Confiteor: I confess . . .

Homily Points

• At the Last Supper, gathered with his closest friends, Jesus offers one last foreshadowing of what is to come. Over the bread he says, "Take it; this is my body." And over the wine, "This is my blood of the covenant, / which will be shed for many." Earlier in the gospel Jesus had told the disciples, "Whoever wishes to come after me must deny himself, take up his cross, and follow me" (Mark 8:34; NABRE). And now we come to the point where we see where this journey ends, in the complete gift of self, just as bread that is broken and wine that is poured out to be consumed by others.

• In her book *Ways to Nurture the Relationship with God,* Scripture scholar and theologian Sofia Cavalletti reflects upon the meaning of Jesus's words at the Last Supper: "What do these words mean? The offering of his whole person; nothing is left out. At the Last Supper, Jesus is expressing the radical, total gift of himself; he could not have communicated it with more explicit words."

• In Holy Week we live into the moment of Jesus's self-gift at the Last Supper and on Calvary. In faith, we know we cannot pass on what we have not received ourselves. Before considering how we are to emulate Jesus in giving each moment of our lives for God and others, we first must be grounded in Jesus's gift of himself to us as a community, and also to each of us individually. May we hear the words of our Lord reverberating deep in our hearts, "Take and eat, take and drink, I desire to give all of myself to you."

Model Universal Prayer (Prayer of the Faithful)

Presider: During his agony in the garden Jesus prays, "Abba, Father, all things are possible to you." With childlike faith in the one who has created us, let us bring our needs before the Lord.

Response: Lord, hear our prayer.

For God's holy church, may it preach the good news of Jesus Christ to the ends of the earth with humility and love . . .

For oppressed peoples all over the world, may their human rights be reinstated and their dignity assured . . .

For all those who have been falsely accused of crimes, may they remain steadfast in the truth that sets captives free . . .

For all gathered here, may we place our gifts and talents at the service of the Lord and dedicate all we say and do to the glory of God . . .

Presider: God of the poor and the broken, Jesus our savior humbled himself and endured death on a cross. Hear our prayers that this Holy Week we might enter into the paschal mystery anew and be transformed by Christ's death and resurrection into servants of his merciful love. We ask this through Jesus our Lord. **Amen.**

COLLECT
Let us pray.

Pause for silent prayer

Almighty ever-living God,
who as an example of humility for the
    human race to follow
caused our Savior to take flesh and submit
    to the Cross,
graciously grant that we may heed his
    lesson of patient suffering
and so merit a share in his Resurrection.
Who lives and reigns with you in the unity
    of the Holy Spirit,
one God, for ever and ever. **Amen.**

FIRST READING
Isa 50:4-7

The Lord God has given me
    a well-trained tongue,
that I might know how to speak to the
    weary
    a word that will rouse them.
Morning after morning
    he opens my ear that I may hear;
and I have not rebelled,
    have not turned back.
I gave my back to those who beat me,
    my cheeks to those who plucked my
      beard;
my face I did not shield
    from buffets and spitting.

The Lord God is my help,
    therefore I am not disgraced;
I have set my face like flint,
    knowing that I shall not be put to
      shame.

RESPONSORIAL PSALM
Ps 22:8-9, 17-18, 19-20, 23-24

℟. (2a) My God, my God, why have you
    abandoned me?

All who see me scoff at me;
    they mock me with parted lips, they
      wag their heads:
"He relied on the Lord; let him deliver him,
    let him rescue him, if he loves him."

℟. My God, my God, why have you
    abandoned me?

Indeed, many dogs surround me,
    a pack of evildoers closes in upon me;
they have pierced my hands and my feet;
    I can count all my bones.

R̰. My God, my God, why have you
    abandoned me?

They divide my garments among them,
    and for my vesture they cast lots.
But you, O Lord, be not far from me;
    O my help, hasten to aid me.

R̰. My God, my God, why have you
    abandoned me?

I will proclaim your name to my brethren;
    in the midst of the assembly I will
        praise you:
"You who fear the Lord, praise him;
    all you descendants of Jacob, give glory
        to him;
    revere him, all you descendants of
        Israel!"

R̰. My God, my God, why have you
    abandoned me?

SECOND READING
Phil 2:6-11

Christ Jesus, though he was in the form
    of God,
    did not regard equality with God
        something to be grasped.
Rather, he emptied himself,
    taking the form of a slave,
    coming in human likeness;
    and found human in appearance,
    he humbled himself,
    becoming obedient to the point of
        death,
        even death on a cross.
Because of this, God greatly exalted him
    and bestowed on him the name
    which is above every name,
    that at the name of Jesus
    every knee should bend,
    of those in heaven and on earth and
        under the earth,
    and every tongue confess that
Jesus Christ is Lord,
    to the glory of God the Father.

About Liturgy

A Very Different Sunday: The assembly today ought to be able to tell from the first instant that this week is unlike any other: vibrant reds abound, palm branches greet their arrival, and, if the first form—the procession commemorating the Lord's entrance into Jerusalem—is done and done well, the assembly is likely gathering in a spot very separate from the church.

If one is creating this procession for what the Missal calls "the principal Mass," it is not worth pursuing unless it is done abundantly well. Simply gathering outside the front doors of the church won't cut it! Gather somewhere distinctly different—perhaps at a school gym, or on an athletic field on campus, or at a park nearby. If the people of God are to process, the journey must be something more than the usual trip from the car in the parking lot to the front doors. Adequate sound reinforcement must be obtained, ministers must be well prepared, and music must be carefully chosen (see below). Lastly, the congregation should be instructed on not just the logistics of the procession, but the theological and liturgical meanings of the procession that begins the holiest week of the church year.

About Processions

A Pilgrimage on Holy Ground: Humans, dependent on factors like age and abilities, have lots of different ways of getting around: crawling, walking, skipping, marching, running—and those are just with our bodies alone, without considering bicycles, cars, trains, planes, ships, and so many other modes of transportation.

Palm Sunday has its own unique entrance procession (as an option), though each Sunday Mass has a procession to begin the liturgy. But there are others too: the procession with the book of the gospels, the procession with the gifts of bread and wine, the communion procession, and the recessional. These movements are practical to be sure—people and things need to get from one place to another—but they are also symbolic, particularly at this time of year. Our faith is itself a journey, where all the ground is holy, where we pass through valleys and over hills. We the church are on the same journey that Christ himself lived. We hear, in part, these words as the liturgy begins: "Today we gather together to herald with the whole Church / the beginning of the celebration / of our Lord's Paschal Mystery, / that is to say, of his Passion and Resurrection. / For it was to accomplish this mystery / that he entered his own city of Jerusalem" (Roman Missal, Palm Sunday 5).

About Music

Music for Procession: Music selected for the procession must be music for traveling and must be easily learned and owned on first or second hearing. It must also be able to be repeated many times over without growing wearisome or "tired." Further, it should be able to be sung unaccompanied or accompanied by instruments one can travel with: guitars, hand percussion, and the like. There are many options for such a piece of music. John Angotti's "Sing Hosanna to Our King" (WLP) has a lot of energy and a receptive melody, as does Dan Schutte's "Hosanna to the Son of David" (OCP).

An issue can arise if the procession becomes too spread out, for instance if a large assembly walks too narrow a path. It is vital that good sound reinforcement be a part of the preparations for today's liturgy, and important that music ministry lead from within. That is, you might prepare a handful of people (a couple instrumentalists, a couple singers) to nominally lead the music, but the remainder of the choir should scatter themselves about the procession at regular intervals. It can be helpful as well to have a visual leader when possible, visible to the whole of the procession, marking time and encouraging participation.

EASTER
TRIDUUM

GOSPEL ACCLAMATION
John 13:34

I give you a new commandment, says the Lord:
love one another as I have loved you.

Gospel John 13:1-15; L39ABC

Before the feast of Passover, Jesus knew
        that his hour had come
    to pass from this world to the Father.
He loved his own in the world and he
        loved them to the end.
The devil had already induced Judas, son
        of Simon the Iscariot, to hand him
        over.
So, during supper,
    fully aware that the Father had
            put everything into his
            power
    and that he had come from God
            and was returning to God,
    he rose from supper and took
            off his outer garments.
He took a towel and tied it around
        his waist.
Then he poured water into a basin
    and began to wash the dis-
            ciples' feet
    and dry them with the towel
            around his waist.
He came to Simon Peter, who said to him,
    "Master, are you going to wash my
            feet?"
Jesus answered and said to him,
    "What I am doing, you do not
            understand now,
    but you will understand later."
Peter said to him, "You will never wash
        my feet."
Jesus answered him,
    "Unless I wash you, you will have no
            inheritance with me."
Simon Peter said to him,
    "Master, then not only my feet, but my
            hands and head as well."
Jesus said to him,
    "Whoever has bathed has no need
            except to have his feet washed,
        for he is clean all over;
        so you are clean, but not all."

Continued in Appendix A, p. 280.
See Appendix A, p. 280, for the other readings.

Reflecting on the Gospel

Key words and phrases: "I have given you a model to follow"; "[Y]ou ought to wash one another's feet."

To the point: This passage from John offers one of the most profound and compelling images of Jesus in the gospels. In washing the disciples' feet Jesus is not just giving service but offering a model of servanthood. Indeed, he is the servant par excellence. In laying aside his outer garments and tying a towel around his waist, Jesus adopts the role of servant. He, who would soon be stripped of those same garments and who would willingly lay down his life in service to a fallen humanity in obedience to the will of the Father, chose to give his disciples an example of the humble service required of those who wish to follow him. There is no clearer expression of the Christian call to service found in all of the gospels. Here, Jesus is explicit on this point, telling his disciples unambiguously, "I have given you a model to follow, so that as I have done for you, you should also do."

How fitting at the Mass of the Lord's Supper that we reenact this simple yet profound gesture. The towel, the basin, and the water remind us of our call to serve. They beckon us to go out and wash the feet of others. They invite us to do as the Master has done. Yet, adding even greater poignancy and deeper significance to this moment, we are told at the beginning of the passage that "Jesus knew that his hour had come." He was "fully aware" that his paschal service had just begun. Here, servanthood and sacrifice would be forever linked at the foot of the cross. So, it certainly is no accident that we enter into this paschal Triduum by imitating Jesus's simple act of service, an act that would take on greater meaning as "he loved them to the end," a fact we commemorate at every Eucharist but enter into with profound remembrance during these sacred days.

Still, the disciples do not seem to grasp its significance. They are confused, embarrassed, and perhaps even a little shocked. In the face of Peter's incomprehension, Jesus tells him, "What I am doing, you do not understand now, but you will understand later." Do we understand? The gospel leaves us with Jesus's question to his disciples: "Do you realize what I have done for you?" It is a question that remains unanswered, open-ended, ongoing. It is a question that hangs in the background throughout the drama of Jesus's arrest, the disciples' abandonment, and Peter's denial of Jesus that very night. And, it is a question that takes on new meaning in light of the paschal events as they unfold. Do we realize what he has done for us? Do we realize that we are called to live the paschal mystery every day through lives of service and sacrificial love following the model that Jesus has given us? And, do we truly realize what it means to wash one another's feet?

To ponder and pray: As we enter into this Sacred Triduum we are reminded of the call to serve. As Jesus who came from the Father prepared to return to the Father, he gave us a model of service and humility to follow the very night he was betrayed. May we strive to imitate his sacrificial love that beckons us to love and serve others as he loved and served. May we heed his call to do as he had done. And, may we never tire of washing feet.

Model Penitential Act

Presider: We gather to celebrate the Lord's Supper. As we prepare to meet Jesus in the Eucharist, let us pause to ask God's pardon and forgiveness for the times we have not acted as the Body of Christ . . . *[pause]*

Lord Jesus, you are the Lamb of God who takes away the sins of the world: Lord, have mercy.

Christ Jesus, you are the high priest who ministers to us at the altar of God: Christ, have mercy.

Lord Jesus, you nourish us with your Body and Blood: Lord, have mercy.

Model Universal Prayer (Prayer of the Faithful)

Presider: In tonight's gospel we hear that Jesus "loved his own in the world and he loved them to the end." Knowing the everlasting compassion of God expressed through Jesus, let us bring our needs before the Lord.

Response: Lord, hear our prayer.

For God's holy church, and especially for parishes without a priest to celebrate the Eucharist, may we be united with them as we pray for priestly vocations . . .

For all the peoples of the world, may the charity and love of God reign in our hearts and transform our societies . . .

For all who go to bed hungry tonight, especially children and the elderly, may they be provided for out of the bounty of their neighbors . . .

For all gathered here, in receiving the Body and Blood of the risen Lord, may we become the Body of Christ alive in the world . . .

Presider: God of charity, at the Last Supper, Jesus, Lord of all, took on the garb of a servant to wash his disciples' feet. Hear our prayers that in emulating Jesus we might become servants to all we meet. We ask this through Christ our Lord. **Amen.**

About Liturgy

Blessing and Consecration: It can be effective, as part of the liturgy this evening, to celebrate the rite of reception of oils from the diocesan chrism Mass. Including this rite helps the faithful stay more connected to the bishop and the whole of the diocese. By having the oils processed in by members of the community connected to their use—for instance those in the RCIA program about to experience the rites of initiation at the Easter Vigil—an even stronger bond develops, connecting many facets of the church life together.

And a bit of liturgical minutiae: while the oil of the catechumens and the oil of the sick were blessed at the chrism Mass, the chrism oil was *consecrated*—set apart for a sacred purpose. We use "consecration" language when we speak of the bread and wine at Mass, when the church's prayer transforms them into a real presence of Christ. Some argue that consecrated chrism oil is the real presence of the Holy Spirit, due to the nature of the prayer of consecration, before which "the Bishop, if appropriate, breathes upon the opening of the vessel of the Chrism" (Order of Blessing the Oil of Catechumens and of the Sick and of Consecrating the Chrism 25).

FOR REFLECTION

• Today's psalm response comes from 1 Corinthians, "Our blessing-cup is a communion with the Blood of Christ." How does your parish's celebration of the Holy Triduum speak to the communion of all within your community?

• St. Paul recounts the words of Jesus at the Last Supper: "This is my body that is for you." How does the Eucharist sustain your faith life?

• Jesus asks his disciples, "Do you realize what I have done for you?" How would you personally answer this question?

Homily Points

• Tonight we celebrate the institution of the Eucharist, the source and summit of our Christian life and our greatest gift. St. Paul, in his first letter to the Corinthians, records Jesus's words at the Last Supper: "This is my body that is for you . . . This cup is the new covenant in my blood." In our time in the history of salvation, we are not able to follow Jesus as he walks along the roads of Israel or to reach out for the hem of his robe when we are in need of healing.

• And yet, Jesus is with us in a way that is just as tangible, just as intimate. We listen to him in the words of Scripture, we feel his touch in the sacraments of the church, we serve him in one another, and we are nourished by him in his Body and Blood.

GOSPEL ACCLAMATION
Phil 2:8-9

Christ became obedient to the point of death,
even death on a cross.
Because of this, God greatly exalted him
and bestowed on him the name which is above
    every other name.

Gospel   John 18:1–19:42;
L40ABC

Jesus went out with his
    disciples across the Kidron
    valley
to where there was a garden,
into which he and his
    disciples entered.
Judas his betrayer also knew
    the place,
because Jesus had often met
    there with his disciples.
So Judas got a band of soldiers
    and guards
from the chief priests and the
    Pharisees
and went there with lanterns,
    torches, and weapons.
Jesus, knowing everything that
    was going to happen to him,
went out and said to them, "Whom are
    you looking for?"
They answered him, "Jesus the Nazorean."
He said to them, "I AM."
Judas his betrayer was also with them.
When he said to them, "I AM,"
    they turned away and fell to the ground.
So he again asked them,
    "Whom are you looking for?"
They said, "Jesus the Nazorean."
Jesus answered,
    "I told you that I AM.
So if you are looking for me, let these
    men go."
This was to fulfill what he had said,
    "I have not lost any of those you gave me."
Then Simon Peter, who had a sword,
    drew it,
    struck the high priest's slave, and cut
        off his right ear.
The slave's name was Malchus.

Continued in Appendix A, pp. 281–282.
See Appendix A, p. 283, for the other readings.

Reflecting on the Gospel
Key words and phrases: "I AM"; "For this I was born and for this I came into the world, to testify to the truth."

To the point: John's account of the passion draws us into the drama of Jesus's crucifixion in a very real way. It is one of the most powerful and compelling portrayals of the events of Good Friday, which is perhaps why the church chose it as the gospel reading for this solemn day. We are confronted with scenes that highlight a very real human tragedy that only serve to reveal the divine mystery as it unfolds. We have Judas accompanying the band of soldiers and guards from the chief priests carrying "lanterns, torches, and weapons," props that only reinforce their ill purpose carried out in the dark of night. We have Peter, hamming it up, drawing a sword and cutting off the ear of the high priest's slave in defense of the very one whom he would just a short while later vehemently deny ever knowing. We have Annas and Caiaphas, whose backstory, we are told, involves intrigue, plotting, and conspiracy, reasoning "it was better that one man should die rather than the people." And, we have a conflicted Pilate, at first appearing indifferent to the case presented before him, telling the chief priests, "Take him yourselves, and judge him according to your law." Although, later, he seems almost sympathetic toward the plight of Jesus, repeatedly saying, "I find no guilt in him," even to the point of trying to release him. Yet, in the end, he is ultimately swayed by his own fear and gives in to the demand of the crowd to crucify Jesus, even though he knows he is condemning an innocent man.

There are the minor characters as well who play their supporting role in this unfolding drama: the temple guard, the Roman soldiers, the crowd. Yet, in the midst of it all, taking center stage, we have Jesus. He gives no long speeches, offers no soliloquies, makes no dramatic gestures. Instead he engages in simple, direct, yet profound dialogue that gives witness to the truth. There is the dialogue between Jesus and the soldiers in the garden. Jesus asks them, "Whom are you looking for?" When they reply, "Jesus the Nazorean," he simply responds, "I AM," uttering the sacred name that reveals his divine origin and purpose. There is the dialogue between Jesus and the high priest. When questioned about his doctrine, Jesus directly states, "I have spoken publicly to the world," openly proclaiming the truth. Then, there is the dialogue with Pilate in the praetorium where Pilate asks Jesus, "Then you are a king?" Jesus powerfully replies, "You say I am a king. For this I was born and for this I came into the world, to testify to the truth." Pilate asks in mock irony, "What is truth?" to the very one who stands before him as the Way, the Truth, and the Life.

Here, we are confronted by the truth since we know that Jesus is, in fact, the crucified and risen Savior. But, at a deeper level we are also confronted with the truth of our own lives as Christians. Do we want to hear the truth by listening to his voice? Are we mere spectators to the events of Good Friday or are we active participants? And, if so, where do we stand? Outside with Peter? At the foot of the cross with Mary? Or, simply among the crowd?

To ponder and pray: Jesus invites us to hear his voice and stand with him at the foot of the cross not only during this Good Friday but throughout our lives as Christians. Are we prepared to stand with him at the foot of the cross? Do we truly hear his voice? And, are we willing to approach the cross today with humility, love, and genuine devotion?

About Liturgy

Cross or Crucifix?: It may at first seem like unnecessary semantics, but on this day when the principal rite of the church is adoration, care should be taken that it is a cross which is adored, and not a crucifix. The Roman Missal, over and over again—in texts the presider says, in rubrics he and the faithful perform, and in the words that are sung—uses the word "cross," and never "crucifix." For instance, when the cross is processed in (or unveiled) these words are sung: "Behold the wood of the Cross, on which hung the salvation of the world." The assembly responds, "Come, let us adore" (Good Friday 15).

Growing up, I know I had the experience of kissing the feet of a corpus on Good Friday, but that's misdirecting the intent of the moment. We are meant to adore and contemplate the cross itself, the instrument of suffering and death. The antiphon the Missal offers gives us insight as to why: "We adore your Cross, O Lord, / we praise and glorify your holy Resurrection, / for behold, because of the wood of a tree / joy has come to the whole world" (Good Friday 20).

COLLECT
Let us pray.

Remember your mercies, O Lord,
and with your eternal protection sanctify your
    servants,
for whom Christ your Son,
by the shedding of his Blood,
established the Paschal Mystery.
Who lives and reigns for ever and ever.
Amen.

or:

O God, who by the Passion of Christ your
    Son, our Lord,
abolished the death inherited from ancient sin
by every succeeding generation,
grant that just as, being conformed to him,
we have borne by the law of nature
the image of the man of earth,
so by the sanctification of grace
we may bear the image of the Man of heaven.
Through Christ our Lord.
Amen.

FOR REFLECTION

• Isaiah's suffering servant song concludes, "[H]e surrendered himself to death." Today we venerate the cross upon which Jesus died. How does this ritual speak to your faith?

• The letter to the Hebrews urges us to "hold fast to our confession." Who do you personally confess Christ to be?

Homily Points

• In the garden of Gethsemane where Jesus is arrested, he instructs soldiers and guards, "[L]et these men go." This is to fulfill Jesus's earlier words in the bread of life discourse, "[T]his is the will of the one who sent me, that I should not lose anything of what he gave me, but that I should raise it [on] the last day" (John 6:39; NABRE).

• In the midst of our sorrow, we call today "good" because on it our savior, embracing the fullness of human experience, entered into death and in so doing released us from its finality. We remember how Jesus the Good Shepherd laid down his life for his sheep, and we are blessed to be members of that flock.

Gospel

Mark 16:1-7; L41B

When the sabbath was over,
  Mary Magdalene, Mary, the mother
    of James, and Salome
  bought spices so that they might go
    and anoint him.
Very early when the sun had risen,
  on the first day of the week, they
    came to the tomb.

They were saying to one another,
  "Who will roll back the stone for us
    from the entrance to the tomb?"
When they looked up,
  they saw that the stone had been
    rolled back;
  it was very large.
On entering the tomb they saw a young
    man
  sitting on the right side, clothed in a
    white robe,
  and they were utterly amazed.
He said to them, "Do not be amazed!
You seek Jesus of Nazareth, the
    crucified.
He has been raised; he is not here.
Behold the place where they laid him.
But go and tell his disciples and Peter,
  'He is going before you to Galilee;
    there you will see him, as he told
    you.'"

See Appendix A, pp. 284–289, for the other readings.

Reflecting on the Gospel

Key words and phrases: "Who will roll back the stone for us from the entrance to the tomb?"; [T]hey were utterly amazed; "He has been raised."

To the point: In this shortest and generally believed by Scripture scholars to be the oldest of the gospel proclamations, we find the most profoundly simple yet most strangely enigmatic of the resurrection narratives, portraying Easter as an event, as a mystery, and as an invitation.

As an event, Mark chooses to focus not on the appearance of the risen Christ but on finding the empty tomb. It is a tangible sign that something extraordinary has happened that defies the ordinary expectations of the women who go there to anoint a dead body. After asking themselves, "Who will roll back the stone for us from the entrance to the tomb?" in order that they may carry out their task of anointing the body of Jesus according to the Jewish custom, we are told that the women are "utterly amazed" after approaching the tomb only to find that the "very large" stone has already been "rolled back" and upon entering the tomb instead of finding the body of Jesus, they find a "young man sitting on the right side, clothed in a white robe." In Matthew's gospel this young man is clearly identified as an angel, but here in Mark he remains ambiguous, puzzling, mysterious. Yet, in spite of their amazement, the women are told by this young man, "Do not be amazed!" While they do not see the risen Jesus, they are instead told, "He has been raised; he is not here." The tomb is empty. Jesus is gone. They are amazed. Moreover, they are promised by this young man that they will see Jesus in Galilee as "he told you."

In confronting this unfathomable, incomprehensible mystery, we are left, along with the women, to ponder the scene laid out before us in this narrative: Who is this young man? Where is he from? Is what he says really true? These and countless other questions loom in the background, unanswered for the women and for us in this seemingly all too brief and perplexingly abrupt gospel passage in its proclamation of the central mystery of our Christian faith: that Christ is risen; he is risen indeed as he said.

However, it is precisely in its brevity and perplexity that this gospel passage serves as an invitation that draws us ever more deeply into the paschal mystery itself. For, in this short passage, we are confronted with our own questions, with our own reactions, with our own amazement at the incredible proclamation of the resurrection of Jesus. What is our reaction? Are we puzzled? Are we amazed? Are we really willing to believe that he has been raised? These questions invite us to reaffirm anew our own Easter faith, our own Easter amazement, our own Easter joy. At this liturgy we are invited to renew our baptismal promises by professing our faith in this amazing proclamation. Do we dare? Do we dare accept the invitation? Do we dare believe? Do we dare risk living as believers? Mark's gospel leaves these questions open-ended for us, inviting us to ponder, to puzzle, and to be amazed.

To ponder and pray: Standing in amazement, the women at the empty tomb are not simply told, "He has been raised," but are commanded to "go and tell his disciples." Their task, their purpose, their whole mission has been completely transformed. No longer are they there to anoint a dead body, but they are there to bear witness to the living Christ, raised from the dead. As we stand with them, we too are called to go out and share the good news: Christ is risen; he is risen indeed.

Model Universal Prayer (Prayer of the Faithful)

Presider: God assures us through the prophet Isaiah, "[M]y love shall never leave you / nor my covenant of peace be shaken." As beloved children of our heavenly Father, let us trustingly place our needs before him.

Response: Lord, hear our prayer.

For God's holy church, immersed in the death and resurrection of the Lord, may it bring God's healing light to places of darkness . . .

For the world that God has made and pronounced "very good," may all the peoples of the earth join together to be faithful stewards of creation . . .

For those who have turned away from God's ways and who find themselves ensnared in wickedness, may they know freedom from sin in the redeeming love of Jesus . . .

For all gathered here in recalling the moment of our baptism, may we be strengthened to live always as children of the light . . .

Presider: God of abundant life, you sent your son Jesus to dwell among us, and in his death and resurrection he has broken the bonds of sin and death. Hear our prayers that we may never tire of sharing his light with others. We ask this through Christ our Lord. **Amen.**

About Liturgy

The Light of Christ: One of the most ignored rubrics in the whole of the Roman Missal may be part of tonight's liturgy: "Then the Deacon places the paschal candle on a large candle stand prepared next to the ambo or in the middle of the sanctuary. And lights are lit throughout the church, except for the altar candles" (Easter Vigil 17).

Liturgy is performative by nature (only to a certain point of course): why turn on all the lights at that moment when the pillar of fire and its light which shatters the darkness has just entered the church, its flame divided but undimmed?

It seems this rubric is a rather old one, dating from the time before electricity, when it would take a rather long time to completely illumine a church, going from lantern to lantern one by one, bringing about a more gradual lighting to the space. In modern times, perhaps there is a lesson here. If your lighting is sophisticated enough to have dimmers, consider bringing up the lights gradually during the chanting of the Easter proclamation. Or, if not too jarring, turn on individual banks of lights every so often to achieve a similar effect.

COLLECT

Let us pray.

Pause for silent prayer

O God, who make this most sacred night radiant
with the glory of the Lord's Resurrection,
stir up in your Church a spirit of adoption,
so that, renewed in body and mind,
we may render you undivided service.
Through our Lord Jesus Christ, your Son,
who lives and reigns with you in the unity of
    the Holy Spirit,
one God, for ever and ever. **Amen.**

FOR REFLECTION

• The Liturgy of the Word begins with the first account of creation. How does your community seek to be faithful stewards of the gifts God has bestowed?

• St. Paul asks the Romans, "Are you unaware that we who were baptized into Christ Jesus / were baptized into his death?" How does his question impact your understanding of baptism?

• At the Easter Vigil our individual candles are lit by sharing the flame of the paschal candle with one another. How are you spreading the light of Christ in your daily life?

Homily Points

• At the Easter Vigil we focus with particular intensity on the symbol of light. The paschal candle is lit from the blessed fire, and then this one flame is in turn shared until all of our candles glow. In the Easter Proclamation we hear: "[A] fire into many flames divided, / yet never dimmed by sharing of its light."

• Within the lighting of many candles from one flame we see the abundance of God's love. As people of God, we never need to act out of scarcity. We lose nothing by sharing the light and love of Jesus with others. Instead, each time it is shared the flame multiplies, bringing light to what is dark and warmth to what is cold. On this holiest of nights we remember and proclaim anew Jesus's victory over death. We also pray and long for a time when all will know the light and warmth of his love.

GOSPEL ACCLAMATION
cf. 1 Cor 5:7b-8a

R︎. Alleluia, alleluia.
Christ, our paschal lamb, has been sacrificed;
let us then feast with joy in the Lord.
R︎. Alleluia, alleluia.

Gospel   John 20:1-9; L42ABC

On the first day of the week,
    Mary of Magdala came to
        the tomb early in the
            morning,
    while it was still dark,
    and saw the stone
        removed from the
            tomb.
So she ran and went to
    Simon Peter
    and to the other disciple
        whom Jesus loved,
        and told them,
    "They have taken the Lord
        from the tomb,
    and we don't know where
        they put him."
So Peter and the other disciple went
    out and came to the tomb.
They both ran, but the other disciple
    ran faster than Peter
    and arrived at the tomb first;
    he bent down and saw the burial
        cloths there, but did not go in.
When Simon Peter arrived after him,
    he went into the tomb and saw the
        burial cloths there,
    and the cloth that had covered his
        head,
    not with the burial cloths but rolled
        up in a separate place.
Then the other disciple also went in,
    the one who had arrived at the tomb
        first,
    and he saw and believed.
For they did not yet understand the
        Scripture
    that he had to rise from the dead.

or Mark 16:1-7; L41B *in Appendix A, p. 290,*

or, at an afternoon or evening Mass
Luke 24:13-35; L46 *in Appendix A, p. 290.*

See Appendix A, p. 291, for the other readings.

Reflecting on the Gospel

All the gospels recall that on the second morning after Jesus was laid in the tomb, Mary Magdalene and other women were the first to arrive at the tomb to care for Jesus's body, but his body was not in the tomb. It would be a strange account to concoct. Why? Scripture scholar James Dunn says, "As is well known, in Middle Eastern society of the time women were not regarded as reliable witnesses: a woman's testimony in court was heavily discounted. And any report that Mary had formerly been demon-possessed (Luke 8:2) would hardly add credibility to any story attributed to her in particular. Why then attribute such testimony to women—unless that was what was remembered as being the case?" (*Jesus Remembered*).

The account of Mary Magdalene as the first witness of the empty tomb was born of a powerful, consistent oral tradition among the earliest disciples. This is not the oral tradition of rote memorization, the sort that memorizes parables, prayers, teachings, and laws, which was also part of first-century Judaism. This is autobiographical memory, in which stories of personal experience are passed on, often colored by the emotional interpretation of those who experienced the events, which shapes the details recalled in the passing on of the accounts. All of those present remember and recount that Mary was there first.

The absence of the body does not necessarily mean that Jesus was raised. There are more ordinary explanations that come to mind: the disciples went to the wrong tomb and the body was somewhere else; they lied about the missing body; or someone stole the body and hid it.

Yet if Jesus's body had been available, it makes sense that those who opposed the teaching of Jesus's resurrection would have found it, or produced it had they stolen it, to the derision and embarrassment of the disciples. If the body had indeed been taken by Jesus's disciples or they had gone to the wrong tomb, the reality of Jesus's body itself would have come to light and the location of his dead body would have put an end to the claims of resurrection. Indeed, his tomb might have become a pilgrimage site, a place of veneration of a great teacher and prophet killed by the Roman authorities.

In John's gospel, Mary Magdalene reports the empty tomb to Peter and the other disciple. The two of them run to the tomb. "Then the other disciple also went in, the one who had arrived at the tomb first, and he saw and believed. For they did not yet understand the Scripture that he had to rise from the dead." The juxtaposition here captures the initial confusion of the empty tomb. The other disciple, also known as the Beloved Disciple, "saw and believed," while Peter and Mary "did not yet understand the Scripture that he had to rise from the dead."

The Beloved Disciple alone initially recognizes the spiritual meaning of the empty tomb, but his understanding will soon be the foundation of the whole church, spurred by later encounters with the risen Lord. The resurrection of Jesus became the central message of the new community of disciples.

The early Christians knew that "[t]hey put him to death by hanging him on a tree" and they knew where Jesus's dead body was laid. When Mary Magdalene and the other disciples encountered the empty tomb, it became the first piece of evidence that "[t]his man God raised on the third day and granted that he be visible, not to all the people, but to us, the witnesses chosen by God in advance." Later, these witnesses would eat and drink "with him after he rose from the dead." Only one last task remained: to bear witness that the empty tomb, the end of Jesus's story, was just the beginning.

Model Penitential Act

Presider: Christ has risen from the grave and conquered sin and death. With joy and thanksgiving, let us turn to him for mercy . . . *[pause]*

Lord Jesus, you are the light that shatters darkness: Lord, have mercy.
Christ Jesus, you are the hope of the sinner and the lost: Christ, have mercy.
Lord Jesus, you are the redeemer of all: Lord, have mercy.

Model Universal Prayer (Prayer of the Faithful)

Presider: Christ our savior is risen and he intercedes for us at the right hand of the Father. In joy let us bring our petitions before the Lord whose mercy is everlasting.

Response: Lord, hear our prayer.

For Christians throughout the world, especially those dwelling in countries antagonistic to Christianity, may they celebrate this holy feast in safety . . .

For nations threatened by and recovering from acts of terror, may hope, peace, and love prevail against every act of violence and hatred . . .

For all who mourn the loss of a loved one, especially parents mourning the death of a child, may they find solace in God's saving power and endless compassion . . .

For all gathered here, in keeping the feast of Easter, may we be infused with a joy that never ends . . .

Presider: God of glory and might, at the empty tomb Mary Magdalene is asked, "Why do you search for the living one among the dead?" Hear our prayers that in our words and actions we may proclaim Jesus Christ risen from the dead to all we encounter. **Amen.**

About Liturgy

A Persistent Easter: Well before Easter arrives, we should ensure that the joy of Easter Day remains throughout the whole octave. As the season continues, consider using the optional sprinkling rite, with care not to conflate the sprinkling with the singing of the Gloria. Lest the Easter liturgies become too "musically top-heavy"—entrance hymn, sprinkling rite, and Gloria within moments of one another—consider utilizing the brief entrance antiphons for the season, paired with a favorite Alleluia of the assembly, or the appropriate *O filii et filiae*.

Are additional flowers ordered for later in the season? If your budget allows, make sure to do so. The vibrant lilies of Easter Day will not last long no matter how well cared for, and the Fifth and Sixth Sundays of Easter (and beyond) should appear just as exuberant as the earliest days of the season.

COLLECT
Let us pray.

Pause for silent prayer

O God, who on this day,
through your Only Begotten Son,
have conquered death
and unlocked for us the path to eternity,
grant, we pray, that we who keep
the solemnity of the Lord's Resurrection
may, through the renewal brought by your Spirit,
rise up in the light of life.
Through our Lord Jesus Christ, your Son,
who lives and reigns with you in the unity of
the Holy Spirit,
one God, for ever and ever. **Amen.**

FOR REFLECTION

• Today is only the beginning of our Easter joy. How will you and your family keep this feast throughout the season of Easter?

• In the first reading Peter tells the gathered crowd, "[Jesus] commissioned us to preach to the people." How do you exercise the ministry of preaching in your own life?

• St. Paul writes to the Colossians, "[Y]our life is hidden with Christ in God." How does this image relate to your own experience of being a Christian?

Homily Points

• After forty days of preparation, fasting, prayer, and works of charity, we arrive at the celebration of Easter. This is our greatest feast of the year, and our joy cannot be contained in only one day. It spills over to fill up the fifty days leading to Pentecost. Today's alleluia verse counsels us, "Christ, our paschal lamb, has been sacrificed; let us then feast with joy in the Lord."

• Christ's resurrection changed human experience. Never before in history had someone risen from the dead, never to die again. It is no wonder that Peter and the beloved disciple stand in the empty tomb amazed and fearful, not understanding what had happened there. In the season of Easter we, too, are invited to live into this mystery that changes everything.

SEASON OF EASTER

SPIRITUALITY

GOSPEL ACCLAMATION
John 20:29

R̸. Alleluia, alleluia.
You believe in me, Thomas, because you have
    seen me, says the Lord;
blessed are those who have not seen me, but still
    believe!
R̸. Alleluia, alleluia.

Gospel John 20:19-31; L44B

On the evening of that first
    day of the week,
    when the doors were
        locked, where
        the disciples
        were,
    for fear of the Jews,
    Jesus came and stood
        in their midst
    and said to them,
        "Peace be with
        you."
When he had said this,
    he showed them his
    hands and his side.
The disciples rejoiced when they
    saw the Lord.
Jesus said to them again, "Peace be with
    you.
As the Father has sent me, so I send you."
And when he had said this, he breathed
    on them and said to them,
    "Receive the Holy Spirit.
Whose sins you forgive are forgiven them,
    and whose sins you retain are retained."

Thomas, called Didymus, one of the
    Twelve,
    was not with them when Jesus came.
So the other disciples said to him, "We
    have seen the Lord."
But he said to them,
    "Unless I see the mark of the nails in
        his hands
    and put my finger into the nailmarks
    and put my hand into his side, I will
        not believe."

Continued in Appendix A, p. 291.

Reflecting on the Gospel

Thomas had not been in the room when the risen Jesus appeared to the disciples, and so has missed out on any personal encounter with him, the words of missioning, and the bestowal of the gifts of peace and forgiveness in the Spirit. John makes Thomas a foil for our own need of these gifts and our struggles with doubt and faith. Often the comments about Thomas concentrate too much on him as a doubter (which he is never called anywhere in the gospels) and too little on his desire to touch the source of life. John's gospel shows him to be the kind of person who blurts out the questions or comments others are too timid or too embarrassed to speak. He is ready to go along with Jesus en route to Lazarus's grave and die with him (John 11:16); and he is honest enough at the Last Supper to say that none of the disciples have any idea where Jesus is heading (John 14:5). The disciples to whom the risen Lord appeared on Easter eve announce the resurrection to Thomas in the same words as Mary Magdalene spoke to them: "We have seen the Lord." And they are just as unsuccessful in convincing Thomas as Mary had been with them. Like all disciples, Thomas needs a personal experience of Jesus before he will believe. Until then, he is locked in his own criterion for faith: he wants Jesus to be "touchable."

So eight days later, on the next "first day of the week" according to the resurrection timeline, the risen Lord of the Sabbath stands again in the midst of his disciples, greets them with his peace, and then turns to the individual who is most in need of this. For eight days Thomas has wrestled with the dark stranger of doubt and is wounded by this struggle. The wounded, risen Jesus and the wounded disciple stand before one another. Jesus invites Thomas to stretch out his hand to the wounds of his hands and side. But there is no physical touching. Jesus's personal presence and self-offering to Thomas touch him and demolish all doubts. Here is "the way, and the truth, and the life" that Thomas is seeking, and he responds with the most profound and personal assent of faith in all the gospels: "My Lord and my God!" For the future generations who will listen to this gospel in the presence of the physically absent Jesus, the last beatitude that Jesus then addresses to Thomas is our greatest hope: "Blessed are those who have not seen and have believed." It is to hand on such life-giving faith, says the evangelist, that he has written his gospel.

In his *Asian Journal*, Thomas Merton wrote: "Faith means doubt. Faith is not the suppression of doubt. It is the overcoming of doubt, and you overcome doubt by going through it. The man of faith who has never experienced doubt is not a person of faith. Consequently, the monk is one who has to struggle in the depths of his being with the presence of doubt, and has to go through what some religions call the Great Doubt, to break through doubt into a certitude which is very, very deep because it is not his own personal certitude; it is the certitude of God Himself, in us."

Christ took his wounds into the grave and did not disown them in his resurrection. Because of his wounds, Jesus is now credibly in touch with wounded humanity: with the wounded in body and spirit, those hurt by society, the victims of domestic and global violence, those suffering from their own addictions, those abused by our disregard and complacency. And we know only too well our own woundedness. Such wounds reveal our need for one another and, therefore, the potential for the building of a compassionate, healing community that witnesses to the love of the Wounded Healer.

Focusing the Gospel

Key words and phrases: "[D]o not be unbelieving, but believe."

To the point: Thomas doubts the appearance of the risen Lord to the rest of the disciples and even challenges, "Unless I see the mark of the nails in his hands / and put my finger into the nailmarks and put my hand into his side, I will not believe." Despite this brusque attitude, Jesus deigns to meet Thomas where he is and arrives once again in the locked room (this time with Thomas present) and invites him, "Put your finger here and see my hands, and bring your hand and put it into my side." All of this is done to change Thomas's doubt to faith, and indeed, Thomas responds to Jesus's invitation by proclaiming, "My Lord and my God!" Jesus desires to meet us where we are on our journey of faith, but he doesn't leave us there. Instead we are invited again and again to deeper relationship with him through the mercy of God.

Connecting the Gospel

to the second reading: Today's second reading from the first letter of St. John also focuses on belief, telling us, "[T]he victory that conquers the world is our faith." Indeed, the faith of Christians is a powerful, audacious thing. We believe in life that is stronger than death, in love that is stronger than evil, in light that is stronger than darkness. This faith in the redeeming grace of God's mercy allows us to continue on in hope even in the face of adversity and seeming defeat. Jesus appears to his closest friends and shows them the nailmarks still present on his hands and the wound where his side was lanced. In encountering the risen Lord, the disciples finally receive the full revelation of Jesus's identity. Before his passion they had come to believe in Jesus the wonderworker, the teacher, the Son of God. Now, they find themselves face-to-face with Jesus, the one who died and rose again, the Lord of life.

to experience: Jesus desires to share this life that is stronger than death with all people of all times and places. When did this good news first come to you and how have you passed it on to others?

Connecting the Responsorial Psalm

to the readings: Aptly, on this feast of Divine Mercy, today's responsorial psalm repeats three times, "His mercy endures forever." In the gospel reading Jesus embodies the mercy of God, drawing near to those who had abandoned him in his greatest suffering with the words, "Peace be with you." Jesus does not rebuke the disciples for their lack of faith or wait for them to seek him out. Instead, he passes through the doors they had locked out of fear and greets them as friends. For their part we are told, "The disciples rejoiced when they saw the Lord."

to psalmist preparation: God's eternal mercy also calls us to joy. How do you express this joy in your ministry?

PROMPTS FOR FAITH-SHARING

Today, we celebrate the Second Sunday of Easter and Divine Mercy Sunday. Where is God calling you to extend mercy to others?

In the first reading we hear that the early community of believers were all of "one heart and mind." Where in your own parish is the community of one mind about issues or values? Where is there division?

The second reading from the first letter of St. John proclaims that "[God's] commandments are not burdensome." At this moment in your faith journey, where are you encountering burden or hardship?

In today's gospel Jesus tells the disciples, "As the Father has sent me, so I send you." Where are you being sent to share Jesus's peace?

CELEBRATION

Model Rite for the Blessing and Sprinkling of Water
Presider: In holy waters, we were baptized into the peace of Christ that surpasses all understanding. May that peace continue to grow in our hearts and take root in our lives . . . *[pause]*
    [continue with The Roman Missal, *Appendix II]*

Homily Points
• We continue the feast of Easter with Divine Mercy Sunday. It's interesting that the first half of the gospel chosen for today is the very same gospel that is read on Pentecost Sunday. In some ways, we could see Jesus's words to the disciples as providing a framework for us as we live out these holy days of Easter joy. Jesus enters the room where the disciples have locked themselves and imparts three messages: "Peace be with you," "As the Father has sent me, so I send you," and "Receive the Holy Spirit" by whose power you may forgive sins.

• Jesus begins with peace and this should be our starting place as well. We cannot be disciples of the Lord unless peace reigns in our hearts. As Christians, we must regularly examine our conscience to discern if our hearts are full of Christ's peace or if they have become bogged down by anger, bitterness, or anxiety. Until we are firmly rooted in peace, we cannot go forth to share the gospel of Jesus. When the good news is preached by ministers who do not embody its message, it becomes distorted.

• Though this is a weighty responsibility, to live in peace so as to truthfully proclaim the risen Lord in word and action, we are not expected to carry the burden alone. Breathing on the disciples, Jesus tells them, "Receive the Holy Spirit." United with the animating power of God's life and love, we become more than we were before. In the Spirit, the anxious become peaceful, the doubting become faithful, and the one who has been wronged finds the power to forgive. So, too, may it be for us as we journey toward Pentecost and seek to live more deeply into the mystery of Christ's death and resurrection.

Model Universal Prayer (Prayer of the Faithful)
Presider: Trusting in the divine mercy of our God, let us place before our Lord and savior the needs and petitions that burden us and the world.

Response: Lord, hear our prayer.

For the church of God, may it be of one heart and one mind in bearing the peace of the risen Lord to the ends of the earth . . .

For nations at war, may politicians and diplomats work tirelessly to end violence and promote justice and goodwill . . .

For those who suffer from addiction and mental illness, may they find strength, courage, and healing in Jesus's merciful heart . . .

For all gathered here, in following the example of the early church, may we share our treasures, both spiritual and material, with those in need . . .

Presider: Peaceful and loving God, in your son you have revealed to us your divine mercy and desire for all people to draw near to you. Hear our prayers that with joy and thanksgiving we might praise you always. We ask this through Christ our Lord. **Amen.**

COLLECT
Let us pray.

Pause for silent prayer

God of everlasting mercy,
who in the very recurrence of the paschal feast
kindle the faith of the people you have made your own,
increase, we pray, the grace you have bestowed,
that all may grasp and rightly understand
in what font they have been washed,
by whose Spirit they have been reborn,
by whose Blood they have been redeemed.
Through our Lord Jesus Christ, your Son,
who lives and reigns with you in the unity of the Holy Spirit,
one God, for ever and ever. **Amen.**

FIRST READING
Acts 4:32-35

The community of believers was of one heart and mind,
    and no one claimed that any of his possessions was his own,
    but they had everything in common.
With great power the apostles bore witness
    to the resurrection of the Lord Jesus,
    and great favor was accorded them all.
There was no needy person among them,
    for those who owned property or houses would sell them,
    bring the proceeds of the sale,
    and put them at the feet of the apostles,
    and they were distributed to each according to need.

RESPONSORIAL PSALM
Ps 118:2-4, 13-15, 22-24

℟. (1) Give thanks to the Lord for he is good, his love is everlasting.
    or:
℟. Alleluia.

Let the house of Israel say,
    "His mercy endures forever."
Let the house of Aaron say,
    "His mercy endures forever."
Let those who fear the LORD say,
    "His mercy endures forever."

℟. Give thanks to the Lord for he is good, his love is everlasting.
    or:
℟. Alleluia.

I was hard pressed and was falling,
    but the LORD helped me.
My strength and my courage is the LORD,
    and he has been my savior.
The joyful shout of victory
    in the tents of the just.

R̸. Give thanks to the Lord for he is good,
    his love is everlasting.
    or:
R̸. Alleluia.

The stone which the builders rejected
    has become the cornerstone.
By the LORD has this been done;
    it is wonderful in our eyes.
This is the day the LORD has made;
    let us be glad and rejoice in it.

R̸. Give thanks to the Lord for he is good,
    his love is everlasting.
    or:
R̸. Alleluia.

SECOND READING
1 John 5:1-6

Beloved:
Everyone who believes that Jesus is the
    Christ is begotten by God,
    and everyone who loves the Father
    loves also the one begotten by him.
In this way we know that we love the
    children of God
    when we love God and obey his
        commandments.
For the love of God is this,
    that we keep his commandments.
And his commandments are not
    burdensome,
    for whoever is begotten by God
        conquers the world.
And the victory that conquers the world is
    our faith.
Who indeed is the victor over the world
    but the one who believes that Jesus is
        the Son of God?

This is the one who came through water
    and blood, Jesus Christ,
    not by water alone, but by water and
        blood.
The Spirit is the one that testifies,
    and the Spirit is truth.

About Liturgy

Scars Are Signs of God's Glory: Think for a moment about a scar you have, and a word or two you might pick to describe the circumstances that led to it. Perhaps words like "accident" or "scary" come to mind, or "embarrassed," "foolish," or even "reckless." But I doubt the word "glorious" comes to mind.

Yet it is on this Second Sunday of Easter each year when we hear about the apostle Thomas and his first encounter with the risen Lord. (I usually refuse to use the typical nickname for him: how would you like to have an everlasting nickname based on the weakest and lowest moment of your life?) Thomas requires the same visual proof the other apostles had of Christ's resurrection and indeed just a little bit more; we all are familiar with the narrative.

Christ's resurrected and glorified body certainly could have been made completely whole again, yet the wounds of the nails and spear persist, and Thomas is able to touch and feel them. "My Lord and my God!" he cries. Christ is truly here a wounded healer—and beyond that, a teacher, a friend, and a brother.

Liturgically, this attention to the "scars" of Christ should call us to his humanity with his divinity, and that we are invited to share that with him, one day. Music should be carefully chosen (see below) to reflect not only the usual attributes on this day of trust and humility, but also of our kinship with Christ and the future glory offered and promised to us. Ritually, today is an opportunity to call particular attention to the fraction rite and the ritual moment often lost in most liturgies.

About the Fraction Rite

One Thing at a Time: On *M*A*S*H*, Charles Emerson Winchester once famously said, "I do one thing at a time, I do it very well, and then I move on." Make sure that, at every liturgy, the fraction rite doesn't become a side note to a lingering sign of peace. Wait for that moment to end before beginning the next, so that the immense symbolism has a chance to express itself fully to a congregation fully aware of the rite. The Missal tells us, "[T]he gesture of the fraction or breaking of bread . . . was quite simply the term by which the Eucharist was known in apostolic times" (GIRM 321), and this eucharistic table is what brings us in one moment to Christ broken on the cross and to a foretaste of the eternal and heavenly banquet. We believe, as we sing in the *Agnus Dei* accompanying the rite, that it is Christ broken on the cross that is the ultimate sign of God's mercy, and only with God in paradise will we know true and divine peace.

About Music

Music of Faith and Glory: Many of us are likely familiar with music whose lyrics at least in part come directly from today's gospel: Haugen's "We Walk by Faith" (GIA), Haas's "Without Seeing You" (GIA), and "O [or 'Ye'] Sons and Daughters." Those wishing to highlight Divine Mercy today will find Booth's "The Jesus Song" (OCP) a perfect contemporary fit.

For music that speaks to kinship and glory, you might reintroduce "Priestly People" (WLP) by Lucien Deiss to your community. "Out of Darkness" (OCP) by Christopher Walker can also festively speak to these concepts, if your performing forces are adequate and well prepared.

APRIL 11, 2021
SECOND SUNDAY OF EASTER
(or of DIVINE MERCY)

SPIRITUALITY

GOSPEL ACCLAMATION
cf. Luke 24:32

℟. Alleluia, alleluia.
Lord Jesus, open the Scriptures to us;
make our hearts burn while you speak to us.
℟. Alleluia, alleluia.

Gospel   Luke 24:35-48; L47B

The two disciples recounted what had taken
    place on the way,
    and how Jesus was made known to them
    in the breaking of bread.

While they were still speaking about this,
    he stood in their midst and said to them,
    "Peace be with you."
But they were startled and terrified
    and thought that they were seeing a ghost.
Then he said to them, "Why are you troubled?
And why do questions arise in your hearts?
Look at my hands and my feet, that it is I
    myself.
Touch me and see, because a ghost does not
    have flesh and bones
    as you can see I have."
And as he said this,
    he showed them his hands and his feet.
While they were still incredulous for joy
    and were amazed,
    he asked them, "Have you anything here
        to eat?"
They gave him a piece of baked fish;
    he took it and ate it in front of them.

He said to them,
    "These are my words that I spoke to you
        while I was still with you,
    that everything written about me in the
        law of Moses
    and in the prophets and psalms must be
        fulfilled."
Then he opened their minds to understand
    the Scriptures.
And he said to them,
    "Thus it is written that the Christ would
        suffer
    and rise from the dead on the third day
    and that repentance, for the forgiveness
        of sins,
    would be preached in his name
    to all the nations, beginning from
        Jerusalem.
You are witnesses of these things."

Reflecting on the Gospel

This Sunday's gospel follows the appearance of the risen Jesus to the two disciples on the way to Emmaus. The Emmaus meal was a welcoming event; the meal with the risen Jesus in Jerusalem will be a missioning event. Despite the witness of the two disciples who have hurried back from Emmaus and the news of Jesus's appearance to Simon, the eleven and their companions are still startled and terrified when Jesus appears among them and greets them with peace. They think he is a ghost! In this gospel of Luke, as in John's narrative last Sunday, Jesus makes clear to them the reality of his glorified human presence, his full embodied existence, by showing them his wounded hands and feet, inviting them to touch him, asking them to give him something to eat, and then taking the piece of grilled fish and eating it before their eyes.

In Luke's Last Supper account, Jesus was among his disciples "as the one who serves" (Luke 22:27; NABRE); now he is among them as one who is to be served. Just seeing with their human eyes is not enough. As Jesus had done in the passion predictions during his ministry, as he had done for the disciples on the way to Emmaus, as the two messengers at the tomb had done for the women on Easter morning, Jesus now opens the eyes of the Jerusalem disciples' hearts so that they may understand the Scriptures. Luke mentions the threefold division of the Hebrew Scriptures: the teaching of Moses (the Pentateuch/Torah), the Prophets, and the Writings (represented by the psalms). These were the Scriptures that had nourished Jesus throughout his life.

Jesus tells his disciples clearly that they cannot stay in this Jerusalem house of ecstatic joy, listening to his words and serving him at table. This experience must burst through the doors in the service of those outside, people of all nations who are waiting to hear the Good News of repentance and forgiveness of their sins. At the first meal with Jesus that is recorded in Luke's gospel, the great banquet that Levi hosted for Jesus, Jesus spoke of the *metanoia* (Luke 5:32), that life-changing repentance that turns one's life around, and which Levi had just experienced in his call to follow Jesus. At that meal, Jesus had addressed the call to repentance to the tax collectors and sinners; at this last meal after his passion and resurrection "the same message had to be preached to all the nations, beginning with Jerusalem. Jesus's passion–resurrection transformed the table of Jesus the prophet into that of Jesus Christ the Lord and made it the springboard for the church's universal mission. Jesus's message at this point in his final discourse looks directly to the story of the church on mission in the Acts of the Apostles" (Eugene LaVerdiere, *Dining in the Kingdom of God*).

This is what the disciples are to witness. And we, who at the Eucharist also sit at the "transformed table" of Jesus, share in the same urgent mission. As individuals and as church, we must admit our own sinfulness, continually turn to Jesus in repentance, and then go out in the strength of the Eucharist we have received to bear credible, outreaching witness of the need for conversion to the following of Jesus in our own small or larger worlds. Many places in our contemporary world are obviously not founded on repentance and forgiveness, but on war and entrenched animosities that we may publicly lament, or rationalize, or even excuse, while at the same time still allowing violence and bitterness to inhabit our hearts. If we are to be disciples who take seriously Jesus's Easter greeting of "Peace be with you" and who offer this peace to one another around the eucharistic table with a present and future intent, we need to create a space in our lives and our hearts where such peace with God and with our sisters and brothers can truly be at home.

Focusing the Gospel

Key words and phrases: "You are witnesses of these things."

To the point: Jesus's work is not complete even after he has risen from the dead. At the time of his dying and rising, his disciples had scattered, their faith crushed and their spirits despairing. In Jesus's resurrection, he conquered death in his own being, but his great desire was not to keep this life for himself but to share it with all. And so for forty days, until his ascension, he appeared to his disciples so they might also know the resurrection and their share in it. During this time, he prepares them for their mission to serve as witnesses until "all the nations" have encountered the gospel. In our Easter joy, we are reminded that this mission is now ours.

Connecting the Gospel

to the first reading: In the first reading Peter takes an opportunity to share the gospel with a crowd that has gathered. They were amazed by his healing of a crippled beggar and in response to their wonder, Peter tells them it is not by his own doing but by "faith in [Jesus's] name" (3:16; NABRE) that the miraculous healing occurred. It is interesting that in this passage Peter echoes the words Jesus speaks in today's gospel when he proclaimed to the disciples, "Thus it is written that the Christ would suffer." Although Jesus has risen from the dead and reigns in glory, Peter does not skirt past the vulnerability of Christ suffering and dying on the cross but instead asserts that in this worldly failure, "God has brought to fulfillment / what he had announced beforehand /through the mouths of all the prophets."

to experience: In his passion and crucifixion, Jesus redeems both pain and death. As Christians, we will not escape the trials that come to each human life, but we will be accompanied through them by the one who underwent them to the fullest extent. The witness to Jesus's life and glory is not complete without witnessing to his passion and death.

Connecting the Responsorial Psalm

to the readings: Today's psalm exhorts us to trust in "the Lord who does wonders for his faithful one." In speaking to the gathered crowd, Peter calls upon "[t]he God of Abraham, the God of Isaac, and the God of Jacob, / the God of our fathers." Throughout the generations we see the mighty works of the Lord in our biblical ancestors and hear about them in the stories told in our communities and families about the saints among us. Though the first verse speaks of "distress" and the need for "pity" from God, the next verses express faith that "the Lord will hear me when I call upon him" and names God as the one who puts "gladness in my heart."

to psalmist preparation: The holy men and women we look to as models in the life of faith show us how to praise God even in the midst of hardship. How do you attempt to do this in your own life?

PROMPTS FOR FAITH-SHARING

Peter rebukes the gathered crowd for Jesus's death, but then acknowledges, "[Y]ou acted out of ignorance." When has ignorance clouded your following of Christ?

The psalmist proclaims, "[T]he Lord does wonders for his faithful one." What wonders have you witnessed in the life of faith?

In the gospel account, the disciples say the risen Lord was made known to them "in the breaking of bread." How do you make meals with friends and family a true time of communion?

Jesus tells the disciples that they are "witnesses" of the good news to be spread to the nations of his life, death, and resurrection. Who are the witnesses in your life who have brought you to deeper faith in Christ?

Model Rite for the Blessing and Sprinkling of Water

Presider: In baptism we were washed clean of sin and freed from its power. May these waters cleanse us anew and strengthen us to follow Jesus all the days of our lives . . . [pause]

    [continue with The Roman Missal, *Appendix II*]

Homily Points

• Beginning last week and continuing this Sunday our second reading is taken from the first letter of St. John. We find one of the letter's major themes when St. John writes, "The way we may be sure that we know him is to keep his commandments." A few verses later, just after the ending of today's reading, this sentiment is stated in slightly different words: "This is the way we may know that we are in union with him: whoever claims to abide in him ought to live [just] as he lived" (2:5b-6; NABRE).

• As Christians, to know the word of God is not only to spend time reading the words of the Bible, praying with them and contemplating them, but also to embody these words in all we do. St. John invites us to a particular imitation of Christ, "to live [just] as he lived." For us, living two thousand years removed from the time when Jesus walked upon the earth, it may seem impossible (and highly inconvenient) to try and replicate Christ's lifestyle with authenticity. Are we to leave home and family to become itinerant preachers with no possessions?

• For a select few this may be the path to holiness, but it is also possible to "live as Jesus lived" by considering the core of his actions—not just the environment in which he performed them. On the Sixth Sunday of Easter we will read from St. John's gospel where Jesus tells us, "This is my commandment: love one another as I love you." In meditating upon how to live as Jesus lived, we could reflect on this question: How did Jesus love us? And then continue to ponder: How do I embody this love?

Model Universal Prayer (Prayer of the Faithful)

Presider: Today's psalm proclaims that the Lord "does wonders for his faithful one." Confident that God knows our needs even before we speak them, let us place our petitions before the Lord.

Response: Lord, hear our prayer.

For bishops, priests, and deacons, may their ministry be characterized by fidelity to the truth and humble service of the lowly . . .

For leaders of nations, may they work together to put an end to torture and inhumane acts against prisoners and captives . . .

For husbands and wives in troubled marriages, may the peace of the Lord bring about reconciliation and understanding . . .

For all gathered here, in the light of the resurrection may we be renewed in joy and hope . . .

Presider: God, Author of life, you raised your Son, Jesus, from the dead and through him offer eternal life to all people. Hear our prayers that nourished by your word, we might bear it to others. We ask this through Christ our Lord. **Amen.**

COLLECT

Let us pray.

Pause for silent prayer

May your people exult for ever, O God,
in renewed youthfulness of spirit,
so that, rejoicing now in the restored glory
    of our adoption,
we may look forward in confident hope
to the rejoicing of the day of resurrection.
Through our Lord Jesus Christ, your Son,
who lives and reigns with you in the unity
    of the Holy Spirit,
one God, for ever and ever. **Amen.**

FIRST READING
Acts 3:13-15, 17-19

Peter said to the people:
"The God of Abraham,
    the God of Isaac, and the God of Jacob,
    the God of our fathers, has glorified his
        servant Jesus,
    whom you handed over and denied in
        Pilate's presence
    when he had decided to release him.
You denied the Holy and Righteous One
    and asked that a murderer be released
        to you.
The author of life you put to death,
    but God raised him from the dead; of
        this we are witnesses.
Now I know, brothers,
    that you acted out of ignorance, just as
        your leaders did;
    but God has thus brought to fulfillment
    what he had announced beforehand
    through the mouth of all the prophets,
    that his Christ would suffer.
Repent, therefore, and be converted, that
    your sins may be wiped away."

RESPONSORIAL PSALM

Ps 4:2, 4, 7-8, 9

R̠. (7a) Lord, let your face shine on us.
or:
R̠. Alleluia.

When I call, answer me, O my just God,
  you who relieve me when I am in
      distress;
  have pity on me, and hear my prayer!

R̠. Lord, let your face shine on us.
or:
R̠. Alleluia.

Know that the LORD does wonders for
    his faithful one;
  the LORD will hear me when I call
      upon him.

R̠. Lord, let your face shine on us.
or:
R̠. Alleluia.

O LORD, let the light of your countenance
    shine upon us!
  You put gladness into my heart.

R̠. Lord, let your face shine on us.
or:
R̠. Alleluia.

As soon as I lie down, I fall peacefully
    asleep,
  for you alone, O LORD,
  bring security to my dwelling.

R̠. Lord, let your face shine on us.
or:
R̠. Alleluia.

SECOND READING

1 John 2:1-5a

My children, I am writing this to you
  so that you may not commit sin.
But if anyone does sin, we have an
    Advocate with the Father,
  Jesus Christ the righteous one.
He is expiation for our sins,
  and not for our sins only but for those
    of the whole world.
The way we may be sure that we know
    him is to keep
  his commandments.
Those who say, "I know him," but do not
    keep his commandments
  are liars, and the truth is not in them.
But whoever keeps his word,
  the love of God is truly perfected in
      him.

About Liturgy

Words into Action: One can employ a variety of words to speak of what liturgy is and how it accomplishes what it does. For instance, the liturgy is catechetical, performative, sacrificial, sustaining, and/or formative (and so much more), depending on which facet one wants to dig deeper into and give closer attention to.

The Scriptures today should remind us to pay attention to how our liturgies are evangelical; that is, how (and how well) do our liturgies preach the good news, both to those we see every week in the pew and to those we have not seen before? Up until now, the good news of Christ's resurrection was primarily shared among friends and relatives, a very close circle of people who surrounded Jesus himself during his three years of ministry. We are at a "hinge" moment of the narrative, and of our Easter season, when in the last line of the gospel Christ reminds the apostles that it is their ministry, foretold by the prophets, to share the joy of the resurrection and forgiveness of sins with all nations. The reading from Acts shows Peter, boldly, doing just that.

We need to consider how we do that ourselves. It is far too simple—some would call it a cop-out—to consider only words, only language when evaluating these efforts. Truly, we need to pay attention to preaching whose content is, at least in part, a proclamation of the risen Christ and to deepening our relationship with him and with the whole body of Christ. So, too, should we give careful attention to hymn texts that speak to the same. But all these words pale in comparison to how it is we preach, and how it is the music ministry is led, how all liturgical ministers exercise their specific roles. If we wish our assemblies to continue living the faith outside the doors of the church building the other six days and twenty-three hours of their week, the church's ministers must show them in action how they do that for that one hour.

The tone of the preaching and presiding must be joyful, without sacrificing reverence. It must seem as if the celebrant has no choice but to proclaim the risen Christ and the difference that that faith and belief makes in day-to-day living. Music must be led invitingly, by action, letting the congregation know not of an invitation to join in singing but a reminder that the sung liturgy is their responsibility! Ministers of music are there principally to aid that song. Texts of both preaching and music must not only themselves evangelize, but spur others on to that same holy activity in the world—not just among their friends and relatives, their closest circle, but among all those who need to hear Good News, every minute of every day.

About Music

Loving Service: A gentle melody that perfectly matches its text is "Partners in the Mission" (WLP) by Peter Hesed. It serves today's Scriptures well by inviting those who sing it to loving service, acknowledging the fear we might have, calmed by Christ's easy and light yoke.

The *Psallite* refrain "Shout to the Ends of the Earth" (Liturgical Press) in a way prefigures the Ascension commission, with bouncy Alleluias that send us forth, people redeemed by the Lord, to proclaim the kingdom of God.

SPIRITUALITY

GOSPEL ACCLAMATION
John 10:14

R℣. Alleluia, alleluia.
I am the good shepherd, says the Lord;
I know my sheep, and mine know me.
R℣. Alleluia, alleluia.

Gospel

John 10:11-18; L50B

Jesus said:
"I am the good shepherd.
A good shepherd lays down his life
  for the sheep.
A hired man, who is not a
  shepherd
  and whose sheep are not his
    own,
  sees a wolf coming and
    leaves the sheep and runs
    away,
  and the wolf catches and
    scatters them.
This is because he works for
  pay and has no concern for
  the sheep.
I am the good shepherd,
  and I know mine and mine know me,
  just as the Father knows me and I
    know the Father;
  and I will lay down my life for the
    sheep.
I have other sheep that do not belong to
  this fold.
These also I must lead, and they will
  hear my voice,
  and there will be one flock, one
    shepherd.
This is why the Father loves me,
  because I lay down my life in order to
    take it up again.
No one takes it from me, but I lay it
  down on my own.
I have power to lay it down, and power
  to take it up again.
This command I have received from my
  Father."

Reflecting on the Gospel

This Sunday's gospel presents us with one of the most loved images of Jesus when he says of himself, "I am the good shepherd." We are sometimes seduced by images of a smiling Middle Eastern shepherd with a cuddly, clean, and fluffy lamb tucked under his arm. Much less romantic and more accurate and robust is the earliest known statue (ca. 60 CE) of the Good Shepherd at Caesarea Maritima in Israel. The legless remnant has a huge, heavy sheep draped around the shepherd's shoulders. To carry such a load would be no easy task! In 1 Samuel, we have another vigorous Old Testament description of a shepherd in the context of King Saul's attempt to dissuade the young David from fighting against the mighty Philistine warrior, Goliath. David argues his case for the fight with a graphic description of how he kept sheep for his father: "[W]henever a lion or bear came to carry off a sheep from the flock, I would chase after it, attack it, and snatch the prey from its mouth. If it attacked me, I would seize it by the throat, strike it, and kill it. . . . The same LORD who delivered me from the claws of the lion and the bear will deliver me from the hand of this Philistine" (17:34-35, 37; NABRE).

As our Good Shepherd, Jesus fights for us, saves us from the gaping jaws of whatever or whoever seeks to grab and destroy our discipleship and wound the little "flock" of the Christian community. He shepherds us with his loving care so that we may "have life and have it more abundantly" (John 10:10; NABRE).

In contrast to the Good Shepherd is the hireling who is concerned primarily with his own self-interest: his reputation, remuneration, and safety. Through the prophets, God had denounced the shepherd leaders of Israel who had prostituted their pastoral ministry. "I myself will pasture my sheep," God promises his people (Ezek 34:15; NABRE; cf. Isa 40:11; Jer 31:10). There are still some political, social, and ecclesial "hired men" with us, but there are also the magnificent shepherds who are willing to lay down their life for their sheep. In *Oscar Romero: Memories in Mosaic*, Maria López collects the memories of two hundred people who had lived, prayed, and worked with such a shepherd—Archbishop Oscar Romero. Here is one:

One morning in rainy season when the skies were heavy with the day's rain, a man in rags, with a shirt full of holes and hair made curly by dust, covered with dust, was cleaning (Romero's) tomb carefully with one of his rags. When he left to go out, I felt I needed to talk to him.
"Why do you do that?"
"Do what?"
"Clean Monseñor's tomb."
"Because he was my father."
"What do you mean . . . ?"
"It's like this. I'm just a poor man, you know? Sometimes I make some money carrying things for people in the market in a little cart. And sometimes I spend it all on liquor and end up lying hungover on the streets. But I never get discouraged. I had a father! I did! He made me feel like a person. Because he loved people like

me and didn't act like we made him sick. He talked to us, he touched us, he asked us questions. He had confidence in us. You could see in his eyes that he cared about me. Like parents love their children. That's why I clean off his tomb, because that's what children do."

As a child, as a son, Jesus the Good Shepherd lives, dies, and is raised to life in the power of the mutual love between him and his Father. Into this love Jesus gathers his disciples so that they may also share in it.

Focusing the Gospel

Key words and phrases: "[T]here will be one flock, one shepherd."

To the point: In today's passage from the parable of the Good Shepherd, we find another insight into Jesus's dream of how the world might be. While "the wolf" attacks the flock in order to "catch and scatter," Jesus is the shepherd who leads not only the flock he is currently tending, but also "other sheep that do not belong to this fold." In gathering the lost and searching for the scattered, Jesus does the work of his Father who desires that all should be found, welcomed, loved, and cherished in the family of God.

Connecting the Gospel

to the first reading: Today's first reading continues where it left off last Sunday, only now Peter and John find themselves arrested and brought before the Sanhedrin. The religious authorities are concerned over the attention and excitement John and Peter have incurred due to their healing of the crippled man at the temple gates. Peter's speech is prompted by the question put to him by the high priest, elders, and scribes, "By what power or by what name have you done this?" (4:7; NABRE). In the gospel, Jesus names himself as the good shepherd who "lays down his life for the sheep." In the first reading Peter identifies Jesus as the savior of all, stating, "There is no salvation through anyone else." In both the gospel and the first reading we come face-to-face with Jesus, the healer, and Jesus, the redeemer. During his life Jesus healed the broken and forgave sinners. Now his work of salvation continues on as his followers heal and forgive, not in their own names, but in the name of "Jesus Christ the Nazorean," the crucified and the risen one.

to experience: As members of God's people, we experience Jesus in the healing touch or word of another and also when we are led by the Spirit to minister to others in Jesus's name. In your path as a disciple, do you find yourself more often as the giver or receiver of this grace?

Connecting the Responsorial Psalm

to the readings: Today's psalm tells us, "Blessed is he who comes in the name of the Lord." We see this lived out in the experiences of Peter and John in the Acts of the Apostles. Filled with the grace of the Holy Spirit newly descended upon them, the two apostles heal a crippled man, stating, "[I]n the name of Jesus Christ the Nazorean, [rise and] walk" (Acts 3:6; NABRE). In today's first reading, their faith does not falter as they are brought before the Sanhedrin due to the crowd's excitement about this healing and about Peter's preaching afterward. In blessing they healed the man, and as *the* blessed they have courage and peace in defending their faith before those who had recently succeeded in bringing Jesus to the cross.

to psalmist preparation: As a cantor, how do you experience your ministry as a blessing done "in the name of the Lord"?

PROMPTS FOR FAITH-SHARING

In the first reading we hear of "a cripple" who was healed in the name of Jesus. What areas in your life are in need of healing at this moment?

Today's responsorial psalm proclaims, "The stone rejected by the builders has become the cornerstone." What examples of this have you seen in your community?

In the reading from the first letter of St. Peter, we find a description of Christ's non-violent response to his persecutors. How do you try to emulate his actions?

In the gospel parable Jesus says, "A good shepherd lays down his life for the sheep." Who are the sheep that you are called to shepherd and how do you give of your life for them?

Model Rite for the Blessing and Sprinkling of Water

Presider: In baptism we were called by name and entered into the sheepfold of the Good Shepherd. By the sprinkling of this water, may we once again perceive how deeply known and loved we are by God, our creator and redeemer . . . *[pause]*
   [continue with The Roman Missal, *Appendix II]*

Homily Points

• In today's first reading, Peter quotes from Psalm 118, "The stone rejected by the builders has become the cornerstone." There is a beautiful pattern to salvation history where God chooses the least to do the greatest work. We find this in Peter, the disciple upon whom Christ founds his church, who denied Jesus three times after promising vehemently that he would never falter in his fidelity. This does not deter Jesus from giving Peter "the keys of the kingdom." Instead, the risen Lord appears to Peter and to the other disciples to give them his peace.

• Jesus's actions should come as no surprise to us. In the gospel for today, Jesus tells us he is "the good shepherd" who "lays down his life for the sheep." Not only does he lay it down, but he does so "in order to take it up again." The resurrected Lord returns to his flock that has been scattered after his crucifixion due to fear and doubt, and restores them to each other and to himself.

• In our reading from the Acts of the Apostles, we find Peter arrested in front of the religious leaders of the time. Instead of denying the Lord or cowering in silence, Peter gives an impassioned defense of his faith in Jesus, telling them, "There is no salvation through anyone else." Peter proudly proclaims Jesus, the one who submitted himself to death on a cross, as the healer of every ill and the redeemer of sinners. Through Jesus's vulnerability to death, he conquered it. Through Peter's failings on his journey of faith, he became the leader the church needed. We, too, are invited into this pattern of salvation, knowing that our weakness becomes strength when given to the Lord.

Model Universal Prayer (Prayer of the Faithful)

Presider: Knowing that we are loved and sustained by Jesus, the Good Shepherd, let us entrust all of our needs to his gracious care.

Response: Lord, hear our prayer.

For all who serve as shepherds to the people of God, emulating the life of Christ may they serve with humility, gathering the scattered and protecting the weak . . .

For elected officials, in their capacity as leaders may they model a respect and reverence for all life from conception to natural death . . .

For all who experience physical or intellectual disability, may their struggles be few and their gifts and talents recognized and treasured in the larger community . . .

For all gathered here, may we be freed from anxieties and needless worry, resting secure in the arms of the Good Shepherd . . .

Presider: God of refuge, by the wounds of Jesus we have been healed. Hear our prayers that we might cling to the example of Christ and find the strength to meet hate with love and violence with peace. We ask this through Christ our Lord. **Amen.**

COLLECT

Let us pray.

Pause for silent prayer

Almighty ever-living God,
lead us to a share in the joys of heaven,
so that the humble flock may reach
where the brave Shepherd has gone before.
Who lives and reigns with you in the unity
      of the Holy Spirit,
one God, for ever and ever. **Amen.**

FIRST READING
Acts 4:8-12

Peter, filled with the Holy Spirit, said:
      "Leaders of the people and elders:
      If we are being examined today
      about a good deed done to a cripple,
      namely, by what means he was saved,
      then all of you and all the people of
            Israel should know
      that it was in the name of Jesus Christ
            the Nazorean
      whom you crucified, whom God raised
            from the dead;
      in his name this man stands before you
            healed.
He is *the stone rejected by you, the
      builders,*
which has become the cornerstone.
There is no salvation through anyone else,
      nor is there any other name under
            heaven
      given to the human race by which we
            are to be saved."

RESPONSORIAL PSALM
Ps 118:1, 8-9, 21-23, 26, 28, 29

℟. (22) The stone rejected by the builders
      has become the cornerstone.
      or:
℟. Alleluia.

Give thanks to the LORD, for he is good,
      for his mercy endures forever
It is better to take refuge in the LORD
      than to trust in man.
It is better to take refuge in the LORD
      than to trust in princes.

℟. The stone rejected by the builders has
      become the cornerstone.
      or:
℟. Alleluia.

I will give thanks to you, for you have
    answered me
  and have been my savior.
The stone which the builders rejected
  has become the cornerstone.
By the LORD has this been done;
  it is wonderful in our eyes.

R⁊. The stone rejected by the builders has
  become the cornerstone.
  or:
R⁊. Alleluia.

Blessed is he who comes in the name of
    the LORD;
  we bless you from the house of the
    LORD.
I will give thanks to you, for you have
    answered me
  and have been my savior.
Give thanks to the LORD, for he is good;
  for his kindness endures forever.

R⁊. The stone rejected by the builders has
  become the cornerstone.
  or:
R⁊. Alleluia.

SECOND READING
1 John 3:1-2

Beloved:
See what love the Father has bestowed
    on us
  that we may be called the children of
    God.
Yet so we are.
The reason the world does not know us
  is that it did not know him.
Beloved, we are God's children now;
  what we shall be has not yet been
    revealed.
We do know that when it is revealed we
  shall be like him,
  for we shall see him as he is.

About Liturgy

Shepherds Who Smell Like Sheep: Though the imagery is not as prevalent in this particular cycle of readings, it is still Good Shepherd Sunday, the gospel reminds us. While we might wish to imagine the Good Shepherd as the one in the famous parable—the one who upon finding the lost sheep lovingly hoists it over his shoulders to bring it back to the other ninety-nine—this is not the shepherd Jesus speaks of today. This Good Shepherd has to protect the flock from wolves, and lays down his life to do so.

While the Good Shepherd at the parish level is of course the pastor, many of us who coordinate liturgical ministries have, in a way, a small subset of that community under our care. Perhaps we are choir directors, those who coordinate and train altar servers, lectors, extraordinary ministers, hospitality ministers, or others. Part of how we exercise leadership in those roles should be as a pastor, as a Good Shepherd does. This can manifest in at least two ways: by leading through service and by truly knowing those whom we serve.

If all we do at rehearsal is learn notes, if all we do at our desk is type up schedules, our ministry is hollow and does not truly serve the ministers. Make sure to share with those you coordinate, especially if they are volunteer ministers, materials that can help them spiritually reflect on their roles and also feed their spirits, which can frequently begin to feel unthanked and unnoticed. Plan retreat days for them; recommission them yearly in a Sunday Eucharist. If they have suggestions or concerns, truly listen to them, sometimes taking time to determine if there is a question or concern "behind" the one expressed. That is, don't just respond to what a specific complaint might be, but take a moment to see what motivates the report, what factors into the person coming to you with the issue at hand.

All of that is easier to do if, like the way Jesus describes himself in today's gospel, we too get to know "our sheep." As above, if the only time you encounter your liturgical ministers is at Mass or at rehearsals or trainings, that too is hollow. In addition to the retreat days mentioned above, plan social gatherings from time to time. Encourage one another to live the gospel by planning days of service together. Above all, be attentive to the needs of each person individually, and encourage the small community to rally around someone—in turn it will be each of us—who needs the loving support of the Christian community. All of this is a small part of truly being a Good Shepherd here and now.

About Music

Singing Easter Psalms: While settings of Psalm 23 abound, don't forget about Psalm 100, "[W]e are his people, the flock he shepherds" (v. 3; NABRE). "All People That on Earth Do Dwell" is a paraphrase of the beginning of that psalm and is found in many hymnals. Francis Patrick O'Brien's "Shepherd of My Heart" (GIA) might be a hidden gem waiting to be uncovered, or rediscovered!

Note, too, that the first reading and psalm bring back the imagery of the rejected cornerstone, so don't be afraid to revisit a favorite Psalm 118 setting from the Easter Vigil or Easter Day celebrations. Tony Alonso has a nice one, "Easter Alleluia" (WLP), which places a paraphrased text into the familiar EASTER HYMN melody.

SPIRITUALITY

GOSPEL ACCLAMATION
John 15:4a, 5b

R̸. Alleluia, alleluia.
Remain in me as I remain in you, says the Lord.
Whoever remains in me will bear much fruit.
R̸. Alleluia, alleluia.

Gospel

John 15:1-8; L53B

Jesus said to his disciples:
"I am the true vine, and
    my Father is the
    vine grower.
He takes away every
    branch in me that
    does not bear fruit,
    and every one that does
    he prunes so that it
    bears more fruit.
You are already pruned
    because of the word
    that I spoke to you.
Remain in me, as I remain
    in you.
Just as a branch cannot bear fruit on
    its own
    unless it remains on the vine,
    so neither can you unless you remain
    in me.
I am the vine, you are the branches.
Whoever remains in me and I in him
    will bear much fruit,
    because without me you can do
    nothing.
Anyone who does not remain in me
    will be thrown out like a branch and
    wither;
    people will gather them and throw
    them into a fire
    and they will be burned.
If you remain in me and my words
    remain in you,
    ask for whatever you want and it will
    be done for you.
By this is my Father glorified,
    that you bear much fruit and become
    my disciples."

Reflecting on the Gospel

Today and next Sunday the gospel readings are from the Last Supper discourse of John. Chronologically, the Last Supper took place before Jesus's death and resurrection, yet we hear them after Easter. This is a reminder that we are not remembering and celebrating events in their strict historical sequence, but that we are immersed in a liturgical mix of time and timelessness; we are celebrating the mystery that is always and everywhere the reality of the resurrection of Jesus. As we listen to the Johannine account of the last meal of Jesus with his disciples, we are, here and now, at the table with Jesus and the community of disciples, tangling our lives with him, the true vine, and with the branches of all the baptized.

We hear much shouting of would-be people of power: fanatical tyrants, political agitators, self-righteous politicians. We may even add to this chorus our own small voices on matters personal, ecclesial, or social. But what Jesus speaks about at table is the power of love and of gentle growth. He gives us another image of the great intimacy and interdependence that exists between himself, his Father, and his disciples: "I am the true vine, and my Father is the vine grower"—and we are the branches.

The vine and vineyard were familiar images to the people of God in the Old Testament. Israel was the vine brought out of Egypt and planted by God the vine grower in its own soil (Ps 80:8-13). So significant was the image of the vine that on one facade of the Jerusalem temple sanctuary was carved an ornamental vine with golden clusters of grapes as big as a human hand. And the early Christian community painted the vine on the walls of the catacombs in memory of Christ, the true vine.

The image of the vine is a radically nonhierarchical image of the people of God, for all the branches are so intertwined that when looking at a vine it is almost impossible to tell where one branch begins and another ends. All tangle together as they grow from the central stock, undifferentiated by anything but their fruitfulness. Such is the relationship of Jesus to the new community that grows from his death and resurrection. Such communities are also to be branching out, hospitable communities that live by and bear fruit through the surging sap of Christ's risen life.

To remain healthy and productive the vine must be pruned by our vine grower God. Those in whom the baptismal sap rises have already been pruned by the words Jesus speaks, but we must continue to accept not only the short, sharp pain of God's snipping from our lives the small and withering infidelities, but also be willing to endure the longer agony of more drastic pruning that is sometimes necessary. This is not to make of the Vine Grower a ruthless tyrant, because what is done is done out of love for the vine. In his passion and death, the Christ who knew no sin was made sin for us (cf. 2 Cor 5:21), and suffered in faithful hope that most drastic pruning of his passion and death so that the branches of the vine, his community, might thrive through his resurrected life.

Sometimes what needs to be pruned in our lives is the parasite runner of individualism that wants to go its own way, or the sucker that feeds on self-interest; both draw life away from the vine. At other times, our vine-dressing God recognizes our potential for greater fruit-bearing, and with this the need for heavy pruning. After such pruning, a vine may bear no fruit for several years, but it remains rooted and waiting, confident in the tending of the Vine Grower, until both are rewarded with a tremendous, bursting yield. When we yield such a harvest of good works, says Jesus, we give glory to the Father and are confirmed in our discipleship.

Focusing the Gospel

Key words and phrases: "I am the vine, you are the branches."

To the point: Last week we pondered the image of Jesus as the Good Shepherd who tenderly cares for his sheep. This week we are given a new image in order to explore our relationship with the Lord, that of a vine and branches. Unlike a shepherd and his sheep, a vine and its branches cleave to each other in such a way that it is impossible to say where one ends and the other begins. This is the closeness Jesus desires to have with each of us—that his life-giving Spirit might flow from him to us as effortlessly as the sap of a healthy vine plant flows through the veins of the branch, allowing it to produce fruit.

Connecting the Gospel

to the second reading: In both the gospel and the second reading from St. John we are given a commandment over and over again: to "remain" in Jesus. Using the image of the true vine, Jesus likens his faithful disciples to branches securely connected to their parent plant. In remaining on the vine they are able to bear fruit, but separated from him they become like branches removed from the plant—without the nutrients brought up from the roots of the vine, they wither.

to experience: Today's gospel invites us to consider how we "remain" in Jesus, the true vine. The second reading from St. John, however, offers us one way to discern our own "remaining." He writes, "Those who keep [Jesus's] commandments, remain in him, and he in them." Instead of thinking of a laundry list of rules when considering the commandments, there is really only one St. John proposes that encompasses all others: the command to "love one another."

Connecting the Responsorial Psalm

to the readings: In today's first reading we continue on with the saga of the early church recorded in the Acts of the Apostles, this time focusing on Paul's journey of faith. In a shocking and dramatic conversion, Paul goes from persecutor of Christians to an apostle of Jesus. Though the other apostles are first afraid to accept him into their midst, they are finally convinced of his change of heart when they hear stories and witness his bold preaching "in the name of the Lord." The responsorial psalm is an apt description of Paul, eager to praise the Lord "in the assembly of your people." We can imagine Paul praying the final verse, "[T]o him my soul shall live," as he dedicates his life to preaching the gospel and sharing with others the salvation he has received.

to psalmist preparation: Within the assembly of God's people, you are blessed to proclaim the praises of the Lord. At this moment in time, where do you find the most joy in your ministry?

PROMPTS FOR FAITH-SHARING

In reading from the Acts of the Apostles, the disciples are at first fearful of Saul. On your journey as a Christian, who have you befriended whom you otherwise wouldn't have known or associated with?

St. John writes, "[L]et us love not in word or speech / but in deed and truth." In following Jesus's command to love others, where do your words not match your actions?

In today's gospel, the command to "remain" in Jesus is issued more than the exhortation to "bear fruit." What spiritual practices help you to "remain" rooted on the true vine?

What "fruits" are evident in yourself, your family, your community that give glory to God?

Model Rite for the Blessing and Sprinkling of Water

Presider: In baptism we have been grafted on to the true vine of Christ. By the sprinkling of this water, may we be strengthened to remain in him always and to bear much fruit for the glory of God . . . *[pause]*

　[continue with The Roman Missal, *Appendix II]*

Homily Points

• In the parable of the True Vine we are given many tools to help us think about the spiritual life. Jesus urges us to "remain" in him, for it is only in "remaining" that we will be able to "bear great fruit." In many ways, this offers us another way to look at morality. It is easy to think we are good people when we do good actions, think good thoughts, and feel good emotions by force of our own will. This is not how Jesus describes the religious life. Instead, he tells us that we will be truly righteous only through our connection with him, "because without me you can do nothing."

• Just as a branch clings to the vine and is able to bear fruit, the fruit of our own spiritual lives comes about not through our own labor, but from our rootedness in the Lord. Today's gospel invites us to ponder how we "remain" firmly connected to Jesus, our true vine. In our uniqueness, our way of "remaining" will very likely be different from those with whom we share our lives. The practice of remaining is not one that anyone can do for another; instead it is deeply personal, even as our remaining on the vine also connects us deeply to all the other branches we share it with.

• Just as Jesus is the vine and we are the branches, we are told that God the Father is "the vine grower." He tends the vine with compassion, pruning as needed to help it flourish. As we continue to live into the Easter mystery of the Lord who calls us to newness of life in him, let us consider how we are being pruned and how we are called to remain.

Model Universal Prayer (Prayer of the Faithful)

Presider: In today's second reading, St. John writes, "[W]e have confidence in God / and receive from him whatever we ask." In perfect trust, let us bring our needs before the Lord.

Response: Lord, hear our prayer.

For God's holy church, by remaining on the true vine may it bear great fruit for the glory of God and the service of all people . . .

For health care workers around the world, may they receive the support necessary to care for the sick and the ailing with skill and compassion . . .

For ex-convicts who have been released from prison, may they find meaningful employment to support themselves and their families . . .

For all gathered here, may we follow Jesus's commandment to love others in word and in deed . . .

Presider: God of peace, with tenderness and compassion you call us away from sin to the fullness of life in your presence. Hear our prayers that by your grace we might build communities where all will flourish and find welcome. We ask this through Christ our Lord. **Amen.**

COLLECT

Let us pray.

Pause for silent prayer

Almighty ever-living God,
constantly accomplish the Paschal
　　Mystery within us,
that those you were pleased to make new
　　in Holy Baptism
may, under your protective care, bear
　　much fruit
and come to the joys of life eternal.
Through our Lord Jesus Christ, your Son,
who lives and reigns with you in the unity
　　of the Holy Spirit,
one God, for ever and ever. **Amen.**

FIRST READING
Acts 9:26-31

When Saul arrived in Jerusalem he tried to
　　join the disciples,
　　but they were all afraid of him,
　　not believing that he was a disciple.
Then Barnabas took charge of him and
　　brought him to the apostles,
　　and he reported to them how he had
　　　　seen the Lord,
　　and that he had spoken to him,
　　and how in Damascus he had spoken
　　　　out boldly in the name of Jesus.
He moved about freely with them in
　　Jerusalem,
　　and spoke out boldly in the name of the
　　　　Lord.
He also spoke and debated with the
　　Hellenists,
　　but they tried to kill him.
And when the brothers learned of this,
　　they took him down to Caesarea
　　and sent him on his way to Tarsus.
The church throughout all Judea, Galilee,
　　and Samaria was at peace.
It was being built up and walked in the
　　fear of the Lord,
　　and with the consolation of the Holy
　　　　Spirit it grew in numbers.

RESPONSORIAL PSALM
Ps 22:26-27, 28, 30, 31-32

℟. (26a) I will praise you, Lord, in the
　　assembly of your people.
　　or:
℟. Alleluia.

I will fulfill my vows before those who fear
　　the LORD.
　　The lowly shall eat their fill;
they who seek the LORD shall praise him:
　　"May your hearts live forever!"

℟. I will praise you, Lord, in the assembly
　　of your people.
　　or:
℟. Alleluia.

All the ends of the earth
  shall remember and turn to the Lord;
all the families of the nations
  shall bow down before him.

R̷. I will praise you, Lord, in the assembly
  of your people.
    or:
R̷. Alleluia.

To him alone shall bow down
  all who sleep in the earth;
before him shall bend
  all who go down into the dust.

R̷. I will praise you, Lord, in the assembly
  of your people.
    or:
R̷. Alleluia.

And to him my soul shall live;
  my descendants shall serve him.
Let the coming generation be told of the
  Lord
  that they may proclaim to a people yet
    to be born
  the justice he has shown.

R̷. I will praise you, Lord, in the assembly
  of your people.
    or:
R̷. Alleluia.

SECOND READING
1 John 3:18-24

Children, let us love not in word or speech
  but in deed and truth.
Now this is how we shall know that we
    belong to the truth
  and reassure our hearts before him
  in whatever our hearts condemn,
  for God is greater than our hearts and
    knows everything.
Beloved, if our hearts do not condemn us,
  we have confidence in God
  and receive from him whatever we ask,
  because we keep his commandments
    and do what pleases him.
And his commandment is this:
  we should believe in the name of his
    Son, Jesus Christ,
  and love one another just as he
    commanded us.
Those who keep his commandments
    remain in him, and he in them,
  and the way we know that he remains
    in us
  is from the Spirit he gave us.

CATECHESIS

About Liturgy

Pruning the Vine: Is the hectic pace brought about by the continuing Eastertide colliding with the month of May starting to take its toll yet? Along with the usual Sunday to Sunday routines, the church asks us to offer mystagogia to the neophytes and to help our younger parishioners encounter the Lord and complete their own initiations through First Eucharist and confirmation. Your parish school might have you preparing for year-end celebrations, a matrimony rush is just about to begin, and of course there are three funerals this week. None of this accounts for any of the off-of-church-property events of the season we all need to attend to this time of year. It can get overwhelming very quickly, with little end in sight. Is that the light at the end of the tunnel, or the train coming to run me over?

Today's gospel offers some lessons for liturgical ministers, especially those charged with great responsibilities of one sort or another this time of year. First, Jesus reminds us that sometimes his Father prunes the vine, so that it may bear more fruit. If you are feeling particularly stretched this year, it may be time for some pruning. A time of stress and anxiety is not conducive to clear-headed decision-making, so consider starting a list, perhaps on a smartphone or a little notebook in a pocket or purse, of your various responsibilities and tasks each day. In a month or two, take a look at that list and try to find opportunities to prune the vine. A reminder: pruning may not be completely up to you, and pruning the vine will almost always initially be painful. Who do you need to speak with about these things? Be prepared for some initial pain in the midst of the pruning as well, trusting the Lord that more abundant fruit lies ahead.

It may be that it seems impossible in your current context to prune the vine. Perhaps you are in a paid ministerial role that is too demanding of time and resources, but yet the job description places all the various responsibilities on your shoulders. Or, perhaps, whether paid or volunteer, you place all of the burden on your own shoulders. If the reasons for that are along the lines of "When I do it myself, I can do it quicker, and I can do it better," it is likely past time to evaluate your ability to delegate, to multitask on projects, and to make better use of the main resource available to you—God's people in your very community.

With some amount of "heavy lifting" at the outset, setting in place a networked, trained, and empowered team of ministry coordinators can very much lighten the load on any one person and help give a sense of ownership and mission to a larger percentage of the parishioners. There are many ways to tackle any responsibility and ensure that an array of ministry goals are met. The path that includes and enlarges the Body of Christ will never be the wrong one to take, if traveled carefully and honestly.

About Music

Music of the Vine: Trevor Thompson has of late given the church much music with some influences from Native Americans. His "Vine and Branches" (OCP) is one of these that not only speaks to today's gospel and epistle, but in its fullness will hearken back to the Triduum, especially Holy Thursday. "We Have Been Told" (GIA) by David Haas is a perennial favorite as well, appropriate for this Sunday or the Sixth Sunday of Easter this year.

SPIRITUALITY

GOSPEL ACCLAMATION
John 14:23

℟. Alleluia, alleluia.
Whoever loves me will keep my word, says the
    Lord,
and my Father will love him and we will come
    to him.
℟. Alleluia, alleluia.

Gospel

John 15:9-17; L56B

Jesus said to his
    disciples:
"As the Father loves me,
    so I also love you.
Remain in my love.
If you keep my
    commandments, you
    will remain in my
    love,
    just as I have kept
        my Father's
        commandments
    and remain in his love.

"I have told you this so
    that my joy may be
    in you
and your joy might be complete.
This is my commandment: love one
    another as I love you.
No one has greater love than this,
    to lay down one's life for one's
        friends.
You are my friends if you do what I
    command you.
I no longer call you slaves,
    because a slave does not know what
        his master is doing.
I have called you friends,
    because I have told you everything I
        have heard from my Father.
It was not you who chose me, but I who
    chose you
    and appointed you to go and bear
        fruit that will remain,
    so that whatever you ask the Father
        in my name he may give you.
This I command you: love one another."

Reflecting on the Gospel

The heartbeat of today's gospel and of the second reading from 1 John is "love." As disciples, we are called to feel this pulse and make our lives beat in rhythm with it. The love commandment that Jesus gives to his disciples depends on God's limitless love for the world (John 3:16). This love is made incarnate and dwells among us in Jesus, the one who is "close to the Father's heart" (John 1:18; NRSV), and so Jesus's own relationship with his Father, his own life and death, become the norm of the costly love he asks of his disciples. This must not be a cramped or grudging love, but joyful and expansive, encompassing the world for which Jesus was sent.

One of the most priceless human gifts is friendship. It allows us to disclose ourselves to and receive from another in complete openness and trust. With a friend we can think aloud; participate in one another's joys and sorrows, hopes and fears; survive loneliness, indifference, hostility. Small wonder, then, that in today's gospel Jesus calls his disciples by this most precious of names: "my friends." Drawn into and abiding in the mutual love of the Father and the Son, disciples are no longer called servants but friends.

The Johannine community was to live as friends and so, throughout his gospel, John introduces us to various occasions of friendship: John the Baptist, the precursor and "the friend of the bridegroom" (John 3:29; NRSV) who, like a best man, hands over the bride Israel to Jesus; the family at Bethany, especially Lazarus, the friend for whom he wept at his grave and for whom Jesus was the tomb breaker (John 11:35-44); Pilate, who at a critical moment preferred to be a friend of Caesar rather than Jesus (John 19:12); the disciple beloved of Jesus (John 13:23; 19:26; 21:7); and Peter, the forgiven friend who will lead and shepherd the community of the forgiven (John 21:44ff.). As we gather around the table of our eucharistic supper, we hear that we have been chosen by Jesus as his friends and commissioned to befriend the world in and with the love he has shown us.

The most startling, profound, yet simple naming of God is proclaimed in the reading from the First Letter of John: "God is love." The letter is addressed to the "[b]eloved," those with whom God has taken the initiative, who are parented by God's love, and this self-giving love is the source of human love. Like today's gospel whose heartbeat is love, so love beats strongly in this reading—named nine times in its four verses. It is love that is expansive and global, yet also intimate and personal, revealed most fully in Jesus, the Son of God and our brother.

In a remarkable photographic event, at the turn of the millennium invitations were sent to 192 countries inviting photographers to submit entries that captured and celebrated the essence of humanity's "Moments of Intimacy, Laughter and Kinship." Ultimately, seventeen thousand photographers from 164 countries entered with over forty thousand photographs. As well as becoming an international traveling exhibition, the winning photographs are published as three incredible books entitled *Family*, *Friendship*, and *Love*. As love always does, the images reach across all continents and races, youth and age, poverty and affluence, to reveal the heart of humanity and, surely, the heart of God.

The viewer has no idea if the God of Jesus Christ is known or unknown to the 6-year-old "policeman" in the slums of Calcutta who is holding up his hand to stop the traffic so that three blind men, their hands on one another's shoulders, can safely cross the road; whether any prayers are being murmured by the 84-year-old woman saying goodbye to her dying 92-year-old friend; or what is the faith of the parents welcoming their womb-wet, wailing newborn. But the Christian gazing on these photographs, or on such realities in our everyday lives, can surely say: "God is love."

Focusing the Gospel

Key words and phrases: "I have told you this so that my joy may be in you."

To the point: Today's gospel comes from Jesus's discourse at the Last Supper in John's gospel. Last Sunday we pondered the first half of the parable of the True Vine, and this week we contemplate the second part. While enjoining his disciples to follow the commandments, love one another, remain in him, and bear fruit for the glory of God, Jesus reminds them that his words are not to burden them with excess worries or tasks, but instead are intended for the fullness of their joy.

Connecting the Gospel

to the first reading: In today's gospel, Jesus commissions the disciples "to go and bear fruit that will remain." For the first ten chapters of the Acts of the Apostles, we find Jesus's followers bringing the good news of his life, death, and resurrection to their fellow Jews, but now, with the baptism of Cornelius and his household in the first reading, a new (and fruitful) ministry is inaugurated to the Gentiles. Though Peter's question ("Can anyone withhold the water for baptizing these people, / who have received the Holy Spirit even as we have?") might seem hypothetical, at the time this baptism brought both a legal and a spiritual risk. Before preaching to Cornelius and his family, Peter tells them, "You know that it is unlawful for a Jewish man to associate with, or visit, a Gentile" (Acts 10:28; NABRE). Fear of disapproval from his fellow Christians or the law does not dissuade Peter from his proclamation of the gospel. He has been enjoined by Jesus to "make disciples of all nations" (Matt 28:19; NABRE) and he will do so.

to experience: In his faithfulness to the actions of the Holy Spirit, Peter welcomes Cornelius, a Roman centurion, and his family into the body of Christ through baptism, proclaiming, "In truth, I see that God shows no partiality. / Rather, in every nation whoever fears him and acts uprightly / is acceptable to him." How does your parish community reflect this attitude of inclusivity and respect for different nationalities, cultures, and ethnicities?

Connecting the Responsorial Psalm

to the readings: Today's psalm invokes us to "[s]ing to the Lord a new song." Peter's actions in the Acts of the Apostles leads to a new age in the life of the church and within the history of salvation as both Jews and Gentiles join together in Jesus to praise and worship the living God.

to psalmist preparation: St. Augustine famously addressed God as the one who is "ever ancient, ever new." Our faith calls us to a dynamic tension between these seemingly opposing truths of our Creator, and away from statically clinging to tradition when God is calling us to newness in the spiritual life. Where is your community being challenged to "sing a new song"?

Model Rite for the Blessing and Sprinkling of Water

Presider: Baptized into the death and resurrection of the Lord, we have become members of the Body of Christ. By the sprinkling of this water, may we be enlivened by his love and confirmed in his charity . . . *[pause]*

    [continue with The Roman Missal, *Appendix II]*

Homily Points

• This Sunday we ponder the second half of Jesus's parable of the True Vine from John's gospel. Jesus speaks these words during the Last Supper as he prepares his disciples for what is to come—the fear and heartache of his passion and death, as well as the mystery of his resurrection. Jesus calls for his disciples to "remain" in him just as a healthy branch is connected to the vine, the source of its sustenance. Today, Jesus's words are even more explicit; not only are we to remain in *him*, Jesus commands his followers: "Remain in my love."

• As Christians, we become like a branch that has withered when we are cut off from the life-giving love of Christ. Without his love to sustain them, our acts of service and commitment to living in righteousness become tinged with bitterness, anxiety, and scrupulosity. Jesus reminds us that his teachings are not intended as a burden but instead are a gift so that "[his] joy might be in [us], and [our] joy might be complete."

• Throughout our lives of faith, Jesus calls us to constant conversion. Continually we must realign ourselves away from darkness and toward light, away from anger and hatred to love, and away from despair and bitterness to hope and joy. Today's Scripture passages offer us a simple way to check in with our progress along the spiritual path. What is the state of our joy? What is the state of our love? If we find ourselves lacking in either of these areas, Jesus offers us an invitation. We need not turn away in shame and guilt, but instead only let ourselves experience the peace of God as we rest in the love of Jesus, the true vine.

Model Universal Prayer (Prayer of the Faithful)

Presider: With concern for the needs of our world and faith in God's healing and saving power, let us bring our petitions before the Lord.

Response: Lord, hear our prayer.

For Christians throughout the world, may they dwell in peace with each other and with members of other faiths . . .

For all areas of the earth affected by natural and human-made disasters, may governments respond with concern for the common good and compassion for victims . . .

For police officers, firefighters, and first responders, may they be safe in the line of duty and find joy and fulfillment in their work . . .

For all gathered here, may Jesus's commandment "Love one another" be the foundation from which all of our actions and words spring forth . . .

Presider: Merciful God, in power and majesty you created the universe and all it contains. Hear our prayers that we might reverently care for all that you have made. We ask this through Christ our Lord. **Amen.**

COLLECT

Let us pray.

Pause for silent prayer

Grant, almighty God,
that we may celebrate with heartfelt
    devotion these days of joy,
which we keep in honor of the risen Lord,
and that what we relive in remembrance
we may always hold to in what we do.
Through our Lord Jesus Christ, your Son,
who lives and reigns with you in the unity
    of the Holy Spirit,
one God, for ever and ever. **Amen.**

FIRST READING

Acts 10:25-26, 34-35, 44-48

When Peter entered, Cornelius met him
    and, falling at his feet, paid him
      homage.
Peter, however, raised him up, saying,
    "Get up. I myself am also a human
      being."

Then Peter proceeded to speak and said,
    "In truth, I see that God shows no
      partiality.
Rather, in every nation whoever fears him
    and acts uprightly
is acceptable to him."

While Peter was still speaking these
    things,
the Holy Spirit fell upon all who were
    listening to the word.
The circumcised believers who had
    accompanied Peter
    were astounded that the gift of the Holy
      Spirit
    should have been poured out on the
      Gentiles also,
    for they could hear them speaking in
      tongues and glorifying God.
Then Peter responded,
    "Can anyone withhold the water for
      baptizing these people,
    who have received the Holy Spirit even
      as we have?"
He ordered them to be baptized in the
    name of Jesus Christ.

RESPONSORIAL PSALM
Ps 98:1, 2-3, 3-4

℟. (cf. 2b) The Lord has revealed to the
 nations his saving power.
 or:
℟. Alleluia.

Sing to the LORD a new song,
 for he has done wondrous deeds;
his right hand has won victory for him,
 his holy arm.

℟. The Lord has revealed to the nations
 his saving power.
 or:
℟. Alleluia.

The LORD has made his salvation known:
 in the sight of the nations he has
 revealed his justice.
He has remembered his kindness and his
 faithfulness
 toward the house of Israel.

℟. The Lord has revealed to the nations
 his saving power.
 or:
℟. Alleluia.

All the ends of the earth have seen
 the salvation by our God.
Sing joyfully to the LORD, all you lands;
 break into song; sing praise.

℟. The Lord has revealed to the nations
 his saving power.
 or:
℟. Alleluia.

SECOND READING
1 John 4:7-10

Beloved, let us love one another,
 because love is of God;
 everyone who loves is begotten by God
 and knows God.
Whoever is without love does not know
 God, for God is love.
In this way the love of God was revealed
 to us:
 God sent his only Son into the world
 so that we might have life through him.
In this is love:
 not that we have loved God, but that he
 loved us
 and sent his Son as expiation for our sins.

*Or, where the Ascension is celebrated on
Sunday, the second reading and gospel for
the Seventh Sunday of Easter may be used
on this Sunday.*

1 John 4:11-16, p. 135.

John 17:11b-19, p. 132.

About Liturgy

Proclaiming the Right Words: The Lectionary begins this week not with a Scripture passage, but with . . . let's call it a warning: "When the Ascension of the Lord is celebrated the following Sunday, the second reading and Gospel from the Seventh Sunday of Easter (see nos. 59–61) may be read on the Sixth Sunday of Easter" (56B).

If you have any responsibility for lectors over this next score of days, it's imperative to clearly communicate the correct readings for each celebration (Sixth Sunday of Easter, Ascension, Seventh Sunday of Easter, and Pentecost Vigil and Pentecost). If you give these ministers some sort of preparatory workbook, your communication becomes even more important. Due to the vagaries of the liturgical calendar from diocese to diocese this time of year, along with the legitimate choices day by day each local parish can make, mishaps can and will occur. These preparation books can be confusing to navigate, as they offer every conceivable option for every place and time. Be clear: which date, which exact Scripture reference, which lectionary number, which page in the preparation workbook—perhaps even include the first few words of each passage. Any amount of seemingly redundant communication, with a few words explaining why you are being so redundant, will help alleviate any possible Sunday morning misadventures.

I would note here that, for the average pew-dweller each Sunday, if you have some sort of participation aid, it would be best for their prayerful participation to stay with whichever readings the booklet lays out for you. Even though it is preferable that the Word of God be listened to—and only listened to—attentively, there is little anyone can do to keep a congregant from reading along in some missalette. In fact, there may be a good reason, such as hearing loss, for them to do so. Choosing to use, for instance, on this Sunday the epistle or gospel from the Seventh Sunday would likely cause more chaos and confusion, even if there are strong pastoral reasons to make such a switch.

About the Lectionary

A Rich Treasury Opened: It is quite significant in our liturgical and spiritual lives that the Lectionary was revised following the decrees of Vatican II. The most relevant of these is this: "The treasures of the bible are to be opened up more lavishly so that a richer fare may be provided for the faithful at the table of God's word. In this way a more significant part of the sacred scriptures will be read to the people over a fixed number of years" (Constitution on the Sacred Liturgy 51).

Comparing our current Lectionary to the preconciliar one, an entire universe of Scripture was opened to our hearing. The former Lectionary contained nearly no Scripture from the Old Testament; of the New Testament, less than 20 percent of verses from the Gospels, Acts, and Epistles were heard during the year—and never anything from Revelation! Today's Lectionary has a three-year Sunday cycle and a two-year weekday cycle, along with readings proper for various feasts and occasions, which present to us over three thousand verses of Scripture from the Old Testament and well over 70 percent of the New Testament.

About Music

Scripture Elsewhere at Mass: Some will note that the Liturgy of the Word is only one place we find Scripture at liturgy: the prayers of the liturgy often have scriptural underpinnings ("[E]nter under my roof . . ." [Matt 8:8; NABRE]) and the various antiphons are almost entirely scriptural as well. While those picking hymnody week to week give much if not sole attention to the Scripture proclaimed, don't forget to also study and pray with the prescribed prayers and antiphons of each celebration. Doing so may provide unexpected insights and point you toward unanticipated musical treasures!

SPIRITUALITY

R꙼. Alleluia, alleluia.
Go and teach all nations, says the Lord;
I am with you always, until the end of the world.
R꙼. Alleluia, alleluia.

Gospel   Mark 16:15-20; L58B

Jesus said to his disciples:
"Go into the whole world
   and proclaim the gospel to every
     creature.
Whoever believes and is baptized will be
   saved;
   whoever does not believe will be
     condemned.
These signs will accompany those who
   believe:
   in my name they will drive out demons,
   they will speak new languages.
They will pick up serpents with their
   hands,
   and if they drink any deadly thing, it
     will not harm them.
They will lay hands on the sick, and they
   will recover."

So then the Lord Jesus, after he spoke to
   them,
   was taken up into heaven
   and took his seat at the right hand of God.
But they went forth and preached
   everywhere,
   while the Lord worked with them
   and confirmed the word through
     accompanying signs.

Reflecting on the Gospel

While the 1969 reform of the church's liturgical calendar retained the feast of the Ascension in the Easter season, the integrity of the fifty postresurrection days, the "Great Sunday," has been restored to the status it enjoyed in the early church. The Ascension is one of the many-faceted Easter jewels that crown the liturgical year, and today's readings reflect this light. In favor of this integrity, in most places the feast of the Ascension has been transferred from the forty-day interrupting marker of "Ascension Thursday" to the Seventh Sunday of Easter, and symbolically the paschal candle is no longer extinguished on the Ascension but continues to be lit until Pentecost Sunday.

In their different ways, all the gospel writers want us to appreciate the threshold moment of Jesus's exaltation into heaven. Luke ends his gospel with one account of the ascension of Jesus happening on the evening of Easter day, and begins the second part of his good news, the Acts of the Apostles, with another account forty days later. Perhaps Luke is using these two accounts to stitch together the farewell reality of Jesus in his glorified humanity (Luke 24:50-53) and the mission of the church, his Body, which in his Spirit must continue his presence and work in the world (Acts 1:9-11). Luke addresses the Acts of the Apostles to "Theophilus" ("Lover of God"), perhaps a patron of the early Christian community. Gathered today around the Word, we are also the intended readers, all called to be "lovers of God."

Mark narrates that Jesus is risen. He has appeared to his followers during forty days—a biblical number symbolic of both fullness and transition—and has instructed them about the promised coming of the Holy Spirit. He explains this coming in baptismal terms. Water had been the baptismal medium of the Baptist, but this new baptism will be in the outpouring of the Holy Spirit. So the disciples wait for this unimagined and unimaginable outpouring, still captive to curiosity about times, dates, the possible relationship of Israel to the kingdom about which Jesus has so often spoken, and an implied hankering for knowledge of their own positions in this kingdom. Jesus deflects their desire for such answers into a concern for mission—the witness to him that the disciples will be called and empowered to give beyond Jerusalem, beyond Judaea and Samaria, to the very ends of the earth. The disciples are still a wounded community, wounded by Judas's treachery, by Peter's betrayal, and by their own cowardice. Yet it is in the midst of such failure, false expectations, and incorrigible personal ambitions and wishes for quick solutions, that Jesus will call them to mission.

For some reason, the Lectionary omits verse 14 from today's reading of the "longer ending" (and third postresurrection appearance of Jesus) of Mark's gospel. It is considered an inspired but later addition to Mark 16:8, for the comfort and strengthening of the communities on mission. And so as we gather liturgically around the table, we may not realize that Jesus's commission to go and proclaim the Good News of his resurrection to the whole of creation is also given to the wounded Eleven "at table." Nor do we hear how Jesus upbraids them for their lack of faith and stubbornness—something that is surely a great consolation for ourselves as wounded, struggling disciples in whom the flame of missionary desire can flicker or even be extinguished. Yet like the Eleven, we are also people entrusted with the mission of proclaiming the gospel now that the physical presence of Jesus has ascended to heaven and is no longer with us. We too are sent to do new wonders, speak new words with the fire of the Spirit on our tongues, offer new healing to our sisters and brothers, and cast out contemporary "demons" from ourselves and others. And all this continues to be "in the name of," in the personal power of Jesus into whose Body we are baptized.

Focusing the Gospel

Key words and phrases: [W]hile the Lord worked with them.

To the point: In today's gospel the disciples are ushered into a new era of the history of salvation. They had grown accustomed to following their friend and teacher as he preached to the crowds of the kingdom of God, and to looking on with astonishment and joy as he healed those broken in mind, body, and spirit. Now they watch as he is "taken up into heaven." Though Jesus has disappeared from sight, his presence has not left them. Now the apostles are the ones who will pray with and lay hands on those who seek healing and forgiveness of sins, and through the power of the Lord "working with them" these things will be accomplished.

Connecting the Gospel

to the first reading: In both the gospel and the first reading, we find an account of the moment of Christ's ascension into heaven. In both passages Jesus commissions the disciples for the work that will give meaning and urgency to the rest of their lives. In the Acts of the Apostles, they are named "witnesses in Jerusalem, / throughout Judea and Samaria, / and to the ends of the earth," while in Mark's gospel Jesus commands his friends to "[g]o into the whole world / and proclaim the gospel to every creature." Although the news of Jesus's life, death, and resurrection will not reach the entire world by the time of the last apostle's death, their preaching, healing, and acts of charity hold the seed, planted in fertile soil, that will lead to far-reaching fruit.

to experience: Now the gospel has been entrusted to us. Despite the widespread nature of Christianity, there are many (oftentimes within our own families and communities) who have not yet fully encountered the living Christ through word and sacrament. How can we witness to Christ's life and love in the way that we live and the words that we speak?

Connecting the Responsorial Psalm

to the readings: The wonders of the risen Lord continue to astonish and amaze the apostles. Not only has Jesus overcome the finality of death, now he is "taken up into heaven" where he "[takes] his seat at the right hand of God." Today's psalm is an apt response for those first apostles, and also for us modern-day disciples, as we reflect on the mystery of the ascension. The psalmist sings, "For the Lord, the Most High, the awesome, / is the great king over all the earth." Due to its everyday use, the term "awesome" might have begun to lose its significance for most of us. Literally, the word means "to inspire awe." Biblically, we can see it as one of the gifts of the Holy Spirit, "awe and wonder," which is sometimes translated as "fear of the Lord."

to psalmist preparation: How do you seek to cultivate a sense of awe and wonder in your own life and especially when encountering the divine?

PROMPTS FOR FAITH-SHARING

In the first reading, Jesus instructs the apostles to return to Jerusalem and "wait for 'the promise of the Father.'" What promise of God's are you waiting on to be fulfilled?

Today's psalm incites us to "[s]ing praise to God, sing praise." What are you currently praising God for in your own life?

In the gospel we hear that Jesus, seated at the right hand of God, continues to "work with" the disciples as they preach and do good works. How do you experience Jesus's presence working with you in ministry?

Model Rite for the Blessing and Sprinkling of Water

Presider: In baptism we were plunged into the life of God the Father, the Son, and the Holy Spirit. By the sprinkling of this water, may we be strengthened to live always as children of the light . . . *[pause]*

    [continue with The Roman Missal, *Appendix II]*

Homily Points

• On the feast of the Ascension we remember Jesus's words to his closest friends before he was taken up to heaven: "Go into the whole world / and proclaim the gospel to every creature." Today these words are addressed to us as the members of the Body of Christ alive in the world. For the apostles, this commissioning meant introducing people to the person of the risen Lord, the vast majority of which had never heard the name Jesus of Nazareth. As they walked this path the apostles met with persecution and (for almost all of them) eventually martyrdom. In a way, for those of us who live in countries where Christianity is a protected religion, our journey as disciples doesn't seem anywhere near as difficult or dangerous.

• In the past two thousand years many places in the world have encountered an initial proclamation of the gospel, and yet in some ways that can be an obstacle for us as we endeavor to be "witnesses" to the good news. While our history includes many saints, there are also those who have repelled others from Christianity by their actions and words. In an interview with a Christian missionary, Mahatma Gandhi was asked, "[T]hough you quote the words of Christ often, why is it that you so adamantly reject becoming his follower?" To this, Gandhi reportedly replied, "Oh, I don't reject your Christ. I love your Christ. It is just that so many of you Christians are so unlike your Christ."

• Jesus has called us to witness to his life, death, and resurrection. Our words about his love that is stronger than hatred and his light that is stronger than darkness will mean nothing if they are not also echoed in the way we live our lives.

Model Universal Prayer (Prayer of the Faithful)

Presider: With praise and thanksgiving for all God has done for us, let us confidently place our needs before him.

Response: Lord, hear our prayer.

For all who preach the gospel, may their words lead others to fullness of life in Christ . . .

For indigenous peoples around the world, may their cultures, languages, and human rights be safeguarded . . .

For all who struggle to pay for necessary medical procedures and medications, may communities and governments work together to care for their needs . . .

For all gathered here, may we take on the role of witness to the risen Lord and joyfully proclaim the good works God has done in our own lives . . .

Presider: God of wisdom, your son Jesus ascended into heaven and sits at your right hand interceding for us. Hear our prayers that the eyes of our hearts might be opened to the riches of your glory and the hope of your call. We ask this through Christ our Lord. **Amen.**

COLLECT

Let us pray.

Pause for silent prayer

Gladden us with holy joys, almighty God,
and make us rejoice with devout
    thanksgiving,
for the Ascension of Christ your Son
is our exaltation,
and, where the Head has gone before in
    glory,
the Body is called to follow in hope.
Through our Lord Jesus Christ, your Son,
who lives and reigns with you in the unity
    of the Holy Spirit,
one God, for ever and ever. **Amen.**

FIRST READING

Acts 1:1-11

In the first book, Theophilus,
    I dealt with all that Jesus did and taught
    until the day he was taken up,
    after giving instructions through the
        Holy Spirit
    to the apostles whom he had chosen.
He presented himself alive to them
    by many proofs after he had suffered,
    appearing to them during forty days
    and speaking about the kingdom of
        God.
While meeting with them,
    he enjoined them not to depart from
        Jerusalem,
    but to wait for "the promise of the
        Father
    about which you have heard me speak;
    for John baptized with water,
    but in a few days you will be baptized
        with the Holy Spirit."

When they had gathered together they
        asked him,
    "Lord, are you at this time going to
        restore the kingdom to Israel?"
He answered them, "It is not for you to
        know the times or seasons
    that the Father has established by his
        own authority.
But you will receive power when the Holy
        Spirit comes upon you,
    and you will be my witnesses in
        Jerusalem,
    throughout Judea and Samaria,
    and to the ends of the earth."
When he had said this, as they were
        looking on,
    he was lifted up, and a cloud took him
        from their sight.

While they were looking intently at the
  sky as he was going,
  suddenly two men dressed in white
    garments stood beside them.
They said, "Men of Galilee,
  why are you standing there looking at
    the sky?
This Jesus who has been taken up from
  you into heaven
  will return in the same way as you have
    seen him going into heaven."

RESPONSORIAL PSALM
Ps 47:2-3, 6-7, 8-9

R. (6) God mounts his throne to shouts of
  joy: a blare of trumpets for the Lord.
  or:
R. Alleluia.

All you peoples, clap your hands,
  shout to God with cries of gladness,
for the LORD, the Most High, the awesome,
  is the great king over all the earth.

R. God mounts his throne to shouts of joy:
  a blare of trumpets for the Lord.
  or:
R. Alleluia.

God mounts his throne amid shouts of joy;
  the LORD, amid trumpet blasts.
Sing praise to God, sing praise;
  sing praise to our king, sing praise.

R. God mounts his throne to shouts of joy:
  a blare of trumpets for the Lord.
  or:
R. Alleluia.

For king of all the earth is God;
  sing hymns of praise.
God reigns over the nations,
  God sits upon his holy throne.

R. God mounts his throne to shouts of joy:
  a blare of trumpets for the Lord.
  or:
R. Alleluia.

SECOND READING
Eph 1:17-23

or Eph 4:1-13

or Eph 4:1-7, 11-13

See Appendix A, p. 292.

CATECHESIS

About Liturgy

Already, Not Yet: At home, a few years ago, my wife and I were getting some land-scaping done. The backyard always was a bit of a jungle—an empty and not well-maintained rectangle that was not real usable space for us. But we were finally able to put some attention and money into it. We re-created a parking space and a gate off the alley, added a storage shed, a patio area of pavers, and had the whole thing leveled and laid down sod. It seemed like we were then done.

But we weren't. My wife has, for many years now, longed for the day when she might have a pool in the backyard again, after spending many of her childhood years with one right off the back deck. Since we both work, generally speaking, for the church, we have limited means, but a small pool is actually not out of the question. Yet it has not arrived even now, and it may still be some time—we will probably have to wait for another round of end-of-the-season sales to get the best deal we can, which will mean another summer without a pool in the backyard.

So, while our backyard appeared to be finished, it really wasn't and won't be, until some unknown time in the future. Life in the church is like that as well—seemingly complete at times, but not really finished yet, and unlikely to be so until some unknown time down the road.

We celebrate now Jesus's ascension and will soon celebrate the coming of the Spirit at Pentecost. Jesus's death and resurrection earned for us a new life and a "New Jeru-salem," but we're not there yet. Jesus's ascension and the arrival of the Spirit show us that same thing—where he has gone, we one day hope to follow—but not yet. "Already, not yet" is one of the overlooked paradoxes of our Christian faith. This odd in-between time is hard to wrap our heads around. To wit: most of us view heaven as the ultimate and final destination of our souls, but that's only because that's what it's been for 2,000 years. Your grandparents (or even parents) might have had to memorize this answer from the Baltimore Catechism once upon a time: "God made me to know Him, to love Him, and to serve Him in this world, *and* to be happy with Him for ever in heaven" (Q6, emphasis added). But wait—isn't that ultimate goal, as recited in the Creed every Sun-day, the resurrection of the dead *and* the life of the world to come?

It feels, sometimes, as if our church has lost that sense of expectation after all this time. Do we, like the early apostles might have, glance up at each passing cloud and wonder, is this the one that is bringing Jesus back to us? When will Christ come again? Is it today? Am I ready? These are the sorts of things we pray over at the end of each church year and into Advent as well—but this is also a perfect time to reexamine our lives and our faith. Are you ready? How can you be more ready? How can we lead our assemblies to more deeply ponder these serious questions?

About Music

Let Music Arise: "Hail the Day That Sees Him (Christ) Rise" is a familiar traditional hymn found in many hymnals; WLP has a rewritten text by Melvin Farrell, "Let the Earth Rejoice and Sing" to the same tune, LLANFAIR. Consider "Rise Up, O Lord" from the *Psallite* (Liturgical Press) collection as well.

SPIRITUALITY

GOSPEL ACCLAMATION
cf. John 14:18

R̸. Alleluia, alleluia.
I will not leave you orphans, says the Lord.
I will come back to you, and your hearts
  will rejoice.
R̸. Alleluia, alleluia.

Gospel

John 17:11b-19; L60B

Lifting up his eyes to heaven,
  Jesus prayed, saying:
"Holy Father, keep them in
    your name that you have
    given me,
  so that they may be one just as
    we are one.
When I was with them I
    protected them in your name
    that you gave me,
  and I guarded them, and none
    of them was lost
  except the son of destruction,
  in order that the Scripture
    might be fulfilled.
But now I am coming to you.
I speak this in the world
  so that they may share my joy
    completely.
I gave them your word, and the world
    hated them,
  because they do not belong to the
    world
  any more than I belong to the world.
I do not ask that you take them out of
    the world
  but that you keep them from the evil
    one.
They do not belong to the world
  any more than I belong to the world.
Consecrate them in the truth. Your
    word is truth.
As you sent me into the world,
  so I sent them into the world.
And I consecrate myself for them,
  so that they also may be consecrated
    in truth."

Reflecting on the Gospel

The first reading captures the meaning of today's liturgical celebration. Matthias, not one of the original followers of Jesus, is chosen to be "a witness to his resurrection." From Easter to Pentecost all the readings in effect present different aspects of what it means to be such a witness.

The gospel concludes the Johannine farewell discourses with a selection from what has been called "the Testament of Jesus," or his "high priestly prayer," one long prayer to his Father, so powerful and so poignant that it should be read in its entirety. The Lectionary excerpt is poorly chosen, since the prayer has three units: Jesus's prayer for himself (17:1-5), for his disciples (vv. 6-19), and for future believers (vv. 20-26). Among nonbiblical Jewish writings slightly earlier or contemporary with the New Testament, there is a collection called *Testaments of the Twelve Patriarchs*, or of Moses, narratives of the deaths of the great founding figures of Israel. These bid farewell to their loved ones, speaking of how God touched their lives and warning them of dangers they face. This literary genre has clearly influenced John 17. We are invited to listen as Jesus, whose death is imminent, gives voice to his deepest hopes for his loved ones.

Jesus prays that the disciples may experience that unity he shares with his Father, that they may share in his joy, and that they will be consecrated in truth. Jesus also prays for their protection in a hostile world. His own life is a paradigm for the lives of believers. He comes from above, from presence with God, to an alien world that does not accept him, and then returns to the Father. The believer, in John, is born from above (1:12-13; 3:3), lives in a hostile and alien world (15:18-19; 16:33; 17:14, 16, 18); and, as Jesus returns to the Father, the destiny of his followers is to be with him (12:26; 14:2-3, 13).

The ambiguity of "the world" echoes throughout John. It was made "through him" (the Word) but did not recognize him (1:10-11). Jesus takes away the sin of the world, and God so loved the world that he gave his only Son; he is the living Bread that will be the life of the world (6:51). Yet "the world" often symbolizes the power of evil organized against Jesus and his followers (see especially 3:19; 15:18-19). Though other New Testament writings have a more positive attitude toward the world, and though the contemporary church is summoned to be engaged in the world and to discern the manifestations of goodness among non-Christians, in John, Jesus and the disciples come to the world not to change it but to challenge its values. The mission should not be lost amid the contemporary change of attitude.

Jesus asks his Father also to "[c]onsecrate them [literally 'make them holy'] in the truth." Holiness in the Bible is not primarily a moral category but is a way of speaking about living in the presence of God. It is more similar to a "zone" or "marked-off area," than a personal disposition. Disciples are to operate in this zone, which is also "in the truth." The Greek term for "truth," *aletheia*, means "unconcealment" or "revelation," removal of a veil, and in John refers principally to the unveiling or revelation of God in the life and teaching of Jesus (1:14,

17; 14:6, "I am the truth"). Jesus prays that the disciples will live in a zone of God's presence (holiness) as they faithfully witness to the truth of his life.

The readings this Sunday before Pentecost provide a bridge between the continued celebration of the resurrection and yearning for God's Spirit, which will come only after the departure of Jesus. Jesus's prayer anticipates the coming of the Spirit of truth (14:7; 15:26). Today—after years of deplorable accounts of sexual and financial abuse in the church—this final wish of Jesus that his Father make the church holy in truth has a dramatic relevance.

Focusing the Gospel

Key words and phrases: "[T]hey may be one just as we are one."

To the point: On both the Fifth and Sixth Sundays of Easter we read from the "Last Supper Discourses" of Jesus (John 13:31–17:26) and today our gospel comes from near the very end of this section in John, when Jesus moves from talking to his disciples into a prayer to God for them and for all "those who will believe in me through their word" (John 17:20; NABRE). Within the prayer Jesus seems to make an impossible request: "[T]hat they may be one just as we are one." Jesus desires his disciples to be unified in the same way he, God the Son, is connected to God, the Father, and to God, the Holy Spirit. This trinitarian fellowship is an outpouring of the life of God from one person of the Trinity to the other, and this is the model Jesus raises up for his human disciples. While this gospel passage might prompt us to work on our relationships with our brothers and sisters in Christ, even more so we must attend to the state of being that is foundational for any unity: being rooted in the love of God.

Connecting the Gospel

to the second reading: At times it can seem like the Christian life asks the impossible of us. Along with forming communities of trinitarian unity, we are also to love each other in the same way that Christ has loved us (John 13:34), and to be perfect as our heavenly father is perfect (Matt 5:48). Lest these humanly unattainable commandments lead us to despair, we must remember that we are never asked to do anything on our own. We can keep the commandments only insofar as we "believe in the love God has for us," as St. John says in today's second reading.

to experience: Only a few verses after today's second reading St. John writes, "We love because he first loved us" (1 John 4:19; NABRE). When the love of God is the foundation from which we "live and move and have our being" (Acts 17:28; NABRE), we can begin to fulfill Jesus's prayer for us that we might live in unity, joy, and truth.

Connecting the Responsorial Psalm

to the readings: Today's psalm proclaims, "As far as the east is from the west, / so far has he put our transgressions from us." As human beings we will falter and stumble on the journey of faith, and yet we are assured of our God's tender love and infinite compassion. We know that as God has done, so we are called to do. In today's gospel Jesus prays that his disciples might be bonded together in unity, filled with complete joy, and "consecrated in truth." All these become possible when we extend the same mercy to others that God has extended to us.

to psalmist preparation: How might God be calling you to practice forgiveness at this moment in your life?

PROMPTS FOR FAITH-SHARING

In the first reading Matthias is chosen to join the apostles as a "witness to [Jesus's] resurrection." In your journey of faith, who have been the most effective witnesses for you of Jesus's light and life?

In today's second reading we hear the familiar statement "God is love." As a Christian, how do you try to live this truth?

In today's gospel, Jesus prays to God that his disciples "may be one just as we are one." What is the biggest obstacle to unity in your parish church? How might God be calling you to address this?

This is our final week of the Easter season. How has your relationship with Jesus been renewed throughout this time of celebration?

Model Rite for the Blessing and Sprinkling of Water

Presider: In the waters of baptism we became sons and daughters of the living God, through the death and resurrection of Christ Jesus. By the sprinkling of these waters may we be sanctified in love and renewed in fidelity . . . *[pause]*

   [continue with The Roman Missal, *Appendix II]*

Homily Points

• In today's gospel, shortly before leaving the upper room with his disciples, Jesus "lift[s] up his eyes to heaven" and prays for those who will be left on the earth when he returns to his Father. Often in the gospels, we hear of Jesus retreating to quiet and deserted places to pray, but far less frequently do we have recorded words of Jesus at prayer. Jesus's words from John's gospel have been known since the sixteenth century as Jesus's "high priestly prayer." Within it he acts as an intercessor and asks that his disciples—both those gathered around him on the evening of the Last Supper and also "those who will believe in me through their word" (John 17:20; NABRE)—might know unity, joy, and truth.

• Today, we could pause to imagine Jesus, seated at the right hand of the Father, continuing to intercede for us, praying for our communities of faith that we might be defined by these same characteristics. Jesus's prayer calls us to be attentive to that which is most essential to the Christian life—being steeped in the love of God, which is the source of all unity, joy, and truth. In the second reading from the first epistle of St. John we are counseled, "God is love, and whoever remains in love / remains in God and God in him."

• If this is the heart of our faith, then any areas of disunity, of falsehood, or of oppressive gloom within ourselves, our families, or our communities call us to a deep examination of conscience. We have been called by name and set apart for a holy purpose: to radiate the love and light of Christ in the world. Let us pray for one another, even as we know Jesus is surely praying for us, that we might be unified and sanctified in the infinite love of God.

Model Universal Prayer (Prayer of the Faithful)

Presider: United as beloved sons and daughters of God, with one voice let us bring our needs and petitions before the Lord.

Response: Lord, hear our prayer.

For God's holy church spread throughout the world, may it be consecrated in truth and fortified against every evil . . .

For the peoples of the earth, in the beautiful diversity that God has made, may every culture and nation embrace the maxim to "love one another" . . .

For children who have been abandoned, abused, and neglected, may the love of God heal their hearts and fill their caregivers with wisdom and compassion . . .

For all gathered here, having journeyed with Jesus from Calvary to the empty tomb, may we witness to his glory in all we say and do . . .

Presider: God, our refuge and our strength, you shield us from evil and lead us into fullness of joy. Hear our prayers that the whole world might know your never-failing love and learn to live in peace. We ask this through Christ our Lord. **Amen.**

COLLECT

Let us pray.

Pause for silent prayer

Graciously hear our supplications, O Lord,
so that we, who believe that the Savior of
    the human race
is with you in your glory,
may experience, as he promised,
until the end of the world,
his abiding presence among us.
Who lives and reigns with you in the unity
    of the Holy Spirit,
one God, for ever and ever. **Amen.**

FIRST READING

Acts 1:15-17, 20a, 20c-26

Peter stood up in the midst of the brothers
    —there was a group of about one
        hundred and twenty persons
    in the one place—.
He said, "My brothers,
    the Scripture had to be fulfilled
    which the Holy Spirit spoke beforehand
    through the mouth of David,
        concerning Judas,
who was the guide for those who
    arrested Jesus.
He was numbered among us
    and was allotted a share in this
        ministry.

"For it is written in the Book of Psalms:
    May another take his office.

"Therefore, it is necessary that one of the
    men
    who accompanied us the whole time
    the Lord Jesus came and went among
        us,
    beginning from the baptism of John
    until the day on which he was taken up
        from us,
    become with us a witness to his
        resurrection."
So they proposed two, Judas called
    Barsabbas,
    who was also known as Justus, and
    Matthias.
Then they prayed,
    "You, Lord, who know the hearts of all,
    show which one of these two you have
        chosen
    to take the place in this apostolic
        ministry
    from which Judas turned away to go to
        his own place."
Then they gave lots to them, and the lot
    fell upon Matthias,
    and he was counted with the eleven
        apostles.

CATECHESIS

RESPONSORIAL PSALM
Ps 103:1-2, 11-12, 19-20

R⫯. (19a) The Lord has set his throne in
    heaven.
    or:
R⫯. Alleluia.

Bless the LORD, O my soul;
    and all my being, bless his holy name.
Bless the LORD, O my soul,
    and forget not all his benefits.

R⫯. The Lord has set his throne in heaven.
    or:
R⫯. Alleluia.

For as the heavens are high above the
    earth,
    so surpassing is his kindness toward
        those who fear him.
As far as the east is from the west,
    so far has he put our transgressions
        from us.

R⫯. The Lord has set his throne in heaven.
    or:
R⫯. Alleluia.

The LORD has established his throne in
    heaven,
    and his kingdom rules over all.
Bless the LORD, all you his angels,
    you mighty in strength, who do his
        bidding.

R⫯. The Lord has set his throne in heaven.
    or:
R⫯. Alleluia.

SECOND READING
1 John 4:11-16

Beloved, if God so loved us,
    we also must love one another.
No one has ever seen God.
Yet, if we love one another, God remains
    in us,
    and his love is brought to perfection in
        us.

This is how we know that we remain in
    him and he in us,
    that he has given us of his Spirit.
Moreover, we have seen and testify
    that the Father sent his Son as savior of
        the world.
Whoever acknowledges that Jesus is the
    Son of God,
    God remains in him and he in God.
We have come to know and to believe in
    the love God has for us.

God is love, and whoever remains in love
    remains in God and God in him.

About Liturgy

Lex Orandi, Lex Credendi: There is a Latin axiom, likely familiar to readers of this volume, that quite briefly explains the integral connection that liturgy has to our faith and beliefs, and how that faith and those beliefs shape our communal prayer: *Lex orandi, lex credendi.* In English, that is often rendered, "The law of prayer is the law of belief." The axiom operates in either transactional direction and can be expressed even more colloquially: we pray what we believe; we believe what we pray.

Most people saw the 2011 Roman Missal translation as a mixed bag of successes and failures. In the collects and other presidential prayers, the retention of Latin grammar and syntax, vocabulary, and word order can make many of these orations nearly unintelligible to listeners without the printed text in front of them.

It's important to allot time for careful study of each Mass's prayers so the faithful can pray and, further, be formed and catechized by these words. Today's collect is an example of this need: "Graciously hear our supplications, O Lord, / so that we, who believe that the Savior of the human race / is with you in your glory, / may experience, as he promised, / until the end of the world, / his abiding presence among us." Statistically, that's one single sentence with forty words, seven commas, and a lot of potential assembly "tuning out" due to unintelligible clauses.

We need to give proclamation of texts like this great care when it comes to the pauses particularly, and it's not as simple as including a short pause for each comma, not when there are that many! One helpful technique is to imagine hearing a voice you know well, perhaps a parent or famous actor, reading the text. Which pauses, what pacing, would help you understand the prayer on a first and only hearing?

Too often these prayers (the collect, prayer over the gifts, and the prayer after Communion) feel a bit like a transitional hinge—that is, something we need liturgically to turn a corner, but not anything of real substance in the liturgy. This is of course dramatically wrong. One other technique to counter this effect, in addition to practicing the orations, is to indicate to the congregation that the invitation "let us pray" is in fact sincere. To achieve this, have the Missal in place and opened to the proper page before that invitation. Following it but before the oration, bow your head silently for several seconds. In short order, the congregation will learn by your lead what this moment in time is for: their own private prayers, soon to be gathered to one by the celebrant.

If we are to pray what we believe and believe what we pray, let us all give these orations the attention and intelligibility they need, and not relegate them to passing moments of overlooked substance.

About Music

Melding Truth and Love: The gospel for this weekend speaks of truth, which can be experienced as cold or hard at times, and the epistle speaks of love, which in certain incarnations can be fickle. Divine truth and divine love are none of those things, perhaps not only because they are divine but because they exist together. Psalm 25 speaks so well to this, in settings such as Tim Manion's "I Lift Up My Soul" (OCP).

SPIRITUALITY

GOSPEL ACCLAMATION
R⁊. Alleluia, alleluia.
Come, Holy Spirit, fill the hearts of your faithful
and kindle in them the fire of your love.
R⁊. Alleluia, alleluia.

Gospel   John 20:19-23; L63B

On the evening of that first day of the
      week,
   when the doors were locked, where the
         disciples were,
   for fear of the Jews,
   Jesus came and stood in their midst
   and said to them, "Peace be with you."
When he had said this, he showed them his
      hands and his side.
The disciples rejoiced when they saw the
      Lord.
Jesus said to them again, "Peace be with
      you.
As the Father has sent me, so I send you."
And when he had said this, he breathed on
      them and said to them,
   "Receive the Holy Spirit.
Whose sins you forgive are forgiven them,
   and whose sins you retain are retained."

or John 15:26-27; 16:12-15

Jesus said to his disciples:
   "When the Advocate comes whom I will
         send you from the Father,
   the Spirit of truth that proceeds from the
         Father,
   he will testify to me.
And you also testify,
   because you have been with me from the
         beginning.

"I have much more to tell you, but you
      cannot bear it now.
But when he comes, the Spirit of truth,
   he will guide you to all truth.
He will not speak on his own,
   but he will speak what he hears,
   and will declare to you the things that are
         coming.
He will glorify me,
   because he will take from what is mine
         and declare it to you.
Everything that the Father has is mine;
   for this reason I told you that he will take
         from what is mine
         and declare it to you."

Reflecting on the Gospel

The gospel read during the Mass on Pentecost day tells us of Jesus's appearance to his apostles in Jerusalem on Easter evening. He is suddenly there, even though the doors were locked, as the evangelist notes; he shows his hands and side to his disciples. Should we not connect this action with the greeting Jesus gives his disciples, "Peace be with you"? This is not an ordinary greeting. In

John's view, it is connected with the wounds, because peace flows from the passion and resurrection. (For Luke, Christ's display of his wounds was a way of assuring the disciples of his identity [see 24:39]; this is not the case for John.)

Now Christ "sends" his disciples. In doing so, he uses the kind of formula we find frequently in the fourth gospel: "As the Father has sent me, so I send you." (See the many other formulas in John that establish a parallel between the activity of the Father in relation to the Son and the activity of the Son in relation to his disciples: for example, 6:57; 10:15; 15:9; 17:18.) For John, however, such formulas express more than a simple parallelism; they do more than affirm the divinity of Christ on the grounds that he acts as the Father acts. They are also a theological statement that believers share in the very life that is common to Father and Son.

The formula ends rather abruptly: "I send you." He is not sending them to a place, but giving them a mission that they must carry out. What is the mission? It is that of forgiving sins, as Christ immediately makes clear. Since, however, Christ draws a parallel between his action in sending the disciples and the Father's action in sending him, he is also telling the disciples that they are to continue the work that Jesus himself has been doing for the reconstruction of the world. They too are to do the Father's work. As Jesus reveals the Father and makes him known, so the disciples are to reveal Jesus and make him known.

St. Luke tells us in today's first reading of how the Spirit came upon the disciples as they were gathered in the upper room. Luke thus puts the coming of the Spirit on Pentecost. John, however, in the gospel reading, speaks of the Spirit being given on Easter evening. Is there contradiction here between Acts and John? Has John conflated Pentecost and Easter? According to some exegetes, John is not conflating the two events, but neither is he distinguishing them; he is interested, rather, in giving expression to the paschal mystery as a unitary whole.

We should note that Luke too has an anticipation of Pentecost inasmuch as he speaks of the apostles having been chosen by Christ "through the holy Spirit" (Acts 1:2; NABRE). It seems more accurate, therefore, to say that these various actions and gifts of the Spirit (including John 20:22) were all a preparation for the definitive coming of the Spirit. When we say that the church was born on Pentecost, we are undoubtedly simplifying somewhat. After all, the church was born from the side of Christ on Calvary, while the various appearances of Christ after his resurrection were so many stages in the formation of the church. The church was born on Calvary and born of his resurrection, no less than she was born of the Spirit on Pentecost. The whole first chapter of the Acts of the Apostles is concerned with this gradual formation that was going on even before the Spirit was poured out on Pentecost.

We may say that St. Luke lays greater emphasis on the historical facts, while John is more concerned with the close connection between Calvary, the resurrection, the appearances, and the gift of the Spirit at Pentecost.

Focusing the Gospel

Key words and phrases: [H]e breathed on them.

To the point: Jesus, the risen Lord, enters the room in which the disciples had barricaded themselves out of fear and offers them two gifts: his peace and the breath of the Holy Spirit. This scene and these words are familiar to us, having pondered them only a few weeks ago on the Second Sunday of Easter. Today, on the feast of Pentecost, we focus on the sharing of the Holy Spirit. Like Adam, brought from lifeless clay to a creature made in the image and likeness of God with a breath, the disciples are also transformed into a new creation. With this new indwelling of the Holy Spirit, they are sharers in the life of Christ who has conquered death and darkness, and they are to bear this life to the world through their preaching, healing, and forgiving.

Connecting the Gospel

to the first and second readings: In the first reading from the Acts of the Apostles, we find a very different description of the arrival of the Holy Spirit. Instead of the gentleness of a breath, the Spirit comes to the disciples as "a strong driving wind" and "tongues of fire." While breath is necessary for life, wind and fire lend themselves to movement and change. Within today's Scripture readings we are given a fuller picture of the Holy Spirit through the diverse ways it is portrayed. Just as God, the Father, and God, the Son, cannot be completed fathomed or contained by our human understanding, it is the same with the Holy Spirit. In the second reading St. Paul writes to the Corinthians to help them recognize the unity within the variety of gifts, services, and workings of the Holy Spirit that are being manifested in their community.

to experience: Whether it is acting as wind, fire, or breath, the Holy Spirit continues to animate and inspire the Body of Christ alive in the world. Which one of these images speaks to your experience of the Holy Spirit moving in your life? How do you perceive the Spirit working now within your life and the life of your community of faith?

Connecting the Responsorial Psalm

to the readings: Today's psalm lifts up another aspect of the Holy Spirit as an agent of renewal in the world. Within the life of creation, we see a pattern of death and rebirth constantly at work. For those of us living in the Northern Hemisphere, we celebrate the Easter season during a time where new life is appearing all around us in the form of plants and newborn birds and animals. Following the dark and cold of the winter months, the warmth and light of spring reminds us that our creator God is constantly at work "renew[ing] the face of the earth."

to psalmist preparation: How are you experiencing or in need of the Holy Spirit's renewing action in your own life right now?

In today's psalm we pray, "Lord, send out your Spirit, and renew the face of the earth." How do your faith community's ministries renew the earth?

St. Paul writes to the Corinthians, "To each individual the manifestation of the Spirit / is given for some benefit." How are you using your gifts to benefit the people of God?

Jesus addresses the disciples, "Peace be with you." How are you in need of the Lord's peace at this moment?

Commissioning the disciples to carry on his ministry, Jesus says, "As the Father has sent me, so I send you." How do these words reverberate with your own faith journey?

CELEBRATION

Model Rite for the Blessing and Sprinkling of Water

Presider: John the Baptist told the people that the one coming after him would baptize with the Holy Spirit and with fire. By the sprinkling of these waters may the purifying fire of the Holy Spirit's love come to rest on each of us . . . *[pause]*

[continue with The Roman Missal, *Appendix II]*

Homily Points

• Along with gifting the disciples with his peace and with the breath of the Holy Spirit, Jesus gives them a new commission: "As the Father has sent me, so I send you." Following Jesus's crucifixion fear had kept the disciples locked away, but now they are sent out to no longer live motivated by self-preservation or success, but in the same way Jesus was sent by his Father—in complete vulnerability, as a sacrifice and a sign of God's love and compassion for the world.

• Throughout the seasons of Lent and Easter, we have been strengthened and fortified by ongoing conversion to the Lord through penance and prayer, and through our celebration of Jesus's triumph over sin and death these last fifty days. Now we, too, are sent forth to live in the world in a different way than we did before. Alive with the breath of the Holy Spirit, we are to use the different gifts and talents we have been given to live out Christ's forgiveness and peace in the world.

• This is not an easy task. To be sent as Jesus was sent means to strip away all of the human armor that we often use to protect ourselves. In St. Paul's letter to the Galatians (today's optional second reading), we are exhorted to renounce "hatreds, rivalry, jealousy, / outbursts of fury, acts of selfishness, / dissensions, factions, occasions of envy . . . and the like." All of these are counter to the nonviolence of Christ who opened his arms on the cross in love and surrender. Today, on this feast of Pentecost, let us again invite the Holy Spirit to renew us in fidelity to follow in Christ's footsteps, the same footsteps that led to the vulnerability of the cross and also the glory of the empty tomb.

Model Universal Prayer (Prayer of the Faithful)

Presider: Renewed by the word of God and animated with the gift of the Holy Spirit, let us confidently bring our needs before the Lord.

Response: Lord, hear our prayer.

For those who undertake the ministry of confessor, may they be granted the gifts of counsel and understanding as they offer tender care to those burdened by sin . . .

For the earth we call home, by the power of the Holy Spirit may our planet be renewed both physically and spiritually . . .

For those who live in fear, may the peace of the Lord free them from all anxieties and grant them the courage to use their talents and gifts for the glory of God . . .

For all gathered here, may our ears be attuned to the direction and guidance of the Holy Spirit as we seek to do God's will in our lives . . .

Presider: God of all blessings, with attentive care you nurture and sustain all that you have created. Hear our prayers that by meeting you in word and sacrament we might be inspired to build a society governed by peace and justice. We ask this through Christ our Lord. **Amen.**

COLLECT
Let us pray.

Pause for silent prayer

O God, who by the mystery of today's
    great feast
sanctify your whole Church in every
    people and nation,
pour out, we pray, the gifts of the Holy Spirit
across the face of the earth
and, with the divine grace that was at work
when the Gospel was first proclaimed,
fill now once more the hearts of believers.
Through our Lord Jesus Christ, your Son,
who lives and reigns with you in the unity
    of the Holy Spirit,
one God, for ever and ever. **Amen.**

FIRST READING
Acts 2:1-11

When the time for Pentecost was fulfilled,
    they were all in one place together.
And suddenly there came from the sky
    a noise like a strong driving wind,
    and it filled the entire house in which
        they were.
Then there appeared to them tongues as
    of fire,
    which parted and came to rest on each
        one of them.
And they were all filled with the Holy Spirit
    and began to speak in different tongues,
    as the Spirit enabled them to proclaim.

Now there were devout Jews from every
    nation under heaven staying in
        Jerusalem.
At this sound, they gathered in a large
    crowd,
    but they were confused
    because each one heard them speaking
        in his own language.
They were astounded, and in amazement
    they asked,
    "Are not all these people who are
        speaking Galileans?
Then how does each of us hear them in
    his native language?
We are Parthians, Medes, and Elamites,
    inhabitants of Mesopotamia, Judea and
        Cappadocia,
    Pontus and Asia, Phrygia and
        Pamphylia,
    Egypt and the districts of Libya near
        Cyrene,
    as well as travelers from Rome,
    both Jews and converts to Judaism,
        Cretans and Arabs,
    yet we hear them speaking in our own
        tongues
    of the mighty acts of God."

RESPONSORIAL PSALM
Ps 104:1, 24, 29-30, 31, 34

R̸. (cf. 30) Lord, send out your Spirit, and
    renew the face of the earth.
    or:
R̸. Alleluia.

Bless the Lᴏʀᴅ, O my soul!
    O Lᴏʀᴅ, my God, you are great indeed!
How manifold are your works, O Lᴏʀᴅ!
    The earth is full of your creatures.

R̸. Lord, send out your Spirit, and renew
    the face of the earth.
    or:
R̸. Alleluia.

If you take away their breath, they perish
    and return to their dust.
When you send forth your spirit, they are
    created,
    and you renew the face of the earth.

R̸. Lord, send out your Spirit, and renew
    the face of the earth.
    or:
R̸. Alleluia.

May the glory of the Lᴏʀᴅ endure forever;
    may the Lᴏʀᴅ be glad in his works!
Pleasing to him be my theme;
    I will be glad in the Lᴏʀᴅ.

R̸. Lord, send out your Spirit, and renew
    the face of the earth.
    or:
R̸. Alleluia.

SECOND READING
1 Cor 12:3b-7, 12-13

or

Gal 5:16-25

SEQUENCE

See Appendix A, p. 293.

About Liturgy

Embracing the Spirit: It can feel, liturgically speaking, that the Holy Spirit, as a person of the Trinity, gets short shrift. It is almost as if the only time we can hear Scripture regarding the Spirit or pray or sing other Spirit-infused texts is on Pentecost or at confirmation Masses. Certainly, there are hundreds (thousands?) of trinitarian doxologies, but a brief passing mention doesn't really level the balance, ultimately.

Perhaps this is partly what's behind two relatively unique aspects of the liturgies of this weekend: the optional extended Pentecost Vigil and the sequence on Pentecost day. Yes, there are other vigils and sequences, but these two deserve special mention.

The Vigil of Pentecost is not especially well known or practiced, but it is unique save for only the Easter Vigil in its celebration. It includes four Old Testament readings, each followed by a psalm or a period of silence. It also delays the Gloria and collect until after the last of these readings, right before the epistle reading. This form of the liturgy creates a natural tie to the Easter Vigil, and like the Easter Vigil readings, which in part trace salvation history, these readings help bring to life the role of the Spirit in the life of the church.

Be sure to alert your congregation if you are implementing this extended vigil for the first time, and take some time to catechize—by bulletin or even by a short announcement before Mass—regarding the form of Mass and the pastoral reasons for its implementation.

The Pentecost sequence is one of only two that are still mandatory in liturgies today. The name itself is a bit odd and comes from the practice a millennium ago of extending the last syllable of the Alleluia before the gospel to allow time for the deacon to arrive at the ambo. The melisma eventually started taking on prose of its own and became known as the sequence because it followed the Alleluia (at that time). Present practice places it before the Gospel Acclamation. The sequence should be sung if at all possible. It can be confusing for an assembly, even following along in a worship aid, so be sure to help them with information, either in print or announced: "Please remain seated and join with one another in singing the Pentecost sequence . . ." The text of the sequence is an invitation for the Holy Spirit to enter into our lives with practical manifestations of divine power and love.

Once the Spirit is "properly" celebrated, there is no particular reason to avoid, during the rest of the liturgical year, any hymns, prayers, or homilies regarding the Spirit and the renewal, healing, zeal, and vigor that the Spirit brings! Seek out these opportunities to regularly recall, reflect, and pray over this oft-overlooked person of the Trinity!

About Music

Singing the Sequence: There are several accessible and effective settings of the Pentecost sequence; some are especially appropriate to bring the Easter season to a fitting conclusion. One setting uses the ODE TO JOY tune and appears in several hymnals; "Come, Holy Spirit, on Us Shine" (WLP) uses the *O FILII ET FILIAE* tune; Rob Glover has a setting (GIA) that naturally folds into the Celtic Alleluia at its finish as a Gospel Acclamation.

ORDINARY
TIME II

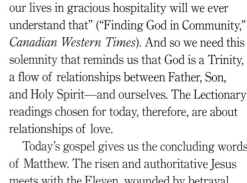

✠ SPIRITUALITY

GOSPEL ACCLAMATION
Rev 1:8

℟. Alleluia, alleluia.
Glory to the Father, the Son, and the
    Holy Spirit;
to God who is, who was, and who is to
    come.
℟. Alleluia, alleluia.

Gospel

Matt 28:16-20; L165B

The eleven disciples went to
    Galilee,
  to the mountain to which Jesus
    had ordered them.
When they all saw him, they
    worshiped, but they
    doubted.
Then Jesus approached and said
    to them,
  "All power in heaven and on
    earth has been given to
    me.
Go, therefore, and make
    disciples of all nations,
  baptizing them in the name of the
    Father,
  and of the Son, and of the Holy
    Spirit,
  teaching them to observe all that I
    have commanded you.
And behold, I am with you always, until
    the end of the age."

Reflecting on the Gospel

Ronald Rolheiser has written: "The most pernicious heresies that block us from properly knowing God are not those of formal dogma, but those of a culture of individualism that invite us to believe that we are self-sufficient, that we can have community and family on our own terms, and that we can have God without dealing with each other. But God is community—and only in opening our lives in gracious hospitality will we ever understand that" ("Finding God in Community," *Canadian Western Times*). And so we need this solemnity that reminds us that God is a Trinity, a flow of relationships between Father, Son, and Holy Spirit—and ourselves. The Lectionary readings chosen for today, therefore, are about relationships of love.

Today's gospel gives us the concluding words of Matthew. The risen and authoritative Jesus meets with the Eleven, wounded by betrayal and failure, still a very human mix of hopeful faith and hesitant doubt, of adoration and indecision. For our consolation, these are the disciples to whom Jesus entrusts the inclusive mission of making disciples of "all nations," without distinction of race or culture. With the authority of the risen Jesus, they are commissioned to baptize "in the name of the Father, and of the Son, and of the Holy Spirit," and to teach these new followers to obey everything that Jesus has revealed to them during his earthly mission. On their first missionary journey (Matt 10:1, 5-8) there had been no command to teach, but now that they have experienced not only Jesus's life but also his death and resurrection, they are equipped to teach the full significance of his instructions. We who have gathered to celebrate the Most Holy Trinity have been baptized and taught, called and schooled by Jesus through the mission of his church. We have been drawn into the divine-human communion of that first "trinitarian" moment of Jesus's baptism by John in the Jordan when the Father, Son, and Holy Spirit were named. Matthew gives us the solemn assurance that Jesus, Immanuel, "God-with-us" (cf. Matt 1:23) as the personal promise of God, will be with the church until the end of human history. His is no "absentee lordship" but a presence of a servant Christ who wishes to liberate rather than dominate. His church, therefore, must also be a humble servant that remembers that its authority is not absolute but is derived from Jesus; a church that identifies with those who are a very human mix of faith and doubt; a church that avoids all triumphalism and insensitivity to the wounded people of our world.

And as we are the church, are *we* this kind of people? When we sign ourselves "in the name of the Father, and of the Son, and of the Holy Spirit," could we sometimes reflect on this rather than making a very perfunctory "brush and babble" gesture? Can we instead have something of the passion of John Donne's "Holy Sonnet XIV," where Donne expresses his faith that, to be truly free, we must be rescued from sin and then taken captive again—but this time by the love of the "three-person'd God": "Batter my heart, three-person'd God; for you / As yet but knock, breathe, shine, and seek to mend; / That I may rise, and stand, o'erthrow me, and bend / Your force, to break, blow, burn, and make me new."

Focusing the Gospel

Key words and phrases: "And behold, I am with you always, until the end of the age."

To the point: Jesus speaks to the disciples shortly before ascending into heaven. From this moment on, their interaction with him will be different. And yet, while Jesus is bodily removed from their presence, his Spirit remains with them, sustaining them, inspiring them, and leading them. Two thousand years later, we bear witness to the continued fulfillment of Jesus's promise. He is "with us always" as we take up his command to bring the good news of his love to the ends of the earth.

Connecting the Gospel

to the first reading: In the book of Deuteronomy, Moses addresses the people on the eve of their entrance into the land of Israel following forty years in the desert. After recounting the history they have lived since their deliverance from slavery in Egypt, Moses exhorts them to "fix in [their] heart[s]" their fundamental belief as a people "that the Lord is God / in the heavens above and on earth below, / and that there is no other." Their adherence to monotheism set the Jewish people apart from the inhabitants of neighboring lands who worshipped many gods. In the gospel, Jesus tells his disciples that they are to initiate people into new life in Christ with the trinitarian formula: "in the name of the Father, and of the Son, and of the Holy Spirit." Although the one God has been revealed to us Christians as Creator, Redeemer, and Sanctifier, we continue to affirm that this triune God is one. The theologian Elizabeth Johnson writes in her book *Quest for the Living God,* "It is all the one God, but we use a triple mode of address to signal the threefold way God has self-communicated in history."

to experience: In your own life of faith and of prayer, how do you most often call upon and experience the Lord who is Father, Son, and Holy Spirit?

Connecting the Responsorial Psalm

to the readings: Today's psalm proclaims "of the kindness of the Lord the earth is full." As Christians, we experience the fullness of God through the mystery of the Most Holy Trinity. We understand God as Father, Son, and Holy Spirit to be a relationship of love that overflows to animate all of creation. Through this love we have been chosen to be God's own and to care for and steward the abundance of creation. In the first reading, our thriving is linked to keeping the "statutes and commandments" of God, for in this way, Moses tells the people, "[Y]ou and your children after you may prosper, / and [you will] have long life on the land / which the Lord, your God, is giving you forever."

to psalmist preparation: How do you make care and enjoyment of creation part of your spiritual life?

PROMPTS FOR FAITH-SHARING

In the first reading from Deuteronomy, Moses urges the people to "fix in [their] hearts" the knowledge of the one God. How do you keep God in the center of your life?

The psalmist proclaims, "[O]f the kindness of the Lord the earth is full." How do you experience God's "kindness" in creation?

St. Paul writes to the Romans, "[Y]ou did not receive a spirit of slavery to fall back into fear, / but you received a Spirit of adoption." How has fear impacted your spiritual life?

Jesus commissions the disciples, "Go, therefore, and make disciples of all nations." How does your parish community join in this work of "making disciples"?

Model Penitential Act

Presider: In his letter to the Romans, St. Paul reminds us that we are all children of God. For the times we have not treated each other as brothers and sisters, let us ask God for pardon and mercy . . . [pause]

Lord Jesus, you are our strength and our shield: Lord, have mercy.

Christ Jesus, you reign in heaven with the Father and the Holy Spirit: Christ, have mercy.

Lord Jesus, you entreat us to spread your gospel to the ends of the earth: Lord, have mercy.

Homily Points

• In today's gospel Jesus speaks the words of the baptismal formula that, since then, have been used for millennia to usher men, women, and children into the life of God. The threefold gift of water is to be imparted "in the name of the Father, and of the Son, and of the Holy Spirit." On this feast of the Most Holy Trinity, we pause to reflect on the mystery of "Trinity" not as a way of *thinking* about God, but as our Christian way of *knowing* God. All theology is rooted in our experience of God, and this is true for the doctrine of the Trinity as well. In her book *Quest for the Living God*, theologian Elizabeth Johnson describes how the early Christian community of the New Testament knew "the saving God in a threefold way as beyond them, with them, and within them that is, as utterly transcendent, as present historically in the person of Jesus, and as present in the Spirit within their community. These were all encounters with only one God."

• In the Trinity we experience God as a continuous outpouring of love, and in our baptism we have been welcomed into the dynamic dance of grace that occurs between the Father, Son, and Holy Spirit. In the first reading from the book of Deuteronomy, Moses enjoins the people to "fix in your heart, that the Lord is God / in the heavens above and on earth below, / and that there is no other."

• Above all, God desires a wholehearted relationship with us that requires our active participation and fidelity. We, too, are called to "fix in [our] hearts" our understanding of God as the one who creates, redeems, and sanctifies us and then sends us forth to bear his life to others.

Model Universal Prayer (Prayer of the Faithful)

Presider: Knowing that our God hears and answers the cries of the vulnerable and weak, let us bring our needs and the needs of others before the Lord.

Response: Lord, hear our prayer.

For bishops, priests, deacons, and lay ministers, may they serve the faithful and the poor in unity of Spirit and with fullness of compassion . . .

For leaders of nations, may they join together to combat the scourge of human trafficking and modern-day slavery throughout the world . . .

For the elderly and infirm who require long-term care, may they know their preciousness in the eyes of God and their importance within the community of faith . . .

For all gathered here, as beloved sons and daughters of God, may we speak for the voiceless and extend empathy and compassion to all who suffer . . .

Presider: Triune God, as Father, Son, and Holy Spirit, you call us to draw closer to you and to each other. Hear our prayers that emboldened by your grace we might preach the gospel of your love and care to the ends of the earth. We ask this through Christ our Lord. **Amen.**

COLLECT

Let us pray.

Pause for silent prayer

God our Father, who by sending into the world
the Word of truth and the Spirit of sanctification
made known to the human race your wondrous mystery,
grant us, we pray, that in professing the true faith,
we may acknowledge the Trinity of eternal glory
and adore your Unity, powerful in majesty.
Through our Lord Jesus Christ, your Son,
who lives and reigns with you in the unity of the Holy Spirit,
one God, for ever and ever. **Amen.**

FIRST READING
Deut 4:32-34, 39-40

Moses said to the people:
"Ask now of the days of old, before your time,
ever since God created man upon the earth;
ask from one end of the sky to the other:
Did anything so great ever happen before?
Was it ever heard of?
Did a people ever hear the voice of God
speaking from the midst of fire, as you did, and live?
Or did any god venture to go and take a nation for himself
from the midst of another nation,
by testings, by signs and wonders, by war,
with strong hand and outstretched arm, and by great terrors,
all of which the LORD, your God,
did for you in Egypt before your very eyes?
This is why you must now know,
and fix in your heart, that the LORD is God
in the heavens above and on earth below,
and that there is no other.
You must keep his statutes and commandments that I enjoin on you today,
that you and your children after you may prosper,
and that you may have long life on the land
which the LORD, your God, is giving you forever."

RESPONSORIAL PSALM

Ps 33:4-5, 6, 9, 18-19, 20, 22

R̸. (12b) Blessed the people the Lord has
    chosen to be his own.

Upright is the word of the LORD,
    and all his works are trustworthy.
He loves justice and right;
    of the kindness of the LORD the earth
        is full.

R̸. Blessed the people the Lord has chosen
    to be his own.

By the word of the LORD the heavens were
    made;
    by the breath of his mouth all their
        host.
For he spoke, and it was made;
    he commanded, and it stood forth.

R̸. Blessed the people the Lord has chosen
    to be his own.

See, the eyes of the LORD are upon those
    who fear him,
    upon those who hope for his kindness,
to deliver them from death
    and preserve them in spite of famine.

R̸. Blessed the people the Lord has chosen
    to be his own.

Our soul waits for the LORD,
    who is our help and our shield.
May your kindness, O LORD, be upon us
    who have put our hope in you.

R̸. Blessed the people the Lord has chosen
    to be his own.

SECOND READING

Rom 8:14-17

Brothers and sisters:
Those who are led by the Spirit of God are
    sons of God.
For you did not receive a spirit of slavery
    to fall back into fear,
    but you received a Spirit of adoption,
    through whom we cry, "Abba, Father!"
The Spirit himself bears witness with our
    spirit
    that we are children of God,
    and if children, then heirs,
    heirs of God and joint heirs with Christ,
    if only we suffer with him
    so that we may also be glorified with
        him.

About Liturgy

The Changing Seasons: Our church calendar, in terms of its Sundays, is seemingly trying to ease us out of Eastertide and return us to Ordinary Time by way of today's celebration of the Trinity as well as next week's solemnity. Eastertide of course ended on Pentecost, with Ordinary Time beginning the following day. However, since these particular feasts fall just after Eastertide, it may be tempting to postpone making the obvious external signs of transition as we might do between other liturgical seasons. It's not uncommon, for instance, to have poinsettias linger into winter Ordinary Time, but surely we take down any Christmas trees and place the nativity scene back into storage at the appropriate time.

Giving our congregations as many clear signs of the passing of liturgical time will, even if only subconsciously, help them come to a fuller understanding of that cycle of seasons and how the various facets of our faith that they reveal intersect with and relate to one another. Even though the celebrant will be wearing white vestments for two more Sundays, and even though there is an obvious connection between the celebrations of Pentecost and Holy Trinity, it is no longer Eastertide, and we should help the faithful in the pews understand that a liturgical transition is happening.

So, in addition to retiring the crosses draped in white and gold, and all of the bountiful reds of Pentecost, this would be a good moment to change which Mass setting you are singing, from a more festive and celebratory setting to one perhaps a bit more subdued or prayerful (in a different way). Perhaps the style of psalmody sung at liturgy can be another change, from metrical to chanted for instance.

Practical considerations, like the availability of personnel to change the art and environment or the lack of rehearsal time for choirs as summer is beginning, certainly may affect such utopian ideals. Still, striving for careful observation of the changing liturgical seasons is praiseworthy and, all things considered, a better approach.

About the Sign of the Cross

Praying with Our Bodies: Just as we begin and end each prayer by making the sign of the cross, so too will our very lives begin and end with that same sign of the cross. It shows to whom we belong: we trace on our bodies and bear in our souls the marks of his same cross. As we speak the names of the persons of the Trinity, we recall that it is not just our prayer, but all that we do that is dedicated to them: "In the name of . . ."

There is a long and varied history of the sign of the cross; suffice it to say here that it is both an ancient gesture and one imbued with significance for all Christians across time and space. St. Athanasius (AD 296–373) said, "By the signing of the holy and life-giving cross, devils and various scourges are driven away. For it is without price and without cost and praises him who can say it."

About Music

Who God Is, Not What God Does: There is of course much hymnody that includes a trinitarian doxology, as previously mentioned, so take some time to locate texts that more fully elaborate on the persons, three-in-one, coequal and eternal. Recall that the persons of the Trinity are defined not by what they do, but only by who they are: each God, related to but not the other two persons. Therefore, avoid texts like "Creator, Redeemer, Sanctifier" if at all possible. Stay with hymns of praise, like "God, We Praise You" (text by Christopher Idle, Hope Publishing).

SPIRITUALITY

GOSPEL ACCLAMATION
John 6:51

℟. Alleluia, alleluia.
I am the living bread that came down from
    heaven,
says the Lord; whoever eats this bread will live
    forever.
℟. Alleluia, alleluia.

Gospel   Mark 14:12-16, 22-26; L168B

On the first day of the Feast of Unleavened
    Bread,
  when they sacrificed the Passover lamb,
  Jesus' disciples said to him,
  "Where do you want us to go
  and prepare for you to eat the Passover?"
He sent two of his disciples and said to
    them,
  "Go into the city and a man will meet you,
  carrying a jar of water.
Follow him.
Wherever he enters, say to the master of
    the house,
  'The Teacher says, "Where is my guest
    room
  where I may eat the Passover with my
    disciples?"'
Then he will show you a large upper room
    furnished and ready.
Make the preparations for us there."
The disciples then went off, entered the
    city,
  and found it just as he had told them;
  and they prepared the Passover.

While they were eating,
  he took bread, said the blessing,
  broke it, gave it to them, and said,
  "Take it; this is my body."
Then he took a cup, gave thanks, and gave
    it to them,
  and they all drank from it.
He said to them,
  "This is my blood of the covenant,
  which will be shed for many.
Amen, I say to you,
  I shall not drink again the fruit of the
    vine
  until the day when I drink it new in the
    kingdom of God."
Then, after singing a hymn,
  they went out to the Mount of Olives.

Reflecting on the Gospel

Sometimes I find myself in a lineup with a bunch of strangers, shuffling down the aisle in church, and I forget that I am standing with my family on the pathway to heaven about to partake of the Body and Blood of Christ offered once for all time for the salvation of the world. Perhaps you have walked down that aisle with me?

The sacrificial nature of the Eucharist is clear from Jesus's words and actions at the Last Supper, but hearing the words of institution over and over can become a part of a rote behavior that obscures their life-giving meaning. In the words of Mark's gospel, "While they were eating, he took bread, said the blessing, broke it, gave it to them, and said, 'Take it; this is my body.' Then he took a cup, gave thanks, and gave it to them, and they all drank from it. He said to them, 'This is my blood of the covenant, which will be shed for many.'"

The primary sacrificial context for the Last Supper comes from the Passover feast in which the meal is situated, but the offering of Jesus's Body and Blood on behalf of "many"—that is, for all people—takes on and reinterprets much more of the sacrificial imagery of the Old Testament. The bread that he broke is a sign of his body, which he will offer in death, the true bread of the presence. The "blood of the covenant" shares in the imagery of the ceremony in Exodus in which Moses sprinkled blood on the people of Israel as a sign of their obedience to the covenant. The phrase "shed for many" draws us inexorably to the Suffering Servant of Isaiah, who pours himself out as an expiation for the sins of the people.

These sacrificial realities are not alien to the Last Supper. They are an inherent part of Jesus's actions, which he interprets for his apostles prior to the crucifixion. But for these understandings to come to the fore, the first Christians had to meditate and reflect on what Jesus had done and what this meant for the continuing life of the church.

The author of the Letter to the Hebrews makes it his mission to explicate and explain what took place on Calvary in light of the Jewish sacrificial system. He explains that Jesus is not only the sacrifice for the sins of the world but also the perfect high priest and that through the offering of himself as the perfect sacrifice, Jesus "is mediator of a new covenant: . . . those who are called may receive the promised eternal inheritance."

Jesus's words over the bread and wine, then sharing it with his disciples, signifies his giving them a share in the atoning power of his death. And that atoning power has as its goal eternal life with Jesus. But it was not just those who sat at the table with Jesus who are able to share in the atoning power of Jesus's sacrifice; Jesus opened the way for all to share in the eternal inheritance.

The Eucharist fulfills the sacrificial system and gives us the ability to share in the power of Christ's atoning death here and now, but it also prepares us for our eternal inheritance. With the rest of God's family, we will share in the messianic banquet. Jesus tells us "many will come from the east and the west, and will recline with Abraham, Isaac, and Jacob at the banquet in the kingdom of heaven" (Matt 8:11; NABRE). Only the true bread of heaven, the perfect High Priest, could offer himself once for all and so pave the way for our entry into the temple made not with hands. So walk with joy toward the temple prepared for us for eternity, as you are about to share a foretaste of the unending banquet.

Focusing the Gospel

Key words and phrases: "[T]his is my body." "This is my blood."

To the point: In his words over the bread and the wine at the Last Supper, Jesus reveals his desire to become a complete self-gift in the sacrifice of his body and blood. Today, this gift is still present to us in the Body and Blood of Jesus consecrated at the altar, consumed by the faithful, and reserved for adoration and worship. In the simple elements of bread and wine, we find the totality of our Lord who humbled himself to take on flesh, suffered, died, and rose again. Here we encounter him with us always as food and drink to nourish, heal, and sustain us "until the end of the age" (Matt 28:20; NABRE).

Connecting the Gospel

to the second reading: In the letter to the Hebrews, Jesus's words and actions at the Last Supper are viewed as that of a great "high priest" who "entered once for all into the sanctuary, / not with the blood of goats and calves, / but with his own blood, thus obtaining eternal redemption."

to experience: We continue to live into this redemption through our own share in the Body and Blood of Christ. Jesus tells the disciples gathered with him at the table, "This is my blood of the covenant, / which will be shed for many." We who have received the Lord in bread and wine are called to become the Body of Christ for others. How does your parish community live out this call?

Connecting the Responsorial Psalm

to the readings: In the first verse of today's psalm, the psalmist asks, "How shall I make a return to the Lord / for all the good he has done for me?" While this line might spur us to consider a multitude of "goods" we have received from God, the original author sought to particularly thank God for his help when "I was caught by the cords of death" (Ps 116:3; NABRE). Now that these cords are "loosed," the faithful one seeks to "offer sacrifice of thanksgiving" in appreciation and recognition of God's care and healing power. Today we celebrate the feast of the Most Holy Body and Blood of Christ. Our "cup of salvation" is the chalice that holds the precious blood of Jesus. In his apostolic exhortation The Joy of the Gospel, Pope Francis urges us to consider the Eucharist, "not as a prize for the perfect but a powerful medicine and nourishment for the weak" (47). As the second reading assures us, "[I]f the blood of goats and bulls / and the sprinkling of a heifer's ashes / can sanctify those who are defiled / so that their flesh is cleansed, / how much more will the blood of Christ . . . cleanse our consciences from dead works / to worship the living God."

to psalmist preparation: How do you experience the Eucharist as a sacrament of healing? Where are you most in need of healing at this moment in your life?

PROMPTS FOR FAITH-SHARING

In the first reading and the gospel, we hear of a covenant made in blood between the people and God. How do you attend to your covenant relationship with God each day?

Today's psalm asks, "How shall I make a return to the Lord / for all the good he has done for me?" What are the greatest gifts you have received from the Lord?

How does your parish community, as the Body of Christ alive in the world, seek to be bread that is broken and wine that is poured out for others?

We know the Eucharist is "the source and summit of Christian life." How is this true in your journey of faith?

Model Penitential Act

Presider: In the first reading, the people of Israel proclaim, "All that the Lord has said, we will heed and do." For the times we have gone against God's commandments and failed to do what is right, let us ask for mercy and pardon . . . *[pause]*

Lord Jesus, you are the Lamb of God who takes away the sins of the world: Lord, have mercy.

Christ Jesus, you are the Son of the living God: Christ, have mercy.

Lord Jesus, you remain with us always in the bread and wine, your Body and Blood: Lord, have mercy.

Homily Points

• In the first reading we find the people of Israel sealing their covenant with the Lord with the blood of animals. They have been freed from slavery in Egypt, formed as God's people through the gift of the Torah on Mount Sinai, and now their sacred relationship with him is ratified with their promise, "All that the Lord has said, we will heed and do." Despite their intentions, throughout the generations the people fall short of their desire to follow God with fidelity. It is the same in our own time. Despite our best intentions as sons and daughters of God, we fail continually in our endeavor to be perfect partners in the covenant.

• And yet, God is not dissuaded from his own faithfulness by our sin and error. In his book *Jesus of Nazareth: Holy Week: From the Entrance into Jerusalem to the Resurrection*, Pope Benedict XVI writes of the divine yearning for a new covenant (expressed through the prophet Jeremiah), a covenant "no longer built upon the perennially fragile fidelity of the human will but that is written indestructibly on men's hearts (cf. Jer 31:33). In other words, the New Covenant must be founded on an obedience that is irrevocable and inviolable." Jesus, fully human and fully divine, takes "all human disobedience upon himself in his obedience even unto death, suffered it right to the end, and conquered it."

• Our participation in the Eucharist binds us to the sacrifice and victory of Jesus. Each time we draw close to the altar to consume his body and blood, we pledge ourselves anew to live out the "new and everlasting covenant," praying fervently that through God's eternal mercy and never-failing love "[he] will place [his] law within [us], and write it upon [our] hearts" (Jer 31:33; NABRE).

Model Universal Prayer (Prayer of the Faithful)

Presider: In the Eucharist, Jesus gives himself to us as bread and wine. Let us turn to the one who satisfies our deepest hunger and place before him our petitions.

Response: Lord, hear our prayer.

For God's holy church, may an increase in priestly vocations make it possible for all of the faithful to partake of the eucharistic banquet . . .

For officials elected to public office, may they enact legislation to combat the evil of racism while promoting the dignity of all human life . . .

For all who suffer from food insecurity, especially children and the elderly, may their needs be provided for today and every day . . .

For all gathered here, as the Body of Christ alive in the world, may we seek to be bread that is broken and wine that is poured out on behalf of others . . .

Presider: Provident and gracious God, you lavishly provide for all of our needs, giving even of your very self in the Body and Blood of your Son, Jesus. Hear our prayers that in feasting at this table we might know your love and bear it to others. We ask this through Christ our Lord. **Amen.**

COLLECT

Let us pray.

Pause for silent prayer

O God, who in this wonderful Sacrament
have left us a memorial of your Passion,
grant us, we pray,
so to revere the sacred mysteries of your
    Body and Blood
that we may always experience in
    ourselves
the fruits of your redemption.
Who live and reign with God the Father
in the unity of the Holy Spirit,
one God, for ever and ever. **Amen.**

FIRST READING

Exod 24:3-8

When Moses came to the people
    and related all the words and
        ordinances of the LORD,
    they all answered with one voice,
    "We will do everything that the LORD
        has told us."
Moses then wrote down all the words of
    the LORD and,
    rising early the next day,
    he erected at the foot of the mountain
        an altar
    and twelve pillars for the twelve tribes
        of Israel.
Then, having sent certain young men of
    the Israelites
    to offer holocausts and sacrifice young
        bulls
    as peace offerings to the LORD,
    Moses took half of the blood and put it
        in large bowls;
    the other half he splashed on the altar.
Taking the book of the covenant, he read
    it aloud to the people,
    who answered, "All that the LORD has
        said, we will heed and do."
Then he took the blood and sprinkled it on
    the people, saying,
    "This is the blood of the covenant
    that the LORD has made with you
    in accordance with all these words of
        his."

RESPONSORIAL PSALM
Ps 116:12-13, 15-16, 17-18

R̸. (13) I will take the cup of salvation, and
    call on the name of the Lord.
    or:
R̸. Alleluia.

How shall I make a return to the Lᴏʀᴅ
    for all the good he has done for me?
The cup of salvation I will take up,
    and I will call upon the name of the
    Lᴏʀᴅ.

R̸. I will take the cup of salvation, and call
    on the name of the Lord.
    or:
R̸. Alleluia.

Precious in the eyes of the Lᴏʀᴅ
    is the death of his faithful ones.
I am your servant, the son of your
    handmaid;
    you have loosed my bonds.

R̸. I will take the cup of salvation, and call
    on the name of the Lord.
    or:
R̸. Alleluia.

To you will I offer sacrifice of
    thanksgiving,
    and I will call upon the name of the
    Lᴏʀᴅ.
My vows to the Lᴏʀᴅ I will pay
    in the presence of all his people.

R̸. I will take the cup of salvation, and call
    on the name of the Lord.
    or:
R̸. Alleluia.

SECOND READING
Heb 9:11-15

OPTIONAL SEQUENCE

See Appendix A, p. 294.

About Liturgy

Source and Summit: Many of us are familiar with the expression "source and summit of our faith." This expression has blossomed and become widely known to a large number of the faithful, particularly over the last two decades or so. A resurgence in eucharistic devotion has brought about an awareness of what the church says and teaches regarding the Eucharist. For instance, we can read in the *Catechism*, "The Eucharist is 'the source and summit of the Christian life'" (1324). It is drawing from the Vatican II text *Lumen Gentium* as it says this, notably regarding the faithful: "Taking part in the Eucharistic sacrifice, the source and summit of the christian life, they offer the divine victim to God and themselves along with him" (11).

Some, though, take what the *Catechism* says (and what other apologists continue to say), and in turn make the statement about only the consecrated host—that it itself is the source and summit of our faith. This is fortified, perhaps in a symbiotic way, by the intense eucharistic devotion of some who, anecdotally and experientially, may value time in adoration over that spent during a eucharistic liturgy!

Note that *Lumen Gentium* above refers specifically to taking part in the eucharistic sacrifice—that is the whole of Mass, not just the consumption of the host. This is bolstered in meaning by *Sacrosanctum Concilium*, when it early on says, "Nevertheless, the liturgy is the summit toward which the activity of the church is directed; it is also the source from which all its power flows. For the goal of apostolic endeavor is that all who are made children of God by faith and Baptism should come together to praise God in the midst of his church, to take part in the sacrifice and to eat the Lord's Supper" (10).

Understanding that it is the liturgy itself—the whole action of the church at prayer—that is source and summit, font and apex, is an integral part of our communal spirituality. It is one that, if it was ever particularly strong, appears to be quickly fading. While we must celebrate our belief in what the eucharistic substances are and what they become (and, in part, the mystery of how they become), this is another significant example of a faith that needs to be expressed better in terms of verbs instead of nouns—that is, it's in the doing and activity of our faith that it becomes alive, not in the objects we rightly revere in wonder and awe.

Note well that all of this is not to say that time spent in adoration is wasted or misdirected; rather, any eucharistic devotion should be understood in a proper place within the whole of the faith, and that time spent pursuing "ocular communion" should make us hunger and thirst for receiving Christ himself into our very beings.

About Music

Both Body and Blood: Note that while the older and still familiar name for this solemnity is Corpus Christi, the current and proper name acknowledges both the body *and blood* of Christ. To that end, consider music that focuses on Jesus's blood and of drinking in his life and love. "Jesus, Wine of Peace" (GIA) by David Haas is one; "Come to Me and Drink" (OCP) by Bob Hurd deserves consideration too.

GOSPEL ACCLAMATION

Matt 11:29ab

R/. Alleluia, alleluia.
Take my yoke upon you, says the Lord;
and learn from me, for I am meek and humble
of heart.
R/. Alleluia, alleluia.

or

1 John 4:10b

R/. Alleluia, alleluia.
God first loved us
and sent his Son as expiation for our
sins.
R/. Alleluia, alleluia.

Gospel

John 19:31-37; L171B

**Since it was preparation day,
in order that the bodies
might not remain on the
cross on the sabbath,
for the sabbath day of that
week was a solemn one,
the Jews asked Pilate that
their legs be broken
and they be taken down.
So the soldiers came and
broke the legs of the first
and then of the other one who was
crucified with Jesus.
But when they came to Jesus and saw
that he was already dead,
they did not break his legs,
but one soldier thrust his lance into
his side,
and immediately blood and water
flowed out.
An eyewitness has testified, and his
testimony is true;
he knows that he is speaking the
truth,
so that you also may come to believe.
For this happened so that the Scripture
passage might be fulfilled:
Not a bone of it will be broken.
And again another passage says:
*They will look upon him whom they
have pierced.***

See Appendix A, p. 295, for the other readings.

Reflecting on the Gospel

On this solemnity and in this graphic gospel reading, there is a powerful juxta-position of violence and gentleness. On the one hand, the gospel text is bloody and violent. On the other hand, the solemnity is gentle and sacred. On one hand, we are confronted by the dead body of Jesus. On the other, we as a church venerate his loving heart. Word and worship are in tension, but totally entwined.

Of course, it is the cross that brings these realities together, one as real and vivid as the other. It is always the cross that brings together the good and bad, the highs and lows, the mysteries of death and life. Today's gospel reading—with its setting entirely on the cross—reminds us of this. Nowhere is Jesus's humanity so exposed and brilliantly illuminated as on the cross. Even John's gospel with its high Christology (its clarity about the divinity of Jesus) shares with us this very human scene about dead bodies, Sabbath deadlines, the breaking of legs, and the thrusting of lances. And it is in the midst of this humanity that we discover the heart of Jesus—a heart that is literally poured out for us.

According to John, Jesus died on "prepa-ration day"—not only the day before the Sabbath, but also the day before the great celebration of Passover. Careful to observe Sabbath regulations, the Jews asked Pilate that the bodies of those who were crucified be taken down so this work would not need to be done on the Sabbath/Passover. In response, the soldiers broke the legs of the two criminals crucified with Jesus in order to speed up their deaths. Jesus was already dead, so they did not break his legs. Instead, one soldier thrust his spear into Jesus's side. We don't know why the soldier in John's ac-count did this, but his action became an occasion for John to reveal more about who Jesus is. First, the reference to "blood and water" flowing out of the side of Jesus symbolizes the very life of Jesus being poured out. Some of the early church fathers (and others) have further interpreted these elements as symbol-izing the church, or baptism and the Eucharist. Second, the fact that Jesus's legs are not broken is interpreted by John as deeply symbolic; he echoes the descrip-tion of the Passover lamb from the book of Exodus: "You shall not break any of its bones" (12:46; NABRE). Jesus is the Paschal Lamb (John 1:29, 36), killed the day before Passover, who quietly and willingly gives his life to free his people. And finally, the piercing of Jesus's side fulfills another prophecy: "*They will look upon him whom they have pierced.*" This is a reference to a passage from the prophet Zechariah about an unknown victim (Zech 12:10). It invites everyone—those at the foot of the cross (both friends and foes of Jesus), the Johannine community, and the modern reader—to look upon this death and take it into their own hearts.

Blood and water are physical, material things. Sacrifice, salvation, and love are spiritual. These physical and spiritual elements meet in the heart of Jesus. On the cross, divine and human are intermingled, and the salvation that only God can offer is extended to all. We are to imitate the heart of our Savior, ex-tending that love, continuing to pour it out of our own hearts and bodies.

Focusing the Gospel

Key words and phrases: They will look upon him whom they have pierced.

To the point: Jesus of Nazareth, in his life, death, and resurrection, reveals the nature of God to us as one so in love with humanity that he willingly suffered and died so as to enter fully into the human experience and redeem it. As we contemplate Jesus's sacred heart, pierced and broken at the crucifixion, we are called to care for those who suffer in our midst. In this way, we console the heart of God that continues to mourn at the pain present in our world.

Model Penitential Act

Presider: In the sacred heart of Jesus we find healing for every ill. Knowing his everlasting love, let us call to mind our sins and ask for mercy . . . *[pause]*

Lord Jesus, you are our strength and our courage: Lord, have mercy.
Christ Jesus, on the cross you bore our sins: Christ, have mercy.
Lord Jesus, your sacred heart calls us to fullness of life: Lord, have mercy.

Model Universal Prayer (Prayer of the Faithful)

Presider: Today's first reading from the prophet Hosea assures us that God's love will never fail. With trust in the one who is our creator and healer, let us bring our needs before the Lord.

Response: Lord, hear our prayer.

For God's holy church, may it serve the poor and vulnerable and spread the gospel with the tender compassion of the sacred heart of Jesus . . .

For teachers and caregivers throughout the world, may they respectfully foster the children in their care and take joy in their work . . .

For those suffering from dementia and Alzheimer's disease, though their memories might fade, may they know peace in God's never-ending love . . .

For all gathered here, may we be rooted and grounded in Jesus's mercy and so empowered to be merciful to those who have harmed us . . .

Presider: God of faithfulness, your love is revealed in the self-giving of your son Jesus. Hear our prayers that the whole earth experience your compassion and in so doing be redeemed. We ask this through Christ our Lord. **Amen.**

About Liturgy

An Unsanitized Heart: The typically drawn heart, at least as usually depicted in greeting cards or on elementary school St. Valentine's Day cards, is a rather sanitized expression of the human organ, vital and, yes, bloody. It is also, frankly, a sanitized expression of what "love" is, or at least the way many people live out love for their family, friends, and spouse.

This devotion is about the Heart of Christ, unsanitized and "real"—pierced by the soldier's lance while on the cross—and a love expressed by that same sacrificial death. For those who are preparing this liturgy, take every opportunity to make Christ's heart and love as "real" as you can. Do the prayers and other texts of liturgy allow for contemplation of Christ and how, in the words of a song by Shannon Cerneka, "love is less about meaning than sacrifice"?

Be careful not to shy away from anything liturgically that, because it is "real" and honest, makes us or those around us uncomfortable. Most likely, it is in this discomfort that Christ is active and speaking to our own sacred hearts.

COLLECT
Let us pray.

Grant, we pray, almighty God,
that we, who glory in the Heart of your
    beloved Son
and recall the wonders of his love for us,
may be made worthy to receive
an overflowing measure of grace
from that fount of heavenly gifts.
Through our Lord Jesus Christ, your Son,
who lives and reigns with you in the unity of
    the Holy Spirit,
one God, for ever and ever. **Amen.**

or:
O God, who in the Heart of your Son,
wounded by our sins,
bestow on us in mercy
the boundless treasures of your love,
grant, we pray,
that, in paying him the homage of our devotion,
we may also offer worthy reparation.
Through our Lord Jesus Christ, your Son,
who lives and reigns with you in the unity of
    the Holy Spirit,
one God, for ever and ever. **Amen.**

FOR REFLECTION

• In the first reading, we are given a picture of God's tenderness toward us as that of one holding an infant up to his cheek. How does this image match your experience of God's love?

• In the gospel passage we find Jesus on the cross, having given his entire life, from first breath to the last, for us and for the Father. Which people in your life model Jesus's self-giving love?

Homily Points

• Today's first reading shows God as a doting parent, stooping to hold a toddler's hands and raising a newborn up to cuddle. The prophet Hosea warns the people of God's impending punishment given their straying from the covenant relationship. And yet, despite his anger, in the end God remembers the people as his beloved firstborn.

• Despite our failings, our God continues to look upon us with the kindness, love, and devotion of a parent. We need only turn back to him and his sacred heart is ready to welcome us home.

SPIRITUALITY

GOSPEL ACCLAMATION
Ry. Alleluia, alleluia.
The seed is the word of God, Christ is the sower.
All who come to him will live forever.
Ry. Alleluia, alleluia.

Gospel

Mark 4:26-34; L92B

Jesus said to the crowds:
  "This is how it is with
      the kingdom of God;
  it is as if a man were to
      scatter seed on the
      land
  and would sleep and rise
      night and day
  and through it all the seed
      would sprout and grow,
  he knows not how.
Of its own accord the land
      yields fruit,
  first the blade, then
      the ear, then the full
      grain in the ear.
And when the grain is ripe, he wields
      the sickle at once,
  for the harvest has come."

He said,
  "To what shall we compare the
      kingdom of God,
  or what parable can we use for it?
It is like a mustard seed that, when it is
      sown in the ground,
  is the smallest of all the seeds on the
      earth.
But once it is sown, it springs up and
      becomes the largest of plants
  and puts forth large branches,
  so that the birds of the sky can dwell
      in its shade."
With many such parables
  he spoke the word to them as they
      were able to understand it.
Without parables he did not speak to
      them,
  but to his own disciples he explained
      everything in private.

Reflecting on the Gospel

Jesus's parables are not nice entertaining little stories. As Jesus proclaims in the first words he speaks according to Mark (Mark 1:14-15), his mission is to announce the Good News of the kingdom, the reigning and transforming presence of God in his person and words, and call the people to faith and repentance. Like all the parables, the two parables of green and growing things we hear today are words of Jesus that tease us into contemplating our own lives and our response to the kingdom.

In the first parable, Jesus compares the growth of the kingdom to the seed that is planted by the farmer who then retires from the scene into the rhythm of his everyday life. Day and night he wakes and sleeps, while the seed, once sown, has its own potential for growth independent of the farmer. The mystery of growth belongs to the seed and the soil, to the gradual "dispossession" of the hard little seed to the nourishing earth, and its consequent unhurried and gradual growth: first the stalk, then the head, then the full grain. The only activity required of the farmer is vigilant patience. In the dispossession that is his incarnation, even Jesus had to accept some unknowing, some surrender of events into his Father's hands (Mark 13:32).

Perhaps we have had the experience with children who have planted their seeds in the garden and, excited about the possibilities of the flowers or vegetables to come, must be dissuaded from regular and disastrous digging down into the earth to see how the growth is proceeding! The farmer must wait confidently on God's good time and providence, and eventually the time of growth and the time of harvesting will intersect. Once we have received the seed of God's word in the soil of our hearts, we must be ready for the dispossession, the gradual unfolding of the seed's potential that will push into our consciousness and transform our lives, making us a plentiful harvest and enabling us to become nourishment for others. Because the growth of the seed is God's secret, it can often happen in what, to our limited human perspective, are the most unlikely places: in the lives of the poor, the despised, the persecuted. This was surely a great consolation to Mark's community, for this was the reality of their lives. It should give the same hope and confidence to Christians today in our personal, communal, or national situations. What seems humanly insignificant, and even a failure, is transformed by God's power, just as the seed of Jesus's life fell into the ground of death to be transformed by his resurrection (cf. John 12:24). This is the great encouragement for disciples as we live between the planting and harvesting into the kingdom of God.

The parable of the mustard seed and its surprising growth is also one of encouragement for struggling communities frustrated or despondent because of what seems the small and insignificant growth of the kingdom of God and its impact on the world around them. Jesus makes use of legitimate poetic license in exaggerating the size of the mustard seed ("the smallest of all the seeds on the earth") and the bush that grows from it ("the largest of plants"), in order to stress the extravagant and disproportionate growth of the kingdom. That God is in all our beginnings and endings is the great and faithful hope of Jesus's disciples. The mustard bush, we are reminded, does not exist only for itself, but it offers a welcoming refuge for the birds of the air who nest in its shade. So the Christian community should spread out its branches in welcome to others, especially to those who are enduring the heat of suffering, who are searching either physically or spiritually for some "shade" or sanctuary.

We often find it hard to be at home and comfortable with mystery; there is still the primeval temptation to be like gods, to know everything, to overreach our God-given humanity. That we have Jesus's word to "explain" to us the deeper meaning of God's action in our lives and our world, is the privilege of Jesus's disciples.

Focusing the Gospel

Key words and phrases: "[T]he smallest of all seeds on the earth . . . becomes the largest of plants."

To the point: We find a familiar refrain in today's gospel where the one that was considered least ("the smallest of all seeds") turns into the greatest ("becomes the largest of plants"). Once again, Jesus calls us to look with new eyes at the world that surrounds us. Just as the tiny mustard seed can grow to provide shelter for "the birds of the sky," we should not underestimate the power and potential of the small to become mighty. This is the way with the kingdom of God, where, as Mary proclaims in the Magnificat, "[God] has put down the mighty from their thrones, and has exalted the lowly."

Connecting the Gospel

to the first and second readings: The first reading from the prophet Eze-kiel contains much of the same imagery that is found in the gospel. Speaking in a "riddle" (Ezek 17:2; NABRE), God proclaims that he will eventually restore the people of Israel, "a tender shoot," from their Babylonian exile to become a "majestic cedar" in which "[b]irds of every kind shall dwell beneath." Just as with the mustard seed, the unassuming, fragile shoot of the cedar will grow to offer welcome and shelter to all. In his second letter to the Corinthians, St. Paul reminds the community that "we walk by faith, not by sight." This faith invites us to recognize the strength of God, working in weakness and fragility, to build a kingdom where all are welcome, cared for, and valued.

to experience: Today's readings invite us to embrace a new perspective, knowing that in the kingdom of God the small and lowly hold the greatest potential for growth and transformation. How have you seen this pattern lived out in your own life?

Connecting the Responsorial Psalm

to the readings: Our responsorial psalm reminds us of the foundation for all prayer: offering thanksgiving to God. Only with eyes of gratitude can we perceive the action of the Lord in our lives from "dawn" to dusk and all "throughout the night." As in the first reading and in the gospel, today's psalm also speaks of plants flourishing, this time palms and cedars, "planted in the house of the Lord." The gospel reminds us of a farmer who scatters seeds on the ground and then waits for them to "sprout and grow, / he knows not how." The farmer trusts that within the depths of the ground the seed is sending down roots that will eventually produce fruit he can see and harvest.

to psalmist preparation: At times it is difficult to witness the action of God's grace within ourselves and others, but today's psalm encourages us that if we are "planted in the house of the Lord," we will flourish and grow. How do you experience your time of prayer and worship in "the house of the Lord" as the soil in which your own faith is planted?

PROMPTS FOR FAITH-SHARING

In both the first reading and the gospel, we are given an image of the small becoming great. Where have you seen this pattern in your own life?

In his second letter to the Corinthians, St. Paul tells the community, "[W]e walk by faith, not by sight." What does this mean for your journey of faith?

In the gospel the mustard seed grows to become a plant that can shelter "the birds of the sky." How does your parish community offer shelter and safe haven for others?

What evidence do you see of the kingdom of God growing in your midst?

Model Penitential Act

Presider: As we prepare our hearts and minds to receive the word of God, let us pause to recall the times we have failed to follow that word in our lives and ask for pardon and mercy . . . *[pause]*

Lord Jesus, you teach us how to walk by faith and not by sight: Lord, have mercy.

Christ Jesus, you champion the meek and the humble: Christ, have mercy.

Lord Jesus, you are the Word of God, sent forth to bear much fruit: Lord, have mercy.

Homily Points

• After the celebration and joy of the Easter season, capped off with the feasts of the Holy Trinity and the Body and Blood of Christ, this Sunday it feels as if we have finally settled back into Ordinary Time. We pick up with the Gospel of Mark in the fourth chapter, where Jesus, after proclaiming the good news, healing various ailments throughout Galilee, and having appointed the twelve apostles, pauses to preach to the crowds about the mystery of the kingdom of God through parables. Both of the parables from today's gospel call to mind an image that would have been very recognizable to Jesus's audience, that of seeds that are sown.

• It is interesting that Jesus expounds on the kingdom of God, something so mysterious and beyond human understanding, by using such mundane imagery. And yet, perhaps that is the very point. Jesus directs our attention to the mysterious growth and transformation that takes place in secret at all times, all over the world, as seeds sprout and grow, fulfilling their purpose in providing nourishment and shelter for others.

• These parables orient us to Ordinary Time as a season dedicated to our own slow but constant growth and transformation as children of God. We take on the work of sowing the seeds of God's word in our own lives and the lives of those around us, but we also trust in the action of the Holy Spirit, bringing the kingdom of God to fruition in and around us, we "[know] not how." Where do you sense the slow work of the Spirit in your own life and community bringing about renewal and transformation?

Model Universal Prayer (Prayer of the Faithful)

Presider: In today's second reading, St. Paul reminds us that "we walk by faith, not by sight." With confidence in our God's generosity and compassion, let us place our needs before him.

Response: Lord, hear our prayer.

For God's church throughout the world, may it provide shelter and welcome for all people of goodwill . . .

For environmentalists and conservationists, may their work and study influence humanity's care for the earth and preservation of natural resources . . .

For migrant workers who plant and harvest, may they labor in safe working conditions and receive a just wage . . .

For all gathered here, may we aspire to please the Lord in all that we do . . .

Presider: God of all goodness, you sent your son Jesus to teach about your kingdom through parables. Hear our prayers that we might plant the seeds of this kingdom and trust in your providence to bring them to fruition. We ask this through Christ our Lord. **Amen.**

COLLECT

Let us pray.

Pause for silent prayer

O God, strength of those who hope in you,
graciously hear our pleas,
and, since without you mortal frailty can
    do nothing,
grant us always the help of your grace,
that in following your commands
we may please you by our resolve and our
    deeds.
Through our Lord Jesus Christ, your Son,
who lives and reigns with you in the unity
    of the Holy Spirit,
one God, for ever and ever. **Amen.**

FIRST READING
Ezek 17:22-24

Thus says the Lord GOD:
    I, too, will take from the crest of the
        cedar,
        from its topmost branches tear off a
            tender shoot,
    and plant it on a high and lofty
        mountain;
        on the mountain heights of Israel I
            will plant it.
    It shall put forth branches and bear
        fruit,
        and become a majestic cedar.
    Birds of every kind shall dwell beneath
        it,
        every winged thing in the shade of
            its boughs.
    And all the trees of the field shall know
        that I, the LORD,
    bring low the high tree,
        lift high the lowly tree,
    wither up the green tree,
        and make the withered tree bloom.
    As I, the LORD, have spoken, so will I do.

RESPONSORIAL PSALM

Ps 92:2-3, 13-14, 15-16

℟. (cf. 2a) Lord, it is good to give thanks
    to you.

It is good to give thanks to the LORD,
    to sing praise to your name, Most High,
to proclaim your kindness at dawn
    and your faithfulness throughout the
        night.

℟. Lord, it is good to give thanks to you.

The just one shall flourish like the palm
        tree,
    like a cedar of Lebanon shall he grow.
They that are planted in the house of the
        LORD
    shall flourish in the courts of our God.

℟. Lord, it is good to give thanks to you.

They shall bear fruit even in old age;
    vigorous and sturdy shall they be,
declaring how just is the LORD,
    my rock, in whom there is no wrong.

℟. Lord, it is good to give thanks to you.

SECOND READING

2 Cor 5:6-10

Brothers and sisters:
We are always courageous,
    although we know that while we are at
        home in the body
    we are away from the Lord,
    for we walk by faith, not by sight.
Yet we are courageous,
    and we would rather leave the body and
        go home to the Lord.
Therefore, we aspire to please him,
    whether we are at home or away.
For we must all appear before the
        judgment seat of Christ,
    so that each may receive recompense,
    according to what he did in the body,
        whether good or evil.

About Liturgy

Ordinary, Extraordinary: This is the Sunday when, during the celebrant's greeting to the assembly or during his homily, we are frequently "welcomed back" to Ordinary Time. As mentioned here on Trinity Sunday, Ordinary Time actually began two Sundays ago, even though vestments were still white in hue, even though we don't actually hear the phrase "Sunday in Ordinary Time" until today.

Along with this misplaced greeting, we will often hear, too, about how it's been months since green vestments have been worn on Sundays, and how after the pinnacle of the year (Easter) and the great feasts of Holy Trinity and the Most Holy Body and Blood of Christ, we are now returning to the ordinary days of the calendar, as if they are somehow lackluster and banal. Some overcorrect for this by speaking about how the time isn't ordinary at all but rather "extraordinary," in that we will spend many weeks, being trained by the readings at Mass, in the practice of being a disciple of the Lord.

While that last bit is true, utilizing the language of "ordinary" and "extraordinary" in this way is a disservice to the faithful. The periods of the liturgical calendar known as Ordinary Time are called that because these Sundays are counted, and for no other reason. You've likely heard of the ordinal numbers: first, second, third, and so on. It is because of these ordinal numbers we get, in English, the name Ordinary Time. Further, to call these days extraordinary is to use that word to mean "amazing" or "remarkable," when, in the lingo of the church, extraordinary typically means "outside of the normal, usual, or prescribed"—for instance, "extraordinary ministers of Holy Communion" are those people outside the normal, usual, prescribed ministers, those who are ordained.

These coming weeks of Ordinary Time, while not Advent, Christmastide, Lent, or Eastertide, are no less vital to the life of the church and our prayer and formation. We should be careful, then, about how we use language to describe the passage of time and seasons in the liturgical year.

About Sitting

A Middle Posture: Perhaps the most "ordinary" posture we humans have is sitting. Whether at a desk in a workplace or relaxing at home, eating a meal, watching a movie or a play in a theater, sitting is perhaps the posture in which we spend most of our days.

It's not the full vulnerability of lying down or the powerful stature of standing; it hovers somewhere in between—not action, not rest—yet it is calm, watchful, alert. If we let it, it can become a posture of receptivity, of openness, of a willingness to hear and understand. We spend much of the Liturgy of the Word in this posture, listening to Scripture, and that Scripture broken open in a well-crafted homily.

For a celebrant, though, we have already seen how his chair is one of dignity and presidential authority when it is used; for a bishop that *cathedra* is so important that the building it occupies is named for it. Let us pray that our servant-leaders are mindful that, when sitting, they too are called to hear and understand the words of Scripture and the needs of the flock they shepherd.

About Music

Seeds of the Kingdom: The Gospel of Mark is not as laden with parables as other gospels, yet today we hear two, both with seeds playing a pivotal role. "Seed, Scattered and Sown" (OCP) is found in several hymnals and would make a thoughtful communion hymn this weekend. A more recent text by Shirley Erena Murray, "A Place at the Table," has settings by Lori True (GIA) and Joy Patterson (WLP) and further paints what the reign of God ought to look like here and now.

JUNE 13, 2021
ELEVENTH SUNDAY
IN ORDINARY TIME

SPIRITUALITY

GOSPEL ACCLAMATION
Luke 7:16

℟. Alleluia, alleluia.
A great prophet has risen in our midst,
God has visited his people.
℟. Alleluia, alleluia.

Gospel

Mark 4:35-41; L95B

On that day, as evening
    drew on, Jesus said
    to his disciples:
    "Let us cross to the
    other side."
Leaving the crowd, they
    took Jesus with
    them in the boat
    just as he was.
And other boats were
    with him.
A violent squall came up and waves
    were breaking over the boat,
    so that it was already filling up.
Jesus was in the stern, asleep on a
    cushion.
They woke him and said to him,
    "Teacher, do you not care that we are
        perishing?"
He woke up,
    rebuked the wind, and said to the
        sea, "Quiet! Be still!"
The wind ceased and there was great
    calm.
Then he asked them, "Why are you
    terrified?
Do you not yet have faith?"
They were filled with great awe and
    said to one another,
    "Who then is this whom even wind
        and sea obey?"

Reflecting on the Gospel

Mark is writing his gospel for a community suffering persecution, Christians who feared that any day they might be overwhelmed by either the waves of their own cowardice and infidelity to Christ, or blown off their Christian course by the fear of imprisonment and death. They could be tempted to believe that Jesus is "asleep" and cares nothing for them. In different contexts, we too are familiar with the storms that can brew in our own hearts. The struggle between fear and faith is a constant theme in Mark's gospel, continuing until the very last verse (Mark 16:8), but that we have a Gospel according to Mark witnesses to the final triumph of faith. Among these disciples are men who know this sea well, and for them to be afraid shows that their fear was humanly well founded. Although they have seen Jesus's power over the chaos that overwhelms people's bodies and minds, this crossing had been Jesus's idea, and their cries to him sound more like accusations of his lack of care for them than proclamations of their faith in him.

In the image of Jesus peacefully asleep in the storm-tossed boat there may be the memory of Jonah fast asleep in the bowels of the ship while God hurled great winds and waves at the vessel carrying the disobedient prophet away from his calling to the conversion of Nineveh (Jonah 1:4-15). Jonah has to re-sort to the much more dramatic and drastic solution of allowing himself to be tossed overboard before God will calm the storm. In contrast, Jesus rises from sleep, and the brief and powerful words of this most obedient prophet of God are enough to restore order out of chaos. Jesus rebukes the wind and the sea in the same way as he had "rebuked" or exorcised the "unclean spirit" and healed the tortured psyche of the man in the synagogue in Mark's account of Jesus's first miracles (Mark 1:23-27; NABRE). And there comes a great calm.

Jesus's authority over the natural world confronts our faith in an unsettling way. As Michael Casey writes: "We do not mind a man forgiving sins, because the supposed effect is invisible and beyond proof. Cures can be dismissed as merely 'psychological.' Our weak faith can dodge the question if there is some possibility of a 'rational' explanation. The nature miracles are different. They confront our faith directly" (*Fully Human, Fully Divine*).

Jesus's authority over the storm reveals him as Lord of Creation, and re-calls the divine authority over the chaotic waters "[i]n the beginning" (Gen 1:1; NABRE) and when God divided the waters to allow the people to pass through from slavery into freedom (Exod 14–15). This divine prerogative is also praised in a number of the psalms, including Psalm 107, which is today's responsorial psalm. But the disciples are looking and not perceiving, listening and not under-standing, despite the privileged instruction Jesus has given them (cf. Mark 4:10-12). Jesus's command of peace and stillness over the wind and waves assures the disciples' safe crossing, but their crossing from fear to faith is at a perilous beginning point. At least Jesus seems to suggest that the journey is possible. "Do you not yet have faith?" But the disciples turn to one another, not to Jesus, with their questions about his identity.

The Jesus who has risen from the sleep of death is the faithful hope of every disciple and postresurrection community. Often the storms sweep down on us as suddenly as the wind and waves on the Sea of Galilee, and we find ourselves unprepared for sickness, for a terminal diagnosis for ourselves or a loved one, for the upheaval of personal relations, the painful work of retrenchment. The mass media brings tragedies into our homes, and we may find ourselves saying: "Teacher, do you not care that we are perishing?" Yet Jesus is present in the storms and will bring us to the shore of new beginnings and new initiatives.

Focusing the Gospel
Key words and phrases: "Why are you terrified? Do you not yet have faith?"

To the point: Jesus's questions to the disciples in the boat seem a bit harsh. Of course they respond with terror when a "violent squall" threatens to sink the small boat they are using to traverse the Sea of Galilee! Jesus's ability to sleep through their travail no doubt astonished and maybe even angered his friends who ask him (perhaps reproachfully), "Teacher, do you not care that we are perishing?" At this moment in the gospel, the disciples do not yet understand that the one who travels alongside them in the boat is actually the God of creation who has become "flesh" and "made his dwelling among [them]" (John 1:14; NABRE). They have known him as Jesus the healer and Jesus the teacher, but now they are introduced to one whom "even wind and sea obey." Only after journeying with Jesus along the road to Jerusalem, encountering him as the resurrected Lord, and receiving the Holy Spirit at Pentecost will the disciples begin to have the faith necessary to leave all fear behind and to dwell in the peace of Christ, "that surpasses all understanding" (Phil 4:7; NABRE).

Connecting the Gospel
to the first reading: The first thirty-seven chapters of the book of Job are filled with dialogues between Job and his friends, who debate and argue the age-old question "[W]hy do the righteous suffer?" And then, in chapter 38 God begins to speak to Job, first asking him, "Where were you when I founded the earth?" (38:4; NABRE). Our first reading begins a few verses after this rhetorical question, establishing God as the creator of all and the one who rules the sea and sky. In some ways, the disciples' question "[D]o you not care that we are perishing?" seems to mirror Job's frustration when he pleads with God, "Your hands have formed me and fashioned me; / will you then turn and destroy me?" (Job 10:8; NABRE). Unlike Job, the disciples receive a quick response as Jesus rouses himself to rebuke the wind and sea and to restore calm to the waters.

to experience: Another prophetic book (Isaiah) reminds us that "as the heavens are higher than the earth, / so are [God's] ways higher than [our] ways, / [God's] thoughts higher than [our] thoughts" (55:9; NABRE). Though God's ways are incomprehensible, we can have faith in his unending love and never-failing presence beside us within any storm (literal or figurative) we encounter.

Connecting the Responsorial Psalm
to the readings: Today's responsorial psalm reminds us of the reason for our hope, the everlasting love of God. In the gospel we see Jesus acting out the words of the psalmist as he "hush[es] the storm to a gentle breeze" and calms "the billows of the sea."

to psalmist preparation: How do you experience God's compassion, protection, and guidance in the midst of life's storms?

PROMPTS FOR FAITH-SHARING

In the first reading God speaks to Job of the work of creation. How does the natural world reveal God's glory and majesty to you?

God addresses Job from the midst of a storm. How have times of suffering led you to grow in faith?

St. Paul tells us, "[W]hoever is in Christ is a new creation." How does your parish call its members to newness of life?

In the gospel Jesus calms the sea and wind, telling them, "Quiet! Be still!" What storms in your life are you being called to entrust to the Lord?

CELEBRATION

Model Penitential Act

Presider: In today's gospel, after calming the storm, Jesus asks his disciples, "Do you not yet have faith?" For the times our own faith has failed, let us ask for mercy and healing . . . *[pause]*

Lord Jesus, you command the wind and the sea: Lord, have mercy.

Christ Jesus, you save the perishing and afraid: Christ, have mercy.

Lord Jesus, you call us to have confidence in your compassion: Lord, have mercy.

Homily Points

• In the first four chapters of Mark's gospel, Jesus causes plenty of confusion and uncertainty among the people he encounters. Within this man the townspeople of Capernaum find something completely new and baffling that leads them to ask, "What is this?" when Jesus casts out an unclean spirit (1:27; NABRE). The scribes and Pharisees question why he eats with tax collectors and sinners (2:16), dares to break the Sabbath (2:24), and has the audacity to forgive sins (2:7). And in today's gospel the disciples, "filled with great awe and fear," turn to each other to ask, "Who then is this whom even wind and sea obey?"

• Slowly Jesus's identity as the Messiah, the son of the living God, is being revealed through his words and actions as he demonstrates his authority over all from spirits, to illness and sin, to the forces of nature. As we continue to journey into Ordinary Time, the time of living and growing in our life of faith, we are confronted with the question, who do we know Jesus to be? Have we experienced him as the Master Teacher, the Redeemer, the Wonder-worker?

• In today's gospel, the disciples do not yet know Jesus well enough to trust that they can turn to him in their moment of peril at sea. Instead, as their boat begins to fill with water, they wake him with the question, "Teacher, do you not care that we are perishing?" Despite their lack of faith, Jesus is quick to calm the wind and sea with a stern rebuke, "Quiet! Be still!" As we continue our own path of discipleship, let us keep turning to Jesus in times of trial and times of joy, knowing he is present in the boat beside us whether we encounter stormy weather or calm seas.

Model Universal Prayer (Prayer of the Faithful)

Presider: With childlike trust in the Father who provides for our every need, let us bring our petitions before the Lord.

Response: Lord, hear our prayer.

For members of the church who have had their faith shaken by scandal and abuse, may their stories be heard and their wounds healed . . .

For the peoples of the world, by the revelation of creation may all come to know the Creator God who loves and sustains them . . .

For fishermen and those who make their living on the sea, in the midst of stormy waters and violent seas may they be protected and led to safe harbor . . .

For all gathered here, in the midst of chaos and conflict may we turn to the Lord of life and trust in his goodness and mercy . . .

Presider: God most high, you have created the earth and all it contains and bestowed it as a gift upon humankind. Hear our prayers that each day we might grow in faith and never cease to praise you for all you have done. We ask this through Christ our Lord. **Amen.**

COLLECT

Let us pray

Pause for silent prayer

Grant, O Lord,
that we may always revere and love your
    holy name,
for you never deprive of your guidance
those you set firm on the foundation of
    your love.
Through our Lord Jesus Christ, your Son,
who lives and reigns with you in the unity
    of the Holy Spirit,
one God, for ever and ever. **Amen.**

FIRST READING

Job 38:1, 8-11

The Lord addressed Job out of the storm
    and said:
Who shut within doors the sea,
    when it burst forth from the womb;
when I made the clouds its garment
    and thick darkness its swaddling bands?
When I set limits for it
    and fastened the bar of its door,
and said: Thus far shall you come but no
    farther,
    and here shall your proud waves be
        stilled!

RESPONSORIAL PSALM

Ps 107:23-24, 25-26, 28-29, 30-31

℟. (1b) Give thanks to the Lord, his love is everlasting.
  or:
℟. Alleluia.

They who sailed the sea in ships,
    trading on the deep waters,
these saw the works of the LORD
    and his wonders in the abyss.

℟. Give thanks to the Lord, his love is everlasting.
  or:
℟. Alleluia.

His command raised up a storm wind
    which tossed its waves on high.
They mounted up to heaven; they sank to
    the depths;
    their hearts melted away in their plight.

℟. Give thanks to the Lord, his love is everlasting.
  or:
℟. Alleluia.

They cried to the LORD in their distress;
    from their straits he rescued them,
he hushed the storm to a gentle breeze,
    and the billows of the sea were stilled.

R̷. Give thanks to the Lord, his love is
everlasting.
    or:
R̷. Alleluia.

They rejoiced that they were calmed,
    and he brought them to their desired
        haven.
Let them give thanks to the LORD for his
        kindness
    and his wondrous deeds to the children
        of men.

R̷. Give thanks to the Lord, his love is
everlasting.
    or:
R̷. Alleluia.

SECOND READING
2 Cor 5:14-17

Brothers and sisters:
The love of Christ impels us,
    once we have come to the conviction
        that one died for all;
    therefore, all have died.
He indeed died for all,
    so that those who live might no longer
        live for themselves
    but for him who for their sake died and
        was raised.

Consequently, from now on we regard no
    one according to the flesh;
    even if we once knew Christ according
        to the flesh,
    yet now we know him so no longer.
So whoever is in Christ is a new creation:
    the old things have passed away;
    behold, new things have come.

✠ CATECHESIS

About Liturgy

Here I Am, Lord: Very few of us experience God in such an obvious, tangible way as do the disciples in today's gospel pericope. As a five-year-old, I saw a sketch of a person with hands raised in prayer in a missalette open in my father's lap. It was accompanied by a caption, which I asked my father to read to me. "Here I am, Lord, I come to do your will" was the caption, quoting Psalm 40 from that Sunday's readings. Without telling anyone, I decided that this image and these words must be teaching me a new way to pray, that by taking this posture and saying these words, I would experience an immediate and clear response from the divine: "Well, today I want you to clean your room, help with the dishes after dinner, and try not to pick on your sister too much . . ."

Monday morning, I went out in the backyard to give it a try. Unsurprisingly, though I had the posture correct and prayed the words with all the fervor any five-year-old could muster, there was no obvious and immediate answer to my declaration. Further, no matter where I stood in the backyard, no matter how often I appealed to God, no answer came.

Prayer, especially the gathered liturgical prayer of the church, doesn't operate like that, typically. This is not to say God is not communicating to us, trying to answer our prayers in accordance with divine will. Inasmuch as we might experience individually God's voice in communal prayer, the whole of the community also experiences God, Christ sharing himself by presences in Word, Eucharist, the priest-celebrant, and the assembly itself (*Sacrosanctum Concilium* 7). The answer to our prayers then, whatever they are, at liturgy is always relationship with God (Word, sacrifice, meal) and with one another (priest and assembly).

About Orans

With Hands Uplifted: The raising of hands is a most ancient prayer practice. The US Conference of Catholic Bishops document Praying with Body, Mind, and Voice states, "Early Christian art frequently depicts the saints and others standing in this posture, offering their prayers and surrendering themselves, with hands uplifted to the Lord, in a gesture that echoes Christ's outstretched arms as he offered himself on the Cross" (*Orans*). The name itself means "prayer," as in the Latin litanic response "ora pro nobis."

There is much debate about whether the orans posture is reserved, always and everywhere, for a priest. The Book of Blessings directs that while the ordained minister speaks words of blessing with arms outstretched, a layperson does so while keeping hands folded (18, together with instructions given in applicable rites). The orans position is prescribed for priests in certain other moments—the eucharistic prayer, presidential prayers—it's never mentioned for a deacon, at least at Eucharist. Some take this to be evidence that the orans posture is meant, always, for the priest alone. Others, employing a different but valid logic, suggest that at appropriate presidential moments, anyone can utilize the orans posture. Many liturgical rites may be rightly led by any layperson, who is not, in any liturgical law that I know of, barred from utilizing orans for presidential prayers (collects, for instance). Some go so far as to suggest the orans posture is okay for anyone anywhere, noting the relative silence of the rubrics when it comes to the assembly (compared to the mountains of rubrics for celebrants and other liturgical ministers).

About Music

Keeeeeeeeeep Singing: "How Can I Keep from Singing?" (Lowry) is almost certainly in your hymnal, and will be well sung by your congregation—if your musical leadership, with confidence, leads the long "keep" at the end of the refrain well.

JUNE 20, 2021
TWELFTH SUNDAY
IN ORDINARY TIME

cf. Luke 1:76

℞. Alleluia, alleluia.
You, child, will be called prophet of the Most
    High,
for you will go before the Lord to prepare his
    way.
℞. Alleluia, alleluia.

Gospel   Luke 1:57-66, 80; L587

When the time arrived for Elizabeth
    to have her child
  she gave birth to a son.
Her neighbors and relatives heard
    that the Lord had shown his great
        mercy toward her,
  and they rejoiced with her.
When they came on the eighth day
    to circumcise the child,
  they were going to call him
        Zechariah after his father,
  but his mother said in reply,
  "No. He will be called John."
But they answered her,
  "There is no one among your
        relatives who has this name."
So they made signs, asking his
    father what he wished him to
    be called.
He asked for a tablet and wrote,
  "John is his name,"
  and all were amazed.
Immediately his mouth was opened, his
    tongue freed,
  and he spoke blessing God.
Then fear came upon all their
    neighbors,
  and all these matters were discussed
    throughout the hill country of Judea.
All who heard these things took them
    to heart, saying,
  "What, then, will this child be?"
For surely the hand of the Lord was
    with him.

The child grew and became strong in
    spirit,
  and he was in the desert until the day
    of his manifestation to Israel.

See Appendix A, p. 296, for the other readings.

Reflecting on the Gospel

Few biblical figures capture the imagination more than John the Baptist. And no wonder! With his camel's hair outfit, diet of locusts and honey, and fiery temperament, John was a colorful figure, a booming prophetic voice, and an all-around force to be reckoned with. Of course, we would expect nothing less from the one who was sent to prepare the way for the Messiah. Something out of the ordinary was in order.

And so we would expect the story of John's birth to be special. The conception itself was miraculous; Elizabeth was barren and elderly, but she conceived a son. The angel Gabriel told Elizabeth's husband Zechariah that the child's name was to be "John," a name that refers to the graciousness of God ("grace" means "gift"). This naming becomes a somewhat humorous part of the story as it unfolds in today's gospel. Elizabeth insists that her baby boy is to be named "John." She is met with great resistance—this is not a family name! We can just imagine the elderly couple's exasperation as the well-meaning people around them insist that the babe should be named after a relative. Finally Zechariah asks for a tablet and writes a note to all of these (un)helpful people: "John is his name." Zechariah and Elizabeth will prevail. They will name the child "John" as they were instructed by the angel, and he will indeed be a "gift" of the gracious God of Israel. Once John is named, Zechariah's mouth opens (he had been struck dumb because he did not initially believe that Elizabeth would conceive), and he immediately begins to bless and praise God.

According to Luke's vivid account, the birth of John stirs up emotions and reactions, from rejoicing to amazement to fear and awe. It seems that even as a baby, John causes an uproar! News of the event spreads across the Judean countryside, and people begin to ask, "What, then, will this child be?" Of course, the miraculous conception of John and the awe and wonder at his birth already foreshadow the coming of the Christ. Jesus's conception will also be miraculous; he will also be the cause of awe and wonder. And those who lay eyes upon him will certainly ask: What will this child be? As Luke's gospel unfolds, it becomes clear that every prophecy in the world could not have prepared the human heart for the likes of John the Baptist or his cousin, Jesus of Nazareth.

In the last verse of our gospel reading, we are told that John grew and became strong, and that he was "in the desert." It is in the stark, empty, quiet desert that John's ministry will explode and the question of the people will be answered: *What will this child become?* He will become the voice crying out in the wilderness, the conscience of Israel, preparing the way for the Messiah and baptizing the people with a baptism of repentance. *What will this child become?* He will be the one who points to Jesus and names him the Lamb of God, who considers himself unworthy to untie the thong of Jesus's sandal, who will decrease so that Jesus might increase. John's life will play out in dramatic fashion from birth to death, but it will always point away from himself and toward Christ. This is why we celebrate John's birth.

Focusing the Gospel

Key words and phrases: "What, then, will this child be?"

To the point: John the Baptist's birth is filled with awe and mystery. Before the angel Gabriel is sent to Nazareth to proclaim Jesus's coming to his mother, Mary, a different angelic message is given to Zechariah: His wife, Elizabeth, who was barren, will conceive and bear a child who will "prepare a people fit for the Lord" (Luke 1:17; NABRE). In today's gospel the acquaintances of Zechariah and Elizabeth are filled with joy and amazement at the birth of their son, but become fearful when Zechariah's tongue is finally "freed" and he speaks, "blessing God." Sometimes, God's actions in our lives lead us to anxious questioning, wondering, where am I being led? In these moments we are invited to rest in the wonder and awe of being in the presence of a God who is so far beyond us. A God who has spoken through the prophets, "I know well the plans I have . . . for your welfare and not for woe" (Jer 29:11; NABRE).

Model Penitential Act

Presider: John the Baptist called sinners to a baptism of repentance as they prepared for the coming of the Son of God. As we prepare to meet Jesus in word and sacrament, let us call to mind our sins so they might be cleansed in God's abundant mercy . . . *[pause]*

Lord Jesus, you are the Son of God and son of David: Lord, have mercy.
Christ Jesus, you are the light of the nations: Christ, have mercy.
Lord Jesus, you came to show sinners the way: Lord, have mercy.

Model Universal Prayer (Prayer of the Faithful)

Presider: Through the intercession of St. John the Baptist, let us bring our needs and the needs of the world before our loving Savior.

Response: Lord, hear our prayer.

For all who minister to the people of God, following in the example of John the Baptist may they point to Jesus in everything they do and say . . .

For leaders of nations, may they protect the dignity of expectant mothers and safeguard the right to health care for women and their unborn children . . .

For all children in the womb, may they grow and develop in safety and security . . .

For all gathered here, may we praise the Lord by honoring and caring for our bodies, knowing that we are "fearfully and wonderfully made" . . .

Presider: Living God, your servant John the Baptist prepared the way for Jesus, our Savior and Lord, by calling upon sinners to repent. Hear our prayers that we might heed his call to conversion in our own lives and each day journey more closely with you. We ask this through Christ our Lord. **Amen.**

About Liturgy

Set Apart; Given a New Name: Names are important. In today's gospel, everyone is astounded that Elizabeth and Zechariah would name their child John, as it wasn't a name in their family history. Knowing, using, and teaching others to use liturgical verbiage is important. Names, in our faith tradition, indicate conversion and consecration, being changed and set apart for sacred purposes.

COLLECT
Let us pray.

Pause for silent prayer

O God, who raised up Saint John the Baptist to make ready a nation fit for Christ the Lord, give your people, we pray, the grace of spiritual joys and direct the hearts of all the faithful into the way of salvation and peace. Through our Lord Jesus Christ, your Son, who lives and reigns with you in the unity of the Holy Spirit, one God, for ever and ever. **Amen.**

FOR REFLECTION

• Through the prophet Isaiah, God says, "I will make you a light to the nations." How do you try to bring light into darkness?

• The psalmist gives God thanks that "I am fearfully, wonderfully made." How do you experience yourself as fearfully and wonderfully made?

• In the gospel we hear how Elizabeth's neighbors and relatives "rejoiced with her." Who are the companions in your life who share both your sorrow and your joy?

Homily Points

• As human beings, we are in a constant process of becoming. From the moment of conception through adolescence, our senses, intellect, and bodies grow and change at an astounding rate. In today's readings we find a proclamation about whose hand guides this growth. In the first reading Isaiah tells us, "The Lord called me from birth, / from my mother's womb he gave me my name." The psalmist proclaims, "You have formed my inmost being; / you knit me in my mother's womb."

• We are continually being called to become a people after "[God's] own heart." On this feast of the Nativity of St. John the Baptist, let us consider the growth in our own lives over this past year and rededicate ourselves to maturing into men, women, and children who bring Christ's light to all those we meet.

SPIRITUALITY

GOSPEL ACCLAMATION
cf. 2 Tim 1:10

℟. Alleluia, alleluia.
Our Savior Jesus Christ destroyed death
and brought life to light through the Gospel.
℟. Alleluia, alleluia.

Gospel   Mark 5:21-43; L98B

When Jesus had crossed again in the
    boat
  to the other side,
  a large crowd gathered around him,
      and he stayed close to the sea.
One of the synagogue officials, named
    Jairus, came forward.
Seeing him he fell at his feet and
    pleaded earnestly with him, saying,
"My daughter is at the point of
    death.
Please, come lay your hands on her
  that she may get well and live."
He went off with him,
  and a large crowd followed him and
    pressed upon him.

There was a woman afflicted with
    hemorrhages for twelve years.
She had suffered greatly at the hands
    of many doctors
  and had spent all that she had.
Yet she was not helped but only grew
    worse.
She had heard about Jesus and came
    up behind him in the crowd
  and touched his cloak.
She said, "If I but touch his clothes, I
    shall be cured."
Immediately her flow of blood dried up.
She felt in her body that she was
    healed of her affliction.
Jesus, aware at once that power had
    gone out from him,
  turned around in the crowd and
    asked, "Who has touched my
    clothes?"

Continued in Appendix A, p. 297, or
Mark 5:21-24, 35b-43 *in Appendix A, p. 297.*

Reflecting on the Gospel

It is to be hoped that the whole of this gospel is proclaimed today, as the option for the shorter version cuts out the portrait of the woman with a hemorrhage that is framed by the two-part narrative of Jairus's daughter. Mark deliberately structures his narrative so that the two stories relate to one another.

Jairus, a synagogue official, appeals not to the synagogue but to Jesus for the healing of his daughter. As Jesus and Jairus are on the way to his house, they are interrupted. A woman who is hemorrhaging, probably from a gynecological cause, worms her way through the crowd and touches his clothes. In first-century Palestine, a menstruating woman was regarded as ritually "unclean," excluded from relationships with her husband, family, friends, and worshiping assembly. Anyone or anything with which she came into contact during those days was also regarded as unclean. For twelve years, Mark tells us, the desperate woman had wasted money on physicians, and becoming even worse she had endured a living death of alienation. Regarded as a "contaminant," she should not even have been out in a pressing crowd; but she is ready now to risk being identified in the desperate hope that if she could only touch Jesus's garment she would be cured. (In Greek, the word translated here as "cured" is also the word for "saved.")

As she touches Jesus, the woman knows immediately that she is healed. In the depths of her body there is a sigh of relief and joy. When Jesus asks, "Who has touched my clothes?" the woman comes forward, falls down "in fear and trembling," but caring nothing now about who hears her story. Then from being nobody's daughter, disowned as wife, or mother, or sister, or friend, she hears herself named by Jesus as "Daughter." Jesus sends her away in peace, for her faith in him has brought not only physical healing that allows her to return after twelve years to her normal everyday relationships, but also establishes a new relationship as a member of the family of faith.

And so as Jesus continues to Jairus's house, now as someone who has violated taboos and been "contaminated" with ritual uncleanness by the woman, word comes that the girl has died. But Jesus encourages Jairus to have the same faith as the woman. When they reach the house, Jesus faces ridicule, scorn, and the ultimate enemy—death. With the girl's parents clinging desperately to the last thread of hope, Jesus takes the girl by the hand and tells her to "arise!" That Mark has retained in this narrative the mother tongue of Jesus and those with him, adds to the precious intimacy of the miracle. After rising from the dead, she begins to walk around, and Jesus tells the young woman's parents to give her something to eat—a sequence of events that parallels the resurrection appearances of Jesus himself and has eucharistic memories for Christian communities gathered as we are today for a meal of thanksgiving and nourishing.

The young woman is, says Mark, twelve years old. Blood now courses again through her body and, at about the age of beginning menstruation, she now has a future and a marriageable hope. The woman who had hemorrhaged for twelve years, whose menstruation was her shame, is also healed and whole. Both women can now go and live their womanhood in peace and wholeness, for God's reigning presence has touched and restored their lives through Jesus. These women announce to us the situation of women throughout the world who, for whatever reason, are still conditioned or condemned to insignificance or abuse; all those women who are still marginalized by society, yet who grasp bravely at other possibilities. Nor can the church opt out of its responsibility. The church's teaching about nondiscrimination needs to be applied to its own affairs. It must refer constantly back to Jesus and his way of relating to women and men in the Scriptures.

Focusing the Gospel

Key words and phrases: "[L]ay your hands on her / that she may get well and live."

To the point: Today's gospel contains the healings of two individuals—one, the daughter of a synagogue official who is "at the point of death," and the other, an unnamed woman who has been "afflicted with hemorrhages for twelve years." Jesus is approached by Jairus, the distraught father of the twelve-year-old girl, who pleads with Jesus that he might come "lay your hands on her / that she may get well and live." The woman with the hemorrhage is equally certain of Jesus's ability to heal with a touch. Through their faith and persistence, both Jairus and the unnamed woman proclaim Jesus to be the one whose presence and touch brings renewal and healing.

Connecting the Gospel

to the first reading: On the Fifth Sunday of Ordinary Time, we read of another healing from the Gospel of Mark where Jesus restores Peter's mother-in-law to health. On that Sunday, the first reading was from the book of Job, the Old Testament book that grapples with the temptation to believe that God deals out misfortune and illness as a punishment for sin. Today's gospel and first reading from the book of Wisdom reiterate that death and destruction are never the will of God.

to experience: We see God's desire for each of us lived out in Jesus's healing of the little girl whom he takes by the hand and commands, "I say to you arise!"
How is Jesus calling you to newness of life at this moment?

Connecting the Responsorial Psalm

to the readings: In its entirety, Psalm 30 is a hymn of praise whose author has been saved from a life-threatening illness. The psalmist writes in the third verse, "O Lord, my God, / I cried out to you for help and you healed me" (30:3; NABRE). For this reason the psalmist praises God, exulting, "You changed my mourning into dancing." In today's gospel, when Jesus arrives at Jairus's house, "weeping and wailing" for Jairus's daughter has already begun. After Jesus heals the girl, the onlookers "were utterly astounded." We can only imagine the rejoicing that must have taken place after having a beloved child restored to life and health.

to psalmist preparation: Throughout life we encounter moments of joy and moments of deep suffering and grief. As you prepare to proclaim Psalm 30, consider how you have experienced God's healing and life-giving presence even when overcome by sorrow. In the midst of life's difficulties, how do you continue to proclaim the goodness of God?

PROMPTS FOR FAITH-SHARING

The first reading from the book of Wisdom reminds us that we have been formed in "the image of [God's] own nature." How does this impact your understanding of God and your understanding of humanity?

The psalmist praises God, "[F]or you have rescued me." How have you experienced God's saving action in your own life?

St. Paul lists several areas of "excelling" to the Corinthians: faith, discourse, knowledge, earnestness, and love. Which one of these do you feel most comfortable with? Which are you being called to grow in?

In the gospel, Jesus tells Jairus, "Do not be afraid; just have faith." Where is fear impacting your ability to trust in God?

163

Model Penitential Act

Presider: In today's gospel, Jesus tells Jairus, the synagogue official, "Do not be afraid; just have faith." Without fear, but with true repentance, let us pause to call to mind our sins and to ask for pardon and mercy . . . *[pause]*

Lord Jesus, you heal the ill and mend the brokenhearted: Lord, have mercy.

Christ Jesus, you are our helper and guide: Christ, have mercy.

Lord Jesus, in you death has been destroyed and life is triumphant: Lord, have mercy.

Homily Points

• In today's gospel reading we encounter two desperate figures. Jairus, the synagogue official, is bereft over his precious daughter's illness and the seeming inevitability of her death. The woman with the hemorrhage is not only afflicted by a serious ailment, but has also "spent all she [has]" in seeking relief from doctors whose care has "not helped" her condition but only made it "[grow] worse." We can deduce that each of these figures has done everything he or she can think to do, and now turns to Jesus for healing beyond what mere humans can produce.

• In some ways, the plight of Jairus and the woman with the hemorrhage can give us insight into our own spiritual lives. Often it is in times of great trial or when we sense we have been pushed to the limits of what we can endure that we turn to God with renewed intensity. Perhaps Jairus and the unnamed woman would have been in the crowd following Jesus and listening to his words even if they had not been facing trials that seemed insurmountable. But because of their desperation for the healing that could only be enacted by the Lord of life, they experience an encounter that certainly would have changed the trajectory of their lives.

• We do not need to go looking for trouble or difficulties in order to draw close to the Lord and it is certainly not God's will that we would suffer, even when this suffering does bring us closer to him. Instead, we may be certain that God is present with us during times of joy and times of grief, tenderly caring for us when we are broken and in need of healing and renewal, as well as when we are standing strong on the foundation of faith.

Model Universal Prayer (Prayer of the Faithful)

Presider: With faith in God's goodness and mercy, let us bring our needs, and the needs of the world, before the Lord.

Response: Lord, hear our prayer.

For bishops, priests, deacons, and lay ministers, may their ministry bring comfort and healing to those who are suffering and in grief . . .

For leaders of nations, may they attend to the needs of their people with humility and justice by standing with the weak and vulnerable . . .

For parents of children who are gravely ill, may they know the comfort of God's tender care and the support of their family and community . . .

For all who are gathered here, by God's grace may we be healed from every ailment of mind, body, and spirit . . .

Presider: God of wholeness, you desire to bring all people into the fullness of your kingdom where peace and joy reside. Hear our prayers that we might be strengthened in faith and empowered to proclaim your good deeds and gracious love to all. We ask this through Christ our Lord. **Amen.**

COLLECT

Let us pray.

Pause for silent prayer

O God, who through the grace of adoption
chose us to be children of light,
grant, we pray,
that we may not be wrapped in the
    darkness of error
but always be seen to stand in the bright
    light of truth.
Through our Lord Jesus Christ, your Son,
who lives and reigns with you in the unity
    of the Holy Spirit,
one God, for ever and ever. **Amen.**

FIRST READING

Wis 1:13-15; 2:23-24

God did not make death,
    nor does he rejoice in the destruction of
        the living.
For he fashioned all things that they might
        have being;
    and the creatures of the world are
        wholesome,
and there is not a destructive drug among
        them
    nor any domain of the netherworld on
        earth,
    for justice is undying.
For God formed man to be imperishable;
    the image of his own nature he made
        him.
But by the envy of the devil, death entered
        the world,
    and they who belong to his company
        experience it.

RESPONSORIAL PSALM
Ps 30:2, 4, 5-6, 11, 12, 13

R̸. (2a) I will praise you, Lord, for you
   have rescued me.

I will extol you, O LORD, for you drew me
   clear
   and did not let my enemies rejoice over
   me.
O LORD, you brought me up from the
   netherworld;
   you preserved me from among those
      going down into the pit.

R̸. I will praise you, Lord, for you have
   rescued me.

Sing praise to the LORD, you his faithful
   ones,
   and give thanks to his holy name.
For his anger lasts but a moment;
   a lifetime, his good will.
At nightfall, weeping enters in,
   but with the dawn, rejoicing.

R̸. I will praise you, Lord, for you have
   rescued me.

Hear, O LORD, and have pity on me;
   O LORD, be my helper.
You changed my mourning into dancing;
   O LORD, my God, forever will I give you
   thanks.

R̸. I will praise you, Lord, for you have
   rescued me.

SECOND READING
2 Cor 8:7, 9, 13-15

Brothers and sisters:
As you excel in every respect, in faith,
   discourse,
   knowledge, all earnestness, and in the
      love we have for you,
   may you excel in this gracious act also.

For you know the gracious act of our Lord
   Jesus Christ,
   that though he was rich, for your sake
      he became poor,
   so that by his poverty you might
      become rich.
Not that others should have relief while
   you are burdened,
   but that as a matter of equality
your abundance at the present time
      should supply their needs,
   so that their abundance may also
      supply your needs,
   that there may be equality.
As it is written:
   Whoever had much did not have more,
      and whoever had little did not have
      less.

About Liturgy

Specifics Are Important: There are so very few Aramaic words of Jesus quoted in the Scriptures directly—not translated into Greek by the evangelists—that when we encounter them, we should recognize there is something important about them, even if what that was centuries and centuries ago is now lost. *"Talitha koum,"* we are told Jesus commanded, when healing Jairus's daughter. These words were, and in some way still are, revered by those who follow the way. It's as if, without these specific words, the girl would not have arisen from what Jesus called her "sleep."

Liturgically speaking, the dialogues that the assembly shares with, at different times, the priest (or other celebrant), the deacon, or the lector seem to operate in the same way. The assembly waits for a certain "call" to know exactly when and with which words to offer their "response." I don't imagine these moments, at least the usual ones from Sunday Mass, need to be listed here. What does need mentioning however, is that it is wise for anyone who begins one of these sorts of "forced dialogues" to avoid tinkering with the texts.

First of all, it is no one's right to change nearly any of the liturgical texts. Infrequently one will find rubrics that advise, "in these or similar words" or some comparable language.

Second, to the point here, changing the prescribed and expected texts typically disrupts not only the dialogue, but the liturgical moment as well. One celebrant I know, following Communion and just before the final blessing and dismissal, greets the congregation with "The Lord *is* with you." It's understandable, when we've all just consumed the body, blood, soul, and divinity of Christ, why one might decide to make that alteration. The change, though, does not give any deference to the antiquity and solemnity of the greeting, that we are not to change liturgical texts, and that anyone in the congregation might not know exactly what to say or do upon hearing those unfamiliar words.

A more obvious example: perhaps you know a priest or deacon who likes to adapt the dismissal to refer back to something from the readings or the homily. One for today might sound like, "Go in peace, to bring Christ's healing and hope to all you meet." Again, with no malice toward the intention, this kind of embellishment not only makes it difficult for the assembly to know when to respond, it also makes their "Thanks be to God" less sensical. Further, if the dismissal is being improvised on the spot, that person should be prepared for any slight pause to be filled with a hesitant "Thanks be to God?" from some percentage of the faithful, as if to ask, "Is that where this goes? I just want to do my part, and do it right!"

Stick with the prescribed texts of the liturgy. It's part of what makes the ritual prayerful and effective; it's certainly a large part of what makes the liturgy "work" as it's intended to.

About Music

Let Music Arise, II: Note that today's gospel of healings, each featuring people of great faith, will be followed next week by Jesus returning to his native place and experiencing a great lack of faith there. Because of this, music selections this week and next should be attentive not only to the healing power of God, but also to the hope and trust people of faith place in Christ, healer and teacher.

John Angotti's "Arise, O Church, Arise" (WLP) with text by Paul Nienaber, SJ, speaks directly to the pivotal gospel narrative and also evocatively describes how people of faith live and evangelize. Consider, too, "I Am the Resurrection" from the *Psallite* collection (Liturgical Press), which speaks to the ultimate rising our faith directs us toward.

JUNE 27, 2021
THIRTEENTH SUNDAY
IN ORDINARY TIME

GOSPEL ACCLAMATION
Matt 16:18

R̸. Alleluia, alleluia.
You are Peter and upon this rock I will build my
    Church,
and the gates of the netherworld shall not
    prevail against it.
R̸. Alleluia, alleluia.

Gospel

Matt 16:13-19; L591

When Jesus went into the
    region of Caesarea
    Philippi
he asked his disciples,
    "Who do people say
        that the Son of
        Man is?"
They replied, "Some
    say John the Baptist,
    others Elijah,
    still others Jeremiah or
    one of the prophets."
He said to them, "But who do
    you say that I am?"
Simon Peter said in reply,
    "You are the Christ, the Son of the
        living God."
Jesus said to him in reply, "Blessed are
    you, Simon son of Jonah.
For flesh and blood has not revealed
    this to you, but my heavenly
    Father.
And so I say to you, you are Peter,
    and upon this rock I will build my
        Church,
    and the gates of the netherworld
        shall not prevail against it.
I will give you the keys to the Kingdom
    of heaven.
Whatever you bind on earth shall be
    bound in heaven;
    and whatever you loose on earth
        shall be loosed in heaven."

See Appendix A, p. 298, for the other readings.

Reflecting on the Gospel

Today's feast, one of the most ancient in the church, celebrates the apostolic careers and martyrdom of two great missionaries of the early church. Persecution and divine rescue permeate the readings. The gospel contains the promise to Peter that he will be a "rock" who will withstand persecution and that he will be given the power of the keys and the power to bind and loose (which later, in Matthew 18:16, will be given to the larger community).

Especially since the First Vatican Council, the Matthean text has been at the center of understanding the Petrine ministry and the basis of *ex cathedra* infallible teaching and universal jurisdiction. Yet the dogmatic definition does not exhaust the richness of Matthew's text. Important in Matthew is the gratuitous revelation to Peter that Jesus is Messiah and Son of God. Throughout Matthew's gospel, Peter is one with little faith who often doubts and even fails but is rescued by the action of Jesus (14:28; 17:24-27). Jesus also stresses that on Peter the rock, he will build *his church*, which will be stronger than the forces of evil. Throughout church history the "rock" has been variously interpreted. The early "typological" and "mother" of all interpretations was that Peter is the symbol of every true, spiritual Christian on whom the church is built (Origen). While this section of Matthew has been a rich source for understanding the Petrine ministry, it has caused suffering and division. In his landmark encyclical On Commitment to Ecumenism, Pope John Paul II stated that "the Catholic Church's conviction that in the ministry of the Bishop of Rome she has preserved, in fidelity to the Apostolic Tradition and the faith of the Fathers, the visible sign and guarantor of unity, constitutes a difficulty for most other Christians, whose memory is marked by certain painful recollections. . . . To the extent that we are responsible for these, I join my Predecessor Paul VI in asking forgiveness." The pope mentioned New Testament passages that speak of the weakness of Peter and Paul (e.g., Luke 22:31-32; John 15–19; 2 Cor 12:9-10), which "show that the Church is founded upon the infinite power of grace." John Paul II envisioned a Petrine ministry characterized by mercy and unity.

Paul, a person of great energy and passion, is called, like the prophet Jeremiah, to proclaim the love and mercy of God manifest in the cross of Christ. He nurtures his communities with a mother's love and guides them like a father (1 Thess 2:7, 11), yet he reacts with a violent outburst, hoping that those who attack the freedom of the gospel "might also castrate themselves" (Gal 5:12; NABRE). Though he recognizes that Peter was the first to see the risen Lord, he does not hesitate to criticize him for duplicity: "[W]hen Cephas came to Antioch, I opposed him to his face because he clearly was wrong" (Gal 2:11; NABRE).

As we celebrate this feast of "the princes of the apostles," we recall the legacy handed down to be a church of apostles and martyrs. We celebrate the gift of the Petrine ministry as a witness of leadership and unity for the churches today, while not forgetting the prophetic witness of Paul. Can the Petrine ministry reach its fullness without a Paul to challenge it? Paul and Peter died most likely during the persecution under Nero about AD 67. Following different courses in life, they join in death as models for us of the cost and glory of following Christ.

Focusing the Gospel

Key words and phrases: "[F]lesh and blood has not revealed this to you, but my heavenly Father."

To the point: Today's gospel lifts up both the human and divine elements that are interwoven in the construction and living of the church. God calls mortals and sinners to collaborate in building his kingdom. While Peter is given authority and is proclaimed the "rock" of the church, he remains a human being in need of ongoing conversion to the will of God. It is the same in our time. The church is holy *through* the grace of God and also in need of constant conversion *by* the grace of God. Let us ask Sts. Peter and Paul to pray for us as we seek to be a church that proclaims Jesus as "the Christ, the Son of the Living God" with all that we say and do.

Model Penitential Act

Presider: Today we celebrate the witness of Sts. Peter and Paul in living the Christian life with fidelity and courage. For the times we have faltered in faith and bravery, let us ask the Lord for pardon and mercy . . . *[pause]*

Lord Jesus, you are the Christ, the son of the living God: Lord, have mercy.
Christ Jesus, you are our refuge and our deliverer: Christ, have mercy.
Lord Jesus, you bring us to the heavenly kingdom: Lord, have mercy.

Model Universal Prayer (Prayer of the Faithful)

Presider: Together with Sts. Peter and Paul, let us lift our minds and voices in prayer and place before the Lord our needs and the needs of our world.

Response: Lord, hear our prayer.

For the pope who shepherds the people of God in the footsteps of St. Peter, may he be granted wisdom to lead the church with faith and charity . . .

For leaders of nations, may they work to end capital punishment and for the reform of prison systems to aid in rehabilitation of prisoners . . .

For persecuted Christians throughout the world, may they remain stalwart in faith and find spaces of refuge to worship God in peace . . .

For all gathered here, like St. Paul may we "keep the faith" even in the midst of trials, challenges, and doubts . . .

Presider: God of saints and martyrs, in the witness of Peter and Paul we find models for our own faith journeys. Hear our prayers that in contemplating the lives of your holy ones, we might be inspired to serve you in truth and love. We ask this through Christ our Lord. **Amen.**

About Liturgy

A Big Church: We don't know everything there is to know about Sts. Peter and Paul, but we do know they frequently disagreed. Indeed, at times their relationship was strained to the point where any one of us might have just given up. Yet it is divine wisdom that pairs these two, liturgically and otherwise, in the hearts and minds of the faithful. The church as we know it would not exist with only one half of this pair. So, too, we must keep in mind the church they helped build is broad and deep, vast and nearly immeasurable in every conceivable direction. If devotional practices to, for instance, Divine Mercy aren't your cup of tea, they do appeal and are helpful to someone you know. So, too, lay-led Liturgy of the Hours, or adoration, or Taizé prayer, or . . . It's a big church, Peter and Paul can remind us, if we allow it to be.

FOR REFLECTION

• How do the lives of the saints inspire you on your own journey of faith?

• St. Paul writes to Timothy, "I have kept the faith." How do you keep the faith in times of trial, challenge, or doubt?

• What is your response to Jesus's question "[W]ho do you say that I am?"

Homily Points

• In today's gospel, Jesus begins by asking the disciples, "Who do people say that the Son of Man is?" After they respond, he probes further: "But who do you say that I am?" In many ways these two questions could be seen as a microcosm of the life of faith. Often, we come to know Jesus through others when they share who they know the Lord to be. This is a necessary first step to discipleship, but it is not the last step.

• Today's gospel emphasizes the necessity of personal faith. As Christians, we are the Body of Christ and we journey toward God together with the saints of our own time and of times before us. But ultimately, each of us must decide for ourselves how we will answer Jesus's question: "Who do you say that I am?"

SPIRITUALITY

Gospel

Mark 6:1-6a; L101B

**Jesus departed from there
and came to his native
place, accompanied by
his disciples.
When the sabbath came
he began to teach in
the synagogue,
and many who
heard him were
astonished.
They said, "Where did
this man get all this?
What kind of wisdom has
been given him?
What mighty deeds are
wrought by his hands!
Is he not the carpenter, the son of
Mary,
and the brother of James and Joses
and Judas and Simon?
And are not his sisters here with us?"
And they took offense at him.
Jesus said to them,
"A prophet is not without honor
except in his native place
and among his own kin and in his
own house."
So he was not able to perform any
mighty deed there,
apart from curing a few sick people
by laying his hands on them.
He was amazed at their lack of faith.**

Reflecting on the Gospel

Viktor Frankl, the Austrian Jewish psychotherapist who endured four years in Nazi death camps, knew by bitter experience that what gives light must endure burning. In *Man's Search for Meaning,* he remembered the light that radiated from those who remained decent human beings in the midst of the darkness of suffering and dehumanizing conditions. Each reading this Sunday is about those who were singed by failure and vulnerability, but who continue to be a guiding light to their communities. Ezekiel is sent by God to the people named as rebels, who are obstinate, defiant, and deaf to God's word. Paul finds himself facing opposition both from those who regard themselves as "super apostles" and who tout around the word of God for their own reputation, and also from the members of the Corinthian church who have fallen under their influence. And Jesus is found to be unacceptable and offensive in his own hometown of Nazareth.

Some cultures speak of the "tall poppy syndrome," the delight that some people have in cutting people down to size—usually a bit smaller than their size—by belittling them through subtle innuendo, and disguising resentment of another person's achievements by damning with faint praise. When Jesus is invited to teach in the Nazareth synagogue on the Sabbath, he fails to live up to the expectations of his hometown. What Jesus spoke to the synagogue assembly we are not told, but they were the authoritative words of the one who has exorcised, healed, raised from the dead, and proclaimed the Good News of the kingdom. But in some way the listeners consider that Jesus's words go against their own comfortable interpretation of family customs or established religion traditions. Here is the Nazareth version of the "tall poppy," so Jesus has to be cut down to the hometown size expected by those who think they know everything about him and his family, and recognize him as a local craftsman.

Jesus embodies the "scandal" of the ordinary, and familiarity breeds contempt in the assembly whose perceptions are limited to the domestic and parochial. They are closed to any surprising presence and action of God that would violate their own expectations and insight, and consider their own wisdom to be superior to that of Jesus. They ask the right questions, but their prejudgment supplies them with the wrong answers, and amazement deteriorates into offense and rejection. If the synagogue assembly is amazed at Jesus and has no faith in him, Mark comments ironically that Jesus is amazed at their lack of faith that leads to Jesus's powerlessness, because for his deeds of power to be effective they must be worked in the context of faith. Jesus has failed to call forth faith where he might have most expected to find it.

That the "Word was made failure and died among us" is the source of our hope, not despair, for as Maria Boulding, OSB, writes: "If you have ever been sickened by the failure of some enterprise into which you put your best efforts and the love of your heart, you are caught up into the fellowship of Christ's death and resurrection, whether or not you thought of your experience in that way. God had dealt with our failure by himself becoming a failure and so healing it from the inside. This is why we can meet him in our failure; it is a sure place for finding him, since he has claimed it. So central is failure to the Easter mystery that a person who has never grappled with it could scarcely claim to be Christ's friend and follower" (*Gateway to Hope*).

We may still be more inclined to listen to those who appear to be prophets on the celebrity circuit rather than those with whom we rub shoulders daily. We need humble ongoing and gospel-based discernment of the authenticity of prophets. Continued success is a dangerous criterion.

Focusing the Gospel

Key words and phrases: He was amazed at their lack of faith.

To the point: Jesus visits his hometown of Nazareth and arrives at the synagogue to teach. At first the people are "astonished" at the wisdom of his words and the tales of mighty deeds that Jesus has performed around Galilee. Quickly though their astonishment turns to suspicion and even anger. The crowd cannot handle the dichotomy they perceive between the ordinary and the extraordinary. How can the boy they witnessed grow up be the same man who now is said to be able to calm the stormy sea with a word and to heal illness with the touch of his hand? In the incarnation, we proclaim Jesus as fully God and fully human. In Nazareth, Jesus's neighbors were unable to look past his humanity to be open to the divinity also present to them. As Christians, how do we challenge our own perceptions and find God within the ordinary events, people, and things in our everyday lives?

Connecting the Gospel

to the first reading: In the gospel Jesus tells those who have taken offense at his words, "A prophet is not without honor except in his native place / and among his own kin and in his own house." In the first reading we encounter another prophet facing difficulty. God commissions the prophet Ezekiel to speak his word to the Israelites. Ezekiel's chances of success do not seem promising, as his prospective hearers are described as "[h]ard of face and obstinate of heart." Nonetheless, God sends Ezekiel, so that "whether they heed or resist . . . they shall know that a prophet has been among them."

to experience: Despite our failure as human beings to consistently respond to God's call with joyful trust, God continues to send messengers bearing his word and calling us to repentance. When have you experienced God's call and responded with an obstinate heart? Despite past refusals, how does God continue to call you to conversion?

Connecting the Responsorial Psalm

to the readings: For the times we have failed to answer the call of God and have instead been "[h]ard of face and obstinate of heart," our psalm offers a prayer of repentance: "Our eyes are fixed on the Lord, pleading for his mercy." In our baptism we have each been called to take up the mantle of "priest, prophet, and king." To be a prophet in the footsteps of Ezekiel and following the way of Christ, we must first listen before we speak. With eyes fixed upon the Lord, we become oriented to God's fidelity, beauty, and truth. As our being is permeated with the word and the presence of the Lord, we are able to prophesy to God's goodness in all that we do and say.

to psalmist preparation: This coming week, how might you rededicate yourself to fixing your eyes on the Lord?

PROMPTS FOR FAITH-SHARING

God sends Ezekiel to prophesy to the people who have become "[h]ard of face and obstinate of heart." When have you experienced these traits in yourself? How did your heart become open to God again?

God tells St. Paul, "My grace is sufficient for you, / for power is made perfect in weakness." What weaknesses have you experienced transformed by God's grace?

In the gospel Jesus proclaims, "A prophet is not without honor except in his native place." Are there prophets in your community whose messages have been dismissed?

We hear how the people in Jesus's hometown are unable to accept his teaching because they know him as "the carpenter, the son of Mary." In your relationship with Christ, how do you balance your understanding of him as fully God and fully human?

Model Penitential Act

Presider: In the first reading, Ezekiel is sent to preach to the people who have become "hard of face and obstinate of heart." For the times our own hardness of heart has separated us from God and his ways, let us ask for pardon and mercy . . . *[pause]*

Lord Jesus, you are the wisdom of God: Lord, have mercy.

Christ Jesus, your power is made perfect in weakness: Christ, have mercy.

Lord Jesus, you are true God and true man: Lord, have mercy.

Homily Points

• Through baptism we have each been anointed "priest, prophet, and king." In today's gospel we see Jesus carrying out his own prophetic ministry, among his friends, neighbors, and family in Nazareth. Despite the wondrous deeds Jesus has done since they last saw him, the people, though first "astonished" at him, quickly become offended. In his book *The Lord*, theologian Romano Guardini asserts that in the rejection of Christ at Nazareth, we find an "outburst of man's irritation against God and the essence of God: holiness." Perhaps it is the same irritation that caused the Israelites in the first reading to become "rebels who rebelled against me . . . [h]ard of face and obstinate of heart."

• This gospel calls us to examine two things. First, how are we exercising our prophetic ministry even when it might lead to rejection and ridicule? And second, how do we respond when we are the one prophecy is intended to reach? Perhaps these two questions are related, for in order to be a prophet of God's word we must first be cleansed and converted by it. The Bible includes numerous examples of false prophets who preach for personal gain by telling their listeners (usually people in power) what they desire to hear. A true prophet never speaks on his or her own account. In the Gospel of John, Jesus responds to a crowd gathered at the temple in Jerusalem who question his authority by telling them, "My teaching is not my own but is from the one who sent me" (7:16; NABRE).

• In order to fulfill our baptismal calling to be prophets, let us rededicate ourselves to being formed, converted, and changed by the word of God. Only in this way may we share this life-giving word of God with others.

Model Universal Prayer (Prayer of the Faithful)

Presider: Knowing that we are loved and cared for by our heavenly Father, let us not hesitate to place before him our needs and the needs of the world.

Response: Lord, hear our prayer.

For preachers of the Good News, having listened intently to the word of God, may they be inspired to share it with truth and fidelity . . .

For journalists throughout the world who risk personal harm in order to expose injustice and the abuse of power, may their safety be ensured . . .

For families that have been wounded through separation and divorce, may all members find healing and support . . .

For all gathered here, may our hearts be opened to God's word and action in our lives . . .

Presider: God of infinite goodness, throughout the ages you have continued to call all people to find shelter and refuge in your love. Hear our prayers that we might embody your peace in the world and help to establish your kingdom of joy. We ask this through Christ our Lord. **Amen.**

COLLECT

Let us pray.

Pause for silent prayer

O God, who in the abasement of your Son
have raised up a fallen world,
fill your faithful with holy joy,
for on those you have rescued from slavery
 to sin
you bestow eternal gladness.
Through our Lord Jesus Christ, your Son,
who lives and reigns with you in the unity
 of the Holy Spirit,
one God, for ever and ever. **Amen.**

FIRST READING
Ezek 2:2-5

As the Lord spoke to me, the spirit entered
 into me
 and set me on my feet,
 and I heard the one who was speaking
 say to me:
 Son of man, I am sending you to the
 Israelites,
 rebels who have rebelled against me;
 they and their ancestors have revolted
 against me to this very day.
Hard of face and obstinate of heart
 are they to whom I am sending you.
But you shall say to them: Thus says the
 Lord God!
And whether they heed or resist—for they
 are a rebellious house—
 they shall know that a prophet has been
 among them.

RESPONSORIAL PSALM
Ps 123:1-2, 2, 3-4

R̸. (2cd) Our eyes are fixed on the Lord,
    pleading for his mercy.

To you I lift up my eyes
    who are enthroned in heaven—
as the eyes of servants
    are on the hands of their masters.

R̸. Our eyes are fixed on the Lord,
    pleading for his mercy.

As the eyes of a maid
    are on the hands of her mistress,
so are our eyes on the LORD, our God,
    till he have pity on us.

R̸. Our eyes are fixed on the Lord,
    pleading for his mercy.

Have pity on us, O LORD, have pity on us,
    for we are more than sated with
        contempt;
our souls are more than sated
    with the mockery of the arrogant,
    with the contempt of the proud.

R̸. Our eyes are fixed on the Lord,
    pleading for his mercy.

SECOND READING
2 Cor 12:7-10

Brothers and sisters:
That I, Paul, might not become too elated,
    because of the abundance of the
        revelations,
    a thorn in the flesh was given to me, an
        angel of Satan,
    to beat me, to keep me from being too
        elated.
Three times I begged the Lord about this,
    that it might leave me,
    but he said to me, "My grace is
        sufficient for you,
    for power is made perfect in weakness."
I will rather boast most gladly of my
    weaknesses,
    in order that the power of Christ may
        dwell with me.
Therefore, I am content with weaknesses,
    insults,
    hardships, persecutions, and
        constraints,
    for the sake of Christ;
    for when I am weak, then I am strong.

About Liturgy

Sending and Receiving: There is an inherent danger in communicating with others. The danger persists whether the communication is face-to-face, over the phone, written words, or emojis—no form of communication is immune. The danger is, no matter how carefully we try to express whatever we wish to communicate, those who receive the communication must interpret what they are receiving and perhaps make inferences and other judgments, depending on the medium, regarding body language, tone, "reading between the lines," and other contextual clues. That is, nearly all of the time, people receiving some form of communication get something at least a little "wrong," and sometimes receive something almost completely different from what we meant to communicate.

There has already been so much real and digital ink spilled over the junction of what we might loosely call religiosity and patriotism that it might seem redundant to add to the conversation here. Topics such as the inclusion of a country's flag in the church sanctuary, or the singing of patriotic melodies—even those that include a mention of God or prayer—at liturgy are well-discussed and easily found on the internet and via other resources.

When it comes to the concept of miscommunication as described earlier, consider now the two examples above in this light: what might these two elements communicate to someone, regardless of what one's intent is, when they are brought to liturgy? What might the presence of an American flag in a sanctuary communicate, for instance, to someone visiting your church from a foreign country: that your particular church is somehow set apart from the church universal because it is American? When praying for our country, via song, or perhaps in the universal prayers (more commonly known as petitions or intercessions), is there something in the way the text is phrased that makes it possible for one to hear "God bless, protect, and guide America—but not those other lands" or "God bless, protect, and guide America—because America and Americans are obviously more exceptional than other lands and peoples"? Once, anecdotally, I read about a "Patriotic Rosary" one parish had prayed prior to a midweek Independence Day Mass some years ago. It included religious words from various political figures of our country's history, including from Robert E. Lee, commander of the Confederate forces during the American Civil War. How might those words have been received, I wondered, by any African Americans who had come by to pray that day?

Independence Day is of course an American celebration, and regardless of where one lives around the globe, there is nothing wrong with praying for one's country and homeland, one's civic leaders and citizens. In crafting our public prayer on civic holidays like this one, we should be particularly mindful of what we might be communicating to every individual gathered by Christ to pray that day, in union and communion with the universal church. Sometimes we communicate more with what is left unsaid, unsung, for good or for ill.

About Music

Music of All Nations: "This Is My Song" is a poignant text and melody (typically FINLANDIA) for moments of liturgical prayer intersecting with civic holidays. More recently, Michael Joncas crafted a text for the same hymn tune, titled "A Place Called Home" (GIA), expressing the dream of a hope-filled society where all humans are treated fairly, with compassion and grace.

SPIRITUALITY

GOSPEL ACCLAMATION
cf. Eph 1:17-18

℟. Alleluia, alleluia.
May the Father of our Lord Jesus Christ
enlighten the eyes of our hearts,
that we may know what is the hope that
belongs to our call.
℟. Alleluia, alleluia.

Gospel

Mark 6:7-13; L104B

Jesus summoned the Twelve and
    began to send them out two by
    two
  and gave them authority over
    unclean spirits.
He instructed them to take nothing
    for the journey
  but a walking stick—
  no food, no sack, no money in
    their belts.
They were, however, to wear sandals
  but not a second tunic.
He said to them,
  "Wherever you enter a house, stay
    there until you leave.
Whatever place does not welcome you
    or listen to you,
  leave there and shake the dust off
    your feet
  in testimony against them."
So they went off and preached
    repentance.
The Twelve drove out many demons,
  and they anointed with oil many who
    were sick and cured them.

Reflecting on the Gospel

Jesus has not been deterred by his rejection at Nazareth and continues to teach among the surrounding villages, but now it is time to send the Twelve to do what he has been doing. When Jesus called these disciples, Mark described them as "those whom he wanted and they came to him" to "be with him" and be sent "forth to preach and to have authority to drive out demons" (Mark 3:13-15; NABRE). We might be excused for wondering if they really are ready, for al-

though they have been with Jesus as he taught, exorcised, and healed, and had experienced his rejection by his hometown synagogue, their main recorded response to him has been the accusation of not caring much about them in the middle of the storm, and impatience with him over the "interruption" of the hemorrhaging woman! But, for our consolation, Jesus is willing to work with flawed disciples, and still dares today to send out men and women like ourselves to be instruments of the healing power and authority of God. What we hear in this gospel is both challenge and consolation to Mark's Christian community and every community that, through baptism, is called and sent on Jesus's own mission.

Now the "see, judge, and act" apprenticeship of the Twelve is to be tested in their first mission. Equipped only with the authority of Jesus's word and the memory of his example, the Twelve are sent out like their ancestors, with exodus urgency—with their walking staffs and sandals, for they are on a new and urgent journey to free enslaved bodies, hearts, and psyches as Jesus has done. They are to travel in pairs, with respect for the Jewish tradition that required that the validity of witness must be verified by at least two people (Deut 17:6; 19:15). There is to be no dallying or packing bags with things that are not really needed and will only become an intolerable burden along the way. Their missionary survival kit consists of the authority of Jesus and his word, the providence of God, and the hospitality of those who will open their hearts and homes to the Twelve. The one tunic they are allowed may also be symbolic of the single-mindedness that Jesus expects of those who, as Paul wrote to the Galatians, "have clothed yourselves with Christ" through baptism (Gal 3:27; NABRE). No matter what the quality of the hospitality offered to them, the disciples are to accept this and stay put. Searching for more congenial accommodation or company is not to be part of their journey. For people to welcome the Twelve, knowing that they have associated with the taboo, marginalized people, will spread the kingdom of compassion, and offer the possibilities of a welcoming reentry into religious and social relationships for the outcasts and shunned who have been healed.

If they are not well received, the disciples are to leave, not responding with any harsh words, but merely with the Jewish symbolic gesture of shaking off from their feet the dust of the unwelcoming place, as Jews did when returning to Israel from foreign soil. All that the inhospitable household was left with was insubstantial dust, rather than the word of God. We all need to be honestly and humbly discerning about when to stay and when to leave a particular mission, "and take upon's the mystery of things, / as if we were God's spies," said King Lear (Shakespeare, *The Tragedy of King Lear*). In the Christian sense, we are to be "God's spies," reconnoitering the possibilities for announcing the reigning presence of God in human lives in our own situations. And we must be prepared to fail, as Jesus and his followers failed, but without turning such failure into a career of self-pity.

Focusing the Gospel

Key words and phrases: Jesus summoned the Twelve and began to send them out.

To the point: In chapter 3 of Mark's gospel Jesus "appointed twelve [whom he also named apostles] that they might be with him and he might send them forth to preach and to have authority to drive out demons" (3:14-15; NABRE). Now, three chapters later the Twelve are given their first mission: to go out "two by two" to preach repentance, drive out demons, and cure the sick. With this first commissioning of the Twelve, we see that Jesus is not intent upon carrying out his work of proclaiming the kingdom of God on his own. Instead he seeks co-workers to join in his efforts. It is the same pattern we see throughout salvation history of God inviting human beings to be his collaborators, and it continues up to today. How are you living out your call to go forth and build the kingdom of God?

Connecting the Gospel

to the first reading: In the first reading, God invites the prophet Amos, who was called "from following the flock," to go and prophesy to God's people. Upset at Amos's words, which he considers demoralizing the people, Amaziah, the priest, demands that Amos return to his own home in the southern kingdom of Judah and there "make [his] bread by prophesying." Amos has a quick response, however: he is not a professional prophet like other "false prophets" of his day who made their living telling those in power what they wished to hear. He only prophesies due to his call from God. Amos is in a very similar position to the twelve apostles. We know that of the Twelve several were fishermen and at least one was a tax collector, but we don't hear of any of them having any particular "religious" credentials that would make them obvious choices to carry out Jesus's mission of spreading the good news to all people.

to experience: At times in our life of discipleship, we might be called to accept challenges that we feel ill-equipped to face. And yet, like Amos and the apostles, the only qualification we need is to discern the will of God in our lives and to respond to it faithfully.

Connecting the Responsorial Psalm

to the readings: In the first verse of today's psalm, the psalmist assures us, "I will hear what God proclaims / the Lord—for he proclaims peace." In the gospel and the first reading, Amos and the Twelve have listened deeply to God's word and now it is time for them to proclaim it to others.

to psalmist preparation: We encounter God's proclamation of peace in many ways: reading the Bible, opening our hearts to God in prayer, and listening to the prophetic voices of others. How do you listen deeply for the voice of God in your life?

PROMPTS FOR FAITH-SHARING

In the first reading Amos retells how God called him from being a shepherd to "prophesying to my people Israel." When in your life of faith have you felt called to speak out against injustice or oppression?

In his letter to the Ephesians, St. Paul writes, "In [Christ] we are also chosen." What does it mean to you to consider yourself "chosen" by God?

In the gospel Jesus sends the disciples out "two by two." Who are your closest collaborators in living the life of discipleship?

Jesus instructs the disciples to only bring the bare necessities with them on their mission. How are you being called to let go of the "non-essentials" as you follow Jesus?

Model Penitential Act

Presider: In today's gospel, Jesus sends out the Twelve, two by two, to proclaim the Good News. For the times in our life of discipleship where our words or actions have not witnessed to God's love and salvation, let us ask for pardon and mercy . . . *[pause]*

Lord Jesus, you consecrate us in faith, hope, and love: Lord, have mercy.

Christ Jesus, you call all people to holiness: Christ, have mercy.

Lord Jesus, you show us the way to life everlasting: Lord, have mercy.

Homily Points

• In today's gospel, Jesus's instructions for the Twelve as he sends them out on mission seem particularly challenging. They are sent into unknown territory and the only accompaniment for their journey will be a walking stick and a fellow apostle. Equipped with the barest of essentials (namely the clothes on their backs), the apostles are nevertheless successful in preaching repentance, driving out demons, and healing the sick. While few of us are likely called to the same asceticism the disciples display on their first mission, today's gospel does lift up for us an important practice: discerning what is most essential.

• Oftentimes as Christians, we might feel like we need to do or acquire numerous things before we are prepared to preach the good news, such as gaining a degree in theology, a ministry certificate, or a better understanding of the Bible. All of these are good, but often they also give us an easy excuse for why we are not yet sharing the good news with others. For the disciples, the only necessities for carrying out their mission were their relationship with Jesus, the commissioner, and also the assistance and fellowship of another apostle.

• This coming week, let's take time to reflect on these essentials in our own lives. How do we intentionally foster our relationship with the Lord and with our co-workers in discipleship? Instead of worrying about acquiring more "stuff" to aid us in ministry, let us grow in trust that the one who has called us will provide everything we need to complete the work he has given us to do.

Model Universal Prayer (Prayer of the Faithful)

Presider: As adopted sons and daughters of God, the Father, with hope and faith, let us bring our needs and the needs of the world before the Lord.

Response: Lord, hear our prayer.

For missionaries who bring the word of God to remote and dangerous areas of the earth, may they preach the word of God in safety . . .

For nations torn apart by war and acts of terror, may the peace of Christ come to dwell in the hearts of all who suffer . . .

For all suffering from depression, anxiety, and mental illness, may they be accompanied on their life journey by empathetic family, friends, and caregivers . . .

For all gathered here, may we heed the Lord's call to leave behind what is non-essential and to follow him on the path of discipleship . . .

Presider: God of all hopefulness, in Jesus you have chosen us to be your sons and daughters and to serve you in all things. Hear our prayers that we might joyfully give our lives to you and to proclaiming the coming of your kingdom. We ask this through Christ our Lord. **Amen.**

COLLECT

Let us pray.

Pause for silent prayer

O God, who show the light of your truth
to those who go astray,
so that they may return to the right path,
give all who for the faith they profess
are accounted Christians
the grace to reject whatever is contrary to
    the name of Christ
and to strive after all that does it honor.
Through our Lord Jesus Christ, your Son,
who lives and reigns with you in the unity
    of the Holy Spirit,
one God, for ever and ever. **Amen.**

FIRST READING
Amos 7:12-15

Amaziah, priest of Bethel, said to Amos,
    "Off with you, visionary, flee to the land
        of Judah!
There earn your bread by prophesying,
    but never again prophesy in Bethel;
    for it is the king's sanctuary and a royal
        temple."
Amos answered Amaziah, "I was no
        prophet,
    nor have I belonged to a company of
        prophets;
    I was a shepherd and a dresser of
        sycamores.
The LORD took me from following the
        flock, and said to me,
    Go, prophesy to my people Israel."

RESPONSORIAL PSALM
Ps 85:9-10, 11-12, 13-14

R̸. (8) Lord, let us see your kindness, and
        grant us your salvation.

I will hear what God proclaims;
    the LORD—for he proclaims peace.
Near indeed is his salvation to those who
        fear him,
    glory dwelling in our land.

R̸. Lord, let us see your kindness, and
        grant us your salvation.

Kindness and truth shall meet;
    justice and peace shall kiss.
Truth shall spring out of the earth,
    and justice shall look down from
        heaven.

R̸. Lord, let us see your kindness, and
        grant us your salvation.

The LORD himself will give his benefits;
  our land shall yield its increase.
Justice shall walk before him,
  and prepare the way of his steps.

R⁊. Lord, let us see your kindness, and
  grant us your salvation.

SECOND READING
Eph 1:3-14

Blessed be the God and Father of our Lord
    Jesus Christ,
  who has blessed us in Christ
  with every spiritual blessing in the
    heavens,
  as he chose us in him, before the
    foundation of the world,
  to be holy and without blemish before
    him.
In love he destined us for adoption to
    himself through Jesus Christ,
  in accord with the favor of his will,
  for the praise of the glory of his grace
  that he granted us in the beloved.

In him we have redemption by his blood,
  the forgiveness of transgressions,
  in accord with the riches of his grace
    that he lavished upon us.
In all wisdom and insight, he has made
    known to us
  the mystery of his will in accord with
    his favor
  that he set forth in him as a plan for the
    fullness of times,
  to sum up all things in Christ, in heaven
    and on earth.

In him we were also chosen,
  destined in accord with the purpose of
    the One
  who accomplishes all things according
    to the intention of his will,
  so that we might exist for the praise of
    his glory,
  we who first hoped in Christ.
In him you also, who have heard the word
    of truth,
  the gospel of your salvation, and have
    believed in him,
  were sealed with the promised Holy
    Spirit,
  which is the first installment of our
    inheritance
  toward redemption as God's possession,
    to the praise of his glory.

or Eph 1:3-10

See Appendix A, p. 299.

About Liturgy

Take, Bless, Break, Share: The eucharistic liturgy can be described using four words that depict the fourfold activity in each Mass: "Take, Bless, Break, Share." These words describe Jesus himself when he feeds the multitudes, when he eats the Last Supper the night before his crucifixion, and when he stops to dine with the two disciples on the road to Emmaus. So it happens at Mass: the presider takes the gifts of bread and wine offered by the community, blesses (consecrates) them, breaks them, and shares them. While some of the significance is lost with the usual practice of distributing small hosts and pouring the wine into separate cups before consecration, the pattern is undeniably there.

That pattern, further, is repeated by Christ with our very selves. We might believe it to be a conscious choice of our own will to arise and make our way to church on Sunday morning—and it is—but it is truly Christ himself who gathers, who takes us into that house of God that we might ourselves be blessed, broken, and shared with the world in need, sent to proclaim the Gospel of the Lord.

"Broken?" you might ask. "How are we 'broken' at Mass? Aren't we there to be made whole, to be made holy?" So we are, but the Lord also expects of us a certain vulnerability. Perhaps we come to Mass already broken by some of our "real life" experiences during the week, perhaps not. But in either and any case, we must allow ourselves, by the prayers, the Scripture, the music, by the multivalent presence of Christ himself, to be ripped apart to be made whole again. Does not the word "surrender" contain the word "rend"? "Rend not your garments, rend your hearts! Turn back your lives to me," says the perhaps familiar Lenten hymn "Led by the Spirit."

Each liturgy is a chance for us to enter into that truest of conversion moments and, like the apostles in today's gospel, be sent out to proclaim, heal, and build the reign of God, in Christ's name.

About Doors

The Jesus Door: Think of all the many doors you might pass through on a given day: front or back doors, sliding doors, revolving doors, barn doors, garage doors, car doors, screen doors, wooden doors . . . Ponder now Jesus as a door, as *the* door. Speaking of us, the faithful, as sheep in a pen, he tells us, "I am the gate. Whoever enters through me will be saved, and will come in and go out and find pasture" (John 10:9; NABRE). Jesus is the door.

Doors often figure prominently in church architecture and liturgy for the very same reasons. The door to the church is a gateway to heaven itself, or at least a foretaste of it. If the physical door allows one entry into the physical church building, the baptismal font, perhaps near those doors, is itself another door into the church of God, built of living stones. Candidates in RCIA are met at those doors, as is a casket, holding the remains of a loved one who in baptism died with Christ, hoping one day to share his glory. "Practically, of course, they [doors] secure the building from the weather and exterior dangers, expressing by their solid strength the safe harbor that lies within" (BLS 97).

As we enter the church by such a door, "taken" by Christ, we are also sent out, "shared" through it, to be Christ's hands and feet, to in turn bring more people to the church, to the door, to salvation itself. Salvation door, kingdom door, the Jesus door.

About Music

Active Discipleship: Bernadette Farrell's "God Has Chosen Me" (OCP) speaks strongly to the active discipleship the Scriptures call us to today.

JULY 11, 2021
FIFTEENTH SUNDAY
IN ORDINARY TIME

SPIRITUALITY

GOSPEL ACCLAMATION
John 10:27

℞. Alleluia, alleluia.
My sheep hear my voice, says the
  Lord;
I know them, and they follow me.
℞. Alleluia, alleluia.

Gospel

Mark 6:30-34; L107B

**The apostles gathered
  together with Jesus
  and reported all they had
  done and taught.
He said to them,
  "Come away by
  yourselves to a
  deserted place and
  rest a while."
People were coming and
  going in great numbers,
  and they had no opportunity even to
  eat.
So they went off in the boat by
  themselves to a deserted place.
People saw them leaving and many
  came to know about it.
They hastened there on foot from all
  the towns
  and arrived at the place before them.**

**When he disembarked and saw the vast
  crowd,
  his heart was moved with pity for
  them,
  for they were like sheep without a
  shepherd;
  and he began to teach them many
  things.**

Reflecting on the Gospel

The prophet Jeremiah sounded a warning over twenty-five hundred years ago, chastening those who would mislead the Lord's flock: "Woe to the shepherds who mislead and scatter the flock of my pasture, says the LORD." It is also a current problem, made tragically clear in the crisis of clergy sex abuse and its mishandling by so many of our bishops, laid bare in the media for all to see. It is a reality that drives people out of parishes, and even from the church.

Each of us is responsible before God for our behavior, but those who have been assigned to care for the people of God, the shepherds who have been asked to guide the sheep, have a heavy burden when the sheep are scattered and driven away due to the actions, or lack of action, by the shepherds. God chastises the shepherds who have "scattered my sheep and driven them away."

Through Jeremiah, God promised that the scattered "remnant of my flock" would be gathered up and good shepherds raised up to guide them. While the historical context of the Babylonian exile is clear in these promises to Israel through the prophet Jeremiah, the eschatological context is also evident in God's promise to "raise up a righteous shoot to David," who "shall reign and govern wisely." This promised Messiah was raised up as the Good Shepherd not just for the people of Israel, but also for all of the sheep who did not belong to that one fold (John 10:16).

And it was through the life of the Good Shepherd that we "who once were far off have become near by the blood of Christ" (Eph 2:13). The shepherd not only protected his sheep, but gave up his own life to bring us to life eternal. This compassion for the flock, both those who knew the voice of the shepherd and those who were not yet aware of their heritage as God's people, enlivened all that Jesus did in his mission. His work was for the life of his flock.

Jesus also raised up shepherds to continue to guide the flock. After being sent out to evangelize, the apostles reported back to Jesus on "all they had done and taught." The Good Shepherd's compassion extended to these protégés, who Jesus knew needed rest, so he took them to a deserted place.

Yet Jesus, when he "saw the vast crowd," did not turn from the flock and focus on the shepherds. Jesus's compassion was poured out on the sheep, "for they were like sheep without a shepherd." Jesus's compassion instead was a model for the shepherds who would continue his mission. In responding to the needs of the flock, Jesus gives us the priorities of the Good Shepherd: serve the people; care for the people; build up the people. These are the priorities not just of the Good Shepherd; they must be the priorities also of the successors to the apostles, who have been called to shepherd the people.

There are no excuses for shepherds who scatter the flock and drive people away. It is not that there is not forgiveness from God for all those who repent, for sin stalks all of the sheep of the flock. But when shepherds are unable to bear the burden of caring for the sheep, protecting the sheep, and even aid in the destruction of the sheep, they will indeed be forgiven when they genuinely repent. Still, even with forgiveness, they must never be allowed to guard the sheep any longer. It is for this reason that Pope Francis has recently established tribunals to deliberate on negligence among bishops.

All of us stumble, but true shepherds do not repeatedly put the sheep, especially the little ones, in harm's way, time after time, year after year, and then claim to be doing the work of the Lord. The Good Shepherd gave himself up for the sheep; woe to those shepherds who give up the sheep to protect themselves.

Focusing the Gospel

Key words and phrases: [H]is heart was moved with pity for them, / for they were like sheep without a shepherd.

To the point: Many places in the Old Testament refer to the people of God as a "flock." Psalm 95 calls the people to worship the Lord stating, "For he is our God, / we are the people he shepherds, / the sheep in his hands" (95:7; NABRE). This image of a shepherd and his sheep would have been a meaningful one to the Israelites. Not only did many of the great leaders of the Hebrew Bible tend sheep (such as Abraham, Moses, and King David), but the people would also be intimately familiar with a shepherd's role in the lives of the sheep. In today's gospel, Jesus looks upon the crowds who have followed him as sheep without a shepherd. They are desperately seeking the nourishment, security, and direction that only Jesus, the Son of God can provide.

Connecting the Gospel

to the first reading: The first reading from the prophet Jeremiah is addressed to the kings and prophets of Israel who have failed in their role as shepherds of God's people. Instead of protecting and guiding the sheep, these individuals have "scattered" and "driven [them] away." In the face of their perfidy, God proclaims, "I myself will gather the remnant of my flock." In John's gospel, Jesus identifies himself as "the good shepherd" (10:11) who will "lay down [his] life for the sheep" (10:15; NABRE). In the final verses of the reading from Jeremiah, we as Christians find another link to Jesus as the one who will "do what is just and right in the land" so that "Judah shall be saved" and "Israel shall dwell in security."

to experience: While we find comfort in knowing that God is our shepherd, today's readings also include warning to those who have abused the power and authority that they hold over others. Who are the people in your life you have been given to shepherd? How do you strive to take on this role with humility, mercy, and justice?

Connecting the Responsorial Psalm

to the readings: Today's psalm is attributed to David, the great king of Israel, who is "tending the sheep" (1 Sam 16:11) when we are first introduced to him in the Bible. This psalm offers details about shepherding that only a shepherd would know. For the shepherd, the welfare of his sheep is a constant preoccupation. He is responsible for their rest and their activity, their nourishment, and their health. In today's gospel, Jesus intends to find a quiet place the apostles could "rest a while." But when he sees the crowds longing to be fed with his life-giving words, he cannot turn his back on them. And so, just as a good shepherd would, he sets about tending to their needs.

to psalmist preparation: How do you experience God's love and care for you as that of a shepherd tending his sheep?

PROMPTS FOR FAITH-SHARING

Through the prophet Jeremiah, God proclaims, "I will appoint shepherds for [my flock] who will shepherd them." Which bishops, priests, deacons, religious and lay ministers have shepherded you well in life?

Today's psalm is the well-beloved Psalm 23. At this moment in your life, which verse calls to you the most?

In his letter to the Ephesians, St. Paul preaches that all become one in Christ. Where are there places of division in your parish community and how might Jesus be calling you to work for unity?

In the gospel Jesus invites the disciples to "[c]ome away by yourselves . . . and rest a while." What spiritual practices do you turn to when facing burnout?

CELEBRATION

Model Penitential Act

Presider: Today's responsorial psalm proclaims, "The Lord is my shepherd; there is nothing I shall want." For the times we have looked for fulfillment and comfort outside of God's love, let us ask for mercy and pardon . . . *[pause]*

Lord Jesus, you are our peace and our salvation: Lord, have mercy.

Christ Jesus, in you we find refuge and fullness of life: Christ, have mercy.

Lord Jesus, you call us to unity: Lord, have mercy.

Homily Points

• Today's gospel reading begins with the twelve apostles returning from their first missionary outing to preach repentance, cast out demons, and heal people through the laying on of hands. Jesus responds to their reports of all that "they had done and taught" by extending an invitation: "Come away by yourselves to a deserted place and rest a while." In this, the disciples are welcomed into Jesus's own pattern of ministry, which is disclosed in the first chapter of Mark. After traveling to Capernaum, preaching in the synagogue, curing a demoniac, and then healing Simon's mother-in-law, Jesus wakes up early the next morning and goes off "to a deserted place" to pray (1:35; NABRE).

• Unfortunately, it seems that both Jesus and his disciples are not granted as much peace as they might have desired. In Capernaum, it is the disciples themselves who pursue Jesus and "finding him [say], 'Everyone is looking for you'" (1:37; NABRE). In today's gospel reading, the crowds see the disciples and Jesus leaving by boat, and they are ready to greet them when they arrive at the place Jesus had intended to be one of quiet and rest.

• Jesus's response to the crowds that clamor for his attention, however, is not resentful or irritated. Instead, looking at the people gathered, he is "moved with pity for them." Today's gospel invites us to consider two aspects of the life of discipleship: How do we take time for necessary prayer and renewal, and how do we respond to the people who come to us seeking help and a listening ear? Though we don't read of it today, it is telling that after having fed the crowd and ministering to them, Jesus once again goes off on his own to pray (6:46). As in all things, Jesus sets an example for us to follow in the life of faith.

Model Universal Prayer (Prayer of the Faithful)

Presider: With confidence and faith in the everlasting love and mercy of our Good Shepherd, let us place our needs before the Lord.

Response: Lord, hear our prayer.

For all those who are called upon to shepherd the church of God, may they tend their people with humility and wisdom . . .

For elected officials, may they work to promote unity among all people and to banish the scourge of racism and prejudice . . .

For the oppressed who hunger and thirst for righteousness, may their voices be heeded by those in positions of power and authority . . .

For all members of this parish community, may we grow in faith, hope, and love as we seek to follow the path of Jesus . . .

Presider: Gracious God, you desired to shepherd your people to everlasting life and so you sent your son to teach us your ways. Hear our prayers that we might cling to his words and so be transformed into a people after your own heart. We ask this through Christ our Lord. **Amen.**

COLLECT

Let us pray.

Pause for silent prayer

Show favor, O Lord, to your servants
and mercifully increase the gifts of your grace,
that, made fervent in hope, faith, and charity,
they may be ever watchful in keeping your commands.
Through our Lord Jesus Christ, your Son,
who lives and reigns with you in the unity of the Holy Spirit,
one God, for ever and ever. **Amen.**

FIRST READING
Jer 23:1-6

Woe to the shepherds
    who mislead and scatter the flock of my pasture,
    says the LORD.
Therefore, thus says the LORD, the God of Israel,
    against the shepherds who shepherd my people:
    You have scattered my sheep and driven them away.
You have not cared for them,
    but I will take care to punish your evil deeds.
I myself will gather the remnant of my flock
    from all the lands to which I have driven them
    and bring them back to their meadow;
    there they shall increase and multiply.
I will appoint shepherds for them who will shepherd them
    so that they need no longer fear and tremble;
    and none shall be missing, says the LORD.

Behold, the days are coming, says the LORD,
    when I will raise up a righteous shoot to David;
    as king he shall reign and govern wisely,
    he shall do what is just and right in the land.
In his days Judah shall be saved,
    Israel shall dwell in security.
This is the name they give him:
    "The LORD our justice."

CATECHESIS

RESPONSORIAL PSALM
Ps 23:1-3, 3-4, 5, 6

R̸. (1) The Lord is my shepherd; there is
    nothing I shall want.

The LORD is my shepherd; I shall not want.
    In verdant pastures he gives me repose;
beside restful waters he leads me;
    he refreshes my soul.

R̸. The Lord is my shepherd; there is
    nothing I shall want.

He guides me in right paths
    for his name's sake.
Even though I walk in the dark valley
    I fear no evil; for you are at my side
with your rod and your staff
    that give me courage.

R̸. The Lord is my shepherd; there is
    nothing I shall want.

You spread the table before me
    in the sight of my foes;
you anoint my head with oil;
    my cup overflows.

R̸. The Lord is my shepherd; there is
    nothing I shall want.

Only goodness and kindness follow me
    all the days of my life;
and I shall dwell in the house of the LORD
    for years to come.

R̸. The Lord is my shepherd; there is
    nothing I shall want.

SECOND READING
Eph 2:13-18

Brothers and sisters:
In Christ Jesus you who once were far off
    have become near by the blood of
        Christ.

For he is our peace, he who made both one
    and broke down the dividing wall of
        enmity, through his flesh,
    abolishing the law with its
        commandments and legal claims,
    that he might create in himself one new
        person in place of the two,
    thus establishing peace,
    and might reconcile both with God,
    in one body, through the cross,
    putting that enmity to death by it.
He came and preached peace to you who
        were far off
    and peace to those who were near,
    for through him we both have access in
        one Spirit to the Father.

About Liturgy

Unintended Consequences: Many parishes designate one liturgy as the "youth Mass," or some similar moniker. Given that Pew Research indicates the age one typically decides to become a "none" in terms of religious affiliation is shockingly low—age thirteen!—these efforts seem sensical if not necessary and urgent. Frequently, a Mass time is created anew when a new youth minister is hired or a new pastor begins ministry at the parish. This Mass is "constructed," in all its pieces, in a way that the parish hopes will appeal to its younger members, typically teens and young adults. Often the Mass falls on a Sunday afternoon or evening; the music is driven by contemporary ensembles and is of recent composition and airplay on the local contemporary Christian radio station; if young people wish to be liturgical ministers, they are assigned to this Mass with their peers; the homilist is urged to be brief and to keep his words relevant to those gathered; the list continues, with some variances place to place.

It must be noted straight away that there is nothing *per se* "wrong" with anything on the above list. None of these efforts will by themselves, nor even in partnership with one another, make for a poor liturgy. The issue is primarily in the naming of the liturgy and focusing the ministry too narrowly.

It is easily argued that youth are in many ways a distinct subculture with needs and worldviews all their own, along with unique methods of communication, being in relationship, and growing in maturity, all very different from any generation that has ever existed before. Yet, we often overlook two questions: does the church need to respond, liturgically, in such a pointed way to that subculture, and are there any unintended consequences of doing so?

Starting with the latter, there certainly are unintended consequences, as any action always has those. The church is universal, we all understand; why should one fragment of the parish, liturgically speaking, be separated out? While a parish's various Sunday liturgies often feature different styles of music, preaching, and presiding, we don't typically name any of the other liturgies demographically. We might talk about a "traditional" Mass, but it's never called, officially, "the forties and up" Mass. (Of course, "traditional" as a descriptor has its own myriad issues.) Fragmenting the parish in any way—be it by age, language, or any other factor—fragments the very Body of Christ, who Paul teaches us all need one another to be whole and, frankly, functional. The youth are effectively separated from the wisdom of the community's elders, and they from the energy and passion of the younger generation.

There are further issues too: part of a faith family learning a completely different repertoire of music with which to pray; some parishioners feeling as if they are excluded from this sort of liturgical expression, even if they prefer it, because they are no longer "young"; more fundamentally, the inference that always develops—that one Mass is "better than" or "worse than" another. Unintended consequences indeed.

It is much better to think of each and every liturgy as an opportunity to make each person feel at home, welcome, and valued. Specific ensembles of music ministry will always minister at a certain Mass time; a certain associate pastor will always preside and preach with the same mannerisms and quirks; but if those with liturgical responsibilities are mindful that the whole of the Body of Christ is in the pews at each liturgy, *and if those in the pews are formed to be just as mindful of the same*, then a parish family will grow together in holiness, wisdom, and truth.

SPIRITUALITY

R⁊. Alleluia, alleluia.
A great prophet has risen in our midst.
God has visited his people.
R⁊. Alleluia, alleluia.

Gospel

John 6:1-15; L110B

**Jesus went across the Sea of
  Galilee.
A large crowd followed him,
  because they saw the signs
    he was performing on the
    sick.
Jesus went up on the mountain,
  and there he sat down with his
    disciples.
The Jewish feast of Passover was
  near.
When Jesus raised his eyes
  and saw that a large crowd was
    coming to him,
  he said to Philip,
  "Where can we buy enough
    food for them to eat?"
He said this to test him,
  because he himself knew what
    he was going to do.
Philip answered him,
  "Two hundred days' wages worth of
    food would not be enough
  for each of them to have a little."
One of his disciples,
  Andrew, the brother of Simon Peter,
    said to him,
  "There is a boy here who has five
    barley loaves and two fish;
  but what good are these for so many?"
Jesus said, "Have the people recline."
Now there was a great deal of grass in
  that place.
So the men reclined, about five thousand
  in number.**

Continued in Appendix A, p. 299.

Reflecting on the Gospel

In the three-year Lectionary cycle, we have no "Year of John." So that the significant John 6 may be proclaimed at some time in the cycle, it is inserted beginning on this Sunday through to the Twenty-First Sunday of Year B.

The account of the feeding of the five thousand is the only miracle recorded in each one of the four gospels. John's narrative is true to his portrait of a more self-sufficient Jesus who knows what is in everyone (cf. John 2:27-28). For John, miracles are "signs" that point to a reality beyond themselves, to the identity and truth of Jesus. It is Passover, but the disciples and the crowds that follow Jesus to a mountain by the side of the Sea of Galilee are a long way from where the religious leaders would expect them to be for this festival, namely, in Jerusalem.

John's account is concerned with how people respond to Jesus. The crowd is enthusiastic about his healing of the sick and they hope that they will get something out of their following of this miracle worker. Although he knows what he will do, Jesus asks Phillip what they should do about buying bread for the people, and Phillip's response is logical: it would cost more than half the annual wage of a laborer to give this number even a few crumbs, and Jesus and his disciples don't have that kind of money! Andrew's response is pragmatic, producing one small boy with five coarse barley loaves and two dried fish, a typical and minimal meal for two poor people, not five thousand! All these responses are inadequate, then as now, for what is most important is not utilitarian satisfaction, not logic or reason, not even the miracle that Jesus will work. The gospel concern is that people see what happens as a "sign" that points to something more and beyond, to who Jesus really is, and how he will satisfy not only empty stomachs but also empty hearts.

Jesus takes the little that is offered to him, and in his hands it becomes an abundant meal. Jewish memories and Christian eucharistic themes (well established in the Johannine communities near the end of the first century) are woven together as Jesus takes the bread, gives thanks, and, unlike the synoptic gospel accounts, distributes both the bread and fish himself. John is not concerned with practical catering logistics, but with the theological emphasis that in this Passover feeding Jesus becomes a personally nourishing presence to each person. This food that he distributes is more precious than the manna, for the people were not to leave any manna until the next day (Exod 16:19-20) because it would decay. Whatever fragments (*ta klásmata*) are left over from the lakeside meal are not perishable; they are to be gathered up (*synágete*) and cared for by the disciples. In the early church, the eucharistic assembly was sometimes spoken of as the "gathering," and the eucharistic bread as the "fragments" (for example, in Didache, 1 Clement, and Ignatius's Letter to Polycarp).

The response of the crowd is to hail Jesus as a prophet, one like that promised in Deuteronomy 18:15, who would usher in the messianic era. Knowing their intent to "carry him off" to manipulate him to their own political and material expectations of what the messiah should be and do, Jesus "withdrew" only to return later for a deeper engagement with the crowd, as we will hear in the continuation of the bread of life discourse on the following Sundays.

We bring to this Eucharist the little that we have, all the fragments of our inadequacies, our successes and failures, our hopes and fears. We offer them to God with the fruits of the earth and the work of human hands, and these small gifts are transformed and offered back to us as the gift of Jesus's sacramental Body and Blood, into whose life we are gathered. This is not logic, pragmatism, or self-satisfaction; this is *eucharistía*, thanksgiving for God's abundant and eternal generosity.

Focusing the Gospel

Key words and phrases: "There is a boy who has five barley loaves and two fish; / but what good are these for so many?"

To the point: The disciples begin this gospel passage focused on the scarcity of resources at hand to satisfy the hunger of the large crowd that has followed Jesus up the mountain. They discount the rations of five loaves and two fish as worthless in the face of the overwhelming need in front of them. On the Eleventh Sunday in Ordinary Time, we read the parables of the kingdom where Jesus equates its growth to a mustard seed becoming a bush able to shelter birds. Once again, this time in a miracle, we see the very small becoming very great. At the end of the gospel, the overflowing abundance of life in God's kingdom is revealed in the "twelve wicker baskets" of leftovers that remain—perhaps one for each of the twelve disciples to carry down the mountain as they contemplate Jesus's ability to take what is ordinary and insignificant and to transform it into a heavenly feast.

Connecting the Gospel

to the first reading: For the next several weeks, as we delve into chapter 6 of John's gospel, the first readings will draw a parallel between Jesus and an Old Testament hero. Today we read of the charismatic prophet Elisha, who miraculously feeds the people of Gilgal who are experiencing a famine (1 Kgs 4:38). In both the first reading and the gospel, "barley loaves" are multiplied to feed a large number of people, and afterward there is some "left over." In the gospel passage it seems the people of Jesus's time are aware that his actions mirror those of God's servants from the past, for they say, "This is truly the Prophet, the one who is to come into the world."

to experience: In John's gospel, Jesus performs signs that reveal to the people his identity as well as the nature of the kingdom of God. How do you experience Jesus and his kingdom as an abundance that can satisfy our deepest hungers?

Connecting the Responsorial Psalm

to the readings: Today's responsorial psalm invites us to trust in the abundance and tenderness of God. This is not just a global or impersonal generosity, but the intimacy of a parent who feeds a child or a caregiver nurturing one who is ill or weak. We are fed by "the hand of the Lord," and in him alone "all our needs" are answered. In today's gospel, Jesus's hands grasp the barley loaves to bless them and distribute them to the hungry crowd.

to psalmist preparation: Over the next few weeks we will delve deeply into Jesus's discourse about the Bread of Life. As you prepare to encounter Jesus in the Eucharist, how do you experience the sacrament as being hand-fed by the Lord of all?

PROMPTS FOR FAITH-SHARING

In both the first reading and the gospel, the people eat their fill and there is some left over. When have you particularly experienced the abundance of God?

Today's psalm proclaims, "Let all your works give you thanks, O Lord, / and let your faithful ones bless you." How do you keep gratitude and thanksgiving central to your life of prayer?

St. Paul instructs the Ephesians to live lives characterized by humility, gentleness, and patience. Which of these is most difficult for you to espouse?

In the Gospel of John, Jesus makes himself known through "signs." What does the sign of the feeding of the five thousand reveal to you about who Jesus is?

Model Penitential Act

Presider: In his letter to the Ephesians, St. Paul exhorts the community to "live in a manner worthy of the call you have received." For the times our own lives have not been characterized by humility, gentleness, and patience, let us ask for pardon and mercy . . . [*pause*]

> Lord Jesus, you are our light and our salvation: Lord, have mercy.
>
> Christ Jesus, you satisfy all who hunger and thirst for righteousness: Christ, have mercy.
>
> Lord Jesus, you have the words of everlasting life: Lord, have mercy.

Homily Points

• Today begins our multi-week detour into the Gospel of John from the narrative of Mark. It begins with the feeding of the five thousand, the fourth of John's seven signs that Jesus performs. This miracle is recounted in all four gospels. John uses it as an introduction to Jesus's bread of life discourse, which will provide the gospels of the next two Sundays. Both the sign of the feeding of the five thousand and Jesus's words about the Bread of Life focus on the Eucharist and inform our understanding of the mystery we partake in.

• Today's readings point to the abundance of the eucharistic meal. In the first reading, the prophet Elisha tells the people, "Thus says the Lord, / 'They shall eat and there shall be some left over.'" In the gospel the leftovers reveal the overflowing generosity of God in that twelve baskets of fragments are collected after everyone has had their fill.

• Throughout the gospel, the disciples are slowly initiated into the abundant nature of the kingdom of God. At first, they seem intent upon persuading Jesus of the futility of even attempting to feed the crowd that has joined them on the mountain. Philip tells Jesus, "Two hundred days' wages worth of food would not be enough / for each of them to have a little." And Simon Peter protests about the rations of five barley loaves and two fish: "[W]hat good are these for so many?" Of course, Jesus is not dissuaded by this seeming scarcity. He is the Bread of Life who has come to feed the world and he invites the disciples to join him in this endeavor. In our own lives as Christians, do we trust in the abundance of God or are our minds and hearts limited by the perception of scarcity?

Model Universal Prayer (Prayer of the Faithful)

Presider: Grateful for God's abundant love and care for us, let us humbly place our needs before the Lord.

Response: Lord, hear our prayer.

For all the members of God's holy church, may the Eucharist unify and nourish us as we journey together on the path of discipleship . . .

For leaders of nations, may their governance be characterized by humility, gentleness, and patience as they seek to serve their people with integrity . . .

For all who hunger on this day, may their needs be met through the generosity of others . . .

For all gathered here, may we never cease to praise the Lord and to give him thanks for his goodness . . .

Presider: God of all blessings, you alone can satisfy our deepest needs and longings. Hear our prayers that we might freely share the lavish gifts you have bestowed upon us. We ask this through Christ our Lord. **Amen.**

COLLECT

Let us pray.

Pause for silent prayer

O God, protector of those who hope in you,
without whom nothing has firm foundation, nothing is holy,
bestow in abundance your mercy upon us
and grant that, with you as our ruler and guide,
we may use the good things that pass
in such a way as to hold fast even now
to those that ever endure.
Through our Lord Jesus Christ, your Son,
who lives and reigns with you in the unity of the Holy Spirit,
one God, for ever and ever. **Amen.**

FIRST READING

2 Kgs 4:42-44

A man came from Baal-shalishah bringing to Elisha, the man of God,
    twenty barley loaves made from the firstfruits,
    and fresh grain in the ear.
Elisha said, "Give it to the people to eat."
But his servant objected,
    "How can I set this before a hundred people?"
Elisha insisted, "Give it to the people to eat.
For thus says the LORD,
    'They shall eat and there shall be some left over.'"
And when they had eaten, there was some left over,
    as the LORD had said.

RESPONSORIAL PSALM

Ps 145:10-11, 15-16, 17-18

R̍. (cf. 16) The hand of the Lord feeds us;
    he answers all our needs.

Let all your works give you thanks, O
    Lord,
    and let your faithful ones bless you.
Let them discourse of the glory of your
    kingdom
    and speak of your might.

R̍. The hand of the Lord feeds us; he
    answers all our needs.

The eyes of all look hopefully to you,
    and you give them their food in due
        season;
you open your hand
    and satisfy the desire of every living
        thing.

R̍. The hand of the Lord feeds us; he
    answers all our needs.

The Lord is just in all his ways
    and holy in all his works.
The Lord is near to all who call upon him,
    to all who call upon him in truth.

R̍. The hand of the Lord feeds us; he
    answers all our needs.

SECOND READING

Eph 4:1-6

Brothers and sisters:
I, a prisoner for the Lord,
    urge you to live in a manner worthy of
        the call you have received,
    with all humility and gentleness, with
        patience,
    bearing with one another through love,
    striving to preserve the unity of the
        spirit through the bond of peace:
    one body and one Spirit,
    as you were also called to the one hope
        of your call;
    one Lord, one faith, one baptism;
    one God and Father of all,
    who is over all and through all and in
        all.

About Liturgy

Cloth and Wineskins—Evaluating Liturgy: In some ways, the next five weeks are a quasi-liturgical season, a retreat the church gives us every three years, to contemplate the importance of the Eucharist in our faith and our lives. We've recently discussed here how the liturgy is the source and summit of the Christian life, and how that expression has been extended not only to the celebration of the Eucharist specifically but also to the Eucharist itself—the consecrated bread and wine become body, blood, soul, and divinity. It's noteworthy, then, that as we begin this five-week time of contemplation on the Bread of Life that the first set of readings points us toward not the food itself, but the action of sharing and feeding on the miraculous feast provided by God.

It's not as if between these two sources and summits—the action of the eucharistic liturgy or the eucharistic objects themselves—that we need to decide which is more important than the other. They are both important, vital in their own ways, and indeed inextricably linked. So says the famous Frank Sinatra hit "Love and Marriage": "You can't have one without the other!"

It is just as vital that we periodically evaluate our liturgies, particularly Eucharist, to ensure our practices conform to the instructions given us and are pastorally connected to the communities that gather in prayer and worship. There are many tools, many questions, many ways in which one might approach such an evaluation; previous editions of this have offered valuable techniques with which to take assessment of our liturgical efforts.

Over the next few weeks, we will approach here our evaluation through the lens of the parable of the cloth and wineskins, found at Luke 5:36-38 (NABRE; as well as in Matthew and Mark). Read the text of the parable, which we'll then break open a bit over the coming weeks: "And he also told them a parable. 'No one tears a piece from a new cloak to patch an old one. Otherwise, he will tear the new and the piece from it will not match the old cloak. Likewise, no one pours new wine into old wineskins. Otherwise, the new wine will burst the skins, and it will be spilled, and the skins will be ruined. Rather, new wine must be poured into fresh wineskins.'"

About Music

Bread, Bread, Bread, Bread, Bread: The five-week stretch of the bread of life discourse can be problematic for those responsible for liturgical music selections week to week. While there is no shortage of eucharistic hymns, many communities know a limited number of them, and, when seeking three or four for a given weekend instead of the more typical one, options can run out quickly. It is critical, then, that a close reading of each text give distinction and nuance to the selections, and that this five-week period be planned as a whole, mindful of the eucharistic journey the readings provide for us every three years.

This first Sunday, the readings of this pilgrimage speak of the miraculous abundance of sustenance the Lord is able to provide for us. Musically, "All Who Hunger" with text by Sylvia Dunstan works well as a gathering hymn and is found, among other iterations, in a lovely setting by Bob Moore (GIA). "Miracle of Grace" by Curtis Stephan (OCP) would give contemporary sound and voice to our sung prayers this weekend.

SPIRITUALITY

GOSPEL ACCLAMATION
Matt 4:4b

℟. Alleluia, alleluia.
One does not live on bread alone, but by every
word that comes forth from the mouth of God.
℟. Alleluia, alleluia.

Gospel

John 6:24-35; L113B

When the crowd saw that
    neither Jesus nor his
    disciples were there,
  they themselves got into boats
  and came to Capernaum
    looking for Jesus.
And when they found him across
    the sea they said to him,
  "Rabbi, when did you get here?"
Jesus answered them and said,
  "Amen, amen, I say to you,
  you are looking for me not because
    you saw signs
  but because you ate the loaves and
    were filled.
Do not work for food that perishes
  but for the food that endures for
    eternal life,
  which the Son of Man will give you.
For on him the Father, God, has set his
    seal."
So they said to him,
  "What can we do to accomplish the
    works of God?"
Jesus answered and said to them,
  "This is the work of God, that you
    believe in the one he sent."
So they said to him,
  "What sign can you do, that we may
    see and believe in you?
What can you do?
Our ancestors ate manna in the desert,
    as it is written:
  *He gave them bread from heaven to
    eat.*"

Continued in Appendix A, p. 299.

Reflecting on the Gospel

After the multiplication of the loaves the crowds hail Jesus as prophet and want to make him king, so he withdraws from them. When they find him, they ask, "[W]hen did you get here [Capernaum]?" The question serves as foil for Jesus to say that they were interested only in the material benefits of the feeding without seeing that it was a symbol of the "food that endures for eternal life" and which the Son of Man will give. Highly condensed in this answer is a summary of the whole ministry of Jesus. He will come to bring eternal life, that is, the fullness of life to people, and this will be brought about through the cross, when the Son of Man who is lifted up will draw all people to himself (John 12:32).

The misunderstanding continues in the next question posed by the crowds, who seek some easy way to perform the works of God (such as the multiplication of loaves). The Johannine Jesus responds with another foundational theme of the gospel: "This is the work of God, that you believe in the one he sent." At the conclusion, in John 20:31, the evangelist will comment, "But these [things] are written that you may [come to] believe that Jesus is the Messiah, the Son of God, and that through this belief you may have life in his name" (NABRE). Believing, which is never a noun in John (that is faith), is the aim of the whole gospel and challenges readers to accept the extraordinary claim that in the very text of the gospel they encounter the transcendent God in the person of the Word made flesh.

Yet another misunderstanding is posed to Jesus, where the crowd seems to oppose this "work" with the gift of manna in the desert (a miraculous work of God), which Jesus again counters by saying that the manna was not a miracle of Moses, but God's gift of bread from heaven, and that God's bread from heaven gives life to the world, and he is the Bread of Life, so that "whoever comes to me will never hunger, and whoever believes in me will never thirst." The next major section of the discourse extends from this saying to its repetition in 6:51, when in clear eucharistic language Jesus will speak of eating his flesh and drinking his blood.

Two major themes are woven into the tapestry of this discourse which help to shape eucharistic theology today. In the Jewish tradition the manna in the desert came to be associated with the giving of the Torah, so that believers are nurtured by God's teaching as were their ancestors in the wilderness, and the wisdom of God is often portrayed by the metaphor of food. Throughout the first section of the discourse (6:24-51), while speaking of the bread of life, Jesus uses language of believing, drawing near, and listening, terms that are associated more with assimilation of wisdom than eating. The full participation in eating the body and drinking the blood of Jesus (6:55-56) follows upon personal commitment and love which draws a person to absorb the teaching of Jesus and imitate his life given for others (John 13:34; 15:12).

John's Jesus today says the bread of God that comes down from heaven "gives life to the *world*" and "whoever comes to me will never hunger, and whoever believes in me will never thirst." Jesus then says, "I will not reject anyone who comes to me." The eucharistic discipline of the church, especially by not exploring more open Eucharist hospitality, is in tension with this Johannine theology. Should people who have been nurtured by the teaching of Jesus be excluded from eucharistic participation? Can Christians be urged to respond fully to John 6:1-51 and be denied the gift of John 6:52-59? Baptized Christians, in the words of the second reading, form a new people "created in God's way in righteousness and holiness of truth." How will they participate in the fullness of this life?

Focusing the Gospel

Key words and phrases: "I am the bread of life."

To the point: The Gospel of John contains seven "I am" statements by Jesus that make known his identity and also connect him to God, the Father who revealed himself to Moses by stating, "I am who I am" (Exod 3:14; NABRE). In today's gospel we find the first of these statements when Jesus tells the gathered crowd, "I am the bread of life; / whoever comes to me will never hunger, / and whoever believes in me will never thirst." The sustenance that Jesus will provide goes beyond the physical needs of the body to something even more essential. This bread which gives "life to the world" will animate heart and soul with charity and love, binding all into the one Body of Christ.

Connecting the Gospel

to the first reading: While last week's gospel alluded to Elisha through the use of barley loaves in the miracle of the feeding of the five thousand, today's gospel is even more concretely connected to the first reading as the gathered people ask Jesus, "What sign can you do, that we may see and believe in you? . . . Our ancestors ate manna in the desert." The first reading from the book of Exodus details how the Lord tells Moses, "I will now rain down bread from heaven for you." After their escape from slavery in the land of Egypt, the Hebrew people renew their relationship with God by spending forty years in the desert. Once again, they learn reliance on God, who provides for their every need—from the gifts of manna, quail, and water to sustain them, to the greatest gift of the law that will guide their lives.

to experience: By revealing himself as the Bread of Life, Jesus invites us also to rely fully on him, stating, "Do not work for food that perishes / but for the food that endures for eternal life." How do you experience the Eucharist as the "source and summit" of your being?

Connecting the Responsorial Psalm

to the readings: Today's psalm recalls the gift of manna in the desert by proclaiming, "The Lord gave them bread from heaven." It is a psalm of faith and hope with the people responding to God's saving acts by promising to "declare to the generation to come / the glorious deeds of the Lord and his strength / and the wonders that he has wrought." As Christians, we also find in today's psalm a reference to Christ, the Bread of Life, who continues to be our heavenly food at the eucharistic banquet.

to psalmist preparation: What are the glorious deeds and wonders the Lord has wrought in your life and how do you proclaim his faithfulness and love to those you meet?

PROMPTS FOR FAITH-SHARING

Today's psalm proclaims, "We will declare to the generation to come / the glorious deeds of the Lord." How do you share your experience of God with the next generation in your family?

St. Paul urges the Ephesians to "be renewed in the spirit of your minds." What area of your life is in need of renewal at this moment?

Jesus instructs the crowd, "Do not work for food that perishes / but for the food that endures for eternal life." How does the Eucharist nourish and strengthen you on the path of discipleship?

Jesus also says, "This is the work of God, that you believe in the one he sent." How do you experience faith as "the work of God"?

185

CELEBRATION

Model Penitential Act

Presider: In today's first reading from the book of Exodus, God provides manna for the people of Israel despite their grumbling. For the times we have rebelled against the Lord and failed to trust in his providence, let us ask for pardon and mercy . . . *[pause]*

Lord Jesus, you are the bread of heaven that gives life to the world: Lord, have mercy.

Christ Jesus, you are the truth that sets us free: Christ, have mercy.

Lord Jesus, you are peace and healing for those in need: Lord, have mercy.

Homily Points

• Today's gospel begins with the crowds who were present at the feeding of the five thousand once again searching for and finding Jesus. In a way, Jesus seems to chide them for their persistence. They are looking for him not because they are seeking spiritual fulfillment but instead because their physical hunger was miraculously sated by the loaves and the fish on the mountainside. Jesus instructs them, "Do not work for food that perishes / but for the food that endures for eternal life."

• In many ways, physical hunger is an apt metaphor for the spiritual life. We need food in order to live, and as Abraham Maslow's hierarchy of needs points out, nothing else matters if we are unable to attain the basic necessities of air, water, food, rest, and health. Only after these key needs have been met can we begin to focus on the ascending exigencies of security, love and belonging, esteem, and finally self-actualization. The people who clamor for Jesus's attention have been initially enthralled by his ability to provide for their physical hunger. Now Jesus asks them to seek something else—not the bread and water that will satisfy for a moment but instead heavenly nourishment that alleviates all hunger and thirst.

• Considering this through the lens of Maslow's pyramid, we could surmise that Jesus wants his followers not only to have the basic necessities of survival, but to have the "bread of life," which nourishes them to be the people God has dreamed them to be (the fullest definition of self-actualization). One need only browse the self-help section of a bookstore to find evidence for our universal desire as humans to become better and more than we are. Jesus points us to the true food, the Eucharist and the word of God, that will nurture us to be fully alive in Christ.

Model Universal Prayer (Prayer of the Faithful)

Presider: In today's gospel, Jesus reveals himself as "the bread of life" who satisfies every hunger. Grateful for God's provision, let us bring our needs before the Lord.

Response: Lord, hear our prayer.

For all who serve at the altar of the Lord, may their ministry be renewed and their hearts strengthened through devotion to the Eucharist . . .

For leaders of nations, may they work together with charity and wisdom to find solutions for hunger and famine worldwide . . .

For those experiencing unemployment and underemployment, may their needs and the needs of their families be attended to as they search for sustainable work . . .

For all gathered here, nourished by the Body and Blood of Jesus, may we go forth to be bread that is broken and wine that is poured out for others . . .

Presider: God of all goodness, you feed us with the bread from heaven and fortify us for eternal life in your kingdom. Hear our prayers that we might always dwell in your presence and be intent on drawing others to you. We ask this through Christ our Lord. **Amen.**

COLLECT

Let us pray.

Pause for silent prayer

Draw near to your servants, O Lord,
and answer their prayers with unceasing kindness,
that, for those who glory in you as their Creator and guide,
you may restore what you have created
and keep safe what you have restored.
Through our Lord Jesus Christ, your Son,
who lives and reigns with you in the unity of the Holy Spirit,
one God, for ever and ever. **Amen.**

FIRST READING
Exod 16:2-4, 12-15

The whole Israelite community grumbled against Moses and Aaron.
The Israelites said to them,
"Would that we had died at the LORD's hand in the land of Egypt,
as we sat by our fleshpots and ate our fill of bread!
But you had to lead us into this desert
to make the whole community die of famine!"

Then the LORD said to Moses,
"I will now rain down bread from heaven for you.
Each day the people are to go out and gather their daily portion;
thus will I test them,
to see whether they follow my instructions or not.

"I have heard the grumbling of the Israelites.
Tell them: In the evening twilight you shall eat flesh,
and in the morning you shall have your fill of bread,
so that you may know that I, the LORD, am your God."

In the evening quail came up and covered the camp.
In the morning a dew lay all about the camp,
and when the dew evaporated, there on the surface of the desert
were fine flakes like hoarfrost on the ground.
On seeing it, the Israelites asked one another, "What is this?"
for they did not know what it was.
But Moses told them,
"This is the bread that the LORD has given you to eat."

RESPONSORIAL PSALM

Ps 78:3-4, 23-24, 25, 54

R℣. (24b) The Lord gave them bread from
heaven.

What we have heard and know,
and what our fathers have declared to
us,
we will declare to the generation to come
the glorious deeds of the LORD and his
strength
and the wonders that he wrought.

R℣. The Lord gave them bread from
heaven.

He commanded the skies above
and opened the doors of heaven;
he rained manna upon them for food
and gave them heavenly bread.

R℣. The Lord gave them bread from
heaven.

Man ate the bread of angels,
food he sent them in abundance.
And he brought them to his holy land,
to the mountains his right hand had
won.

R℣. The Lord gave them bread from
heaven.

SECOND READING

Eph 4:17, 20-24

Brothers and sisters:
I declare and testify in the Lord
that you must no longer live as the
Gentiles do,
in the futility of their minds;
that is not how you learned Christ,
assuming that you have heard of him
and were taught in him,
as truth is in Jesus,
that you should put away the old self of
your former way of life,
corrupted through deceitful desires,
and be renewed in the spirit of your
minds,
and put on the new self,
created in God's way in righteousness
and holiness of truth.

About Liturgy

Wineskins, Old and New: Returning to the parable of the cloth and wineskins (see last week's "About Liturgy" section), let us turn our attention to evaluating our eucharistic liturgies through the lenses this pericope offers.

The more well-known portion of this parable is the second half, that of the wine and wineskins. While many of us are probably familiar with wine, it is likely that none of us have similar familiarity with wineskins. What were they, why were they used, and why shouldn't one put new wine into old wineskins?

Wineskins, as the name suggests, were made from animal hides, often from a goat, and were used to hold and transport various liquids of Jesus's time. Usually wine was only partly fermented when poured into wineskins. The continuing fermentation process would produce gasses that would in turn stretch the wineskin. Old wineskins had been previously stretched and could stretch no further if new wine was poured into them. So, though it's not mentioned in Luke's presentation of the parable, in the telling of it in Mark's and Matthew's gospels, new wine in old wineskins would cause the skins to burst and the wine to spill, destroying everything.

In every workplace, ministry, or home, there are always certain practices and behaviors that exist, because, "well, that's how we've always done it." In a church built partly on 2,000 years of tradition, many such practices and behaviors can be expected. In many cases, it might only take two or three years, not 2,000, for something to become "a tradition." These traditions are, for the present moment, our wineskins to which we will turn a critical eye.

In evaluating elements of our liturgies that are traditions of any length, we should first consider whether the tradition is in place because of years of accumulated wisdom (of people, of institutions) or because of a certain amount of lethargy and inertia, which makes change difficult. Likely, it's not one or the other but some combination of both. That is, these "wineskins of tradition," are they still useful, pliable, resilient? Are these wineskins of our own making or given to us from outside? Is the wine originally placed in them still there, or are the wineskins dry? What was the wine originally poured into them? If the skins are dry, should they be thrown out or could they be reused somehow? What about new wine; into what should that be poured; where will new wineskins come from?

More about these questions next week!

About Music

Reliance on God: The distinctiveness of today's readings is one of dependence, relying on God completely for sustenance. This is elaborated in the Lord's Prayer: "Give us this day our daily bread." This prayer asks for only what is needed today and no more, and petitions the Lord to provide it. This sort of complete dependence is something most of us are not well versed in or, typically, willing to accept.

Steve Janco's "The Hand of the Lord Feeds Us" (WLP) borrows last week's psalm refrain, but the verses speak not so much to abundance but to how only the divine presence can feed, nurture, and sustain us. Another selection that speaks to God's providence is the *Psallite* (Liturgical Press) refrain "Finest Food! Choicest Wine!" "We Belong to You" by Trevor Thompson (OCP), while not explicitly eucharistic, speaks to our dependence on God throughout the everyday moments of our lives.

SPIRITUALITY

GOSPEL ACCLAMATION
John 6:51

R̸. Alleluia, alleluia.
I am the living bread that came down from
   heaven, says the Lord;
whoever eats this bread will live forever.
R̸. Alleluia, alleluia.

Gospel

John 6:41-51; L116B

The Jews murmured about Jesus
   because he said,
   "I am the bread that came down
      from heaven,"
   and they said,
   "Is this not Jesus, the son of
      Joseph?
Do we not know his father and
   mother?
Then how can he say,
   'I have come down from
      heaven'?"
Jesus answered and said to them,
   "Stop murmuring among yourselves.
No one can come to me unless the
   Father who sent me draw him,
   and I will raise him on the last day.
It is written in the prophets:
   They shall all be taught by God.
Everyone who listens to my Father and
   learns from him comes to me.
Not that anyone has seen the Father
   except the one who is from God;
   he has seen the Father.
Amen, amen, I say to you,
   whoever believes has eternal life.
I am the bread of life.
Your ancestors ate the manna in the
   desert, but they died;
   this is the bread that comes down
      from heaven
   so that one may eat it and not die.
I am the living bread that came down
   from heaven;
   whoever eats this bread will live
      forever;
   and the bread that I will give is my
      flesh for the life of the world."

Reflecting on the Gospel

In the continuation of the reading from John 6 there is movement to another level of understanding of what Jesus means by "bread": from material bread, to the bread that is the work of faith, and now to the bread that is Jesus himself. We should not be too eager to hurry on to eucharistic references—not yet (on this, see Raymond E. Brown, *The Gospel According to John I–XII*, The Anchor Bible, 272–73). The challenge to the people is to recognize Jesus as the revelation of God's word. When they come to him and accept to be taught his wisdom,

his words become a source of life. In his person and words, Jesus sets before the people a feast that will be nourishment for eternal life.

The religious leaders (named as "the Jews," the fourth evangelist's selective terminology for those who oppose Jesus) are foolishly certain that they know all about him because they know his parentage. They have closed the ears of their hearts to anything Jesus has said about "my Father" and the unique relationship of this Father and Son. They are not ready for a surprising God, for a God who can be present in the prosaic and ordinary, present in this man who claims to have been sent by God, to speak the words of God, to have seen God, and who has the temerity to endorse himself by the teaching of the prophets (e.g., Isa 54:13) and compare himself more favorably with some of the wonderful events of Israel's past, such as the feeding with the manna that was God's gift from heaven. From speaking of "this bread" of his teaching, Jesus now unambiguously points to himself: "I am the living bread that came down from heaven," says Jesus. The manna was sustenance for a time but Jesus's revelation will nourish for eternity; the manna fell from heaven but, as John proclaimed at the beginning of his gospel, Jesus is the Word who was with God and was God from the beginning, and who came from the place close to the Father's heart to make God known in our human flesh (John 1:1, 14, 18).

Today's gospel concludes with Jesus speaking of the bread he will give for the life of the world as "my flesh." There may be some eucharistic hints here, but the word "flesh" (*sarx*) refers first of all to Jesus's humanity, his way of being in the world and his self-gift to the world. This is his mission, a consequence of the Father's love for the world (John 3:16), that will lead him into his death and resurrection for the life of the world. How this relates to the Eucharist will be further revealed as we listen to the bread of life discourse on the following two Sundays.

There are always options available to us in our journey of faith. Like Elijah, we may feel it would be easier to opt out, perhaps with a struggle, perhaps with a whimper, and often because there is no "angel" around to help us. Or we may join the ranks of the murmurers, resistant to new ideas, new wisdom, new interpretations, even if from the highest teaching authority in the church—an ecumenical council such as Vatican II. Or we may continue to do the hard work of faith and come to Jesus to feed on his word and wisdom, given to us especially in the Scriptures, in the eucharistic Liturgy of the Word, and in our personal *lectio divina*.

Focusing the Gospel

Key words and phrases: "Is this not Jesus the son of Joseph? / Do we not know his father and mother?"

To the point: Today's gospel begins with the same protestations against Jesus that the people gathered at the synagogue in Nazareth leveled on the Fourteenth Sunday in Ordinary Time. In that Gospel from Mark, the crowd's initial astonishment at Jesus's words quickly becomes irritation as they ask one another, "Is he not the carpenter, the son of Mary?" In these gospels we come face-to-face with what theologians call "the scandal of the incarnation." At times, it is too much for our human psyches to comprehend the ability and decision of the infinite and divine to take on the form of the finite and mortal. Within Jesus who walked the dusty roads of Israel, just as within the bread of life at the Eucharist, we find the true presence of the living God, longing for relationship with us, if only we have the eyes to see.

Connecting the Gospel

to the first reading: In the first reading, the prophet Elijah is strengthened for his journey to the mountain of God by eating and drinking food provided by an angel. This is the third prophet we have encountered from the Old Testament in as many weeks. These Old Testament heroes foreshadow the actions of the Son of God, and also call us to imitate them in our own lives as those who have been anointed priests, prophets, and kings in baptism. Elijah begins this passage overcome with despair to the point of praying for death. Instead of granting his request, God sends heavenly nourishment.

to experience: How do you experience the Eucharist as food that nourishes and strengthens you in the face of life's difficulties?

Connecting the Responsorial Psalm

to the readings: This is our second Sunday reading from the bread of life discourse in John's gospel and considering the Eucharist as the food that sustains and nurtures us for eternal life. Today's responsorial psalm invites us to "[t]aste and see the goodness of the Lord." Our God wants us to know him with all our senses. It was not enough for God to reveal himself to us through creation or even in the human body of Jesus Christ. Throughout the ages, the resurrected Lord is made present to us in a way that we both taste and see as the Eucharist, the Bread that is Jesus's "flesh for the life of the world." For this reason, we "bless the Lord at all times."

to psalmist preparation: Consider the gift of the Eucharist in your life. When did you first receive this sacrament and how has your relationship with the Lord grown over the years of being invited to feast at the Lord's table?

PROMPTS FOR FAITH-SHARING

In the first reading, Elijah tells God, "This is enough, O Lord!" In the life of faith, when have you struggled with despair and what gave you the strength to continue on?

Today's responsorial psalm invites us to "[t]aste and see the goodness of the Lord." What memories do you have of the first time you encountered the risen Lord in the Eucharist?

In the second reading, St. Paul urges the Ephesians to "be kind to one another, compassionate, / forgiving one another as God has forgiven you in Christ." How do you strive to treat those who have harmed you with compassion and forgiveness?

In the gospel Jesus quotes the prophets: "They shall all be taught by God." In the life of faith, how do you continue to be open to learning more and more?

Model Penitential Act

Presider: In today's second reading, St. Paul urges the Ephesians to "be imitators of God, as beloved children, and [to] live in love." For the times our words and actions have not mirrored the life of Christ, let us ask for pardon and mercy . . . *[pause]*

　　Lord Jesus, you gave your flesh for the life of the world: Lord, have mercy.

　　Christ Jesus, you call us to draw near to you in your Body and Blood: Christ, have mercy.

　　Lord Jesus, you heal the afflicted and strengthen the weak: Lord, have mercy.

Homily Points

• In last week's gospel, Jesus proclaimed, "I am the bread of life; / whoever comes to me will never hunger, / and whoever believes in me will never thirst." Today we hear Jesus becoming even more explicit about his meaning when he tells the crowd, "[T]he bread that I will give is my flesh for the life of the world." Considering how the Gospel of John does not contain an institution narrative for the Last Supper, scripture scholar Raymond Brown has suggested that this line might be the Johannine eucharistic formula, similar to "This is my body which will be given for you" (Luke 22:19; NABRE).

• When we as Catholics meditate on the bread of life discourse, we are inevitably led to consider the role of the Eucharist in our lives of faith. This line in particular, "the bread that I will give is my flesh for the life of the world," highlights the paschal nature of this sacrament. Pope Benedict XVI tells us, "[O]nly through the cross and through the transformation that it effects does this flesh become accessible to us, drawing us up into the process of transformation" (*Jesus of Nazareth* 270).

• The immensity of Jesus's love and vulnerability on the cross is present within the eucharistic feast, and when we come forward to receive the Body of Christ, we also say "amen" to becoming this Body in all that we say and do. As Elijah does in the first reading, at times we may be tempted to despair when life's challenges and difficulties get to be too much. It is in these moments, however, that our Lord desires to feed us with himself, giving us his very flesh so we might be nourished and strengthened on this journey to eternal life.

Model Universal Prayer (Prayer of the Faithful)

Presider: In his goodness and love, the Lord desires to satisfy our hunger and quench our thirst through the gift of his Body and Blood. With confidence let us bring our needs before him.

Response: Lord, hear our prayer.

For God's holy church, through the Eucharist may we be brought together as one Body unified in love and compassion . . .

For diplomats and peacekeepers around the world, may their efforts to promote the well-being of all bear abundant fruit . . .

For all children who have been orphaned or abandoned, may they know the love of God, the Father of all, and the security and safety of forever homes . . .

For all gathered here around the table of the Lord, may our ears be opened to the wisdom of God's word and our spirits strengthened through heavenly food . . .

Presider: Abundant God, you sent your son Jesus to preach forgiveness of sins and newness of life. Hear our prayers that we might dwell in the love of Christ all the days of our lives and express that love through word and deed to all we meet. We ask this through Jesus, our brother and savior. **Amen.**

COLLECT

Let us pray.

Pause for silent prayer

Almighty ever-living God,
whom, taught by the Holy Spirit,
we dare to call our Father,
bring, we pray, to perfection in our hearts
the spirit of adoption as your sons and
　　daughters,
that we may merit to enter into the
　　inheritance
which you have promised.
Through our Lord Jesus Christ, your Son,
who lives and reigns with you in the unity
　　of the Holy Spirit,
one God, for ever and ever. **Amen.**

FIRST READING

1 Kgs 19:4-8

Elijah went a day's journey into the desert,
　　until he came to a broom tree and sat
　　　　beneath it.
He prayed for death, saying:
　　"This is enough, O Lord!
Take my life, for I am no better than my
　　fathers."
He lay down and fell asleep under the
　　broom tree,
　　but then an angel touched him and
　　　　ordered him to get up and eat.
Elijah looked and there at his head was a
　　hearth cake
　　and a jug of water.
After he ate and drank, he lay down again,
　　but the angel of the Lord came back a
　　　　second time,
　　touched him, and ordered,
　　"Get up and eat, else the journey will be
　　　　too long for you!"
He got up, ate, and drank;
　　then strengthened by that food,
　　he walked forty days and forty nights
　　　　to the mountain of God, Horeb.

CATECHESIS

RESPONSORIAL PSALM

Ps 34:2-3, 4-5, 6-7, 8-9

R̸. (9a) Taste and see the goodness of the
Lord.

I will bless the LORD at all times;
    his praise shall be ever in my mouth.
Let my soul glory in the LORD;
    the lowly will hear me and be glad.

R̸. Taste and see the goodness of the
Lord.

Glorify the LORD with me,
    let us together extol his name.
I sought the LORD, and he answered me
    and delivered me from all my fears.

R̸. Taste and see the goodness of the
Lord.

Look to him that you may be radiant with
    joy,
    and your faces may not blush with
      shame.
When the afflicted man called out, the
    LORD heard,
    and from all his distress he saved him.

R̸. Taste and see the goodness of the
Lord.

The angel of the LORD encamps
    around those who fear him and delivers
      them.
Taste and see how good the LORD is;
    blessed the man who takes refuge in
      him.

R̸. Taste and see the goodness of the
Lord.

SECOND READING

Eph 4:30–5:2

Brothers and sisters:
Do not grieve the Holy Spirit of God,
    with which you were sealed for the day
      of redemption.
All bitterness, fury, anger, shouting, and
    reviling
    must be removed from you, along with
      all malice.
And be kind to one another,
    compassionate,
    forgiving one another as God has
      forgiven you in Christ.

So be imitators of God, as beloved
    children, and live in love,
    as Christ loved us and handed himself
      over for us
    as a sacrificial offering to God for a
      fragrant aroma.

About Liturgy

Wine, Old and New: New wine and old wineskins—as we continue our exploration of this parable and evaluating our eucharistic liturgies (a process that began with the July 25 writings here), we turn our attention to wine, both old and new.

Wine is, firstly, the fruit of the vine and work of human hands, we hear at liturgy. The grapes themselves are created by and gifted to us by God, and, after our labors, we return this gift to God, part of our communal meal and sacrifice. Wine is, too, a symbol of life and joy outside of our faith experience; it is a symbol of exuberance and vitality, of joy and promise.

Following from last week, if we examine our liturgies through the lens of this parable, if we further liken the liturgical traditions of our communities to the old wineskins of the parable, then we next need to ask ourselves questions about the wine of our communities. These questions and answers are necessarily connected to the leading questions about wineskins last week.

Often, when this parable is referenced in discussing the present church, the new wine is understood to represent the people who comprise the church, often the younger generations. Is this true for your community? Every Christian community has members of various ages. Or, for you, does the new wine signify a shift of culture and language in your congregation? It could even be that the new wine is the relative aging of your parishioners or some other demographic shifting.

We might also ponder "new wine" liturgically with a desire to pastorally minister to a particular segment of our community, be this subculture new to us or from a longer history. In this approach, the new wine might be desired practices of multilingual or multicultural liturgy, which may or may not conform well to liturgical rubrics (wineskins) that seem to leave little room for adaptation or outright change. Who, or what, is our wine? Is the wine new, or just new to us? Where can we find or create new liturgical wineskins? As we asked last week, are the old wineskins but trash, or is there a way to reuse the skins themselves or their material?

To be continued in two weeks!

About Music

God's Sustenance: As we look for something in this Sunday's readings to distinguish them from the surrounding Sundays, let us note the emphasis on the Bread of Life sustaining us, and in a way different from other foods. This bread not only sustains us physically until tomorrow, but "whoever eats this bread will live forever." This Bread of Life is abundant, is one we must depend on, and is one that gives eternal life.

Two hymns titled "I Am the Bread of Life" have lyrics that draw from various parts of the bread of life discourse but speak especially well to the eternal life Jesus offers and on which we focus this Sunday. Given that next Sunday we miss some of this text due to Assumption falling on a Sunday, this is a perfect Sunday for either hymn. Sr. Suzanne Toolan's setting (GIA, but found in many hymnals) is most familiar and should be simple for your summertime music ministers to prepare. The other is by Tom Booth and Steve Angrisano (OCP), and, with lyrics like "I am the hope in night" and "I am the door wide open," speaks more specifically to those longing for the hope of eternal life and the companionship of the divine.

SPIRITUALITY

GOSPEL ACCLAMATION
℟. Alleluia, alleluia.
Mary is taken up to heaven;
a chorus of angels exults.
℟. Alleluia, alleluia.

Gospel   Luke 1:39-56; L622

Mary set out
  and traveled to the hill country in haste
  to a town of Judah,
  where she entered the house of
    Zechariah
  and greeted Elizabeth.
When Elizabeth heard Mary's greeting,
  the infant leaped in her womb,
  and Elizabeth, filled with the Holy
    Spirit,
  cried out in a loud voice and said,
  "Blessed are you among women,
  and blessed is the fruit of your womb.
And how does this happen to me,
  that the mother of my Lord should
    come to me?
For at the moment the sound of your
    greeting reached my ears,
  the infant in my womb leaped for joy.
Blessed are you who believed
  that what was spoken to you by the
    Lord
  would be fulfilled."

And Mary said:

"My soul proclaims the greatness of
    the Lord;
  my spirit rejoices in God my Savior
  for he has looked with favor on his
    lowly servant.
From this day all generations will call
    me blessed:
  the Almighty has done great things
    for me,
  and holy is his Name.
He has mercy on those who fear him
  in every generation.
He has shown the strength of his arm,
  and has scattered the proud in their
    conceit.

Continued in Appendix A, p. 299.

Reflecting on the Gospel

The assumption of Mary into heaven, an event that is not described in the biblical tradition, has nevertheless been a part of the church's tradition since the early centuries. It emerged out of reflection among the faithful on the profound role Mary had in the salvation of all humanity, especially in her openness and faithfulness to God. Her openness and faithfulness to God were most profoundly witnessed in her bearing and giving birth to the Son of God, her son Jesus. It

was understood that her role in the divine plan warranted her being taken bodily to heaven, to be in the home of God, the one to whom she gave a home in God's earthly sojourn.

Some have seen support for the church's teaching regarding Mary in the image of the "woman clothed with the sun" in Revelation. The woman certainly could stand for Mary, since the woman "gave birth to a son, a male child, destined to rule all the nations with an iron rod." But like so many images in Revelation, the symbol is polyvalent, having more than one referent. Remember, the woman had "on her head a crown of twelve stars," which could signify the twelve tribes of Israel or the twelve apostles, so referencing the church. Later, the woman "fled into the desert where she had a place prepared by God." The Lectionary omits the conclusion of the verse: "that there she might be taken care of for twelve hundred and sixty days" (NABRE)—most certainly a reference to the church, as the "twelve hundred and sixty days" refers to a symbolic number in Daniel regarding a period of three and a half years before the time of the end.

The point is that Mary is in heaven with her Lord and she is not simply the stuff of legendary, mythic, or symbolic numbers. She was an actual flesh and blood woman, chosen above all people, male or female, to play the most significant human role in the divine salvific plan. We should never lose track of her humanity. There is this temptation to dehumanize her, but this pays no justice to her faithfulness or to Mary as a model woman, someone women and men can follow as exemplary in trust and joy.

When Mary heard the word from the angel, she went to confide in another woman, not in the men of her family. She traveled "in haste" to the Judean hill country to see her relative Elizabeth. It was Elizabeth to whom Mary entrusted her momentous news and Elizabeth, far from questioning Mary, was open to Mary and her greeting. The Holy Spirit filled Elizabeth and she cried out, "Blessed are you among women, and blessed is the fruit of your womb. And how does this happen to me, that the mother of my Lord should come to me?"

Elizabeth was there for Mary, open to her joy and faithfulness, open to being with her and listening to her story. It was in response to Elizabeth's belief, recall, that Mary recited the *Magnificat*. In this song of praise, Mary speaks of her joy at being chosen, of being blessed in spite of being what she calls "lowly." More significantly, Mary places her own role in the context of God's promises and faithfulness to the people of Israel and the lowly and forgotten of the world. So often the lowly and the forgotten in the world are comprised of women, like Mary and Elizabeth, whose roles are denigrated and whose bodies bear the brunt of abuse and pain.

Mary did not just stop by to talk to Elizabeth; she needed to stay with Elizabeth and so "Mary remained with her about three months and then returned to her home." They were women together because though Mary had been called and chosen for a role unique among women, had been set apart to return bodily to God's kingdom, she needed another woman, a friend and relative, to talk to, to be with, to share her story.

Focusing the Gospel

Key words and phrases: "Blessed are you who believed / that what was spoken to you by the Lord / would be fulfilled."

To the point: In today's gospel, Mary finds confirmation for the angel Gabriel's proclamation that she would bear a son. Through the Holy Spirit, Elizabeth knows from the sound of Mary's greeting that this young kinswoman is also, in fact, "the mother of [the] Lord." In Mary we find a model of discipleship. Mary accepts her role as the mother of Jesus with humility and profound trust. The word of God, planted within the rich soil of Mary's soul, grows and flowers throughout her life as, with every breath, she lives out her response to Gabriel's message, "May it be done to me according to your word" (Luke 1:38; NABRE).

Connecting the Gospel

to the second reading: Elizabeth greets Mary with the words, "Blessed are you among women, / and blessed is the fruit of your womb." In the second reading from St. Paul's First Letter to the Corinthians, Jesus is also described as "fruit," this time as the "firstfruits of those who have fallen asleep." In being identified as the firstfruits of the harvest of salvation, we can deduce that there are more fruits to come. As "those who belong to Christ," we hold fast to the promise that our Lord has conquered death and desires to share everlasting life with all people of goodwill.

to experience: On feast of the Assumption, we celebrate (as our gospel acclamation reminds us) how "Mary is taken up to heaven [while] a chorus of angels exults." In Mary, the model disciple, we also find God's blueprint for each of our lives: that we might bear Christ to the world and then live with him forever in the kingdom of heaven.

Connecting the Responsorial Psalm

to the readings: Today's psalm, which commemorates a royal wedding, is fitting for this day when we celebrate Mary, the Queen of Heaven, the Mother of God. The third verse describes the wedding guests who are "borne in with gladness and joy." We also encounter joy in the gospel when John the Baptist leaps within the womb of his mother, Elizabeth. John's joy signals the presence of Jesus, the one who is Emmanuel, God with us. We partake of this joy every time we draw near to the risen Lord in word and sacrament, or whenever his love is mediated to us through the compassion and service of another.

to psalmist preparation: Today, how do you experience the joy of the Lord as you celebrate the feast of the Assumption?

PROMPTS FOR FAITH-SHARING

In the first reading from Revelation, the woman who has given birth flees "into the desert / where she had a place prepared by God." Where do you go to find solace and peace?

In the second reading St. Paul tells the Corinthians, "[J]ust as in Adam all die, / so in Christ shall all be brought to life." How has your Christian faith led you to a fuller life in the Spirit?

In the Hail Mary, we pray the greeting Elizabeth offers Mary, "Blessed are you among women, / and blessed is the fruit of your womb." How have the Hail Mary and other Marian devotions and prayers nurtured your spiritual life?

John the Baptist leaps for joy when he senses the nearness of Jesus in the Virgin Mary's womb. Where do you experience the greatest joy in your journey of discipleship?

Model Penitential Act

Presider: Mary's *Magnificat* begins, "My soul proclaims the greatness of the Lord." Conscious of God's divinity and our own humanity, let us pause to ask the Lord for pardon and mercy . . . *[pause]*

Lord Jesus, you have conquered sin and death: Lord, have mercy.

Christ Jesus, you call us to fullness of joy in your presence: Christ, have mercy.

Lord Jesus, you are Son of God and son of Mary: Lord, have mercy.

Homily Points

• For the past three Sundays the gospels have focused on the feeding of the five thousand and the bread of life discourse in John's gospel. Next week we'll return again to consider the crowd's response to Jesus's proclamation, "I am the living bread that came down from heaven," but for today we make a detour to celebrate the feast of the Assumption with the Gospel of Luke's visitation of Mary to Elizabeth. We can surmise that since Mary was newly pregnant, there was nothing about her appearance to suggest that she would be with child, and yet, through the power of the Holy Spirit and the joyful leap of her own unborn child, Elizabeth intuits that she is in the presence of "the mother of my Lord."

• In this moment of salvation history, the eternal and infinite God has come to dwell in the womb of a young Jewish woman, and in her visit to Elizabeth, Mary, bearing the life of God, becomes a mobile tabernacle. The *Catechism of the Catholic Church* tells us, "For the first time in the plan of Salvation and because his Spirit had prepared her, the Father found the dwelling place where his Son and his Spirit could dwell among men" (721).

• As the model of discipleship, Mary offers us the ideal of what we are all called to be—those who bear Christ to the world. In the Eucharist we consume the body and blood of our Lord and also dedicate ourselves to be living tabernacles. On today's feast we celebrate Mary's assumption into heaven, confident in her prayers that we might one day join her there as members of the Body of Christ.

Model Universal Prayer (Prayer of the Faithful)

Presider: Through the intercession of Mary, mother of the church, let us entrust our needs, and the needs of our world, to the Lord.

Response: Lord, hear our prayer.

For all who minister to the poor and the oppressed, inspired by the *Magnificat*, may they tend to the lowly with respect, justice, and compassion . . .

For leaders of nations, may they embrace the humility of Mary as they labor to advance the common good . . .

For those who grieve the loss of loved ones, may they be comforted and sustained by the Lord of life . . .

For all gathered here, with joy may we bear the presence of the risen Lord to all we encounter . . .

Presider: Glorious God, you have given us the Virgin Mary as our own mother and as a model for our lives of discipleship. Hear our prayer that through her intercession we may daily take up our crosses to follow you with fidelity and devotion. We ask this through Christ our Lord. **Amen.**

COLLECT

Let us pray.

Pause for silent prayer

Almighty ever-living God,
who assumed the Immaculate Virgin
    Mary, the Mother of your Son,
body and soul into heavenly glory,
grant, we pray,
that, always attentive to the things that are
    above,
we may merit to be sharers of her glory.
Through our Lord Jesus Christ, your Son,
who lives and reigns with you in the unity
    of the Holy Spirit,
one God, for ever and ever. **Amen.**

FIRST READING

Rev 11:19a; 12:1-6a, 10ab

God's temple in heaven was opened,
    and the ark of his covenant could be
        seen in the temple.

A great sign appeared in the sky, a woman
    clothed with the sun,
    with the moon under her feet,
    and on her head a crown of twelve
        stars.
She was with child and wailed aloud in
    pain as she labored to give birth.
Then another sign appeared in the sky;
    it was a huge red dragon, with seven
        heads and ten horns,
    and on its heads were seven diadems.
Its tail swept away a third of the stars in
    the sky
    and hurled them down to the earth.
Then the dragon stood before the woman
    about to give birth,
    to devour her child when she gave birth.
She gave birth to a son, a male child,
    destined to rule all the nations with an
        iron rod.
Her child was caught up to God and his
    throne.
The woman herself fled into the desert
    where she had a place prepared by God.

Then I heard a loud voice in heaven say:
    "Now have salvation and power come,
    and the Kingdom of our God
    and the authority of his Anointed
        One."

CATECHESIS

RESPONSORIAL PSALM

Ps 45:10, 11, 12, 16

R̶. (10bc) The queen stands at your right hand, arrayed in gold.

The queen takes her place at your right hand in gold of Ophir.

R̶. The queen stands at your right hand, arrayed in gold.

Hear, O daughter, and see; turn your ear, forget your people and your father's house.

R̶. The queen stands at your right hand, arrayed in gold.

So shall the king desire your beauty; for he is your lord.

R̶. The queen stands at your right hand, arrayed in gold.

They are borne in with gladness and joy; they enter the palace of the king.

R̶. The queen stands at your right hand, arrayed in gold.

SECOND READING

1 Cor 15:20-27

Brothers and sisters:
Christ has been raised from the dead,
    the firstfruits of those who have fallen
        asleep.
For since death came through man,
    the resurrection of the dead came also
        through man.
For just as in Adam all die,
    so too in Christ shall all be brought to
        life,
    but each one in proper order:
    Christ the firstfruits;
    then, at his coming, those who belong
        to Christ;
    then comes the end,
    when he hands over the Kingdom to his
        God and Father,
    when he has destroyed every
        sovereignty
    and every authority and power.
For he must reign until he has put all his
    enemies under his feet.
The last enemy to be destroyed is death,
    for "he subjected everything under his
        feet."

About Liturgy

Music of Mary at Liturgy: The bread of life discourse is liturgically interrupted this Sunday by the solemnity of the Assumption. A continuing discussion is the appropriateness of including Marian hymns at Eucharist. Many see no issue with the practice; some decry any Marian hymns at a liturgy focused on Christ and the paschal mystery.

In practice, there are three judgments—liturgical, pastoral, and musical—which taken as a whole answer the question, "Is this particular piece of music appropriate for use in this particular liturgy?" (Sing to the Lord [STL] 126). The pastoral judgment, broadly speaking, focuses on the community, and the musical judgment focuses on the characteristics of the piece of music itself. So let us turn to the GIRM and STL to inform our liturgical evaluation of the four or five places hymns are frequently used at Mass.

The function of the entrance chant or song is to "open the celebration, foster the unity of those who have been gathered, introduce their thoughts to the mystery of the liturgical season or festivity, and accompany the procession of the priest and ministers" (STL 142; GIRM 47). STL continues, regarding the preparation of the gifts, "The norms on the manner of singing are the same as for the Entrance Chant" (173). The communion song strives "to express the communicants' union in spirit by means of the unity of their voices, to show joy of heart, and to highlight more clearly the 'communitarian' nature of the procession to receive Communion" (STL 189; GIRM 86). Some places have a tradition of a song after Communion: "'When the distribution of Communion is finished, as circumstances suggest, the priest and faithful spend some time praying privately. If desired, a psalm or other canticle of praise or a hymn may also be sung by the entire congregation' (GIRM 88). The song after Communion should focus the assembly on the mystery of the Holy Communion in which it participates" (STL 196). Since the recessional is not mentioned in liturgical rubrics, it is not possible to mention similar guidelines regarding its purpose or content, though STL offers, "[W]hen it is a custom, all may join in a hymn or song after the dismissal" (199).

Given the broad guidance offered above, it seems (to me) that the only time where most Marian hymns would not be a good fit would be at Communion and the song after Communion. There surely, though, is wide leeway given to scriptural Marian texts, like settings of the *Magnificat* or content from Psalm 45 (the prescribed psalm for Assumption) or from Revelation.

It would also be wise to ensure that the texts of any Marian music used during liturgy do point to Christ, the Trinity, or some facet of the paschal mystery. "On This Day, O Beautiful Mother," for instance, in most iterations, is only focused on the Blessed Mother. Even "Immaculate Mary," in many versions, gives only a passing reference to Christ and our redemption. Newer hymns often do a better job of allowing Mary to magnify the Lord: "I Sing a Maid" (GIA) with text by M. D. Ridge allows Mary to watch Christ's life and for us to honor her as his mother.

Further, it is almost never appropriate to bring Marian music to liturgical celebrations outside of Marian feasts. So, too, prayers that, even if scriptural, are principally devotional (such as the Hail Mary) should typically never be included in any liturgy, either spoken or sung.

AUGUST 15, 2021
THE ASSUMPTION OF THE BLESSED VIRGIN MARY

✠ SPIRITUALITY

GOSPEL ACCLAMATION
John 6:63c, 68c

℟. Alleluia, alleluia.
Your words, Lord, are Spirit and life;
you have the words of everlasting life.
℟. Alleluia, alleluia.

Gospel

John 6:60-69; L122B

Many of Jesus' disciples who
  were listening said,
 "This saying is hard; who can
  accept it?"
Since Jesus knew that his
  disciples were murmuring
  about this,
  he said to them, "Does this
  shock you?
What if you were to see the
  Son of Man ascending
  to where he was before?
It is the spirit that gives life,
  while the flesh is of no avail.
The words I have spoken to you
  are Spirit and life.
But there are some of you who do not
  believe."
Jesus knew from the beginning the
  ones who would not believe
  and the one who would betray him.
And he said,
 "For this reason I have told you that
  no one can come to me
  unless it is granted him by my
  Father."

As a result of this,
  many of his disciples returned to
  their former way of life
  and no longer accompanied him.
Jesus then said to the Twelve, "Do you
  also want to leave?"
Simon Peter answered him, "Master, to
  whom shall we go?
You have the words of eternal life.
We have come to believe
  and are convinced that you are the
  Holy One of God."

Reflecting on the Gospel

The time of decision-making has come for those listening to Jesus's bread of life discourse. It is not only his opponents, but his followers, his own disciples, who are scandalized by his words. They complain that it is an intolerable teaching, too hard, too offensive to accept. They have been nourished at the table of Torah wisdom and are not prepared to accept any new spiritual food. Surprisingly, after all the talk about "flesh," Jesus now says that it has nothing to offer. But here Jesus is saying that from a purely *human* point of view (especially one's own) what he has been saying makes no sense. He will not conform to the expectations of those who want to judge him according to their own superficial experiences. Jesus descended from heaven to speak the words of spirit and life in a way no one else can (cf. John 3:31-36), but some of those listening to him would like to see him ascend to heaven as the Jewish tradition held that their revelatory ancestor Moses had ascended. Jesus leaves his followers free, neither asking them to stay nor giving them permission to go. Their choice, this crisis moment, is personally theirs . . . and ours.

Then Jesus asks those who are still with him one of the most moving of gospel questions: "Do you also want to leave?" It is Simon Peter who answers, and for the first time in John's gospel someone explicitly accepts Jesus for the most foundational and significant of reasons: because he is the Holy One of God who offers them the words of eternal life. Today's Lectionary portion finishes here, no doubt to conclude the bread of life discourse on a positive note, but we also need to hear the last two verses, to realize that even at the moment of this profession of profound faith (John 6:71-72), the church is haunted by the reality of betrayal that lurks in the background and is always a tragic possibility for any of Jesus's disciples. One night Peter will huddle in the dark corner of denial, and Judas will betray his master. To continue with Jesus is an ongoing struggle with the possibility of right or wrong decisions for or against him.

There are times when we, too, may have felt like walking away from the Eucharist: tired of words about it that seem empty of spirit and life, bored with poor celebrations of it, some of us leaving because change is too slow, others because it is too fast. Basically, we are like the people listening to Jesus in this gospel, and like the community for whom John wrote his gospel: we can be tempted to want Jesus to conform to our expectations of how he should be present in and to his church in word and sacrament; we are intolerant of his willingness to be present in the poverty of so many eucharistic liturgies—which is not to say that we do not do all we can to have good liturgies. But perhaps our greatest betrayal is our failure to realize that when we are not in communion with our sisters and brothers we fail to be in communion with the Body of Christ. Peter's response—"Master, to whom shall we go?"—faces us with the memory of the Servant Jesus who went to death, who gave his full human reality, his body and blood, for us, so that we might share in his eternal risen life.

Focusing the Gospel

Key words and phrases: "The words I have spoken to you are Spirit and life."

To the point: Today's gospel reading concludes the discourse on the bread of life. The crowd following Jesus was confused by his proclamation "[U]nless you eat the flesh of the Son of Man and drink his blood, you do not have life within you" (John 6:53; NABRE). This is hardly surprising. Was this nomadic preacher really inciting them to *cannibalism*? Their outrage and astonishment led many of Jesus's disciples to "return to their former way of life." In the Christian faith we realize there are many things we might not fully understand or comprehend. As the Lord reminds us through the prophet Isaiah, "For as the heavens are higher than the earth, / so are my ways higher than your ways" (55:9; NABRE). Instead of rejecting the Lord's words and actions that we might not understand, we are called to meditate on them and even to struggle with them until we are blessed with the nourishment and insight they bear.

Connecting the Gospel

to the first reading: Today's first reading comes from the final chapter of the book of Joshua, which began with the death of Moses and the entry of the people into the land promised to their ancestors. Gathering all the people together, Joshua relays their history beginning with Terah, the father of Abraham, who "served other gods" (24:2; NABRE). Now that the people have been freed from slavery, entrusted with the gift of the Law, and have settled into the Promised Land, Joshua calls them once again to ratify their covenant with the Lord by rejecting the "gods your Fathers served beyond the River" and "the gods of the Amorites in whose country you are now dwelling." The choice he places before them seems to foreshadow the words of Jesus in the gospel when he asks the disciples, "Do you also want to leave?"

to experience: Within any authentic relationship there is always freedom of choice. In today's readings both Joshua and Jesus call upon the people to exercise this freedom by once again declaring their fidelity to God. How have you been called to rededicate your life to Jesus through your journey of faith?

Connecting the Responsorial Psalm

to the readings: Today's psalm once again directs our attention to the Eucharist (as have the psalms from the Seventeenth, Eighteenth, and Nineteenth Sundays of Ordinary Time). In fact, today we return again to Psalm 34 with its beloved refrain, "Taste and see the goodness of the Lord." In our gospel, Jesus tells the crowd, "The words I have spoken to you are Spirit and life." Not only does Jesus wish to nourish us with his Body and Blood in the Eucharist, but also with the words of truth he speaks to all who would listen.

to psalmist preparation: How does the word of God nourish and strengthen you in the life of faith?

Model Penitential Act

Presider: In today's gospel we hear of many disciples who, shocked at Jesus's words, return to their former way of life. For the times we have failed to live Christ's teachings with integrity, let us ask for pardon and mercy . . . *[pause]*

Lord Jesus, you call us to holiness: Lord, have mercy.

Christ Jesus, you satisfy our deepest longings: Christ, have mercy.

Lord Jesus, you have the words of everlasting life: Lord, have mercy.

Homily Points

• For the past several weeks as we've journeyed through chapter 6 of John's gospel we've encountered Jesus as the one who can relieve physical hunger (in the feeding of the five thousand) and as the nourishment necessary for fullness of life. Today's gospel and first reading call us to make a choice, just as the people of Israel did when Joshua, shortly before his death, gathered them together in an invitation to rededicate themselves to serving the Lord. This choice is also placed before the Twelve when Jesus asks them, "Do you also want to leave?"

• A life of discipleship is not easy. We are called to accept teachings that are difficult and commandments that, at times, may seem impossible. Jesus asks us to love our enemies (Matt 5:43-45), turn the other cheek (Matt 5:39), and embrace the same vulnerability and humility that he embodied on the cross. To any one of these requests we might be tempted to say, "This saying is hard; who can accept it?" And yet, Jesus reminds us today that these words, which cause consternation and challenge us to be more than we ever thought possible, are "Spirit and life."

• Peter models a response of perfect faith to Jesus's question, "Do you also want to leave?" Theologian Roman Guardini writes in his book *The Lord*, "[Peter] does not say: We understand what you mean, but: We hold fast to your hand. Your words are words of life, whether we understand them or not." Each day, as disciples of Jesus, we are given a choice: "Do you also want to leave?" May our response be that of Peter's and the Israelites' who proclaim with certainty, "[W]e will serve the Lord, for he is our God."

Model Universal Prayer (Prayer of the Faithful)

Presider: Having been nourished by the Word of God, with trust and faithfulness, let us bring our needs before the Lord.

Response: Lord, hear our prayer.

For God's church spread throughout the world, together may we continue to grow in holiness and fidelity to Jesus's teachings . . .

For medical professionals worldwide who labor to care for the sick and the elderly, may they be protected from disease and find rest and renewal to continue their service . . .

For all who are homeless this day, may they find food, shelter, and the assistance necessary to dwell in safety . . .

For all gathered here, may we be renewed in faith and in our commitment to live a life of discipleship . . .

Presider: God of justice and compassion, you hear the cries of all people in need. Hear our prayers that we might selflessly care for our brothers and sisters and so work to bring about your kingdom of love and peace. We ask this through Christ our Lord. **Amen.**

COLLECT

Let us pray.

Pause for silent prayer

O God, who cause the minds of the faithful
to unite in a single purpose,
grant your people to love what you
    command
and to desire what you promise,
that, amid the uncertainties of this world,
our hearts may be fixed on that place
where true gladness is found.
Through our Lord Jesus Christ, your Son,
who lives and reigns with you in the unity
    of the Holy Spirit,
one God, for ever and ever. **Amen.**

FIRST READING

Josh 24:1-2a, 15-17, 18b

Joshua gathered together all the tribes of
    Israel at Shechem,
    summoning their elders, their leaders,
    their judges, and their officers.
When they stood in ranks before God,
    Joshua addressed all the people:
    "If it does not please you to serve the
        Lord,
    decide today whom you will serve,
    the gods your fathers served beyond the
        River
or the gods of the Amorites in whose
        country you are now dwelling.
As for me and my household, we will
    serve the Lord."

But the people answered,
    "Far be it from us to forsake the Lord
    for the service of other gods.
For it was the Lord, our God,
    who brought us and our fathers up out
        of the land of Egypt,
    out of a state of slavery.
He performed those great miracles before
        our very eyes
    and protected us along our entire
        journey
    and among the peoples through whom
        we passed.
Therefore we also will serve the Lord, for
    he is our God."

RESPONSORIAL PSALM

Ps 34:2-3, 16-17, 18-19, 20-21

R. (9a) Taste and see the goodness of the
    Lord.

I will bless the Lord at all times;
    his praise shall be ever in my mouth.
Let my soul glory in the Lord;
    the lowly will hear me and be glad.

R. Taste and see the goodness of the Lord.

The LORD has eyes for the just,
    and ears for their cry.
The LORD confronts the evildoers,
    to destroy remembrance of them from
        the earth.

R℣. Taste and see the goodness of the Lord.

When the just cry out, the LORD hears them,
    and from all their distress he rescues
        them.
The LORD is close to the brokenhearted;
    and those who are crushed in spirit he
        saves.

R℣. Taste and see the goodness of the Lord.

Many are the troubles of the just one,
    but out of them all the LORD delivers him;
he watches over all his bones;
    not one of them shall be broken.

R℣. Taste and see the goodness of the Lord.

SECOND READING
Eph 5:21-32

Brothers and sisters:
Be subordinate to one another out of
        reverence for Christ.
Wives should be subordinate to their
        husbands as to the Lord.
For the husband is head of his wife
    just as Christ is head of the church,
    he himself the savior of the body.
As the church is subordinate to Christ,
    so wives should be subordinate to their
        husbands in everything.
Husbands, love your wives,
    even as Christ loved the church
    and handed himself over for her to
        sanctify her,
    cleansing her by the bath of water with
        the word,
    that he might present to himself the
        church in splendor,
    without spot or wrinkle or any such thing,
    that she might be holy and without
        blemish.
So also husbands should love their wives
    as their own bodies.
He who loves his wife loves himself.
For no one hates his own flesh
    but rather nourishes and cherishes it,
    even as Christ does the church,
    because we are members of his body.
*For this reason a man shall leave his father
        and his mother
    and be joined to his wife,
    and the two shall become one flesh.*
This is a great mystery,
    but I speak in reference to Christ and
        the church.

or Eph 5:2a, 25-32 in Appendix A, p. 300.

About Liturgy

Patching the Rips and Tears: Returning one last time to the parable of the cloth and wineskins (a journey which began four Sundays ago), sharper readers will note that as we use this text as a lens to evaluate our liturgies, we have completely ignored half of the pericope—that of the cloth used to patch a cloak.

As we have given our liturgies a closer examination, we have thus far used only the imagery of the new wine and old wineskins: what, in our liturgical practices, do these represent; what is our next effort to be, given any new insights and revelations?

An example of a common use of this phrase in ministry was recently discussed in this space: a "new wineskin" of a "youth Mass" created for the "new wine" of the up-and-coming younger generation (see "About Liturgy," July 18). The writings there expounded a bit upon the values and missteps in pursuing such a liturgy.

Consider the first half of the parable now. If one uses a new piece of fabric to patch a hole, that new fabric will have not yet shrunk. If it shrinks after patching a rip or hole, it is likely only to reopen that tear and make it worse. So, while it is true that new wine needs new wineskins, it is simultaneously true that rips and holes in fabric should not be repaired with something new but rather with a piece of fabric that is more aged and has had a chance to shrink first.

When we think of our liturgies, then, and our communities that gather in prayer, we must be not only mindful of where the new wine and old wineskins are, but also of where the holes—the gaps in our communities and practices—are and what bit of time-tested fabric we might use to mend the tear. That is, sometimes something new is needed, and sometimes something new might only make matters worse.

The trick is to discern through prayer, conversations, careful observation, and prudent discernment what the right ministerial course of action is. Is it a reinvigoration of priest-led adoration and benediction, or is it youth-led Liturgy of the Hours? Is it incorporating more Latin text and chant into Mass, or is it investing in more contemporary musical resources?

Once again, we must realize that ours is a "both/and" faith, and as with the parable of the cloth and wineskins, most often our answers must be held together: both adoration and vespers (perhaps at the same time!), both chant and Christian contemporary music (perhaps at the same Mass!).

In this way, finally, let us also evaluate our evaluations. It's sometimes simple but incorrect to label everything liturgical as either a "right" or a "wrong"—even though, to be sure, some things are with certainty either right or wrong. But if our evaluations utilize only this binary choice, we should learn a lesson from this parable. Our faith, with liturgy and Eucharist as source and summit, is too important not to.

About Music

Responding to the Bread of Life: While the readings of the bread of life discourse that were replaced last week spoke of union and community, the readings today offer our response to Christ's difficult teachings and the abundance, reliance, sustenance, and union given to us: belief. "Master, to whom shall we go? You have the words of eternal life."

"Journey of Faith" by Delores Dufner (WLP) to the familiar tune LOBE DEN HERREN is a strong statement of that pilgrimage of belief we all share, toward transformation and redemption. Consider, too, *Psallite's* "My Grace Is Enough" (Liturgical Press) for a similar sentiment expressed from the divine perspective.

AUGUST 22, 2021
TWENTY-FIRST SUNDAY
IN ORDINARY TIME

SPIRITUALITY

GOSPEL ACCLAMATION
James 1:18

R℣. Alleluia, alleluia.
The Father willed to give us birth by the word
of truth
that we may be a kind of firstfruits of his
creatures.
R℣. Alleluia, alleluia.

Gospel   Mark 7:1-8, 14-15, 21-23;
L125B

When the Pharisees with some
scribes who had come from
Jerusalem
gathered around Jesus,
they observed that some of his
disciples ate their meals
with unclean, that is, unwashed,
hands.
—For the Pharisees and, in fact, all
Jews,
do not eat without carefully washing
their hands,
keeping the tradition of the elders.
And on coming from the marketplace
they do not eat without purifying
themselves.
And there are many other things that
they have traditionally observed,
the purification of cups and jugs and
kettles and beds.—
So the Pharisees and scribes questioned
him,
"Why do your disciples not follow the
tradition of the elders
but instead eat a meal with unclean
hands?"
He responded,
"Well did Isaiah prophesy about you
hypocrites, as it is written:
*This people honors me with their
lips,
but their hearts are far from me;
in vain do they worship me,
teaching as doctrines human
precepts.*
You disregard God's commandment but
cling to human tradition."

Continued in Appendix A, p. 300.

Reflecting on the Gospel

Today's gospel proclaims an encounter of Jesus with some of his opponents, named as "Pharisees with some scribes who had come from Jerusalem." Jerusalem was the center of formal opposition to Jesus by those who were fearful of the loss of personal power, overly concerned with the externals of religious appearances, or devoted to censorious inquiry into minor deviations from the established way of doing things religious while ignoring more serious matters.

In this sense, every religious group, in the present as well as the past, has those who "come from Jerusalem"—self-appointed custodians of the orthodox faith.

Traditions are necessary for the identity of any group, both secular (think of sports teams!) and religious. As Eugene LaVerdiere writes: "Traditions are tenacious and important, but they are not absolute, and their value can be questioned. Traditions spring from a particular history. They nourish a community's ideals, and they in turn are nourished by those ideals. When a life context that inspired a set of traditions dies or is drastically altered, traditions it once sustained become lifeless and meaningless. That does not mean they are immediately abandoned" (*The Beginning of the Gospel*).

The life context of the early Markan church was being drastically altered by the numbers of Gentiles who were entering into the Christian community. Tension inevitably arose between these new converts and the Christians whose faith had been nourished in the rich soil of Judaism. Many of the latter felt that the traditions they held dear, and that were reconcilable with following Jesus, had been carelessly trampled down or uprooted by the Gentile Christians to whom such traditions meant little or nothing.

On the other hand, the Gentile Christians felt coerced by what, to them, were meaningless laws and rituals. To reconcile both groups in baptismal freedom and love was an ongoing challenge for community leaders. The "tradition of the elders," rightly understood, were not an attempt to bury the commands of God under suffocating trivia, but rather to aerate the whole of Jewish life with mindfulness of the people's identity and responsibilities as God's people. For the sake of the non-Jewish readers, Mark enumerates some of the traditional rituals of washing that are observed.

Jesus responds to the Pharisees' challenge about the behavior of his disciples with a quotation from the prophet Isaiah, addressing them as "hypocrites." Out of the strong Jewish prophetic tradition of self-criticism, Isaiah spoke of religious practices that were on the lips but not in the heart as a superficial and external playacting at true religion. The Pharisees have fallen into the same religious trap of absolutizing their own human traditions of outward observance, not the commands of God. What should be washed is not so much pots and pans and hands, but their own hearts. External rituals have value only insofar as they encourage or express the dedication of our hearts. Before we eat as a eucharistic community, are our hearts clean?

Finally, Jesus tells his disciples that what truly defiles a person does not come from without, from the food that we take into our bodies; what defiles a person is the moral impurity and ethical evil that is first savored in the heart, not in the mouth. As if to emphasize that he is not setting aside God's tradition, Jesus enumerates a catalogue of vices, all of which are either directly proscribed in the Ten Commandments or indirectly related to them. Nineteen centuries later, another Jew would make a choice against "defilement" and for purity of heart in the tradition of true religion. Etty Hillesum, a young Jewish Dutch woman living in Nazi-occupied Amsterdam, and soon to die in Auschwitz at the age of twenty-nine, wrote in her extraordinary diary: "Every atom of hate we add to this world makes it more inhospitable . . . and every act of loving perfects it" (*Etty: A Diary 1941–1943*).

Focusing the Gospel

Key words and phrases: "You disregard God's commandment but cling to human tradition."

To the point: Within all four gospels, we often find Jesus at odds with the religious authorities of his day, particularly the Pharisees, scribes, and Sadducees. It is important to recognize that Jesus did not have a problem with these groups in general; it was only when their strongly held beliefs went against the requirements of charity that he would issue a rebuke. In today's gospel, Jesus quotes the prophet Isaiah, accusing those who "[honor] me with their lips, / but their hearts are far from me; / in vain do they worship me, / teaching as doctrines human precepts." In the religious life it is easy to become caught up in rules and regulations. As humans, we characteristically take comfort in knowing what is right and wrong. Jesus calls us, however, to discern which teachings come from God and which are the invention of human tradition. While the latter might change, the former are the bedrock of our faith.

Connecting the Gospel

to the first reading: Today's first reading, which comes from the book of Deuteronomy, is set on the eve of Moses's death and the people's entry into the Promised Land. On this momentous occasion Moses offers the people his parting words of wisdom, in particular enjoining them to follow the law of the Lord. As this law is a gift that reveals God's closeness to the people of Israel, it is also to be guarded and preserved just as it was revealed. Moses warns the people, "[Y]ou shall not add to what I command you nor subtract from it." In the gospel, Jesus accuses the Pharisees of yielding to the temptation to add to God's law by conflating "human tradition" with divine commandment.

to experience: In your own life of faith, when have you been tempted to add to God's commandments or to place undue emphasis on human rules? How might Jesus be calling you to greater fidelity to the essentials of our Christian faith?

Connecting the Responsorial Psalm

to the readings: The spirit of the law is encapsulated in today's psalm. To follow the Lord is to "walk blamelessly and do justice," by embracing truth and charity in word and action. The first reading from Deuteronomy lauds the law as the bringer of wisdom and justice that also proves to the nations the closeness of God to the people of Israel. In today's gospel, Jesus reminds the Pharisees of the most important purpose of the law: to bring hearts close to God. While sin separates us from God and others, doing justice leads us to "live in the presence of the Lord."

to psalmist preparation: How are you being called to live God's law with fidelity and courage?

PROMPTS FOR FAITH-SHARING

In the first reading Moses invites the people to ponder, "[W]hat great nation has statutes and decrees / that are as just as this whole law / which I am setting before you today?" How is God's law a gift in your life?

The psalm lifts up the just person as one who "thinks the truth in his heart / and slanders not with his tongue." How do you endeavor to be truthful in all your words and deeds?

The second reading from the letter of St. James reminds us that true religion is "to care for orphans and widows in their affliction / and to keep oneself unstained by the world." Who has modeled this purity of religion for you?

In the gospel, Jesus quotes the prophet Isaiah who condemned hypocrites who honor God with their lips, "but their hearts are far from [God]." What spiritual practices keep your heart close to God?

CELEBRATION

Model Penitential Act

Presider: In today's gospel Jesus teaches that "[n]othing that enters one from the outside can defile that person; / but the things that come out from within are what defile." Conscious of our own sinfulness, let us ask the Lord for healing and mercy . . . *[pause]*

Lord Jesus, you are pure of heart and constant in charity: Lord, have mercy.

Christ Jesus, you answer all who call upon you in need: Christ, have mercy.

Lord Jesus, you are our hope and our salvation: Lord, have mercy.

Homily Points

• Today's second reading comes from the letter of St. James. We will be journeying with this epistle for the next five weeks of Ordinary Time. Some have likened this letter to the Old Testament's wisdom literature. It is considered a "universal letter" written to the entirety of the early church instead of to a specific community or person, and as such, it provides insight to help us in our own daily lives of discipleship. Today's reading begins by reminding us of the gracious God who supplies us with "every perfect gift" and in "whom there is no alteration or shadow caused by change."

• Knowing the constancy and generosity of our God, the great gift-giver, we are invited to "humbly welcome the word that has been planted in you." James's metaphor to gardening is an apt one for the spiritual life. To flourish as Christians, we need to nourish and protect the seed of faith that we have received. But this is not all. James continues by invoking us to "[b]e doers of the word and not hearers only."

• St. Francis of Assisi famously stated, "Preach the gospel at all times, and if necessary use words." While our call to evangelization definitely requires the use of words, this quote—and James's injunction—remind us that our words mean nothing if they are not supported and lived out by our actions. It is not enough to hear the words of God. We must allow these words to become fully rooted within us; when they do, our whole lives change. We become more loving, more giving, more humble, more Christlike. This week let us consider, how do we receive the word of God as the greatest gift in our lives? And after receiving this gift, how do we strive to enact these words in all that we do and say?

Model Universal Prayer (Prayer of the Faithful)

Presider: Today's second reading reminds us that "all good giving and every perfect gift is from above." With gratitude for all our God has done for us, let us turn to him with our needs and the needs of our world.

Response: Lord, hear our prayer.

For members of God's holy church spread throughout the world, may we care for the oppressed and needy while living lives of holiness and purity . . .

For lawmakers and law enforcers, may the recognition of the preciousness and dignity of every human life guide them in building a just society . . .

For those who face persecution due to religion, gender, race, or sexual orientation, may their human rights be protected and their contributions to their communities celebrated . . .

For all gathered here, may we heed St. James's call to be "doers of the word and not hearers only" and be intent upon carrying out the will of God in our lives . . .

Presider: Father of lights, you sent your only Son to enlighten our darkness with words of salvation and truth. Hear our prayers that we might be ever attentive to his voice leading us along the path of holiness and peace. We ask this through Christ our Lord. **Amen.**

COLLECT

Let us pray.

Pause for silent prayer

God of might, giver of every good gift,
put into our hearts the love of your name,
so that, by deepening our sense of
     reverence,
you may nurture in us what is good
and, by your watchful care,
keep safe what you have nurtured.
Through our Lord Jesus Christ, your Son,
who lives and reigns with you in the unity
     of the Holy Spirit,
one God, for ever and ever. **Amen.**

FIRST READING
Deut 4:1-2, 6-8

Moses said to the people:
     "Now, Israel, hear the statutes and
          decrees
     which I am teaching you to observe,
     that you may live, and may enter in and
          take possession of the land
     which the LORD, the God of your
          fathers, is giving you.
In your observance of the commandments
     of the LORD, your God,
     which I enjoin upon you,
     you shall not add to what I command
          you nor subtract from it.
Observe them carefully,
     for thus will you give evidence
     of your wisdom and intelligence to the
          nations,
     who will hear of all these statutes and
          say,
     'This great nation is truly a wise and
          intelligent people.'
For what great nation is there
     that has gods so close to it as the LORD,
          our God, is to us
     whenever we call upon him?
Or what great nation has statutes and
          decrees
     that are as just as this whole law
     which I am setting before you today?"

RESPONSORIAL PSALM

Ps 15:2-3, 3-4, 4-5

℟. (1a) The one who does justice will live in the presence of the Lord.

Whoever walks blamelessly and does justice;
  who thinks the truth in his heart
  and slanders not with his tongue.

℟. The one who does justice will live in the presence of the Lord.

Who harms not his fellow man,
  nor takes up a reproach against his neighbor;
by whom the reprobate is despised,
  while he honors those who fear the LORD.

℟. The one who does justice will live in the presence of the Lord.

Who lends not his money at usury
  and accepts no bribe against the innocent.
Whoever does these things
  shall never be disturbed.

℟. The one who does justice will live in the presence of the Lord.

SECOND READING

Jas 1:17-18, 21b-22, 27

Dearest brothers and sisters:
All good giving and every perfect gift is from above,
  coming down from the Father of lights,
  with whom there is no alteration or shadow caused by change.
He willed to give us birth by the word of truth
  that we may be a kind of firstfruits of his creatures.

Humbly welcome the word that has been planted in you
  and is able to save your souls.

Be doers of the word and not hearers only, deluding yourselves.

Religion that is pure and undefiled before God and the Father is this:
  to care for orphans and widows in their affliction
  and to keep oneself unstained by the world.

About Liturgy

Relationships or Rules?: A few years ago, while I was music directing a musical at a nearby high school, it came time for sound checks before the opening night performance. The actors had to keep talking for as long as a minute each while we did the checks; most spoke of mundane things like what they ate for breakfast. One, though, told the following joke to fill the needed time:

> A priest, a minister, and a rabbi want to see who's best at their job. So, each one goes into the woods, finds a bear, and attempts to convert it. Later, they all get together to report how things had gone.
> The priest begins: "When I found the bear, I read to him from the catechism and sprinkled him with holy water. Next week is his First Communion."
> "I found a bear by the stream," says the minister, "and preached God's holy Word. The bear was so mesmerized that he let me baptize him."
> These two both look down at the rabbi, who is lying on a gurney in a body cast. "Looking back," he says, "maybe I shouldn't have started with the circumcision."

It's a pretty good joke, I think, but it also has a relevant point for those of us who evangelize, especially via the liturgy, in different times and places. From the very beginning, our missionary efforts recognized that step one was always to enter into a human relationship with the people and culture being visited, and to make sure their human needs were being met. If those with whom we hope to share the Good News don't know us and trust us as friends, any words we share will be hollow and distrusted. If those with whom we hope to share the Good News are hungry, poorly clothed, or need shelter, these basic human needs will preclude them from hearing any other message.

In the joke, I wouldn't say that the priest or the minister start from a place of relationship and trust, but the rabbi (in this case) seems to have just jumped in with the rituals of his faith. The readings for this Sunday are focused on observances of laws, and as liturgists, we can get caught up in how well the minutiae of each rubric are being followed. How much time do we spend, as liturgists, meeting needs and building relationship, and how much time do we spend on catechesis, Bible study, worship, and the like? It's likely that many of those we meet have "needs" not related to hunger or housing insecurity, but rather to relationship: being understood, sensing one's own belonging. Said another way, people won't care what you know until they know you care. This remains true for any of us in the church—the most missionary, evangelistic thing we can do as church is to let others know we care. Tertullian, in the second and third centuries, wrote that the early Christians' lives of love were so pronounced that others would declare, "See how they love one another." So may it be for us today.

About the Sign of Peace

Christ Breaking Through: The GIRM tells us, "There follows the Rite of Peace, by which the Church entreats peace and unity for herself and for the whole human family, and the faithful express to each other their ecclesial communion and mutual charity before communicating in the Sacrament" (82). There is a restlessness within, and sometimes a reluctance to the rite, but Christ always breaks through, strangers bonded, by touch and word, in divine peace.

About Music

The Word Within: Bob Moore's "The Word Is in Your Heart" (GIA) sings well and emphasizes the holy word dwelling within and guiding our speech and actions in love.

AUGUST 29, 2021
TWENTY-SECOND SUNDAY IN ORDINARY TIME

SPIRITUALITY

GOSPEL ACCLAMATION
cf. Matt 4:23

℟. Alleluia, alleluia.
Jesus proclaimed the Gospel of the kingdom
and cured every disease among the people.
℟. Alleluia, alleluia.

Gospel

Mark 7:31-37; L128B

Again Jesus left the district
    of Tyre
    and went by way of
        Sidon to the Sea
        of Galilee,
    into the district of
        the Decapolis.
And people brought
    to him a deaf man
    who had a speech
        impediment
    and begged him to
        lay his hand on
        him.
He took him off by
    himself away from the crowd.
He put his finger into the man's ears
    and, spitting, touched his tongue;
    then he looked up to heaven and
        groaned, and said to him,
    "Ephphatha!"—that is, "Be
        opened!"—
And immediately the man's ears were
    opened,
    his speech impediment was removed,
    and he spoke plainly.
He ordered them not to tell anyone.
But the more he ordered them not to,
    the more they proclaimed it.
They were exceedingly astonished and
    they said,
    "He has done all things well.
He makes the deaf hear and the mute
    speak."

Reflecting on the Gospel

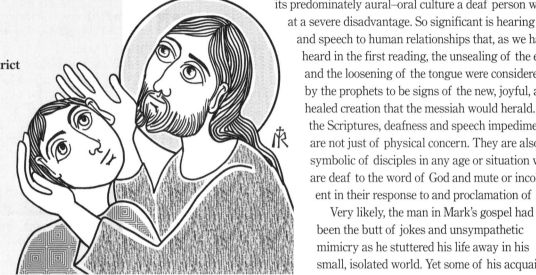

In the gospel, Jesus seems to make an involved and impractical journey into the Decapolis ("ten cities") that were previously under Jewish control but had become Gentile territory. Mark, however, is not concerned with geography but with announcing the boundary-breaking mission of Jesus, the Messiah for all nations. "They," the anonymous crowds that we can presume are Gentiles, bring to Jesus a man who is deaf and has an impediment in his speech, two obviously related disabilities. First-century Decapolis was not a world of computerized hearing aids or bionic ears, and in its predominately aural–oral culture a deaf person was at a severe disadvantage. So significant is hearing and speech to human relationships that, as we have heard in the first reading, the unsealing of the ears and the loosening of the tongue were considered by the prophets to be signs of the new, joyful, and healed creation that the messiah would herald. In the Scriptures, deafness and speech impediments are not just of physical concern. They are also symbolic of disciples in any age or situation who are deaf to the word of God and mute or incoherent in their response to and proclamation of it.

Very likely, the man in Mark's gospel had been the butt of jokes and unsympathetic mimicry as he stuttered his life away in his small, isolated world. Yet some of his acquaintances are compassionate enough to bring him to Jesus, begging Jesus to speak to the man in the only language he can understand—the language of touch. Jesus takes him away from the crowd, and even from his helpful companions. Perhaps this is because of Jesus's delicate consideration for the man, lest the amazed babble of the crowd at his cure is too overwhelming as his first hearing experience; or perhaps it is to ensure that the first words the man hears are the words of the Word.

The actions of Jesus are unusual and described in detail. Instead of the simple taking by the hand or laying on of hands in the miracles he worked in Jewish territory, there are fingers in the man's ears, touching of the man's tongue with Jesus's spittle, looking up to heaven, and sighing. Such folkloric actions resemble those of first-century faith healers and seem to be an "inculturation" of Jesus's miracle working in non-Jewish territory, a considerate translation into gestures that would have been familiar to a Gentile. Then Jesus speaks a single word: *"Ephphatha!"* and speaks it in his Aramaic mother tongue. Mark courteously translates it for us: "Be opened!" but the fact that he retained the Aramaic adds a note of privilege and respect to the human words of Jesus. It would not have been such an unintelligible word or a magical incantation in the Decapolis where many spoke a kind of Aramaic dialect. But it is more important that not only the deaf man hears this word, but that all who come to Jesus recognize this as the command to us of the most open One—open to God's will, open to healing of the suffering of our brothers and sisters.

What happens next is a new creation, such as that hoped for by Isaiah in the first reading. With open ears and unshackled tongue, the man speaks plainly—to Jesus, for they are on their own. Here is a model of discipleship that is recalled in the baptismal rite of every Christian. As the child's or adult's ears and mouth are touched by the minister of the sacrament, these words accompany the action in what is still called the Ephphatha rite: "May the Lord Jesus, / who made the deaf to hear and the mute to speak, / grant that you may soon receive his word with your ears / and profess the faith with your lips, / to the glory and praise of God the Father" (Order of Baptism 65). Throughout our lives we need to come to Jesus or be brought to him by the compassion of others, for the healing of whatever is an impediment to our baptismal commitment.

Focusing the Gospel

Key words and phrases: And immediately the man's ears were opened.

To the point: Once again we see the efficacy of God's word at work. Jesus commands, "*'Ephphatha!'*—that is, 'Be opened!'" And immediately what he has commanded comes to pass. The man who previously was limited in both hearing and speech now is able to do both. In each of the gospel miracles, we discover something new about Jesus. He has authority over sickness and health, life and death, as well as over the cosmos and all of creation. In Jesus we find God's dreams for the world enacted: the blind see, the lame walk, the deaf hear, the sick are healed, and the outcast are restored to society.

Connecting the Gospel

to the first reading: The crowd rejoices in Jesus's healing of the deaf man not only for the man's sake, but also because within this moment they recognize the fulfillment of Isaiah's prophecy from the first reading. Isaiah foretells a time when "the ears of the deaf [will] be cleared" and "the tongue of the mute will sing." This chapter of Isaiah speaks of Israel's deliverance and is believed to have been written during the Babylonian exile. At this time of desolation in the history of Israel, God offers words of comfort and consolation: Though their plight might be difficult at the moment, this is not the final will of the Lord.

to experience: God instructs Isaiah, "Say to those whose hearts are frightened: / Be strong, fear not!" Where are you most in need of this reassuring message in your own life?

Connecting the Responsorial Psalm

to the readings: The triumphant nature of Psalm 146 calls us to praise and worship the Lord who "shall reign forever." Similar to the prophecy from Isaiah, within this psalm we are given insight into God's dreams for the world. God envisions and intends a social order where the hungry are filled, the captives freed, the blind see, the bowed down are raised, and the stranger, widow, and orphan are sustained. Not only are these comforting images to bring us consolation in times of grief and suffering, they are also a call to action. As the Body of Christ, we are meant to help bring about this kingdom where justice and mercy reign.

to psalmist preparation: Today's psalm contains good news for the poor, the hungry, and the oppressed—and also a warning for the wicked whose ways God will "thwart." These Scripture passages that champion the vulnerable and weak of society invite us to discern where we stand on social issues. Are we in tune with the needs of the poorest of the poor or do we align ourselves with the powerful? This week, consider how today's psalm might call you to ongoing conversion as a disciple of Christ.

PROMPTS FOR FAITH-SHARING

The prophet Isaiah speaks of God's desire and intention to heal every ill. Where are you in need of healing?

God instructs Isaiah, "Say to those whose hearts are frightened: / Be strong, fear not!" Where has fear crept into your life and how might you give this anxiety over to God?

St. James urges his community to show no partiality based on wealth or social standing. How does your parish seek to treat all as equals in God's eyes?

In the gospel, Jesus heals a deaf man through touch and the words "*'Ephphatha!'* —that is, 'Be opened!'" In what ways is Jesus calling you to be more open to his wisdom and word?

205

Model Penitential Act

Presider: In today's first reading, God instructs the prophet Isaiah, "Say to those whose hearts are frightened: / Be strong, fear not!" Confident in our God's compassion and never-ending mercy, let us pause to call to mind our sins . . . *[pause]*

Lord Jesus, you came to save us: Lord, have mercy.

Christ Jesus, you choose the poor to be heirs to your kingdom: Christ, have mercy.

Lord Jesus, you open the eyes of the blind and the ears of the deaf: Lord, have mercy.

Homily Points

• In 1950, St. Teresa of Calcutta founded the Missionaries of Charity, an order of religious sisters that seeks to care for the dying and destitute of the world. In her book *In the Heart of the World*, St. Teresa described her spirituality: "Seeking the face of God in everything, everyone, all the time, and his hand in every happening; this is what it means to be contemplative in the heart of the world. Seeing and adoring the presence of Jesus, especially in the lowly appearance of bread, and in the distressing disguise of the poor." So often, it can be difficult for us to recognize Jesus in the people in front of us, especially if their "distressing disguise" is one of poverty or of mental or physical illness. And yet, within these "poorest of the poor" we find the beloved of God.

• In the second reading, St. James urges the early Christian community to examine their habit of treating the rich and the poor differently. He accuses them of making "distinctions" based on social class and thus becoming "judges with evil designs." St. James points to God's habit of choosing "those who are poor in the world" as the ones who are "to be rich in faith and heirs to the kingdom." Throughout salvation history, God invites the vulnerable and powerless to be his greatest collaborators—from David, a lowly shepherd boy, the youngest of seven brothers who becomes the king of Israel, to Mary, a young peasant woman who bears the Son of God to the world.

• In the gospel, Jesus heals the deaf man by using the word *"Ephphatha!"* meaning "Be opened!" We might also make this our prayer, that in everything our Lord might open our senses to find him and serve him in all those we meet.

Model Universal Prayer (Prayer of the Faithful)

Presider: With trust in God's desire to lead us to fullness of life in his presence, let us place before him our needs and the needs of others.

Response: Lord, hear our prayer.

For God's holy church, may it be an instrument of peace and healing in the world . . .

For leaders of nations, may they attend to the growing divide between the rich and the poor and seek to create a society where all might thrive . . .

For those suffering from a terminal illness and for their families, friends, and caregivers, may they be comforted by the Lord of life and lifted up by loving communities . . .

For members of this parish community, may we entrust God with all our fears and anxieties so as to live in the peace of Christ . . .

Presider: God of abundant blessings, through word and sacrament you nourish and strengthen us to be the people you call us to be. Hear our prayers that we might know your love and, in knowing it, share it with all we meet. We ask this through Christ our Lord. **Amen.**

COLLECT

Let us pray.

Pause for silent prayer

O God, by whom we are redeemed and
    receive adoption,
look graciously upon your beloved sons
    and daughters,
that those who believe in Christ
may receive true freedom
and an everlasting inheritance.
Through our Lord Jesus Christ, your Son,
who lives and reigns with you in the unity
    of the Holy Spirit,
one God, for ever and ever. **Amen.**

FIRST READING

Isa 35:4-7a

Thus says the LORD:
    Say to those whose hearts are
        frightened:
        Be strong, fear not!
    Here is your God,
        he comes with vindication;
    with divine recompense
        he comes to save you.
    Then will the eyes of the blind be
        opened,
        the ears of the deaf be cleared;
    then will the lame leap like a stag,
        then the tongue of the mute will sing.
    Streams will burst forth in the desert,
        and rivers in the steppe.
    The burning sands will become pools,
        and the thirsty ground, springs of
            water.

RESPONSORIAL PSALM
Ps 146:6-7, 8-9, 9-10

℟. (1b) Praise the Lord, my soul!
or:
℟. Alleluia.

The God of Jacob keeps faith forever,
    secures justice for the oppressed,
    gives food to the hungry.
The Lord sets captives free.

℟. Praise the Lord, my soul!
or:
℟. Alleluia.

The Lord gives sight to the blind;
    the Lord raises up those who were
        bowed down.
The Lord loves the just;
    the Lord protects strangers.

℟. Praise the Lord, my soul!
or:
℟. Alleluia.

The fatherless and the widow the Lord
    sustains,
    but the way of the wicked he thwarts.
The Lord shall reign forever;
    your God, O Zion, through all
        generations.
Alleluia.

℟. Praise the Lord, my soul!
or:
℟. Alleluia.

SECOND READING
Jas 2:1-5

My brothers and sisters, show no
        partiality
    as you adhere to the faith in our
        glorious Lord Jesus Christ.
For if a man with gold rings and fine
        clothes
    comes into your assembly,
    and a poor person in shabby clothes
        also comes in,
    and you pay attention to the one
        wearing the fine clothes
    and say, "Sit here, please,"
    while you say to the poor one, "Stand
        there," or "Sit at my feet,"
    have you not made distinctions among
        yourselves
    and become judges with evil designs?

Listen, my beloved brothers and sisters.
Did not God choose those who are poor in
        the world
    to be rich in faith and heirs of the
        kingdom
    that he promised to those who love him?

About Liturgy

Two Expressions of One Rite?: Today's readings speak to an openness of senses, which in turn open our very selves to new experiences and new world views. As we take in new sights and sounds, our horizons expand, and old experiences inform our reception of new, and new experiences can reshape our insights from the former ones. Perhaps this is partly what Pope Benedict XVI had in mind fourteen years ago, regarding the rites of the church, principally Eucharist.

Summorum Pontificum, released on July 7, 2007, became church law on September 14, 2007, the feast of the Exaltation of the Holy Cross. The document, with an accompanying letter, seeks to update and clarify the liturgical occasions on which the Tridentine rite of 1962 may be used. It greatly liberalizes access to this rite in all forms—not just Eucharist, but all rites of the church, within certain guidelines. Both the actual document and its accompanying letter emphasize the continuity of the two rites—that following the axiom *lex orandi, lex credendi*, the two exist not as different forms of prayer: "Rather, it is a matter of a twofold use of one and the same rite" (6).

Yet there are very obvious differences between the two rites, most dramatically observed at Eucharist. Earlier we discussed the larger amount of Scripture the current rite presents to the faithful over time; there are also many additional eucharistic prayers, wider allowances for distribution of Holy Communion under both species, and several other changes throughout the liturgy.

Regarding specifically postures of the eucharistic rite, the principal variance occurs during the reception of Communion—both that of the individual at the moment of reception and that of the community throughout the distribution of Communion. In the older rite, reception of Communion took place directly on the tongue while kneeling; in the new rite, reception takes place on the tongue or in the hand while standing. In the older rite, the community's posture during distribution was kneeling except while moving to the altar rail; in the newer rite, the community also kneels (or in some instances stands), but those in motion are deemed to be processing to the altar, and that procession is much more theologically developed than before.

Given what we know about the significance of posture both individually and as a community and, most importantly, posture's ability to communicate with God and with one another and posture's ability to create (or destroy) group identity; given what we know about the history and anthropology of varying prayer postures and their theological significance; and given the mandates of Vatican II, what conclusions can we draw regarding our present postures at Eucharist, both the variety of postures in our ordinary rite and the differing postures exhibited by the ordinary and extraordinary rites?

Perhaps it is clear—whether one agrees with the current rubric or would wish for some alteration or a return to any of various former practices—that a communal posture ought to be known, understood, and effected as much as pastorally possible. To this end, it seems that one Roman rite can be expressed in only one way, and not in two (or more?) ways as Pope Benedict and *Summorum Pontificum* suggest. While unity does not necessarily demand uniformity, body as symbol is important and necessary both to our spiritual lives and to our communal identity as Christians.

About Music

With Opened Eyes: I suspect many readers will be familiar with Jesse Manibusan's "Open My Eyes" (OCP) and of course "Amazing Grace," found in nearly all hymnals. A lesser-known hymn choice would be "O Christ, the Healer, We Have Come" (Hope), which pairs nicely with ERHALT UNS, HERR.

SEPTEMBER 5, 2021
TWENTY-THIRD SUNDAY IN ORDINARY TIME

SPIRITUALITY

℟. Alleluia, alleluia.
May I never boast except in the cross of our Lord
through which the world has been
    crucified to me and I to the world.
℟. Alleluia, alleluia.

Gospel

Mark 8:27-35; L131B

Jesus and his disciples set out
    for the villages of Caesarea
        Philippi.
Along the way he asked his
    disciples,
    "Who do people say that I am?"
They said in reply,
    "John the Baptist, others Elijah,
    still others one of the prophets."
And he asked them,
    "But who do you say that I am?"
Peter said to him in reply,
    "You are the Christ."
Then he warned them not to tell
    anyone about him.

He began to teach them
    that the Son of Man must suffer greatly
    and be rejected by the elders, the chief
        priests, and the scribes,
    and be killed, and rise after three days.
He spoke this openly.
Then Peter took him aside and began to
    rebuke him.
At this he turned around and, looking at
    his disciples,
    rebuked Peter and said, "Get behind
    me, Satan.
You are thinking not as God does, but as
    human beings do."

He summoned the crowd with his
    disciples and said to them,
    "Whoever wishes to come after me
        must deny himself,
    take up his cross, and follow me.
For whoever wishes to save his life will
    lose it,
    but whoever loses his life for my sake
    and that of the gospel will save it."

Reflecting on the Gospel

Jesus bluntly rebukes Peter, telling him, "You are thinking not as God does, but as human beings do." Mark does not tell us what Peter had actually said to Jesus, but given that Jesus has just disclosed that "the Son of Man must suffer greatly and be rejected by the elders, the chief priests, and the scribes, and be killed, and rise after three days," it is not a stretch to believe that Peter rejected the need for the Son of Man to suffer and die. Jesus's divinely ordained and freely chosen destiny is, in this context, God's "thinking."

And what is human beings' "thinking"? What is the thinking that draws us away from God's ways and desires? Although human "thinking" in itself is not necessarily negative—avoiding suffering and death is not inherently wrong—what seems to be the case is that whenever (divine) values and (human) preferences come into conflict, one chooses God's thinking. Values and preferences are not always at odds, but when they are, the choice must be made for the things of God.

What things did Peter tell Jesus to choose? When we reflect on Peter telling Jesus to choose human "thinking," it is hard to avoid considering the concrete temptations Satan offered Jesus in the synoptic gospel narratives, since it is Jesus who raises the specter of Satan here in Caesarea Philippi. It seems likely that Jesus does not consider Peter as Satan, but that the temptations Peter offers in the guise of helping Jesus are connected to the temptations of Satan that we know from Matthew and Luke—that is, the basic temptations that underlie all "human thinking."

In the temptation accounts, Jesus is offered the power to satisfy all his earthly hungers, the power to presume upon God's will and favor, and the power over all kingdoms. Wealth, authority, and fame—what more could a person want? Did Peter tempt Jesus with a plea for him not to die at the hands of foreign oppressors, the Romans, but to institute God's kingdom by conquering them militarily and installing himself as king? While it is impossible to know precisely what temptation Peter called upon Jesus to accept, it is not too much to believe that he asked him to act on his power and authority and bring about the kingdom of God in a way that aligned with "human thinking," that involved shows of force, might, and revenge.

When Peter identified Jesus as the Messiah, he must have had particular ideas not just of what this meant for the Messiah, God's Anointed One, but for those who were the Messiah's closest friends, his apostles and disciples. Whatever kingdom Peter's mind conjured, it probably did not involve denying himself and taking up his cross to follow Jesus or losing his life for the gospel. What kind of kingdom is that? Feel for Peter for a moment. What kind of ridiculous kingdom is built on the broken body of a defeated Messiah?

This is the kingdom of "God's thinking," the kingdom of paradox. Tomáš Halík, the Czech priest and theologian, says, "If we have never had the feeling that what Jesus wants of us is absurd, crazy, and impossible, then we've probably either been too hasty in taming or diluting the radical nature of his teaching by means of soothing intellectualizing interpretations, or (mostly naïvely, illusorily, or even hypocritically) we have too easily forgotten just to what extent—in our thinking, customs, and actions—we are rooted 'in this world' where totally different rules apply" (*Night of the Confessor*).

Jesus offers us the things of God, the things in which we save our lives by losing them and build a kingdom whose divine power is seen as human weakness.

Focusing the Gospel

Key words and phrases: "Whoever wishes to come after me must deny himself, / take up his cross, and follow me."

To the point: Nearly halfway through Mark's gospel, we come to Jesus's first prediction of his passion. After Peter confesses Jesus to be "the Christ," Jesus immediately reveals an important truth about who "the Christ" is—one who will undergo suffering and even death in following the will of God. And this is not all: those who would follow Jesus will also find this path in front of them, one of sacrifice and even suffering on the way to eternal life. Jesus seems to place this revelation in front of the disciples as a challenge. They know Jesus the wonder-worker and the wise teacher. Now they are introduced to Jesus the suffering servant who will undergo rejection and death. Do they dare to continue following in his footsteps, knowing where this path will lead them?

Connecting the Gospel

to the first reading: The first reading from the prophet Isaiah comes from one of the segments of this book designated as the "song of the suffering servant." In these sections of Isaiah, we find a prefiguring of the humility and vulnerability of Christ who will not shy away from the violence and torture that ends his mortal life. And yet, the servant in Isaiah knows, as Jesus does, that even in enduring "buffets and spitting . . . I shall not be put to shame." When Peter rebukes Jesus for predicting his own passion, we could intuit that he is not concerned for the physical pain Jesus will undergo, but rather for the disgrace of such a death. He has just proclaimed this man to be "the Christ," the anointed one of God. Surely this is not the way God's own Son will meet his end!

to experience: The first reading and the gospel invite us to shape our perspective to think not as human beings do but as God does. Those who cling to the truth and devote their lives to faithful discipleship can proclaim with the suffering servant, "The Lord is my help, / therefore I am not disgraced."

Connecting the Responsorial Psalm

to the readings: In today's gospel Jesus predicts not only his passion, but also his resurrection. Just as Peter does, when we read that "the Son of Man must suffer greatly / be rejected by the elders, the chief priests, and the scribes, / and be killed, and rise after three days," we might focus on the dark events of this narrative rather than the outcome. Death is not the end here. Today's responsorial psalm can be prayed as our own affirmation of life coming from death in the resurrection. No matter what events befall us we believe, "I will walk before the Lord, in the land of the living."

to psalmist preparation: How does belief in the resurrection affect the way you live?

PROMPTS FOR FAITH-SHARING

The prophet Isaiah writes, "The Lord is my help, / therefore I am not disgraced." When has your faith helped you to stand firm in the face of derision?

St. James reminds us, "[F]aith of itself, / if it does not have works, is dead." How do you put your faith into action each day?

Once again, we encounter Jesus's question to the disciples: "But who do you say that I am?" At this moment in your journey of faith, how would you answer this question?

How do you understand Jesus's words "whoever wishes to save his life will lose it, / but whoever loses his life for my sake / and that of the gospel will save it"?

CELEBRATION

Model Penitential Act

Presider: In today's gospel, Jesus rebukes Peter for "thinking not as God does, but as human beings do." For the times our own thoughts have been counter to the divine wisdom of God, let us pause to ask for pardon and mercy . . . *[pause]*

Lord Jesus, you are our help and our salvation: Lord, have mercy.

Christ Jesus, you show sinners the road of repentance: Christ, have mercy.

Lord Jesus, you call us to take up our cross and follow you: Lord, have mercy.

Homily Points

• Today, Jesus asks the disciples a deeply personal question: "Who do you say that I am?" Peter answers for the group by proclaiming, "You are the Christ." Peter and the other disciples began this journey as ordinary men who were called from their everyday labors to follow an itinerant preacher. During their time with Jesus, they have sat as his feet as he proclaimed the good news that the kingdom of God has drawn near, watched as he healed those who are ill, and witnessed him casting out demons. Their discipleship is based not on a printed set of beliefs, but on their relationship with the Lord.

• This is true for each of us as well. Christianity is not about following doctrines or adhering to a certain set of rules; instead it is a covenant relationship with the Lord of life. Throughout our lives of discipleship, our own answers to this question "Who do you say that I am?" will change. At times we might know Jesus best as the one who performs wonders in our own lives, or perhaps as the great teacher whose words bring us wisdom. At other times Jesus will be the comforter who walks with us in times of grief, or perhaps the just judge who calls us to repentance and growth.

• This question "Who do you say that I am?" is found in each of the Synoptic Gospels. We celebrate Peter's first confession of faith that this is "the Christ" even as we confront this question ourselves today. We live a communal faith that is also deeply personal. Each one of us must answer for ourselves, who do we say Jesus is and how do we live out this belief with every moment of our lives?

Model Universal Prayer (Prayer of the Faithful)

Presider: Knowing that our God is always near to those who are brokenhearted and in need, let us confidently place before him our intentions.

Response: Lord, hear our prayer.

For bishops, priests, deacons, religious and lay ministers, may they be strengthened in their resolve to take up their crosses and follow the Lord daily . . .

For teachers and educators throughout the world, may their work bear fruit in the minds and hearts of their students . . .

For those struggling with learning disabilities, may they persevere in the path of knowledge and be richly rewarded for their efforts . . .

For all gathered here, as we pray for those in need let us recommit ourselves to putting this concern into action in our everyday life . . .

Presider: Gracious and glorious God, you have created us for yourself and "our hearts are restless until they rest in you." Hear our prayers that with courage and faith we might follow your Son on the path of salvation. We ask this through Christ our Lord. **Amen.**

COLLECT

Let us pray.

Pause for silent prayer

Look upon us, O God,
Creator and ruler of all things,
and, that we may feel the working of your
    mercy,
grant that we may serve you with all our
    heart.
Through our Lord Jesus Christ, your Son,
who lives and reigns with you in the unity
    of the Holy Spirit,
one God, for ever and ever. **Amen.**

FIRST READING
Isa 50:4c-9a

The Lord GOD opens my ear that I may
    hear;
and I have not rebelled,
    have not turned back.
I gave my back to those who beat me,
    my cheeks to those who plucked my
        beard;
my face I did not shield
    from buffets and spitting.

The Lord GOD is my help,
    therefore I am not disgraced;
I have set my face like flint,
    knowing that I shall not be put to
        shame.
He is near who upholds my right;
    if anyone wishes to oppose me,
    let us appear together.
Who disputes my right?
    Let that man confront me.
See, the Lord GOD is my help;
    who will prove me wrong?

RESPONSORIAL PSALM
Ps 116:1-2, 3-4, 5-6, 8-9

R̶. (9) I will walk before the Lord, in the
    land of the living.
    or:
R̶. Alleluia.

I love the LORD because he has heard
    my voice in supplication,
because he has inclined his ear to me
    the day I called.

R̶. I will walk before the Lord, in the land
    of the living.
    or:
R̶. Alleluia.

The cords of death encompassed me;
   the snares of the netherworld seized
      upon me;
   I fell into distress and sorrow,
and I called upon the name of the Lord,
   "O Lord, save my life!"

R︎. I will walk before the Lord, in the land
   of the living.
   or:
R︎. Alleluia.

Gracious is the Lord and just;
   yes, our God is merciful.
The Lord keeps the little ones;
   I was brought low, and he saved me.

R︎. I will walk before the Lord, in the land
   of the living.
   or:
R︎. Alleluia.

For he has freed my soul from death,
   my eyes from tears, my feet from
      stumbling.
I shall walk before the Lord
   in the land of the living.

R︎. I will walk before the Lord, in the land
   of the living.
   or:
R︎. Alleluia.

SECOND READING
Jas 2:14-18

What good is it, my brothers and sisters,
   if someone says he has faith but does
      not have works?
Can that faith save him?
If a brother or sister has nothing to wear
   and has no food for the day,
   and one of you says to them,
   "Go in peace, keep warm, and eat well,"
   but you do not give them the necessities
      of the body,
   what good is it?
So also faith of itself,
   if it does not have works, is dead.

Indeed someone might say,
   "You have faith and I have works."
Demonstrate your faith to me without
      works,
   and I will demonstrate my faith to you
      from my works.

About Liturgy

In Christ There Is No East or West: In today's gospel, Christ asks his apostles, "But who do you say that I am?" Liturgically, it is worth pondering a similar question from time to time: imagine Christ asking, about the assembly, the minister, the liturgical furnishings, the ritual objects, the liturgy itself, "*Where* do you say that I am?"

One effect of *Summorum Pontificum*, discussed last week, is that the Tridentine rite and the *novus ordo* exert some influence on one another, for good or ill. One example of such influence is presiders, while celebrating the current rite, choosing to face *ad orientem*, "to the east," for presidential prayers addressed to God the Father. Some describe this as the priest turning his back on the congregation, which falsely describes the true motive, which is to face East or at least to what has been coined "liturgical east."

In short, the theology behind this is to allow the entire congregation, together with the presider *in persona Christi capitas*, to face the same way to God the Father. There are often appeals to it being an ancient and broad practice, which while perhaps true neglect the actuality of a rather varied liturgical practice across both time and space.

The typical present practice of the priest facing the assembly throughout the liturgy is frequently termed *versus populum,* which many find a theologically unhelpful descriptor—but perhaps it is at least accurate. Many times, "liturgical east" is not actual east in many (if not most) of our sacred spaces, and, in a church that values the real over artificial, it seems we should all actually either face true east or not even bother with this practice. Another issue is that facing *ad orientem* tries to, in a sense, limit God geographically—as if God is confined to one particular spot, as if one can't face God while facing one's neighbor, created in the image and likeness of God, a temple of the Holy Spirit.

And while Christ, too, is bound by neither time nor space, *Sacrosanctum Concilium* tells us that Christ is uniquely present in the liturgy in four ways: the gathered assembly, the proclaimed Word, the presiding minister, and uniquely in the Eucharist (7). Further, in the context of liturgy the altar itself *is* Christ. Not only does *Built of Living Stones* remind us of this (see "About the Altar" from December 13, Third Sunday of Advent), but one of the prefaces for the eucharistic prayer during the Easter season states that Christ is "the Priest, the Altar, and the Lamb of sacrifice" (Roman Missal, Preface V of Easter).

So if the assembly and priest gather around an altar at Mass, we are all already facing Christ: in one another, in the altar, in the consecrated bread and wine elevated above that altar and then soon consumed by all gathered. The last verse of the widely known hymn "In Christ There Is No East or West" by John Oxenham (1908) puts it quite succinctly: "In Christ now meet both east and west; / in him meet south and north. / All Christly souls are one in him / throughout the whole wide earth."

About Music

Take Up Your Cross: In addition to this hymn, the theme of discipleship is so strong that it in turn prompts two hymns which share the title "Take Up Your Cross." The first has text by Charles W. Everest and is in found in many hymnals with a variety of tunes. A newer song of the same title mentioned earlier this year is by Jaime Cortez (OCP) and draws lyrics more directly from today's gospel.

SEPTEMBER 12, 2021
TWENTY-FOURTH SUNDAY
IN ORDINARY TIME

SPIRITUALITY

R︠. Alleluia, alleluia.
God has called us through the Gospel
to possess the glory of our Lord Jesus Christ.
R︠. Alleluia, alleluia.

Gospel

Mark 9:30-37; L134B

Jesus and his disciples left from there
and began a journey through
Galilee,
but he did not wish anyone to know
about it.
He was teaching his disciples and
telling them,
"The Son of Man is to be handed
over to men
and they will kill him,
and three days after his death
the Son of Man will rise."
But they did not understand the
saying,
and they were afraid to question
him.

They came to Capernaum and, once
inside the house,
he began to ask them,
"What were you arguing about on the
way?"
But they remained silent.
They had been discussing among
themselves on the way
who was the greatest.
Then he sat down, called the Twelve,
and said to them,
"If anyone wishes to be first,
he shall be the last of all and the
servant of all."
Taking a child, he placed it in their midst,
and putting his arms around it, he
said to them,
"Whoever receives one child such as
this in my name, receives me;
and whoever receives me,
receives not me but the One who sent
me."

Reflecting on the Gospel

On one occasion after the composer Robert Schumann had played a very difficult étude, one of his listeners asked him to explain the piece. Schumann replied by sitting down at the piano and playing the same étude a second time. This Sunday's gospel may seem to be like Schumann's reply—a repeat performance for disciples who appear not to have heard much of what Jesus told them in his first passion prediction. But Mark also plays some significant variations on the theme of the gospel we heard

last Sunday. The crowds have gone, and Jesus is journeying with his disciples, focusing his full attention on them—and they need it! In the verses immediately before this reading they have rather accusingly asked Jesus why *they* could not cure the epileptic boy, to which Jesus's response implies that it was because of their lack of prayer and faith (see Mark 9:18-19).

Jesus again names himself as the Son of Man, with memories of the Daniel figure (Dan 7:13-14) who comes to announce the end of one age and the beginning of another. Jesus looks beyond his earlier reference to rejection by the elders, the chief priests, and the scribes, and says that he will be "handed over to men" to be put to death, and in three days will rise again. Silence, dense and dumb, descends on the disciples. This time not even Peter summons up an argument. They don't understand what Jesus is saying and, what is worse, they are afraid to ask and learn what Jesus means—and what might be the implications for them if they keep on following a master who seems headed for suffering. We too know the temptation in difficult times to stop questioning and questing, and to hope that the disturbing problems will go away and leave us to a complacent life in our comfort zones.

Jesus will not allow this, so when they are alone together, "inside the house," he questions the Twelve who, "on the way" of increasingly obtuse discipleship, have miraculously found their tongues in order to argue with one another about which one of them is the greatest! The silence thickens. It is as though the disciples have been deaf to everything that Jesus has said about his vulnerability and powerlessness. So Jesus sits down, taking up the position of a rabbinical teacher, and calls the Twelve to himself just as he had done initially (Mark 3:13). They need to be shocked out of their competitiveness and power-seeking, not by reprimand but by reversal, by action that will proclaim that, in the reign of God, to be first is to be last of all and servant of all. Gloomy silence gives way to astonishment when Jesus does what would be almost inconceivable in first-century Palestinian culture, where children, along with women and slaves, had almost no social status. In front of his twelve adult male disciples, Jesus wraps his arms around a disregarded child. Only one other time in the New Testament is such an intimate gesture mentioned—in the father's welcoming embrace of the returning Prodigal Son (Luke 15:20). Here "inside the house," a symbol of the domestic church, is a parable in action which teaches that what should characterize the ecclesial household is inclusion and equality, not exclusion and superiority.

In Jesus's day to extend hospitality to such little ones would be considered ridiculous because, although hospitality was such a significant Middle Eastern virtue, so was the return of hospitality. What could a child offer in return? But Jesus is teaching his disciples that these are the very "little ones" who are to be welcomed down through the ages: the ones who have no social status, no vote value, those whose human dignity is ignored or violated. To welcome them is to forge a link in the chain of what binds together those who offer such hospitality with Jesus and his Father.

Focusing the Gospel

Key words and phrases: "If anyone wishes to be first, / he shall be the last of all and the servant of all."

To the point: In today's gospel, when the disciples do not understand Jesus's second prediction of his passion, they turn to arguing about something that is far easier for them to comprehend: who among them is "the greatest." Once again the disciples are displaying natural human behavior. It is easy for us to get caught up in competition, whether consciously or subconsciously, by comparing ourselves with others. But Jesus has no time for these petty arguments. Among his followers there must be a new preoccupation—not *who* is the greatest but *how* can one be of service.

Connecting the Gospel

to the second reading: Today is the rare Sunday where the second reading perfectly reflects the themes of the gospel. St. James writes, "Where jealousy and selfish ambition exist, / there is disorder and every foul practice." Were the disciples to continue to focus on their own merits and how they stack up against others', they would have no energy left to follow Christ.

to experience: When our lives become centered on personal gain and prestige, our interest turns inward. Others become competitors to be bested rather than brothers and sisters in Christ to be served and cared for. Cardinal Merry del Val wrote a beautiful prayer called the Litany of Humility. The last line resonates with Jesus's message to the disciples and St. James's letter to the early church: "That others become holier than I, provided that I may become as holy as I should, Jesus, grant me the grace to desire it." May this be our prayer too.

Connecting the Responsorial Psalm

to the readings: We find the humility that Jesus expects from his followers expressed in today's responsorial psalm. Rather than boasting of one's accomplishments and self-sufficiency, the psalmist points to the One who holds all human life in his hands, singing, "The Lord upholds my life." In today's gospel Jesus calls a child forward, telling the disciples, "Whoever receives one child such as this in my name, receives me." Jesus lavishes attention on the child not because of his or her innocence or spiritual capacity, but because of the child's utter dependence on others. In our own day and age, children continue to be the most vulnerable of society, relying on others for food, shelter, affection, and education. As Christians, we are called to serve the vulnerable and to be willing to be vulnerable ourselves.

to psalmist preparation: Instead of focusing on our own supposed "greatness," we must shift our gaze to the One who is our "helper" and sustainer, the One who is worthy of all praise. How do you embrace humility as part of your spiritual path?

PROMPTS FOR FAITH-SHARING

Today's psalm proclaims, "God is my helper; / the Lord sustains my life." How have you sensed the Lord's presence in times of need?

St. James questions the community he writes to: "Where do the wars / and where do the conflicts among you come from?" What are the origins of tensions within your own community and how are you called to bring peace?

In the gospel the disciples argue about who is the "greatest." At times a comparative attitude (rather than a contributive one) can hamper our efforts to build the kingdom of God. When has this been true in your life?

Jesus places a child in the midst of the disciples and tells them, "Whoever receives one child such as this in my name, receives me." How does your parish community minister to children?

Model Penitential Act

Presider: In today's gospel the disciples argue over who is "the greatest." For the times our own pride and arrogance have blinded us to the gifts and talents of others, let us ask for pardon and mercy . . . *[pause]*

Lord Jesus, you are our peace and our salvation: Lord, have mercy.

Christ Jesus, you sustain the poor and lift up the lowly: Christ, have mercy.

Lord Jesus, you call us to humbly serve others: Lord, have mercy.

Homily Points

• In today's gospel Jesus tells the disciples, "Whoever receives one child such as this in my name, receives me." Jesus calls them away from their petty and destructive argument of who among them is "the greatest" and instead asks them to look outside of themselves and their fragile egos.

• In these middle chapters of Mark's gospel, Jesus predicts his passion three times. Each time the disciples refuse to accept his words. Peter rebukes Jesus (8:32), the Twelve commence jockeying for position in a hierarchy they have erected in their own minds (9:34), and James and John demand to be given places to sit at Jesus's right and left hand when he enters into his glory (10:37). Each time Jesus redirects the disciples' attention from glory and power to servanthood, as he tells James and John, "[W]hoever wishes to be great among you will be your servant" (10:43; NABRE).

• If the Twelve needed to hear this message again and again, how often must we have it repeated in our lives? Jesus calls us to a radical new way of life. We are to renounce every form of control over others, to refuse privilege, and to leave behind competition, for there is no place for any of these in the kingdom of God. This is difficult. We seem to be hardwired to seek success and to desire the good opinion of others. But Jesus gives us a simple practice to help us on our path of ongoing conversion. When we empty ourselves of pride and jealous grasping, space opens up for us to receive the gift of Christ found in every person, especially the poor, the weak, and the vulnerable.

Model Universal Prayer (Prayer of the Faithful)

Presider: With open hearts and grateful spirits, let us place our prayers before the Lord.

Response: Lord, hear our prayer.

For bishops, priests, deacons, religious and lay ministers, with humility and joy may they serve and lead the people of God . . .

For leaders of nations, may they set aside all selfish ambition and political rivalries in order to uphold the common good . . .

For children throughout the world, especially those who have been abandoned, abused, and neglected, may they dwell in safety and security knowing the love of their Creator . . .

For all gathered here, may we be given the grace to look upon all we meet with compassion and so be instruments of peace in our families and communities . . .

Presider: God of wisdom, your constant presence brings us comfort and inspires us to live lives of holiness. Hear our prayers that we might be cleansed of every sin that separates us from you and so be bearers of your light and life to the world. We ask this through Christ our Lord. **Amen.**

COLLECT

Let us pray.

Pause for silent prayer

O God, who founded all the commands of
    your sacred Law
upon love of you and of our neighbor,
grant that, by keeping your precepts,
we may merit to attain eternal life.
Through our Lord Jesus Christ, your Son,
who lives and reigns with you in the unity
    of the Holy Spirit,
one God, for ever and ever. **Amen.**

FIRST READING

Wis 2:12, 17-20

The wicked say:
    Let us beset the just one, because he is
        obnoxious to us;
        he sets himself against our doings,
    reproaches us for transgressions of the
        law
        and charges us with violations of our
            training.
    Let us see whether his words be true;
        let us find out what will happen to
            him.
    For if the just one be the son of God,
        God will defend him
        and deliver him from the hand of his
            foes.
    With revilement and torture let us put
        the just one to the test
        that we may have proof of his
            gentleness
        and try his patience.
    Let us condemn him to a shameful
        death;
        for according to his own words, God
            will take care of him.

RESPONSORIAL PSALM
Ps 54:3-4, 5, 6-8

℟. (6b) The Lord upholds my life.

O God, by your name save me,
 and by your might defend my cause.
O God, hear my prayer;
 hearken to the words of my mouth.

℟. The Lord upholds my life.

For the haughty have risen up against me,
 the ruthless seek my life;
 they set not God before their eyes.

℟. The Lord upholds my life.

Behold, God is my helper;
 the Lord sustains my life.
Freely will I offer you sacrifice;
 I will praise your name, O LORD, for its
  goodness.

℟. The Lord upholds my life.

SECOND READING
Jas 3:16–4:3

Beloved:
Where jealousy and selfish ambition exist,
 there is disorder and every foul practice.
But the wisdom from above is first of all
  pure,
 then peaceable, gentle, compliant,
 full of mercy and good fruits,
 without inconstancy or insincerity.
And the fruit of righteousness is sown in
  peace
 for those who cultivate peace.

Where do the wars
 and where do the conflicts among you
  come from?
Is it not from your passions
 that make war within your members?
You covet but do not possess.
You kill and envy but you cannot obtain;
 you fight and wage war.
You do not possess because you do not
  ask.
You ask but do not receive,
 because you ask wrongly, to spend it on
  your passions.

About Liturgy

A Visible Sign: Disorder, wars, conflict, envy, passions: all words from the epistle this Sunday, a Sunday where the epistle feels much more a part of a unified Liturgy of the Word than is usual, given how the Lectionary is structured. Where do these troubles come from, and why do they seem so persistent? Perhaps a quick "case study" might be useful here.

Have you ever noticed how at the Holy Thursday Mass of the Lord's Supper, the gospel reading is not what it seems like it ought to be? One would think we would hear one of the evangelists tell about the Passover meal, the last supper Christ shared with his apostles. Rather, in the epistle that night we hear Paul describe how the tradition of that meal was handed down to him. Then, in the gospel, we hear a narrative unique to John—Christ's humble washing of the apostles' feet.

John's gospel doesn't even include a narrative about the last supper meal the way the Synoptics do. Some see the significance of this—that the description of the meal is replaced with this story of the foot washing—as one which instructs the early Christian community to live lives of solidarity and service, both important tenets of contemporary Catholic social teaching. In fact, the whole evening, if one listens from a certain vantage point, is linked to issues of social justice: liberation, solidarity, service, and so on.

Many have often wondered why foot washing didn't "make the cut," so to speak, when the church finally focused in upon seven "Big S" sacraments. It seems like it would meet the usual requirements and definitions of one. For instance, St. Augustine's primal and simple definition, "a visible sign of an invisible grace," paired with the typical sacramental need for form and matter do seem to describe foot washing well.

Pause for a moment and imagine if, when preparing for First Communion, young people learned about and prepared for foot washing alongside the more usual catechetical and spiritual pursuits. How much more linked, then, would we as a church find our reception of Eucharist to the command we are given just a few minutes later: Go in peace, glorifying the Lord by your life. Eucharist, as much as it is thanksgiving, is also service, solidarity, and our freedom. May we recognize it as such the next time we gather around the table, and may it sow peace and righteousness among us all!

About Reconciliation

Eyelash to Eyelash: Normally this space has been reserved for brief discussions about liturgical postures, gestures, and furnishings, so it may initially seem that a paragraph or two on reconciliation is, by that metric, out of place. On a weekend where the Scripture urges us to pursue peace with one another, it is useful to examine a bit of the etymology of the word itself.

Taking "reconciliation" to its Latin roots syllable by syllable, "re" means again, and "con" means with, and "cilia" is the Latin word for eyelash. So then "re-con-cilia-tion" is a posture, "to again be eyelash to eyelash with [someone]." What a beautiful image of the invisible grace found in this sacrament!

About Music

Service and Peace: This would be a wonderful opportunity for your assemblies to sing "The Servant Song" by Richard Gillard, found in many hymnals. Consider, too, David Hass's "Prayer of Peace" (GIA) and "My Plans for You Are Peace" from *Psallite* (Liturgical Press).

SEPTEMBER 19, 2021
TWENTY-FIFTH SUNDAY IN ORDINARY TIME

SPIRITUALITY

GOSPEL ACCLAMATION
cf. John 17:17b, 17a

R⁊. Alleluia, alleluia.
Your word, O Lord, is truth;
consecrate us in the truth.
R⁊. Alleluia, alleluia.

Gospel

Mark 9:38-43, 45, 47-48; L137B

At that time, John said to Jesus,
  "Teacher, we saw someone
      driving out demons in your
      name,
  and we tried to prevent him
      because he does not follow
      us."
Jesus replied, "Do not prevent
      him.
There is no one who performs a
      mighty deed in my name
  who can at the same time speak
      ill of me.
For whoever is not against us is
      for us.
Anyone who gives you a cup of
      water to drink
  because you belong to Christ,
  amen, I say to you, will surely
      not lose his reward.

"Whoever causes one of these little ones
      who believe in me to sin,
  it would be better for him if a great
      millstone
  were put around his neck
  and he were thrown into the sea.
If your hand causes you to sin, cut it off.
It is better for you to enter into life maimed
      than with two hands to go into Gehenna,
      into the unquenchable fire.
And if your foot causes you to sin, cut it off.
It is better for you to enter into life crippled
      than with two feet to be thrown into
          Gehenna.
And if your eye causes you to sin, pluck it
      out.
Better for you to enter into the kingdom of
      God with one eye
  than with two eyes to be thrown into
          Gehenna,
  where 'their worm does not die, and the
      fire is not quenched.'"

Reflecting on the Gospel

"But they're not one of us!" is an exclusive catch-cry that can be raised in many contexts, from the bullying on the school playground to that in the much more serious social, political, and religious arenas. Just consider, say these cryers: migrants will take our jobs, asylum seekers will threaten our security, community housing in our street for people with disabilities will lower our property values, ecumenism and contact with other religions will dilute our faith! And those who hold these views consider that they have a monopoly on wisdom and insight!

In the gospel proclaimed today we hear exclusion spoken from the midst of the Twelve. John is their indignant spokesman, informing Jesus that a man who "does not follow us" is "driving out demons in your name." The real issue from John's point of view is not that this man is *not following Jesus*—after all, he is doing his healing acts in Jesus's name, which implies some faith in Jesus; the problem is that he is *not following the Twelve!* They tried to stop him, apparently unsuccessfully, since they make an implicit appeal to Jesus to do something about it. Jesus responds to John's indignation by telling him that they should see such a person not as a competitor but as a companion along the way, even if he is not physically traveling with the Twelve, because "whoever is not against us is for us." Work for the kingdom is not to be the jealously guarded preserve only of the disciples who are physically accompanying him.

Jesus expands on what being "with" him means. In a land where the availability of water can mean the difference between life and death, offering someone a cup of water symbolizes the simple but generous hospitality that should characterize a Christian disciple, for doing this to another is doing it to Christ. Those who are aiming to be "the biggest and the best," even religiously, can too easily overlook or disparage the service of the "little ones" of great faith: the behind-the-scenes workers in a parish; those who seem to have the gift of a spontaneously positive response to everyday relationships and crises; the people who welcome demands on their time without fuss and with unfailing generosity. "Little ones" may also refer to those who are young in faith, new members of the Christian community. As a parish, how hospitable have we continued to be toward those who were baptized at Easter, or have we forgotten them and the drama of the Great Night? How inclusive are our attitudes to people who are entering from surprising—and even from what some "established" Christians might consider unwelcome and scandalous—quarters or lifestyles?

Strong feelings evoke strong language, and the Markan Jesus uses vivid images to heighten the impact of his words about the sin and scandal of those who are a stumbling block to the faith of others. Rather than concentrate on criticizing those whom we consider "outsiders," disciples need to be self-critical. The harsh words about self-mutilation are to be taken figuratively, not literally. It would be better, says Jesus, to go through life physically handicapped than to give scandal by our sinfulness and so become spiritually maimed and unfit for the kingdom of God. The final image of "Gehenna" (or "hell") refers to what was a valley just outside the city of Jerusalem, and once the site of Canaanite human sacrifice. The Israelites had converted this into a garbage dump where the stench of the burning refuse became a constant reminder of corruption and a symbol of punishment. The alternative is the life of the new heavens and the new earth, the Isaian memory that probably lies behind this verse (see Isa 66:22-24). As we have prayed in the responsorial Psalm 19, it is only by trusting in God's guidance as do the simple, those who are wise enough to know their own frailty, that we can live wisely, truthfully, and reverently.

Focusing the Gospel

Key words and phrases: "If your hand causes you to sin, cut it off. / It is better for you to enter into life maimed / than with two hands to go into Gehenna."

To the point: Today's gospel contains harsh teachings. We don't read the words of this gospel literally, but rather look for the meaning Jesus wishes to convey. The hand, foot, and eye are all singled out as possible agents of sin. We are given these tools to help build the kingdom of God, yet at times we use them for purposes that go against God's plan, such as stealing, looking upon another with envy or contempt, or causing bodily harm to others. Jesus seems to be inviting us to consider what situations or possessions tempt us toward sin in our everyday lives. Are there ways that we might remove these events or items from our lives so as to live in greater freedom and holiness?

Connecting the Gospel

to the second reading: The second reading from St. James's letter warns against excess riches as another path that leads to sin. Instead of using the blessings of wealth to care for others and to bring about a more just society, St. James condemns those who have made money from the "withheld wages" of workers and "have lived on earth in luxury and pleasure" without thought for others. Just as a hand, foot, or eye that sins can lead to corruption of the person, the ill-gotten gains of the wealthy bring about corrosion and rot.

to experience: Both Jesus and St. James hold us to a high standard. As Christians, we are called to examine our lives regularly and when we find sinfulness taking root, to decisively weed out the tendencies that tempt us to stray from the path of holiness.

Connecting the Responsorial Psalm

to the readings: Today's psalm combines praise and repentance. Rather than a burden, the law of the Lord is hailed as a gift that brings refreshment, wisdom, and purity to those who seek to walk in its ways. And yet, even for one who takes delight in God's law, divine assistance is necessary. The psalmist requests the Lord to "[c]leanse me from my unknown faults" and to "restrain" him or her "from wanton sin."

to psalmist preparation: In this psalm we find that holiness is first of all about love of God. When we worship God with our whole hearts, minds, and spirits, our one desire is to remain in close relationship with him. Anything that might separate us from this intimacy with God is rightly seen as an evil to be rejected at once. How does living within the precepts of the Lord bring joy to your own heart?

PROMPTS FOR FAITH-SHARING

In the first reading Moses tells Joshua, "Would that all the people of the Lord were prophets!" Who are some of the modern-day prophets calling us to holiness at this time in history?

How do you exercise prophetic ministry in your life of discipleship?

In the second reading, St. James condemns the corrosive power of wealth built on the suffering of others. How does your parish community speak out for the rights of workers and the dignity of the poor?

In the gospel, Jesus instructs the disciples to sever ties with anything that causes them to sin. At this moment in your life, are you being called to give up a practice or possession that separates you from God?

Model Penitential Act

Presider: In all things Jesus calls us to live in holiness. For the times we have not lived up to this call, let us ask for healing and mercy . . . *[pause]*

Lord Jesus, you desire to show us the way of salvation: Lord, have mercy.

Christ Jesus, you defend the weak and champion the poor: Christ, have mercy.

Lord Jesus, in you we find peace and fullness of compassion: Lord, have mercy.

Homily Points

• In today's gospel, the disciples become concerned after witnessing a stranger "driving out demons" in Jesus's name. But Jesus stops them from interfering, telling them, "[W]hoever is not against us is for us." A similar occurrence happens in the first reading when two men, Eldad and Medad, who were not present when God bestowed the spirit of prophecy upon the seventy elders, receive the spirit anyway. At first, Joshua, Moses's aide, is incensed. But Moses challenges him: "Are you jealous for my sake? / Would that all the people of the Lord were prophets!"

• Within the disciples' and Joshua's response we find a common human tendency: trying to own or control something that does not belong to us. In these instances, it is God's generosity that the disciples and Joshua desire to police. Jesus's and Moses's responses, however, point to the uncontrollable nature of God's will. We are laborers in the vineyard of the Lord, not managers who question or judge the worthiness of our fellow workers.

• Once again, we are called to renounce the temptation to competition and the hunger to be better than others. Our prayer should be that of Moses—that all the people of the Lord might be prophets—not that our parish community, our family, or ourselves as individuals might be recognized as the "best" Christians. By rejoicing in and welcoming the talents of others, we embrace the humility of Christ who "did not regard equality with God / something to be grasped. / Rather he emptied himself, / taking the form of a slave" (Phil 2:6-7; NABRE). The kingdom of God arises in our midst when people develop their talents fully, not for their own glory, but for the good of all and as an act of praise to the Lord.

Model Universal Prayer (Prayer of the Faithful)

Presider: Having been nourished by the word of God, let us confidently place our intentions before the Lord, knowing that he hears the cries of those in need.

Response: Lord, hear our prayer.

For all the people of God, in word and action may we exercise our prophetic ministry to speak out against injustice . . .

For leaders of nations, may they protect the rights of workers and devote resources to fighting oppression in its many forms . . .

For vulnerable children and adults, may their dignity and safety be assured and their gifts to society celebrated . . .

For all members of this parish community, may we work together in harmony to create spaces where all are welcomed and valued . . .

Presider: God of peace and love, in creation we find your bounty and your glory revealed to us. Hear our prayers that we might follow your law with joy and in so doing build your kingdom of justice and mercy. We ask this through Christ our Lord. **Amen.**

COLLECT

Let us pray.

Pause for silent prayer

O God, who manifest your almighty power
above all by pardoning and showing
    mercy,
bestow, we pray, your grace abundantly
    upon us
and make those hastening to attain your
    promises
heirs to the treasures of heaven.
Through our Lord Jesus Christ, your Son,
who lives and reigns with you in the unity
    of the Holy Spirit,
one God, for ever and ever. **Amen.**

FIRST READING

Num 11:25-29

The Lord came down in the cloud and
    spoke to Moses.
Taking some of the spirit that was on
    Moses,
    the Lord bestowed it on the seventy
        elders;
    and as the spirit came to rest on them,
        they prophesied.

Now two men, one named Eldad and the
    other Medad,
    were not in the gathering but had been
        left in the camp.
They too had been on the list, but had not
    gone out to the tent;
    yet the spirit came to rest on them also,
    and they prophesied in the camp.
So, when a young man quickly told Moses,
    "Eldad and Medad are prophesying in
        the camp,"
    Joshua, son of Nun, who from his youth
        had been Moses' aide, said,
"Moses, my lord, stop them."
But Moses answered him,
    "Are you jealous for my sake?
Would that all the people of the Lord were
    prophets!
Would that the Lord might bestow his
    spirit on them all!"

RESPONSORIAL PSALM

Ps 19:8, 10, 12-13, 14

℟. (9a) The precepts of the Lord give joy
    to the heart.

The law of the Lord is perfect,
    refreshing the soul;
the decree of the Lord is trustworthy,
    giving wisdom to the simple.

℟. The precepts of the Lord give joy to
    the heart.

The fear of the LORD is pure,
  enduring forever;
the ordinances of the LORD are true,
  all of them just.

R̸. The precepts of the Lord give joy to
  the heart.

Though your servant is careful of them,
  very diligent in keeping them,
yet who can detect failings?
  Cleanse me from my unknown faults!

R̸. The precepts of the Lord give joy to
  the heart.

From wanton sin especially, restrain your
  servant;
  let it not rule over me.
Then shall I be blameless and innocent
  of serious sin.

R̸. The precepts of the Lord give joy to
  the heart.

SECOND READING
Jas 5:1-6

Come now, you rich, weep and wail over
  your impending miseries.
Your wealth has rotted away, your clothes
  have become moth-eaten,
  your gold and silver have corroded,
  and that corrosion will be a testimony
    against you;
  it will devour your flesh like a fire.
You have stored up treasure for the last
  days.
Behold, the wages you withheld from the
  workers
  who harvested your fields are crying
    aloud;
  and the cries of the harvesters
  have reached the ears of the Lord of
    hosts.
You have lived on earth in luxury and
  pleasure;
  you have fattened your hearts for the
    day of slaughter.
You have condemned;
  you have murdered the righteous one;
  he offers you no resistance.

About Liturgy

Preaching and Leading: Growing up, when the neighborhood kids played lawn darts, they were truly lawn "darts" and really quite dangerous. And my neighbor Wade, a year younger than me, was very, very bad at lawn darts. Thankfully, his mother supervised our matches. One time, Wade offered a particularly bad throw: it went not at all in the direction of the target hoop lying on the ground, but ninety degrees over to the right. He was on the verge of a tantrum about it when his mother tightly hugged him from behind and offered probably the only words of consolation she could come up with in a hurry: "Oh, but honey—look how deep it went into the ground!"

The attempt here, it seems, was to change what it meant to be successful in the game. No longer was getting the dart in the target the fundamental measure of achievement, but it was diminished and placed next to something really rather unimportant: how deeply the dart burrowed into the ground.

Today's Scripture passages point to ministers of the church preaching, evangelizing, and healing—as they should—and others wondering from whom these people, sometimes unknown to them, got such a mandate. In the Old Testament passage, Moses, realizing that the Holy Spirit was upon Eldad and Medad, answers, "Would that all the people of the LORD were prophets! Would that the LORD might bestow his spirit on them all!"

Liturgically, at Mass, only ordained ministers may preach a homily. The *Catechism* teaches, "The grace of the Holy Spirit proper to this sacrament [ordination] is configuration to Christ as Priest, Teacher, and Pastor, of whom the ordained is made a minister" (1585). The church points to this as indication that the charism for preaching is given at ordination and is part of the ontological change that occurs there.

It is true that those who are not ordained may preach the Word in many other ways; it is also true that those who are not ordained may offer leadership to the church in many other ways. By virtue of baptism, we are all priest, prophet, and king, and it is true that we need not be priests to have influence in the church.

For many of our faithful, the only time they experience the teaching of the church, hear the proclamation of the Word, and observe church leadership is in the eucharistic liturgy. When offering to the laity only options to preach and teach outside of Mass, and when arguing that these opportunities are sufficient if not equivalent to the preaching in the Mass, some people sound to me rather like Wade's mother: "Look how deep it went into the ground!"

While not arguing for any change to liturgical norms nor suggesting that anyone ignore existing norms, imagine what liturgy would be like if the voices of an infinitely broader experience and perspective were able to be heard. "Would that all the people of the LORD were prophets! Would that the LORD might bestow his spirit on them all!" How can we lift up the voices of the faithful all around us, especially those intentionally kept silent and marginalized? There are certainly prayer opportunities, like Liturgy of the Hours, for laity to preach. How might those gathered at the eucharistic table be presented a wider collection of voices more regularly?

About Music

We Are Chosen: Bernadette Farrell's "God Has Chosen Me" (OCP) puts on the assembly's lips words of their own calling by Christ to be preachers, teachers, and healers. Omer Westendorf's "Sent Forth by God's Blessing" (WLP) to the tune ASH GROVE is in many hymnals and joyfully sends the faithful into the world to live the gospel in word and deed.

SEPTEMBER 26, 2021
TWENTY-SIXTH SUNDAY
IN ORDINARY TIME

SPIRITUALITY

GOSPEL ACCLAMATION
1 John 4:12

R℣. Alleluia, alleluia.
If we love one another, God remains in us
and his love is brought to perfection in us.
R℣. Alleluia, alleluia.

Gospel

Mark 10:2-16; L140B

The Pharisees approached
    Jesus and asked,
    "Is it lawful for a
        husband to divorce
        his wife?"
They were testing him.
He said to them in reply,
    "What did Moses
        command you?"
They replied,
    "Moses permitted a husband
        to write a bill of divorce
    and dismiss her."
But Jesus told them,
    "Because of the hardness of your hearts
    he wrote you this commandment.
But from the beginning of creation, *God*
    made them male and female.
For this reason a man shall leave his father
    and mother
    and be joined to his wife,
    and the two shall become one flesh.
So they are no longer two but one flesh.
Therefore what God has joined together,
    no human being must separate."
In the house the disciples again questioned
    Jesus about this.
He said to them,
    "Whoever divorces his wife and marries
        another
    commits adultery against her;
    and if she divorces her husband and
        marries another,
    she commits adultery."

Continued in Appendix A, p. 300, or
Mark 10:2-12 *in Appendix A, p. 300.*

Reflecting on the Gospel

Some Pharisees come to Jesus to confront him over his interpretation of Scripture and, specifically, how he understood the matter of divorce. Jesus throws the question back to them by asking what the Mosaic Law commanded. The Pharisees reply that a man is permitted to give his wife a bill of divorce and send her away. Jesus shifts the discussion away from this law (Deut 24:1-4), the interpretations of which could range from the permissive to the stringent. He goes beyond the question "Is it lawful?" and beyond legalistic arguments to the plan of God for relationships between men and women. The focus then becomes marriage, not divorce.

The prophet Malachi had denounced divorce, appealing to the creation story that we have heard in the first reading (Mal 2:13-17). Jesus also takes a prophetic, countercultural stance, and refers to this same Torah text. This encounter with the Pharisees comes in the section of Mark's gospel where the focus is on the cost of discipleship, as proclaimed the last three Sundays, and fidelity in marriage is never a cheap grace. Jesus refers to Moses's concession about divorce as something that was allowed because of a sickness of the heart or cardiosclerosis, to give a literal translation of "hardness of . . . heart." The same words are used to describe their ancestors' wilderness rebellion in Psalm 95:8-9. In the divine plan for whole and healthy human relations in marriage, God did not intend divorce, says Jesus.

"In the house" with his disciples, Jesus expands his teaching, probably reflecting the Markan concern to strengthen the marriage commitment in the Christian communities in the Greco-Roman world where divorce was common, and women could also divorce their husbands. Jesus's message is not only uncompromising, it is also countercultural, passing a subtle judgment on the double standard that allows one course of action for men but denies the same for women. Not only does a woman who has been divorced by her husband and marries another man commit adultery; it also works the other way, says Jesus. That he should accuse of adultery a *man* who divorced his wife and marries another woman, offended patriarchal honor! But both the man and the woman have equal rights and responsibilities to God's plan for their unity in "one flesh."

Jesus's teaching on marriage and divorce flows directly into the description of his blessing of the young children, and once again we see the obtuseness of the disciples. Their selective memory has forgotten the words and action of Jesus when he placed and embraced a little child in their midst as a sign of their responsibility to and love of the insignificant and unimportant ones (Mark 9:36-37). They "rebuke" the people, presumably the children's parents, and most likely their mothers, just as Peter had "rebuked" Jesus, had tried to exorcise him of his ideas about suffering and death (Mark 8:32; NABRE). Once again Jesus turns the rebuke back on the disciples in an attempt to rid them of their spirit of preoccupation with power and status. The disciples' stern, dismissive words to the people bringing the children to Jesus contrast with Jesus's words of gentle encouragement to those who want him to touch their children, to have contact with Jesus's own holy person and have him call down on them the blessing of God. Jesus again embraces the children, hugging to himself those who are helpless and dependent.

We should not hear this gospel as a sentimental romanticizing or idealizing of children, but as an embrace of Jesus for all those who have no status, no claims to make, no power to wield, and so are receptive to the great gift that is offered—the kingdom of God. With what have we been touched: with the distorted hope of the disciples for power, or with willingness to be "little ones" who are open to and receptive of the reigning presence of God?

Focusing the Gospel

Key words and phrases: "Is it lawful for a husband to divorce his wife?"

To the point: The Pharisees approach Jesus with a question but the narrator of Mark's gospel comments that they are not truly curious about Jesus's answer, but instead are "testing him." Jesus's answer to their query about divorce goes back to the foundations of creation when God ordained the unity of husband and wife. Jesus ends with the retort, "What God has joined together, / no human being must separate." Jesus upholds the hierarchy of truth, placing God's law above human commandments that have been fashioned due to "hardness of heart." In our lives, we know we are called to perfection and yet, as human beings, we often fall short. Though we might not carry out the ideal of God's dreams for us, he never ceases to call us back to covenant relationship with him.

Connecting the Gospel

to the first reading: In today's first reading from the book of Genesis, we hear proclaimed the very segment of Scripture that Jesus quotes in the gospel reading. It is interesting to put this verse in context. In the second story of creation, God creates woman from the rib of man in order to provide a "suitable partner" for him. The man does not find the companionship he seeks with the animals and birds of creation, but only with the one who is "bone of my bones and flesh of my flesh." This reading offers a truth about the beautiful unity of marriage and a truth about humanity: men and women need each other. God has formed us for relationship with those who are like us and yet different from us.

to experience: God's dream for the world is one of ultimate communion, where both the vertical aspect of the covenant with God and the horizontal aspect of the covenant with other human beings are kept faithfully. How do you strive to build healthy relationships with those who are different from you?

Connecting the Responsorial Psalm

to the readings: Today's gospel reading focuses on both the importance of marriage and the importance of children. Whatever our vocation—whether to ordained or consecrated life, single life, or marriage—as human beings we crave community. In today's psalm, the blessings of the Lord are seen tangibly present in a family gathered around a household table, and prosperity is to live a long life and eventually see "your children's children."

to psalmist preparation: Whatever your vocation, who is the family that gathers around your table and how do you find God in communion with others?

PROMPTS FOR FAITH-SHARING

In the first reading we find the famous line from Genesis: "[A] man leaves his father and mother, / and clings to his wife, / and the two of them become one flesh." In your life, which couples have modeled marital unity and mutual service for you?

We also hear, "It is not good for the man to be alone." How important is community and companionship in your life of faith?

In the letter to the Hebrews, we encounter the theme of perfection being brought on by suffering. How have you experienced suffering as a means to greater holiness?

Jesus tells the disciples, "[W]hoever does not accept the kingdom of God like a child / will not enter it." What aspects of childhood do you think Jesus is referring to that adults are meant to emulate?

221

Model Penitential Act

Presider: Today's gospel acclamation reminds us that "[i]f we love one another, God remains in us and his love is brought to perfection in us." For the times we have failed to love as Jesus does, let us pause to ask for pardon and mercy . . . *[pause]*

Lord Jesus, you call us to childlike faith: Lord, have mercy.

Christ Jesus, in you we are purified and strengthened: Christ, have mercy.

Lord Jesus, you are our hope and our joy: Lord, have mercy.

Homily Points

• In today's gospel, Jesus chides the disciples who are intent on discouraging parents from bringing their children to him, stating, "Let the children come to me; / do not prevent them, for the kingdom of God belongs to such as these." This proclamation comes as no shock to us. Jesus is constantly lifting up the poor, vulnerable, and weak as important members of his community. But today Jesus does more. After affirming children's place in the kingdom of God, Jesus lifts them up as the spiritual model for adults.

• In particular Jesus points to a child's ability to "receive" the kingdom of God as a necessary attribute for anyone wishing to enter this kingdom. And so, for a moment, let us consider how a young child receives. Upon being given a gift, a child often responds with delight and eagerness. Once the gift is opened, the child's joy grows in wishing to use the gift right away.

• At times, as adults, we might receive gifts in this way. But oftentimes other feelings creep in beyond eagerness, delight, and joy. We might be concerned whether we "deserve" the gift we have been given, or perhaps we worry about what we will give in return to make the relationship "even" between us and the gift giver. This is not the way one receives a gift such as the kingdom of heaven. There is nothing we can do to deserve such a gift and nothing we could give in return that would "equal out" our relationship with God. This week, let us ponder how we might receive the gift of God's kingdom with childlike wonder, awe, and joyful thanksgiving that prompts us to eagerly live each day as kingdom people.

Model Universal Prayer (Prayer of the Faithful)

Presider: Assured of God's never-ending mercy and care for us, let us place before him our needs and petitions.

Response: Lord, hear our prayer.

For God's holy church, may it embrace the spirituality of childhood so as to lead all people to wonder and awe in the Lord's presence . . .

For legislators and other elected officials, may they enact and support policies that reinforce the dignity and holiness of family life . . .

For those in troubled marriages or who are kept apart due to travel, deployment, or illness, may the God of love bring grace and healing . . .

For all gathered here, may we walk in the ways of the Lord and give him glory with every word and action . . .

Presider: God of holiness, in following your law we are invited into fullness of life. Hear our prayers that we might grow in fidelity and charity each day so as to become the people you call us to be. We ask this through Christ our Lord. **Amen.**

COLLECT

Let us pray.

Pause for silent prayer

Almighty ever-living God,
who in the abundance of your kindness
surpass the merits and the desires of
    those who entreat you,
pour out your mercy upon us
to pardon what conscience dreads
and to give what prayer does not dare to
    ask.
Through our Lord Jesus Christ, your Son,
who lives and reigns with you in the unity
    of the Holy Spirit,
one God, for ever and ever. **Amen.**

FIRST READING
Gen 2:18-24

The Lord God said: "It is not good for the
    man to be alone.
I will make a suitable partner for him."
So the Lord God formed out of the ground
    various wild animals and various birds
        of the air,
    and he brought them to the man to see
        what he would call them;
    whatever the man called each of them
        would be its name.
The man gave names to all the cattle,
    all the birds of the air, and all wild
        animals;
    but none proved to be the suitable
        partner for the man.

So the Lord God cast a deep sleep on the
    man,
    and while he was asleep,
    he took out one of his ribs and closed
        up its place with flesh.
The Lord God then built up into a woman
    the rib
    that he had taken from the man.
When he brought her to the man, the man
    said:
"This one, at last, is bone of my bones
        and flesh of my flesh;
    this one shall be called 'woman,' for
        out of 'her man' this one has been
        taken."
That is why a man leaves his father and
    mother
    and clings to his wife,
    and the two of them become one flesh.

RESPONSORIAL PSALM
Ps 128:1-2, 3, 4-5, 6

R̸. (cf. 5) May the Lord bless us all the
    days of our lives.

Blessed are you who fear the LORD,
    who walk in his ways!
For you shall eat the fruit of your
    handiwork;
    blessed shall you be, and favored.

R̸. May the Lord bless us all the days of
    our lives.

Your wife shall be like a fruitful vine
    in the recesses of your home;
your children like olive plants
    around your table.

R̸. May the Lord bless us all the days of
    our lives.

Behold, thus is the man blessed
    who fears the LORD.
The LORD bless you from Zion:
    may you see the prosperity of
        Jerusalem
    all the days of your life.

R̸. May the Lord bless us all the days of
    our lives.

May you see your children's children.
    Peace be upon Israel!

R̸. May the Lord bless us all the days of
    our lives.

SECOND READING
Heb 2:9-11

Brothers and sisters:
He "for a little while" was made "lower
    than the angels,"
    that by the grace of God he might taste
        death for everyone.

For it was fitting that he,
    for whom and through whom all things
        exist,
    in bringing many children to glory,
    should make the leader to their
        salvation perfect through suffering.
He who consecrates and those who are
    being consecrated
    all have one origin.
Therefore, he is not ashamed to call them
    "brothers."

About Liturgy

More than the Black and Red: Fr. Godfrey Diekmann, OSB, wrote these words, originally in Latin, in his 1964 diary: "O God, who through the Order of Rubricists has impeded the way to heaven, we pray that you give to us who have been buried under this sea of red, another way to eternal life."

He wrote these words (a "Prayer Against Rubricists") while at Vatican II, considering the Tridentine rite and looking forward to the liturgical reforms that had just begun and were to come. In this Sunday's gospel, the Pharisees try to trap Jesus by asking his opinion on Judaic laws of divorce and marriage, much like it seems Fr. Diekmann felt trapped by the red rubrics of the Missal of the time, themselves liturgical laws to be followed and obeyed.

Today, too—whether we are liturgists, other ministers of the church, or the assembly in the pews—we can sometimes feel trapped by the letters of the liturgical laws. Sometimes it can seem as if these instructions were written long ago and for a place of worship very different from the ones we minister in and know today—and frequently that appraisal is based in reality!

"Say the black, do the red" is a frequent mantra among some liturgists: remain true to the Missal and only the words and rubrics within, and with that, good liturgy will simply come to be. While we ought to be most reluctant to change these words and rubrics, to create a rite that the faithful can truly enter into, participate in fully, and by which they can be sanctified, much more needs to be planned and created than is contained in any missal.

The second portion of today's gospel offers wisdom here. Many long for their children to be touched by Jesus, and he welcomes them, embraces them, saying that the kingdom of God belongs to such as these. Jesus here is, probably, not speaking about children who are pure or simplistic, but rather children who are powerless and rely on their parents for everything—shelter, food, love, and more. So, too, the kingdom of God belongs to those who rely on God for everything. If we place our reliance both on black and red words in a missal but perhaps more so on God who reaches out to embrace us, then our liturgies might reach out and embrace all the faithful with shelter, sustenance, and love.

About Touch

Connection and Trust: Human beings were created to be in community, in relationship with one another—that is one important facet of what it means to be created in the image and likeness of God, God who is Trinity, community, and relationship.

An especially important component of human relationship is that of touch. Poet and novelist Margaret Atwood tells us, "Touch comes before sight, before speech. It is the first language and the last, and it always tells the truth" (*The Blind Assassin*). Laura Guerrero, who cowrote *Close Encounters: Communication in Relationships*, states, "We feel more connected to someone if they touch us."

This is why touch is an integral part to many of our sacraments: the anointings in baptism, confirmation, holy orders, and anointing of the sick, for instance. In the sacrament of matrimony, the celebrant instructs the couple to join their right hands while pronouncing the vows. More than just a handshake, this human touch is a symbol of connection, trust, and the truth of what is being expressed: that the love being witnessed at a marriage is reflective of the self-sacrificial love that Christ has for the church.

About Music

Love: Music about love should form the core of a parish repertoire this weekend. Consider "God Is Love" by David Haas (GIA).

✚ SPIRITUALITY

GOSPEL ACCLAMATION
Matt 5:3

℟. Alleluia, alleluia.
Blessed are the poor in spirit,
for theirs is the kingdom of heaven.
℟. Alleluia, alleluia.

Gospel

Mark 10:17-30; L143B

**As Jesus was setting out on a journey, a
    man ran up,**
   **knelt down before him, and asked
       him,**
   **"Good teacher, what must I do to
       inherit eternal life?"**
**Jesus answered him, "Why do you
    call me good?**
No one is good but God alone.
You know the commandments:
    You shall not kill;
    *you shall not commit
        adultery;*
    you shall not steal;
    *you shall not bear false
        witness;*
    you shall not defraud;
    honor your father and your mother."
He replied and said to him,
   **"Teacher, all of these I have observed
       from my youth."**
**Jesus, looking at him, loved him and said
    to him,**
   "You are lacking in one thing.
**Go, sell what you have, and give to the
    poor**
   and you will have treasure in heaven;
   then come, follow me."
At that statement his face fell,
   **and he went away sad, for he had many
       possessions.**

**Jesus looked around and said to his
    disciples,**
   **"How hard it is for those who have
       wealth**
   to enter the kingdom of God!"
The disciples were amazed at his words.

Continued in Appendix A, p. 301, or
Mark 10:17-27 *in Appendix A, p. 301.*

Reflecting on the Gospel

On the way to Jerusalem, Jesus continues to make radical demands of those who want to be his disciples. Last Sunday it was about marriage; today it is about money. We meet a man who has a sense of his own mortality and a hope for eternal life. He comes eagerly and respectfully to Jesus. The eternal life that the man is seeking is the gift of God. Then Jesus places the man within his own faith tradition, quoting to him some of the Ten Commandments, with the Markan addition of "you shall not defraud." The man replies that he has kept all these commandments.

Jesus gazes at the man and loves him so much that he gives him the radical answer that his radical question deserved. Jesus asks him to discard everything, to extend his love of God to the poor by selling all he owns and giving the money from this transaction to them, leaving himself dependent on nothing but treasure in heaven, and then come and follow Jesus. To stand bare and dispossessed before the God who is good, with radical trust in God's gifts, is the way to the eternal life for which the man had approached Jesus. But then a shadow falls over the bright landscape of this encounter of eager love. The man is shocked by Jesus's reply, and instead of following he goes away "sad, for he had many possessions."

There is certainly much of which we can be possessive—ambitions, relationships, social status—but Mark does not want us to leave the question of wealth and material riches too quickly. It is surely significant, especially for disciples in affluent social situations, that this portion of the gospel continues with two more conversations: one with the disciples who are with Jesus and have witnessed his meeting with the rich man, and the other with Peter who wants to clarify the disciples' situation.

Just as Jesus had looked at the man, he now looks around at his disciples with the same look of penetrating love—and he looks at us, his church. He tells us that riches are a great obstacle to entering the kingdom of God, and calls us "[c]hildren," reminding us that we must have a sense of our dependence on God for all good gifts. To drive his point home, Jesus makes an exaggerated and metaphorical comparison. For a rich person to enter heaven is as difficult as a camel getting through the eye of a needle! The disciples do not have the wisdom of the first reading, and are still caught in the convention that sees riches as a sign of God's blessing; so, more astonished than ever, they ask one another: "Then who can be saved?" But only Jesus can answer them. It may be humanly impossible, he says, but nothing is impossible to God. It may take a miracle for a rich person to be saved—but trust God to work this, because before God we are all beggars of love and salvation.

Then Peter, typically, asks his question, What about us? Peter and the disciples have left what they had to follow Jesus, but such dispossession is not a matter of just one leaving, as Mark's gospel will show. The disciples are finding it hard to leave their preconceptions about the messiah, about suffering, about who should be first and last; and in Gethsemane the disciples will leave everything not to follow Jesus, but to run away from him (Mark 14:50-53).

Jesus assures Peter that those who do give up the "everything" of possessions and relationships for the sake of following him and the gospel with which he identifies himself, will receive a hundredfold: new relationships in the new family of Jesus's followers, new possessions that are the fruit of doing and hearing the word of God and, the most cherished possession of all, the eternal life they had witnessed the man was seeking. But with all these benefits will come persecution, for no disciple can escape the cross.

Focusing the Gospel

Key words and phrases: "[H]e went away sad, for he had many possessions."

To the point: In today's gospel we find another call story. Jesus invites the young man who asks him, "[W]hat must I do to inherit eternal life?" to "[g]o, sell what you have, and give to the poor / and you will have treasure in heaven; then come, follow me." Unlike Simon and Andrew, James and John, in the first chapter of Mark's gospel, the young man does not immediately leave everything to follow Jesus when he is called. Instead, he sadly walks away from the Lord of life. There is a longing within this young man to leave behind the material things that hold him hostage and to find a deeper purpose, but he is not yet ready to break the ties that bind him to his former life. Perhaps, later on in his life, this same sorrow will lead him back to Jesus, once he discovers the truth St. Augustine so succinctly expressed: "You have made us for yourself, O Lord, and our heart is restless until it rests in you."

Connecting the Gospel

to the second reading: Today's reading from the letter to the Hebrews seems to encapsulate the rich young man's experience with Jesus perfectly: "[T]he word of God is living and effective, / sharper than any two-edged sword, / penetrating between soul and spirit, joints and marrow, / and able to discern reflections and thoughts of the heart." In his conversation with the living Word, the young man's goodwill is found wanting. Although he desires to lead a life of holiness by keeping the commandments, he is unwilling to let go of everything to follow Jesus.

to experience: In our own lives of faith, the word of God calls us to constant conversion. Holding up the Scriptures as a mirror, we find where we are in need of repentance and transformation. Despite this, we need not despair, for though it is impossible for human beings to enter the kingdom of God on their own, "[a]ll things are possible for God."

Connecting the Responsorial Psalm

to the readings: Today's responsorial psalm calls upon the generosity of God to "[f]ill us with your love, O Lord, and we will sing for joy!" In Christ, not only are we called to become more than we previously were, but we are also given the help and strength necessary for transformation. Only with God's wisdom and compassion are we able to "number our days aright" and to know what is truly worthy of our time, attention, and labors. When we understand the preciousness of life in Christ, all else becomes unimportant and it is easy to leave behind that which saps our energies and leads us away from God's love.

to psalmist preparation: Where do you find your deepest joy? How does this guide you to a closer relationship with Jesus?

PROMPTS FOR FAITH-SHARING

In the first reading, prudence and wisdom are lifted up as more important than riches or power. In what areas of life are you in need of God's gifts of wisdom and right judgment?

The psalmist sings, "Fill us at daybreak with your kindness, / that we may shout for joy and gladness all our days." What brings you the deepest joy at this moment in your life?

The author of Hebrews writes, "[T]he word of God is living and effective." How do you engage with the word of God daily in your life of faith?

Today's gospel provides a good example of a man whose possessions "own him" rather than him owning his possessions. How might God be calling you to give up certain material things in order to gain greater freedom in the spiritual life?

CELEBRATION

Model Penitential Act

Presider: In today's gospel, Jesus invites a young man to leave all he has to "come and follow me." For the times we have clung to what we know instead of stepping into the freedom of discipleship, let us ask for pardon and mercy . . . *[pause]*

Lord Jesus, in you we find wisdom and fullness of life: Lord, have mercy.

Christ Jesus, you sustain and strengthen us to do your will: Christ, have mercy.

Lord Jesus, you look upon us with love and tenderness: Lord, have mercy.

Homily Points

• Jesus's interaction with the rich young man does not seem to burst with "good news." After seeking out Jesus and asking him how he might inherit eternal life, the young man ends up leaving in sadness. He is unable to give up his possessions in order to follow Jesus as a disciple. And yet, perhaps within this seemingly tragic sentence, "he went away sad," we catch an echo of salvation hidden in the young man's grief.

• We know this young man is a seeker. The sense of lack in his life is what brings him to Jesus in the first place. Though he has many possessions, youth and perhaps health, and family (all of the things the world counts as good), something is missing. He has kept the law, but he knows there is more, and he approaches Jesus searching for the "more" that he cannot even define. Although he leaves his interaction with Jesus feeling sad, this sadness may be the very thing that will eventually lead him back again in the ongoing process of conversion that we all engage in every day.

• In our own lives of discipleship, we know our relationship with Jesus cannot be reduced to checking off good deeds or avoiding bad ones. Instead, the life of faith often requires finding, losing, and finding again our heart's greatest desire—to join the one who calls us by name in building the kingdom of God. At times on this journey of faith, we might find ourselves walking away sad, unable yet to give a full and resounding "yes" to Jesus. When this happens, may these emotions be the key to true discernment of where, and in whom, our true happiness resides.

Model Universal Prayer (Prayer of the Faithful)

Presider: Our God knows our deepest desires and greatest needs. With trust and hope we place our petitions before him.

Response: Lord, hear our prayer.

For the church throughout the world, in action and word may it uphold the dignity of every human life and lead others to care for the poor and vulnerable . . .

For migrants and refugees fleeing from war, persecution, and natural disasters, may they travel in safety and find warm welcome in host countries . . .

For parents who struggle to provide the basic necessities for their children, may they find support and compassion within their communities . . .

For all gathered here, may we be given the wisdom to know what is right and the courage to act on our convictions . . .

Presider: God of blessing, you look upon all of your creation with love and tenderness. Hear our prayers that we might serve you by protecting the weak and caring for the vulnerable. We ask this through Christ our Lord. **Amen.**

COLLECT

Let us pray.

Pause for silent prayer

May your grace, O Lord, we pray,
at all times go before us and follow after
and make us always determined
to carry out good works.
Through our Lord Jesus Christ, your Son,
who lives and reigns with you in the unity
	of the Holy Spirit,
one God, for ever and ever. **Amen.**

FIRST READING
Wis 7:7-11

I prayed, and prudence was given me;
	I pleaded, and the spirit of wisdom
		came to me.
I preferred her to scepter and throne,
and deemed riches nothing in comparison
		with her,
	nor did I liken any priceless gem to her;
because all gold, in view of her, is a little
		sand,
	and before her, silver is to be accounted
		mire.
Beyond health and comeliness I loved her,
and I chose to have her rather than the
		light,
	because the splendor of her never yields
		to sleep.
Yet all good things together came to me in
	her company,
	and countless riches at her hands.

RESPONSORIAL PSALM

Ps 90:12-13, 14-15, 16-17

R̦. (14) Fill us with your love, O Lord, and we will sing for joy!

Teach us to number our days aright,
   that we may gain wisdom of heart.
Return, O LORD! How long?
   Have pity on your servants!

R̦. Fill us with your love, O Lord, and we will sing for joy!

Fill us at daybreak with your kindness,
   that we may shout for joy and gladness
      all our days.
Make us glad, for the days when you
      afflicted us,
   for the years when we saw evil.

R̦. Fill us with your love, O Lord, and we will sing for joy!

Let your work be seen by your servants
   and your glory by their children;
and may the gracious care of the Lord our
      God be ours;
   prosper the work of our hands for us!
   Prosper the work of our hands!

R̦. Fill us with your love, O Lord, and we will sing for joy!

SECOND READING

Heb 4:12-13

Brothers and sisters:
Indeed the word of God is living and
      effective,
   sharper than any two-edged sword,
   penetrating even between soul and
         spirit, joints and marrow,
   and able to discern reflections and
         thoughts of the heart.
No creature is concealed from him,
   but everything is naked and exposed to
         the eyes of him
   to whom we must render an account.

About Liturgy

Sacred Music—A Two-Edged Sword: Picture a young boy, about four years old—yes, me—sitting in a small-town Minnesota church on a Saturday night, with his sister and his parents. A few minutes before Mass began, I noticed that the pew holders contained a new book, brown and orange, the same size as the missalettes they were right next to. I don't recall the exact conversation, but I know I asked Dad what they were, what they were doing there, and he told me that the folks who helped us sing each week had decided we needed more music.

Some of you will immediately know I'm speaking of the original *Glory & Praise* hymnal, packed with liturgical songs by the St. Louis Jesuits and several other composers of the time. One of my earliest church memories, if not the first, is hoping at Mass that we would sing the "long" and "fancy" amen at the end of the eucharistic prayer, the one with the "alleluias" and "forever and evers" in it. Perhaps you know it.

Growing up in the era of the church completely post Vatican II, I have no personal familiarity, and therefore no nostalgia, about the preconciliar liturgy, and in particular its music. I know of the music; I find it, at various times, intensely beautiful, evocative, and perhaps even mystical. Other times I find it poorly performed; not engaging at all of my voice, mind, heart, or spirit; and in fact off-putting to a sacred experience of prayer.

Liturgical music today is meant, subjectively, to be music that is beautiful, to be able to carry the weight of the theological texts it bears, and to engage the assembly, both externally and internally. There is such liturgical music from almost every land and every age. No matter what time or place liturgical music comes from, that music has to be "done" well. Those in positions of musical leadership must be able, to the best of their abilities, to approach the task at hand. Music must be performed not like in a concert hall, but with the demands of the liturgy in mind. Some places, I know, who favor preconciliar musical styles, resort to paying not only a music director, but also nearly all of the other music ministers, typically singers. Some places, I know, who favor contemporary music, hire outside guitar players, bass players, and drummers. Should not, rather, the musical leadership, and even the choice of what music is appropriate for the liturgy of that worshiping community, come from within?

That's what the folks in the rural parish I grew up in were doing. Most small churches don't have monetary resources, only the talents of those already in the community. By ten years old, I was playing the Stations of the Cross during Lent, and the next year I was being mentored into playing Mass, a few months later playing on my own, with a small team of cantors there with me. And I was playing many of those same pieces from the *Glory & Praise* books, as well as many other pieces, both newer and older.

What is sacred music? What should it be? There are many church documents that point the way, and a whole heck of a lot of arguing about it these days, people setting up camp typically in the musical genre where they feel most at home. Like in today's Letter to the Hebrews, a two-edged sword often musically penetrates and divides the one Body of Christ. Sacred music to me is this: beautiful, profound, engaging, and led well. Surely we could all get on board there as a common starting point?

SPIRITUALITY

GOSPEL ACCLAMATION
Mark 10:45

R7. Alleluia, alleluia.
The Son of Man came to serve
and to give his life as a ransom for many.
R7. Alleluia, alleluia.

Gospel   Mark 10:35-45; L146B

James and John, the sons of Zebedee, came
    to Jesus and said to him,
    "Teacher, we want you to do for us
        whatever we ask of you."
He replied, "What do you wish me to do for
    you?"
They answered him, "Grant that in your
    glory
    we may sit one at your right and the other
        at your left."
Jesus said to them, "You do not know what
    you are asking.
Can you drink the cup that I drink
    or be baptized with the baptism with
        which I am baptized?"
They said to him, "We can."
Jesus said to them, "The cup that I drink,
    you will drink,
    and with the baptism with which I am
        baptized, you will be baptized;
    but to sit at my right or at my left is not
        mine to give
    but is for those for whom it has been
        prepared."
When the ten heard this, they became
    indignant at James and John.
Jesus summoned them and said to them,
    "You know that those who are recognized
        as rulers over the Gentiles
    lord it over them,
    and their great ones make their authority
        over them felt.
But it shall not be so among you.
Rather, whoever wishes to be great among
    you will be your servant;
    whoever wishes to be first among you will
        be the slave of all.
For the Son of Man did not come to be
    served
    but to serve and to give his life as a
        ransom for many."

or Mark 10:42-45 in Appendix A, p. 301.

Reflecting on the Gospel

No one in Mark's gospel approaches Jesus as arrogantly as James and John in today's reading. But perhaps our criticism of these two disciples who, with Peter, comprise the most intimate core of the Twelve, needs to be modified if we are honest with ourselves. How often do we, too, approach Jesus with self-centered demands about our own plans rather than with deep faith in *his* plans for us?

It is as though James and John have not heard one word of what Jesus has told them about the suffering and death that await him in Jerusalem. All that they are concerned about is what Jesus can make happen for them when he comes into his "glory." What they want, they tell him, are the two best places next to him, on his right and on his left. Perhaps it is Jesus's deep sorrow at the obtuseness of the brothers' request that tempers his response to them. He answers with the images of "cup" and "baptism." In the Old Testament, the cup was a rich and ambivalent symbol. It could refer not only to overflowing joy and communion with God (Ps 23:5) and God's salvation (Ps 116:13), but also to the draining of the painful cup of punishment (Ps 11:6; Isa 51:17; Jer 49:12).

In his passion Jesus will gulp down the sins of the world, drain the cup of suffering and wrath so that it may be refilled with the joy of salvation. Can the brothers drink this same cup? The baptism of which Jesus speaks is his total submersion in the flood of suffering and death. Can James and John go with him into these depths of his passion? Again, before we pass judgment on them, we need to ask ourselves if we accept the consequences of our sacramental baptism—a baptism into Christ's death so that we may rise with him in newness of life (cf. Rom 6:3-4). In the mention of the cup, do Christian communities hear and obey that echo of the Eucharist that also initiates us into participation into the self-giving of Jesus and a sharing in his thirst for justice? The paradox of Jesus's Good News must be constantly repeated: that there can be no glory without a share in his suffering.

The failure of his disciples to understand him, his mission, or his relationship to his Father, was an aspect of Jesus's suffering. Their desertion on the eve of his passion would add to the bitterness of the cup he would drink, would be another flood of pain sweeping over him. Power and triumphalism, the desire for first places in the kingdom, have nothing to do with Christian leadership, yet into the hands of these frail and failing human beings Jesus entrusts the Christian community that would, in the power of his love and forgiveness, struggle through to resurrection with him. This is both our challenge and our consolation.

The other ten disciples, who were so glum and dumb when confronted by Jesus's earlier prediction of his passion, regain their voices to argue and bicker among themselves, angry over James and John's approach to Jesus. We might suspect that this reaction is not so much because of the inappropriateness of the brothers' approach, but more because these two had beaten the other ten to it! Knowing that earthly ambition (transferred to heaven!) and competitiveness were what the disciples had in their sights, Jesus calls them together to try to teach them, yet again, what is to be the foundation of their identity: the service of others that reflects the self-sacrificing service of Jesus. Kingdom greatness is the gift for those who make no claim to power and status. The demand of James and John—"Teacher, we want you to do for us whatever we ask of you"—needs to be transformed for and by all disciples into this: Teacher, we want to do for you and for many whatever *you* ask of *us*.

Focusing the Gospel

Key words and phrases: "For the Son of Man did not come to be served / but to serve and to give his life as a ransom for many."

To the point: The last line of today's gospel succinctly defines the mystery and the import of the incarnation. In the person of Jesus, the infinite God took on flesh and came to earth to dwell among people, to heal their ills, and to give his life so that death would not be the ultimate end of human beings. Once again the disciples, specifically James and John in this case, are concerned about glory and prestige. Jesus tells them that true greatness does not lie in lording power over another, but instead in taking on the mantle of servanthood, just as he has done.

Connecting the Gospel

to the first reading: Today's first reading from the prophet Isaiah is another section of the song of the suffering servant. Though crushed "in infirmity," through acceptance of his affliction, the servant will "justify many, and their guilt he shall bear." In the plight of the suffering servant we see a foreshadowing of Christ's passion, death, and resurrection, which Jesus predicts for a third and final time just before James and John request to sit at the Lord's side when he enters into his glory. This prediction includes more detail than the prior two. Jesus tells the disciples, "[T]he Son of Man will be handed over to the chief priests and the scribes, and they will condemn him to death and hand him over to the Gentiles who will mock him, spit upon him, scourge him, and put him to death, but after three days he will rise" (10:33-34; NABRE).

to experience: Though our God does not will suffering for suffering's sake, within Jesus's passion and the song of the suffering servant we find that, as children of God, we are given the ability to accept unavoidable affliction and to offer it up to God as a means of redemptive love—leading to our own salvation and that of the world.

Connecting the Responsorial Psalm

to the readings: In the second reading, the author of the letter to the Hebrews assures us that we have nothing to fear since "we do not have a high priest / who is unable to sympathize with our weaknesses, / but one who has similarly been tested in every way, / yet without sin." In Jesus's ability to empathize with our human struggles, we find another reason to agree with the psalmist's proclamation: "Upright is the word of the Lord, / and all his works are trustworthy." In the midst of life's trials, we turn to the Lord "who is our help and our shield."

to psalmist preparation: In your own life, how have you experienced the Lord as "trustworthy" in times of hardship?

PROMPTS FOR FAITH-SHARING

The psalmist sings "of the kindness of the Lord the earth is full." How have you experienced God's kindness in creation recently?

Today's psalm also proclaims, "Our soul waits for the Lord, / who is our help and our shield." In what areas of life are you in need of the Lord's help and protection?

The author of the letter to the Hebrews urges us to "confidently approach the throne of grace." How do you pray with confidence?

Jesus tells the disciples, "[T]he Son of Man did not come to be served / but to serve." Who is a model of Christian servanthood in your life?

Model Penitential Act

Presider: The author of the letter to the Hebrews urges us to "confidently approach the throne of grace / to receive mercy and to find grace for timely help." Burdened by our sins, let us turn to the Lord for healing . . . *[pause]*

Lord Jesus, you are our help and our shield: Lord, have mercy.

Christ Jesus, you show us the way of humility and service: Christ, have mercy.

Lord Jesus, you gave your life as a ransom for many: Lord, have mercy.

Homily Points

• In Mark's gospel, as Jesus nears Jerusalem, there is a sense that the disciples are still hoping for a tangible victory that will usher in Jesus's earthly kingship. Jesus predicts his passion, death, and resurrection three times in this gospel. On the Twenty-Fourth and Twenty-Fifth Sundays of Ordinary Time, we read the first and second predictions. The third comes right before James and John's request in today's gospel reading. This prediction offers even more details of how Jesus's passion will play out, noting how the Son of Man will be mocked, spit upon, and scourged (10:34). The path to Jesus's glory lies in the shadow of the cross. And this is true not only for him, but also for those who choose to follow him.

• Despite having just heard Jesus's prediction of the ignominious death that awaits him, James and John still dare to ask to have privileged seats when Jesus enters into his glory. Again and again, Jesus teaches his disciples that true greatness lies not in power, prestige, and authority but in the humble service one can offer to another. This lesson is difficult to learn, however, and it seems that the disciples (like us) need constant reminders to let go of the desire for personal gain.

• When word of James and John's request causes consternation among the Twelve, Jesus warns his disciples that they have embarked on a new path—they are not like the Gentile rulers who lord it over their subjects, to "make their authority over them felt." Instead Jesus invites them to take their ambition for greatness and turn that energy into service. This is the way of the Son of Man who "did not come to be served / but to serve and to give his life as a ransom for many."

Model Universal Prayer (Prayer of the Faithful)

Presider: Trusting in God's never-ending mercy and compassion, let us place our needs before the Lord.

Response: Lord, hear our prayer.

For bishops, priests, deacons, religious and lay ministers, with humility may they seek to emulate the servanthood of Christ as they minister to others . . .

For leaders of nations, may they work to abolish the death penalty, ensure the rights of prisoners, and support the rehabilitation of criminals . . .

For victims of modern-day slavery and human trafficking, may their freedom be restored and their emotional, physical, and psychological wounds healed . . .

For all gathered here, may we be renewed in our commitment to follow Christ along the path of salvation . . .

Presider: God of justice and mercy, you sent your son to embody your love and to give his life as a ransom for many. Hear our prayers that each day we might notice your kindness revealed in creation, and seek to praise and glorify you with every breath. We ask this through Christ our Lord. **Amen.**

COLLECT

Let us pray.

Pause for silent prayer

Almighty ever-living God,
grant that we may always conform our
     will to yours
and serve your majesty in sincerity of
     heart.
Through our Lord Jesus Christ, your Son,
who lives and reigns with you in the unity
     of the Holy Spirit,
one God, for ever and ever. **Amen.**

FIRST READING
Isa 53:10-11

The LORD was pleased
     to crush him in infirmity.

If he gives his life as an offering for sin,
     he shall see his descendants in a long
          life,
     and the will of the LORD shall be
          accomplished through him.

Because of his affliction
     he shall see the light in fullness of days;
through his suffering, my servant shall
     justify many,
     and their guilt he shall bear.

RESPONSORIAL PSALM
Ps 33:4-5, 18-19, 20, 22

℟. (22) Lord, let your mercy be on us, as
    we place our trust in you.

Upright is the word of the Lord,
    and all his works are trustworthy.
He loves justice and right;
    of the kindness of the Lord the earth
      is full.

℟. Lord, let your mercy be on us, as we
    place our trust in you.

See, the eyes of the Lord are upon those
    who fear him,
    upon those who hope for his kindness,
to deliver them from death
    and preserve them in spite of famine.

℟. Lord, let your mercy be on us, as we
    place our trust in you.

Our soul waits for the Lord,
    who is our help and our shield.
May your kindness, O Lord, be upon us
    who have put our hope in you.

℟. Lord, let your mercy be on us, as we
    place our trust in you.

SECOND READING
Heb 4:14-16

Brothers and sisters:
Since we have a great high priest who has
    passed through the heavens,
    Jesus, the Son of God,
    let us hold fast to our confession.
For we do not have a high priest
    who is unable to sympathize with our
      weaknesses,
    but one who has similarly been tested in
      every way,
    yet without sin.
So let us confidently approach the throne
    of grace
    to receive mercy and to find grace for
      timely help.

About Liturgy

Making Mistakes: We all make mistakes from time to time, and the liturgy is no exception. Sometimes our mistakes arise from misunderstandings or a lack of preparation, sometimes they are brought about by factors outside our (or anyone's) control, and sometimes there seems to be no rhyme or reason to them! Particularly regarding these last sorts of mistakes, they can be a powerful reminder that liturgy is both a divine action and simultaneously the "work of the people"—a very human liturgy, simply, isn't human if it is without mistakes.

My mother died on March 17, which most of us know as St. Patrick's Day. In 2008, March 17 also happened to be Monday of Holy Week, which meant I celebrated the Triduum that year back home at St. Dionysius Church in Tyler, Minnesota. Tyler is in the New Ulm diocese, which is a rural, mission diocese. The church's pastor at the time, Fr. Sam, was from Guatemala originally, and to this day he continues to serve in various parishes of the diocese, well-liked wherever he is assigned. At the time of my mother's funeral, he had been speaking English for only three years. Given that fact, his command of the language, a difficult one for many who have reason to learn it as a second language, was extraordinary—but not perfect.

The first glimpse of his occasional lapses with his newly learned language occurred on Good Friday, as he was voicing the words of Jesus in the proclamation of the passion. Simon Peter, early in John's telling of the passion, had just cut off Malchus's ear, during Jesus's arrest. I'm not sure if Peter's *scabbard* had fallen off in all the ruckus, but Jesus, through Fr. Sam, calmly but sternly told Peter to "put your sword into the *cupboard.* Shall I not drink the cup that the Father gave me?" (John 18:11; NABRE, *nearly*).

Due to the rites of Holy Week, the vigil service for my mother wasn't until Easter Sunday night. Probably with very little time to prepare, this missionary pastor ably led us through the service. He arose to proclaim the gospel, familiar to us all, and in a calm-but-stern voice warned us: Be prepared. Jesus told his disciples, "*Guard* your *lions* and light your lamps" (Luke 12:35; NABRE *nearly*).

While Fr. Sam had good reason to misspeak, the apostles make verbal mistake upon mistake without any such justification in today's gospel: presumptions, arguments, boasting, dreams of grandeur and power. Jesus must teach them that "whoever wishes to be great among you will be your servant; whoever wishes to be first among you will be the slave of all." That is, Jesus teaches them humility. May our mistakes at liturgy be reminders of that same humility and a reminder that the liturgy is truly where the human meets the divine.

About Kneeling

Humility at Prayer: Our kneeling at prayer, be it at church, at our bedside, or by a young child, can communicate many different affects and values. Piety, penance, adoration, and supplication are but a few, and kneeling might mean any one or several of these, depending on context.

Notably, at Eucharist, the postures of those gathered at prayer have varied broadly over time and space, sometimes with the assembly and the presider sharing a common posture, and in more recent times a dissimilar posture. At least partly because of this, in some ways, kneeling has come also to represent theologies of humility and differentiation.

When kneeling in humility, we can recognize, rightly, that God is God and that we are not. Yet St. Augustine's thought that God does not need any outward sign of gesture or posture for our hearts to be open to God is reflected in the many diverse postures the assembly enacts during any given liturgy.

OCTOBER 17, 2021
TWENTY-NINTH SUNDAY
IN ORDINARY TIME

SPIRITUALITY

GOSPEL ACCLAMATION
cf. 2 Tim 1:10

℟. Alleluia, alleluia.
Our Savior Jesus Christ destroyed death
and brought life to light through the Gospel.
℟. Alleluia, alleluia.

Gospel

Mark 10:46-52; L149B

As Jesus was leaving Jericho
　　with his disciples and a
　　sizable crowd,
　　Bartimaeus, a blind man,
　　　　the son of Timaeus,
　　sat by the roadside
　　　　begging.
On hearing that it was Jesus
　　of Nazareth,
　　he began to cry out and
　　　　say,
　　"Jesus, son of David, have
　　　　pity on me."
And many rebuked him,
　　telling him to be silent.
But he kept calling out all the more,
　　"Son of David, have pity on me."
Jesus stopped and said, "Call him."
So they called the blind man, saying to
　　him,
　　"Take courage; get up, Jesus is
　　　　calling you."
He threw aside his cloak, sprang up,
　　and came to Jesus.
Jesus said to him in reply, "What do
　　you want me to do for you?"
The blind man replied to him, "Master,
　　I want to see."
Jesus told him, "Go your way; your
　　faith has saved you."
Immediately he received his sight
　　and followed him on the way.

Reflecting on the Gospel

Bartimaeus is sitting at the side of the road, not going anywhere, as Jesus and his disciples approach. They are going somewhere, on the way to Jerusalem. When he hears that Jesus of Nazareth is passing by, hope begins to germinate in the dust that is his own broken self as well as his sitting and begging place. Exiled into destitution by his blindness, probably fallen out of family favor ("Timaeus" means "respected one") because of the mistaken idea that physical disability was also indicative of a moral taint, Bartimaeus begs for more than alms. With the eyes of faith he shouts out to Jesus, using not only his everyday name but also a messianic title: "Jesus, son of David, have pity on me"! The crowd tosses Bartimaeus the rebuke and scorn that are so often earned by those who have the courage to profess their faith, especially if they are regarded as unimportant, marginalized people. The blind Bartimaeus cannot find his way to Jesus; only his longing again reaches out to him across the distance, begging Jesus to have mercy on him.

And even in the crowd Jesus is aware of the individual, of the tattered man who is eager for personal contact with him. For that, Jesus will take the time and interrupt his journey. Jesus's command to the crowd, "Call him," combined with the persistence of Bartimaeus, seems to transform them from rebuking to encouraging Bartimaeus, and their voices become a kind of resurrection chorus that urges him to have courage, rise up, and answer Jesus's call. Bartimaeus's response is not only an exultant physical leap, but also a leap of faith. He throws away his cloak, his last poor shred of possessions that, for a beggar, served as coat, sleeping bag, and scrappy collecting rug for the few coins tossed his way. Nothing now matters to Bartimaeus, not even his dusty "bit of turf" that, like every beggar, he would have guarded so jealously. Bartimaeus is about to be newly clothed with the identity of a follower of Jesus, an eager beggar of the abundant riches that can be expected as a disciple.

Jesus asks this beggar "outsider" the identical question that we heard him ask the two privileged "insider" disciples in last Sunday's gospel: "What do you want me to do for you?" The contrast of Bartimaeus's response with theirs is both poignant and prophetic. Blinded by self-aggrandizement to the demands of following a suffering and servant Messiah, the disciples had asked for the best places in the kingdom. Ambition and possessiveness will soon cause them to leave everything to run away from Jesus, but Bartimaeus, aware of his poverty and disability, asks for nothing but that he may see, addressing Jesus reverently as *Rabbouni*, "Master." This address is only used one other time in the New Testament—when Mary Magdalene recognizes her risen Lord (John 20:16). Jesus knows that the blind man already has the seeing eyes of faith, and he tells Bartimaeus that it is this faith that now restores his physical sight. "Go your way; your faith has saved you," says Jesus. No longer confined to groping his blind way around the place, Bartimaeus can "go" wherever he wants to, but his choice is to follow Jesus "on the way," the way that leads to Jerusalem, the city of passion, death, and resurrection.

Are we aware of our own blindness, of our inability to recognize Jesus who is passing through our everyday lives? From the depths of our spiritual poverty and disabilities, do we urgently ask for insightful faith so that we recognize who Jesus really is? Or are we reluctant to leave even the small, secure territory of our reputation or material comfort that we have staked out for ourselves and push forward to Jesus, ready to enter with him into whatever "Jerusalem" he will lead us into, with his promise of a share in his passion, death . . . and resurrection?

Focusing the Gospel

Key words and phrases: He kept calling out all the more.

To the point: Shortly before entering Jerusalem, Jesus passes through Jericho and heals a blind man who is begging on the side of the road. At first when Bartimaeus calls out "Jesus, son of David, have pity on me," he is rebuked by others in the crowd. Perhaps they think that Bartimaeus isn't worthy of Jesus's attention, or maybe they doubt Jesus can do anything for this man. But Bartimaeus is not dissuaded. He continues to cry out to Jesus and is heard by the Lord. In the face of others' doubt and derision, Bartimaeus believes that he is worthy of healing and that Jesus is capable of restoring his sight. And this is what Jesus does.

Connecting the Gospel

to the first reading: In the first reading Jeremiah prophesies with hope that the people who have been sent into exile will be eventually gathered together and returned home by the Lord. In this reading, God is named the deliverer who restores the remnant of Israel to the promised land. No person is left out from this deliverance, including the "blind and the lame, / the mothers and those with children." In the gospel Jesus, the deliverer, restores sight to the eyes of a blind man. In fact, this is what Jesus's name means, as given to him by the angel in the Gospel of Matthew, who tells Joseph, "[Y]ou are to name him Jesus, for he will save his people."

to experience: How have you experienced Jesus's healing power in your life? If Jesus stood in front of you today and asked, "What do you want me to do for you?" how would you respond?

Connecting the Responsorial Psalm

to the readings: Today's psalm echoes the gladness of Jeremiah's prophecy. The people who have been restored to their homeland sing, "The Lord has done great things for us; we are filled with joy." In today's readings we see God's saving power in the life of a nation and in the life of an individual in need of healing. Our God continues to interact with us this way. We are saved in community as the people of God, the Body of Christ, but we are also cared for as beloved sons and daughters. We continue to read the Sacred Scriptures to remember the history of God's redemptive relationship with people throughout the ages, but also because it calls us to recognize God's movement in our own lives. Today's psalm reminds us that though we might at times "sow in tears," we will eventually "reap rejoicing."

to psalmist preparation: In your life of faith, how do you celebrate and remember the great things God has done for you?

PROMPTS FOR FAITH-SHARING

Today's psalm tells us, "Those that sow in tears / shall reap rejoicing." How have you experienced this in your life?

The letter to the Hebrews says that a "high priest . . . is able to deal patiently with the ignorant and the erring." How do you treat others with compassion, especially those you disagree with?

The disciples tell Bartimaeus, "Take courage; get up, Jesus is calling you." How have you experienced the call of Jesus in your life?

Where are you in need of courage at this moment on your journey of faith?

Model Penitential Act

Presider: As we prepare to meet the Lord in word and sacrament, let us call to mind our sins and turn to our God for pardon and mercy . . . *[pause]*

Lord Jesus, you heal the blind and the lame: Lord, have mercy.

Christ Jesus, you are near to the brokenhearted: Christ, have mercy.

Lord Jesus, you are the high priest who pleads for us at the right hand of the Father: Lord, have mercy.

Homily Points

• Today's gospel issues a personal appeal to each of us: "Take courage; get up, Jesus is calling you." The blind beggar, Bartimaeus, calls out to Jesus from the side of the road as Jesus passes through Jericho. He continues to call, "Jesus . . . have pity on me," even after being rebuked by others in the crowd. And then when Jesus issues the command, "[C]all him," the message of the crowd becomes different: "Take courage; get up, Jesus is calling you."

• As the savior and the Lord, Jesus calls us to be more than we are at this moment. Though he loves us exactly as we are, he also dreams that we will embrace the "fullness of life." And this fullness of life requires conversion and change. It seems the crowd knows this. When Bartimaeus is called forth, he draws near to an encounter that will transform everything in his life. He will stop being someone who must rely on others to lead him and provide for his needs and become an individual who can make his own choices and chart his own course.

• When Bartimaeus stands in front of Jesus, the Lord asks him, "What do you want me to do for you?" And when Bartimaeus responds, "I want to see," Jesus immediately restores his sight. Jesus's parting words to Bartimaeus are, "Go your way." But instead, Bartimaeus follows Jesus on the road that leads to Jerusalem and Jesus's passion, death, and resurrection. Doubtless, in the days to come as he witnesses the man who had healed him be arrested, tortured, and put to death, Bartimaeus will need the courage that he relied on to stand up, throw off his beggar's cloak, and make his request of Jesus. It is the same courage we all need to answer Jesus's call and to follow him on the path that leads to life eternal.

Model Universal Prayer (Prayer of the Faithful)

Presider: In today's gospel Jesus asks Bartimaeus, "What do you want me to do for you?" Confident in his care for us, let us not hesitate to place our needs before the Lord.

Response: Lord, hear our prayer.

For God's holy church, may all members listen for the voice of the Lord calling them to fullness of life . . .

For firefighters, police officers, and other first responders, may they carry out their work in safety and be sustained in their life of service to others . . .

For those who grieve the loss of a loved one, may they know the compassionate love and comfort of God's embrace . . .

For all who gather here, may we be healed from every spiritual blindness, so as to focus our gaze on Christ . . .

Presider: God of creation, your glory is present in all you have made. Hear our prayers that we might serve you with fidelity and love our neighbors as ourselves. We ask this through Christ our Lord. **Amen.**

COLLECT

Let us pray.

Pause for silent prayer

Almighty ever-living God,
increase our faith, hope, and charity,
and make us love what you command,
so that we may merit what you promise.
Through our Lord Jesus Christ, your Son,
who lives and reigns with you in the unity
of the Holy Spirit,
one God, for ever and ever. **Amen.**

FIRST READING

Jer 31:7-9

Thus says the LORD:
Shout with joy for Jacob,
exult at the head of the nations;
proclaim your praise and say:
The LORD has delivered his people,
the remnant of Israel.
Behold, I will bring them back
from the land of the north;
I will gather them from the ends of the
world,
with the blind and the lame in their
midst,
the mothers and those with child;
they shall return as an immense throng.
They departed in tears,
but I will console them and guide them;
I will lead them to brooks of water,
on a level road, so that none shall
stumble.
For I am a father to Israel,
Ephraim is my firstborn.

RESPONSORIAL PSALM
Ps 126:1-2, 2-3, 4-5, 6

℟. (3) The Lord has done great things for
us; we are filled with joy.

When the Lord brought back the captives
of Zion,
we were like men dreaming.
Then our mouth was filled with laughter,
and our tongue with rejoicing.

℟. The Lord has done great things for us;
we are filled with joy.

Then they said among the nations,
"The Lord has done great things for
them."
The Lord has done great things for us;
we are glad indeed.

℟. The Lord has done great things for us;
we are filled with joy.

Restore our fortunes, O Lord,
like the torrents in the southern desert.
Those that sow in tears
shall reap rejoicing.

℟. The Lord has done great things for us;
we are filled with joy.

Although they go forth weeping,
carrying the seed to be sown,
they shall come back rejoicing,
carrying their sheaves.

℟. The Lord has done great things for us;
we are filled with joy.

SECOND READING
Heb 5:1-6

Brothers and sisters:
Every high priest is taken from among men
and made their representative before
God,
to offer gifts and sacrifices for sins.
He is able to deal patiently with the
ignorant and erring,
for he himself is beset by weakness
and so, for this reason, must make sin
offerings for himself
as well as for the people.
No one takes this honor upon himself
but only when called by God,
just as Aaron was.
In the same way,
it was not Christ who glorified himself
in becoming high priest,
but rather the one who said to him:
You are my son:
this day I have begotten you;
just as he says in another place:
You are a priest forever
according to the order of
Melchizedek.

About Liturgy

Know Who You Are: "Master, I want to see." So often we wish we could help our assemblies see themselves for who they actually are: the Body of Christ, the principal choir of the liturgy, the fully and consciously engaged and active people of God. We do have some opportunity to tell them these things, in the preaching or in careful music selection. What is even more powerful, though, is when we have the ability to *show* them that they are (or at least can be) all of those things.

Consider the way that hymns are announced in most parishes: "Please join us in singing hymn number . . ." This phrasing, without being explicit, informs the assembly that the choir will be taking care of the singing, thank you, but feel free to join in if you wish. If it seems like that might be perhaps far too picky of an interpretation on an inconsequential moment, briefly consider an alternative.

Contrast this more typical announcement with something like "Please join with one another in singing hymn number . . ." That way of phrasing the announcement— "with one another"—without offering any longer explanation, reminds the assembly of all the things they are, mentioned above. The choir is there to support, to assist, but not to replace the assembly's vital role in liturgy. Given the repetitive nature of these invitations, the reinforcement of this message will be persistent and effective.

Further, you can pair this formative message with an approach to music ministry that avoids over-amplification of the singers and instruments, and occasionally even eliminates that support. Those in the assembly will then be able to hear their own voice and know better the important role they play in the celebration of the liturgy. If at first such changes seem daunting and without success, consider for how long the prior practice had been in place—inertia is strong, and it might take several weeks or months (or longer!) for any noticeable results. Know that the goal is worth it, though, helping the assembly see themselves, with eyes of faith, as they truly are.

About Watching

The Mirror of the World: In this section of writing, on the First Sunday of Advent, we reflected on "Stillness" and its importance in the liturgy, as well as the increasing difficulty we have of simply being still. A critical skill to develop or maintain in pursuit of stillness is that of watching.

In stillness, if we allow time for observation and contemplation, we begin to recognize the activity and interconnectedness of the world—and the liturgy—around us. We are not ourselves responsible for every action, yet we are, even in observant stillness, a part of all that lives and moves and has being. The external prayer informs and illumines our internal prayer. As if looking into a mirror, the movements of others reflect our own inner stirrings, and the liturgy reflects all of life—the living liturgy becomes life itself.

About Music

Seeing Healing around Us: "Eye Has Not Seen" by Marty Haugen (GIA) has the beautiful line, "To those who see with eyes of faith, the Lord is ever near . . ." and would be a beautiful text for an assembly this weekend. Consider, too, "Your Hands, O Lord, in Days of Old" found in many hymnals, for a text more focused on the healing power of Christ. The *Psallite* (Liturgical Press) refrain "I Know I Shall See the Goodness of the Lord" effectively quotes Psalm 27 for a simple and beautiful sung prayer.

OCTOBER 24, 2021
THIRTIETH SUNDAY
IN ORDINARY TIME

SPIRITUALITY

GOSPEL ACCLAMATION
John 14:23

R7. Alleluia, alleluia.
Whoever loves me will keep my word,
says the Lord; and my Father will love
    him
and we will come to him.
R7. Alleluia, alleluia.

Gospel

Mark 12:28b-34; L152B

One of the scribes came to Jesus
    and asked him,
    "Which is the first of all the
        commandments?"
Jesus replied, "The first is this:
    Hear, O Israel!
    The Lord our God is Lord
        alone!
    You shall love the Lord your
        God with all your heart,
    with all your soul,
    with all your mind,
    and with all your strength.
The second is this:
    You shall love your neighbor as
        yourself.
There is no other commandment
    greater than these."
The scribe said to him, "Well said,
    teacher.
You are right in saying,
    'He is One and there is no other than
    he.'
And 'to love him with all your heart,
    with all your understanding,
    with all your strength,
    and to love your neighbor as
        yourself'
is worth more than all burnt offerings
    and sacrifices."
And when Jesus saw that he answered
    with understanding,
he said to him,
    "You are not far from the kingdom of
    God."
And no one dared to ask him any more
    questions.

Reflecting on the Gospel
The conclusion to the Pontifical Biblical Commission's 2002 document, The Jewish People and Their Sacred Scriptures in the Christian Bible, states: "Without the Old Testament, the New Testament would be an incomprehensible book, a plant deprived of its roots and destined to dry up and wither" (84). This Sunday's gospel bears witness to Jesus's deep insertion into the traditions of his Jewish people and the intrinsic relationship of the two Testaments.

The Austrian psychotherapist Viktor Frankl recalled what he said was perhaps the deepest experience he had in the Auschwitz concentration camp. On arrival, he was made to surrender the manuscript of his first book on psychotherapy. Stripped also of his own clothes, naked and shaved, he was handed the worn-out rags of an inmate who had already been sent to the gas chambers. Then he describes what happened next: "Instead of the many pages of my manuscript, I found in a pocket of the newly acquired coat one single page torn out of a Hebrew prayer book, containing the main Jewish prayer, *Shema Yisrael.* How should I have interpreted such a 'coincidence' other than as a challenge to live my thoughts instead of merely putting them onto paper?" (*Man's Search for Meaning*).

In the verses immediately before today's gospel we learn that Jesus is in the temple (cf. Mark 11:27), confronted by the heckling and casuistry of the leaders of the religious establishment. There is not much love around as they question his authority. One scribe, however, stands attentively on the margins, obedient to the primary command of Judaism to "Hear." In Jesus's words he hears truthfulness and integrity, and the ensuing encounter that the scribe initiates by coming up to Jesus is a model for searching faith. The scribe's question—"Which is the first of all the commandments?"—is not intended to provoke argument but is a sincere quest for truth, and dialogue, not debate, is the result. Jesus answers the scribe by quoting the verses of the *Shema* we have heard in the first reading, but then he adds to this Leviticus 19:18: "*You shall love your neighbor as yourself.*" The scribe had asked Jesus for one "first of all" commandment; Jesus responds with two commandments that bind together love of God, of neighbor, and of self. Following Jesus's words there is a moment of rare intimacy, of agreement between him and the scribe, between the old law and the new. Then the scribe comments that the love of God and neighbor, which Jesus has joined, should take precedence over any sacrificial cult or ritual empty of such love. In the scribe's words are an echo of the prophetic words that cry out for justice: "I desire steadfast love and not sacrifice, / the knowledge of God rather than burnt offerings" (Hos 6:6; NRSV; cf. Amos 5:23-24; Mic 6:6-8). Jesus affirms his insight as one that brings him close to the reigning presence of God.

This meeting of Jesus and the scribe becomes an enactment of the great commandment of love. They treat each other as neighbors, transcending party politics and religious differences, crossing the dividing line between "you" and "us." In the sea of hostility that Mark describes in this chapter of his gospel, the mutual affirmation of Jesus and the scribe is like an island of reconciliation. It surely has much to say to us, as individuals or communities, about the course we should set in daily relationships or in ecumenical and interfaith dialogue, for "law can lose its heart; ritual can lose its reason; a relationship can lose its love" (Fred B. Craddock and others, *Preaching Through the Christian Year, Year B*). With Mark, we should know only too well that Judaism has no monopoly on such distortions of faith.

Focusing the Gospel

Key words and phrases: "You are not far from the kingdom of God."

To the point: In today's gospel a scribe asks Jesus, "Which is the first of all the commandments?" In his response, Jesus tells him that love of God and love of neighbor comprise the essence of morality, explaining, "There is no other commandment greater than these." Although our Christian faith can at times lead to complex conversations about ethics and the discernment of proper action, Jesus gives us a litmus test that all of our decisions must pass in order to be considered godly: they must have love at their heart. When all of our words and deeds are motivated by love of God and love of neighbor, we will truly be living as members of the kingdom of God.

Connecting the Gospel

to the first reading: In the gospel reading, Jesus quotes Moses's decree to the people: "Hear, O Israel! The Lord is our God, the Lord alone!" In the ancient world, monotheism set the Jewish people apart from their neighboring countries. Instead of entertaining the idea that there might be many gods (some bad and some good) who control the cosmos and must be appeased by various acts of worship and sacrifice, the Jews proclaimed there was only one God, and this one God desired wholehearted love and devotion above other acts of worship. The love God desires is not for him alone, but for all the people he has created. By quoting both love of God and love of neighbor as the greatest commandments, Jesus affirms we cannot have one without the other. God cannot be loved without loving his creation, and in loving creation we adore and worship the Creator.

to experience: Moses urges the people, "Take to heart these words which I enjoin on you today." How do you live the command to love God and love neighbor with your whole heart?

Connecting the Responsorial Psalm

to the readings: Moses tells the people, "[Y]ou shall love the LORD, your God, . . . with all your soul, and with all your strength." Today's responsorial psalm points to the Lord as the source of this strength. God is hailed as rock, fortress, and deliverer. Our strength comes from the firm foundation of the covenant relationship with our Creator. All good gifts we receive from the Lord, including the ability to love and serve him with fidelity. When our faith wavers or our love weakens, we can always turn to the One who is our shield, salvation, and stronghold for help and renewal.

to psalmist preparation: Where are you in need of God's strength to help you live with fidelity the commandments to love God and love neighbor?

PROMPTS FOR FAITH-SHARING

In the first reading, Moses urges the people to "[t]ake to heart these words which I enjoin on you today." Which verses from the Bible do you hold close to your heart?

The psalmist sings, "I love you Lord, my strength." When in your life have you most relied on the strength of the Lord?

In the gospel, Jesus quotes the first commandment as loving "the Lord your God with all your heart, / with all your soul, / with all your mind, / and with all your strength." Who in your life exemplifies this all-encompassing fidelity to God?

Jesus continues, "The second is this: / You shall love your neighbor as yourself." When do you find this most difficult?

Model Penitential Act

Presider: Today's gospel contain the great commandments to love God and love neighbor. For the times we have failed in loving God and others, let us pause to ask for pardon and mercy . . . *[pause]*

Lord Jesus, you are our strength and our hope: Lord, have mercy.

Christ Jesus, you intercede for us at the right hand of God: Christ, have mercy.

Lord Jesus, you show us the way to the kingdom of God: Lord, have mercy.

Homily Points

• German painter Franz Marc said, "The spiritual life is the discerning of what is essential from what is not." Today's readings point to what is most essential to living out our discipleship in Christ: love. During the last days before his death and resurrection, Jesus spends his time preaching and teaching in the temple in Jerusalem. In today's gospel a scribe asks Jesus, "Which is the first of all the commandments?"

• Jesus responds with the Shema, the ancient Jewish proclamation of faith in the one God, and devotion to loving God with "all your heart, / with all your soul, / with all your mind, / and with all your strength." While this is the first commandment, Jesus follows it immediately with a second: "You shall love your neighbor as yourself." Within these two phrases, we find the beating heart of what it means to live life in Christ. In only a few days, Jesus will be arrested, tortured, and then put to death. Despite the miracles he has performed throughout his public ministry, Jesus does not use heavenly power to protect himself from pain or to harm his tormentors. Instead, Jesus's life ends as it was lived—in a complete gift of love to the Father.

• In the journey of faith, we are constantly called to grow in our love of God and love of others. Rather than a sentimental or fleeting fancy, the love we are called to demands everything from us: all of our time, energy, and strength of will. As we continue on the path of discipleship, let us be attentive to the quality of our love for God and others and always devoted to living more deeply into the self-giving love Jesus modeled on the cross.

Model Universal Prayer (Prayer of the Faithful)

Presider: With trust in God, our rock and our salvation, let us place our needs and the needs of others before the Lord.

Response: Lord, hear our prayer.

For preachers of the Good News, may their words and actions inspire others to love of God and love of neighbor . . .

For the nations of the world, may they live in harmony with each other and work together to find solutions for natural disasters and those caused by human activities . . .

For spiritual seekers and those who are questioning their faith and religion, may the wisdom of God guide them in their search and lead them to the light of Christ . . .

For all gathered here around the table of the Lord, may the word of God be written on our hearts so that we might live it with fidelity and bear it to others . . .

Presider: God of knowledge and truth, you sent your son, Jesus, to reveal to us the path of salvation. Hear our prayers that together with all of creation we might embrace your will and work to build your kingdom. We ask this through Christ our Lord. **Amen.**

COLLECT

Let us pray.

Pause for silent prayer

Almighty and merciful God,
by whose gift your faithful offer you
right and praiseworthy service,
grant, we pray,
that we may hasten without stumbling
to receive the things you have promised.
Through our Lord Jesus Christ, your Son,
who lives and reigns with you in the unity
        of the Holy Spirit,
one God, for ever and ever. **Amen.**

FIRST READING

Deut 6:2-6

Moses spoke to the people, saying:
    "Fear the LORD, your God,
    and keep, throughout the days of your
        lives,
    all his statutes and commandments
        which I enjoin on you,
    and thus have long life.
Hear then, Israel, and be careful to observe
        them,
    that you may grow and prosper the
        more,
    in keeping with the promise of the
        LORD, the God of your fathers,
    to give you a land flowing with milk
        and honey.

"Hear, O Israel! The LORD is our God, the
        LORD alone!
Therefore, you shall love the LORD, your
        God,
    with all your heart,
    and with all your soul,
    and with all your strength.
Take to heart these words which I enjoin
        on you today."

RESPONSORIAL PSALM
Ps 18:2-3, 3-4, 47, 51

R/. (2) I love you, Lord, my strength.

I love you, O LORD, my strength,
   O LORD, my rock, my fortress, my
     deliverer.

R/. I love you, Lord, my strength.

My God, my rock of refuge,
   my shield, the horn of my salvation, my
     stronghold!
Praised be the LORD, I exclaim,
   and I am safe from my enemies.

R/. I love you, Lord, my strength.

The LORD lives! And blessed be my rock!
   Extolled be God my savior,
you who gave great victories to your king
   and showed kindness to your anointed.

R/. I love you, Lord, my strength.

SECOND READING
Heb 7:23-28

Brothers and sisters:
The levitical priests were many
   because they were prevented by death
     from remaining in office,
   but Jesus, because he remains forever,
   has a priesthood that does not pass
     away.
Therefore, he is always able to save those
   who approach God through him,
   since he lives forever to make
     intercession for them.

It was fitting that we should have such a
   high priest:
   holy, innocent, undefiled, separated
     from sinners,
   higher than the heavens.
He has no need, as did the high priests,
   to offer sacrifice day after day,
   first for his own sins and then for those
     of the people;
   he did that once for all when he offered
     himself.
For the law appoints men subject to
   weakness to be high priests,
   but the word of the oath, which was
     taken after the law,
   appoints a son,
   who has been made perfect forever.

About Liturgy

Truly Hearing the Word: Today's readings quote a prayer that for Judaism holds a spot not unlike what the Lord's Prayer holds for Christianity: the Sh'ma. "Hear, O Israel . . ." it begins, before describing the unity of God and that our God is truly the only God.

Perhaps you are a music director or sit on a team charged with helping pick music week to week for liturgy. Sometimes the particular task can become repetitive or even mundane. "What music did we do three years ago?" is a question that can easily arise, even though we—and the people we minister to—are different people now, with different experiences that will shape how we hear Scripture differently and will cause us to bring to prayer a different assortment of needs and desires.

Here, then, is a sample method of reflecting on Scripture with a specific goal of music selection. It is based very loosely on *lectio divina*, a traditional monastic practice of scriptural reading, meditation, and prayer that does not treat Scripture as texts to be studied, but as words alive and active. You can do this alone or with a group; this description imagines a small collection of people reflecting and praying together. Such reflection engages the imagination of the listener and allows for unexpected insights into faith. It can be done in one sitting or can be adapted to cover the course of a week.

As you begin your Scripture reflection, instruct those gathered to listen for one word or a short phrase that speaks or "clings" to them and touches their heart that day. Explain that it doesn't matter what word they select (even if it is the word "the") but that it is important to select one. Then ask someone to slowly and clearly proclaim the Scripture reading. After ten seconds of silence, invite participants to say their word silently to themselves three times.

After another ten seconds of silence, invite all to focus on their specific word as they listen to the Scripture passage proclaimed a second time. Then invite them to create an image that includes their word. This does not have to be, nor even should it be, connected directly to the Scripture passage. They can imagine a painting or photo, any other form of art, or a real or fictional scenario where the word or concept is on display. They could also create, draw, or paint an image, depending on time constraints. Let imaginations and talents be free!

After this, ask the reader to again proclaim the Scripture for a third time, and after ten seconds of silence, invite the listeners say their word to themselves three times. Now, invite the participants to connect their image (imaginary or real) to the Scripture passage they just heard. Offer substantial time here for reflection and prayer. Eventually, ask all to share any new insights they have discovered from this time of meditation. Some may offer their thoughts immediately, or there may be some silence. Resist the urge to fill the emptiness with leading questions or your own thoughts. Someone will speak soon enough, and prayerful conversations can begin.

Be prepared to offer any clarifying questions as you listen, or to solicit questions from the group, but let everyone express themselves fully and "piggyback" off on one another's ideas and reflections. You might be amazed at the deep level of faith and holiness this simple form of reflection can offer!

About Music

Where There Is Love: Any favorite setting of Ubi Caritas would be appropriate today; you probably already have one in your repertoire. If not, add one and return to it next Holy Thursday! Consider, too, "Love the Lord Your God" from *Psallite* (Liturgical Press).

OCTOBER 31, 2021
THIRTY-FIRST SUNDAY
IN ORDINARY TIME

GOSPEL ACCLAMATION
Matt 11:28

R︎. Alleluia, alleluia.
Come to me, all you who labor and are burdened,
and I will give you rest, says the Lord.
R︎. Alleluia, alleluia.

Gospel

Matt 5:1-12a; L667

When Jesus saw the
     crowds, he went up the
     mountain,
and after he had sat down,
     his disciples came to
     him.
He began to teach them,
     saying:

"Blessed are the poor in
     spirit,
     for theirs is the Kingdom
          of heaven.
Blessed are they who
     mourn,
     for they will be
          comforted.
Blessed are the meek,
     for they will inherit the
          land.
Blessed are they who hunger and
     thirst for righteousness,
     for they will be satisfied.
Blessed are the merciful,
     for they will be shown mercy.
Blessed are the clean of heart,
     for they will see God.
Blessed are the peacemakers,
     for they will be called children of
          God.
Blessed are they who are persecuted
     for the sake of righteousness,
     for theirs is the Kingdom of
          heaven.
Blessed are you when they insult you
     and persecute you
     and utter every kind of evil against
          you falsely because of me.
Rejoice and be glad,
     for your reward will be great in
          heaven."

See Appendix A, p. 302, for the other readings.

240

Reflecting on the Gospel

The call for Christians to live up to their baptismal call ought to be a constant reminder that not only are we called *to be* saints, but, as St. Paul says, we *are* saints, however imperfectly we are running the race to the heavenly goal. It is not just that we do not share in the eternal joy of heaven now, but that we know how often we fall short of the goal of holiness that Jesus called us to in this life, whether in purity of heart, mercy, righteousness, or peacefulness.

But we have exemplars, for we live in communion with the saints, who share in the fullness of God's life presently. As the *Catechism of the Catholic Church* says, "[S]ome of his disciples are pilgrims on earth. Others have died and are being purified, while still others are in glory, contemplating 'in full light, God himself triune and one, exactly as he is'" (954). The feast of All Saints is a necessary reminder for us whenever we doubt that God could make a saint of you or me. Sainthood is our purpose and destiny.

Those saints in heaven share the life for which we are being prepared, but they are not simply models for us; they intercede on our behalf. The Revelation of John promises us that the saints are "a great multitude" who worship God, calling us home. In 1 John, we are told that as saints, "we are God's children now; what we shall be has not yet been revealed. We do know that when it is revealed we shall be like him, for we shall see him as he is." This is the glorious future, in which some members of the family, children of God like us, already share and in which they mediate for us.

But if we are encouraged to recognize that we are saints even now, how do we make certain we will be saints also then, sharing eternal life with our brothers and sisters in the presence of God, seeing God as God is, like God, for eternity? As with so much of the Christian life, sainthood is a study in the mundane and the ordinary, done with great love of God and neighbor. Jesus, the one and only teacher, instructs us in the Beatitudes, offering us "the paradoxical promises that sustain hope in the midst of tribulations" (*Catechism* 1717). The paradox, as with so much of the kingdom, is that sainthood confounds and confuses the ways of the world, counseling behavior that others see as foolishness.

Jesus offers that his followers are "[b]lessed" (or "happy," which is another suitable translation of *makarios*) when they walk Christ's path of discipleship. In spite of persecution, being reviled, or even mourning, the follower of Jesus is "happy" when showing mercy, making peace, and thirsting for righteousness. "Rejoice and be glad, for your reward will be great in heaven." The "happy" are the saints who are destined for the divine reward, whose lives show that they yearn to share in communion with the saints in heaven.

But to be a saint, as Jesus encourages us, is to live the happy life now, in which virtue allows us to participate in the life of God with joy. Life in the kingdom of God is the goal, but the Beatitudes allow us to participate in that life now with God and all the saints.

Focusing the Gospel
Key words and phrases: "Rejoice and be glad, / for your reward will be great in heaven."

To the point: Throughout the year we celebrate the saints whose names we know. Today we celebrate all of the saints in heaven whose devotion and service gave glory to God and yet whose names have been lost to history. Though they are unknown to us by name, we are connected with all of these holy men and women in the Body of Christ as we gather together to celebrate the Eucharist. We rejoice that this great crowd of witnesses continues to bless us with prayers of love and support as we seek to live lives deserving of sainthood.

Model Rite for the Blessing and Sprinkling of Water
Presider: In our baptism we became members of the Body of Christ along with all the saints who have gone before us. May this water remind us of the day of redemption and cleanse us of every sin . . . *[pause]*
   [continue with The Roman Missal*, Appendix II]*

Model Universal Prayer (Prayer of the Faithful)
Presider: Together with the saints in heaven, let us confidently entrust our needs to the Lord of compassion.

Response: Lord, hear our prayer.

For all members of God's holy church, as we celebrate the feast of all saints may we be inspired by the lives of those who have gone before us . . .

For elected officials, may they work tirelessly to promote the dignity of all people, especially the unborn and the elderly . . .

For people throughout the world who face religious persecution, may their human rights be safeguarded . . .

For all gathered here, each day may we grow in holiness and faith as we strive to live in a manner fitting for the children of God . . .

Presider: God of joy, in the lives of the saints we see your love and mercy take on flesh. Hear our prayers that we might follow their example and live our lives in service to you and others. We ask this through Christ our Lord. **Amen.**

About Liturgy
Seeing God's Face: Who is the holiest person, living or alive, you have ever met? Describe this individual. What is it about him or her that causes you to see such holiness? Take a minute, too, and call to mind this person's face: his or her smile, eyes, wrinkles perhaps, hair . . . The Ten Commandments include a prohibition on making graven images, both so idol worship could be avoided and so an image of God might not be created that limits who God is. Words and images are limiting: as much as they help us explore holiness, they can also confine the completeness that God is. How striking, then, that today's psalm implores God, "[T]his is the people that longs to see your face." As Christians, we believe that God took on flesh: Jesus, truly God and truly man, God with a face.

On All Saints' Day, we remember the communion of saints—who were, are, and are yet to be—and our own call to sainthood. Are we able to see holiness, to see Christ's face, to see a saint's face, in every person we meet?

COLLECT
Let us pray.

Pause for silent prayer

Almighty ever-living God,
by whose gift we venerate in one celebration the merits of all the Saints,
bestow on us, we pray,
through the prayers of so many intercessors,
an abundance of the reconciliation with you for which we earnestly long.
Through our Lord Jesus Christ, your Son,
who lives and reigns with you in the unity of
   the Holy Spirit,
one God, for ever and ever. **Amen.**

FOR REFLECTION

• Our responsorial psalm today is "Lord, this is the people that longs to see your face." How do you experience this longing for God in your daily life?

• How do the Beatitudes exemplify for you what it is to be a Christian?

• Which saint has been a model for your spiritual path?

Homily Points
• On All Saints' Day, we meditate and ponder the Beatitudes. Like Moses, the great lawgiver, Jesus goes up a mountain, and there he preaches to the disciples a series of seemingly contradictory statements. How can the meek inherit the land, or how can one be considered blessed when facing insult and persecution? And yet, this is the way of the Lord, a very different wisdom than generally accepted by the world.

• When we turn our attention to the lives of the saints, we see this wisdom take on flesh. The saints are people who love God with their whole heart, soul, and strength, and in this love their lives become an expression of the Beatitudes and a model for all of us to follow.

GOSPEL ACCLAMATION
See John 6:40

This is the will of my Father, says the Lord,
that everyone who sees the Son and believes
in him
may have eternal life.

Gospel   John 6:37-40; L668

Jesus said to the crowds:
"Everything that the Father gives me
will come to me,
and I will not reject anyone who
comes to me,
because I came down from heaven
not to do my own will
but the will of the one who sent me.
And this is the will of the one who
sent me,
that I should not lose anything of
what he gave me,
but that I should raise it on the
last day.
For this is the will of my Father,
that everyone who sees the Son and
believes in him
may have eternal life,
and I shall raise him on the last day."

See Appendix A, p. 303, for the other readings.

*or any other readings from L668 or any readings
from the Masses for the Dead (L1011–1016)*

242

Reflecting on the Gospel

What is God's will? We've all asked ourselves that question many times throughout our lives. Searching for the answer can be overwhelming, discouraging, and confusing. But in today's gospel, Jesus answers this question for us with confidence and precision: "[T]his is the will of the one who sent me, that I should not lose anything of what he gave me." Is it really that simple? Yes, it is.

On All Souls' Day we remember and make present in our minds and hearts those who have gone before us. We honor their memories, and we entrust their souls to the embrace of God. This solemnity is therefore a celebration of trust—the kind of trust we read about in 1 Timothy 2:4—a firm belief that God "wills everyone to be saved" (NABRE).

Today's gospel reading is one of many examples from John's gospel of Jesus speaking as though he knows the very mind of God. Of course, the prologue to John's gospel tells us that "the Word was with God, / and the Word was God" (1:1; NABRE), and that the Word is Jesus (1:17). So we know that Jesus has the intimate knowledge—the "credentials"—to tell us who God is and what God thinks. Thus every word Jesus speaks about the Father is authentic revelation.

Today's brief excerpt from John is also a remarkable example of the shared "work" of the Father and the Son in this gospel. Jesus says elsewhere in the gospel, "My food is to do the will of the one who sent me and to finish his work" and "My Father is at work until now, so I am at work" (4:34; 5:17; NABRE). Today's reading clarifies the nature of this work as *salvation*. The Father and Son work together as one (see 10:30). They have one mission: eternal life for those who believe in the Son. Note that if the Father and Son are truly one, then to believe in the Son is to believe in the Father. To believe in Jesus is to believe in God.

The movement described in this passage is cosmic and beautiful. The Father sends the Son to do his will. The Son, in perfect obedience, tells "the crowds" that he has not come to do his "own will" but that of the Father. In carrying out the Father's will, the Son will demonstrate unconditional love and mercy: "I will not reject anyone who comes to me," he promises. Jesus then makes a bold claim: not only will he welcome all who come to him, but he will "raise [them] on the last day." Imagine what these words must have sounded like to the crowds. In those crowds were all kinds of people—believers, unbelievers, Jews, Gentiles, old, young, cynical, and naïve. Here was a human being claiming that he could "raise" other human beings! Preposterous! Of course, as believing Christians, we know that this claim is only as "preposterous" as Jesus's claim that he could raise himself. Later in the gospel, Jesus will tell another crowd that he has the power to lay down his own life and to "take it up again" (10:18; NABRE). The work of the Father and the Son begins with the Son's own resurrection. And in John's gospel, Jesus is fully in control and all-powerful, like the Father. He does lay down his life. And he does raise it up again.

This is all the assurance we need. We have given our loved ones into the eternal, loving, all-powerful, and in-control embrace of the Father and the Son. And we believe that the shared will and work of the Father and the Son is to hold forever—to save—those who have gone before us who believe: "I will not reject anyone who comes to me."

Focusing the Gospel

Key words and phrases: "I should not lose anything of what he gave me, but that I should raise it on the last day."

To the point: In his death and resurrection, Jesus has conquered death forever and opened up the way to eternal life. This is the will of God, the Father, that all might be saved and come to dwell in heavenly glory. Today we pray for the souls of the deceased, that they might be purified and found worthy of God, who desires nothing more than to welcome them into his kingdom of peace and joy in his presence.

Model Penitential Act

Presider: Knowing the grace and mercy of our God, let us humbly pause to call to mind our sins and to ask the Lord for pardon and healing . . . *[pause]*

Lord Jesus, you guard the souls of the just: Lord, have mercy.

Christ Jesus, you enlighten the darkness of grief and despair: Christ, have mercy.

Lord Jesus, you are our hope and our salvation: Lord, have mercy.

Model Universal Prayer (Prayer of the Faithful)

Presider: Trusting in the abounding and everlasting grace of God, our Father, let us confidently place our needs before the Lord.

Response: Lord, hear our prayer.

For God's holy church, may it be a sign of hope for those who are despairing and a refuge for all who mourn . . .

For leaders of nations, may they work together to bring an end to the production of chemical and nuclear weapons . . .

For those who are approaching the hour of death, with trust in God's mercy and confidence in his love, may they know the peace that surpasses understanding . . .

For all gathered here, in praying for the souls of the dead may we recommit ourselves to lives of holiness and service . . .

Presider: Ever-living God, you sent your son, Jesus, to reveal to us your will that he "not lose anything" given into his hand, but instead "should raise it on the last day." Hear our prayers that with trust in your promises, we might comfort those who grieve and joyfully await the day of your coming. We ask this through Christ our Lord. **Amen.**

About Liturgy

A Mass of Remembrance: A wonderful custom at many parishes is to have, on November 2 or at least early in the month, a liturgy to which are invited the families of church members who have been buried in the preceding year. More generally, anyone in the parish community who has lost a loved one in the last year is also invited.

At that liturgy, the names of the deceased can be remembered in prayer. A beautiful musical way to do so is with the "Lux Aeterna Litany" by Chris de Silva (OCP), perhaps at the preparation of the gifts. You may also be able to create a display somewhere, perhaps reminiscent of a Jacob's ladder, for people gathered to place photos of loved ones, near your book of the dead. Consider creating, artfully, a votive candle to light during the liturgy from the paschal candle, which families can take home with them. One other nice touch, if time and resources allow, is to have a communal meal before or after the liturgy, where those gathered can become more aware of the unity and healing Christ brings us all in times of grief and pain.

COLLECT (from the first Mass)
Let us pray.

Pause for silent prayer

Listen kindly to our prayers, O Lord,
and, as our faith in your Son,
raised from the dead, is deepened,
so may our hope of resurrection for your
    departed servants
also find new strength.
Through our Lord Jesus Christ, your Son,
who lives and reigns with you in the unity of
    the Holy Spirit,
one God, for ever and ever. **Amen.**

FOR REFLECTION

• Who do you especially pray for on this commemoration of all souls?

• How has belief in the resurrection of the dead affected the way you live your life?

• How do you incorporate the spiritual practice of praying for the dead into your life of faith?

Homily Points

• In one of the second readings, St. Paul writes to the Romans, "Hope does not disappoint." We gather together today filled with hope in the one who desires to reconcile all people to himself. Paul especially points to God's infinite grace, in that "while we were still sinners Christ died for us."

• We are loved extravagantly and with infinite mercy and compassion. Our God desires to forgive all who repent of the wrong they have done and to welcome them into his eternal glory. And so with hope, we pray for our beloved dead and entrust their souls to the love of God.

SPIRITUALITY

R̸. Alleluia, alleluia.
Blessed are the poor in spirit,
for theirs is the kingdom of heaven.
R̸. Alleluia, alleluia.

Gospel

Mark 12:38-44; L155B

In the course of his teaching
  Jesus said to the crowds,
  "Beware of the scribes,
    who like to go around
      in long robes
    and accept greetings in the
      marketplaces,
    seats of honor in
      synagogues,
    and places of honor at
      banquets.
They devour the houses of
    widows and, as a pretext,
    recite lengthy prayers.
They will receive a very severe
    condemnation."

He sat down opposite the treasury
    and observed how the crowd put
      money into the treasury.
Many rich people put in large sums.
A poor widow also came and put in two
    small coins worth a few cents.
Calling his disciples to himself, he said
    to them,
    "Amen, I say to you, this poor widow
      put in more
    than all the other contributors to the
      treasury.
For they have all contributed from their
    surplus wealth,
    but she, from her poverty, has
      contributed all she had,
    her whole livelihood."

or Mark 12:41-44 in Appendix A, p. 304.

Reflecting on the Gospel

The scribes about whom Jesus speaks in today's gospel are very different from the truth-seeking scribe of last week, and so a reminder to us not to be universally sweeping in our judgments of any group of people. The scribes about whom Jesus warns his disciples are probably the more significant temple lawyers preoccupied with their own status and with being recognized publicly as people of moral substance. They paraded outwardly what they believed to be their religious superiority, expecting substantial honors and salutations while, in reality, their inner lives were insubstantial and hypocritical. Jesus has hard words for their failure in social justice toward widows for whom the scribes often acted as legal agents, managing their affairs to their own scribal advantage when these women had no husband or adult male relative to care for them. Widows bereft of family support were easy victims of such financial abuse that tragically compounded the physical and social abuse they could suffer. Instead of receiving the compassion commanded by the Mosaic teaching and the prophets (e.g., Exod 22:22; Deut 27:19; Isa 1:17; Zech 7:10), widows often found themselves destitute victims of fraud at the hands of the unscrupulous whom they may have trusted, scribes included.

Jesus is described as sitting "opposite the treasury," and so opting to teach in the woman's court of the temple. In this area were thirteen trumpet-shaped receptacles to receive alms for the upkeep of the temple. In the temple, devoid of paper money, it was the large donations that reverberated loudly through the court to trumpet the generosity of the donor. But Jesus listens with the ear of his heart to the whisper of the two small coins dropped in by the poor widow. She gives two *lepta*, the least valuable coins in circulation at the time, and worth about one sixty-fourth of a *denarius* or "a few cents," the average daily wage of an unskilled laborer. And the widow gives *two* coins, not just one. The narrative seems to suggest that the widow is not bitter over her misfortune or her possible defrauding; for her, the upkeep of the temple, the holy place of the Presence, is her first priority.

Jesus's condemnation of the unscrupulous scribes is part of his public teaching, but then he calls his disciples to himself to impress on them the significance of the widow's action. We have already seen Jesus calling the attention of his disciples to children, defenseless "little ones" (Mark 9:36-37, 42; cf. 10:14-16; NABRE); have heard how Bartimaeus tossed away everything to go to Jesus. Now Jesus solemnly points to the widow as one who gives God "all she had, her whole livelihood."

We should not read into this gospel a romanticization of poverty nor a condemnation of large donations. It is the motivation behind gifts, large or small, that is important. To give out of our surplus may be useful for taxation purposes, or a generous donation may be great publicity for the corporate business image; contributing to costly buildings or supporting grandiose schemes may often have the aim of making a name for the donor, regardless of the consequences, especially for the poor. We may be able to think of times and places when the church is not exempt from such temptations. It is acting out of love, the motivation that is not economic, promotional, or ostentatious, that makes the difference in the eyes of God.

In both Testaments, the widow is an icon of what we call today the feminization of poverty. Tragically, what imposes impoverished widowhood on millions of contemporary women is not the religious establishment but genocide, war, HIV/AIDS. Poor widowed grandmothers are caring for their grandchildren who have been orphaned by these scourges, and the United Nations Commission on the Status of Women states that the majority of the more than one billion people who live on a dollar a day or less are women.

Focusing the Gospel

Key words and phrases: "Beware of the scribes, who like to go around in long robes / and accept greetings in the marketplaces, / seats of honor in synagogues, / and places of honor at banquets."

To the point: In the gospel Jesus issues a strong condemnation of religious leaders who delight in the privileges accorded to them because of their station. Their love of human accolades corrupts their actions—instead of serving the beloved of God (the poor and the weak), they "devour the houses of widows." In our own day and within our own church community, power continues to corrupt those who are seduced by its glamour and prestige. If our intent is to follow Christ, we must keep our hearts centered on humble service of God and others and be wary of the temptations that come with positions of honor.

Connecting the Gospel

to the first reading: Both the gospel and the first reading focus on the generosity of two destitute widows. In the first book of Kings, a widow makes the prophet Elijah a cake out of the last handful of flour and bit of oil she had reserved for herself and her son. In the gospel, Jesus lifts up the sacrificial giving of a widow who places "a few cents" in the temple treasury. Although these women have little, they give freely of what they do possess. This contrasts with the actions of the scribes who Jesus condemns. Their hunger for more power and wealth causes them to take from those who have less, instead of giving generously from their own abundance.

to experience: In your own life experience, has it been easier for you to share when you have an abundance or when resources are scarce?

Connecting the Responsorial Psalm

to the readings: Today's psalm lifts up the privileged place of the oppressed, captive, hungry, and blind, as well as of the stranger, the widow, and the fatherless in the eyes of God. These individuals, who are so often pushed to the margins of society where they can be ignored by those who do not know their struggles, are at the center of God's attention and care. In the first reading and the gospel, we also see how God values the contributions of those considered powerless. Elijah calls upon a widow to feed him when he enters Zarephath, and Jesus lauds the contribution of the poor widow, who gives "all she had, / her whole livelihood."

to psalmist preparation: How do you and your faith community support the poor and oppressed? And how do you welcome and celebrate the gifts they bring?

PROMPTS FOR FAITH-SHARING

In the first reading a widow offers hospitality to the prophet Elijah. What place does hospitality hold in your ministry?

As we near the end of the liturgical year, our thoughts turn to Jesus's second coming. How are you preparing yourself to greet the Lord at the end of your life?

When have you witnessed someone giving not from their surplus, but from their lack?

How do you strive to be charitable and generous to those in need?

Model Penitential Act

Presider: In today's gospel, Jesus lifts up the example of the widow who gives all she has. For the times we have failed in generosity of spirit, let us ask for pardon and mercy . . . [pause]

Lord Jesus, you are close to the meek and the brokenhearted: Lord, have mercy.

Christ Jesus, you nourish us with the bread from heaven: Christ, have mercy.

Lord Jesus, you hear the cries of the poor: Lord, have mercy.

Homily Points

• Once again, in today's gospel, Jesus invites the disciples to see not as human beings do, but as God does. Whereas humans often lavish attention on those who are able to donate large sums of money from their wealth and abundance, Jesus lifts up the model of the poor widow whose donation to the temple might only amount to "a few cents" but that symbolizes a giving of all she has, "her whole livelihood." Jesus tells the disciples, "[T]his poor widow has put in more / than all the other contributors to the treasury."

• Jesus's words give us insight into the mind of God, where the wealthy and poor are equal, and the generosity of one is not greater than that of another, even though the monetary value may differ. It also sharpens our eyes to recognize the many small and humble actions that happen around us each and every day. St. Teresa of Calcutta famously stated, "Not all of us can do great things. But we can do small things with great love." It seems that to God, the small things done with great love are really the most important actions.

• Each day we are given the opportunity to generously give of ourselves as the widow does in today's gospel: to sit with an aging parent or care for small children, to stop and talk with the panhandler on the side of the road, or to simply offer a kind word to someone who is having a difficult day. All of these seemingly insignificant expressions of love and service are what creates the kingdom of God in the here and now. And we can be certain that our Lord sees and appreciates all of them.

Model Universal Prayer (Prayer of the Faithful)

Presider: With faith in God's fidelity and constant care, let us bring our needs and the needs of others before the Lord.

Response: Lord, hear our prayer.

For all those who minister in the name of Jesus, may they be strengthened with wisdom and understanding and protected from every evil . . .

For all who are affected by famine throughout the world, may their needs be provided for and their hunger satisfied . . .

For those who experience homelessness, may they find shelter and know safety this day . . .

For all gathered here, may we eagerly await the return of the Lord and tirelessly work to build his kingdom of peace and joy here on earth . . .

Presider: God of goodness, you graciously hear the prayers of all those in need. Hear our prayers that we might be always attentive to the needs of others and quick to share from the abundance of blessings you have bestowed upon us. We ask this through Christ our Lord. **Amen.**

COLLECT

Let us pray.

Pause for silent prayer

Almighty and merciful God,
graciously keep from us all adversity,
so that, unhindered in mind and body
    alike,
we may pursue in freedom of heart
the things that are yours.
Through our Lord Jesus Christ, your Son,
who lives and reigns with you in the unity
    of the Holy Spirit,
one God, for ever and ever. **Amen.**

FIRST READING

1 Kgs 17:10-16

In those days, Elijah the prophet went to
    Zarephath.
As he arrived at the entrance of the city,
    a widow was gathering sticks there; he
        called out to her,
"Please bring me a small cupful of
        water to drink."
She left to get it, and he called out after
    her,
"Please bring along a bit of bread."
She answered, "As the Lord, your God,
    lives,
    I have nothing baked; there is only a
        handful of flour in my jar
and a little oil in my jug.
Just now I was collecting a couple of
    sticks,
    to go in and prepare something for
        myself and my son;
    when we have eaten it, we shall die."
Elijah said to her, "Do not be afraid.
Go and do as you propose.
But first make me a little cake and bring
    it to me.
Then you can prepare something for
    yourself and your son.
For the Lord, the God of Israel, says,
    'The jar of flour shall not go empty,
    nor the jug of oil run dry,
    until the day when the Lord sends rain
        upon the earth.'"
She left and did as Elijah had said.
She was able to eat for a year, and he and
    her son as well;
    the jar of flour did not go empty,
    nor the jug of oil run dry,
    as the Lord had foretold through Elijah.

RESPONSORIAL PSALM
Ps 146:7, 8-9, 9-10

℟. (1b) Praise the Lord, my soul!
or:
℟. Alleluia.

The LORD keeps faith forever,
    secures justice for the oppressed,
    gives food to the hungry.
The LORD sets captives free.

℟. Praise the Lord, my soul!
or:
℟. Alleluia.

The LORD gives sight to the blind;
    the LORD raises up those who were
        bowed down.
The LORD loves the just;
    the LORD protects strangers.

℟. Praise the Lord, my soul!
or:
℟. Alleluia.

The fatherless and the widow he sustains,
    but the way of the wicked he thwarts.
The LORD shall reign forever;
    your God, O Zion, through all
        generations. Alleluia.

℟. Praise the Lord, my soul!
or:
℟. Alleluia.

SECOND READING
Heb 9:24-28

Christ did not enter into a sanctuary made
        by hands,
    a copy of the true one, but heaven itself,
    that he might now appear before God
        on our behalf.
Not that he might offer himself repeatedly,
    as the high priest enters each year into
        the sanctuary
    with blood that is not his own;
    if that were so, he would have had to
        suffer repeatedly
    from the foundation of the world.
But now once for all he has appeared at
        the end of the ages
    to take away sin by his sacrifice.
Just as it is appointed that human beings
        die once,
    and after this the judgment, so also
        Christ,
    offered once to take away the sins of
        many,
    will appear a second time, not to take
        away sin
    but to bring salvation to those who
        eagerly await him.

About Liturgy

You Who Do Through: Jesus warns the crowds in today's gospel to beware of the scribes who, among other things, "as a pretext recite lengthy prayers." While they perhaps, because their profession gave them repeated access to all of Scripture, had reason (or at least an excuse) to be so long-winded, some of us, too, especially in moments of improvised prayer, tend to go on and on. Likely this is because such moments of prayer lack structure, often sprung on us at the last moment: "Fred, you work for the church; why don't you say the meal blessing for Grandma's surprise birthday luncheon?" Sometimes it's because we're nervous as well.

There is no wrong way to pray. Please repeat after me: *There is no wrong way to pray.* However, the liturgy offers us another pattern to follow, found in most of the presidential prayers (even if obscured by curious syntax), and it is an easy way to create spur-of-the-moment prayers: YOU—WHO—DO—THROUGH.

YOU: *Name God.* It can be as simple as "Lord" or "God" or something more elaborate like "Good and Gracious God" or "God of Wisdom and Understanding." Think about what you want to pray for and then think about how that can connect with God. For example, if you are going to pray, broadly, about "love," you might use, "Loving God."

WHO: *Name something that God has already done for us.* What would you say to thank and praise God or offer God a compliment? What do you want to ask God in prayer? Now think of something similar that God has already done or is doing. Your answer to that question becomes your WHO. Back to our "love" example, "Loving God, who answers all our needs."

DO: *This is the point in the prayer where we ask or petition God to do something for us.* At meals, we might ask a blessing on our food and pray for those who have prepared it and for those who are hungry and do not have food. We can ask God to bless all these people and ask to make something happen—like to bring an end to world famine or to give us more courage to be a better witness, or anything else we want God to DO. Often, the WHO relates to the DO. "Loving God, who answers all our needs, we ask you to guide and strengthen us as we care for those who are in need."

THROUGH: *Typically, we ask our prayers through Jesus Christ, because that is our connection to God.* We are baptized, saved, and set free through Jesus, who is one with God. Some familiar ways to express this relationship are, "We ask this through Christ our Lord" or more simply, "Through Christ our Lord." Or use your creativity, but be sure that you pray "through Jesus Christ," who is Lord forever and ever. Amen. You get the idea.

So, a typical YOU-WHO-DO-THROUGH prayer might read like this:

> Loving God,
> who answers all our needs,
> we ask you to guide and strengthen us
> as we care for those who are in need.
> We ask this through our Lord Jesus Christ, your Son. Amen.

Look and listen for this format in the collects, prayers over the gifts, and prayers after Communion at Mass, and remember YOU—WHO—DO—THROUGH when it is next your turn to publicly improvise prayer.

About Music

Music of Sacrifice: Today's gospel offers an image of a woman who gives not of her surplus wealth, but sacrificially from "her whole livelihood." Connecting that kind of giving to our gifts offered at Mass is imperative. An obscure text with delightful tune, "What You Gave Us for Our Taking" prays well that linking of sacrifices.

NOVEMBER 7, 2021
THIRTY-SECOND SUNDAY
IN ORDINARY TIME

✝ SPIRITUALITY

GOSPEL ACCLAMATION
Luke 21:36

℟. Alleluia, alleluia.
Be vigilant at all times
and pray that you have the strength to
stand before the Son of Man.
℟. Alleluia, alleluia.

Gospel

Mark 13:24-32; L158B

Jesus said to his disciples:
"In those days after that
tribulation
the sun will be darkened,
and the moon will not give its
light,
and the stars will be falling
from the sky,
and the powers in the heavens
will be shaken.

"And then they will see 'the Son
of Man coming in the clouds'
with great power and glory,
and then he will send out the angels
and gather his elect from the four
winds,
from the end of the earth to the end
of the sky.

"Learn a lesson from the fig tree.
When its branch becomes tender and
sprouts leaves,
you know that summer is near.
In the same way, when you see these
things happening,
know that he is near, at the gates.
Amen, I say to you,
this generation will not pass away
until all these things have taken
place.
Heaven and earth will pass away,
but my words will not pass away.

"But of that day or hour, no one knows,
neither the angels in heaven, nor the
Son, but only the Father."

Reflecting on the Gospel

When Jesus outlines the apocalyptic scenario found in the Gospel of Mark, he warns, "But of that day or hour, no one knows, neither the angels in heaven, nor the Son, but only the Father." Patristic discussion of this verse focused on what this admission indicated about Jesus's divinity and the relationship between Jesus's divine and human knowledge, but in context the intent of this saying points to the need for vigilance and perseverance regarding the coming end, since no one knows when it will occur.

But Jesus also tells us in Mark that "this generation will not pass away until all these things have taken place." The sense of imminence here is profound, though later Christians would argue whether Jesus meant the generation of his disciples or the generation of all human beings, while others discussed whether "all these things" referred to Jesus's death and resurrection, the destruction of Jerusalem, or "'the Son of Man coming in the clouds' with great power and glory," which is the clearest meaning.

The themes of imminent preparation for the end, the *eschaton*, and the fact that no one knows when the end will occur, therefore, have been joined in Christianity from the earliest days, maintaining a tension between what has been accomplished (realized eschatology) and what is still to come (future eschatology).

Whether we understand, or believe we understand, much about the last things—not only when these things will occur but what sort of process we go through in death; what the interim period between our death and the resurrection is like, the process of purgatory; what the heavenly life is like, whether it takes place on a renewed earth or in a heavenly, otherworldly domain—these mysteries will in many ways remain mysteries on this side of death and appear to us as vague and incomplete.

We have the assurances of revelation, however, that there is a world to come and that it may come in fullness at any time. In an odd way, though, the dramatic and mythic apocalyptic scenarios of the coming end can be distractions from the realities to which they point: death, judgment, heaven, and hell—the four last things. How? Calculating the end times and whether the apocalypse will play out now or then, in this way or that, can draw us away from preparation for our own end.

For death is coming for each of us, whether we will confront it in our own personal *eschaton* or in the cosmic apocalyptic drama as described in the Gospel of Mark. Even if "the end" does not occur in our lifetime, and even if another group of end-time prophets falsely calculate Jesus's return and offer precise dates that do not come to pass, we will still come to our end. How are we preparing for it?

For this is not just a future reality. This is our life to live now and then. It is incumbent upon us to live for God, to begin the process of righteous living now that will be brought to perfection then, at the time of the end. Our time is short, even from the perspective of human history, but especially in the scope of eternity, and it can end at any time.

But as Jesus tells us, the time of the end is the coming of the Son of Man, the time of the fullness of revelation—the time, that is, when God makes all things new. And though it is true that apocalyptic scenarios speak of persecution and torment, this is not the final story, though modern apocalyptic movies, books, and video games give an inordinate and theologically unsound emphasis to darkness and desperation. Death can create fear for us, as do judgment and hell, but we were created for one last thing, heaven, to be like and to be with God. Jesus encourages us to prepare now, for this is the time to get ready for whatever happens and whenever it takes place.

Focusing the Gospel

Key words and phrases: "But of that day or hour, no one knows, / neither the angels in heaven, nor the Son, but only the Father."

To the point: As we near the end of the liturgical year, our readings turn to the end of times when we hear the "powers in the heaven will be shaken" and we "will see the Son of Man coming in the clouds." Though Christ's early followers believed his return was imminent, in the almost two thousand years since these words were spoken, the timetable remains shrouded in mystery. What we do know for sure is that each of us will eventually arrive at the end of our mortal life and meet our Lord face-to-face. This week let us ponder how we have lived our lives up to this point. In light of the uncertainty of time allotted for us in this life, how would you like to live in this coming year?

Connecting the Gospel

to the first reading: In the first reading, Daniel also prophesies about the end of times. There is consolation and warning in Daniel's words. He says the "wise shall shine brightly," while "others shall be an everlasting horror and disgrace." We know our God has given us free will, and for those who have decided to reject a relationship with him, the Lord will not force them to spend eternity with him. We should not read these words, however, as evidence that our God is capricious in wrath. While evil has no place in God's everlasting kingdom, God is quick to help those who seek out his mercy, healing, and strength when combating their own sin.

to experience: In your walk of faith, where do you need help in living more fully as a child of the light?

Connecting the Responsorial Psalm

to the readings: Today's psalm offers us comfort and hope as we consider the final judgment awaiting each of us. Our Lord is perfectly just and perfectly merciful, and in his mercy he holds us safe, where we might abide "in confidence" knowing the Lord "will not abandon my soul to the netherworld, / nor . . . suffer your faithful one to undergo corruption." When we rely on the Lord as our "inheritance" and dedicate our lives to serving and loving him, we need not fear "everlasting horror and disgrace." We hold fast to the words Jesus has spoken, knowing that "[h]eaven and earth will pass away, / but [his] words will not pass away."

to psalmist preparation: Today's psalm looks forward to "fullness of joy in [God's] presence." How does the joy of God fill your life at this moment?

PROMPTS FOR FAITH-SHARING

In the first reading Daniel prophesies that "the wise shall shine brightly / like the splendor of the firmament." How is your faith community faithful to and enlightened by the wisdom of God?

The psalmist sings of "fullness of joys in [God's] presence." How joyful is your spiritual life at this moment in time?

The author of Hebrews tells us that Jesus "has made perfect forever those who are being consecrated." How do you experience yourself as "consecrated" through your discipleship in Christ?

Jesus tells us, "Heaven and earth will pass away, / but my words will not pass away." How does the word of God provide an anchor for your life?

Model Penitential Act

Presider: Jesus Christ, our high priest, intercedes for us constantly at the right hand of God. Trusting in his mercy, let us pause to call to mind our sins . . . *[pause]*

Lord Jesus, you give us the light of wisdom and the joy of salvation: Lord, have mercy.

Christ Jesus, you are the eternal Word: Christ, have mercy.

Lord Jesus, you lead us on the path to life: Lord, have mercy.

Homily Points

• Today's second reading from the letter to the Hebrews details how Jesus, our High Priest, "offered one sacrifice for sins, / and took his seat forever at the right hand of God." In this one offering, "he has made perfect forever those who are being consecrated." When we read the apocalyptic literature in the Bible that deals with the end of times (such as is found in our first reading and our gospel today), we might become fearful. How could anyone hope to be worthy to enter into God's eternal glory?

• And yet, the author of Hebrews reminds us that it is not our doing that brings about salvation. Instead, Jesus—in his life, death, and resurrection—has conquered mortality, crushed evil, and now offers us his very own light and life so that we might enter into the joys of his salvation.

• When we focus on our own actions, we might easily become discouraged. On our own, we are not perfect, not sinless, not holy. It is only when we are united with the sacrifice of Christ that we become perfected in his all-encompassing love. The spiritual life does require something of us: our wholehearted "yes" to being transformed by life in Christ and our determination to follow him on the journey of discipleship. Today's psalm assures us that when we do this, we have nothing to fear, for the Lord is our "inheritance." And what an inheritance God has planned for his faithful ones!

Model Universal Prayer (Prayer of the Faithful)

Presider: As we await the coming of the kingdom of God in its fullness, let us bring our needs and the needs of the world before the Lord.

Response: Lord, hear our prayer.

For God's holy church, may it evangelize with joy, trusting in the power of God's word to bring all to salvation . . .

For countries torn apart by civil war and unrest, may fighting cease and peace reign . . .

For those suffering from illnesses of the mind and body, may they be sustained by the grace of God and comforted through the care of their community . . .

For all members of this parish community, especially those who are unable to join us due to illness and infirmity, may we be united in the bonds of charity . . .

Presider: God of power and might, you have created us for yourself and called us to fullness of life. Hear our prayers that we might be attentive to your voice and always ready to serve you in word and deed. We ask this through Christ our Lord. **Amen.**

Let us pray.

Pause for silent prayer

Grant us, we pray, O Lord our God,
the constant gladness of being devoted
    to you,
for it is full and lasting happiness
to serve with constancy
the author of all that is good.
Through our Lord Jesus Christ, your Son,
who lives and reigns with you in the unity
    of the Holy Spirit,
one God, for ever and ever. **Amen.**

Dan 12:1-3

In those days, I, Daniel,
    heard this word of the Lord:
"At that time there shall arise
    Michael, the great prince,
    guardian of your people;
it shall be a time unsurpassed in distress
    since nations began until that time.
At that time your people shall escape,
    everyone who is found written in the
        book.

"Many of those who sleep in the dust of
        the earth shall awake;
    some shall live forever,
    others shall be an everlasting horror
        and disgrace.

"But the wise shall shine brightly
    like the splendor of the firmament,
and those who lead the many to justice
    shall be like the stars forever."

RESPONSORIAL PSALM

Ps 16:5, 8, 9-10, 11

R̸. (1) You are my inheritance, O Lord!

O LORD, my allotted portion and my cup,
    you it is who hold fast my lot.
I set the LORD ever before me;
    with him at my right hand I shall not be
        disturbed.

R̸. You are my inheritance, O Lord!

Therefore my heart is glad and my soul
        rejoices,
    my body, too, abides in confidence;
because you will not abandon my soul to
        the netherworld,
    nor will you suffer your faithful one to
        undergo corruption.

R̸. You are my inheritance, O Lord!

You will show me the path to life,
    fullness of joys in your presence,
    the delights at your right hand forever.

R̸. You are my inheritance, O Lord!

SECOND READING

Heb 10:11-14, 18

Brothers and sisters:
Every priest stands daily at his ministry,
    offering frequently those same sacrifices
        that can never take away sins.
But this one offered one sacrifice for sins,
    and took his seat forever at the right
        hand of God;
    now he waits until his enemies are made
        his footstool.
For by one offering
    he has made perfect forever those who
        are being consecrated.

Where there is forgiveness of these,
    there is no longer offering for sin.

About Liturgy

Dressing with Dignity: In the rite of baptism, those gathered hear the celebrant say these words regarding the white garment and the candle lit from the Easter candle just after the baptismal washing and anointing:

> N., you have become a new creation
> and have clothed yourself in Christ.
> May this white garment be a sign to you of your Christian dignity.
> With your family and friends to help you by word and example,
> bring it unstained into eternal life. (Order of Baptism 99)

> Parents and godparents,
> this light is entrusted to you to be kept burning brightly,
> so that your child, enlightened by Christ,
> may walk always as a child of the light
> and, persevering in the faith,
> may run to meet the Lord when he comes
> with all the Saints in the heavenly court. (Order of Baptism 100)

Thus, the white garment—an alb—and the dignity and purity it represents is inextricably linked to what the light of the candle represents: a burning and zealous faith, the light of Christ for all to see. The dignity of our baptism must be lived in an obvious and public way.

Some see the alb as only a priestly garment—meaning, to them, of the ordained priesthood—but it is in fact a garment of the "priesthood of the baptized" and the public faith we are all called to by our initiation into the church. Some are bothered when laypeople wear an alb in some liturgical ministry, be it as a lector, a choir member, a presider at an appropriate moment, etc., because they believe a layperson is "pretending" to be an ordained minister. It's worth noting that at nearly any Sunday Mass we see altar servers in albs and rarely if ever are complaints raised about their liturgical attire. Others are bothered because whether or not lay ministers' vest might present publicly a different ecclesiology—or at least a differing anthropology of church and Christian community—is it hierarchical or egalitarian, is it (to use not especially helpful or descriptive terminology) "high" or "low" church, or other similar concerns?

Certainly, we must be able to differentiate between what is objectively "right" or "wrong," and then what we might subjectively agree or disagree with, or find appropriate or inappropriate in a given circumstance. Properly catechized, there can be something wonderful (and itself catechetical) about a layperson wearing an alb, publicly showing one's Christian dignity to the whole of the Christian community at prayer.

About Light and Candles

We Bear Christ's Light: Even on the brightest Sunday morning, when the church is bathed in light, we light candles. In the lifeless, taciturn darkness of night we light candles. Burning brightly, they remind us that we, too, bear the light of Christ, given us at our baptism, shining brightly on a pedestal, not hidden under a basket. Light helps us to see: Christ, the light of the nations, and the glory of our people.

About Music

The Second Coming Is Coming: As the race to the end of the liturgical year continues, our attention remains fixed on the Parousia. "In the Day of the Lord" by M. D. Ridge (OCP) would be an appropriate and energetic opening or closing hymn.

NOVEMBER 14, 2021
THIRTY-THIRD SUNDAY IN ORDINARY TIME

SPIRITUALITY

GOSPEL ACCLAMATION
Mark 11:9, 10

℟. Alleluia, alleluia.
Blessed is he who comes in the name of the
Lord!
Blessed is the kingdom of our father David that
is to come!
℟. Alleluia, alleluia.

Gospel

John 18:33b-37; L161B

Pilate said to Jesus,
   "Are you the King of the Jews?"
Jesus answered, "Do you say this on
      your own
   or have others told you about me?"
Pilate answered, "I am not a Jew, am I?
Your own nation and the chief priests
      handed you over to me.
What have you done?"
Jesus answered, "My kingdom does not
      belong to this world.
If my kingdom did belong to this world,
   my attendants would be fighting
   to keep me from being handed over
      to the Jews.
But as it is, my kingdom is not here."
So Pilate said to him, "Then you are a
      king?"
Jesus answered, "You say I am a king.
For this I was born and for this I came
      into the world,
   to testify to the truth.
Everyone who belongs to the truth
   listens to my voice."

Reflecting on the Gospel

Is our God cozy or cosmic? That is the large and exciting question that challenges us on this last Sunday of the liturgical year as we celebrate the solemnity of Christ the King. It is the celebration of the climax, not only of this year of grace, but also of the end, the omega point of the mystery toward which we orient our lives.

The gospel proclaims that in Jesus the reigning presence of God comes among us in the flesh. Rather than Jesus being put on trial by Pilate, it is the Roman governor who is put on trial by the eloquent Word who stands before him bound as a prisoner. "Are you the King of the Jews?" asks Pilate, understanding kingship as political, with possibly religious implications, and therefore wary of any claim that could be a challenge to absolute Roman authority. Jesus replies with a question that seeks to confront Pilate with his own personal commitment as opposed to what "others" tell him about Jesus. The issue is no longer Jesus's guilt or innocence, but whether Pilate will respond to the truth of Jesus's kingship. Three times Jesus speaks of what his kingdom is not. It is not of this world in the sense that it neither takes its origin from here, nor is it an earthly kingdom that would be a rival to Caesar and Roman imperialism. But it does belong *in* this world and its followers do have a role to play in human affairs of justice. Like Jesus, his followers are not power brokers or mercenaries defending their own "kingdoms" of political or religious power; violence, exploitation, and opportunism have no part in the following of Jesus.

"Then you are a king?" pushes Pilate, and Jesus responds to what Pilate has called him by speaking of what his power really is: the power of the truth John proclaimed in the Prologue: "And the Word became flesh / and made his dwelling among us, / and we saw his glory, / the glory as of the Father's only Son, / full of grace and truth" (John 1:14; NABRE). The life, death, and resurrection of Jesus testify to this truth, and all who listen to Jesus and commit themselves to his wisdom will belong to the truth and to his kingdom. Pilate can make no sense of this. His world is more concerned with illusions of grandeur than with truth.

On this day we all stand not before Pilate but with him, to be interrogated by Christ the King. What power do we seek and how would we like to get it? Do we excuse ourselves of manipulating and exploiting others for the sake of safeguarding our own status or progress? How often do we strike out with the violent word or the cutting silence? Timothy Radcliffe queries whether our fascination with the countless TV shows and books that are concerned with the "naked" something or other, with either self-revelation or the exposure of others, is an indicator of a frustrated hunger for truth? He goes on to comment that in Dante's *Inferno* "the icy heart of hell was kept for those who undermined the human community of truth: the liars, the fraudulent, the flatterers, the forgers, and worst of all the traitors" (*What is the Point of Being a Christian?*). Do we belong to the community of truth that listens to and follows Jesus?

Behind Christ is the God who reveals himself in Christ, the "I AM" who is the Alpha and the Omega, the Beginning and the End, the Almighty, who is not the cozy God but the dynamic, transforming, and cosmic God, the only one whose mystery is big enough to show us a new way into the experience of the holy and large truth when we are disenchanted by unholy minutiae and legalisms.

Focusing the Gospel

Key words and phrases: "For this I was born and for this I came into the world, / to testify to the truth."

To the point: Jesus stands before Pontius Pilate, accused of proclaiming himself "King of the Jews" and therefore threatening Caesar's rule of the land of Israel. This is not the nature of Jesus's kingship, however. He has no designs on political control and yet, his power extends over every nation of the earth. Earlier in John's gospel, in the Last Supper discourses, Jesus revealed to his disciples, "I am the way and the truth and the life" (14:6; NABRE). Jesus's kingship is written into the laws of reality as certainly as the sun rises and sets each day. Jesus tells Pilate, "I came into the world, / to testify to the truth. / Everyone who belongs to the truth listens to my voice." In our lives as disciples of Christ, we are called to proclaim the reality of Jesus's kingship in word and deed. In this way we hold fast to the truth that Jesus came to testify to.

Connecting the Gospel

to the first and second readings: Both the first and second readings comment on the kingship of the Lord. Daniel prophesies about "the one like a Son of man" whose "dominion is an everlasting dominion / that shall not be taken away." The book of Revelation contains the line, "'I am the Alpha and the Omega,' says the Lord God, / 'the one who is and who was and who is to come, the almighty.'" In these readings we find that Jesus, as true God and true man, is not bound by the laws of time and space. He is the second person of the Trinity, and as such reigns in past, present, and future with the Father and the Holy Spirit.

to experience: On this feast of Christ the King of the Universe, how is your life affected by living it under the kingship of Jesus?

Connecting the Responsorial Psalm

to the readings: Today's responsorial psalm sings to the Lord, who "is king, he is robed in majesty." Our praise and worship of God, the almighty, gives us hope and trust in the world God has made, which is "firm / not to be moved." God's decrees ground us, as well, on the path of salvation as we strive for holiness that "befits your house, / O Lord." While we proclaim Jesus king of creation, we also know that his kingdom goes beyond our lived reality. Jesus explains to Pilate, "My kingdom does not belong to this world." And so, as subjects of this king, we are called beyond ourselves, to grow and develop as children of God who devote their lives to service and to love.

to psalmist preparation: In this coming liturgical year, how would you like to rededicate your life to Jesus, king of the universe?

PROMPTS FOR FAITH-SHARING

Today is the last Sunday before beginning the new liturgical year. What have been your spiritual triumphs and struggles this past year?

Next Sunday we enter into the season of Advent. What Advent practices are you planning to embrace as you prepare for Christmas?

Jesus tells Pilate, "Everyone who belongs to the truth listens to my voice." What role does a commitment to truth have in your spiritual life?

On this feast of Christ the King of the Universe, how is your life affected by living it under the kingship of Jesus?

Model Penitential Act

Presider: On this feast of Christ the King of the Universe, let us prepare to welcome Jesus in word and sacrament by first calling to mind our sins and asking the Lord for pardon and mercy . . . *[pause]*

 Lord Jesus, you are the Alpha and the Omega: Lord, have mercy.

 Christ Jesus, you lead us in truth and justice: Christ, have mercy.

 Lord Jesus, you are the eternal King: Lord, have mercy.

Homily Points

• Each year we round out the liturgical cycle with the feast of Christ the King of the Universe. Today's gospel focuses on the otherworldly aspect of Christ's kingship. Jesus is arrested by his own people but the chief priests are not able to put him to death, since executions are under the discretion of their Roman oppressors. For this reason, Jesus is brought to Pontius Pilate, the Roman governor. Jesus's captors tell Pilate that Jesus poses a threat to Caesar, given that he has proclaimed himself "King of the Jews."

• Just as Pilate does in today's gospel, we are called to consider the identity of Jesus, the king. In his life, death, and resurrection, Jesus gives us a contradictory portrait of kingship. As king of the universe, he controls the wind and the waves, heals illness, multiplies bread and fish, and casts out demons. And yet, this same king is born among animals, placed in a manger, and then is given a criminal's death on the cross. He lives an ordinary life in the village of Nazareth for thirty years and when he begins his public ministry, he lives as an itinerant preacher who has "nowhere to rest his head" (Matt 8:20; NABRE).

• Perhaps most anathema to our ordinary perception of kingship, Jesus does not demand special treatment, instead stating his mission as one of service and the self-gift of his life to the world. Our understanding of Jesus affects every aspect of how we, as his disciples, live our lives. We worship Jesus, the king of the universe, who humbled himself to die on a cross and rose in glory three days later. Let us proclaim the truth of who he is with every word we speak and every action we undertake.

Model Universal Prayer (Prayer of the Faithful)

Presider: With praise for the greatness of the Lord and thanksgiving for all he has accomplished in our lives, let us place before him our petitions.

Response: Lord, hear our prayer.

For all members of the church, may our lives reflect and proclaim the kingship of Jesus . . .

For leaders of nations, may they work together to protect the resources and beauty of the earth

For those whose lives have become enslaved to sin, through the kingship of Jesus may the bonds of evil be broken and may they step into the freedom of a child of God . . .

For all gathered here, may the work of our hands be prospered as we commit ourselves to service of God and others . . .

Presider: God of mercy and love, each time we pray the Our Father we ask that your kingdom might come in its fullness. Hear our prayers that we might proclaim the kingship of Jesus in word and deed and so build the kingdom here on earth. We ask this through Christ our Lord. **Amen.**

COLLECT

Let us pray.

Pause for silent prayer

Almighty ever-living God,
whose will is to restore all things
in your beloved Son, the King of the
 universe,
grant, we pray,
that the whole creation, set free from
 slavery,
may render your majesty service
and ceaselessly proclaim your praise.
Through our Lord Jesus Christ, your Son,
who lives and reigns with you in the unity
 of the Holy Spirit,
one God, for ever and ever. **Amen.**

FIRST READING

Dan 7:13-14

As the visions during the night continued,
 I saw
 one like a Son of man coming,
  on the clouds of heaven;
 when he reached the Ancient One
  and was presented before him,
 the one like a Son of man received
  dominion, glory, and kingship;
 all peoples, nations, and languages
  serve him.
His dominion is an everlasting dominion
 that shall not be taken away,
 his kingship shall not be destroyed.

RESPONSORIAL PSALM

Ps 93:1, 1-2, 5

R℣. (1a) The Lord is king; he is robed in
majesty.

The LORD is king, in splendor robed;
robed is the LORD and girt about with
strength.

R℣. The Lord is king; he is robed in
majesty.

And he has made the world firm,
not to be moved.
Your throne stands firm from of old;
from everlasting you are, O LORD.

R℣. The Lord is king; he is robed in
majesty.

Your decrees are worthy of trust indeed;
holiness befits your house,
O LORD, for length of days.

R℣. The Lord is king; he is robed in
majesty.

SECOND READING

Rev 1:5-8

Jesus Christ is the faithful witness,
the firstborn of the dead and ruler of
the kings of the earth.
To him who loves us and has freed us
from our sins by his blood,
who has made us into a kingdom,
priests for his God and Father,
to him be glory and power forever and
ever. Amen.

Behold, he is coming amid the clouds,
and every eye will see him,
even those who pierced him.
All the peoples of the earth will lament
him.
Yes. Amen.

"I am the Alpha and the Omega," says the
Lord God,
"the one who is and who was and who
is to come, the almighty."

About Liturgy

We Belong to Christ: For several years now, Americans (and truly many peoples around the globe) have been debating with others and within themselves which political candidates they felt could next best lead their citizens—according to the Constitution, our values, our beliefs, and many other measuring sticks. The aftermath of many election days has left many heads spinning, hearts confused and broken, and brings uncertainty into many lives. This solemnity should remind us, though, of two things.

First, during Christ's passion and crucifixion, Christ reminds Pilate, "My kingdom does not belong to this world," and "For this I was born and for this I came into the world, to testify to the truth." Jesus continues to show us through his passion that his definition of kingship is upside down from what most of us would believe it to be: someone who is sneered at and reviled, and someone who serves the repentant—and indeed everyone—with love and compassion, giving of himself in humility to the point of death of a cross.

Many people today are at times angry, scared, hateful, and desolate. But again, just like Christ's kingdom is not of this world, neither is his peace. Anyone who believes any political candidate of any time and place can, by himself or herself alone, truly bring God's peace to earth is probably incorrect. Christ is the source of those things and needs his whole body on earth to make them real for all of creation.

Second, today's passage from Revelation ends with the Lord God reminding us, "Jesus Christ is . . . the firstborn of the dead and ruler of the kings of the earth. To him who loves us and has freed us from our sins by his blood, who has made us into a kingdom, . . . to him be glory and power forever and ever. Amen."

What does this mean for us today? Simply, it means we belong to Christ who is eternal. We are not created by our government, our identity is ultimately much more than any world leader can give us, and our lives are owed to Christ and Christ only. It is his kingdom we strive to build, and his peace we try to bring. In that regard, no matter who wins any election, we all have work to do. At our liturgies, we must strive to—in the words attributed to a few different saints—pray as if it all depends on God, and act as if it all depends on us. What can you do or enact at your upcoming liturgies to help others pray as a citizen of God's kingdom of truth and self-sacrificing love? What can you do or enact at your upcoming liturgies to bring God's peace to someone in need?

About Music

Music of Kingship and Crown: There certainly is no shortage of music appropriate for today's solemnity! When choosing selections, a particular mindfulness must be present to ensure the texts speak not only of Christ, reigning in heavenly splendor, but also of Christ who chose no such title for himself on earth but rather chose a crown of thorns. So, while perhaps utilizing traditional favorites like "Crown Him with Many Crowns" or "To Jesus Christ, Our Sovereign King," both found in many hymnals, also ensure that hymns like "Amazing Love" (Hillsong) or perhaps "At the Name of Jesus" in either the traditional setting or the gospel-feel version by Christopher Walker (OCP) are part of your assembly's sung prayer this weekend.

GOSPEL ACCLAMATION
1 Thess 5:18

R⁄. Alleluia, alleluia.
In all circumstances, give thanks,
for this is the will of God for you in Christ Jesus.
R⁄. Alleluia, alleluia.

Gospel

Luke 17:11-19; L947.6

**As Jesus continued his
journey to Jerusalem,
he traveled through
Samaria and
Galilee.
As he was entering a
village, ten lepers met
him.
They stood at a distance
from him and raised
their voices, saying,
"Jesus, Master! Have
pity on us!"
And when he saw them,
he said,
"Go show yourselves to
the priests."
As they were going they
were cleansed.
And one of them, realizing he had been
healed,
returned, glorifying God in a loud
voice;
and he fell at the feet of Jesus and
thanked him.
He was a Samaritan.
Jesus said in reply,
"Ten were cleansed, were they not?
Where are the other nine?
Has none but this foreigner returned to
give thanks to God?"
Then he said to him, "Stand up and go;
your faith has saved you."**

See Appendix A, p. 304, for the other readings.

Additional reading choices may be found in the
Lectionary for Mass, *vol. IV, "In Thanksgiving to
God," nos. 943–947.*

Reflecting on the Gospel

Today's reading has a clear message—it is right and good to give thanks to God. In this story from the "journey section" of Luke's gospel (Jesus is journeying to Jerusalem, where he knows he will die), Jesus enters a village where ten people with leprosy ask him for mercy. They call Jesus by his name and the title "Master," clearly recognizing his authority and his ability to heal them. Indeed, that authority is confirmed when with a mere phrase from the lips of Jesus—

"Go show yourselves to the priests"—the lepers are healed. Here is where Luke's masterful storytelling gives us much to consider. He writes that one of the (former) lepers "realiz[ed] he had been healed." While it's hard to imagine that the other nine did *not* realize such a major change in their own situation, Luke singles out this one with the description: "realizing he had been healed." The lepers are simply healed as they walk away. It seems that the cleansing was so subtle that only one even noticed as it happened.

Essentially, we are being told that this particular leper is the perceptive one. He is aware. And that awareness is oriented not only to himself, but toward God. At some point along the way, the other nine must have realized that they were healed. But their perception, their awareness, remained inward-focused: I am healed! I have my life back! But for this one: I am healed! Glory to God! Indeed, Luke's imagination-inducing narrative tells us that this one returned to Jesus, "glorifying God." And this was no tepid glory-giving! It was done "in a loud voice" as he "fell at the feet of Jesus." This act of giving thanks (*eucharistein*)—and giving all the glory to God—was done with this man's whole body, the body that had been healed by a few simple words (and certainly a deeply compassionate intention) from Jesus.

We are told that this man was a Samaritan. The significance of this is that the Samaritans were looked down upon in the Jewish society of Jesus's time and place. They were thought to be not quite as religious, or not the "right kind" of religious. But it was this man that gave thanks. It was this man that glorified God in a loud voice. And so it was the Samaritan that was declared "saved" by Jesus!

Notice that Jesus does not humbly shy away from the former leper's thanks. He does not tell the man to tone down his dramatic and loud praise of God. Instead he says to the man, "Where are the other nine?" In other words, Why aren't the others doing the same as you? This is not because Jesus loved to hear people thanking him or wanted to see them falling at his feet. Rather, Jesus knows that it is right and good to give thanks. Authentic gratitude means that we have realized the good in our lives. We are perceptive and aware. And it means that when we perceive the good, we don't keep it to ourselves. We turn outward, to the giver of the blessings. We return to the one who has healed us. We glorify God in a loud voice. We fall at the feet of Jesus and thank him. This is salvation—it is the right and good relationship between ourselves and God, the giver of all that is good.

Focusing the Gospel

Key words and phrases: One of them, realizing he had been healed, returned, glorifying God.

To the point: The story of the lepers who are healed reminds us of an important lesson in gratitude: in order to be grateful, we must foster awareness of the gifts we receive. Each moment of every day there are countless things we could be grateful for. When we open our eyes to the bounteous gifts of God (from those we find in creation, to the gift of other people, and the gifts of our own talents and abilities), we could easily live our lives as a litany of thanksgiving. In this spirituality of thanksgiving, we are reminded constantly of who sustains our life and animates it with joy and meaning.

Model Penitential Act

Presider: The lepers who meet Jesus plead, "Jesus, Master! Have pity on us!" Assured of our Lord's compassion and mercy, let us bring before him the places in our lives that are in need of pardon and healing . . . *[pause]*

Lord Jesus, you show us hope and thanksgiving: Lord, have mercy.
Christ Jesus, you are slow to anger and quick to forgive: Christ, have mercy.
Lord Jesus, you are worthy of all gratitude and praise: Lord, have mercy.

Model Universal Prayer (Prayer of the Faithful)

Presider: With hearts filled with gratitude for the many blessings God has bestowed upon us, let us lift up our petitions to the Lord.

Response: Lord, hear our prayer.

For God's holy church, in word and deed may it never cease to praise the Lord of life and to offer hospitality and care for all those in need . . .

For nations rich in resources, may they find ways to share their abundance with countries suffering from natural disasters and economic hardship . . .

For those who are far from family and friends this holiday, or are grieving the loss of a loved one, may they know the love of supportive community . . .

For all gathered here, may we embrace the practice of gratitude in our daily lives . . .

Presider: God of every good gift, in your generosity you shower us with blessings. Hear our prayers that we might recognize your presence in everyone we meet and offer hospitality. We ask this through Christ our Lord. **Amen.**

About Liturgy

Thanks at the Table: Giving thanks is itself a holy activity, and the Thanksgiving holiday commemorates, at least in part, those long ago seeking religious freedom. Consider introducing this custom in your community: at a morning Mass, include a blessing of bread, which parishioners bring from home and later share at a dinner table. Distribute cards prepared with text to use at the family dinner table when the bread is broken and shared. Include a prayer of blessing over the bread and the meal, along with a question or two for family members to answer when receiving the bread. Questions could include "How do you see God in what you are thankful for today?" or "What actions might you do this coming week to show God your gratitude not in words but in how you live?"

FOR REFLECTION

• Considering the events of this past year, what are you most thankful for today?

• How do you seek to make gratitude a daily part of your spiritual practice?

• Today's first reading from Sirach prays, "May [God] grant you joy of heart / and may peace abide among you." Which areas in your life are in need of the Lord's peace?

Homily Points

• In the first reading from the book of Sirach, we find the blessing, "May God grant you joy of heart / and may peace abide among you." We could say that joy and peace are two fruits of a grateful spirit. When we pause to reflect on our blessings and give thanks for them, we realize anew how much there is within our lives to spark joy.

• In thanking God for our blessings, we also realize the abundance in which we live. There is no need for greed, jealousies, or envy of another's wealth or good fortune when we contemplate our own giftedness. As we end this liturgical year, may we recommit ourselves to living lives of gratitude that foster joy and peace throughout the coming year.

Readings *(continued)*

The Immaculate Conception of the Blessed Virgin Mary, *December 8, 2020*

Gospel (cont.)
Luke 1:26-38; L689

He will be great and will be called Son of the Most High,
    and the Lord God will give him the throne of David his father,
    and he will rule over the house of Jacob forever,
    and of his Kingdom there will be no end."
But Mary said to the angel,
    "How can this be,
    since I have no relations with a man?"
And the angel said to her in reply,
    "The Holy Spirit will come upon you,
    and the power of the Most High will overshadow you.
Therefore the child to be born
    will be called holy, the Son of God.

And behold, Elizabeth, your relative,
    has also conceived a son in her old age,
    and this is the sixth month for her who was called barren;
    for nothing will be impossible for God."
Mary said, "Behold, I am the handmaid of the Lord.
May it be done to me according to your word."
Then the angel departed from her.

FIRST READING
Gen 3:9-15, 20

After the man, Adam, had eaten of the tree,
    the LORD God called to the man and asked
        him, "Where are you?"
He answered, "I heard you in the garden;
    but I was afraid, because I was naked,
    so I hid myself."
Then he asked, "Who told you that you were
        naked?
You have eaten, then,
    from the tree of which I had forbidden you
        to eat!"
The man replied, "The woman whom you put
        here with me—
    she gave me fruit from the tree, and so I
        ate it."
The LORD God then asked the woman,
    "Why did you do such a thing?"
The woman answered, "The serpent tricked
    me into it, so I ate it."

Then the LORD God said to the serpent:
    "Because you have done this, you shall be
        banned
        from all the animals
        and from all the wild creatures;
    on your belly shall you crawl,
        and dirt shall you eat
        all the days of your life.
    I will put enmity between you and the
        woman,
        and between your offspring and hers;
    he will strike at your head,
        while you strike at his heel."

The man called his wife Eve,
    because she became the mother of all the
        living.

RESPONSORIAL PSALM
Ps 98:1, 2-3ab, 3cd-4

R̸. (1a) Sing to the Lord a new song, for he has
    done marvelous deeds.

Sing to the LORD a new song,
    for he has done wondrous deeds;
His right hand has won victory for him,
    his holy arm.

R̸. Sing to the Lord a new song, for he has
    done marvelous deeds.

The LORD has made his salvation known:
    in the sight of the nations he has revealed
        his justice.
He has remembered his kindness and his
        faithfulness
    toward the house of Israel.

R̸. Sing to the Lord a new song, for he has
    done marvelous deeds.

All the ends of the earth have seen
    the salvation by our God.
Sing joyfully to the LORD, all you lands;
    break into song; sing praise.

R̸. Sing to the Lord a new song, for he has
    done marvelous deeds.

SECOND READING
Eph 1:3-6, 11-12

Brothers and sisters:
Blessed be the God and Father of our Lord
        Jesus Christ,
    who has blessed us in Christ
    with every spiritual blessing in the heavens,
    as he chose us in him, before the foundation
        of the world,
    to be holy and without blemish before him.
In love he destined us for adoption to himself
        through Jesus Christ,
    in accord with the favor of his will,
    for the praise of the glory of his grace
    that he granted us in the beloved.

In him we were also chosen,
    destined in accord with the purpose of the
        One
    who accomplishes all things according to
        the intention of his will,
    so that we might exist for the praise of his
        glory,
    we who first hoped in Christ.

Gospel (cont.)
Matt 1:1-25; L13ABC

Asaph became the father of Jehoshaphat,
   Jehoshaphat the father of Joram,
   Joram the father of Uzziah.
Uzziah became the father of Jotham,
   Jotham the father of Ahaz,
   Ahaz the father of Hezekiah.
Hezekiah became the father of Manasseh,
   Manasseh the father of Amos,
   Amos the father of Josiah.
Josiah became the father of Jechoniah and his brothers
   at the time of the Babylonian exile.

After the Babylonian exile,
   Jechoniah became the father of Shealtiel,
   Shealtiel the father of Zerubbabel,
   Zerubbabel the father of Abiud.
Abiud became the father of Eliakim,
   Eliakim the father of Azor,
   Azor the father of Zadok.
Zadok became the father of Achim,
   Achim the father of Eliud,
   Eliud the father of Eleazar.
Eleazar became the father of Matthan,
   Matthan the father of Jacob,
   Jacob the father of Joseph, the husband of Mary.
Of her was born Jesus who is called the Christ.

Thus the total number of generations
   from Abraham to David
   is fourteen generations;
   from David to the Babylonian exile,
   fourteen generations;
   from the Babylonian exile to the Christ,
   fourteen generations.

Now this is how the birth of Jesus Christ came about.
When his mother Mary was betrothed to Joseph,
   but before they lived together,
   she was found with child through the Holy Spirit.
Joseph her husband, since he was a righteous man,
   yet unwilling to expose her to shame,
   decided to divorce her quietly.
Such was his intention when, behold,
   the angel of the Lord appeared to him in a dream and said,
   "Joseph, son of David,
   do not be afraid to take Mary your wife into your home.
For it is through the Holy Spirit
   that this child has been conceived in her.
She will bear a son and you are to name him Jesus,
   because he will save his people from their sins."
All this took place to fulfill
   what the Lord had said through the prophet:
      Behold, the virgin shall conceive and bear a son,
         and they shall name him Emmanuel,
      which means "God is with us."
When Joseph awoke,
   he did as the angel of the Lord had commanded him
   and took his wife into his home.
He had no relations with her until she bore a son,
   and he named him Jesus.

or Matt 1:18-25

This is how the birth of Jesus Christ came about.
When his mother Mary was betrothed to Joseph,
   but before they lived together,
   she was found with child through the Holy Spirit.
Joseph her husband, since he was a righteous man,
   yet unwilling to expose her to shame,
   decided to divorce her quietly.
Such was his intention when, behold,
   the angel of the Lord appeared to him in a dream and said,
   "Joseph, son of David,
   do not be afraid to take Mary your wife into your home.
For it is through the Holy Spirit
   that this child has been conceived in her.
She will bear a son and you are to name him Jesus,
   because he will save his people from their sins."
All this took place to fulfill
   what the Lord had said through the prophet:
      Behold, the virgin shall conceive and bear a son,
         and they shall name him Emmanuel,
      which means "God is with us."
When Joseph awoke,
   he did as the angel of the Lord had commanded him
   and took his wife into his home.
He had no relations with her until she bore a son,
   and he named him Jesus.

The Nativity of the Lord, *December 25, 2020 (Vigil Mass)*

FIRST READING
Isa 62:1-5

For Zion's sake I will not be silent,
   for Jerusalem's sake I will not be quiet,
until her vindication shines forth like the
    dawn
   and her victory like a burning torch.

Nations shall behold your vindication,
   and all the kings your glory;
you shall be called by a new name
   pronounced by the mouth of the LORD.
You shall be a glorious crown in the hand of
    the LORD,
   a royal diadem held by your God.
No more shall people call you "Forsaken,"
   or your land "Desolate,"
but you shall be called "My Delight,"
   and your land "Espoused."
For the LORD delights in you
   and makes your land his spouse.
As a young man marries a virgin,
   your Builder shall marry you;
and as a bridegroom rejoices in his bride
   so shall your God rejoice in you.

RESPONSORIAL PSALM
Ps 89:4-5, 16-17, 27, 29

R̦. (2a) For ever I will sing the goodness of
   the Lord.

I have made a covenant with my chosen one,
   I have sworn to David my servant:
forever will I confirm your posterity
   and establish your throne for all
    generations.

R̦. For ever I will sing the goodness of the
   Lord.

Blessed the people who know the joyful shout;
   in the light of your countenance, O LORD,
    they walk.
At your name they rejoice all the day,
   and through your justice they are exalted.

R̦. For ever I will sing the goodness of the
   Lord.

He shall say of me, "You are my father,
   my God, the rock, my savior."
Forever I will maintain my kindness toward
    him,
   and my covenant with him stands firm.

R̦. For ever I will sing the goodness of the
   Lord.

SECOND READING
Acts 13:16-17, 22-25

When Paul reached Antioch in Pisidia and
    entered the synagogue,
   he stood up, motioned with his hand, and
    said,
    "Fellow Israelites and you others who are
     God-fearing, listen.
The God of this people Israel chose our
    ancestors
   and exalted the people during their sojourn
    in the land of Egypt.
With uplifted arm he led them out of it.
Then he removed Saul and raised up David
    as king;
   of him he testified,
   'I have found David, son of Jesse, a man
    after my own heart;
   he will carry out my every wish.'
From this man's descendants God, according
    to his promise,
   has brought to Israel a savior, Jesus.
John heralded his coming by proclaiming a
    baptism of repentance
   to all the people of Israel;
   and as John was completing his course, he
    would say,
   'What do you suppose that I am? I am not
    he.
Behold, one is coming after me;
   I am not worthy to unfasten the sandals of
    his feet.'"

The Nativity of the Lord, *December 25, 2020 (Mass during the Night)*

Gospel (cont.)
Luke 2:1-14; L14ABC

Now there were shepherds in that region living in the fields
   and keeping the night watch over their flock.
The angel of the Lord appeared to them
   and the glory of the Lord shone around them,
   and they were struck with great fear.
The angel said to them,
   "Do not be afraid;
   for behold, I proclaim to you good news of great joy
   that will be for all the people.
For today in the city of David
   a savior has been born for you who is Christ and Lord.
And this will be a sign for you:
   you will find an infant wrapped in swaddling clothes
   and lying in a manger."
And suddenly there was a multitude of the heavenly host with the
    angel,
   praising God and saying:
    "Glory to God in the highest
     and on earth peace to those on whom his favor rests."

The Nativity of the Lord, *December 25, 2020 (Mass during the Night)*

FIRST READING
Isa 9:1-6

The people who walked in darkness
    have seen a great light;
upon those who dwelt in the land of gloom
    a light has shone.
You have brought them abundant joy
    and great rejoicing,
as they rejoice before you as at the harvest,
    as people make merry when dividing spoils.
For the yoke that burdened them,
    the pole on their shoulder,
and the rod of their taskmaster
    you have smashed, as on the day of Midian.
For every boot that tramped in battle,
    every cloak rolled in blood,
    will be burned as fuel for flames.
For a child is born to us, a son is given us;
    upon his shoulder dominion rests.
They name him Wonder-Counselor, God-Hero,
    Father-Forever, Prince of Peace.
His dominion is vast
    and forever peaceful,
from David's throne, and over his kingdom,
    which he confirms and sustains
by judgment and justice,
    both now and forever.
The zeal of the LORD of hosts will do this!

RESPONSORIAL PSALM
Ps 96:1-2, 2-3, 11-12, 13

℟. (Luke 2:11) Today is born our Savior,
    Christ the Lord.

Sing to the LORD a new song;
    sing to the LORD, all you lands.
Sing to the LORD; bless his name.

℟. Today is born our Savior, Christ the Lord.

Announce his salvation, day after day.
    Tell his glory among the nations;
    among all peoples, his wondrous deeds.

℟. Today is born our Savior, Christ the Lord.

Let the heavens be glad and the earth rejoice;
    let the sea and what fills it resound;
    let the plains be joyful and all that is in
      them!
Then shall all the trees of the forest exult.

℟. Today is born our Savior, Christ the Lord.

They shall exult before the LORD, for he
    comes;
    for he comes to rule the earth.
He shall rule the world with justice
    and the peoples with his constancy.

℟. Today is born our Savior, Christ the Lord.

SECOND READING
Titus 2:11-14

Beloved:
The grace of God has appeared, saving all
    and training us to reject godless ways and
      worldly desires
    and to live temperately, justly, and devoutly
      in this age,
    as we await the blessed hope,
    the appearance of the glory of our great
      God
    and savior Jesus Christ,
    who gave himself for us to deliver us from
      all lawlessness
    and to cleanse for himself a people as his
      own,
    eager to do what is good.

The Nativity of the Lord, *December 25, 2020 (Mass at Dawn)*

FIRST READING
Isa 62:11-12

See, the LORD proclaims
    to the ends of the earth:
say to daughter Zion,
    your savior comes!
Here is his reward with him,
    his recompense before him.
They shall be called the holy people,
    the redeemed of the LORD,
and you shall be called "Frequented,"
    a city that is not forsaken.

RESPONSORIAL PSALM
Ps 97:1, 6, 11-12

℟. A light will shine on us this day: the Lord
    is born for us.

The LORD is king; let the earth rejoice;
    let the many isles be glad.
The heavens proclaim his justice,
    and all peoples see his glory.

℟. A light will shine on us this day: the Lord
    is born for us.

Light dawns for the just;
    and gladness, for the upright of heart.
Be glad in the LORD, you just,
    and give thanks to his holy name.

℟. A light will shine on us this day: the Lord
    is born for us.

SECOND READING
Titus 3:4-7

Beloved:
When the kindness and generous love
    of God our savior appeared,
not because of any righteous deeds we had
      done
    but because of his mercy,
he saved us through the bath of rebirth
    and renewal by the Holy Spirit,
whom he richly poured out on us
    through Jesus Christ our savior,
so that we might be justified by his grace
    and become heirs in hope of eternal life.

Gospel (cont.)
John 1:1-18; L16ABC

And the Word became flesh
  and made his dwelling among us,
  and we saw his glory,
  the glory as of the Father's only Son,
  full of grace and truth.

John testified to him and cried out, saying,
  "This was he of whom I said,
  'The one who is coming after me ranks ahead of me
  because he existed before me.'"
From his fullness we have all received,
  grace in place of grace,
  because while the law was given through Moses,
  grace and truth came through Jesus Christ.
No one has ever seen God.
The only Son, God, who is at the Father's side,
  has revealed him.

or John 1:1-5, 9-14

In the beginning was the Word,
  and the Word was with God,
  and the Word was God.
He was in the beginning with God.

All things came to be through him,
  and without him nothing came to be.
What came to be through him was life,
  and this life was the light of the human race;
the light shines in the darkness,
  and the darkness has not overcome it.
The true light, which enlightens everyone, was coming into the world.

He was in the world,
  and the world came to be through him,
  but the world did not know him.
He came to what was his own,
  but his own people did not accept him.

But to those who did accept him
  he gave power to become children of God,
  to those who believe in his name,
  who were born not by natural generation
  nor by human choice nor by a man's decision
  but of God.

And the Word became flesh
  and made his dwelling among us,
  and we saw his glory,
  the glory as of the Father's only Son,
  full of grace and truth.

FIRST READING
Isa 52:7-10

How beautiful upon the mountains
  are the feet of him who brings glad tidings,
announcing peace, bearing good news,
  announcing salvation, and saying to Zion,
  "Your God is King!"

Hark! Your sentinels raise a cry,
  together they shout for joy,
for they see directly, before their eyes,
  the LORD restoring Zion.
Break out together in song,
  O ruins of Jerusalem!
For the LORD comforts his people,
  he redeems Jerusalem.
The LORD has bared his holy arm
  in the sight of all the nations;
all the ends of the earth will behold
  the salvation of our God.

RESPONSORIAL PSALM
Ps 98:1, 2-3, 3-4, 5-6

R̞. (3c) All the ends of the earth have seen the
  saving power of God.

Sing to the LORD a new song,
  for he has done wondrous deeds;
his right hand has won victory for him,
  his holy arm.

R̞. All the ends of the earth have seen the
  saving power of God.

The LORD has made his salvation known:
  in the sight of the nations he has revealed
  his justice.
He has remembered his kindness and his
  faithfulness
  toward the house of Israel.

R̞. All the ends of the earth have seen the
  saving power of God.

All the ends of the earth have seen
  the salvation by our God.
Sing joyfully to the LORD, all you lands;
  break into song; sing praise.

R̞. All the ends of the earth have seen the
  saving power of God.

Sing praise to the LORD with the harp,
  with the harp and melodious song.
With trumpets and the sound of the horn
  sing joyfully before the King, the LORD.

R̞. All the ends of the earth have seen the
  saving power of God.

SECOND READING
Heb 1:1-6

Brothers and sisters:
In times past, God spoke in partial and
  various ways
  to our ancestors through the prophets;
in these last days, he has spoken to us
  through the Son,
  whom he made heir of all things
  and through whom he created the universe,
  who is the refulgence of his glory,
  the very imprint of his being,
  and who sustains all things by his mighty
  word.
When he had accomplished purification
  from sins,
  he took his seat at the right hand of the
  Majesty on high,
  as far superior to the angels
  as the name he has inherited is more
  excellent than theirs.

For to which of the angels did God ever say:
  *You are my son; this day I have begotten
  you?*
Or again:
  *I will be a father to him, and he shall be a
  son to me?*
And again, when he leads the firstborn into
  the world, he says:
  Let all the angels of God worship him.

Gospel (cont.)

Luke 2:22-40; L17B

He came in the Spirit into the temple;
and when the parents brought in the child Jesus
to perform the custom of the law in regard to him,
he took him into his arms and blessed God, saying:
"Now, Master, you may let your servant go
in peace, according to your word,
for my eyes have seen your salvation,
which you prepared in sight of all the peoples,
a light for revelation to the Gentiles,
and glory for your people Israel."
The child's father and mother were amazed at what was said about
him;
and Simeon blessed them and said to Mary his mother,
"Behold, this child is destined
for the fall and rise of many in Israel,
and to be a sign that will be contradicted
—and you yourself a sword will pierce—
so that the thoughts of many hearts may be revealed."
There was also a prophetess, Anna,
the daughter of Phanuel, of the tribe of Asher.
She was advanced in years,
having lived seven years with her husband after her marriage,
and then as a widow until she was eighty-four.
She never left the temple,
but worshiped night and day with fasting and prayer.
And coming forward at that very time,
she gave thanks to God and spoke about the child
to all who were awaiting the redemption of Jerusalem.

When they had fulfilled all the prescriptions
of the law of the Lord,
they returned to Galilee,
to their own town of Nazareth.
The child grew and became strong, filled with wisdom;
and the favor of God was upon him.

or Luke 2:22, 39-40

When the days were completed for their purification
according to the law of Moses,
the parents of Jesus took him up to Jerusalem
to present him to the Lord.

When they had fulfilled all the prescriptions
of the law of the Lord,
they returned to Galilee,
to their own town of Nazareth.
The child grew and became strong, filled with wisdom;
and the favor of God was upon him.

SECOND READING

or Col 3:12-17

Brothers and sisters:
Put on, as God's chosen ones, holy and beloved,
heartfelt compassion, kindness, humility,
gentleness, and patience,
bearing with one another and forgiving one
another,
if one has a grievance against another;
as the Lord has forgiven you, so must you
also do.
And over all these put on love,
that is, the bond of perfection.
And let the peace of Christ control your
hearts,
the peace into which you were also called in
one body.
And be thankful.
Let the word of Christ dwell in you richly,
as in all wisdom you teach and admonish
one another,
singing psalms, hymns, and spiritual songs
with gratitude in your hearts to God.
And whatever you do, in word or in deed,
do everything in the name of the Lord
Jesus,
giving thanks to God the Father through
him.

The Holy Family of Jesus, Mary, and Joseph, *December 27, 2020*

FIRST READING
Gen 15:1-6; 21:1-3

The word of the Lord came to Abram in a
vision, saying:
"Fear not, Abram!
I am your shield;
I will make your reward very great."
But Abram said,
"O Lord God, what good will your gifts be,
if I keep on being childless
and have as my heir the steward of my
house, Eliezer?"
Abram continued,
"See, you have given me no offspring,
and so one of my servants will be my heir."
Then the word of the Lord came to him:
"No, that one shall not be your heir;
your own issue shall be your heir."
The Lord took Abram outside and said,
"Look up at the sky and count the stars, if
you can.
Just so," he added, "shall your descendants be."
Abram put his faith in the Lord,
who credited it to him as an act of
righteousness.

The Lord took note of Sarah as he had said
he would;
he did for her as he had promised.
Sarah became pregnant and bore Abraham a
son in his old age,
at the set time that God had stated.
Abraham gave the name Isaac to this son of his
whom Sarah bore him.

RESPONSORIAL PSALM
Ps 105:1-2, 3-4, 6-7, 8-9

R̸. (7a, 8a) The Lord remembers his covenant
for ever.

Give thanks to the Lord, invoke his name;
make known among the nations his deeds.
Sing to him, sing his praise,
proclaim all his wondrous deeds.

R̸. The Lord remembers his covenant for ever.

Glory in his holy name;
rejoice, O hearts that seek the Lord!
Look to the Lord in his strength;
constantly seek his face.

R̸. The Lord remembers his covenant for ever.

You descendants of Abraham, his servants,
sons of Jacob, his chosen ones!
He, the Lord, is our God;
throughout the earth his judgments prevail.

R̸. The Lord remembers his covenant for ever.

He remembers forever his covenant
which he made binding for a thousand
generations
which he entered into with Abraham
and by his oath to Isaac.

R̸. The Lord remembers his covenant for ever.

SECOND READING
Heb 11:8, 11-12, 17-19

Brothers and sisters:
By faith Abraham obeyed when he was called
to go out to a place
that he was to receive as an inheritance;
he went out, not knowing where he was to
go.
By faith he received power to generate,
even though he was past the normal age
—and Sarah herself was sterile—
for he thought that the one who had made
the promise was trustworthy.
So it was that there came forth from one man,
himself as good as dead,
descendants as numerous as the stars in
the sky
and as countless as the sands on the
seashore.
By faith Abraham, when put to the test,
offered up Isaac,
and he who had received the promises was
ready to offer
his only son,
of whom it was said,
"Through Isaac descendants shall bear
your name."
He reasoned that God was able to raise even
from the dead,
and he received Isaac back as a symbol.

Solemnity of Mary, the Holy Mother of God, *January 1, 2021*

FIRST READING
Num 6:22-27

The Lord said to Moses:
"Speak to Aaron and his sons and tell them:
This is how you shall bless the Israelites.
Say to them:
The Lord bless you and keep you!
The Lord let his face shine upon
you, and be gracious to you!
The Lord look upon you kindly and
give you peace!
So shall they invoke my name upon the
Israelites,
and I will bless them."

RESPONSORIAL PSALM
Ps 67:2-3, 5, 6, 8

R̸. (2a) May God bless us in his mercy.

May God have pity on us and bless us;
may he let his face shine upon us.
So may your way be known upon earth;
among all nations, your salvation.

R̸. May God bless us in his mercy.

May the nations be glad and exult
because you rule the peoples in equity;
the nations on the earth you guide.

R̸. May God bless us in his mercy.

May the peoples praise you, O God;
may all the peoples praise you!
May God bless us,
and may all the ends of the earth fear him!

R̸. May God bless us in his mercy.

SECOND READING
Gal 4:4-7

Brothers and sisters:
When the fullness of time had come, God sent
his Son,
born of a woman, born under the law,
to ransom those under the law,
so that we might receive adoption as sons.
As proof that you are sons,
God sent the Spirit of his Son into our
hearts,
crying out, "Abba, Father!"
So you are no longer a slave but a son,
and if a son then also an heir, through God.

The Epiphany of the Lord, *January 3, 2021*

Gospel (cont.)
Matt 2:1-12; L20ABC

After their audience with the king they set out.
And behold, the star that they had seen at its rising preceded them,
    until it came and stopped over the place where the child was.
They were overjoyed at seeing the star,
    and on entering the house
      they saw the child with Mary his mother.
They prostrated themselves and did him homage.
Then they opened their treasures
    and offered him gifts of gold, frankincense, and myrrh.
And having been warned in a dream not to return to Herod,
    they departed for their country by another way.

The Baptism of the Lord, *January 10, 2021*

FIRST READING
Isa 55:1-11

Thus says the LORD:
All you who are thirsty,
    come to the water!
You who have no money,
    come, receive grain and eat;
come, without paying and without cost,
    drink wine and milk!
Why spend your money for what is not bread,
    your wages for what fails to satisfy?
Heed me, and you shall eat well,
    you shall delight in rich fare.
Come to me heedfully,
    listen, that you may have life.
I will renew with you the everlasting
      covenant,
    the benefits assured to David.
As I made him a witness to the peoples,
    a leader and commander of nations,
so shall you summon a nation you knew not,
    and nations that knew you not shall run
      to you,
because of the LORD, your God,
    the Holy One of Israel, who has glorified
      you.

Seek the LORD while he may be found,
    call him while he is near.
Let the scoundrel forsake his way,
    and the wicked man his thoughts;
let him turn to the LORD for mercy;
    to our God, who is generous in forgiving.
For my thoughts are not your thoughts,
    nor are your ways my ways, says the LORD.
As high as the heavens are above the earth
    so high are my ways above your ways
    and my thoughts above your thoughts.

For just as from the heavens
    the rain and snow come down
and do not return there
    till they have watered the earth,
    making it fertile and fruitful,
giving seed to the one who sows
    and bread to the one who eats,
so shall my word be
    that goes forth from my mouth;
my word shall not return to me void,
    but shall do my will,
    achieving the end for which I sent it.

RESPONSORIAL PSALM
Isa 12:2-3, 4bcd, 5-6

℟. (3) You will draw water joyfully from the
springs of salvation.

God indeed is my savior;
    I am confident and unafraid.
My strength and my courage is the LORD,
    and he has been my savior.
With joy you will draw water
    at the fountain of salvation.

℟. You will draw water joyfully from the
springs of salvation.

Give thanks to the LORD, acclaim his name;
    among the nations make known his deeds,
    proclaim how exalted is his name.

℟. You will draw water joyfully from the
springs of salvation.

Sing praise to the LORD for his glorious
      achievement;
    let this be known throughout all the earth.
Shout with exultation, O city of Zion,
    for great in your midst
    is the Holy One of Israel!

℟. You will draw water joyfully from the
springs of salvation.

SECOND READING
1 John 5:1-9

Beloved:
Everyone who believes that Jesus is the Christ
    is begotten by God,
    and everyone who loves the Father
    loves also the one begotten by him.
In this way we know that we love the children
    of God
    when we love God and obey his
      commandments.
For the love of God is this,
    that we keep his commandments.
And his commandments are not burdensome,
    for whoever is begotten by God conquers
      the world.
And the victory that conquers the world is
    our faith.
Who indeed is the victor over the world
    but the one who believes that Jesus is the
      Son of God?

This is the one who came through water and
    blood, Jesus Christ,
    not by water alone, but by water and
      blood.
The Spirit is the one who testifies,
    and the Spirit is truth.
So there are three that testify,
    the Spirit, the water, and the blood,
    and the three are of one accord.
If we accept human testimony,
    the testimony of God is surely greater.
Now the testimony of God is this,
    that he has testified on behalf of his Son.

Ash Wednesday, *February 17, 2021*

FIRST READING
Joel 2:12-18

Even now, says the LORD,
  return to me with your whole heart,
  with fasting, and weeping, and mourning;
Rend your hearts, not your garments,
  and return to the LORD, your God.
For gracious and merciful is he,
  slow to anger, rich in kindness,
  and relenting in punishment.
Perhaps he will again relent
  and leave behind him a blessing,
Offerings and libations
  for the LORD, your God.

Blow the trumpet in Zion!
  proclaim a fast,
  call an assembly;
Gather the people,
  notify the congregation;
Assemble the elders,
  gather the children
  and the infants at the breast;
Let the bridegroom quit his room
  and the bride her chamber.
Between the porch and the altar
  let the priests, the ministers of the LORD,
    weep,
And say, "Spare, O LORD, your people,
  and make not your heritage a reproach,
  with the nations ruling over them!
Why should they say among the peoples,
  'Where is their God?'"

Then the LORD was stirred to concern for his
    land
  and took pity on his people.

RESPONSORIAL PSALM
Ps 51:3-4, 5-6ab, 12-13, 14, and 17

R̸. (see 3a) Be merciful, O Lord, for we have
    sinned.

Have mercy on me, O God, in your goodness;
  in the greatness of your compassion wipe
    out my offense.
Thoroughly wash me from my guilt
  and of my sin cleanse me.

R̸. Be merciful, O Lord, for we have sinned.

For I acknowledge my offense,
  and my sin is before me always:
"Against you only have I sinned,
  and done what is evil in your sight."

R̸. Be merciful, O Lord, for we have sinned.

A clean heart create for me, O God,
  and a steadfast spirit renew within me.
Cast me not out from your presence,
  and your Holy Spirit take not from me.

R̸. Be merciful, O Lord, for we have sinned.

Give me back the joy of your salvation,
  and a willing spirit sustain in me.
O Lord, open my lips,
  and my mouth shall proclaim your praise.

R̸. Be merciful, O Lord, for we have sinned.

SECOND READING
2 Cor 5:20–6:2

Brothers and sisters:
We are ambassadors for Christ,
  as if God were appealing through us.
We implore you on behalf of Christ,
  be reconciled to God.
For our sake he made him to be sin who did
    not know sin,
  so that we might become the righteousness
    of God in him.

Working together, then,
  we appeal to you not to receive the grace of
    God in vain.
For he says:

In an acceptable time I heard you,
  and on the day of salvation I helped you.

Behold, now is a very acceptable time;
  behold, now is the day of salvation.

Third Sunday of Lent, *March 7, 2021*

Gospel (cont.)
John 2:13-25; L29B

But he was speaking about the temple of his body.
Therefore, when he was raised from the dead,
  his disciples remembered that he had said this,
  and they came to believe the Scripture
  and the word Jesus had spoken.

While he was in Jerusalem for the feast of Passover,
  many began to believe in his name
  when they saw the signs he was doing.
But Jesus would not trust himself to them because he knew them all,
  and did not need anyone to testify about human nature.
He himself understood it well.

RESPONSORIAL PSALM

Ps 19:8, 9, 10, 11

R℟. (John 6:68c) Lord, you have the words of
  everlasting life.

The law of the LORD is perfect,
  refreshing the soul;
the decree of the LORD is trustworthy,
  giving wisdom to the simple.

R℟. Lord, you have the words of everlasting life.

The precepts of the LORD are right,
  rejoicing the heart;
the command of the LORD is clear,
  enlightening the eye.

R℟. Lord, you have the words of everlasting life.

The fear of the LORD is pure,
  enduring forever;
the ordinances of the LORD are true,
  all of them just.

R℟. Lord, you have the words of everlasting life.

They are more precious than gold,
  than a heap of purest gold;
sweeter also than syrup
  or honey from the comb.

R℟. Lord, you have the words of everlasting life.

SECOND READING

1 Cor 1:22-25

Brothers and sisters:
Jews demand signs and Greeks look for
    wisdom,
  but we proclaim Christ crucified,
  a stumbling block to Jews and foolishness
    to Gentiles,
  but to those who are called, Jews and
    Greeks alike,
Christ the power of God and the wisdom
  of God.
For the foolishness of God is wiser than
  human wisdom,

and the weakness of God is stronger than
  human strength.

FIRST READING

Exod 17:3-7

In those days, in their thirst for water,
  the people grumbled against Moses,
  saying, "Why did you ever make us leave
    Egypt?
Was it just to have us die here of thirst
  with our children and our livestock?"
So Moses cried out to the LORD,
  "What shall I do with this people?
A little more and they will stone me!"
The LORD answered Moses,
  "Go over there in front of the people,
  along with some of the elders of Israel,
  holding in your hand, as you go,
  the staff with which you struck the river.
I will be standing there in front of you on the
    rock in Horeb.
Strike the rock, and the water will flow from it
  for the people to drink."
This Moses did, in the presence of the elders
  of Israel.
The place was called Massah and Meribah,
  because the Israelites quarreled there
  and tested the LORD, saying,
  "Is the LORD in our midst or not?"

RESPONSORIAL PSALM

Ps 95:1-2, 6-7, 8-9

R℟. (8) If today you hear his voice, harden not
  your hearts.

Come, let us sing joyfully to the LORD;
  let us acclaim the Rock of our salvation.
Let us come into his presence with
    thanksgiving;
  let us joyfully sing psalms to him.

R℟. If today you hear his voice, harden not
  your hearts.

Come, let us bow down in worship;
  let us kneel before the LORD who made us.
For he is our God,
  and we are the people he shepherds, the
    flock he guides.

R℟. If today you hear his voice, harden not
  your hearts.

Oh, that today you would hear his voice:
  "Harden not your hearts as at Meribah,
  as in the day of Massah in the desert,
Where your fathers tempted me;
  they tested me though they had seen my
    works."

R℟. If today you hear his voice, harden not
  your hearts.

SECOND READING

Rom 5:1-2, 5-8

Brothers and sisters:
Since we have been justified by faith,
  we have peace with God through our Lord
    Jesus Christ,
  through whom we have gained access by
    faith
  to this grace in which we stand,
  and we boast in hope of the glory of God.

And hope does not disappoint,
  because the love of God has been poured
    out into our hearts
  through the Holy Spirit who has been given
    to us.
For Christ, while we were still helpless,
  died at the appointed time for the ungodly.
Indeed, only with difficulty does one die for a
    just person,
  though perhaps for a good person one
    might even find courage to die.
But God proves his love for us
  in that while we were still sinners Christ
    died for us.

Gospel

John 4:5-42; L28A

Jesus came to a town of Samaria called Sychar,
  near the plot of land that Jacob had given to his son Joseph.
Jacob's well was there.
Jesus, tired from his journey, sat down there at the well.
It was about noon.

A woman of Samaria came to draw water.
Jesus said to her,
  "Give me a drink."
His disciples had gone into the town to buy food.
The Samaritan woman said to him,
  "How can you, a Jew, ask me, a Samaritan woman, for a drink?"
—For Jews use nothing in common with Samaritans.—
Jesus answered and said to her,

"If you knew the gift of God
and who is saying to you, 'Give me a drink,'
you would have asked him
and he would have given you living water."
The woman said to him,
  "Sir, you do not even have a bucket and the cistern is deep;
  where then can you get this living water?
Are you greater than our father Jacob,
  who gave us this cistern and drank from it himself
  with his children and his flocks?"
Jesus answered and said to her,
  "Everyone who drinks this water will be thirsty again;
  but whoever drinks the water I shall give will never thirst;

the water I shall give will become in him
a spring of water welling up to eternal life."
The woman said to him,
"Sir, give me this water, so that I may not be thirsty
or have to keep coming here to draw water."

Jesus said to her,
"Go call your husband and come back."
The woman answered and said to him,
"I do not have a husband."
Jesus answered her,
"You are right in saying, 'I do not have a husband.'
For you have had five husbands,
and the one you have now is not your husband.
What you have said is true."
The woman said to him,
"Sir, I can see that you are a prophet.
Our ancestors worshiped on this mountain;
but you people say that the place to worship is in Jerusalem."
Jesus said to her,
"Believe me, woman, the hour is coming
when you will worship the Father
neither on this mountain nor in Jerusalem.
You people worship what you do not understand;
we worship what we understand,
because salvation is from the Jews.
But the hour is coming, and is now here,
when true worshipers will worship the Father in Spirit and truth;
and indeed the Father seeks such people to worship him.
God is Spirit, and those who worship him
must worship in Spirit and truth."
The woman said to him,
"I know that the Messiah is coming, the one called the Christ;
when he comes, he will tell us everything."
Jesus said to her,
"I am he, the one speaking with you."

At that moment his disciples returned,
and were amazed that he was talking with a woman,
but still no one said, "What are you looking for?"
or "Why are you talking with her?"
The woman left her water jar
and went into the town and said to the people,
"Come see a man who told me everything I have done.
Could he possibly be the Christ?"
They went out of the town and came to him.
Meanwhile, the disciples urged him, "Rabbi, eat."
But he said to them,
"I have food to eat of which you do not know."
So the disciples said to one another,
"Could someone have brought him something to eat?"
Jesus said to them,
"My food is to do the will of the one who sent me
and to finish his work.
Do you not say, 'In four months the harvest will be here'?
I tell you, look up and see the fields ripe for the harvest.
The reaper is already receiving payment
and gathering crops for eternal life,
so that the sower and reaper can rejoice together.
For here the saying is verified that 'One sows and another reaps.'
I sent you to reap what you have not worked for;
others have done the work,

and you are sharing the fruits of their work."

Many of the Samaritans of that town began to believe in him
because of the word of the woman who testified,
"He told me everything I have done."
When the Samaritans came to him,
they invited him to stay with them;
and he stayed there two days.
Many more began to believe in him because of his word,
and they said to the woman,
"We no longer believe because of your word;
for we have heard for ourselves,
and we know that this is truly the savior of the world."

or
John 4:5-15, 19b-26, 39a, 40-42; L28A

Jesus came to a town of Samaria called Sychar,
near the plot of land that Jacob had given to his son Joseph.
Jacob's well was there.
Jesus, tired from his journey, sat down there at the well.
It was about noon.

A woman of Samaria came to draw water.
Jesus said to her,
"Give me a drink."
His disciples had gone into the town to buy food.
The Samaritan woman said to him,
"How can you, a Jew, ask me, a Samaritan woman, for a drink?"
—For Jews use nothing in common with Samaritans.—
Jesus answered and said to her,
"If you knew the gift of God
and who is saying to you, 'Give me a drink,'
you would have asked him
and he would have given you living water."
The woman said to him,
"Sir, you do not even have a bucket and the cistern is deep;
where then can you get this living water?
Are you greater than our father Jacob,
who gave us this cistern and drank from it himself
with his children and his flocks?"
Jesus answered and said to her,
"Everyone who drinks this water will be thirsty again;
but whoever drinks the water I shall give will never thirst;
the water I shall give will become in him
a spring of water welling up to eternal life."
The woman said to him,
"Sir, give me this water, so that I may not be thirsty
or have to keep coming here to draw water.

"I can see that you are a prophet.
Our ancestors worshiped on this mountain;
but you people say that the place to worship is in Jerusalem."
Jesus said to her,
"Believe me, woman, the hour is coming
when you will worship the Father
neither on this mountain nor in Jerusalem.
You people worship what you do not understand;
we worship what we understand,
because salvation is from the Jews.
But the hour is coming, and is now here,
when true worshipers will worship the Father in Spirit and truth;
and indeed the Father seeks such people to worship him.

Gospel (cont.)
John 4:5-42; L28A

God is Spirit, and those who worship him
    must worship in Spirit and truth."
The woman said to him,
    "I know that the Messiah is coming, the one called the Christ;
    when he comes, he will tell us everything."
Jesus said to her,
    "I am he, the one who is speaking with you."

Many of the Samaritans of that town began to believe in him.
When the Samaritans came to him,
    they invited him to stay with them;
    and he stayed there two days.
Many more began to believe in him because of his word,
    and they said to the woman,
    "We no longer believe because of your word;
    for we have heard for ourselves,
    and we know that this is truly the savior of the world."

SECOND READING
Eph 2:4-10

Brothers and sisters:
God, who is rich in mercy,
    because of the great love he had for us,
    even when we were dead in our
        transgressions,
    brought us to life with Christ—by grace
        you have been saved—,
    raised us up with him,
    and seated us with him in the heavens in
        Christ Jesus,
    that in the ages to come
he might show the immeasurable riches of
    his grace
    in his kindness to us in Christ Jesus.
For by grace you have been saved through
    faith,
    and this is not from you; it is the gift of
        God;
    it is not from works, so no one may boast.
For we are his handiwork, created in Christ
    Jesus for the good works
    that God has prepared in advance,
    that we should live in them.

FIRST READING
1 Sam 16:1b, 6-7, 10-13a

The Lord said to Samuel:
    "Fill your horn with oil, and be on your
        way.
I am sending you to Jesse of Bethlehem,
    for I have chosen my king from among his
        sons."

As Jesse and his sons came to the sacrifice,
    Samuel looked at Eliab and thought,
    "Surely the Lord's anointed is here before
        him."
But the Lord said to Samuel:
    "Do not judge from his appearance or from
        his lofty stature,
    because I have rejected him.

Not as man sees does God see,
    because man sees the appearance
    but the Lord looks into the heart."
In the same way Jesse presented seven sons
        before Samuel,
    but Samuel said to Jesse,
    "The Lord has not chosen any one of
        these."
Then Samuel asked Jesse,
    "Are these all the sons you have?"
Jesse replied,
    "There is still the youngest, who is tending
        the sheep."
Samuel said to Jesse,
    "Send for him;
    we will not begin the sacrificial banquet
        until he arrives here."
Jesse sent and had the young man brought to
        them.
He was ruddy, a youth handsome to behold
    and making a splendid appearance.
The Lord said,
    "There—anoint him, for this is the one!"
Then Samuel, with the horn of oil in hand,
    anointed David in the presence of his
        brothers;
    and from that day on, the spirit of the Lord
        rushed upon David.

RESPONSORIAL PSALM
Ps 23:1-3a, 3b-4, 5, 6

R⁄. (1) The Lord is my shepherd; there is
    nothing I shall want.

The Lord is my shepherd; I shall not want.
    In verdant pastures he gives me repose;
beside restful waters he leads me;
    he refreshes my soul.

R⁄. The Lord is my shepherd; there is nothing
    I shall want.

He guides me in right paths
    for his name's sake.

Even though I walk in the dark valley
    I fear no evil; for you are at my side
with your rod and your staff
    that give me courage.

R⁄. The Lord is my shepherd; there is nothing
    I shall want.

You spread the table before me
    in the sight of my foes;
you anoint my head with oil;
    my cup overflows.

R⁄. The Lord is my shepherd; there is nothing
    I shall want.

Only goodness and kindness follow me
    all the days of my life;
and I shall dwell in the house of the Lord
    for years to come.

R⁄. The Lord is my shepherd; there is nothing
    I shall want.

SECOND READING
Eph 5:8-14

Brothers and sisters:
You were once darkness,
    but now you are light in the Lord.
Live as children of light,
    for light produces every kind of goodness
    and righteousness and truth.
Try to learn what is pleasing to the Lord.
Take no part in the fruitless works of
        darkness;
    rather expose them, for it is shameful even
        to mention
    the things done by them in secret;
    but everything exposed by the light
        becomes visible,
    for everything that becomes visible is light.
Therefore, it says:
    "Awake, O sleeper,
    and arise from the dead,
    and Christ will give you light."

Gospel

John 9:1-41; L31A

As Jesus passed by he saw a man blind from birth.
His disciples asked him,
"Rabbi, who sinned, this man or his parents,
that he was born blind?"
Jesus answered,
"Neither he nor his parents sinned;
it is so that the works of God might be made visible through him.
We have to do the works of the one who sent me while it is day.
Night is coming when no one can work.
While I am in the world, I am the light of the world."
When he had said this, he spat on the ground
and made clay with the saliva,
and smeared the clay on his eyes, and said to him,
"Go wash in the Pool of Siloam"—which means Sent—.
So he went and washed, and came back able to see.

His neighbors and those who had seen him earlier as a beggar said,
"Isn't this the one who used to sit and beg?"
Some said, "It is,"
but others said, "No, he just looks like him."
He said, "I am."
So they said to him, "How were your eyes opened?"
He replied,
"The man called Jesus made clay and anointed my eyes
and told me, 'Go to Siloam and wash.'
So I went there and washed and was able to see."
And they said to him, "Where is he?"
He said, "I don't know."

They brought the one who was once blind to the Pharisees.
Now Jesus had made clay and opened his eyes on a sabbath.
So then the Pharisees also asked him how he was able to see.
He said to them,
"He put clay on my eyes, and I washed, and now I can see."
So some of the Pharisees said,
"This man is not from God,
because he does not keep the sabbath."
But others said,
"How can a sinful man do such signs?"
And there was a division among them.
So they said to the blind man again,
"What do you have to say about him,
since he opened your eyes?"
He said, "He is a prophet."

Now the Jews did not believe
that he had been blind and gained his sight
until they summoned the parents of the one who had gained his
sight.
They asked them,
"Is this your son, who you say was born blind?
How does he now see?"
His parents answered and said,
"We know that this is our son and that he was born blind.
We do not know how he sees now,
nor do we know who opened his eyes.
Ask him, he is of age;
he can speak for himself."

His parents said this because they were afraid of the Jews,
for the Jews had already agreed
that if anyone acknowledged him as the Christ,
he would be expelled from the synagogue.
For this reason his parents said,
"He is of age; question him."

So a second time they called the man who had been blind
and said to him, "Give God the praise!
We know that this man is a sinner."
He replied,
"If he is a sinner, I do not know.
One thing I do know is that I was blind and now I see."
So they said to him,
"What did he do to you?
How did he open your eyes?"
He answered them,
"I told you already and you did not listen.
Why do you want to hear it again?
Do you want to become his disciples, too?"
They ridiculed him and said,
"You are that man's disciple;
we are disciples of Moses!
We know that God spoke to Moses,
but we do not know where this one is from."
The man answered and said to them,
"This is what is so amazing,
that you do not know where he is from, yet he opened my eyes.
We know that God does not listen to sinners,
but if one is devout and does his will, he listens to him.
It is unheard of that anyone ever opened the eyes of a person born
blind.
If this man were not from God,
he would not be able to do anything."
They answered and said to him,
"You were born totally in sin,
and are you trying to teach us?"
Then they threw him out.

When Jesus heard that they had thrown him out,
he found him and said, "Do you believe in the Son of Man?"
He answered and said,
"Who is he, sir, that I may believe in him?"
Jesus said to him,
"You have seen him,
and the one speaking with you is he."
He said,
"I do believe, Lord," and he worshiped him.
Then Jesus said,
"I came into this world for judgment,
so that those who do not see might see,
and those who do see might become blind."

Some of the Pharisees who were with him heard this
and said to him, "Surely we are not also blind, are we?"
Jesus said to them,
"If you were blind, you would have no sin;
but now you are saying, 'We see,' so your sin remains."

Fourth Sunday of Lent, *March 14, 2021*

Gospel (cont.)

or
John 9:1, 6-9, 13-17, 34-38; L31A

As Jesus passed by he saw a man blind from birth.
He spat on the ground and made clay with the saliva,
    and smeared the clay on his eyes, and said to him,
    "Go wash in the Pool of Siloam"—which means Sent—.
So he went and washed, and came back able to see.

His neighbors and those who had seen him earlier as a beggar said,
    "Isn't this the one who used to sit and beg?"
Some said, "It is,"
    but others said, "No, he just looks like him."
He said, "I am."

They brought the one who was once blind to the Pharisees.
Now Jesus had made clay and opened his eyes on a sabbath.
So then the Pharisees also asked him how he was able to see.
He said to them,
    "He put clay on my eyes, and I washed, and now I can see."
So some of the Pharisees said,
    "This man is not from God,
    because he does not keep the sabbath."

But others said,
    "How can a sinful man do such signs?"
And there was a division among them.
So they said to the blind man again,
    "What do you have to say about him,
    since he opened your eyes?"
He said, "He is a prophet."

They answered and said to him,
    "You were born totally in sin,
    and are you trying to teach us?"
Then they threw him out.

When Jesus heard that they had thrown him out,
    he found him and said, "Do you believe in the Son of Man?"
He answered and said,
    "Who is he, sir, that I may believe in him?"
Jesus said to him,
    "You have seen him,
    and the one speaking with you is he."
He said,
    "I do believe, Lord," and he worshiped him.

Saint Joseph, Spouse of the Blessed Virgin Mary, *March 19, 2021*

Gospel
Matt 1:16, 18-21, 24a; L543

Jacob was the father of Joseph, the husband of Mary.
Of her was born Jesus who is called the Christ.

Now this is how the birth of Jesus Christ came about.
When his mother Mary was betrothed to Joseph,
    but before they lived together,
    she was found with child through the Holy Spirit.
Joseph her husband, since he was a righteous man,
    yet unwilling to expose her to shame,
    decided to divorce her quietly.
Such was his intention when, behold,
    the angel of the Lord appeared to him in a dream and said,
    "Joseph, son of David,
    do not be afraid to take Mary your wife into your home.
For it is through the Holy Spirit
    that this child has been conceived in her.
She will bear a son and you are to name him Jesus,
    because he will save his people from their sins."
When Joseph awoke,
    he did as the angel of the Lord had commanded him
    and took his wife into his home.

FIRST READING
2 Sam 7:4-5a, 12-14a, 16

The LORD spoke to Nathan and said:
"Go, tell my servant David,
    'When your time comes and you rest with
        your ancestors,
    I will raise up your heir after you, sprung
        from your loins,
    and I will make his kingdom firm.
It is he who shall build a house for my name.
And I will make his royal throne firm forever.
I will be a father to him,
    and he shall be a son to me.
Your house and your kingdom shall endure
        forever before me;
    your throne shall stand firm forever.'"

Saint Joseph, Spouse of the Blessed Virgin Mary, *March 19, 2021*

RESPONSORIAL PSALM
Ps 89:2-3, 4-5, 27 and 29

R⁷. (37) The son of David will live for ever.

The promises of the LORD I will sing forever,
  through all generations my mouth will
    proclaim your faithfulness,
For you have said, "My kindness is
    established forever";
  in heaven you have confirmed your
    faithfulness.

R⁷. The son of David will live for ever.

"I have made a covenant with my chosen one;
  I have sworn to David my servant:
Forever will I confirm your posterity
  and establish your throne for all
    generations."

R⁷. The son of David will live for ever.

"He shall say of me, 'You are my father,
  my God, the Rock, my savior.'
Forever I will maintain my kindness toward
    him,
  and my covenant with him stands firm."

R⁷. The son of David will live for ever.

SECOND READING
Rom 4:13, 16-18, 22

Brothers and sisters:
It was not through the law
  that the promise was made to Abraham
    and his descendants
  that he would inherit the world,
  but through the righteousness that comes
    from faith.
For this reason, it depends on faith,
  so that it may be a gift,
and the promise may be guaranteed to all
    his descendants,
  not to those who only adhere to the law
  but to those who follow the faith of
    Abraham,
  who is the father of all of us, as it is
    written,
  I have made you father of many nations.
He is our father in the sight of God,
  in whom he believed, who gives life to the
    dead
  and calls into being what does not exist.
He believed, hoping against hope,
  that he would become *the father of many
    nations,*
  according to what was said, *Thus shall your
    descendants be.*
That is why *it was credited to him as
    righteousness.*

Fifth Sunday of Lent, *March 21, 2021*

Gospel (cont.)
John 12:20-33; L35B

The crowd there heard it and said it was thunder;
  but others said, "An angel has spoken to him."
Jesus answered and said,
  "This voice did not come for my sake but for yours.
Now is the time of judgment on this world;
  now the ruler of this world will be driven out.
And when I am lifted up from the earth,
  I will draw everyone to myself."
He said this indicating the kind of death he would die.

FIRST READING
Ezek 37:12-14

Thus says the Lord GOD:
  O my people, I will open your graves
  and have you rise from them,
  and bring you back to the land of Israel.
Then you shall know that I am the LORD,
  when I open your graves and have you rise
    from them,
  O my people!
I will put my spirit in you that you may live,
  and I will settle you upon your land;
  thus you shall know that I am the LORD.
I have promised, and I will do it, says the
  LORD.

RESPONSORIAL PSALM
Ps 130:1-2, 3-4, 5-6, 7-8

R̷. (7) With the Lord there is mercy and
    fullness of redemption.

Out of the depths I cry to you, O LORD;
    LORD, hear my voice!
Let your ears be attentive
    to my voice in supplication.

R̷. With the Lord there is mercy and fullness
    of redemption.

If you, O LORD, mark iniquities,
    LORD, who can stand?
But with you is forgiveness,
    that you may be revered.

R̷. With the Lord there is mercy and fullness
    of redemption.

I trust in the LORD;
    my soul trusts in his word.
More than sentinels wait for the dawn,
    let Israel wait for the LORD.

R̷. With the Lord there is mercy and fullness
    of redemption.

For with the LORD is kindness
    and with him is plenteous redemption;
and he will redeem Israel
    from all their iniquities.

R̷. With the Lord there is mercy and fullness
    of redemption.

SECOND READING
Rom 8:8-11

Brothers and sisters:
Those who are in the flesh cannot please God.
But you are not in the flesh;
    on the contrary, you are in the spirit,
    if only the Spirit of God dwells in you.
Whoever does not have the Spirit of Christ
    does not belong to him.
But if Christ is in you,
    although the body is dead because of sin,
    the spirit is alive because of righteousness.
If the Spirit of the One who raised Jesus from
    the dead dwells in you,
    the One who raised Christ from the dead
    will give life to your mortal bodies also,
    through his Spirit dwelling in you.

Gospel
John 11:1-45; L34A

Now a man was ill, Lazarus from Bethany,
    the village of Mary and her sister Martha.
Mary was the one who had anointed the Lord with perfumed oil
    and dried his feet with her hair;
    it was her brother Lazarus who was ill.
So the sisters sent word to Jesus saying,
    "Master, the one you love is ill."
When Jesus heard this he said,
    "This illness is not to end in death,
    but is for the glory of God,
    that the Son of God may be glorified through it."
Now Jesus loved Martha and her sister and Lazarus.
So when he heard that he was ill,
    he remained for two days in the place where he was.
Then after this he said to his disciples,
    "Let us go back to Judea."
The disciples said to him,
    "Rabbi, the Jews were just trying to stone you,
    and you want to go back there?"
Jesus answered,
    "Are there not twelve hours in a day?
If one walks during the day, he does not stumble,
    because he sees the light of this world
But if one walks at night, he stumbles,
    because the light is not in him."
He said this, and then told them,
    "Our friend Lazarus is asleep,
    but I am going to awaken him."
So the disciples said to him,
    "Master, if he is asleep, he will be saved."
But Jesus was talking about his death,
    while they thought that he meant ordinary sleep.
So then Jesus said to them clearly,
    "Lazarus has died.
And I am glad for you that I was not there,
    that you may believe.
Let us go to him."

So Thomas, called Didymus, said to his fellow disciples,
    "Let us also go to die with him."

When Jesus arrived, he found that Lazarus
    had already been in the tomb for four days.
Now Bethany was near Jerusalem, only about two miles away.
And many of the Jews had come to Martha and Mary
    to comfort them about their brother.
When Martha heard that Jesus was coming,
    she went to meet him;
    but Mary sat at home.
Martha said to Jesus,
    "Lord, if you had been here,
    my brother would not have died.
But even now I know that whatever you ask of God,
    God will give you."
Jesus said to her,
    "Your brother will rise."
Martha said to him,
    "I know he will rise,
    in the resurrection on the last day."
Jesus told her,
    "I am the resurrection and the life;
    whoever believes in me, even if he dies, will live,
    and everyone who lives and believes in me will never die.
Do you believe this?"
She said to him, "Yes, Lord.
I have come to believe that you are the Christ, the Son of God,
    the one who is coming into the world."

When she had said this,
    she went and called her sister Mary secretly, saying,
    "The teacher is here and is asking for you."
As soon as she heard this,
    she rose quickly and went to him.
For Jesus had not yet come into the village,
    but was still where Martha had met him.
So when the Jews who were with her in the house comforting her
    saw Mary get up quickly and go out,

they followed her,
  presuming that she was going to the tomb to weep there.
When Mary came to where Jesus was and saw him,
  she fell at his feet and said to him,
    "Lord, if you had been here,
    my brother would not have died."
When Jesus saw her weeping and the Jews who had come with her
      weeping,
  he became perturbed and deeply troubled, and said,
    "Where have you laid him?"
They said to him, "Sir, come and see."
And Jesus wept.
So the Jews said, "See how he loved him."
But some of them said,
    "Could not the one who opened the eyes of the blind man
    have done something so that this man would not have died?"

So Jesus, perturbed again, came to the tomb.
It was a cave, and a stone lay across it.
Jesus said, "Take away the stone."
Martha, the dead man's sister, said to him,
    "Lord, by now there will be a stench;
    he has been dead for four days."
Jesus said to her,
    "Did I not tell you that if you believe
    you will see the glory of God?"
So they took away the stone.
And Jesus raised his eyes and said,
    "Father, I thank you for hearing me.
I know that you always hear me;
    but because of the crowd here I have said this,
    that they may believe that you sent me."
And when he had said this,
    he cried out in a loud voice,
    "Lazarus, come out!"
The dead man came out,
    tied hand and foot with burial bands,
    and his face was wrapped in a cloth.
So Jesus said to them,
    "Untie him and let him go."

Now many of the Jews who had come to Mary
  and seen what he had done began to believe in him.

Gospel
John 11:3-7, 17, 20-27, 33b-45; L34A

The sisters of Lazarus sent word to Jesus saying,
  "Master, the one you love is ill."
When Jesus heard this he said,
  "This illness is not to end in death,
  but is for the glory of God,
  that the Son of God may be glorified through it."
Now Jesus loved Martha and her sister and Lazarus.
So when he heard that he was ill,
  he remained for two days in the place where he was.
Then after this he said to his disciples,
  "Let us go back to Judea."

When Jesus arrived, he found that Lazarus
  had already been in the tomb for four days.

When Martha heard that Jesus was coming,
  she went to meet him;
  but Mary sat at home.
Martha said to Jesus,
  "Lord, if you had been here,
  my brother would not have died.
But even now I know that whatever you ask of God,
  God will give you."
Jesus said to her,
  "Your brother will rise."
Martha said,
  "I know he will rise,
  in the resurrection on the last day."
Jesus told her,
  "I am the resurrection and the life;
  whoever believes in me, even if he dies, will live,
  and everyone who lives and believes in me will never die.
Do you believe this?"
She said to him, "Yes, Lord.
I have come to believe that you are the Christ, the Son of God,
  the one who is coming into the world."

He became perturbed and deeply troubled, and said,
  "Where have you laid him?"
They said to him, "Sir, come and see."
And Jesus wept.
So the Jews said, "See how he loved him."
But some of them said,
  "Could not the one who opened the eyes of the blind man
  have done something so that this man would not have died?"

So Jesus, perturbed again, came to the tomb.
It was a cave, and a stone lay across it.
Jesus said, "Take away the stone."
Martha, the dead man's sister, said to him,
  "Lord, by now there will be a stench;
  he has been dead for four days."
Jesus said to her,
  "Did I not tell you that if you believe
  you will see the glory of God?"
So they took away the stone.
And Jesus raised his eyes and said,
  "Father, I thank you for hearing me.
I know that you always hear me;
  but because of the crowd here I have said this,
  that they may believe that you sent me."
And when he had said this,
  he cried out in a loud voice,
  "Lazarus, come out!"
The dead man came out,
  tied hand and foot with burial bands,
  and his face was wrapped in a cloth.
So Jesus said to them,
  "Untie him and let him go."

Now many of the Jews who had come to Mary
  and seen what he had done began to believe in him.

The Annunciation of the Lord, *March 25, 2021*

FIRST READING
Isa 7:10-14; 8:10

The LORD spoke to Ahaz, saying:
Ask for a sign from the LORD, your God;
    let it be deep as the nether world, or high as
        the sky!
But Ahaz answered,
  "I will not ask! I will not tempt the LORD!"
Then Isaiah said:
    Listen, O house of David!
Is it not enough for you to weary people,
    must you also weary my God?
Therefore the Lord himself will give you this
        sign:
    the virgin shall be with child, and bear a
        son,
    and shall name him Emmanuel,
    which means "God is with us!"

RESPONSORIAL PSALM
Ps 40:7-8a, 8b-9, 10, 11

R̸. (8a and 9a) Here I am, Lord; I come to do
    your will.

Sacrifice or offering you wished not,
    but ears open to obedience you gave me.
Holocausts and sin-offerings you sought not;
    then said I, "Behold, I come."

R̸. Here I am, Lord; I come to do your will.

"In the written scroll it is prescribed for me,
To do your will, O God, is my delight,
    and your law is within my heart!"

R̸. Here I am, Lord; I come to do your will.

I announced your justice in the vast assembly;
    I did not restrain my lips, as you, O LORD,
    know.

R̸. Here I am, Lord; I come to do your will.

Your justice I kept not hid within my heart;
    your faithfulness and your salvation I have
    spoken of;
I have made no secret of your kindness and
    your truth
    in the vast assembly.

R̸. Here I am, Lord; I come to do your will.

SECOND READING
Heb 10:4-10

Brothers and sisters:
It is impossible that the blood of bulls and
    goats
    takes away sins.
For this reason, when Christ came into the
    world, he said:

    "Sacrifice and offering you did not desire,
        but a body you prepared for me;
    in holocausts and sin offerings you took no
        delight.
    Then I said, 'As is written of me in the
        scroll,
    behold, I come to do your will, O God.'"

First Christ says, "Sacrifices and offerings,
    holocausts and sin offerings,
    you neither desired nor delighted in."
These are offered according to the law.
Then he says, "Behold, I come to do your will."
He takes away the first to establish the second.
By this "will," we have been consecrated
    through the offering of the Body of Jesus
        Christ once for all.

Palm Sunday of the Lord's Passion, *March 28, 2021*

Gospel (cont.) at the procession with palms

Some of the bystanders said to them,
  "What are you doing, untying the colt?"
They answered them just as Jesus had told them to,
  and they permitted them to do it.
So they brought the colt to Jesus
  and put their cloaks over it.
And he sat on it.
Many people spread their cloaks on the road,
  and others spread leafy branches
  that they had cut from the fields.
Those preceding him as well as those following kept crying out:
  "Hosanna!
    Blessed is he who comes in the name of the Lord!
    Blessed is the kingdom of our father David that is to come!
  Hosanna in the highest!"

Gospel at Mass
Mark 14:1–15:47; L38B

The Passover and the Feast of Unleavened Bread
  were to take place in two days' time.
So the chief priests and the scribes were seeking a way
  to arrest him by treachery and put him to death.
They said, "Not during the festival,
  for fear that there may be a riot among the people."

When he was in Bethany reclining at table
  in the house of Simon the leper,
  a woman came with an alabaster jar of perfumed oil,
  costly genuine spikenard.
She broke the alabaster jar and poured it on his head.
There were some who were indignant.
"Why has there been this waste of perfumed oil?
It could have been sold for more than three hundred days' wages
  and the money given to the poor."
They were infuriated with her.
Jesus said, "Let her alone.
Why do you make trouble for her?
She has done a good thing for me.
The poor you will always have with you,
  and whenever you wish you can do good to them,
  but you will not always have me.
She has done what she could.
She has anticipated anointing my body for burial.
Amen, I say to you,
  wherever the gospel is proclaimed to the whole world,
  what she has done will be told in memory of her."

Then Judas Iscariot, one of the Twelve,
  went off to the chief priests to hand him over to them.
When they heard him they were pleased and promised to pay him money.
Then he looked for an opportunity to hand him over.

On the first day of the Feast of Unleavened Bread,
  when they sacrificed the Passover lamb,

his disciples said to him,
"Where do you want us to go
and prepare for you to eat the Passover?"
He sent two of his disciples and said to them,
"Go into the city and a man will meet you,
carrying a jar of water.
Follow him.
Wherever he enters, say to the master of the house,
'The Teacher says, "Where is my guest room
where I may eat the Passover with my disciples?"'
Then he will show you a large upper room furnished and ready.
Make the preparations for us there."
The disciples then went off, entered the city,
and found it just as he had told them;
and they prepared the Passover.

When it was evening, he came with the Twelve.
And as they reclined at table and were eating, Jesus said,
"Amen, I say to you, one of you will betray me,
one who is eating with me."
They began to be distressed and to say to him, one by one,
"Surely it is not I?"
He said to them,
"One of the Twelve, the one who dips with me into the dish.
For the Son of Man indeed goes, as it is written of him,
but woe to that man by whom the Son of Man is betrayed.
It would be better for that man if he had never been born."

While they were eating,
he took bread, said the blessing,
broke it, and gave it to them, and said,
"Take it; this is my body."
Then he took a cup, gave thanks, and gave it to them,
and they all drank from it.
He said to them,
"This is my blood of the covenant,
which will be shed for many.
Amen, I say to you,
I shall not drink again the fruit of the vine
until the day when I drink it new in the kingdom of God."
Then, after singing a hymn,
they went out to the Mount of Olives.

Then Jesus said to them,
"All of you will have your faith shaken, for it is written:
I will strike the shepherd,
and the sheep will be dispersed.
But after I have been raised up,
I shall go before you to Galilee."
Peter said to him,
"Even though all should have their faith shaken,
mine will not be."
Then Jesus said to him,
"Amen, I say to you,
this very night before the cock crows twice
you will deny me three times."
But he vehemently replied,
"Even though I should have to die with you,
I will not deny you."
And they all spoke similarly.

Then they came to a place named Gethsemane,
and he said to his disciples,

"Sit here while I pray."
He took with him Peter, James, and John,
and began to be troubled and distressed.
Then he said to them, "My soul is sorrowful even to death.
Remain here and keep watch."
He advanced a little and fell to the ground and prayed
that if it were possible the hour might pass by him;
he said, "Abba, Father, all things are possible to you.
Take this cup away from me,
but not what I will but what you will."
When he returned he found them asleep.
He said to Peter, "Simon, are you asleep?
Could you not keep watch for one hour?
Watch and pray that you may not undergo the test.
The spirit is willing but the flesh is weak."
Withdrawing again, he prayed, saying the same thing.
Then he returned once more and found them asleep,
for they could not keep their eyes open
and did not know what to answer him.
He returned a third time and said to them,
"Are you still sleeping and taking your rest?
It is enough. The hour has come.
Behold, the Son of Man is to be handed over to sinners.
Get up, let us go.
See, my betrayer is at hand."

Then, while he was still speaking,
Judas, one of the Twelve, arrived,
accompanied by a crowd with swords and clubs
who had come from the chief priests,
the scribes, and the elders.
His betrayer had arranged a signal with them, saying,
"The man I shall kiss is the one;
arrest him and lead him away securely."
He came and immediately went over to him and said,
"Rabbi." And he kissed him.
At this they laid hands on him and arrested him.
One of the bystanders drew his sword,
struck the high priest's servant, and cut off his ear.
Jesus said to them in reply,
"Have you come out as against a robber,
with swords and clubs, to seize me?
Day after day I was with you teaching in the temple area,
yet you did not arrest me;
but that the Scriptures may be fulfilled."
And they all left him and fled.
Now a young man followed him
wearing nothing but a linen cloth about his body.
They seized him,
but he left the cloth behind and ran off naked.

They led Jesus away to the high priest,
and all the chief priests and the elders and the scribes came together.
Peter followed him at a distance into the high priest's courtyard
and was seated with the guards, warming himself at the fire.
The chief priests and the entire Sanhedrin
kept trying to obtain testimony against Jesus
in order to put him to death, but they found none.
Many gave false witness against him,
but their testimony did not agree.
Some took the stand and testified falsely against him,

alleging, "We heard him say,
'I will destroy this temple made with hands
and within three days I will build another
not made with hands.'"
Even so their testimony did not agree.
The high priest rose before the assembly and questioned Jesus,
saying, "Have you no answer?
What are these men testifying against you?"
But he was silent and answered nothing.
Again the high priest asked him and said to him,
"Are you the Christ, the son of the Blessed One?"
Then Jesus answered, "I am;
and 'you will see the Son of Man
seated at the right hand of the Power
and coming with the clouds of heaven.'"
At that the high priest tore his garments and said,
"What further need have we of witnesses?
You have heard the blasphemy.
What do you think?"
They all condemned him as deserving to die.
Some began to spit on him.
They blindfolded him and struck him and said to him, "Prophesy!"
And the guards greeted him with blows.

While Peter was below in the courtyard,
one of the high priest's maids came along.
Seeing Peter warming himself,
she looked intently at him and said,
"You too were with the Nazarene, Jesus."
But he denied it saying,
"I neither know nor understand what you are talking about."
So he went out into the outer court.
Then the cock crowed.
The maid saw him and began again to say to the bystanders,
"This man is one of them."
Once again he denied it.
A little later the bystanders said to Peter once more,
"Surely you are one of them; for you too are a Galilean."
He began to curse and to swear,
"I do not know this man about whom you are talking."
And immediately a cock crowed a second time.
Then Peter remembered the word that Jesus had said to him,
"Before the cock crows twice you will deny me three times."
He broke down and wept.

As soon as morning came,
the chief priests with the elders and the scribes,
that is, the whole Sanhedrin, held a council.
They bound Jesus, led him away, and handed him over to Pilate.
Pilate questioned him,
"Are you the king of the Jews?"
He said to him in reply, "You say so."
The chief priests accused him of many things.
Again Pilate questioned him,
"Have you no answer?
See how many things they accuse you of."
Jesus gave him no further answer, so that Pilate was amazed.

Now on the occasion of the feast he used to release to them
one prisoner whom they requested.
A man called Barabbas was then in prison
along with the rebels who had committed murder in a rebellion.

The crowd came forward and began to ask him
to do for them as he was accustomed.
Pilate answered,
"Do you want me to release to you the king of the Jews?"
For he knew that it was out of envy
that the chief priests had handed him over.
But the chief priests stirred up the crowd
to have him release Barabbas for them instead.
Pilate again said to them in reply,
"Then what do you want me to do
with the man you call the king of the Jews?"
They shouted again, "Crucify him."
Pilate said to them, "Why? What evil has he done?"
They only shouted the louder, "Crucify him."
So Pilate, wishing to satisfy the crowd,
released Barabbas to them and, after he had Jesus scourged,
handed him over to be crucified.

The soldiers led him away inside the palace,
that is, the praetorium, and assembled the whole cohort.
They clothed him in purple and,
weaving a crown of thorns, placed it on him.
They began to salute him with, "Hail, King of the Jews!"
and kept striking his head with a reed and spitting upon him.
They knelt before him in homage.
And when they had mocked him,
they stripped him of the purple cloak,
dressed him in his own clothes,
and led him out to crucify him.

They pressed into service a passer-by, Simon,
a Cyrenian, who was coming in from the country,
the father of Alexander and Rufus,
to carry his cross.

They brought him to the place of Golgotha
—which is translated Place of the Skull—.
They gave him wine drugged with myrrh,
but he did not take it.
Then they crucified him and divided his garments
by casting lots for them to see what each should take.
It was nine o'clock in the morning when they crucified him.
The inscription of the charge against him read,
"The King of the Jews."
With him they crucified two revolutionaries,
one on his right and one on his left.
Those passing by reviled him,
shaking their heads and saying,
"Aha! You who would destroy the temple
and rebuild it in three days,
save yourself by coming down from the cross."
Likewise the chief priests, with the scribes,
mocked him among themselves and said,
"He saved others; he cannot save himself.
Let the Christ, the King of Israel,
come down now from the cross
that we may see and believe."
Those who were crucified with him also kept abusing him.

At noon darkness came over the whole land
until three in the afternoon.
And at three o'clock Jesus cried out in a loud voice,
"Eloi, Eloi, lema sabachthani?"

which is translated,
"My God, my God, why have you forsaken me?"
Some of the bystanders who heard it said,
"Look, he is calling Elijah."
One of them ran, soaked a sponge with wine, put it on a reed
and gave it to him to drink saying,
"Wait, let us see if Elijah comes to take him down."
Jesus gave a loud cry and breathed his last.

Here all kneel and pause for a short time.

The veil of the sanctuary was torn in two from top to bottom.
When the centurion who stood facing him
saw how he breathed his last he said,
"Truly this man was the Son of God!"
There were also women looking on from a distance.
Among them were Mary Magdalene,
Mary the mother of the younger James and of Joses,
and Salome.
These women had followed him when he was in Galilee
and ministered to him.
There were also many other women
who had come up with him to Jerusalem.

When it was already evening,
since it was the day of preparation,
the day before the sabbath, Joseph of Arimathea,
a distinguished member of the council,
who was himself awaiting the kingdom of God,
came and courageously went to Pilate
and asked for the body of Jesus.
Pilate was amazed that he was already dead.
He summoned the centurion
and asked him if Jesus had already died.
And when he learned of it from the centurion,
he gave the body to Joseph.
Having bought a linen cloth, he took him down,
wrapped him in the linen cloth,
and laid him in a tomb that had been hewn out of the rock.
Then he rolled a stone against the entrance to the tomb.
Mary Magdalene and Mary the mother of Joses
watched where he was laid.

or Mark 15:1-39; L38B

As soon as morning came,
the chief priests with the elders and the scribes,
that is, the whole Sanhedrin, held a council.
They bound Jesus, led him away, and handed him over to Pilate.
Pilate questioned him,
"Are you the king of the Jews?"
He said to him in reply, "You say so."
The chief priests accused him of many things.
Again Pilate questioned him,
"Have you no answer?
See how many things they accuse you of."
Jesus gave him no further answer, so that Pilate was amazed.

Now on the occasion of the feast he used to release to them
one prisoner whom they requested.
A man called Barabbas was then in prison
along with the rebels who had committed murder in a rebellion.
The crowd came forward and began to ask him
to do for them as he was accustomed.

Pilate answered,
"Do you want me to release to you the king of the Jews?"
For he knew that it was out of envy
that the chief priests had handed him over.
But the chief priests stirred up the crowd
to have him release Barabbas for them instead.
Pilate again said to them in reply,
"Then what do you want me to do
with the man you call the king of the Jews?"
They shouted again, "Crucify him."
Pilate said to them, "Why? What evil has he done?"
They only shouted the louder, "Crucify him."
So Pilate, wishing to satisfy the crowd,
released Barabbas to them and, after he had Jesus scourged,
handed him over to be crucified.

The soldiers led him away inside the palace,
that is, the praetorium, and assembled the whole cohort.
They clothed him in purple and,
weaving a crown of thorns, placed it on him.
They began to salute him with, "Hail, King of the Jews!"
and kept striking his head with a reed and spitting upon him.
They knelt before him in homage.
And when they had mocked him,
they stripped him of the purple cloak,
dressed him in his own clothes,
and led him out to crucify him.

They pressed into service a passer-by, Simon,
a Cyrenian, who was coming in from the country,
the father of Alexander and Rufus,
to carry his cross.

They brought him to the place of Golgotha
—which is translated Place of the Skull—.
They gave him wine drugged with myrrh,
but he did not take it.
Then they crucified him and divided his garments
by casting lots for them to see what each should take.
It was nine o'clock in the morning when they crucified him.
The inscription of the charge against him read,
"The King of the Jews."
With him they crucified two revolutionaries,
one on his right and one on his left.
Those passing by reviled him,
shaking their heads and saying,
"Aha! You who would destroy the temple
and rebuild it in three days,
save yourself by coming down from the cross."
Likewise the chief priests, with the scribes,
mocked him among themselves and said,
"He saved others; he cannot save himself.
Let the Christ, the King of Israel,
come down now from the cross
that we may see and believe."
Those who were crucified with him also kept abusing him.

At noon darkness came over the whole land
until three in the afternoon.
And at three o'clock Jesus cried out in a loud voice,
"Eloi, Eloi, lema sabachthani?"
which is translated,
"My God, my God, why have you forsaken me?"

Some of the bystanders who heard it said,
  "Look, he is calling Elijah."
One of them ran, soaked a sponge with wine, put it on a reed
  and gave it to him to drink saying,
  "Wait, let us see if Elijah comes to take him down."
Jesus gave a loud cry and breathed his last.

Here all kneel and pause for a short time.

The veil of the sanctuary was torn in two from top to bottom.
When the centurion who stood facing him
  saw how he breathed his last he said,
  "Truly this man was the Son of God!"

Holy Thursday Evening Mass of the Lord's Supper, *April 1, 2021*

Gospel (cont.)
John 13:1-15; L39ABC

For he knew who would betray him;
  for this reason, he said, "Not all of you are clean."

So when he had washed their feet
  and put his garments back on and reclined at table again,
  he said to them, "Do you realize what I have done for you?

You call me 'teacher' and 'master,' and rightly so, for indeed I am.
If I, therefore, the master and teacher, have washed your feet,
  you ought to wash one another's feet.
I have given you a model to follow,
  so that as I have done for you, you should also do."

FIRST READING
Exod 12:1-8, 11-14

The Lord said to Moses and Aaron in the land
  of Egypt,
  "This month shall stand at the head of
  your calendar;
  you shall reckon it the first month of the
  year.
Tell the whole community of Israel:
  On the tenth of this month every one of
  your families
  must procure for itself a lamb, one apiece
  for each household.
If a family is too small for a whole lamb,
  it shall join the nearest household in
  procuring one
  and shall share in the lamb
  in proportion to the number of persons
  who partake of it.
The lamb must be a year-old male and
  without blemish.
You may take it from either the sheep or the
  goats.
You shall keep it until the fourteenth day of
  this month,
  and then, with the whole assembly of Israel
  present,
  it shall be slaughtered during the evening
  twilight.
They shall take some of its blood
  and apply it to the two doorposts and the
  lintel
  of every house in which they partake of
  the lamb.

That same night they shall eat its roasted
  flesh
  with unleavened bread and bitter herbs.

"This is how you are to eat it:
  with your loins girt, sandals on your feet
  and your staff in hand,
  you shall eat like those who are in flight.
It is the Passover of the Lord.
For on this same night I will go through
  Egypt,
  striking down every firstborn of the land,
  both man and beast,
  and executing judgment on all the gods of
  Egypt—I, the Lord!
But the blood will mark the houses where you
  are.
Seeing the blood, I will pass over you;
  thus, when I strike the land of Egypt,
  no destructive blow will come upon you.

"This day shall be a memorial feast for you,
  which all your generations shall celebrate
  with pilgrimage to the Lord, as a perpetual
  institution."

RESPONSORIAL PSALM
Ps 116:12-13, 15-16bc, 17-18

℟. (cf. 1 Cor 10:16) Our blessing-cup is a
  communion with the Blood of Christ.

How shall I make a return to the Lord
  for all the good he has done for me?
The cup of salvation I will take up,
  and I will call upon the name of the Lord.

℟. Our blessing-cup is a communion with the
  Blood of Christ.

Precious in the eyes of the Lord
  is the death of his faithful ones.
I am your servant, the son of your handmaid;
  you have loosed my bonds.

℟. Our blessing-cup is a communion with the
  Blood of Christ.

To you will I offer sacrifice of thanksgiving,
  and I will call upon the name of the Lord.
My vows to the Lord I will pay
  in the presence of all his people.

℟. Our blessing-cup is a communion with the
  Blood of Christ.

SECOND READING
1 Cor 11:23-26

Brothers and sisters:
I received from the Lord what I also handed
  on to you,
  that the Lord Jesus, on the night he was
  handed over,
  took bread, and, after he had given thanks,
  broke it and said, "This is my body that is
  for you.
Do this in remembrance of me."
In the same way also the cup, after supper,
  saying,
  "This cup is the new covenant in my blood.
Do this, as often as you drink it, in
  remembrance of me."
For as often as you eat this bread and drink
  the cup,
  you proclaim the death of the Lord until he
  comes.

Gospel (cont.)
John 18:1–19:42; L40ABC

Jesus said to Peter,
  "Put your sword into its scabbard.
Shall I not drink the cup that the Father gave me?"

So the band of soldiers, the tribune, and the Jewish guards seized Jesus,
  bound him, and brought him to Annas first.
He was the father-in-law of Caiaphas,
  who was high priest that year.
It was Caiaphas who had counseled the Jews
  that it was better that one man should die rather than the people.

Simon Peter and another disciple followed Jesus.
Now the other disciple was known to the high priest,
  and he entered the courtyard of the high priest with Jesus.
But Peter stood at the gate outside.
So the other disciple, the acquaintance of the high priest,
  went out and spoke to the gatekeeper and brought Peter in.
Then the maid who was the gatekeeper said to Peter,
  "You are not one of this man's disciples, are you?"
He said, "I am not."
Now the slaves and the guards were standing around a charcoal fire
  that they had made, because it was cold,
  and were warming themselves.
Peter was also standing there keeping warm.

The high priest questioned Jesus
  about his disciples and about his doctrine.
Jesus answered him,
  "I have spoken publicly to the world.
I have always taught in a synagogue
  or in the temple area where all the Jews gather,
  and in secret I have said nothing. Why ask me?
Ask those who heard me what I said to them.
They know what I said."
When he had said this,
  one of the temple guards standing there struck Jesus and said,
  "Is this the way you answer the high priest?"
Jesus answered him,
  "If I have spoken wrongly, testify to the wrong;
  but if I have spoken rightly, why do you strike me?"
Then Annas sent him bound to Caiaphas the high priest.

Now Simon Peter was standing there keeping warm.
And they said to him,
  "You are not one of his disciples, are you?"
He denied it and said,
  "I am not."
One of the slaves of the high priest,
  a relative of the one whose ear Peter had cut off, said,
  "Didn't I see you in the garden with him?"
Again Peter denied it.
And immediately the cock crowed.

Then they brought Jesus from Caiaphas to the praetorium.
It was morning.
And they themselves did not enter the praetorium,
  in order not to be defiled so that they could eat the Passover.
So Pilate came out to them and said,
  "What charge do you bring against this man?"
They answered and said to him,
  "If he were not a criminal,

we would not have handed him over to you."
At this, Pilate said to them,
  "Take him yourselves, and judge him according to your law."
The Jews answered him,
  "We do not have the right to execute anyone,"
  in order that the word of Jesus might be fulfilled
  that he said indicating the kind of death he would die.
So Pilate went back into the praetorium
  and summoned Jesus and said to him,
  "Are you the King of the Jews?"
Jesus answered,
  "Do you say this on your own
  or have others told you about me?"
Pilate answered,
  "I am not a Jew, am I?
Your own nation and the chief priests handed you over to me.
What have you done?"
Jesus answered,
  "My kingdom does not belong to this world.
If my kingdom did belong to this world,
  my attendants would be fighting
  to keep me from being handed over to the Jews.
But as it is, my kingdom is not here."
So Pilate said to him,
  "Then you are a king?"
Jesus answered,
  "You say I am a king.
For this I was born and for this I came into the world,
  to testify to the truth.
Everyone who belongs to the truth listens to my voice."
Pilate said to him, "What is truth?"

When he had said this,
  he again went out to the Jews and said to them,
  "I find no guilt in him.
But you have a custom that I release one prisoner to you at Passover.
Do you want me to release to you the King of the Jews?"
They cried out again,
  "Not this one but Barabbas!"
Now Barabbas was a revolutionary.

Then Pilate took Jesus and had him scourged.
And the soldiers wove a crown out of thorns and placed it on his head,
  and clothed him in a purple cloak,
  and they came to him and said,
  "Hail, King of the Jews!"
And they struck him repeatedly.
Once more Pilate went out and said to them,
  "Look, I am bringing him out to you,
  so that you may know that I find no guilt in him."
So Jesus came out,
  wearing the crown of thorns and the purple cloak.
And he said to them, "Behold, the man!"
When the chief priests and the guards saw him they cried out,
  "Crucify him, crucify him!"
Pilate said to them,
  "Take him yourselves and crucify him.
I find no guilt in him."

The Jews answered,
  "We have a law, and according to that law he ought to die,
  because he made himself the Son of God."
Now when Pilate heard this statement,
  he became even more afraid,
  and went back into the praetorium and said to Jesus,
  "Where are you from?"
Jesus did not answer him.
So Pilate said to him,
  "Do you not speak to me?
Do you not know that I have power to release you
  and I have power to crucify you?"
Jesus answered him,
  "You would have no power over me
  if it had not been given to you from above.
For this reason the one who handed me over to you
  has the greater sin."
Consequently, Pilate tried to release him; but the Jews cried out,
  "If you release him, you are not a Friend of Caesar.
Everyone who makes himself a king opposes Caesar."

When Pilate heard these words he brought Jesus out
  and seated him on the judge's bench
  in the place called Stone Pavement, in Hebrew, Gabbatha.
It was preparation day for Passover, and it was about noon.
And he said to the Jews,
  "Behold, your king!"
They cried out,
  "Take him away, take him away! Crucify him!"
Pilate said to them,
  "Shall I crucify your king?"
The chief priests answered,
  "We have no king but Caesar."
Then he handed him over to them to be crucified.

So they took Jesus, and, carrying the cross himself,
  he went out to what is called the Place of the Skull,
  in Hebrew, Golgotha.
There they crucified him, and with him two others,
  one on either side, with Jesus in the middle.
Pilate also had an inscription written and put on the cross.
It read,
  "Jesus the Nazorean, the King of the Jews."
Now many of the Jews read this inscription,
  because the place where Jesus was crucified was near the city;
  and it was written in Hebrew, Latin, and Greek.
So the chief priests of the Jews said to Pilate,
  "Do not write 'The King of the Jews,'
  but that he said, 'I am the King of the Jews.'"
Pilate answered,
  "What I have written, I have written."

When the soldiers had crucified Jesus,
  they took his clothes and divided them into four shares,
  a share for each soldier.
They also took his tunic, but the tunic was seamless,
  woven in one piece from the top down.
So they said to one another,
  "Let's not tear it, but cast lots for it to see whose it will be,"

in order that the passage of Scripture might be fulfilled that says:
  They divided my garments among them,
    and for my vesture they cast lots.
This is what the soldiers did.
Standing by the cross of Jesus were his mother
  and his mother's sister, Mary the wife of Clopas,
  and Mary of Magdala.
When Jesus saw his mother and the disciple there whom he loved
  he said to his mother, "Woman, behold, your son."
Then he said to the disciple,
  "Behold, your mother."
And from that hour the disciple took her into his home.

After this, aware that everything was now finished,
  in order that the Scripture might be fulfilled,
  Jesus said, "I thirst."
There was a vessel filled with common wine.
So they put a sponge soaked in wine on a sprig of hyssop
  and put it up to his mouth.
When Jesus had taken the wine, he said,
  "It is finished."
And bowing his head, he handed over the spirit.

Here all kneel and pause for a short time.

Now since it was preparation day,
  in order that the bodies might not remain
    on the cross on the sabbath,
  for the sabbath day of that week was a solemn one,
  the Jews asked Pilate that their legs be broken
  and that they be taken down.
So the soldiers came and broke the legs of the first
  and then of the other one who was crucified with Jesus.
But when they came to Jesus and saw that he was already dead,
  they did not break his legs,
  but one soldier thrust his lance into his side,
  and immediately blood and water flowed out.
An eyewitness has testified, and his testimony is true;
  he knows that he is speaking the truth,
  so that you also may come to believe.
For this happened so that the Scripture passage might be fulfilled:
  Not a bone of it will be broken.
And again another passage says:
  They will look upon him whom they have pierced.

After this, Joseph of Arimathea,
  secretly a disciple of Jesus for fear of the Jews,
  asked Pilate if he could remove the body of Jesus.
And Pilate permitted it.
So he came and took his body.
Nicodemus, the one who had first come to him at night,
  also came bringing a mixture of myrrh and aloes
  weighing about one hundred pounds.
They took the body of Jesus
  and bound it with burial cloths along with the spices,
  according to the Jewish burial custom.
Now in the place where he had been crucified there was a garden,
  and in the garden a new tomb, in which no one had yet been buried.
So they laid Jesus there because of the Jewish preparation day;
  for the tomb was close by.

Friday of the Passion of the Lord (Good Friday), *April 2, 2021*

FIRST READING
Isa 52:13–53:12

See, my servant shall prosper,
    he shall be raised high and greatly exalted.
Even as many were amazed at him—
    so marred was his look beyond human
        semblance
    and his appearance beyond that of the sons
        of man—
so shall he startle many nations,
    because of him kings shall stand
        speechless;
for those who have not been told shall see,
    those who have not heard shall ponder it.

Who would believe what we have heard?
    To whom has the arm of the LORD been
        revealed?
He grew up like a sapling before him,
    like a shoot from the parched earth;
there was in him no stately bearing to make
        us look at him,
    nor appearance that would attract us to him.
He was spurned and avoided by people,
    a man of suffering, accustomed to infirmity,
one of those from whom people hide their
        faces,
    spurned, and we held him in no esteem.

Yet it was our infirmities that he bore,
    our sufferings that he endured,
while we thought of him as stricken,
    as one smitten by God and afflicted.
But he was pierced for our offenses,
    crushed for our sins;
upon him was the chastisement that makes
        us whole,
    by his stripes we were healed.
We had all gone astray like sheep,
    each following his own way;
but the LORD laid upon him
    the guilt of us all.

Though he was harshly treated, he submitted
    and opened not his mouth;
like a lamb led to the slaughter
    or a sheep before the shearers,
    he was silent and opened not his mouth.
Oppressed and condemned, he was taken away,
    and who would have thought any more of
        his destiny?
When he was cut off from the land of the
        living,
    and smitten for the sin of his people,
a grave was assigned him among the wicked
    and a burial place with evildoers,
though he had done no wrong
    nor spoken any falsehood.
But the LORD was pleased
    to crush him in infirmity.

If he gives his life as an offering for sin,
    he shall see his descendants in a long life,
    and the will of the LORD shall be
        accomplished through him.

Because of his affliction
    he shall see the light
        in fullness of days;
through his suffering, my servant shall justify
        many,
    and their guilt he shall bear.
Therefore I will give him his portion among
        the great,
    and he shall divide the spoils with the
        mighty,
because he surrendered himself to death
    and was counted among the wicked;
and he shall take away the sins of many,
    and win pardon for their offenses.

RESPONSORIAL PSALM
Ps 31:2, 6, 12-13, 15-16, 17, 25

R̸. (Luke 23:46) Father, into your hands I
    commend my spirit.

In you, O LORD, I take refuge;
    let me never be put to shame.
In your justice rescue me.
Into your hands I commend my spirit;
    you will redeem me, O LORD, O faithful God.

R̸. Father, into your hands I commend my
    spirit.

For all my foes I am an object of reproach,
    a laughingstock to my neighbors, and a
        dread to my friends;
    they who see me abroad flee from me.
I am forgotten like the unremembered dead;
    I am like a dish that is broken.

R̸. Father, into your hands I commend my
    spirit.

But my trust is in you, O LORD;
    I say, "You are my God.
In your hands is my destiny; rescue me
    from the clutches of my enemies and my
        persecutors."

R̸. Father, into your hands I commend my
    spirit.

Let your face shine upon your servant;
    save me in your kindness.
Take courage and be stouthearted,
    all you who hope in the LORD.

R̸. Father, into your hands I commend my
    spirit.

SECOND READING
Heb 4:14-16; 5:7-9

Brothers and sisters:
Since we have a great high priest who has
    passed through the heavens,
    Jesus, the Son of God,
    let us hold fast to our confession.
For we do not have a high priest
    who is unable to sympathize with our
        weaknesses,
    but one who has similarly been tested in
        every way,
    yet without sin.
So let us confidently approach the throne of
        grace
    to receive mercy and to find grace for
        timely help.

In the days when Christ was in the flesh,
    he offered prayers and supplications with
        loud cries and tears
    to the one who was able to save him from
        death,
    and he was heard because of his reverence.
Son though he was, he learned obedience from
    what he suffered;
    and when he was made perfect,
    he became the source of eternal salvation
    for all who obey him.

FIRST READING

Gen 1:1–2:2

In the beginning, when God created the
heavens and the earth,
the earth was a formless wasteland, and
darkness covered the abyss,
while a mighty wind swept over the waters.

Then God said,
"Let there be light," and there was light.
God saw how good the light was.
God then separated the light from the
darkness.
God called the light "day," and the darkness
he called "night."
Thus evening came, and morning followed—
the first day.

Then God said,
"Let there be a dome in the middle of the
waters,
to separate one body of water from the
other."
And so it happened:
God made the dome,
and it separated the water above the dome
from the water below it.
God called the dome "the sky."
Evening came, and morning followed—the
second day.

Then God said,
"Let the water under the sky be gathered
into a single basin,
so that the dry land may appear."
And so it happened:
the water under the sky was gathered into
its basin,
and the dry land appeared.
God called the dry land "the earth,"
and the basin of the water he called "the
sea."
God saw how good it was.
Then God said,
"Let the earth bring forth vegetation:
every kind of plant that bears seed
and every kind of fruit tree on earth
that bears fruit with its seed in it."
And so it happened:
the earth brought forth every kind of plant
that bears seed
and every kind of fruit tree on earth
that bears fruit with its seed in it.
God saw how good it was.
Evening came, and morning followed—the
third day.

Then God said:
"Let there be lights in the dome of the sky,
to separate day from night.
Let them mark the fixed times, the days and
the years,

and serve as luminaries in the dome of the
sky,
to shed light upon the earth."
And so it happened:
God made the two great lights,
the greater one to govern the day,
and the lesser one to govern the night;
and he made the stars.
God set them in the dome of the sky,
to shed light upon the earth,
to govern the day and the night,
and to separate the light from the darkness.
God saw how good it was.
Evening came, and morning followed—the
fourth day.

Then God said,
"Let the water teem with an abundance of
living creatures,
and on the earth let birds fly beneath the
dome of the sky."
And so it happened:
God created the great sea monsters
and all kinds of swimming creatures with
which the water teems,
and all kinds of winged birds.
God saw how good it was, and God blessed
them, saying,
"Be fertile, multiply, and fill the water of
the seas;
and let the birds multiply on the earth."
Evening came, and morning followed—the
fifth day.

Then God said,
"Let the earth bring forth all kinds of living
creatures:
cattle, creeping things, and wild animals of
all kinds."
And so it happened:
God made all kinds of wild animals, all
kinds of cattle,
and all kinds of creeping things of the
earth.
God saw how good it was.
Then God said:
"Let us make man in our image, after our
likeness.
Let them have dominion over the fish of the
sea,
the birds of the air, and the cattle,
and over all the wild animals
and all the creatures that crawl on the
ground."
God created man in his image;
in the image of God he created him;
male and female he created them.
God blessed them, saying:
"Be fertile and multiply;
fill the earth and subdue it.
Have dominion over the fish of the sea, the
birds of the air,

and all the living things that move on the
earth."
God also said:
"See, I give you every seed-bearing plant all
over the earth
and every tree that has seed-bearing fruit
on it to be your food;
and to all the animals of the land, all the
birds of the air,
and all the living creatures that crawl on
the ground,
I give all the green plants for food."
And so it happened.
God looked at everything he had made, and he
found it very good.
Evening came, and morning followed—the
sixth day.

Thus the heavens and the earth and all their
array were completed.
Since on the seventh day God was finished
with the work he had been doing,
he rested on the seventh day from all the
work he had undertaken.

or

Gen 1:1, 26-31a

In the beginning, when God created the
heavens and the earth,
God said: "Let us make man in our image,
after our likeness.
Let them have dominion over the fish of the
sea,
the birds of the air, and the cattle,
and over all the wild animals
and all the creatures that crawl on the
ground."
God created man in his image;
in the image of God he created him;
male and female he created them.
God blessed them, saying:
"Be fertile and multiply;
fill the earth and subdue it.
Have dominion over the fish of the sea, the
birds of the air,
and all the living things that move on the
earth."
God also said:
"See, I give you every seed-bearing plant all
over the earth
and every tree that has seed-bearing fruit
on it to be your food;
and to all the animals of the land, all the
birds of the air,
and all the living creatures that crawl on
the ground,
I give all the green plants for food."
And so it happened.
God looked at everything he had made, and
found it very good.

RESPONSORIAL PSALM

Ps 104:1-2, 5-6, 10, 12, 13-14, 24, 35

R͡. (30) Lord, send out your Spirit, and renew
 the face of the earth.

Bless the Lᴏʀᴅ, O my soul!
 O Lᴏʀᴅ, my God, you are great indeed!
You are clothed with majesty and glory,
 robed in light as with a cloak.

R͡. Lord, send out your Spirit, and renew the
 face of the earth.

You fixed the earth upon its foundation,
 not to be moved forever;
with the ocean, as with a garment, you
 covered it;
 above the mountains the waters stood.

R͡. Lord, send out your Spirit, and renew the
 face of the earth.

You send forth springs into the watercourses
 that wind among the mountains.
Beside them the birds of heaven dwell;
 from among the branches they send forth
 their song.

R͡. Lord, send out your Spirit, and renew the
 face of the earth.

You water the mountains from your palace;
 the earth is replete with the fruit of your
 works.
You raise grass for the cattle,
 and vegetation for man's use,
producing bread from the earth.

R͡. Lord, send out your Spirit, and renew the
 face of the earth.

How manifold are your works, O Lᴏʀᴅ!
 In wisdom you have wrought them all—
the earth is full of your creatures.
 Bless the Lᴏʀᴅ, O my soul!

R͡. Lord, send out your Spirit, and renew the
 face of the earth.

or

Ps 33:4-5, 6-7, 12-13, 20 and 22

R͡. (5b) The earth is full of the goodness of
 the Lord.

Upright is the word of the Lᴏʀᴅ,
 and all his works are trustworthy.
He loves justice and right;
 of the kindness of the Lᴏʀᴅ the earth is full.

R͡. The earth is full of the goodness of the Lord.

By the word of the Lᴏʀᴅ the heavens were
 made;
 by the breath of his mouth all their host.
He gathers the waters of the sea as in a flask;
 in cellars he confines the deep.

R͡. The earth is full of the goodness of the Lord.

Blessed the nation whose God is the Lᴏʀᴅ,
 the people he has chosen for his own
 inheritance.
From heaven the Lᴏʀᴅ looks down;
 he sees all mankind.

R͡. The earth is full of the goodness of the Lord.

Our soul waits for the Lᴏʀᴅ,
 who is our help and our shield.
May your kindness, O Lᴏʀᴅ, be upon us
 who have put our hope in you.

R͡. The earth is full of the goodness of the Lord.

SECOND READING

Gen 22:1-18

God put Abraham to the test.
He called to him, "Abraham!"
"Here I am," he replied.
Then God said:
 "Take your son Isaac, your only one, whom
  you love,
 and go to the land of Moriah.
There you shall offer him up as a holocaust
 on a height that I will point out to you."
Early the next morning Abraham saddled his
 donkey,
 took with him his son Isaac and two of his
  servants as well,
 and with the wood that he had cut for the
  holocaust,
 set out for the place of which God had told
  him.

On the third day Abraham got sight of the
 place from afar.
Then he said to his servants:
 "Both of you stay here with the donkey,
 while the boy and I go on over yonder.
We will worship and then come back to you."
Thereupon Abraham took the wood for the
 holocaust
 and laid it on his son Isaac's shoulders,
 while he himself carried the fire and the
  knife.
As the two walked on together, Isaac spoke to
 his father Abraham:
 "Father!" Isaac said.
"Yes, son," he replied.
Isaac continued, "Here are the fire and the
 wood,
 but where is the sheep for the holocaust?"
"Son," Abraham answered,
 "God himself will provide the sheep for the
  holocaust."
Then the two continued going forward.

When they came to the place of which God
 had told him,
 Abraham built an altar there and arranged
  the wood on it.

Next he tied up his son Isaac,
 and put him on top of the wood on the
  altar.
Then he reached out and took the knife to
 slaughter his son.
But the Lᴏʀᴅ's messenger called to him from
 heaven,
 "Abraham, Abraham!"
"Here I am," he answered.
"Do not lay your hand on the boy," said the
 messenger.
"Do not do the least thing to him.
I know now how devoted you are to God,
 since you did not withhold from me your
  own beloved son."
As Abraham looked about,
 he spied a ram caught by its horns in the
  thicket.
So he went and took the ram
 and offered it up as a holocaust in place of
  his son.
Abraham named the site Yahweh-yireh;
 hence people now say, "On the mountain
  the Lᴏʀᴅ will see."

Again the Lᴏʀᴅ's messenger called to
 Abraham from heaven and said:
 "I swear by myself, declares the Lᴏʀᴅ,
 that because you acted as you did
 in not withholding from me your beloved
  son,
 I will bless you abundantly
 and make your descendants as countless
 as the stars of the sky and the sands of the
  seashore;
 your descendants shall take possession
 of the gates of their enemies,
 and in your descendants all the nations of
  the earth
  shall find blessing—
 all this because you obeyed my command."

or

Gen 22:1-2, 9a, 10-13, 15-18

God put Abraham to the test.
He called to him, "Abraham!"
"Here I am," he replied.
Then God said:
 "Take your son Isaac, your only one, whom
  you love,
 and go to the land of Moriah.
There you shall offer him up as a holocaust
 on a height that I will point out to you."

When they came to the place of which God
 had told him,
 Abraham built an altar there and arranged
  the wood on it.
Then he reached out and took the knife to
 slaughter his son.

But the LORD's messenger called to him from heaven,
"Abraham, Abraham!"
"Here I am," he answered.
"Do not lay your hand on the boy," said the messenger.
"Do not do the least thing to him.
I know now how devoted you are to God,
since you did not withhold from me your own beloved son."
As Abraham looked about,
he spied a ram caught by its horns in the thicket.
So he went and took the ram
and offered it up as a holocaust in place of his son.

Again the LORD's messenger called to Abraham from heaven and said:
"I swear by myself, declares the LORD,
that because you acted as you did
in not withholding from me your beloved son,
I will bless you abundantly
and make your descendants as countless
as the stars of the sky and the sands of the seashore;
your descendants shall take possession
of the gates of their enemies,
and in your descendants all the nations of the earth
shall find blessing—
all this because you obeyed my command."

RESPONSORIAL PSALM
Ps 16:5, 8, 9-10, 11

R∕. (1) You are my inheritance, O Lord.

O LORD, my allotted portion and my cup,
you it is who hold fast my lot.
I set the LORD ever before me;
with him at my right hand I shall not be disturbed.

R∕. You are my inheritance, O Lord.

Therefore my heart is glad and my soul rejoices,
my body, too, abides in confidence;
because you will not abandon my soul to the netherworld,
nor will you suffer your faithful one to undergo corruption.

R∕. You are my inheritance, O Lord.

You will show me the path to life,
fullness of joys in your presence,
the delights at your right hand forever.

R∕. You are my inheritance, O Lord.

THIRD READING
Exod 14:15–15:1

The LORD said to Moses, "Why are you crying out to me?
Tell the Israelites to go forward.
And you, lift up your staff and, with hand outstretched over the sea,
split the sea in two,
that the Israelites may pass through it on dry land.
But I will make the Egyptians so obstinate
that they will go in after them.
Then I will receive glory through Pharaoh and all his army,
his chariots and charioteers.
The Egyptians shall know that I am the LORD,
when I receive glory through Pharaoh
and his chariots and charioteers."

The angel of God, who had been leading Israel's camp,
now moved and went around behind them.
The column of cloud also, leaving the front,
took up its place behind them,
so that it came between the camp of the Egyptians
and that of Israel.
But the cloud now became dark, and thus the night passed
without the rival camps coming any closer together all night long.
Then Moses stretched out his hand over the sea,
and the LORD swept the sea
with a strong east wind throughout the night
and so turned it into dry land.
When the water was thus divided,
the Israelites marched into the midst of the sea on dry land,
with the water like a wall to their right and to their left.

The Egyptians followed in pursuit;
all Pharaoh's horses and chariots and charioteers went after them
right into the midst of the sea.
In the night watch just before dawn
the LORD cast through the column of the fiery cloud
upon the Egyptian force a glance that threw it into a panic;
and he so clogged their chariot wheels
that they could hardly drive.
With that the Egyptians sounded the retreat before Israel,
because the LORD was fighting for them against the Egyptians.

Then the LORD told Moses, "Stretch out your hand over the sea,
that the water may flow back upon the Egyptians,
upon their chariots and their charioteers."
So Moses stretched out his hand over the sea,
and at dawn the sea flowed back to its normal depth.
The Egyptians were fleeing head on toward the sea,
when the LORD hurled them into its midst.
As the water flowed back,
it covered the chariots and the charioteers
of Pharaoh's whole army
which had followed the Israelites into the sea.
Not a single one of them escaped.
But the Israelites had marched on dry land
through the midst of the sea,
with the water like a wall to their right and to their left.
Thus the LORD saved Israel on that day
from the power of the Egyptians.
When Israel saw the Egyptians lying dead on the seashore
and beheld the great power that the LORD
had shown against the Egyptians,
they feared the LORD and believed in him
and in his servant Moses.

Then Moses and the Israelites sang this song to the LORD:
I will sing to the LORD, for he is gloriously triumphant;
horse and chariot he has cast into the sea.

RESPONSORIAL PSALM
Exod 15:1-2, 3-4, 5-6, 17-18

R∕. (1b) Let us sing to the Lord; he has covered himself in glory.

I will sing to the LORD, for he is gloriously triumphant;
horse and chariot he has cast into the sea.
My strength and my courage is the LORD,
and he has been my savior.
He is my God, I praise him;
the God of my father, I extol him.

R∕. Let us sing to the Lord; he has covered himself in glory.

The LORD is a warrior,
LORD is his name!
Pharaoh's chariots and army he hurled into the sea;
the elite of his officers were submerged in the Red Sea.

R∕. Let us sing to the Lord; he has covered himself in glory.

The flood waters covered them,
  they sank into the depths like a stone.
Your right hand, O Lord, magnificent in
    power,
  your right hand, O Lord, has shattered the
    enemy.

R⁊. Let us sing to the Lord; he has covered
  himself in glory.

You brought in the people you redeemed
  and planted them on the mountain of your
    inheritance—
the place where you made your seat, O Lord,
  the sanctuary, Lord, which your hands
    established.
The Lord shall reign forever and ever.

R⊼. Let us sing to the Lord; he has covered
  himself in glory.

FOURTH READING
Isa 54:5-14

The One who has become your husband is
    your Maker;
  his name is the Lord of hosts;
your redeemer is the Holy One of Israel,
  called God of all the earth.
The Lord calls you back,
  like a wife forsaken and grieved in spirit,
  a wife married in youth and then cast off,
  says your God.
For a brief moment I abandoned you,
  but with great tenderness I will take you
    back.
In an outburst of wrath, for a moment
  I hid my face from you;
but with enduring love I take pity on you,
  says the Lord, your redeemer.
This is for me like the days of Noah,
  when I swore that the waters of Noah
  should never again deluge the earth;
so I have sworn not to be angry with you,
  or to rebuke you.
Though the mountains leave their place
  and the hills be shaken,
my love shall never leave you
  nor my covenant of peace be shaken,
  says the Lord, who has mercy on you.
O afflicted one, storm-battered and
    unconsoled,
  I lay your pavements in carnelians,
  and your foundations in sapphires;
I will make your battlements of rubies,
  your gates of carbuncles,
  and all your walls of precious stones.
All your children shall be taught by the Lord,
  and great shall be the peace of your children.

In justice shall you be established,
  far from the fear of oppression,
  where destruction cannot come near you.

RESPONSORIAL PSALM
Ps 30:2, 4, 5-6, 11-12, 13

R⊼. (2a) I will praise you, Lord, for you have
  rescued me.

I will extol you, O Lord, for you drew me clear
  and did not let my enemies rejoice over me.
O Lord, you brought me up from the
    netherworld;
  you preserved me from among those going
    down into the pit.

R⊼. I will praise you, Lord, for you have
  rescued me.

Sing praise to the Lord, you his faithful ones,
  and give thanks to his holy name.
For his anger lasts but a moment;
  a lifetime, his good will.
At nightfall, weeping enters in,
  but with the dawn, rejoicing.

R⊼. I will praise you, Lord, for you have
  rescued me.

Hear, O Lord, and have pity on me;
  O Lord, be my helper.
You changed my mourning into dancing;
  O Lord, my God, forever will I give you
    thanks.

R⊼. I will praise you, Lord, for you have
  rescued me.

FIFTH READING
Isa 55:1-11

Thus says the Lord:
All you who are thirsty,
  come to the water!
You who have no money,
  come, receive grain and eat;
come, without paying and without cost,
  drink wine and milk!
Why spend your money for what is not bread,
  your wages for what fails to satisfy?
Heed me, and you shall eat well,
  you shall delight in rich fare.
Come to me heedfully,
  listen, that you may have life.
I will renew with you the everlasting covenant,
  the benefits assured to David.
As I made him a witness to the peoples,
  a leader and commander of nations,
so shall you summon a nation you knew not,
  and nations that knew you not shall run
    to you,

because of the Lord, your God,
  the Holy One of Israel, who has glorified
    you.

Seek the Lord while he may be found,
  call him while he is near.
Let the scoundrel forsake his way,
  and the wicked man his thoughts;
let him turn to the Lord for mercy;
  to our God, who is generous in forgiving.
For my thoughts are not your thoughts,
  nor are your ways my ways, says the Lord.
As high as the heavens are above the earth,
  so high are my ways above your ways
  and my thoughts above your thoughts.

For just as from the heavens
  the rain and snow come down
and do not return there
  till they have watered the earth,
  making it fertile and fruitful,
giving seed to the one who sows
  and bread to the one who eats,
so shall my word be
  that goes forth from my mouth;
my word shall not return to me void,
  but shall do my will,
  achieving the end for which I sent it.

RESPONSORIAL PSALM
Isa 12:2-3, 4, 5-6

R⊼. (3) You will draw water joyfully from the
  springs of salvation.

God indeed is my savior;
  I am confident and unafraid.
My strength and my courage is the Lord,
  and he has been my savior.
With joy you will draw water
  at the fountain of salvation.

R⊼. You will draw water joyfully from the
  springs of salvation.

Give thanks to the Lord, acclaim his name;
  among the nations make known his deeds,
  proclaim how exalted is his name.

R⊼. You will draw water joyfully from the
  springs of salvation.

Sing praise to the Lord for his glorious
    achievement;
  let this be known throughout all the earth.
Shout with exultation, O city of Zion,
  for great in your midst
  is the Holy One of Israel!

R⊼. You will draw water joyfully from the
  springs of salvation.

SIXTH READING
Bar 3:9-15, 32–4:4

Hear, O Israel, the commandments of life:
    listen, and know prudence!
How is it, Israel,
    that you are in the land of your foes,
    grown old in a foreign land,
defiled with the dead,
    accounted with those destined for the
        netherworld?
You have forsaken the fountain of wisdom!
    Had you walked in the way of God,
    you would have dwelt in enduring peace.
Learn where prudence is,
    where strength, where understanding;
that you may know also
    where are length of days, and life,
    where light of the eyes, and peace.
Who has found the place of wisdom,
    who has entered into her treasuries?

The One who knows all things knows her;
    he has probed her by his knowledge—
the One who established the earth for all time,
    and filled it with four-footed beasts;
he who dismisses the light, and it departs,
    calls it, and it obeys him trembling;
before whom the stars at their posts
    shine and rejoice;
when he calls them, they answer, "Here we are!"
    shining with joy for their Maker.
Such is our God;
    no other is to be compared to him:
he has traced out the whole way of
        understanding,
    and has given her to Jacob, his servant,
    to Israel, his beloved son.

Since then she has appeared on earth,
    and moved among people.
She is the book of the precepts of God,
    the law that endures forever;
all who cling to her will live,
    but those will die who forsake her.
Turn, O Jacob, and receive her:
    walk by her light toward splendor.
Give not your glory to another,
    your privileges to an alien race.
Blessed are we, O Israel;
    for what pleases God is known to us!

RESPONSORIAL PSALM
Ps 19:8, 9, 10, 11

R⁊. (John 6:68c) Lord, you have the words of
    everlasting life.

The law of the LORD is perfect,
    refreshing the soul;
the decree of the LORD is trustworthy,
    giving wisdom to the simple.

R⁊. Lord, you have the words of everlasting life.

The precepts of the LORD are right,
    rejoicing the heart;
the command of the LORD is clear,
    enlightening the eye.

R⁊. Lord, you have the words of everlasting life.

The fear of the LORD is pure,
    enduring forever;
the ordinances of the LORD are true,
    all of them just.

R⁊. Lord, you have the words of everlasting life.

They are more precious than gold,
    than a heap of purest gold;
sweeter also than syrup
    or honey from the comb.

R⁊. Lord, you have the words of everlasting life.

SEVENTH READING
Ezek 36:16-17a, 18-28

The word of the LORD came to me, saying:
    Son of man, when the house of Israel lived
        in their land,
    they defiled it by their conduct and deeds.
Therefore I poured out my fury upon them
    because of the blood that they poured out
        on the ground,
    and because they defiled it with idols.
I scattered them among the nations,
    dispersing them over foreign lands;
    according to their conduct and deeds I
        judged them.
But when they came among the nations
    wherever they came,
    they served to profane my holy name,
    because it was said of them: "These are the
        people of the LORD,
    yet they had to leave their land."
So I have relented because of my holy name
    which the house of Israel profaned
    among the nations where they came.
Therefore say to the house of Israel: Thus
        says the Lord GOD:
    Not for your sakes do I act, house of Israel,
    but for the sake of my holy name,
    which you profaned among the nations to
        which you came.
I will prove the holiness of my great name,
    profaned among the nations,
    in whose midst you have profaned it.
Thus the nations shall know that I am the
        LORD, says the Lord GOD,
    when in their sight I prove my holiness
        through you.
For I will take you away from among the nations,
    gather you from all the foreign lands,
    and bring you back to your own land.
I will sprinkle clean water upon you
    to cleanse you from all your impurities,
    and from all your idols I will cleanse you.

I will give you a new heart and place a new
        spirit within you,
    taking from your bodies your stony hearts
    and giving you natural hearts.
I will put my spirit within you and make you
        live by my statutes,
    careful to observe my decrees.
You shall live in the land I gave your fathers;
    you shall be my people, and I will be your
        God.

RESPONSORIAL PSALM
Ps 42:3, 5; 43:3, 4

R⁊. (42:2) Like a deer that longs for running
    streams, my soul longs for you, my God.

Athirst is my soul for God, the living God.
    When shall I go and behold the face of God?

R⁊. Like a deer that longs for running streams,
    my soul longs for you, my God.

I went with the throng
    and led them in procession to the house of God,
amid loud cries of joy and thanksgiving,
    with the multitude keeping festival.

R⁊. Like a deer that longs for running streams,
    my soul longs for you, my God.

Send forth your light and your fidelity;
    they shall lead me on
and bring me to your holy mountain,
    to your dwelling-place.

R⁊. Like a deer that longs for running streams,
    my soul longs for you, my God.

Then will I go in to the altar of God,
    the God of my gladness and joy;
then will I give you thanks upon the harp,
    O God, my God!

R⁊. Like a deer that longs for running streams,
    my soul longs for you, my God.

or

Isa 12:2-3, 4bcd, 5-6

R⁊. (3) You will draw water joyfully from the
    springs of salvation.

God indeed is my savior;
    I am confident and unafraid.
My strength and my courage is the LORD,
    and he has been my savior.
With joy you will draw water
    at the fountain of salvation.

R⁊. You will draw water joyfully from the
    springs of salvation.

Give thanks to the LORD, acclaim his name;
    among the nations make known his deeds,
    proclaim how exalted is his name.

R⁊. You will draw water joyfully from the
    springs of salvation.

Sing praise to the Lord for his glorious
  achievement;
    let this be known throughout all the earth.
Shout with exultation, O city of Zion,
    for great in your midst
    is the Holy One of Israel!

℟. You will draw water joyfully from the
  springs of salvation.

or

Ps 51:12-13, 14-15, 18-19

℟. (12a) Create a clean heart in me, O God.

A clean heart create for me, O God,
    and a steadfast spirit renew within me.
Cast me not out from your presence,
    and your Holy Spirit take not from me.

℟. Create a clean heart in me, O God.

Give me back the joy of your salvation,
    and a willing spirit sustain in me.
I will teach transgressors your ways,
    and sinners shall return to you.

℟. Create a clean heart in me, O God.

For you are not pleased with sacrifices;
    should I offer a holocaust, you would not
    accept it.
My sacrifice, O God, is a contrite spirit;
    a heart contrite and humbled, O God, you
    will not spurn.

℟. Create a clean heart in me, O God.

EPISTLE
Rom 6:3-11

Brothers and sisters:
Are you unaware that we who were baptized
    into Christ Jesus
    were baptized into his death?
We were indeed buried with him through
    baptism into death,
    so that, just as Christ was raised from the
    dead
    by the glory of the Father,
    we too might live in newness of life.

For if we have grown into union with him
    through a death like his,
    we shall also be united with him in the
    resurrection.
We know that our old self was crucified with
    him,
    so that our sinful body might be done away
    with,
    that we might no longer be in slavery to sin.
For a dead person has been absolved from sin.
If, then, we have died with Christ,
    we believe that we shall also live with him.
We know that Christ, raised from the dead,
    dies no more;
    death no longer has power over him.
As to his death, he died to sin once and for all;
    as to his life, he lives for God.
Consequently, you too must think of
    yourselves as being dead to sin
    and living for God in Christ Jesus.

RESPONSORIAL PSALM
Ps 118:1-2, 16-17, 22-23

℟. Alleluia, alleluia, alleluia.

Give thanks to the Lord, for he is good,
    for his mercy endures forever.
Let the house of Israel say,
    "His mercy endures forever."

℟. Alleluia, alleluia, alleluia.

The right hand of the Lord has struck with
    power;
    the right hand of the Lord is exalted.
I shall not die, but live,
    and declare the works of the Lord.

℟. Alleluia, alleluia, alleluia.

The stone which the builders rejected
    has become the cornerstone.
By the Lord has this been done;
    it is wonderful in our eyes.

℟. Alleluia, alleluia, alleluia.

Gospel
Mark 16:1-7; L41B

When the sabbath was over,
    Mary Magdalene, Mary, the mother of James, and Salome
    bought spices so that they might go and anoint him.
Very early when the sun had risen,
    on the first day of the week, they came to the tomb.
They were saying to one another,
    "Who will roll back the stone for us
    from the entrance to the tomb?"
When they looked up,
    they saw that the stone had been rolled back;
    it was very large.

On entering the tomb they saw a young man
    sitting on the right side, clothed in a white robe,
    and they were utterly amazed.
He said to them, "Do not be amazed!
You seek Jesus of Nazareth, the crucified.
He has been raised; he is not here.
Behold the place where they laid him.
But go and tell his disciples and Peter,
    'He is going before you to Galilee;
    there you will see him, as he told you.'"

or, at an afternoon or evening Mass

Gospel
Luke 24:13-35; L46

That very day, the first day of the week,
    two of Jesus' disciples were going
    to a village seven miles from Jerusalem called Emmaus,
    and they were conversing about all the things that had occurred.
And it happened that while they were conversing and debating,
    Jesus himself drew near and walked with them,
    but their eyes were prevented from recognizing him.
He asked them,
    "What are you discussing as you walk along?"
They stopped, looking downcast.
One of them, named Cleopas, said to him in reply,
    "Are you the only visitor to Jerusalem
    who does not know of the things
    that have taken place there in these days?"
And he replied to them, "What sort of things?"
They said to him,
    "The things that happened to Jesus the Nazarene,
    who was a prophet mighty in deed and word
    before God and all the people,
    how our chief priests and rulers both handed him over
    to a sentence of death and crucified him.
But we were hoping that he would be the one to redeem Israel;
    and besides all this,
    it is now the third day since this took place.
Some women from our group, however, have astounded us:
    they were at the tomb early in the morning
    and did not find his body;
    they came back and reported
    that they had indeed seen a vision of angels
    who announced that he was alive.

Then some of those with us went to the tomb
    and found things just as the women had described,
    but him they did not see."
And he said to them, "Oh, how foolish you are!
How slow of heart to believe all that the prophets spoke!
Was it not necessary that the Christ should suffer these things
    and enter into his glory?"
Then beginning with Moses and all the prophets,
    he interpreted to them what referred to him
    in all the Scriptures.
As they approached the village to which they were going,
    he gave the impression that he was going on farther.
But they urged him, "Stay with us,
    for it is nearly evening and the day is almost over."
So he went in to stay with them.
And it happened that, while he was with them at table,
    he took bread, said the blessing,
    broke it, and gave it to them.
With that their eyes were opened and they recognized him,
    but he vanished from their sight.
Then they said to each other,
    "Were not our hearts burning within us
    while he spoke to us on the way and opened the Scriptures to us?"
So they set out at once and returned to Jerusalem
    where they found gathered together
    the eleven and those with them who were saying,
    "The Lord has truly been raised and has appeared to Simon!"
Then the two recounted
    what had taken place on the way
    and how he was made known to them in the breaking of the bread.

FIRST READING
Acts 10:34a, 37-43

Peter proceeded to speak and said:
    "You know what has happened all over Judea,
    beginning in Galilee after the baptism
    that John preached,
    how God anointed Jesus of Nazareth
    with the Holy Spirit and power.
He went about doing good
    and healing all those oppressed by the devil,
    for God was with him.
We are witnesses of all that he did
    both in the country of the Jews and in
        Jerusalem.
They put him to death by hanging him on a tree.
This man God raised on the third day and
        granted that he be visible,
    not to all the people, but to us,
    the witnesses chosen by God in advance,
    who ate and drank with him after he rose
        from the dead.
He commissioned us to preach to the people
    and testify that he is the one appointed by God
    as judge of the living and the dead.
To him all the prophets bear witness,
    that everyone who believes in him
    will receive forgiveness of sins through his
        name."

RESPONSORIAL PSALM
Ps 118:1-2, 16-17, 22-23

R̶/. (24) This is the day the Lord has made; let
    us rejoice and be glad.
    or:
R̶/. Alleluia.

Give thanks to the Lᴏʀᴅ, for he is good,
    for his mercy endures forever.
Let the house of Israel say,
    "His mercy endures forever."

R̶/. This is the day the Lord has made; let us
    rejoice and be glad.
    or:
R̶/. Alleluia.

"The right hand of the Lᴏʀᴅ has struck with
        power;
    the right hand of the Lᴏʀᴅ is exalted.
I shall not die, but live,
    and declare the works of the Lᴏʀᴅ."

R̶/. This is the day the Lord has made; let us
    rejoice and be glad.
    or:
R̶/. Alleluia.

The stone which the builders rejected
    has become the cornerstone.
By the Lᴏʀᴅ has this been done;
    it is wonderful in our eyes.

R̶/. This is the day the Lord has made; let us
    rejoice and be glad.
    or:
R̶/. Alleluia.

SECOND READING
1 Cor 5:6b-8

Brothers and sisters:
Do you not know that a little yeast leavens all
        the dough?
Clear out the old yeast,
    so that you may become a fresh batch of
        dough,
    inasmuch as you are unleavened.
For our paschal lamb, Christ, has been
        sacrificed.
Therefore, let us celebrate the feast,
    not with the old yeast, the yeast of malice
        and wickedness,
    but with the unleavened bread of sincerity
        and truth.

or

Col 3:1-4

Brothers and sisters:
If then you were raised with Christ, seek what
        is above,
    where Christ is seated at the right hand of
        God.
Think of what is above, not of what is on
        earth.
For you have died, and your life is hidden with
        Christ in God.
When Christ your life appears,
    then you too will appear with him in glory.

SEQUENCE

Victimae paschali laudes
Christians, to the Paschal Victim
    Offer your thankful praises!
A Lamb the sheep redeems;
    Christ, who only is sinless,
    Reconciles sinners to the Father.
Death and life have contended in that combat
        stupendous:
    The Prince of life, who died, reigns
        immortal.
Speak, Mary, declaring
    What you saw, wayfaring.
"The tomb of Christ, who is living,
    The glory of Jesus' resurrection;
Bright angels attesting,
    The shroud and napkin resting.
Yes, Christ my hope is arisen;
    To Galilee he goes before you."
Christ indeed from death is risen, our new life
        obtaining.
    Have mercy, victor King, ever reigning!
    Amen. Alleluia.

Gospel (cont.)
John 20:19-31; L44B

Now a week later his disciples were again inside
    and Thomas was with them.
Jesus came, although the doors were locked,
    and stood in their midst and said, "Peace be with you."
Then he said to Thomas, "Put your finger here and see my hands,
    and bring your hand and put it into my side,
    and do not be unbelieving, but believe."
Thomas answered and said to him, "My Lord and my God!"

Jesus said to him, "Have you come to believe because you have seen me?
Blessed are those who have not seen and have believed."

Now Jesus did many other signs in the presence of his disciples
    that are not written in this book.
But these are written that you may come to believe
    that Jesus is the Christ, the Son of God,
    and that through this belief you may have life in his name.

SECOND READING
Eph 1:17-23

Brothers and sisters:
May the God of our Lord Jesus Christ, the
    Father of glory,
  give you a Spirit of wisdom and revelation
  resulting in knowledge of him.
May the eyes of your hearts be enlightened,
  that you may know what is the hope that
      belongs to his call,
    what are the riches of glory
    in his inheritance among the holy ones,
    and what is the surpassing greatness of
        his power
    for us who believe,
    in accord with the exercise of his great might,
    which he worked in Christ,
    raising him from the dead
    and seating him at his right hand in the
        heavens,
    far above every principality, authority,
        power, and dominion,
    and every name that is named
    not only in this age but also in the one to
        come.
And he put all things beneath his feet
  and gave him as head over all things to the
      church,
    which is his body,
    the fullness of the one who fills all things in
        every way.

or

Eph 4:1-13

Brothers and sisters,
I, a prisoner for the Lord,
  urge you to live in a manner worthy of the
      call you have received,
  with all humility and gentleness, with
      patience,
  bearing with one another through love,
  striving to preserve the unity of the Spirit
  through the bond of peace:
  one body and one Spirit,
  as you were also called to the one hope of
      your call;
  one Lord, one faith, one baptism;
  one God and Father of all,
  who is over all and through all and in all.

But grace was given to each of us
  according to the measure of Christ's gift.
Therefore, it says:
    *He ascended on high and took prisoners
        captive;*
    he gave gifts to men.
What does "he ascended" mean except that he
    also descended
  into the lower regions of the earth?
The one who descended is also the one who
    ascended
  far above all the heavens,
  that he might fill all things.

And he gave some as apostles, others as
    prophets,
  others as evangelists, others as pastors and
      teachers,
  to equip the holy ones for the work of
      ministry,
  for building up the body of Christ,
  until we all attain the unity of faith
  and knowledge of the Son of God, to
      mature to manhood,
  to the extent of the full stature of Christ.

or

Eph 4:1-7, 11-13

Brothers and sisters,
I, a prisoner for the Lord,
  urge you to live in a manner worthy of the
      call you have received,
  with all humility and gentleness, with
      patience,
  bearing with one another through love,
  striving to preserve the unity of the Spirit
  through the bond of peace:
  one body and one Spirit,
  as you were also called to the one hope of
      your call;
  one Lord, one faith, one baptism;
  one God and Father of all,
  who is over all and through all and in all.

But grace was given to each of us
  according to the measure of Christ's gift.

And he gave some as apostles, others as
    prophets,
  others as evangelists, others as pastors and
      teachers,
  to equip the holy ones for the work of
      ministry,
  for building up the body of Christ,
  until we all attain the unity of faith
  and knowledge of the Son of God, to
      mature to manhood,
  to the extent of the full stature of Christ.

SECOND READING
1 Cor 12:3b-7, 12-13

Brothers and sisters:
No one can say, "Jesus is Lord," except by the
     Holy Spirit.

There are different kinds of spiritual gifts but
     the same Spirit;
     there are different forms of service but the
          same Lord;
     there are different workings but the same
          God
     who produces all of them in everyone.
To each individual the manifestation of the
     Spirit
     is given for some benefit.

As a body is one though it has many parts,
     and all the parts of the body, though many,
          are one body,
     so also Christ.
For in one Spirit we were all baptized into one
     body,
     whether Jews or Greeks, slaves or free
          persons,
     and we were all given to drink of one Spirit.

or

Gal 5:16-25

Brothers and sisters, live by the Spirit
     and you will certainly not gratify the desire
          of the flesh.
For the flesh has desires against the Spirit,
     and the Spirit against the flesh;
     these are opposed to each other,
     so that you may not do what you want.
But if you are guided by the Spirit, you are
     not under the law.
Now the works of the flesh are obvious:
     immorality, impurity, lust, idolatry,
     sorcery, hatreds, rivalry, jealousy,
     outbursts of fury, acts of selfishness,
     dissensions, factions, occasions of envy,
     drinking bouts, orgies, and the like.
I warn you, as I warned you before,
     that those who do such things will not
          inherit the kingdom of God.
In contrast, the fruit of the Spirit is love, joy,
     peace,
     patience, kindness, generosity,
     faithfulness, gentleness, self-control.
Against such there is no law.
Now those who belong to Christ Jesus have
     crucified their flesh
     with its passions and desires.
If we live in the Spirit, let us also follow the
     Spirit.

SEQUENCE

Veni, Sancte Spiritus
Come, Holy Spirit, come!
And from your celestial home
     Shed a ray of light divine!
Come, Father of the poor!
Come, source of all our store!
     Come, within our bosoms shine.
You, of comforters the best;
You, the soul's most welcome guest;
     Sweet refreshment here below;
In our labor, rest most sweet;
Grateful coolness in the heat;
     Solace in the midst of woe.
O most blessed Light divine,
Shine within these hearts of yours,
     And our inmost being fill!
Where you are not, we have naught,
Nothing good in deed or thought,
     Nothing free from taint of ill.
Heal our wounds, our strength renew;
On our dryness pour your dew;
     Wash the stains of guilt away:
Bend the stubborn heart and will;
Melt the frozen, warm the chill;
     Guide the steps that go astray.
On the faithful, who adore
And confess you, evermore
     In your sevenfold gift descend;
Give them virtue's sure reward;
Give them your salvation, Lord;
     Give them joys that never end. Amen.
     Alleluia.

SECOND READING

Heb 9:11-15

Brothers and sisters:
When Christ came as high priest
    of the good things that have come to be,
    passing through the greater and more
        perfect tabernacle
    not made by hands, that is, not belonging to
        this creation,
    he entered once for all into the sanctuary,
    not with the blood of goats and calves
    but with his own blood, thus obtaining
        eternal redemption.
For if the blood of goats and bulls
    and the sprinkling of a heifer's ashes
    can sanctify those who are defiled
    so that their flesh is cleansed,
    how much more will the blood of Christ,
    who through the eternal Spirit offered
        himself unblemished to God,
    cleanse our consciences from dead works
    to worship the living God.

For this reason he is mediator of a new
    covenant:
    since a death has taken place for
    deliverance
    from transgressions under the first
    covenant,
    those who are called may receive the
    promised eternal inheritance.

OPTIONAL SEQUENCE

Lauda Sion

Laud, O Zion, your salvation,
Laud with hymns of exultation,
    Christ, your king and shepherd true:

Bring him all the praise you know,
He is more than you bestow.
    Never can you reach his due.

Special theme for glad thanksgiving
Is the quick'ning and the living
    Bread today before you set:

From his hands of old partaken,
As we know, by faith unshaken,
    Where the Twelve at supper met.

Full and clear ring out your chanting,
Joy nor sweetest grace be wanting,
    From your heart let praises burst:

For today the feast is holden,
When the institution olden
    Of that supper was rehearsed.

Here the new law's new oblation,
By the new king's revelation,
    Ends the form of ancient rite:

Now the new the old effaces,
Truth away the shadow chases,
    Light dispels the gloom of night.

What he did at supper seated,
Christ ordained to be repeated,
    His memorial ne'er to cease:

And his rule for guidance taking,
Bread and wine we hallow, making
    Thus our sacrifice of peace.

This the truth each Christian learns,
Bread into his flesh he turns,
    To his precious blood the wine:

Sight has fail'd, nor thought conceives,
But a dauntless faith believes,
    Resting on a pow'r divine.

Here beneath these signs are hidden
Priceless things to sense forbidden;
    Signs, not things are all we see:

Blood is poured and flesh is broken,
Yet in either wondrous token
    Christ entire we know to be.

Whoso of this food partakes,
Does not rend the Lord nor breaks;
    Christ is whole to all that taste:

Thousands are, as one, receivers,
One, as thousands of believers,
    Eats of him who cannot waste.

Bad and good the feast are sharing,
Of what divers dooms preparing,
    Endless death, or endless life.

Life to these, to those damnation,
See how like participation
    Is with unlike issues rife.

When the sacrament is broken,
Doubt not, but believe 'tis spoken,
    That each sever'd outward token
        doth the very whole contain.

Nought the precious gift divides,
Breaking but the sign betides
    Jesus still the same abides,
        still unbroken does remain.

The shorter form of the sequence begins here.

Lo! the angel's food is given
To the pilgrim who has striven;
    See the children's bread from heaven,
        which on dogs may not be spent.

Truth the ancient types fulfilling,
Isaac bound, a victim willing,
    Paschal lamb, its lifeblood spilling,
        manna to the fathers sent.

Very bread, good shepherd, tend us,
Jesu, of your love befriend us,
    You refresh us, you defend us,
    Your eternal goodness send us
In the land of life to see.

You who all things can and know,
Who on earth such food bestow,
    Grant us with your saints, though lowest,
    Where the heav'nly feast you show,
Fellow heirs and guests to be. Amen. Alleluia

FIRST READING

Hos 11:1, 3-4, 8c-9

Thus says the LORD:
When Israel was a child I loved him,
 out of Egypt I called my son.
Yet it was I who taught Ephraim to walk,
 who took them in my arms;
I drew them with human cords,
 with bands of love;
I fostered them like one
 who raises an infant to his cheeks;
Yet, though I stooped to feed my child,
 they did not know that I was their healer.

My heart is overwhelmed,
 my pity is stirred.
I will not give vent to my blazing anger,
 I will not destroy Ephraim again;
For I am God and not a man,
 the Holy One present among you;
 I will not let the flames consume you.

RESPONSORIAL PSALM

Isa 12:2-3, 4, 5-6

R⁊. (3)You will draw water joyfully from the
 springs of salvation.

God indeed is my savior;
 I am confident and unafraid.
My strength and my courage is the LORD,
 and he has been my savior.
With joy you will draw water
 at the fountain of salvation.

R⁊. You will draw water joyfully from the
 springs of salvation.

Give thanks to the LORD, acclaim his name;
 among the nations make known his deeds,
 proclaim how exalted is his name.
R⁊. You will draw water joyfully from the
 springs of salvation.

Sing praise to the LORD for his glorious
 achievement;
 let this be known throughout all the earth.
Shout with exultation, O city of Zion,
 for great in your midst
 is the Holy One of Israel!
R⁊. You will draw water joyfully from the
 springs of salvation.

SECOND READING

Eph 3:8-12, 14-19

Brothers and sisters:
To me, the very least of all the holy ones, this
 grace was given,
 to preach to the Gentiles the inscrutable
 riches of Christ,
 and to bring to light for all what is the plan
 of the mystery
 hidden from ages past in God who created
 all things,
 so that the manifold wisdom of God
 might now be made known through the
 church
 to the principalities and authorities in the
 heavens.
This was according to the eternal purpose
 that he accomplished in Christ Jesus our
 Lord,
in whom we have boldness of speech
 and confidence of access through faith in
 him.

For this reason I kneel before the Father,
 from whom every family in heaven and on
 earth is named,
 that he may grant you in accord with the
 riches of his glory
 to be strengthened with power through his
 Spirit in the inner self,
 and that Christ may dwell in your hearts
 through faith;
 that you, rooted and grounded in love,
 may have strength to comprehend with all
 the holy ones
 what is the breadth and length and height
 and depth,
 and to know the love of Christ which
 surpasses knowledge,
 so that you may be filled with all the
 fullness of God.

FIRST READING

Isa 49:1-6

Hear me, O coastlands,
  listen, O distant peoples.
The LORD called me from birth,
  from my mother's womb he gave me my
    name.
He made of me a sharp-edged sword
  and concealed me in the shadow of his arm.
He made me a polished arrow,
  in his quiver he hid me.
You are my servant, he said to me,
  Israel, through whom I show my glory.

Though I thought I had toiled in vain,
  and for nothing, uselessly, spent my
    strength,
yet my reward is with the LORD,
  my recompense is with my God.
For now the LORD has spoken
  who formed me as his servant from the
    womb,
that Jacob may be brought back to him
  and Israel gathered to him;
and I am made glorious in the sight of the
    LORD,
  and my God is now my strength!
It is too little, he says, for you to be my
    servant,
  to raise up the tribes of Jacob,
  and restore the survivors of Israel;
I will make you a light to the nations,
  that my salvation may reach to the ends of
    the earth.

RESPONSORIAL PSALM

Ps 139:1b-3, 13-14ab, 14c-15

R̄. (14a) I praise you, for I am wonderfully
    made.

O LORD, you have probed me, you know me;
  you know when I sit and when I stand;
  you understand my thoughts from afar.
My journeys and my rest you scrutinize,
  with all my ways you are familiar.

R̄. I praise you, for I am wonderfully made.

Truly you have formed my inmost being;
  you knit me in my mother's womb.
I give you thanks that I am fearfully,
    wonderfully made;
  wonderful are your works.

R̄. I praise you, for I am wonderfully made.

My soul also you knew full well;
  nor was my frame unknown to you
When I was made in secret,
  when I was fashioned in the depths of the
    earth.

R̄. I praise you, for I am wonderfully made.

SECOND READING

Acts 13:22-26

In those days, Paul said:
"God raised up David as their king;
  of him God testified,
    I have found David, son of Jesse, a man
      after my own heart;
    he will carry out my every wish.
From this man's descendants God, according
    to his promise,
  has brought to Israel a savior, Jesus.
John heralded his coming by proclaiming a
    baptism of repentance
  to all the people of Israel;
  and as John was completing his course, he
    would say,
  'What do you suppose that I am? I am not
    he.
Behold, one is coming after me;
  I am not worthy to unfasten the sandals of
    his feet.'

"My brothers, sons of the family of Abraham,
  and those others among you who are God-
    fearing,
  to us this word of salvation has been sent."

Gospel (cont.)
Mark 5:21-43; L98B

But his disciples said to Jesus,
 "You see how the crowd is pressing upon you,
  and yet you ask, 'Who touched me?'"
And he looked around to see who had done it.
The woman, realizing what had happened to her,
 approached in fear and trembling.
She fell down before Jesus and told him the whole truth.
He said to her, "Daughter, your faith has saved you.
Go in peace and be cured of your affliction."

While he was still speaking,
 people from the synagogue official's house arrived and said,
 "Your daughter has died; why trouble the teacher any longer?"
Disregarding the message that was reported,
 Jesus said to the synagogue official,
 "Do not be afraid; just have faith."
He did not allow anyone to accompany him inside
 except Peter, James, and John, the brother of James.
When they arrived at the house of the synagogue official,
 he caught sight of a commotion,
 people weeping and wailing loudly.
So he went in and said to them,
 "Why this commotion and weeping?
The child is not dead but asleep."
And they ridiculed him.
Then he put them all out.
He took along the child's father and mother
 and those who were with him
 and entered the room where the child was.
He took the child by the hand and said to her, *"Talitha koum,"*
 which means, "Little girl, I say to you, arise!"
The girl, a child of twelve, arose immediately and walked around.
At that they were utterly astounded.
He gave strict orders that no one should know this
 and said that she should be given something to eat.

or Mark 5:21-24, 35b-43; L98B

When Jesus had crossed again in the boat
 to the other side,
 a large crowd gathered around him, and he stayed close to the sea.
One of the synagogue officials, named Jairus, came forward.
Seeing him he fell at his feet and pleaded earnestly with him, saying,
 "My daughter is at the point of death.
Please, come lay your hands on her
 that she may get well and live."
He went off with him,
 and a large crowd followed him and pressed upon him.

While he was still speaking, people from the synagogue official's house
  arrived and said,
 "Your daughter has died; why trouble the teacher any longer?"
Disregarding the message that was reported,
 Jesus said to the synagogue official,
 "Do not be afraid; just have faith."
He did not allow anyone to accompany him inside
 except Peter, James, and John, the brother of James.
When they arrived at the house of the synagogue official,
 he caught sight of a commotion,
 people weeping and wailing loudly.
So he went in and said to them,
 "Why this commotion and weeping?
The child is not dead but asleep."
And they ridiculed him.
Then he put them all out.
He took along the child's father and mother
 and those who were with him
 and entered the room where the child was.
He took the child by the hand and said to her, *"Talitha koum,"*
 which means, "Little girl, I say to you, arise!"
The girl, a child of twelve, arose immediately and walked around.
At that they were utterly astounded.
He gave strict orders that no one should know this
 and said that she should be given something to eat.

FIRST READING
Acts 12:1-11

In those days, King Herod laid hands upon
   some members of the Church to harm
   them.
He had James, the brother of John, killed by
   the sword,
   and when he saw that this was pleasing to
      the Jews
   he proceeded to arrest Peter also.
—It was the feast of Unleavened Bread.—
He had him taken into custody and put in
   prison
   under the guard of four squads of four
      soldiers each.
He intended to bring him before the people
   after Passover.
Peter thus was being kept in prison,
   but prayer by the Church was fervently
      being made
   to God on his behalf.

On the very night before Herod was to bring
   him to trial,
   Peter, secured by double chains,
   was sleeping between two soldiers,
   while outside the door guards kept watch
      on the prison.
Suddenly the angel of the Lord stood by him,
   and a light shone in the cell.
He tapped Peter on the side and awakened
   him, saying,
   "Get up quickly."
The chains fell from his wrists.
The angel said to him, "Put on your belt and
   your sandals."
He did so.
Then he said to him, "Put on your cloak and
   follow me."
So he followed him out,
   not realizing that what was happening
      through the angel was real;
   he thought he was seeing a vision.
They passed the first guard, then the second,
   and came to the iron gate leading out to the
      city,
   which opened for them by itself.
They emerged and made their way down an
   alley,
   and suddenly the angel left him.
Then Peter recovered his senses and said,
   "Now I know for certain
   that the Lord sent his angel
   and rescued me from the hand of Herod
   and from all that the Jewish people had
      been expecting."

RESPONSORIAL PSALM
Ps 34:2-3, 4-5, 6-7, 8-9

R̸. (8) The angel of the Lord will rescue those
   who fear him.

I will bless the Lord at all times;
   his praise shall be ever in my mouth.
Let my soul glory in the Lord;
   the lowly will hear me and be glad.

R̸. The angel of the Lord will rescue those
   who fear him.

Glorify the Lord with me,
   let us together extol his name.
I sought the Lord, and he answered me
   and delivered me from all my fears.

R̸. The angel of the Lord will rescue those
   who fear him.

Look to him that you may be radiant with joy,
   and your faces may not blush with shame.
When the poor one called out, the Lord heard,
   and from all his distress he saved him.

R̸. The angel of the Lord will rescue those
   who fear him.

The angel of the Lord encamps
   around those who fear him, and delivers
      them.
Taste and see how good the Lord is;
   blessed the man who takes refuge in him.

R̸. The angel of the Lord will rescue those
   who fear him.

SECOND READING
2 Tim 4:6-8, 17-18

I, Paul, am already being poured out like a
   libation,
   and the time of my departure is at hand.
I have competed well; I have finished the race;
   I have kept the faith.
From now on the crown of righteousness
   awaits me,
   which the Lord, the just judge,
   will award to me on that day, and not only
      to me,
   but to all who have longed for his
      appearance.

The Lord stood by me and gave me strength,
   so that through me the proclamation might
      be completed
   and all the Gentiles might hear it.
And I was rescued from the lion's mouth.
The Lord will rescue me from every evil threat
   and will bring me safe to his heavenly
      Kingdom.
To him be glory forever and ever. Amen.

Fifteenth Sunday in Ordinary Time, *July 11, 2021*

SECOND READING
Eph 1:3-10

Blessed be the God and Father of our Lord
    Jesus Christ,
  who has blessed us in Christ
  with every spiritual blessing in the heavens,
  as he chose us in him, before the foundation
    of the world,
  to be holy and without blemish before him.
In love he destined us for adoption to himself
    through Jesus Christ,
  in accord with the favor of his will,
  for the praise of the glory of his grace
  that he granted us in the beloved.

In him we have redemption by his blood,
  the forgiveness of transgressions,
  in accord with the riches of his grace that
    he lavished upon us.
In all wisdom and insight, he has made
    known to us
  the mystery of his will in accord with his
    favor
  that he set forth in him as a plan for the
    fullness of times,
  to sum up all things in Christ, in heaven
    and on earth.

Seventeenth Sunday in Ordinary Time, *July 25, 2021*

Gospel (cont.)
John 6:1-15; L110B

Then Jesus took the loaves, gave thanks,
  and distributed them to those who were reclining,
  and also as much of the fish as they wanted.
When they had had their fill, he said to his disciples,
  "Gather the fragments left over,
  so that nothing will be wasted."
So they collected them,
  and filled twelve wicker baskets with fragments
  from the five barley loaves
  that had been more than they could eat.
When the people saw the sign he had done, they said,
  "This is truly the Prophet, the one who is to come into the world."
Since Jesus knew that they were going to come and carry him off
  to make him king,
  he withdrew again to the mountain alone.

Eighteenth Sunday in Ordinary Time, *August 1, 2021*

Gospel (cont.)
John 6:24-35; L113B

So Jesus said to them,
  "Amen, amen, I say to you,
  it was not Moses who gave the bread from heaven;
  my Father gives you the true bread from heaven.
For the bread of God is that which comes down from heaven
  and gives life to the world."

So they said to him,
  "Sir, give us this bread always."
Jesus said to them,
  "I am the bread of life;
  whoever comes to me will never hunger,
  and whoever believes in me will never thirst."

The Assumption of the Blessed Virgin Mary, *August 15, 2021*

Gospel (cont.)
Luke 1:39-56; L622

  He has cast down the mighty from their thrones,
    and has lifted up the lowly.
  He has filled the hungry with good things,
    and the rich he has sent away empty.
  He has come to the help of his servant Israel
    for he has remembered his promise of mercy,
    the promise he made to our fathers,
    to Abraham and his children forever."

Mary remained with her about three months
  and then returned to her home.

Twenty-First Sunday in Ordinary Time, *August 22, 2021*

SECOND READING
Eph 5:2a, 25-32

Brothers and sisters:
Live in love, as Christ loved us.
Husbands, love your wives,
    even as Christ loved the church
    and handed himself over for her to sanctify
        her,
    cleansing her by the bath of water with the
        word,
    that he might present to himself the church
        in splendor,
    without spot or wrinkle or any such thing,
    that she might be holy and without blemish.

So also husbands should love their wives as
    their own bodies.
He who loves his wife loves himself.
For no one hates his own flesh
    but rather nourishes and cherishes it,
    even as Christ does the church,
    because we are members of his body.
*For this reason a man shall leave his father
    and his mother and be joined to his wife,
and the two shall become one flesh.*
This is a great mystery,
    but I speak in reference to Christ and the
        church.

Twenty-Second Sunday in Ordinary Time, *August 29, 2021*

Gospel (cont.)
Mark 7:1-8, 14-15, 21-23; L125B

He summoned the crowd again and said to them,
    "Hear me, all of you, and understand.
Nothing that enters one from outside can defile that person;
    but the things that come out from within are what defile.

"From within people, from their hearts,
    come evil thoughts, unchastity, theft, murder,
    adultery, greed, malice, deceit,
    licentiousness, envy, blasphemy, arrogance, folly.
All these evils come from within and they defile."

Twenty-Seventh Sunday in Ordinary Time, *October 3, 2021*

Gospel (cont.)
Mark 10:2-16; L140B

And people were bringing children to him that he might touch them,
    but the disciples rebuked them.
When Jesus saw this he became indignant and said to them,
    "Let the children come to me;
    do not prevent them, for the kingdom of God belongs to such as these.
Amen, I say to you,
    whoever does not accept the kingdom of God like a child
    will not enter it."
Then he embraced them and blessed them,
    placing his hands on them.

or Mark 10:2-12; L140B

The Pharisees approached Jesus and asked,
    "Is it lawful for a husband to divorce his wife?"
They were testing him.
He said to them in reply, "What did Moses command you?"

They replied,
    "Moses permitted a husband to write a bill of divorce
    and dismiss her."
But Jesus told them,
    "Because of the hardness of your hearts
    he wrote you this commandment.
But from the beginning of creation, *God made them male and female.*
*For this reason a man shall leave his father and mother
    and be joined to his wife,
    and the two shall become one flesh.*
So they are no longer two but one flesh.
Therefore what God has joined together,
    no human being must separate."
In the house the disciples again questioned Jesus about this.
He said to them,
    "Whoever divorces his wife and marries another
    commits adultery against her;
    and if she divorces her husband and marries another,
    she commits adultery."

Gospel (cont.)
Mark 10:17-30; L143B

So Jesus again said to them in reply,
  "Children, how hard it is to enter the kingdom of God!
It is easier for a camel to pass through the eye of a needle
  than for one who is rich to enter the kingdom of God."
They were exceedingly astonished and said among themselves,
  "Then who can be saved?"
Jesus looked at them and said,
  "For human beings it is impossible, but not for God.
All things are possible for God."
Peter began to say to him,
  "We have given up everything and followed you."
Jesus said, "Amen, I say to you,
  there is no one who has given up house or brothers or sisters
  or mother or father or children or lands
  for my sake and for the sake of the gospel
  who will not receive a hundred times more now in this present age:
  houses and brothers and sisters
  and mothers and children and lands,
  with persecutions, and eternal life in the age to come."

or Mark 10:17-27

As Jesus was setting out on a journey, a man ran up,
  knelt down before him, and asked him,
  "Good teacher, what must I do to inherit eternal life?"
Jesus answered him, "Why do you call me good?
No one is good but God alone.
You know the commandments: *You shall not kill;*
  you shall not commit adultery;
  you shall not steal;
  you shall not bear false witness;
  you shall not defraud;
  honor your father and your mother."
He replied and said to him,
  "Teacher, all of these I have observed from my youth."
Jesus, looking at him, loved him and said to him,
  "You are lacking in one thing.
Go, sell what you have, and give to the poor
  and you will have treasure in heaven; then come, follow me."
At that statement his face fell,
  and he went away sad, for he had many possessions.

Jesus looked around and said to his disciples,
  "How hard it is for those who have wealth
  to enter the kingdom of God!"
The disciples were amazed at his words.
So Jesus again said to them in reply,
  "Children, how hard it is to enter the kingdom of God!
It is easier for a camel to pass through the eye of a needle
  than for one who is rich to enter the kingdom of God."
They were exceedingly astonished and said among themselves,
  "Then who can be saved?"
Jesus looked at them and said,
  "For human beings it is impossible, but not for God.
All things are possible for God."

Gospel
Mark 10:42-45; L146B

Jesus summoned the Twelve and said to them,
  "You know that those who are recognized as rulers over the Gentiles
  lord it over them,
  and their great ones make their authority over them felt.
But it shall not be so among you.
Rather, whoever wishes to be great among you will be your servant;
  whoever wishes to be first among you will be the slave of all.
For the Son of Man did not come to be served
  but to serve and to give his life as a ransom for many."

FIRST READING
Rev 7:2-4, 9-14

I, John, saw another angel come up from the East,
holding the seal of the living God.
He cried out in a loud voice to the four angels
who were given power to damage the land and the sea,
"Do not damage the land or the sea or the trees
until we put the seal on the foreheads of the servants of our God."
I heard the number of those who had been marked with the seal,
one hundred and forty-four thousand marked
from every tribe of the children of Israel.

After this I had a vision of a great multitude,
which no one could count,
from every nation, race, people, and tongue.
They stood before the throne and before the Lamb,
wearing white robes and holding palm branches in their hands.
They cried out in a loud voice:

"Salvation comes from our God,
who is seated on the throne,
and from the Lamb."

All the angels stood around the throne
and around the elders and the four living creatures.
They prostrated themselves before the throne,
worshiped God, and exclaimed:

"Amen. Blessing and glory, wisdom and thanksgiving,
honor, power, and might
be to our God forever and ever. Amen."

Then one of the elders spoke up and said to me,
"Who are these wearing white robes, and where did they come from?"
I said to him, "My lord, you are the one who knows."
He said to me,
"These are the ones who have survived the time of great distress;
they have washed their robes
and made them white in the Blood of the Lamb."

RESPONSORIAL PSALM
Ps 24:1bc-2, 3-4ab, 5-6

℞. (cf. 6) Lord, this is the people that longs to see your face.

The LORD's are the earth and its fullness;
the world and those who dwell in it.
For he founded it upon the seas
and established it upon the rivers.

℞. Lord, this is the people that longs to see your face.

Who can ascend the mountain of the LORD?
or who may stand in his holy place?
One whose hands are sinless, whose heart is clean,
who desires not what is vain.

℞. Lord, this is the people that longs to see your face.

He shall receive a blessing from the LORD,
a reward from God his savior.
Such is the race that seeks him,
that seeks the face of the God of Jacob.

℞. Lord, this is the people that longs to see your face.

SECOND READING
1 John 3:1-3

Beloved:
See what love the Father has bestowed on us
that we may be called the children of God.
Yet so we are.
The reason the world does not know us
is that it did not know him.
Beloved, we are God's children now;
what we shall be has not yet been revealed.
We do know that when it is revealed we shall be like him,
for we shall see him as he is.
Everyone who has this hope based on him makes himself pure,
as he is pure.

FIRST READING
Dan 12:1-3; L1011.7

In those days, I, Daniel, mourned
 and heard this word of the Lord:
At that time there shall arise
 Michael, the great prince,
 guardian of your people;
It shall be a time unsurpassed in distress
 since nations began until that time.
At that time your people shall escape,
 everyone who is found written in the book.

Many of those who sleep in the dust of the
 earth shall awake;
Some shall live forever,
 others shall be an everlasting horror and
 disgrace.
But the wise shall shine brightly
 like the splendor of the firmament,
And those who lead the many to justice
 shall be like the stars forever.

RESPONSORIAL PSALM
Ps 27:1, 4, 7, and 8b, and 9a, 13-14; L1013.3

℟. (1a) The Lord is my light and my
 salvation.
 or:
℟. (13) I believe that I shall see the good
 things of the Lord in the land of the
 living.

The Lord is my light and my salvation;
 whom should I fear?
The Lord is my life's refuge;
 of whom should I be afraid?

℟. The Lord is my light and my salvation.
 or:
℟. I believe that I shall see the good things of
 the Lord in the land of the living.

One thing I ask of the Lord;
 this I seek:
To dwell in the house of the Lord
 all the days of my life,
That I may gaze on the loveliness of the Lord
 and contemplate his temple.

℟. The Lord is my light and my salvation.
 or:
℟. I believe that I shall see the good things of
 the Lord in the land of the living.

Hear, O Lord, the sound of my call;
 have pity on me and answer me.
Your presence, O Lord, I seek.
 Hide not your face from me.

℟. The Lord is my light and my salvation.
 or:
℟. I believe that I shall see the good things of
 the Lord in the land of the living.

I believe that I shall see the bounty of the
 Lord
 in the land of the living.
Wait for the Lord with courage;
 be stouthearted, and wait for the Lord.

℟. The Lord is my light and my salvation.
 or:
℟. I believe that I shall see the good things of
 the Lord in the land of the living.

SECOND READING
Rom 6:3-9; L1014.3

Brothers and sisters:
Are you unaware that we who were baptized
 into Christ Jesus
 were baptized into his death?
We were indeed buried with him through
 baptism into death,
 so that, just as Christ was raised from the
 dead
 by the glory of the Father,
 we too might live in newness of life.

For if we have grown into union with him
 through a death like his,
 we shall also be united with him in the
 resurrection.
We know that our old self was crucified with
 him,
 so that our sinful body might be done away
 with,
 that we might no longer be in slavery to sin.
For a dead person has been absolved from sin.
If, then, we have died with Christ,
 we believe that we shall also live with him.
We know that Christ, raised from the dead,
 dies no more;
 death no longer has power over him.

Thirty-Second Sunday in Ordinary Time, *November 7, 2021*

Gospel
Mark 12:41-44

Jesus sat down opposite the treasury
and observed how the crowd put money into the treasury.
Many rich people put in large sums.
A poor widow also came and put in two small coins worth a few cents.
Calling his disciples to himself, he said to them,
"Amen, I say to you, this poor widow put in more
than all the other contributors to the treasury.
For they have all contributed from their surplus wealth,
but she, from her poverty, has contributed all she had,
her whole livelihood."

Thanksgiving Day, *November 25, 2021*

FIRST READING
Sir 50:22-24; L943.2

And now, bless the God of all,
who has done wondrous things on earth;
Who fosters people's growth from their
mother's womb,
and fashions them according to his will!
May he grant you joy of heart
and may peace abide among you;
May his goodness toward us endure in Israel
to deliver us in our days.

RESPONSORIAL PSALM
Ps 138:1-2a, 2bc-3, 4-5; L945.3

R̸. (2bc) Lord, I thank you for your
faithfulness and love.

I will give thanks to you, O Lord, with all of
my heart,
for you have heard the words of my mouth;
in the presence of the angels I will sing
your praise;
I will worship at your holy temple.

R̸. Lord, I thank you for your faithfulness and
love.

I will give thanks to your name,
Because of your kindness and your truth.
When I called, you answered me;
you built up strength within me.

R̸. Lord, I thank you for your faithfulness and
love.

All the kings of the earth shall give thanks to
you, O Lord,
when they hear the words of your mouth;
And they shall sing of the ways of the Lord:
"Great is the glory of the Lord."

R̸. Lord, I thank you for your faithfulness and
love.

SECOND READING
1 Cor 1:3-9; L944.1

Brothers and sisters:
Grace to you and peace from God our Father
and the Lord Jesus Christ.

I give thanks to my God always on your
account
for the grace of God bestowed on you in
Christ Jesus,
that in him you were enriched in every way,
with all discourse and all knowledge,
as the testimony to Christ was confirmed
among you,
so that you are not lacking in any spiritual
gift
as you wait for the revelation of our Lord
Jesus Christ.
He will keep you firm to the end,
irreproachable on the day of our Lord Jesus
Christ.
God is faithful,
and by him you were called to fellowship
with his Son, Jesus Christ our Lord.

Lectionary Pronunciation Guide

Lectionary Word	Pronunciation	Lectionary Word	Pronunciation	Lectionary Word	Pronunciation
Aaron	EHR-uhn	Asaph	AY-saf	Candace	kan-DAY-see
Abana	AB-uh-nuh	Asher	ASH-er	Capernaum	kuh-PERR-nay-uhm
Abednego	uh-BEHD-nee-go	Ashpenaz	ASH-pee-naz	Cappadocia	kap-ih-DO-shee-u
Abel-Keramin	AY-b'l-KEHR-uh-mihn	Assyria	a-SIHR-ee-uh	Carmel	KAHR-muhl
Abel-meholah	AY-b'l-mee-HO-lah	Astarte	as-TAHR-tee	carnelians	kahr-NEEL-yuhnz
Abiathar	uh-BAI-uh-ther	Attalia	at-TAH-lee-uh	Cenchreae	SEHN-kree-ay
Abiel	AY-bee-ehl	Augustus	uh-GUHS-tuhs	Cephas	SEE-fuhs
Abiezrite	ay-bai-EHZ-rait	Azariah	az-uh-RAI-uh	Chaldeans	kal-DEE-uhnz
Abijah	uh-BAI-dzhuh	Azor	AY-sawr	Chemosh	KEE-mahsh
Abilene	ab-uh-LEE-neh	Azotus	uh-ZO-tus	Cherubim	TSHEHR-oo-bihm
Abishai	uh-BIHSH-ay-ai	Baal-shalishah	BAY-uhl-shuh-	Chislev	KIHS-lehv
Abiud	uh-BAI-uhd		LAI-shuh	Chloe	KLO-ee
Abner	AHB-ner	Baal-Zephon	BAY-uhl-ZEE-fuhn	Chorazin	kor-AY-sihn
Abraham	AY-bruh-ham	Babel	BAY-bl	Cilicia	sih-LIHSH-ee-uh
Abram	AY-br'm	Babylon	BAB-ih-luhn	Cleopas	KLEE-o-pas
Achaia	uh-KAY-yuh	Babylonian	bab-ih-LO-nih-uhn	Clopas	KLO-pas
Achim	AY-kihm	Balaam	BAY-lm	Corinth	KAWR-ihnth
Aeneas	uh-NEE-uhs	Barabbas	beh-REH-buhs	Corinthians	kawr-IHN-thee-uhnz
Aenon	AY-nuhn	Barak	BEHR-ak	Cornelius	kawr-NEE-lee-uhs
Agrippa	uh-GRIH-puh	Barnabas	BAHR-nuh-buhs	Crete	kreet
Ahaz	AY-haz	Barsabbas	BAHR-suh-buhs	Crispus	KRIHS-puhs
Ahijah	uh-HAI-dzhuh	Bartholomew	bar-THAHL-uh-myoo	Cushite	CUHSH-ait
Ai	AY-ee	Bartimaeus	bar-tih-MEE-uhs	Cypriot	SIH-pree-at
Alexandria	al-ehg-ZAN-dree-uh	Baruch	BEHR-ook	Cyrene	sai-REE-nee
Alexandrian	al-ehg-ZAN-dree-uhn	Bashan	BAY-shan	Cyreneans	sai-REE-nih-uhnz
Alpha	AHL-fuh	Becorath	bee-KO-rath	Cyrenian	sai-REE-nih-uhn
Alphaeus	AL-fee-uhs	Beelzebul	bee-EHL-zee-buhl	Cyrenians	sai-REE-nih-uhnz
Amalek	AM-uh-lehk	Beer-sheba	BEE-er-SHEE-buh	Cyrus	SAI-ruhs
Amaziah	am-uh-ZAI-uh	Belshazzar	behl-SHAZ-er	Damaris	DAM-uh-rihs
Amminadab	ah-MIHN-uh-dab	Benjamin	BEHN-dzhuh-mihn	Damascus	duh-MAS-kuhs
Ammonites	AM-uh-naitz	Beor	BEE-awr	Danites	DAN-aits
Amorites	AM-uh-raits	Bethany	BEHTH-uh-nee	Decapolis	duh-KAP-o-lis
Amos	AY-muhs	Bethel	BETH-el	Derbe	DER-bee
Amoz	AY-muhz	Bethesda	beh-THEHZ-duh	Deuteronomy	dyoo-ter-AH-num-mee
Ampliatus	am-plee-AY-tuhs	Bethlehem	BEHTH-leh-hehm	Didymus	DID-I-mus
Ananias	an-uh-NAI-uhs	Bethphage	BEHTH-fuh-dzhee	Dionysius	dai-o-NIHSH-ih-uhs
Andronicus	an-draw-NAI-kuhs	Bethsaida	behth-SAY-ih-duh	Dioscuri	dai-O-sky-ri
Annas	AN-uhs	Beth-zur	behth-ZER	Dorcas	DAWR-kuhs
Antioch	AN-tih-ahk	Bildad	BIHL-dad	Dothan	DO-thuhn
Antiochus	an-TAI-uh-kuhs	Bithynia	bih-THIHN-ih-uh	dromedaries	DRAH-muh-dher-eez
Aphiah	uh-FAI-uh	Boanerges	bo-uh-NER-dzheez	Ebed-melech	EE-behd-MEE-lehk
Apollos	uh-PAH-luhs	Boaz	BO-az	Eden	EE-dn
Appius	AP-ee-uhs	Caesar	SEE-zer	Edom	EE-duhm
Aquila	uh-KWIHL-uh	Caesarea	zeh-suh-REE-uh	Elamites	EE-luh-maitz
Arabah	EHR-uh-buh	Caiaphas	KAY-uh-fuhs	Eldad	EHL-dad
Aram	AY-ram	Cain	kayn	Eleazar	ehl-ee-AY-zer
Arameans	ehr-uh-MEE-uhnz	Cana	KAY-nuh	Eli	EE-lai
Areopagus	ehr-ee-AH-puh-guhs	Canaan	KAY-nuhn	*Eli Eli Lema*	AY-lee AY-lee luh-MAH
Arimathea	ehr-uh-muh-THEE-uh	Canaanite	KAY-nuh-nait	*Sabachthani*	sah-BAHK-
Aroer	uh-RO-er	Canaanites	KAY-nuh-naits		tah-nee

Lectionary Word	Pronunciation	Lectionary Word	Pronunciation	Lectionary Word	Pronunciation
Eliab	ee-LAI-ab	Gilead	GIHL-ee-uhd	Joppa	DZHAH-puh
Eliakim	ee-LAI-uh-kihm	Gilgal	GIHL-gal	Joram	DZHO-ram
Eliezer	ehl-ih-EE-zer	Golgotha	GAHL-guh-thuh	Jordan	DZHAWR-dn
Elihu	ee-LAI-hyoo	Gomorrah	guh-MAWR-uh	Joseph	DZHO-zf
Elijah	ee-LAI-dzhuh	Goshen	GO-shuhn	Joses	DZHO-seez
Elim	EE-lihm	Habakkuk	huh-BAK-uhk	Joshua	DZHAH-shou-ah
Elimelech	ee-LIHM-eh-lehk	Hadadrimmon	hay-dad-RIHM-uhn	Josiah	dzho-SAI-uh
Elisha	ee-LAI-shuh	Hades	HAY-deez	Jotham	DZHO-thuhm
Eliud	ee-LAI-uhd	Hagar	HAH-gar	Judah	DZHOU-duh
Elizabeth	ee-LIHZ-uh-bth	Hananiah	han-uh-NAI-uh	Judas	DZHOU-duhs
Elkanah	el-KAY-nuh	Hannah	HAN-uh	Judea	dzhou-DEE-uh
Eloi Eloi Lama	AY-lo-ee AY-lo-ee	Haran	HAY-ruhn	Judean	dzhou-DEE-uhn
Sabechthani	LAH-mah sah-	Hebron	HEE-bruhn	Junia	dzhou-nih-uh
	BAHK-tah-nee	Hermes	HER-meez	Justus	DZHUHS-tuhs
Elymais	ehl-ih-MAY-ihs	Herod	HEHR-uhd	Kephas	KEF-uhs
Emmanuel	eh-MAN-yoo-ehl	Herodians	hehr-O-dee-uhnz	Kidron	KIHD-ruhn
Emmaus	eh-MAY-uhs	Herodias	hehr-O-dee-uhs	Kiriatharba	kihr-ee-ath-AHR-buh
Epaenetus	ee-PEE-nee-tuhs	Hezekiah	heh-zeh-KAI-uh	Kish	kihsh
Epaphras	EH-puh-fras	Hezron	HEHZ-ruhn	Laodicea	lay-o-dih-SEE-uh
ephah	EE-fuh	Hilkiah	hihl-KAI-uh	Lateran	LAT-er-uhn
Ephah	EE-fuh	Hittite	HIH-tait	Lazarus	LAZ-er-uhs
Ephesians	eh-FEE-zhuhnz	Hivites	HAI-vaitz	Leah	LEE-uh
Ephesus	EH-fuh-suhs	Hophni	HAHF-nai	Lebanon	LEH-buh-nuhn
Ephphatha	EHF-uh-thuh	Hor	HAWR	Levi	LEE-vai
Ephraim	EE-fray-ihm	Horeb	HAWR-ehb	Levite	LEE-vait
Ephrathah	EHF-ruh-thuh	Hosea	ho-ZEE-uh	Levites	LEE-vaits
Ephron	EE-frawn	Hur	her	Leviticus	leh-VIH-tih-kous
Epiphanes	eh-PIHF-uh-neez	hyssop	HIH-suhp	Lucius	LOO-shih-uhs
Erastus	ee-RAS-tuhs	Iconium	ai-KO-nih-uhm	Lud	luhd
Esau	EE-saw	Isaac	AI-zuhk	Luke	look
Esther	EHS-ter	Isaiah	ai-ZAY-uh	Luz	luhz
Ethanim	EHTH-uh-nihm	Iscariot	ihs-KEHR-ee-uht	Lycaonian	lihk-ay-O-nih-uhn
Ethiopian	ee-thee-O-pee-uhn	Ishmael	ISH-may-ehl	Lydda	LIH-duh
Euphrates	yoo-FRAY-teez	Ishmaelites	ISH-mayehl-aits	Lydia	LIH-dih-uh
Exodus	EHK-so-duhs	Israel	IHZ-ray-ehl	Lysanias	lai-SAY-nih-uhs
Ezekiel	eh-ZEE-kee-uhl	Ituraea	ih-TSHOOR-ree-uh	Lystra	LIHS-truh
Ezra	EHZ-ruh	Jaar	DZHAY-ahr	Maccabees	MAK-uh-beez
frankincense	FRANGK-ihn-sehns	Jabbok	DZHAB-uhk	Macedonia	mas-eh-DO-nih-uh
Gabbatha	GAB-uh-thuh	Jacob	DZHAY-kuhb	Macedonian	mas-eh-DO-nih-uhn
Gabriel	GAY-bree-ul	Jairus	DZH-hr-uhs	Machir	MAY-kihr
Gadarenes	GAD-uh-reenz	Javan	DZHAY-van	Machpelah	mak-PEE-luh
Galatian	guh-LAY-shih-uhn	Jebusites	DZHEHB-oo-zaits	Magdala	MAG-duh-luh
Galatians	guh-LAY-shih-uhnz	Jechoniah	dzhehk-o-NAI-uh	Magdalene	MAG-duh-lehn
Galilee	GAL-ih-lee	Jehoiakim	dzhee-HOI-uh-kihm	magi	MAY-dzhai
Gallio	GAL-ih-o	Jehoshaphat	dzhee-HAHSH-uh-fat	Malachi	MAL-uh-kai
Gamaliel	guh-MAY-lih-ehl	Jephthah	DZHEHF-thuh	Malchiah	mal-KAI-uh
Gaza	GAH-zuh	Jeremiah	dzhehr-eh-MAI-uh	Malchus	MAL-kuhz
Gehazi	gee-HAY-zai	Jericho	DZHEHR-ih-ko	Mamre	MAM-ree
Gehenna	geh-HEHN-uh	Jeroham	dzhehr-RO-ham	Manaen	MAN-uh-ehn
Genesis	DZHEHN-uh-sihs	Jerusalem	dzheh-ROU-suh-lehm	Manasseh	man-AS-eh
Gennesaret	gehn-NEHS-uh-reht	Jesse	DZHEH-see	Manoah	muh-NO-uh
Gentiles	DZHEHN-tailz	Jethro	DZHEHTH-ro	Mark	mahrk
Gerasenes	DZHEHR-uh-seenz	Joakim	DZHO-uh-kihm	Mary	MEHR-ee
Gethsemane	gehth-SEHM-uh-ne	Job	DZHOB	Massah	MAH-suh
Gideon	GIHD-ee-uhn	Jonah	DZHO-nuh	Mattathias	mat-uh-THAI-uhs

Lectionary Word	Pronunciation	Lectionary Word	Pronunciation	Lectionary Word	Pronunciation
Matthan	MAT-than	Parmenas	PAHR-mee-nas	Sabbath	SAB-uhth
Matthew	MATH-yoo	Parthians	PAHR-thee-uhnz	Sadducees	SAD-dzhoo-seez
Matthias	muh-THAI-uhs	Patmos	PAT-mos	Salem	SAY-lehm
Medad	MEE-dad	Peninnah	pee-NIHN-uh	Salim	SAY-lim
Mede	meed	Pentecost	PEHN-tee-kawst	Salmon	SAL-muhn
Medes	meedz	Penuel	pee-NYOO-ehl	Salome	suh-LO-mee
Megiddo	mee-GIH-do	Perez	PEE-rehz	Salu	SAYL-yoo
Melchizedek	mehl-KIHZ-eh-dehk	Perga	PER-guh	Samaria	suh-MEHR-ih-uh
Mene	MEE-nee	Perizzites	PEHR-ih-zaits	Samaritan	suh-MEHR-ih-tuhn
Meribah	MEHR-ih-bah	Persia	PER-zhuh	Samothrace	SAM-o-thrays
Meshach	MEE-shak	Peter	PEE-ter	Samson	SAM-s'n
Mespotamia	mehs-o-po-TAY-mih-uh	Phanuel	FAN-yoo-ehl	Samuel	SAM-yoo-uhl
Micah	MAI-kuh	Pharaoh	FEHR-o	Sanhedrin	san-HEE-drihn
Midian	MIH-dih-uhn	Pharisees	FEHR-ih-seez	Sarah	SEHR-uh
Milcom	MIHL-kahm	Pharpar	FAHR-pahr	Sarai	SAY-rai
Miletus	mai-LEE-tuhs	Philemon	fih-LEE-muhn	saraph	SAY-raf
Minnith	MIHN-ihth	Philippi	fil-LIH-pai	Sardis	SAHR-dihs
Mishael	MIHSH-ay-ehl	Philippians	fih-LIHP-ih-uhnz	Saul	sawl
Mizpah	MIHZ-puh	Philistines	fih-LIHS-tihnz	Scythian	SIH-thee-uihn
Moreh	MO-reh	Phinehas	FEHN-ee-uhs	Seba	SEE-buh
Moriah	maw-RAI-uh	Phoenicia	fee-NIHSH-ih-uh	Seth	sehth
Mosoch	MAH-sahk	Phrygia	FRIH-dzhih-uh	Shaalim	SHAY-uh-lihm
myrrh	mer	Phrygian	FRIH-dzhih-uhn	Shadrach	SHAY-drak
Mysia	MIH-shih-uh	phylacteries	fih-LAK-ter-eez	Shalishah	shuh-LEE-shuh
Naaman	NAY-uh-muhn	Pi-Hahiroth	pai-huh-HAI-rahth	Shaphat	Shay-fat
Nahshon	NAY-shuhn	Pilate	PAI-luht	Sharon	SHEHR-uhn
Naomi	NAY-o-mai	Pisidia	pih-SIH-dih-uh	Shealtiel	shee-AL-tih-ehl
Naphtali	NAF-tuh-lai	Pithom	PAI-thahm	Sheba	SHEE-buh
Nathan	NAY-thuhn	Pontius	PAHN-shus	Shebna	SHEB-nuh
Nathanael	nuh-THAN-ay-ehl	Pontus	PAHN-tus	Shechem	SHEE-kehm
Nazarene	NAZ-awr-een	Praetorium	pray-TAWR-ih-uhm	shekel	SHEHK-uhl
Nazareth	NAZ-uh-rehth	Priscilla	PRIHS-kill-uh	Shiloh	SHAI-lo
nazirite	NAZ-uh-rait	Prochorus	PRAH-kaw-ruhs	Shinar	SHAI-nahr
Nazorean	naz-aw-REE-uhn	Psalm	Sahm	Shittim	sheh-TEEM
Neapolis	nee-AP-o-lihs	Put	puht	Shuhite	SHOO-ait
Nebuchadnezzar	neh-byoo-kuhd-NEHZ-er	Puteoli	pyoo-TEE-o-lai	Shunammite	SHOO-nam-ait
Negeb	NEH-gehb	Qoheleth	ko-HEHL-ehth	Shunem	SHOO-nehm
Nehemiah	nee-hee-MAI-uh	qorban	KAWR-bahn	Sidon	SAI-duhn
Ner	ner	Quartus	KWAR-tuhs	Silas	SAI-luhs
Nicanor	nai-KAY-nawr	Quirinius	kwai-RIHN-ih-uhs	Siloam	sih-LO-uhm
Nicodemus	nih-ko-DEE-muhs	Raamses	ray-AM-seez	Silvanus	sihl-VAY-nuhs
Niger	NAI-dzher	Rabbi	RAB-ai	Simeon	SIHM-ee-uhn
Nineveh	NIHN-eh-veh	Rabbouni	ra-BO-nai	Simon	SAI-muhn
Noah	NO-uh	Rahab	RAY-hab	Sin (desert)	sihn
Nun	nuhn	Ram	ram	Sinai	SAI-nai
Obed	O-behd	Ramah	RAY-muh	Sirach	SAI-rak
Olivet	AH-lih-veht	Ramathaim	ray-muh-THAY-ihm	Sodom	SAH-duhm
Omega	o-MEE-guh	Raqa	RA-kuh	Solomon	SAH-lo-muhn
Onesimus	o-NEH-sih-muhs	Rebekah	ree-BEHK-uh	Sosthenes	SAHS-thee-neez
Ophir	O-fer	Rehoboam	ree-ho-BO-am	Stachys	STAY-kihs
Orpah	AWR-puh	Rephidim	REHF-ih-dihm	Succoth	SUHK-ahth
Pamphylia	pam-FIHL-ih-uh	Reuben	ROO-b'n	Sychar	SI-kar
Paphos	PAY-fuhs	Revelation	reh-veh-LAY-shuhn	Syene	sai-EE-nee
		Rhegium	REE-dzhee-uhm	Symeon	SIHM-ee-uhn
		Rufus	ROO-fuhs	synagogues	SIHN-uh-gahgz

Lectionary Word	Pronunciation	Lectionary Word	Pronunciation	Lectionary Word	Pronunciation
Syrophoenician	SIHR-o fee-NIHSH-ih-uhn	Timon	TAI-muhn	Zebedee	ZEH-beh-dee
Tabitha	TAB-ih-thuh	Titus	TAI-tuhs	Zebulun	ZEH-byoo-luhn
Talitha koum	TAL-ih-thuh-KOOM	Tohu	TO-hyoo	Zechariah	zeh-kuh-RAI-uh
Tamar	TAY-mer	Trachonitis	trak-o-NAI-tis	Zedekiah	zeh-duh-KAI-uh
Tarshish	TAHR-shihsh	Troas	TRO-ahs	Zephaniah	zeh-fuh-NAI-uh
Tarsus	TAHR-suhs	Tubal	TYOO-b'l	Zerah	ZEE-ruh
Tekel	TEH-keel	Tyre	TAI-er	Zeror	ZEE-rawr
Terebinth	TEHR-ee-bihnth	Ur	er	Zerubbabel	zeh-RUH-buh-behl
Thaddeus	THAD-dee-uhs	Urbanus	er-BAY-nuhs	Zeus	zyoos
Theophilus	thee-AH-fih-luhs	Uriah	you-RAI-uh	Zimri	ZIHM-rai
Thessalonians	theh-suh-LO-nih-uhnz	Uzziah	yoo-ZAI-uh	Zion	ZAI-uhn
Theudas	THU-duhs	Wadi	WAH-dee	Ziph	zihf
Thyatira	thai-uh-TAI-ruh	Yahweh-yireh	YAH-weh-yer-AY	Zoar	ZO-er
Tiberias	tai-BIHR-ih-uhs	Zacchaeus	zak-KEE-uhs	Zorah	ZAWR-uh
Timaeus	tai-MEE-uhs	Zadok	ZAY-dahk	Zuphite	ZUHF-ait
		Zarephath	ZEHR-ee-fath		